THE ROUTLEDGE HISTORY OF AMERICAN SPORT

The Routledge History of American Sport provides the first comprehensive overview of historical research in American sport from the early Colonial period to the present day. Considering sport through innovative themes and topics such as the business of sport, material culture and sport, the political uses of sport, and gender and sport, this text offers an interdisciplinary analysis of American leisure. Rather than moving chronologically through American history or considering the historical origins of each sport, these topics are dealt with organically within thematic chapters, emphasizing the influence of sport on American society.

The volume is divided into eight thematic sections that include detailed original essays on particular facets of each theme. Focusing on how sport has influenced the history of women, minorities, politics, the media, and culture, these thematic chapters survey the major areas of debate and discussion. The volume offers a comprehensive view of the history of sport in America, pushing the field to consider new themes and approaches as well.

Including a roster of contributors renowned in their fields of expertise, this ground-breaking collection is essential reading for all those interested in the history of American sport.

Linda J. Borish is Associate Professor in the History Department and for Gender & Women's Studies Department at Western Michigan University. She has presented and published her work nationally and internationally.

David K. Wiggins is a professor and co-director of the Center for the Study of Sport and Leisure in Society at George Mason University.

Gerald R. Gems is a past president of the North American Society for Sport History, the current vice-president of the International Society for the History of Physical Education and Sport, and a Fulbright Scholar, who has presented his work in 29 countries.

THE ROUTLEDGE HISTORIES

The Routledge Histories is a series of landmark books surveying some of the most important topics and themes in history today. Edited and written by an international team of world-renowned experts, they are the works against which all future books on their subjects will be judged.

THE ROUTLEDGE HISTORY OF SEX AND THE BODY
Edited by Kate Fisher and Sarah Toulalan

THE ROUTLEDGE HISTORY OF WESTERN EMPIRES
Edited by Robert Aldrich and Kirsten McKenzie

THE ROUTLEDGE HISTORY OF FOOD
Edited by Carol Helstosky

THE ROUTLEDGE HISTORY OF TERRORISM
Edited by Randall D. Law

THE ROUTLEDGE HISTORY OF MEDIEVAL CHRISTIANITY
Edited by Robert Swanson

THE ROUTLEDGE HISTORY OF GENOCIDE
Edited by Cathie Carmichael and Richard C. Maguire

THE ROUTLEDGE HISTORY OF AMERICAN FOODWAYS
Edited by Michael Wise and Jennifer Jensen Wallach

THE ROUTLEDGE HISTORY OF RURAL AMERICA
Edited by Pamela Riney-Kehrberg

THE ROUTLEDGE HISTORY OF DISEASE
Edited by Mark Jackson

THE ROUTLEDGE HISTORY OF AMERICAN SPORT
Edited by Linda J. Borish, David K. Wiggins, and Gerald R. Gems

THE ROUTLEDGE HISTORY OF AMERICAN SPORT

Edited by
Linda J. Borish, David K. Wiggins, and Gerald R. Gems

LONDON AND NEW YORK

First published 2017 by Routledge

2 Park Square, Milton Park, Abingdon, Oxfordshire OX14 4RN
52 Vanderbilt Avenue, New York, NY 10017

Routledge is an imprint of the Taylor & Francis Group, an informa business

First issued in paperback 2019

Library of Congress Cataloging-in-Publication Data
Names: Borish, Linda J., 1961– author.
Title: The Routledge history of American sport / co-edited by Linda J. Borish, David K. Wiggins, Gerald R. Gems.
Description: New York : Routledge, 2016. | Series: The Routledge histories.
Identifiers: LCCN 2016015432 | ISBN 9781138786752 (hardback) | ISBN 9781315767123 (ebook)
Subjects: LCSH: Sports—United States—History. | Sports—Social aspects—United States—History.
Classification: LCC GV583 .R68 2016 | DDC 796.0973—dc23
LC record available at https://lccn.loc.gov/2016015432

ISBN: 978-1-138-78675-2 (hbk)
ISBN: 978-1-138-32757-3 (pbk)

Typeset in Times New Roman
by Apex CoVantage, LLC

Dedicated to all those who have contributed to the growth and importance of sport history as an academic discipline.

CONTENTS

CONTRIBUTORS

Amy Bass is Professor of History and Director of the Honors Program at The College of New Rochelle. She is the author of *Not the Triumph But the Struggle: The 1968 Olympic Games and the Making of the Black Athlete*, among other titles. A frequent contributor to organizations such as Slate, Salon, and CNN Opinion, she received an Emmy Award in 2012 for her work with NBC at the London Olympic Games.

Adam Berg is a PhD Candidate in Kinesiology at Penn State University with a specialization in the history and philosophy of sport. He is the author of " 'To Conquer Myself': The New Strenuosity and the Emergence of Thru-Hiking on the Appalachian Trail in the 1970s," *Journal of Sport History*, 42, no. 1 (2015): 1–19. He is currently working on a dissertation about the 1976 Denver Olympics.

John D. Bloom is an Associate Professor in the Department of History and Philosophy at Shippensburg University of Pennsylvania. He is the author of books on sports and culture in the United States, including *A House of Cards: Baseball Card Collecting and Popular Culture*, *To Show What an Indian Can Do: Sports at Native American Boarding Schools*, and *There You Have It: The Life, Legacy, and Legend of Howard Cosell*. He has also edited, with Michael Nevin Willard, *Sports Matters: Race, Recreation, and Culture*.

Linda J. Borish is Associate Professor in the History Department and for Gender & Women's Studies Department at Western Michigan University. Borish's publications in sport history, women's and gender history, and American Jewish history include chapters in *Sports in Chicago; Sports and the American Jew; Jews in the Gym: Judaism, Sports, and Athletics;* and *A Companion to American Sport History*, and scholarly articles in the *Journal of Sport History*, *The International Journal of the History of Sport*, *Rethinking History: The Journal of Theory and Practice*, and others. Borish co-authored *Sports in American History: From Colonization to Globalization* (2008), with Gerald Gems and Gertrud Pfister. Borish is Executive Producer/Historian of the "Jewish Women in American Sport: Settlement Houses to the Olympics" documentary film (2007) and is a Research Associate of The Hadassah-Brandeis Institute. She served as a book reviews editor for the *Journal of Sport History*.

Adrian Burgos, Jr., is Professor of History at the University of Illinois, specializing in US Latino history, sport history, and urban history. He holds a PhD from the University of Michigan (2000) and a BA from Vassar College (1993). He is the author of *Cuban Star: How One Negro League Owner Changed the Face of Baseball* (Hill & Wang, 2011) and *Playing America's Game: Baseball, Latinos, and the Color Line* (University of California

Press, 2007), which won the Latina/o Book Award from the Latin American Studies Association, and was named a Seymour Medal finalist from the Society of American Baseball Research.

Richard C. Crepeau, author of *NFL Football: A History of America's New National Pastime*, is a Professor of History at the University of Central Florida. He has been working in the area of sport history for over 40 years and has published numerous articles on the history of baseball, intercollegiate athletics, and sport literature. He is author of *Baseball: America's Diamond Mind, 1919–1941* and has been writing "On Sport and Society" an online column for the Sport Literature Association for the past 24 years in which he comments on the role of sport in American life, now available at the Huffington Post.

Braham Dabscheck, Senior Fellow, Faculty of Law, University of Melbourne, conducts research into the economic, historical, legal, and industrial relations aspects of professional sport across the globe. His publications include "Sporting Equality: Labour Market vs. Product Market Control," *The Journal of Industrial Relations*, June 1975; ' "Defensive Manchester": A History of the Professional Footballers' Association," in R. I. Cashman and M. M. McKernan (eds.), *The Making of Sporting Traditions*, 1979; "Sport, Human Rights and Industrial Relations," *Australian Journal of Human Rights*, September 2000; "Reading Baseball: Books, Biographies and the Business of the Game, 2011"; and "Sweated Labour, Literally Speaking: The Case of Australian Jockeys," in Y. H. Lee and R. Fort (eds.), *The Sports Business in the Pacific Rim: Economics and Policy*, 2015. He is past president of the Australian Society for Sports History.

Margaret (Maggie) J. Daniels is the Academic Program Coordinator of Tourism and Events Management at George Mason University. She has conducted collaborative research with the National Park Service regarding tourism within the National Mall and Memorial Parks since 2006.

Richard O. Davies is Distinguished Professor of History, Emeritus, at the University of Nevada, Reno. His recent publications include *Sports in American Life: A History* (2016, 3rd ed.) and *The Main Event: Boxing in Nevada From the Mining Camps to the Las Vegas Strip* (2014).

Mark Dyreson is a faculty member in the history and philosophy of sport program at Penn State University. An academic editor for *The International Journal of the History of Sport* and a fellow in the U.S. National Academy of Kinesiology, he has published extensively, including *Making the American Team: Sport, Culture and the Olympic Experience* (1998) and *Crafting Patriotism for Global Domination: America at the Olympic Games* (2009). He is co-editor (with Jaime Schultz) of *American National Pastimes—A History* (2015) and (with Wray Vamplew) of a four-volume series entitled *Sports History: Issues, Debates and Challenges* (2016).

Chris Elzey teaches in the History and Art History Department at George Mason University in Fairfax, Virginia. He also oversees the Sport and American Culture minor at George Mason. He is the co-editor of *DC Sports: The Nation's Capital at Play*.

Sarah K. Fields is an Acting Associate Dean and Associate Professor at the University of Colorado Denver. She is the author of *Female Gladiators: Gender, Law, and Contact Sport in America* (University of Illinois, 2005) and *Game Faces: Sport Celebrity and the*

Laws of Reputation (University of Illinois, 2016). She is the co-editor of *Sport and the Law: Historical and Cultural Intersections* (University of Arkansas, 2014).

Joel S. Franks teaches Asian American Studies and American Studies at San Jose State University. He has published several articles and books, including *Crossing Sidelines, Crossing Cultures: Sport and Asian Pacific American Cultural Citizenship* (2000), *Whose Baseball?: The National Pastime and Cultural Diversity in California, 1859–1941* (2001), *Hawaiian Sporting Experiences in the Twentieth Century* (2002), *Democracy in America: A History (2008)*, *Asian Pacific Americans and Baseball* (2008), *The Barnstorming Hawaiian Travelers: A Multiethnic Baseball Team Tours the Mainland, 1912–1916* (2012), and *Asian American Basketball: A Century of Sport, Community, and Culture* (2016).

Gerald R. Gems is the author of more than 200 publications, including 18 books. He is a past president of the North American Society for Sport History, the current vice-president of the International Society for the History of Physical Education and Sport, and a Fulbright Scholar, who has presented his work in 29 countries. He is an honorary member of the Bangladesh Institute of Sport Sciences and serves on the editorial board of several journals, as well as serving as the book reviews editor of the *Journal of Sport History*. His research addresses factors of social class, race, ethnicity, and religion relative to sporting practices.

Dennis Gildea is a professor of communications at Springfield College, the birthplace of basketball. A former sportswriter, he is the author of *Hoop Crazy: The Lives of Clair Bee and Chip Hilton* (University of Arkansas Press, 2013).

Annette R. Hofmann is full professor for Sports Studies at the Ludwigsburg University of Education in Germany. She is the president of the International Society for the History of Sport and Physical Education (ISHPES) and vice-president of the German Gymnastic Federation (Deutsche Turner-Bund), the biggest sports for all association. She is an academic editor of *The International Journal of the History of Sport* and book reviews editor of the *Journal of Sport History*. She holds several other positions on national and international academic boards. She published about 30 papers on the American Turners, among them the book *The History of the American Turners from Its Beginnings to 1999* (2010). She is a co-editor of *License to Jump: A Story of Women's Ski Jumping* (2015).

Brian M. Ingrassia is assistant professor of history at West Texas A&M University. He is author of *The Rise of Gridiron University: Higher Education's Uneasy Alliance with Big-Time Football* (University Press of Kansas, 2012), which won the North American Society for Sport History monograph award. He has published articles in scholarly venues such as *The Journal of the Gilded Age and Progressive Era*.

Rita Liberti is a professor in the Department of Kinesiology at Cal State East Bay in Hayward, California, where she also serves as the Director of the Center for Sport & Social Justice. She has published widely on twentieth-century sport history with a focus on the athletic experiences of African American women enrolled at historically black colleges and universities. Recently she co-authored *(Re)Presenting Wilma Rudolph* (Syracuse University, 2015). In addition, Liberti's co-edited volume on San Francisco Bay area sport history (University of Arkansas) is to be published in 2017.

Charles H. Martin is Professor of History at the University of Texas at El Paso, where he teaches courses on recent American history, Texas history, and civil rights history. He is the author of *Benching Jim Crow: The Rise and Fall of the Color Line in Southern College Sports, 1890–1980* (2010), and *The Angelo Herndon Case and Southern Justice* (1976).

Donald J. Mrozek is Professor of History at Kansas State University and is the beneficiary of his department's NEH History Professorship and George M. Kren History Research Fund. He first taught a course in sport history in 1973, his second year at his university. It has been a regular part of departmental offerings ever since. His book *Sport and American Mentality, 1880–1910* was published by the University of Tennessee Press in 1983 and remains in print. He co-edited *Sports Periodicals* (1977). Mrozek also specializes in American military history, and he uses cultural history techniques to the study of both the American military and sport in America.

John Nauright is Professor and Chair, Department of Kinesiology, Health Promotion and Recreation at the University of North Texas. He has also been Visiting Professor at Lomonosov Moscow State University; University of Ghana; and University of the West Indies, Barbados. He is the author and editor of 20 books on global sport, including the award-winning four-volume *Sport Around the World: History, Culture and Practice* (2012); *Beyond C.L.R. James: Race and Ethnicity in Sport; Long Run to Freedom: Sport, Cultures and Identities in South Africa* (2014); and the 2017 *Routledge Handbook of Global Sports and Sporting Entrepreneurs*.

Roberta J. Park is a Professor Emeritus at the University of California, Berkeley. Among the books that she has published (with others) are *Mapping an Empire of American Sport: Expansion, Assimilation and Resistance* (2013); *Women, Sport, Society: Further Reflections Reaffirming Mary Wollstonecraft* (2011); *Sport and Exercise Science: Essays in the History of Sports Medicine* (1992); and *From Fair Sex to Feminism: Sport and the Socialization of Women in the Industrial and Post-Industrial Eras* (1987). She has published more than 90 articles. Among the more recent are "Play, Games and Cognitive Development: Late 19th and Early 20th Century Physicians, Neurologists, Psychologists and Others Already Knew What Researchers Are Proclaiming Today" (*The International Journal of the History of Sport*, 2014); "Soldiers May Fall But Athletes Never: Sport as an Antidote to Nervous Diseases and National Decline in America, 1865–1905" (*International Journal of the History of Sport*, 2012); and "Physicians, Scientists, Exercise, and Athletics in Britain and America from the 1867 Boat Race to the Four-Minute Mile" (*Sport in History*, 2011).

Robert Pruter is the reference and government documents librarian at Lewis University, Romeoville, Illinois. He is a contributor to the *Journal of Sport History*, *The International Journal of the History of Sport*, and other history journals and is the author of *The Rise of High School Sports in America and the Search for Control, 1880–1930*, published by the Syracuse University Press in 2013.

Steven A. Riess is a Bernard Brommel Research Professor, emeritus, Department of History, Northern Illinois University. He is the author of *Sports in Industrial America, 1850–1920*, 2nd ed., rev. (2013); *The Sport of Kings and the Kings of Crime. Horse Racing, Politics, and Crime in New York, 1865–1913* (2011); *Touching Base: Professional Baseball and American Culture in the Progressive Era*, rev. ed., (1999); and *City Games: The Evolution* *of American Society and the Rise of Sports* (1989). He edited *A Companion to American Sport History*, which won the North American Society for Sport History prize in 2015 for the best anthology in sport history.

Robert E. Rinehart is an Associate Professor in Te Oranga School of Human Development and Movement Studies at the University of Waikato in Aotearoa/New Zealand. He has recently co-written (with Richard Pringle and Jayne Caudwell) *Sport and the Social Significance of Pleasure* (Routledge, 2015).

Tom Rorke is a sport historian currently researching early women's ice hockey in the United States and Canada. He has degrees in sociology and history from Carleton University in Ottawa, and as of 2016 is a PhD Candidate in the Department of Kinesiology at the Pennsylvania State University.

Macintosh Ross is an Assistant Professor of Sport Management at Keystone College in La Plume, Pennsylvania. His research focuses primarily on masculinity and boxing in nineteenth-century America. His most recent work, entitled "Prize Fighting and Sparring on the Pacific Coast: The Pugilistic Culture of Late Antebellum and Civil War Era California," appeared in the winter 2015 edition of *Journal of the West*.

Jaime Schultz is an Associate Professor of Kinesiology and Women's Studies at Pennsylvania State University. She received her PhD in the Cultural Studies of Sport from the University of Iowa. She has published many journal articles and book chapters on the subject of women in sport, as well as authoring or editing three books: *Moments of Impact: Injury, Racialized Memory, and Reconciliation in College Football* (University of Nebraska Press, 2016); *American National Pastimes—A History* (Routledge, 2015; co-edited with Mark Dyreson); and *Qualifying Times: Points of Change in U.S. Women's Sport* (University of Illinois Press, 2014). She is the associate editor for the *Journal of Sport History* and serves on several editorial boards.

Amanda N. Schweinbenz is Associate Professor at Laurentian University, and her primary area of focus is gender in sport throughout history. More specifically, Schweinbenz examines how heteronormative concepts of gender have framed and shaped people's participation in sport throughout history, with a particular interest in the Olympic Games. Her early work focused on the history of women's competitive international rowing, but more recently her research interests have broadened to examine parasport and the technologies of the body.

Jason Shurley is an Associate Professor and Director of Kinesiology at Concordia University in Austin, Texas. His research has primarily dealt with the history of the strength and conditioning profession and the history of sports medicine in the United States.

Ronald A. Smith, Professor Emeritus at Penn State University, has been affiliated with the university since 1968 with a focus on college sport history. He pioneered the early history of college athletics with his *Sports and Freedom: The Rise of Big-Time College Athletics* (Oxford, 1988). Books in the twenty-first century include *Play-by-Play: Radio, Television, and Big-Time College Sport* (Johns Hopkins, 2001), *Pay for Play: A History of Big-Time College Athletic Reform* (University of Illinois, 2011), and *Wounded Lions: Joe Paterno, Jerry Sandusky, and the Crises in Penn State Athletics* (University of Illinois, 2016). His "Far More than Commercialism: American University Stadium Building from

Harvard's Innovation to Stanford's 'Dirt Bowl,'" is included in Mark Dyreson and Robert Trumbour (eds.), *The Rise of Stadiums in Modern United States: Cathedrals of Sport* (Routledge, 2010). He was secretary-treasurer of the North American Society for Sport History from its beginning in 1972 until 2015.

John Soares, a former Fulbright Visiting Research Chair in North American Studies at Carleton University in Ottawa, teaches history at the University of Notre Dame. He has published extensively on international ice hockey during the Cold War, including Cold War International History Project's Working Paper 68, *Difficult to Draw a Balance Sheet: Ottawa Views the 1974 Canada-USSR Hockey Series*; a chapter in the University Press of Kentucky anthology, *Diplomatic Games: Sport, Statecraft and International Relations Since 1945*; and his Routledge Prize–winning article in the August 2013 *The International Journal of Sport History*.

Ryan Swanson is an Assistant Professor of History in the Honors College at the University of New Mexico. His primary research areas are sports, reconstruction, and segregation. He has written numerous articles and also serves as the director of the Lobo Scholars Program. This program is a joint venture between the UNM Honors College and Athletics Department designed to serve very high-achieving student-athletes. Swanson's first book, *When Baseball Went White: Reconstruction, Reconciliation, and Dreams of a National Pastime*, was published by the University of Nebraska Press in 2014. The book explores how baseball became segregated after the Civil War.

Jan Todd, the Roy J. McLean Fellow in Sport History, is president-elect of the North American Society of Sport History. Todd teaches in the Department of Kinesiology and Health Education at the University of Texas at Austin where she directs both the doctoral program in Physical Culture and Sport Studies and the Sport Management master's and undergraduate degree programs. She is also the co-founder (with her husband Terry Todd) of the H.J. Lutcher Stark Center for Physical Culture and Sports. She has written two books and more than 100 scholarly and popular articles.

Robert C. Trumpbour is Associate Professor of Communications at Pennsylvania State University, Altoona College. He authored and edited *The New Cathedrals: Politics and Media in the History of Stadium Construction* (Syracuse University Press, 2007), *Cathedrals of Sport: The Rise of Stadiums in the Modern United States* (Routledge, 2010), and *The Eighth Wonder of the World: The Life of Houston's Iconic Astrodome* (University of Nebraska Press, 2016). He is active in the North American Society for Sport History, The Association for Education in Journalism and Mass Communication, and The Society for American Baseball Research. He has worked for CBS and Westwood One in various capacities.

Wanda Ellen Wakefield is an Associate Professor of History at SUNY College at Brockport where she also teaches in the Delta College program. She is the author of *Playing to Win: Sports and the American Military, 1898–1945* (SUNY, 1997), "Reclaiming the Slopes: Sport and Tourism in Post Austria" and "All Downhill from Here: The Sliding Sports and the Amateur Sports Act of 1978." Recently her research interests have focused on the winter sports and the Cold War.

Kevin B. Wamsley is currently the Academic Vice-President and Provost of St. Francis Xavier University in Antigonish, Nova Scotia, Canada. His research expertise has focused specifically on gender relations in sport, the history of violence in sport, sport and the state, the Olympic Games, and Canadian sport history. He is co-author of *Sport in Canada: A History* (2005), now in its fourth edition, and co-editor of *Global Olympics: Historical and Sociological Studies of the Modern Olympic Games* (2017). He is co-editor of *OLYMPIKA: The International Journal of Olympic Studies*.

Brenda P. Wiggins is an associate professor of Recreation Management and co-coordinates the graduate program in Sport and Recreation Studies at George Mason University. Her presentations have included application of the International Classification of Functioning for Disability and Health, interpretative analysis of constraints and negotiations among people with disabilities, and staff retention in a summer camp for children and teens with disabilities. She co-authored a book chapter in the 2015 *Recreational Therapy for Specific Diagnoses and Conditions* published by Idyll Arbor, Inc., and has served for over a decade on the Therapeutic Recreation Advisory Board of Fairfax County.

David K. Wiggins is a professor and co-director of the Center for the Study of Sport and Leisure in Society at George Mason University. Primarily interested in the history of African American participation in sport, he has published numerous essays in scholarly journals, written book chapters, and edited or authored many anthologies and monographs. Among his books are *Glory Bound: Black Athletes in a White America* (1997), *The Unlevel Playing Field: A Documentary History of the African American Experience in Sport* (2003), *Rivals: Legendary Matchups That Made Sports History* (2010), *Out of the Shadows: A Biographical History of African American Athletes* (2006), *DC Sports: The Nation's Capital at Play* (2015), and *Philly Sports: A History of Teams, Games, and Athletes from Rocky's Town* (2016). He is on the editorial review boards for several scholarly journals, is former editor of *Quest* and the *Journal of Sport History*, and is an active fellow in the National Academy of Kinesiology.

Ralph C. Wilcox is Professor, Provost, and Executive Vice-President at the University of South Florida where he provides strategic direction and leadership for one of America's largest top-tier research universities. He graduated from the University of Exeter in the United Kingdom and went on to earn postgraduate degrees from Washington State University and the University of Alberta, Canada, where he was appointed an Izaak Walton Killam Memorial Scholar. He is a Fellow of the American Council on Education. He has published his work widely in the field of cultural studies and globalization, including *Sport in the Global Village* (FIT Press, 1994) and *Sporting Dystopias: The Making and Meaning of Urban Sport Cultures*, with Andrews, Pitter, and Irwin (SUNY Press, 2003).

ACKNOWLEDGMENTS

The development of *The Routledge History of American Sport* has truly been a collaborative endeavor. The co-editors worked closely in the intellectual labors and shared enthusiasm to produce this innovative book. Numerous colleagues at Routledge provided vital assistance and guidance from the initial interest in the book proposal to the submission of the manuscript. Editorial Assistant Daniel Finaldi shared his valuable expertise in preparing the book and offered many suggestions, which greatly enhanced the quality of the volume. History Editor Margo C. Irvin provided her full support for the project and gave welcome encouragement along the way. Linda J. Borish thanks José A. Brandão, Chair of the History Department at Western Michigan University, for supporting her work on this project. Colleague James P. Cousins has continually encouraged her to teach courses in American sport history and shares his interest in her historical work on the study of sport; colleague Larry J. Simon has continuously shown interest in her research on gender and ethnicity and patiently listened to her talk about her work in sport history over the years. So, too, colleague Mitch Kachun has shown interest in her scholarship and consistently encouraged her inclusion of new courses in American sport history in the History Department curriculum. Linda J. Borish gratefully acknowledges the loving support and wisdom of her parents, who have always been very helpful in her efforts in researching and teaching American sport history. David K. Wiggins would like to thank his wife Brenda, sons Jordan and Spencer, and daughter-in-law Courtney for their continued support and encouragement. The copyediting has been skillfully headed by Lisa McCoy, who demonstrated her proficiency to improve the book.

Co-editors David K. Wiggins and Gerald R. Gems put in numerous hours editing, revising, and mentoring to make the book a better product. The academic insight and sound advice of the co-editors in innumerable discussions has yielded an enhanced publication. Both of them thoroughly enjoyed contributing to this project and are appreciative of having the opportunity to contribute to the body of knowledge in American sport history.

The co-editors are grateful for the important contributions of the authors, a community of outstanding and productive and talented scholars in sport history, who have written chapters that provide crucial insights on various topics in the history of American sport. Ultimately, the authors have helped to produce a collaborative project yielding essential content and interpretations about sport in American history. We are deeply appreciative of the spirit of community in which authors shared their expertise for *The Routledge History of American Sport*.

Linda J. Borish
David K. Wiggins
Gerald R. Gems

INTRODUCTION

Linda J. Borish, David K. Wiggins, and Gerald R. Gems

The Routledge History of American Sport provides a comprehensive approach to historical research in American sport from the early Colonial period to the present day through an analysis of particular themes and topics. Most monographs, survey texts, and some encyclopedias of American sport history utilize a traditional chronological framework that yields valuable information, yet underexplore newer themes in American sport history. Although certain groups of people may be included in such historical studies of American sport, a chronological format and emphasis on specific sports like baseball, football, boxing, and basketball seemingly provides limited coverage of minorities and women in gender, race, and ethnic perspectives. The increasing importance of American sport history for scholars, teachers, and an enthusiastic public makes *The Routledge History of American Sport* a critical addition to the historical literature. American sport history, a significant part of American history since the 1970s and taught in many colleges and universities in the United States and globally, offers a rich area for highlighting new and provocative essays on this topic. This volume contributes to the field with a collection of critical essays by a diverse group of outstanding scholars, analyzing significant topics comprising the field of American sport history with an emphasis on integrating gender, race, ethnicity, religion, and social class. In large measure, this book will add to the impressive list of Routledge Handbooks of History.

The Routledge History of American Sport provides the first volume in the Routledge Handbooks of History listings on sport, and a need exists for such a book. No book like this has been developed yet with such a thematic scholarly focus on substantial topics in the field, drawing on primary and secondary resources in chapters on America's sporting past. *The Routledge History of American Sport* is intended to be an essential reference work for scholars and researchers, as well as advanced undergraduate and graduate students interested in the exciting field of sport in American history. This volume provides greater insight into the ways in which sport illuminates other components of American culture.

The Routledge History of American Sport includes 33 chapters organized thematically and topically in eight sections. Each chapter includes historiographical and primary source interpretations to portray valuable historical material on American sport. Taken together, these chapters yield deep insight into the history of American sport. The last section of the book also includes a list of Suggested Further Readings, offering valuable historical resources for those seeking additional knowledge about the topics addressed by the authors of each chapter.

Part I, "Introduction to American Sport History: Perspectives and Prospects," includes three chapters that examine the importance of American sport history as a disciplinary field of study. The chapters analyze the historiographical trends and significant new areas of research and address aspects of teaching, therefore identifying sport history as an important component of American history.

Part II, "Sport and Education," includes four chapters that critically examine the intersections of sport and education at various levels of competition among both men and women. The authors in this section discuss the role of sport in educational settings and the values as well as scandals linked with sport in educational contexts. The section investigates the Progressive Era, growth in organized sport, youth sports, interscholastic sports, and intercollegiate sport.

Part III, "Race, Ethnicity, American Sport, and Identity," includes eight chapters with the authors of each chapter exploring the intersections among race, ethnicity, and American sport and how diverse groups of men and women have shaped American sporting experiences. Particular attention is paid to religion and social class and how these factors influenced the development and pattern of sport among various ethnic and racial groups in the American past. Beginning with the sporting experiences of Native Americans, the chapters in this section address the experiences of African Americans, Latino Americans, Irish Americans, German Americans, Italian Americans, American Jews, and Asian Americans.

Part IV, "Gender and American Sport," includes four chapters that explore the gendered sporting practices of women and men and how gender is a critical factor in the American sporting experience over time. The chapters in this section address the impact of Title IX and the role of sport and sexuality in American culture.

Part V, "The Business of Sport," includes five chapters that investigate the interplay between business and various forms of sport in American society. In particular, these chapters examine the business of sport and how commercial interests have always influenced what people have played and how sport has been structured and promoted. The authors discuss both the interconnection between business and sport and how this relationship has changed over time. Such topics as the media and television, the role of entrepreneurs and baseball unions, the growth of professional sport, and the cultural development of sport films and sport tourism provide a thoughtful look at the business of sport in American life.

Part VI, "Material Culture and Sport," includes three chapters that examine the physical body, sporting places, technology, and contested sites of sport in American culture. The chapters analyze artifacts and spaces of sport, as well as ways the human body has been altered in sport at times with various technological elements, some legal some illegal. In large part, these chapters analyze the ways artifacts, the body, and the built environment have influenced American sporting practices. The themes covered include social class, gender, technology, and cultural spaces.

Part VII, "Social Movements and Political Uses of Sport," includes three chapters that explore the symbiotic as well as contested relationships between sport and politics. The focus of this section centers on sport and politics in the context of the Olympic Games, military sport, the Cold War, and international relations. These chapters show the political meanings of sport in diverse contexts.

Part VIII, the concluding section of the book titled, "Facets of Sport in Recent American Culture," consists of three chapters that delve into some critical issues in the history of American sport and important changes and recent innovations that have affected sport both nationally and internationally. Among the topics covered are alternative and extreme sports, radicals and critics of sport, and globalization. The totality of the chapters in *The Routledge History of American Sport* provide a truly thought-provoking examination of the rich field of the history of American sport from various historical approaches. The co-editors anticipate that the chapters in this volume will bring additional discussion to the stimulating study of sport in American history.

Part I

INTRODUCTION TO AMERICAN SPORT HISTORY

Perspectives and Prospects

1

THEORY AND METHOD IN AMERICAN SPORT HISTORY

John Soares

Introduction

In a 1983 historiographical essay, Melvin Adelman recalled writing a decade earlier about "scholarly developments in American sport history." In Adelman's recollection, writing that earlier essay had been "interesting but not . . . arduous" because at the time, "the number of scholarly works on this subject was quite limited." In the intervening decade, Adelman had observed a "tremendous explosion in the number of studies on sport from different disciplinary perspectives." Adelman celebrated this development as "one of many indicators of the progress made in the study of American sport history."[1]

This increase in scholarship on American sport history has only gained momentum in the years since. By 1997 American sport history had advanced to the point where S.W. Pope edited a volume with contributions from a number of established scholars in the field entitled *The New American Sport History*.[2] Sport historians have long had their own organization, the North American Society for Sport History (NASSH), and its publishing outlet, the *Journal of Sport History*. Historians of American sport have published in other academic journals, sport-related publications like *The International Journal of the History of Sport* and *Sport History Review*, and journals of other specialized subfields, including *The Journal of the Gilded Age and Progressive Era*, *The Journal of Urban History*, *Diplomatic History*, and *Rethinking History: The Journal of Theory and Practice*, among others. Scholars working on American sport have published monographs with some of the most respected academic publishers, including the Oxford University and Harvard University presses.

In producing this body of work, historians of American sport have developed varied intellectual approaches that have been influenced by, and influenced, scholarship in such varied historical subfields as social, cultural, intellectual, economic, political, urban, ethnic, Western, African American, and diplomatic history. Numerous authors and works illustrate this: Donald Mrozek's work on Native American games has shaped our understanding of the American West.[3] Influential works by Adelman, Stephen Hardy, and Steven Riess illuminate connections between sport and the development of American cities.[4] A number of scholars have examined the links between sport and race, religion, or ethnicity. Examples of this include the prize-winning scholarship of Samuel Regalado on Latinos.[5] The work of such scholars as Jules Tygiel, David Wiggins, Michael Lomax, and Charles Martin has explored the connections between race and sport in the case of African Americans.[6] John Bloom has done important work on sport and Native Americans.[7] Sport historians have examined the influence of sport on approaches to gender, such as in Gerald Early's placing of sport and race in the context of cultural constructions of African American masculinity.[8] Many historians, including Susan Cahn, Martha Verbrugge, Jaime Schultz, and Susan Ware, have looked at women, gender, and sport.[9]

Specific sports, too, have come in for close examination. Scholars writing on baseball form a Who's Who in American history; Michael Oriard has written extensively on football, and Elliott Gorn and Gerald Gems have looked at boxing.[10] The Olympics, and American participation in them, have drawn coverage from scholars like Allen Guttmann and Mark Dyreson.[11] Historians dealing with sport have examined U.S. connections with the world; Thomas Zeiler and Gems have published on sport and American imperialism, and Sayuri Guthrie Shimizu on sport and U.S.-Japanese relations.[12] Historians also have examined more specialized topics, like David Zang's work on sports "in the age of Aquarius," Andrew Zimbalist on the economics of professional sport, or Robert Trumpbour on municipal funding of sports stadiums.[13]

The varied intellectual backgrounds of sport historians contribute to the richness of this work. A number of sport historians have been trained in or held faculty appointments in departments outside history, including health and physical education, English, and economics. In fact, some key contributions to sport history have been made by historians who might not even classify themselves as historians of sport.

This wealth of scholarship has spawned a number of theoretical and methodological approaches. The purpose of this essay is to consider some of the most influential of these, offer some illustrative examples, and consider some of the sources and methods historians have used to inform sport history. It is not, and does not claim to be, an exhaustive historiographical treatment of the large and growing body of sport history literature. In some of the most significant theoretical developments, sport historians have wrestled with questions about modernization, social control, the ideology of American sport, and sport as a means of inclusion or exclusion. Sport historians dealing with social control theory have been influenced by Marxist and neo-Marxist arguments. Ideologically, sport historians have speculated as to whether the United States should be considered a "sporting republic" with an ideology of sport. Sport historians also have explored American sport in comparative perspective, embracing "international" and "transnational" approaches. In much writing, sport historians have wrestled with questions of race, class, and gender that also have occupied colleagues in other areas of history. In rendering their varied interpretations, sport historians have often done work that is conceptually synthetic, even while engaged in primary-source research and the production of monographic treatments of topics.

Theory in American Sport History

Modernization has offered an important theoretical approach to sport history, typically without any Whiggish interpretation that modernization invariably means moral progress. Allen Guttmann argued that sport developed distinctive characteristics, which distinguished it from the sports of classical antiquity and from other premodern games and pastimes. Mel Adelman emphasized sport's progression from informally organized games played under loose rules, with local competition and limited public information or record keeping, to modern sport, defined by formal sports played under standardized rules with national (or international) competition, and the development of specialization within both the sports themselves and the communications media that report on them.[14] In challenging this emphasis on modernity,

Donald Mrozek specifically focused on the enduring significance of Native American games and rituals.[15]

Sport historians covering a clearly modern period, most notably those writing about the Progressive Era, have wrestled with the question of whether sport has served chiefly as a form of social control or social uplift. Proponents of social control theory, influenced by Robert Wiebe's classic *The Search for Order*, have emphasized the role of sport for political, economic, and social elites in the late nineteenth century, as these elites attempted to deal with the consequences of dramatic technological growth, concentrations of economic power, the influx of immigrants, and a growing industrial working class and the possibilities that all of this threatened a revolutionary transformation of American society.[16] Sport could serve as an avenue by which the wealthy and politically powerful asserted and maintained control over working classes. Many industrial workers were immigrants from European autocracies, often Catholics or Jews, whose fitness for citizenship in a democratic society was frequently doubted by native-born Protestants. Sport could promote the separation of the wealthy from the masses through activities like golf and yachting that were too expensive or required specialized facilities available only to the wealthy through private clubs. Working-class sport also could contribute to social control by "educating" workers to respect various forms of authority, with obedience to the rules on the playing field and their enforcement by referees being analogous to respect for workplace rules and the authority of company officials.[17]

Although sport might control workers by separating and limiting them, sport also could be a means of uplift. Well-intentioned reformers used sport to promote working-class health and well-being. Sport also could serve, like programs of the Settlement House movement, as a way to promote the assimilation and "Americanness" of immigrants—and to encourage them to abandon the ways of the old country. Influential scholars, though, have found the dichotomy between social control and social uplift too limiting. Roy Rosenzweig, for example, in his study of public parks in Worcester, Massachusetts, explicitly rejected the idea that "inert and totally pliable . . . workers uncritically accepted the park programs handed down by an omnipotent ruling class."[18] Rather than serving as a form of uplift or control, then, sport could be a site of negotiation and contestation among classes, interests, and stakeholders.

As this engagement with social control theory suggests, sport historians have been concerned about the exercise of power and hegemony in sport. Marxist theory posits that working-class sports are designed to keep the labor force fit and productive, and provide some recompense for work that became increasingly tedious as the United States grew more industrialized. In the process, according to Marxist theory, sport contributes to the repression by ruling circles of workers as well as women, African Americans, and other groups. Modern American sport, in this telling, is also a means by which elites also promote "militarism, nationalism and imperialism."[19]

Critiques of sport's role in perpetuating class divisions and elite control are buttressed by elites' obvious establishment of rules of amateurism to exclude workers and by the elites' hypocrisies in applying those rules. Expense and the necessary access to facilities for golf, tennis, yachting, and equestrian sports would keep the working class out of many upper-class pastimes, but rules governing amateurism could exclude workers even from economically affordable sports like track and field.[20] Early intercollegiate sport took shape at elite, exclusive universities like Harvard, Yale, and Princeton. Class exclusivity was necessarily part of its development. Professional baseball, too, fit into a paradigm of elite control and exploitation. The National Association of Base Ball Players, established in 1858, was supplanted by the National League of Professional Base Ball Clubs in 1876. The shift from organization by players to organization by clubs indicated the growing power of owners in the sport. Owners used their power to defeat players' early efforts to organize and imposed the reserve clause that effectively bound each player to an individual club as long as the club wished to keep him; the reserve clause remained in force until the mid-1970s. In the late 1800s, Albert Spalding sought to establish himself as a sporting goods baron in an age of "robber barons."[21] All of these developments connect sport to larger trends in economic, labor, and political history in the late nineteenth century, an era marked by growing concentrations of wealth and economic and political power, the difficulties labor and farmers faced in trying to improve their situation, and American elites' increasing appetite for participation in the imperial ventures of the European powers in Asia.

Further linkage between sport and power was evident in late nineteenth- and early twentieth-century concerns about the softening of American youth, especially upper-class youth. They had no toughening test like the Civil War and were seen as coddled by the comfortable life of elites in a prosperous industrialized society. Mark Dyreson identified an additional worry among late nineteenth- and early twentieth-century Americans: that "modernization threatened the commonweal on which the republican experiment depended" and that the nation's future as a republic might be in jeopardy. For Americans worried about declining toughness or the loss of community and common purpose, sport could serve as a unifying force. Dyreson argued that late nineteenth-century Americans created a "sporting republic" and that "Sport and the political philosophy of republicanism have been directly connected." Leaders consciously used sport as a "social technology" to shape the nation, build community, and promote honesty and good citizenship. Dyreson focused on U.S. Olympic teams, but late nineteenth- and early twentieth-century Americans found other ways to use sport for national purposes. College football and an emphasis on amateur boxing fit in with efforts by the likes of Theodore Roosevelt to encourage "manly" men who would play hard but by the rules—in sport, as in life.[22] This concern about the toughness of American men would be a recurrent source of concern into the twentieth century and especially during the Cold War years.[23]

Sport, then, could contribute to elite control and toughen upper-class men for the rigors of national (and world) leadership. In an open, democratic society, it also could be part of an American ideology of sport that promoted inclusiveness and opportunity. Inclusiveness and opportunity, of course, were quite the opposite of the experiences with sport by many people outside of the mostly white, male, Protestant upper classes. Just as racial segregation was imposed by law, owners and other leaders in sport developed various "gentlemen's agreements" that precluded African Americans from participating in many sports, no matter how qualified. These agreements resulted in the exclusion of African Americans who had once participated in the early days of their professional sport, like Moses Fleetwood "Fleet" Walker in baseball and Fritz Pollard in football.[24] Because individuals could play such influential roles in sport, biography has been a popular approach for many historians, including David Zang's work on Walker and John Carroll's life of Pollard.[25]

The ideology of sport could promote inclusion, but even when it did historians had to wrestle with the complexity and ambiguity of that process. An illustrative example of this involved the 1951 basketball team at Crispus Attucks High School in Indianapolis. A segregated, African American school in a northern city, previously prohibited from playing in the state tournament even though individual African American athletes from integrated schools could compete, Attucks was finally allowed into the state tournament. The team advanced to the state semifinals, winning support from white Indianapolis residents. Yet Attucks' chances for a state championship that year were undone largely by the team's employment of a slow-paced, more polite style of play, specifically to win approval from white Hoosiers. In later years, though, Attucks would return. Playing a more aggressive, up-tempo style and featuring future pro superstar Oscar Robertson, Attucks won multiple state titles.[26]

The development of baseball's Negro Leagues and intercollegiate football and basketball teams at historically black colleges and universities (HBCUs), were powerful testimony to sport's appeal across artificially created boundaries. When white coaches, managers, and owners became willing to seek victory over racial purity, the Negro Leagues and HBCUs had produced numbers of athletes who could more than hold their own with the best white professionals. Championships won by the Cleveland Browns in football, Brooklyn Dodgers in baseball, and Boston Celtics and University of San Francisco in basketball demonstrated the possibilities for teams willing to integrate. By the 1960s, Grambling State University, an HBCU, had more alumni playing in the National Football League (NFL) than any other university except Notre Dame.[27] Some white Southerners began to waver in their support of segregation when continuation of the practice threatened to reduce Southern universities to isolated backwaters in college football. As one Louisiana State University (LSU) fan put it, "I'm all for racial segregation unless it interferes with something important[,] like football."[28]

The possibility of sport to promote certain forms of inclusiveness, and the terms on which athletes accepted it, were not limited to African Americans. A variety of ethnic, racial, or gender groups faced these issues, and their acculturation and assimilation processes have received attention from sport history scholars. For example, Gerald Gems has described Italian immigrants and their children constructing an Italian American identity for themselves through sport.[29] Samuel Regalado has analyzed how baseball players from Latin America have made a major contribution to the development of the game in recent years, overcoming linguistic and cultural differences, and a long legacy of suspicion, condescension, and outright hostility in the process.[30] His work has fostered a wealth of new research into the Latin American experience.[31]

Small steps forward and intense resistance were part of the slow progress made in creating opportunities for women, even after Title IX committed the federal government to ending gender discrimination in higher education.[32] Proponents of greater opportunity for women in society more generally saw sports as a means to promote women's strength and fitness in a framework that could promote greater respect, while forces of resistance tried to channel women into less demanding forms of leisure that reinforced stereotypes of feminine weakness. Those trying to limit opportunities for women, sometimes including other women, often did so in the name of protecting women's health and fertility.[33] For example, Linda Borish's work on Jewish women and settlement houses showed how sport could help Jewish women carve out opportunities for themselves in an unwelcoming society, through their experiences in Jewish and non-Jewish organizations and the high-level athletic achievement of some American Jewish women in the 1920s–1930s.[34] Similarly, Julie Byrne's *O God of Players: The Story of the Immaculata Mighty Macs* is an innovative study dealing with community, competition, and the Catholic religion in women's basketball.[35]

Catholics, in fact, were one of the most notable groups for whom sport played an important role in shaping their identity and helping them win acceptance. They were long disparaged by native-born Protestants as slavish devotees of a foreign dictator whose fitness for citizenship and loyalty to the United States were, at best, problematic. As Murray Sperber has pointed out, Notre Dame football served as a vehicle that enabled Catholics to win vicarious victories over anti-Catholic segments of American society. Notre Dame football also helped convince Protestant Americans that Catholics were loyal citizens. Hollywood mythmaking about Notre Dame's legendary football coach in *Knute Rockne All-American* deployed traditional, national-unity tropes that also were part of *The Jackie Robinson Story*. In addition, publicity about the World War II combat heroics of former Notre Dame football star and assistant coach Jack Chevigny further solidified perceptions of Catholics as loyal Americans.[36]

While considering American sport, historians do not look at the United States in isolation. They increasingly embrace comparative perspectives and consider American developments in the context of other nations. For example, "football" has a very different meaning in the United States than it does in most of the rest of the world, inviting consideration of American exceptionalism. Andrei Markovits has connected America's football "exceptionalism" to its lack of a popular socialist political party.[37] A consideration of the nineteenth-century evolution of football games into Association football (soccer) and rugby undercuts perceptions of American exceptionalism. Canada and Australia also embraced their own brands of football that developed from rugby. Thus, the United States has important similarities to other former British imperial possessions that were populated (at least initially) by British settlers who (often brutally) supplanted and marginalized indigenous populations. In fact, there is much to be gained by a consideration of the United States in comparison to Canada. The two countries share a language, have similar cultures, and top professional leagues in a number of sports have teams on both sides of the border. Race and sport offer one fruitful nexus for transnational comparison with Canada. For example, Neil Longley, Todd Crosset, and Steve Jefferson found a surprising persistence of racial animus north of the border when African Americans played in the Canadian Football League, despite the fact that some cities and teams were welcoming of African American stars.[38]

Systems for talent development offer another useful avenue to take in considering American sport history in international, comparative perspective, especially given how many Americans think the U.S. system of school sports teams is an international norm. The American system of sports competition in the public schools originated logically enough in Christian reformers' efforts to promote healthy mind, body, and spirit. Robert Pruter examined early efforts to use these sports as means of promoting social order.[39] Establishment of interscholastic leagues, like the Public Schools Athletic League created in New York City by Luther Gulick, combined with the growing popularity of intercollegiate sports in the late nineteenth century, helped set in place a system in which secondary schools produced the top athletes in their age group, some of whom would graduate to intercollegiate competition. As early as the construction of Harvard Stadium (1903) and Yale Bowl (1912), colleges and universities began treating their athletics programs as lucrative entertainment enterprises. When professional football and basketball became increasingly popular after World War II, secondary schools, colleges, and universities were effectively in place to serve as talent development programs for the pros in ways that often appeared disconnected from, if not antithetical to, their primary educational missions.[40]

The international context of American sport also helps illuminate the complexity of sport and cultural ties with other nations. Canada again is instructive, especially in the case of Andrew Holman's study of "the Canadian hockey player problem" in mid-twentieth-century U.S. college hockey. Players from American high school and prep school programs were often less skilled than players from Canada's intensive system of junior leagues for teenage players. Coaches at American colleges often recruited Canadian players, leading to concern on both sides of the border: Americans worried that Canadian players were "stealing" roster spots at U.S. universities away from American boys, and Canadians worried that U.S. colleges recruiting north of the border were part of a much more pervasive pattern of American exploitation of Canada's resources.[41]

In addition to wrestling with theoretical questions about hegemony and modernization and considering American sport in an international perspective, sport historians in recent decades have wrestled with the pace of change in modern sports. Scholars like Benjamin Rader have argued that the vast expansion in money and media coverage—the growth in sport as an entertainment enterprise—has been so dramatic that the years since 1990 should be considered "a revolutionary moment."[42] Challenging that interpretation are scholars like Stephen Hardy, who argues that the changes in recent years follow from earlier professionalization and growth in owners' power and accordingly are better understood as "continued *evolution* and not revolution."[43] Also dissenting from Rader's view was Linda Borish, who conceded changes were "no doubt . . . dramatic" but that opportunities for women in sport and sport-related fields like broadcasting remain so limited that the label revolutionary does not apply.[44]

Whether wrestling with these theoretical issues or not, sport historians pursue a variety of methodological approaches, often bringing influences from other fields of history or social sciences. Although sport historians engage in primary-source research, their approach is often synthetic in a topical sense: sport historians tend to produce work that synthesizes different approaches, topics, and methodologies. For example, in analyzing the Spalding baseball world tour of 1888–1889, Thomas Zeiler combines issues of race, imperialism, economic history, and the emergence of robber barons, all in a book about baseball. In another example, Kurt Edward Kemper in *College Football and American Culture in the Cold War Era* combines social, cultural, intellectual, and sport history as he examines segregation, sectional differences (and similarities), post-Sputnik anxieties about U.S. physical and intellectual "softness," and the power of mythology about football in American life, all in a work largely focused on the selection process for the 1962 Rose Bowl. These are just two of the almost limitless examples of the kinds of syntheses produced by sport historians, using a range of sources and methodologies.

Sources and Methodology

In developing these interpretations, sport historians utilize a number of sources. Sport historians rely to a greater degree than their colleagues in some fields on newspapers and magazines. In part this stems from the open, public nature of sporting competitions: many organizers deliberately courted public attention, including media coverage, for reasons of prestige or finance. Thus, these contests were often staged in large arenas and were covered and commented upon as they happened in the communications media of the day. The development of microfilm and microfiche and the subsequent emergence of various online archives and databases like ProQuest Historical Newspapers ensure easy access to media coverage of many athletes and sporting events.

A second factor influencing sport historians' extensive use of media coverage of sport is the role of the media in shaping public understandings of the sporting events and the meaning spectators attach to them. In examining professional football, Michael Oriard has concluded that "when the subject is the NFL's public image, what actually happens is less important than what the media reports as happening. Image and brand are about perception—what we think about when we think about football."[45] This logic applies to most other sports with a significant popular following. The growing importance of money and media attention in recent sports developments has expanded the journalistic sources useful to sport historians. Oriard points out that in studying the NFL, he found that "the financial sections" of newspapers, "along with publications such as *Financial World*, *Forbes*, and *Street & Smith's SportsBusiness Journal*, have become essential reading."[46] Historians studying other leagues and other sports also recognize the connection between image and brand and the importance of business journalism as a source.

For the sport historian, then, newspaper and magazine sources offer a potentially rich vein of contemporary observation of events in question. Use of these sources, though, must be judicious. As Melvin Adelman pointed out in his study of sport in New York, sports journalists

> were not neutral observers. Their reports were colored by their reliance on the good will of sports promoters, their occasional vested interest in sports, either directly or indirectly, and because they shared the class and ethnic prejudices of their period. At times they were also given to sensational journalism, and their judgments suffered no doubt from the all-too-common problem of drawing hasty conclusions in the rush to make a deadline.[47]

Sport historians, of course, also use some of the traditional memoir and manuscript sources common to other subfields of history. Promoters, owners, coaches, leagues, and federations sometimes have particularly valuable records. So, too, politicians, policymakers, reformers, intellectuals, diplomats, and others who have dealt with sport. In researching his magisterial history of college football, John Sayle Watterson found the role of universities like Harvard and Yale in the early years of college football meant their libraries' special collections contained much material of interest to historians of intercollegiate football.[48] The LA84 Foundation, at both its website and its library in Los Angeles, serves as a valuable source of sport materials, especially on the Olympics. In the University of Notre Dame's Hesburgh Library, the Joyce Sports Collection includes a number of manuscript collections valuable to sport historians. And there are other repositories that may be of value to the enterprising scholar. For example, in her work on Jewish American women, Borish uses original resources at the Center for Jewish History and the American Jewish Historical Society. In his books on boxing and sport and Italian Americans, Gems found materials in the Chicago History Museum and among oral history materials in special collections at the University of Illinois at Chicago. He also found material in the Bishop Bernard J. Sheil papers at the Catholic Archdiocese of Chicago Archives, in addition to ethnic-specific materials in the Chicago History Museum, the Florence Roselli Library at Casa Italia, and among the holdings of the Italian American Renaissance Foundation Library in New Orleans.[49]

Government documents of various kinds also furnish useful source material for historians. In his work on sport in Boston, for example, Stephen Hardy used annually published city documents, including the aptly named City Documents and School Documents, and *Reports of the Proceedings of the City Council*. He also used reports produced annually by the state's labor statistics bureau.[50] Michael Lomax used federal census data in his work on African American baseball.[51] Riess and Gems found material from the Chicago Foreign Language Press Survey produced during the New Deal. Riess also used congressional materials from investigations of organized crime and antitrust issues.[52] Historians considering the intersection of sport and foreign policy use State Department records from the National

Archives and Records Administration and material from presidential libraries. Damion Thomas' *Globetrotting* considers the role of African American athletes in U.S. foreign policy, using documents from U.S. Information Agency files, papers of Eisenhower administration officials and committees, and the administration's central files.[53] In producing his interpretation of the 1980 U.S.-led Olympic boycott, Nicholas Evan Sarantakes mined a number of government sources at the National Archives and the Jimmy Carter Presidential Library, in addition to U.S. congressional, British Parliamentary and U.S. and British Olympic records.[54]

Conclusion

In a book published in 1998—the year after *The New American Sport History* came out—Mark Dyreson pointed out,

> Most Americans know more about sport and sports than they do about politics, science, religion or their own Constitution. . . . Still, even though sport has become the most important institution through which many Americans deliberate political, racial, ethical, and social questions, scholars too rarely take sport seriously.[55]

Three years earlier Elliott Gorn and Michael Oriard had written a *Chronicle of Higher Education* essay making the intellectual case for "Taking Sports Seriously."[56]

Sport historians, despite their accomplishments, worry about not being taken seriously by their colleagues. Although sport history was the subject of a "state of the field" essay and forum in *The Journal of American History* in 2014, many sport historians believed "overall, little movement had taken place toward the acceptance of sport history as a legitimate and important field."[57] In part this is understandable: a survey of job postings at the *Chronicle of Higher Education* or the H-Net website indicates that in most years there is not a single history department looking to fill a post with a sport historian. Even though many historians of American sport have tenured academic positions at respected colleges and universities, some practitioners in the field feel they are underappreciated because they work on sport. Yet others recognize the variety and diversity of approaches as a strength. As this chapter has attempted to show, in so many areas of American history, those who study sport have made important contributions. And as our work in recent years has demonstrated, the richness of sport history's theoretical and methodological approaches promises that it will continue to make important contributions in the future.

Notes

1 Melvin L. Adelman, "Academicians and American Athletics: A Decade of Progress," *Journal of Sport History* 10, no. 1 (1983): 80.
2 S.W. Pope, ed., *The New American Sport History: Recent Approaches and Perspectives* (Urbana: University of Illinois Press, 1997).
3 Donald J. Mrozek, "Thoughts on Indigenous Sport: Moving Beyond the Model of Modernity," *Journal of the West* 22, no. 1 (1983): 3–9.
4 Melvin L. Adelman, *A Sporting Time: New York City and the Rise of Modern Athletics, 1820–70* (Urbana: University of Illinois Press, 1986); Stephen Hardy, *How Boston Played: Sport, Recreation and Community, 1865–1915* (Boston: Northeastern University Press, 1982); and Steven A. Riess, *City Games: The Evolution of American Urban Society and the Rise of Sports* (Urbana: University of Illinois Press, 1989).

5 Samuel O. Regalado, *Viva Baseball! Latin Major Leaguers and Their Special Hunger* 3rd ed. (Urbana: University of Illinois Press, 2008).

6 For some examples of this influential scholarship, see Jules Tygiel, *Baseball's Great Experiment: Jackie Robinson and His Legacy* exp. ed. (New York: Oxford University Press, 1997); Charles H. Martin, *Benching Jim Crow: The Rise and Fall of the Color Line in Southern College Sports, 1890–1980* (Urbana: University of Illinois Press, 2010); David K. Wiggins, *Glory Bound: Black Athletes in a White America* (Syracuse: Syracuse University Press, 1997); Patrick B. Miller and David K. Wiggins, eds., *Sport and the Color Line: Black Athletes and Race Relations in Twentieth-Century America* (New York: Routledge, 2004); David K. Wiggins and Patrick B. Miller, *The Unlevel Playing Field: A Documentary History of the African-American Experience in Sport* (Urbana: University of Illinois Press, 2005); and Michael E. Lomax, *Black Baseball Entrepreneurs, 1860–1901: Operating by Any Means Necessary* (Syracuse: Syracuse University Press, 2003).

7 John Bloom, *To Show What an Indian Can Do: Sports at Native American Boarding Schools* (Minneapolis: University of Minnesota Press, 2000).

8 Gerald Early, *This Is Where I Came in: Black America in the 1960s* (Lincoln: University of Nebraska Press, 2003); and Early, *A Level Playing Field: African American Athletes and the Republic of Sports* (Cambridge: Harvard University Press, 2011).

9 See, for example, Susan K. Cahn, *Coming on Strong: Gender and Sexuality in Women's Sport* 2nd. ed. (Urbana: University of Illinois Press, 2015); Jaime Schultz, *Qualifying Times: Points of Change in U.S. Women's Sport* (Urbana: University of Illinois Press, 2014); Martha H. Verbrugge, *Active Bodies: A History of Women's Physical Education in Twentieth-Century America* (New York: Oxford University Press, 2012); Susan Ware, *Game, Set, Match: Billie Jean King and the Revolution in Women's Sports* (Chapel Hill: University of North Carolina Press, 2011); Jean O'Reilly and Susan K. Cahn, eds., *Women and Sports in the United States: A Documentary Reader* (Boston: Northeastern University Press, 2007); and Martha H. Verbrugge, *Able-Bodied Womanhood: Personal Health and Social Change in Nineteenth-Century Boston* (New York: Oxford University Press, 1988).

10 For some recent examples of Michael Oriard's extensive writings on football, see Michael Oriard, *Bowled Over: Big-Time College Football from the Sixties to the BCS Era* (Chapel Hill: University of North Carolina Press, 2009); and Michael Oriard, *Brand NFL: Making & Selling America's Favorite Sport* (Chapel Hill: University of North Carolina Press, 2007). On boxing, see Elliott J. Gorn, *The Manly Art: Bare-Knuckle Prize Fighting in America* (Ithaca: Cornell University Press, 1986); and Gerald R. Gems, *Boxing: A Concise History of the Sweet Science* (Lanham: Rowman & Littlefield, 2014).

11 Allen Guttmann, *The Olympics: A History of the Modern Games* (Urbana: University of Illinois Press, 1992); and Mark Dyreson, *Making the American Team: Sport, Culture and the Olympic Experience* (Urbana: University of Illinois Press, 1998).

12 Thomas W. Zeiler, *Ambassadors in Pinstripes: The Spalding World Baseball Tour and the Birth of the American Sport Empire* (Lanham: Rowman & Littlefield, 2006); Gerald R. Gems, *The Athletic Crusade: Sport and American Cultural Imperialism* (Lincoln: University of Nebraska Press, 2006); and Sayuri Guthrie-Shimizu, *Transpacific Field of Dreams: How Baseball Linked the United States and Japan in Peace and War* (Chapel Hill: University of North Carolina, 2012).

13 David W. Zang, *Sports Wars: Athletes in the Age of Aquarius* (Fayetteville: University of Arkansas Press, 2001); Andrew S. Zimbalist, *Baseball and Billions: A Probing Look Inside the Big Business of Our National Pastime* (New York: Basic Books, 1992); and Robert C. Trumpbour, *The New Cathedrals: Politics and Media in the History of Stadium Construction* (Syracuse: Syracuse University Press, 2007).

14 Melvin L. Adelman, "The First Modern Sport in America: Harness Racing in New York City, 1825–1870, *Journal of Sport History* 8, no. 1 (1981): 5–32.

15 Mrozek, "Thoughts on Indigenous Sport."

16 Robert H. Wiebe, *The Search for Order, 1877–1920* (New York: Hill & Wang, 1967).

17 This discussion of social control theory is shaped by a reading of Adelman, "Academicians and American Athletics."

18 Roy Rosenzweig, "Middle-Class Parks and Working Class Play: The Struggle Over Recreational Space in Worcester, Massachusetts, 1870–1910," *Radical History Review* 21 (1979): 32.

19 For a discussion of Marxist (and neo-Marxist) interpretations of sport, see Allen Guttmann, *From Ritual to Record: The Nature of Modern Sports* (New York: Columbia University Press, 1978), 59–69.

20 For the "blatant . . . class bias" of the early International Olympic Committee (IOC), see Guttmann on early Olympic officials "exempt[ing] equestrians and yachtsmen and equestrians, i.e., themselves, from the ban on valuable prizes." Guttmann, *Sports: The First Five Millennia* (Amherst: University of Massachusetts Press, 2004), 262.

21 Zeiler, *Ambassadors in Pinstripes*. Also see Peter Levine, *A.G. Spalding and the Rise of Baseball: The Promise of American Sport* (New York: Oxford University Press, 1985).

22 Dyreson, *Making the American Team*, esp. 2–18.

23 See, for example, Jeffrey Montez de Oca, " 'The Muscle Gap': Physical Education and U.S. Fears of a Depleted Masculinity, 1954–63," in *East Plays West: Sport and the Cold War*, ed. Stephen Wagg and David Andrews (London: Routledge, 2007), 123–148; and Kurt Edward Kemper, *College Football and American Culture in the Cold War Era* (Urbana: University of Illinois Press, 2009).

24 Fleet Walker played Major League Baseball in 1884; Pollard played (and coached) pro football in the 1920s.

25 David Zang, *Fleet Walker's Divided Heart: The Life of Baseball's First Black Major Leaguer* (Lincoln: University of Nebraska Press, 1995); John M. Carroll, *Fritz Pollard: Pioneer in Racial Advancement* (Urbana: University of Illinois Press, 1992). Among other recent or influential examples of sports biography are Theresa Runstedtler, *Jack Johnson, Rebel Sojourner: Boxing in the Shadow of the Global Color Line* (Berkeley: University of California Press, 2012); Randy Roberts, *Joe Louis: Hard Times Man* (New Haven: Yale University Press, 2010); Russell Sullivan, *Rocky Marciano: The Rock of His Times* (Urbana: University of Illinois Press, 2002); Mark Kurlansky, *Hank Greenberg: The Hero Who Didn't Want to Be One* (New Haven: Yale University, 2011); and Susan E. Cayleff, *Babe: The Life and Legend of Babe Didrikson Zaharias* (Urbana: University of Illinois Press, 1995).

26 Richard B. Pierce, "More Than a Game: The Political Meaning of Basketball in Indianapolis," *Journal of Urban History* 27, no. 3 (2000): 3–23.

27 "Grambling Tigers Have Reached Lofty Heights," *Chicago Daily Defender*, November 15, 1969, 34 (obtained via ProQuest Historical Newspapers).

28 Quoted in Kemper, *College Football and American Culture in the Cold War Era*, 80.

29 Gerald R. Gems, *Sport and the Shaping of Italian-American Identity* (Syracuse: Syracuse University Press, 2013).

30 See, for example, Regalado, *Viva Baseball!*

31 See, for example, Adrian Burgos, Jr., *Cuban Star: How One Negro-League Owner Changed the Face of Baseball* (New York: Hill and Wang, 2011); Adrian Burgos, Jr., *Playing America's Game: Baseball, Latinos, and the Color Line* (Berkeley: University of California Press, 2007); Jorge Iber, ed., *More Than Just Peloteros: Sport and U.S. Latino Communities* (Lubbock: Texas Tech University Press, 2014); and Jorge Iber and Samuel O. Regalado, eds., *Mexican Americans and Sports: A Reader on Athletics and Barrio Life* (College Station: Texas A&M University Press, 2007).

32 Welch Suggs, *A Place on the Team: The Triumph and Tragedy of Title IX* (Princeton: Princeton University Press, 2005); Jennifer Hargreaves, *Heroines of Sport: The Politics of Difference and Identity* (London: Routledge, 2000); Susan Ware, *Title IX: A Brief History with Documents* (Boston: Bedford/St. Martins, 2007).

33 In addition to works cited elsewhere herein, readers interested in evolving scholarship on women in sport might see Susan K. Cahn, "From the 'Muscle Moll' to the 'Butch' Ballplayer: Mannishness, Lesbianism, and Homophobia in U.S. Women's Sport," *Feminist Studies* 19, no. 2 (Summer 1993): 343–368; Martha H. Verbrugge, *Able-Bodied Womanhood: Personal Health and Social Change in Nineteenth Century Boston* (New York: Oxford University Press, 1988). For an example of an early twentieth century woman acting to hinder opportunities for women, see Gregory Kent Stanley, " '. . . And Not to Make Athletes of Them': Banning Women's Sports at the University of Kentucky, 1902–24," *Register of the Kentucky Historical Society* 93, no. 4 (1995): 422–445.

34 Linda J. Borish, "Settlement Houses to Olympic Stadiums: Jewish American Women, Sports and Social Change, 1880s–1930s," *International Sports Studies* 22, no. 1 (2000): 5–24; and Linda J. Borish, " 'Athletic Activities of Various Kinds': Physical Health and Sport Programs for Jewish

American Women," *Journal of Sport History* 26 (1999): 240–270; and Linda J. Borish, " 'An Interest in Physical Well-Being Among the Feminine Membership': Sporting Activities for Women at Young Men's and Young Women's Hebrew Associations," *American Jewish History* 87 (1999): 61–93.

35 Julie Byrne, *O God of Players: The Story of the Immaculata Mighty Macs* (New York: Columbia University Press, 2003).

36 Murray Sperber, *Shake Down The Thunder: The Creation of Notre Dame Football* (Bloomington: Indiana University Press, 2002); and Murray Sperber, *Onward to Victory: The Crises That Shaped College Sports* (New York: Henry Holt, 1998), 256–257.

37 Andrei Markovits, "The Other 'American Exceptionalism'—Why Is There No Soccer in the United States?," *Praxis International* 8, no. 2 (1988): 125–150.

38 Neil Longley, Todd Crosset, and Steve Jefferson, "The Migration of African-Americans to the Canadian Football League During the 1950s: An Escape from Racism?," *The International Journal of the History of Sport* 25, no. 10 (2008): 1374–1397.

39 Robert Pruter, *The Rise of American High School Sports and the Search For Control, 1880–1930* (Syracuse: Syracuse University Press, 2013).

40 Ronald A. Smith notes some of the early hypocrisies in big-time college sport in Smith, *Sports & Freedom: The Rise of Big-Time College Athletics* (New York: Oxford University Press, 1988). He has considered long-running efforts at reform in Smith, *Pay for Play: A History of Big-Time College Athletic Reform* (Urbana: University of Illinois Press, 2011). Murray Sperber has critiqued the connection between sports and higher education in such books as *College Sports Inc.: The Athletic Department vs. The University* (New York: Henry Holt, 1990) and *Beer and Circus: How Big-Time College Sports Is Crippling Undergraduate Education* (New York: Owl Books, 2000).

41 Andrew C. Holman, "The Canadian Hockey Player Problem: Cultural Reckoning and National Identities in American Collegiate Sport, 1947–80," *The Canadian Historical Review* 88, no. 3 (2007): 439–468.

42 Benjamin G. Rader, "A Revolutionary Moment in Recent American Sports History," *Journal of Sport History* 36, no. 3 (2009): 315.

43 Stephen Hardy, "Evolutions in American Sport," *Journal of Sport History* 36, no. 3 (2009): 345, original emphasis.

44 Linda J. Borish, "Transformations in Recent American Sport History," *Journal of Sport History* 36, no. 3 (2009): 350–351.

45 Oriard, *Brand NFL*, 6.

46 Ibid., 6.

47 Adelman, *A Sporting Time*, 369.

48 John Sayle Watterson, *College Football: History, Spectacle, Controversy* (Baltimore: Johns Hopkins University Press, 2000), 461.

49 Gems, *Boxing*; and Gems, *Sport and the Shaping of Italian-American Identity*.

50 Hardy, *How Boston Played*.

51 Lomax, *Black Baseball Entrepreneurs, 1860–1901*.

52 Riess, *City Games*.

53 Damion Thomas, *Globetrotting: African American Athletes and Cold War Politics* (Urbana: University of Illinois Press, 2012).

54 Nicholas Evan Sarantakes, *Dropping the Torch: Jimmy Carter, the Olympic Boycott and the Cold War* (Cambridge: Cambridge University Press, 2011).

55 Dyreson, *Making the American Team*, 1.

56 "Elliott J. Gorn and Michael Oriard, "Taking Sports Seriously," *Chronicle of Higher Education*, March 24, 1995. http://chronicle.com.proxy.library.nd.edu/article/Taking-Sports-Seriously/83703/

57 Amy Bass, "State of the Field: Sports History and the Cultural Turn," *The Journal of American History* 101, no. 1 (2014): 148. Also see essays in that forum by Lisa Doris Alexander, Susan Cahn, Daniel Nathan, and Randy Roberts.

2

NEW DIRECTIONS AND FUTURE CONSIDERATIONS IN AMERICAN SPORT HISTORY

Jaime Schultz

Since the turn of the twenty-first century, sport historians have published multiple historiographic commentaries. In promulgating their own ideas for new directions and future considerations, these scholars have proposed linguistic, cultural, postmodern, visual, material, literary, spatial, and affective "turns." They have contested the merits of theory, reflexivity, empiricism, inventive forms of representation, and the directions from which to view historical change. They have advocated for methodological approaches that range from quantification to deconstruction, for greater attention to new media and technology, for cross-cultural and multilingual investigations; for hybridity with other sport-focused sub-disciplines; and for the importance of ethics. There seems no lack of paths sport historians might take as they travel ahead.[1]

What also emerges in these periodic "progress reports," as S.W. Pope and John Nauright call them, is that sport historians spend a good deal of time focused on their field—looking backward, forward, and inward.[2] In doing so, they frequently, and with varying degrees of success, place ontological and epistemological orientations in contradistinction with one another. At their worst, they pit individual scholars against one another. Although Matthew L. McDowell contends that "*internal* arguments" can be read as "a sign of health, rather than weakness," in sport history these disputes have, of late, become relatively stagnant and rarely get us "beyond the stultifying dogmatism of the 'debates' (yes, sneer marks)," contends Malcolm Maclean.[3]

To my mind, these discussions too often broker in what turn out to be false dichotomies: modern and postmodern, constructionist and deconstructionist (I leave out reconstructionists—those mythical troglodytes of historical practice), social and cultural, and even empiricism and analysis. To be sure, there are considerable and political distinctions between the terms, but the ways they play out in sport history assessment discourse frequently rely on oversimplification, misidentification, the construction of "straw persons," and unnecessary and unproductive hierarchies.[4]

This is not a process in which I want to engage. Instead, my intent here is to survey the vibrancy of the field in the new millennium, identify a select number of "gaps" that deserve greater attention, and contemplate where sport history might "belong" in the future, if, indeed, sport history even exists. I take this approach because I am not comfortable prognosticating.

The new directions and future considerations of American sport history depend on where historians of American sport choose to go.[5] To that end, I have no desire to try to determine who counts as a sport historian (or historian of sport, for that matter). For the purpose of this chapter, sport historians are scholars who work to understand sport (broadly defined) in and of the past. They can be trained in any discipline, housed in a multitude of departments, reside at a variety of institutions, and work as independent scholars. Sport historians produce everything from descriptive encyclopedic accounts to densely theoretical analyses, and to exclude, for any reason, those who investigate the sporting past from this invented community of sport historians does damage to the field. The study of sport has long suffered the slings and arrows of academic snobbery, and to turn that disdain inward would only result in self-inflicted wounds. And to those scholars who, for whatever reason, dismiss the title of sport historian, I hope they will rethink that position for they would find themselves in exceedingly good company.

Bulk or Flourish?

I begin by borrowing from Nancy Struna's 1984 question on the status of the history of women in sport: Is sport history "flourishing" or is it simply "increasing in bulk"?[6] In a word, yes. It has achieved "critical mass," according to Rob Ruck, and there is safety in numbers.[7] But safety should not lead to complacency. Take Martin Johnes' 2004 calculation in which he found 12 English-language journals specific to sport history (this includes *The International Journal of the History of Sport*, which currently produces 18 issues per year). Without question, the pages of these publications contain important research, but there is another side to it: "Arguably," Johnes continues, "the existence of too many journals encourages lower standards of scholarship."[8] Bulk.

In the same regard, various university presses devote either book series or substantial attention to sport, a smattering of which includes Mercer University, Rutgers University Press, Syracuse University, Temple University, University of Arkansas, University of California, University of Illinois, University of Missouri, University of Nebraska, University of Tennessee, University of Texas, and Oxford University Press. Commercial publishers, too, such as Human Kinetics, McFarland, Routledge, and Rowman and Littlefield, continue to put out a dizzying array of sport history texts. This suggests that there is a considerable pool of scholars writing about the history of sport, as well as a sizeable market for their products. Still, as historian Paul Ward gauges, "the quality of some sport history in academic journals and edited collections is not high."[9] I imagine this is true of any (sub)discipline, but I think sport history can—it must—do better.

Unfortunately, several learned colleagues do not foresee much improvement. In 2010, Daniel A. Nathan speculated that what will happen to sport history "over the next 10 to 15 years can be articulated (perhaps too glibly) in four words: "*more of the same*."[10] Allen Tomlinson and Christopher Young assert that sport historians have "little to say in relation to wider interpretive debate or conceptual analysis. This has held back the potential of the subfield and allowed innovative and pioneering approaches to go unchallenged for too long."[11] Douglas Booth apparently agrees, for he concludes his 2005 *The Field* by arguing that for too many sport historians there is "a tendency toward conformity and a stifling of experimentation."[12] Mike Cronin's withering critique is particularly dispiriting. Empiricism, he projects, "will remain the dominant methodology of sport history," for it "survives on a self-sustaining diet of the mediocre which induces a discipline wide state of inertia."[13] If these gloomy forecasts prove accurate, sport history will not wither on the vine, but neither will it flourish.

Minding Gaps

Tony Mason once asked, "is the filling of gaps . . . merely the last refuge of the historical scoundrel?"[14] I worry that identifying these gaps may be equally opportunistic. Nevertheless, there do seem to be a quite a few unexplored, or at least underexplored, areas in the history of sport. Questions of ability and disability, for instance, must be asked more often and with greater urgency. The same is true when it comes to sexuality. Analyses of the sporting endeavors of children rarely appear in sport history publications. And although things are improving, the discipline still has a long way to go when it comes to questions of race-ethnicity and moving past what Adrian Burgos Jr. identifies as "the lingering influence that the black-white paradigm has enjoyed in shaping the popular narrative about race and sport in U.S. society."[15]

At the same time, Carlo Rotella argues that scholars should take caution not to reduce their investigations to "race, race, race." As an analytic tool, Rotella continues, " 'race, race, race' is a stepping stone, a midpoint and not an endpoint."[16] To his critique I would add that although we are three decades past pressing calls for intersectional analyses, too many sport historians still operate within a "single-axis framework."[17] Looking ahead, sport historians could also do more to go beyond crafting romantic narratives in which heroic "firsts" overcome racialized oppressions. Identifying barrier breakers and understanding the processes of breaking barriers are important projects, and they should continue, but more nuanced understandings need to consider the physical practices of racial and ethnic groups as they relate to agency, autonomy, resourcefulness, community, expression, meaning, identity, and historical change.

Sport historians might also view their subjects from different vantage points. Considering the influence of social history on the study of sport, it is no surprise that E.P. Thompson's advocacy for "history from below" continues to hold a place of prominence. Yet, Mike Huggins argues that focusing on the working class has led to "forms of inverted snobbery" to the extent that the "exploration of the complex ways in which sport developed *within* the middle classes . . . is as yet oddly neglected."[18] This is particularly true in Britain where, according to John Lowerson, sport history remains "glued to working-class experiences."[19] But Lowerson fails to mention that it is primarily working-class men on whom scholars have trained their historical lenses. The physical culture of working-class women, on both sides of the Atlantic, remains woefully understudied.

In addition to history from below and, as Huggins might put it, history at the middle, there are alternative perspectives to consider. Since at least the mid-1960s anthropologists have promoted the concept of "studying up." In 1974, for example, Laura Nader asked, "What if, in reinventing anthropology, anthropologists were to study the colonizers rather than the colonized, the culture of power rather than the culture of the powerless, the culture of affluence rather than the culture of poverty."[20] Sport historians have certainly explored similar dynamics but could expand this line of thinking into deconstructing whiteness, as just one possibility. They could follow the path of sociologist Michael A. Messner, who in 1996 proposed "studying 'up' in the power structure." In particular, Messner took on the topic of heterosexuality in sport "not to reify it, but rather to expose its constructedness, its internal differentiation and contradiction."[21] And for Colin Howell, directionality comes from multiple angles, including "from the margins—sideways, downwards, and upwards," all of which "helps to expose the fissured categories of class, gender, race, and ethnicity and challenges the often unexamined assumptions embedded in nationalist history."[22]

Nationalist history is another topic that warrants mention because, for the most part, sport historians remain tethered to the nation-state paradigm. This attention has been uneven. As Wray Vamplew noted in 2013, "The *Journal of Sport History*, which is the official outlet for NASSH [the North American Society for Sport History], has yet to publish an article on Mexico, and all comparative work were restricted to the United States and Canada." In pointing out sport history's shortcomings, Vamplew calls for more "intracontinal" research.[23]

Others promote the importance of looking across continental and national boundaries. British sport historians have done extensive work on questions of sport and empire, but, as Steven W. Pope observes, "the topic has been virtually out of bounds for their American counterparts." Instead, he argues, they "have been seduced by the interpretive talisman that is *American exceptionalism.*"[24] Although scholars such as Mark Dyreson, Barbara Keys, and Gerald Gems have forged impressive inroads when it comes to sport and imperialism, Pope makes a persuasive case for more work in this area.[25]

In fact, multiple historians, including Lynn Hunt, recommend a "transnational turn" within the cognate discipline.

> Like other innovative approaches before it, transnational history promises to offer not just fresh perspectives on the past but truer accounts of it: it puts Africa and Asia back into the study of African and Asian Americans, the influence of competing empires back into the history of the early United States, the colonized back into the study of imperialism, diasporic peoples back into the study of trade networks, and so on. It also offers a way to make sense of globalization, whether by contesting the notion or breaking it down into manageable components.[26]

What would a transnational sport history look like if scholars took into account "the study of discontinuities in the experiences of, and displacements of location in, the lives of their subjects as a result of migration, exile, war, and the like"?[27]

Theoretical insights will help with many of these issues, but theory has produced undue anxiety within the ranks of sport history (and, it seems, history in general). I suspect that skeptics see theory as inductive—as something that prescribes a certain way of looking at the evidence as opposed to a more deductive process of sifting through it. There are cynics who perceive theory as presentist, as reductive, as tantamount to jargon spewing and name dropping, as a descent into discourse or a portal to nihilism. But sports studies scholars John Horne, Alan Tomlinson, Garry Whannel, and Kath Woodward warn that "history without adequate conceptualisation or theorisation can be little more than a form of antiquarianism—an important retrieval of the past, but decontextualised, an academic and anodyne version of the heritage industry."[28]

In recent years, the push for theory aligns with agitation surrounding the various "turns" identified, often problematically and without distinction, as postmodern, poststructural, cultural, and linguistic, the last of which, according to Joan Wallach Scott, has become "a stand-in for theory more broadly."[29] The linguistic turn, writes Sylvia Schafer, "clearly discomfited a large number of historians, especially historians whose commitment to materialist explanations of the past remained in the wake of a more general turn away from Marxism."[30] Thus, many express relief that the linguistic turn is "over," that it has "run its course," and has been "relegated to a niche in history's crypt."[31] In this line of thinking, Schafer continues,

"Poststructuralist theory, and by implication, the critical feminist theory with which it shares certain questions, belongs in the past because historians are moving on to new and newly important subject matter." But Schafer rightly worries if "this slippage between the theoretical and the topical underscores the discipline's now naturalized valorization of *the new* for its own sake." Moreover, taking off in hot pursuit of the latest "gap" to fill should not preclude "asking hard but still important epistemological questions about writing, difference, and the archive."[32] It is a mistake to think of a conceptual, philosophical, and political engagement with theory as something from which to turn away when the next turn comes.

There is no shortage of ways in which sport history might grow, topically, epistemologically, or otherwise. A faction of scholars will always produce internal, even insular, histories of sport. Others will offer richly contextualized accounts that situate sport within broader historical frameworks. If sport history is to prosper, however, scholars must go beyond situating sport as a practice influenced by its milieu—"as something *reflecting* or *illustrating* other historical processes," writes Jeffrey Hill (original emphasis). It is imperative that historians view sport as "something capable of exerting social and cultural influence; of being a process, a language, a system of meaning through which we know the world."[33] This applies to both sport and its historical study, for as Howell asks, "if history does not have emancipatory potential then what is its value?"[34] Hill provides an answer: "if the study of sport and leisure is not 'political' in the broadest sense of the term, then it isn't worth a damn."[35]

A Sense of Belonging

Genealogically speaking, sport history is a hybrid discipline, begat in the late 1960s from the uneasy coupling of physical education and history. Over time, scholars from a range of specialisms have grafted their own branches to that emergent family tree, contributing a great deal to its health and prolificacy. North American sport historians are certainly not bound by membership in the North American Society for Sport History, but a quick look at those who belong to the organization shows a range of disciplinary affiliations. In 2014 there were 388 individual NASSH members; Internet searches revealed the departmental homes of 320. Among them, 136 members (42.5 percent) held employment in physical education, kinesiology, sport studies, and similarly titled fields (e.g., human kinetics, sport management, exercise science, human development). An additional 101 affiliates (31.5 percent) came from history departments. Rounding out the top three were 25 members from American Studies or Canadian Studies departments, who constituted 8 percent of the total (see Table 2.1).[36]

Out of curiosity, I applied the same identification system to winners of the annual NASSH book award, meant to represent the best "research and writing in the field of sports history."[37] Of those who won the award for best monograph (including co-authors), 44 percent came from history, 22 percent from kinesiology (or other programs of its ilk), 11 percent from American Studies, and 11 percent were independent scholars (see Table 2.2). I want to be careful about reading too much into the data—about assuming which disciplines produce the "best" sport history, but the numbers are unavoidably suggestive. What I think is more interesting is that many of the winners were not or are not members of NASSH and that NASSH members do not win similar awards from organizations outside of sport history.

The historical study of sport itself is not at issue here. Sport "hardly needs to prove its credentials as a valid, profitable and necessary object of serious historical study," contend Kay Schiller and Christopher Young (who, as co-authors, won the NASSH book award in 2011).[38]

Table 2.1 There were 388 NASSH members in 2014. This chart only includes those 320 members whose departmental homes could be identified by Internet search.

Departmental Home of NASSH Members, 2014	*Number*
Physical Education, Kinesiology, Human Kinetics, Sport Studies, Sport Science, etc.	136
History	101
American and Canadian Studies	25
Communications	7
Library, Archives, Historical Society	7
Education	6
Independent Scholar	5
English	2
Film Studies	2
African American and Latin American Studies	2
Other Departments (Administration and Development, Anatomy, Business, Engineering, French, High School, Preparatory School, Physical Therapy, Sociology, etc.)	27

Table 2.2 NASSH has granted 26 awards during this time (no award given in 1998; co-winners in 2006). The chart includes authors who have won more than one award, co-authors, and authors with more than one departmental home. A complete list of winners can be found at www.nassh.org/NASSH/content/awards.

Departmental Home NASSH Monograph Award Winners, 1989–2014	*Number*
History	12
Kinesiology	6
Independent Scholar	3
American Studies	3
English	1
Dutch and German	1
Preparatory School	1

As Paul Ward writes, "To ignore it, or to be academically snobbish about its study, leaves a tremendous gap in our understanding of how many people have filled their time and thoughts."[39] (Most) historians no longer consider sport the intellectual equivalent of athlete's foot, the jock itch of academe. It is therefore important to distinguish between attitudes toward *sport* and attitudes toward *sport history*, which according to Tony Collins, has yet to gain "a place at the top table of history."[40]

How many sport historians have submitted an essay to a journal devoted to mainstream history, or even multidisciplinary outlets, only to be rejected with the recommendation that they "consider a sport-specific journal"? Too many, I suspect.[41] The response suggests at least three critiques: 1) work done in sport history is of insufficient quality to merit publication in mainstream journals; 2) editors of mainstream journals view sport history publications as outlets for sub-par work; and 3) sport history is still a marginalized subdiscipline of little interest or value to broader parent disciplines. None of those answers, or combination thereof, are pleasant to entertain.

In response, a handful of scholars propose that sport history should be absorbed into the broader historical discipline, rather than letting it stand alone and insecure as a subfield—seemingly more "shanty town" than the usual "ghetto" metaphor. "One of the first and arguably most important ways to expand the field and avoid isolation," argues Lisa Doris Alexander, "is to integrate sports history into a general history curriculum."[42] Amy Bass similarly asks "should sports history seamlessly evolve and thus disappear into the concentrations of cultural, diplomatic, and social history?" Her answer seems to lean toward yes, but with an interesting twist, for she concludes that sport history "does not need the broader field, nor its approval, as much as the broader field might need it." This turns the conversation on its head, I think, but it still locates sport history within history proper.

Not all historians are comfortable with this location. Writing in 1999, Stephen Hardy expressed

> concerns over the increasing refrains about sports history *really* being a subfield of social and cultural history. Nothing should be further from the truth. If sports history—at least in its academic form—is to thrive and have a future, it must have a space of its own.

Hardy is emphatic: "Sports history must be its own field, with (at the least) its own set of questions. It may draw upon models and methods from other fields, but it should not simply be a test site for 'weightier' questions."[43]

But if sport history is to remain "its own field," as Hardy protests, within which academic discipline should sport historians feather their nests? If they are to be among other sport- or body-minded colleagues, then there are some challenges to consider. As Nancy Struna asked in 1997, "whither sport historians, and sport history, in departments of exercise/sport science or kinesiology?" She continues:

> Even now the number of practicing sport historians has diminished. Many scholars who contributed to the field in the 1970s and 1980s have retired, and more will follow shortly. Only a few of these people are being replaced, as departments choose either to abandon sport history or to assign other faculty to teach history courses who have little or no preparation in history.[44]

In fact, Struna, once in Kinesiology at the University of Maryland, left for the seemingly greener pastures of American Studies. Maryland's Kinesiology Department does not currently boast a specialist in sport history, though the current program does not preclude its study. Even so, Struna's assessment seems even more relevant today than it was almost two decades ago.

There are comparable stories at other institutions. Ohio State University has essentially dissolved its Sport Humanities Department—a place that employed and produced some of the best sport historians in the field. The same is true at the University of Iowa, where the once vibrant Health and Sport Studies Department now operates within American Studies. This is not necessarily a bad thing. Professors and graduate students there will continue to generate excellent studies about the sporting past, but, still, there is something lost. Throughout North America there remain assorted sport-focused graduate programs, but those specific to sport history are few and far between.

Even in supportive, inclusive departments oriented to the multidisciplinary study of physical activity, historians may feel as though their work is neither respected nor valued. The formula the National Academy of Kinesiology (NAK) uses to rank its graduate programs is illustrative. Journal publications account for 20 percent of faculty productivity; books account for just 5 percent, so do presentations.[45] The message is clear: a book, the coin of the realm in historical research, is weighted the same as a conference presentation. It is worth one-quarter as much as a journal article.

The demoralizing calculus may have grim consequences. In both overt and subtle ways, administrators encourage sport historians to publish more articles in peer-reviewed journals at the expense of producing books and, possibly, at the quality of their scholarship. Pascal Delheye writes that at his own institution, Katholieke Universiteit Leuven in Belgium, publishing in journals without impact factors (such as *The Journal of Sport History*) or contributing chapters to edited books "is advised against (because, in economic terms, it is an opportunity cost)."[46] It is no different in the United States. A department looking to improve its NAK ranking may not hire sport historians; biological, physical, and social scientists tend to churn out journal articles with greater frequency. Even more, scientifically oriented researchers are more likely to secure funding, which, incidentally, accounts for 26 percent of faculty evaluation in the NAK ranking.

Canadian sport history seems to be in similar straits. Educational reform in Québec, for example, spelled the end of many history courses in programs of physical education.[47] Fred Mason explains that The Canadian Council of University Physical Education and Physical Educators, which certifies undergraduate kinesiology programs, requires a minimum of two courses in the "social science and/or humanities area." It requires six courses in scientific disciplines and four with laboratory components.[48] This imbalance is indicative of the increasing scientization and biomedicalization of these departments and the subsequent devaluation of the humanities.

It bears mention that although studying history in a department of something akin to "sport studies" elicits frustration, it also offers tremendous benefits. Martin Polley notes the "fascinating interplay" that comes from working within a multidisciplinary field focused on similar objects of study.[49] But multidisciplinarity and even cross-disciplinarity falls short, argues Diane L. Gill: "*Inter*-disciplinary implies actual connections among subareas, and an interdisciplinary kinesiology that integrates subdisciplinary knowledge is essential."[50] Ideally, as David L. Andrews asserts, kinesiology "requires a complementary synthesis of epistemologies if it is to realize its diverse and multifaceted empirical project."[51]

Patricia Vertinsky leads the ranks of those who advocate for integrative research. Importantly, she writes, sport historians have much to contribute to scientific understandings of the body:

> They can illustrate how scientific discourse and common sense have tended to combine to naturalize the truth about the body such that its historical context and its significance in the constitution of human relationships have been obscured. They can help scientists understand that while the bodies they study appear natural—a biological entity—they have also been constituted in particular ways in response to social and cultural arrangements and beliefs.[52]

It is not enough to pronounce the many ways in which history can benefit kinesiology's scientific and social scientific epistemes, however. As Douglas Hochstetler advises, while "it could be argued that scientists could learn from the humanities, the situation cuts both ways."[53] In these situations, it is incumbent upon historians to understand the work of their scientific colleagues. Kinesiology departments, as locations that can house and, ideally, assimilate academia's "three cultures" (natural sciences, social sciences, and humanities), may well provide a model for higher education.[54] A more pragmatic approach to filling "gaps" may be to find ways that will increase history's currency within departments of kinesiology. Sport historians may therefore have to take (may *want* to take), as I have argued elsewhere, a kinesiological turn.[55]

When this happens, then, what does the *sport* in sport history come to mean? For many of its disciples, sport has always been an expansive term that encompasses a variety of corporeal practices. To exert "greater definitional rigor" with regard to *sport*, as Guttmann argues (as "non-utilitarian physical contests," or John Loy's "institutionalized games" or David Sansone's, "ritual sacrifice of physical energy," or what Peter Donnelly calls "prolympic" sport) is to simultaneously discount the physical activities of too many groups and individuals.[56] Feminist scholars, critical race theorists, and anthropologists, in particular, have noted the ways in which sport is an exclusionary term.[57] Consequently, Roberta Park considers "sport history to be a category term that includes, at least, agonistic athletics, vigorous recreational pursuits and physical education, and intersects with aspects of medicine, biology, social reform and a host of other topics."[58]

Other scholars have proposed alternative phrasing. Jennifer Hargreaves and Patricia Vertinsky suggest a (re)turn to "physical culture," which they define as "those activities where the body itself—its anatomy, its physicality, and importantly its forms of movement—is the very purpose, the raison d'être, of the activity."[59] It is a proposal that seems to be gaining traction. Tempering Alan Ingham's sponsorship of a department of physical culture as a possible solution to kinesiology's "tribal warfare," Andrews advocates for "Physical Cultural Studies."[60] In "a *sea of empty signifiers*," he writes, "*sport* is arguably one of the most-highly contested and least useful nouns with which to frame an area of study."[61]

For these and other reasons, Colin Tatz has insisted that "sports history really needs a new name, or a recasting."[62] Because sport historians concern themselves with more than sport, as traditionally defined, should they change the name of the field? Should the name remain but be marked with an asterisk to indicate its porous borders? Or should sport history shore up those borders to maintain its distinctiveness? Vanessa Heggie, who identifies as a historian of medicine, wonders at the lack of debate about such a fundamental issue. It is easy to see the distress any name change or debates to that effect would provoke, but, as Heggie continues, "If the broadening of terms of reference seems like a loss of identity, then it is time to go back to the philosophical roots of the discipline and reconsider the meaning of sport in light of twenty-first-century scholarship; it is clearly no longer about white, male, Anglo-centric competitive games and athletics." I am not advocating for one side or another—on any of these issues—but Heggie makes a point worth considering.

Whereas Colin Tatz called for recasting of sport history as we know it, Amy Bass questions the field's very existence. In 2014 Bass organized a forum on sport history in the *Journal of American History*, marking a rare occasion in which a "mainstream" publication devoted significant space to sport. In her audaciously titled "The Last Word on the State of Sports History" she works her way to the following point: "Maybe there is no such thing as sports history." She qualifies that she is "not denying the work," but is instead "wondering if the category simply no longer works, if it ever did. The study of sports does require its own sphere of knowledge, but does it have a method and a unifying framework?"[63] I admit to a visceral reaction upon reading her words, but if sport historians are to push forward, they—we—need to engage seriously with questions of identity, coherence, and purpose. We have to ask and wrestle with the uncomfortable.

State-of-the field essays are important enterprises, but only if they eventually coax us to a better place. The problem is, as Susan Cahn identifies, "In fifteen years of vigorously debating the health of the field, there has been no dramatic change in the production or legitimacy of sports history."[64] So maybe it is time to stop assessing what has been done and get on with the exciting process of doing. Douglas Booth maintains that the "real problem for those practitioners grappling with a new model for sport history is the lack of exemplars."[65] Perhaps what the field needs at this particular moment is more history and less historiography. I am painfully aware of the hypocrisy of writing such a statement in an overtly historiographical chapter, but there are gaps to fill, directions to take, theories to engage, disciplines to disrupt, and legitimacy to be claimed if sport history is to flourish.

Notes

1 Although historiographical essays on the status of sport history appear at least as early as 1979, I am concerned here with those assessments published since 2000. Murray G., Phillips, ed., *Deconstructing Sport History: A Postmodern Analysis* (Albany, NY: SUNY Press, 2006); Douglas Booth, "Escaping the Past? The Cultural Turn and Language in Sport History," *Rethinking History: The Journal of Theory and Practice* 8, no. 1 (2004): 103–125; idem. *The Field: Truth and Fiction in Sport History* (London: Routledge, 2005), 212–221; idem, "Theory," in *Routledge Companion to Sports History*, ed. S.W. Pope and John Nauright (London: Routledge, 2010), 12–33; idem, "Politics, Ethics, Affects: Reflections on a Historiographic Turn," in *Critical Sport Histories: Paradigms, Power and the Postmodern Turn*, ed. Richard Pringle and Murray Phillips (Morgantown, WV: Fitness Information Technology, 2013); Mike Huggins, "The Sporting Gaze: Towards A Visual Turn in Sports History–Documenting Art and Sport," *Journal of Sport History* 35, no. 2 (2008): 311–329; Linda J. Borish and Murray Phillips, "Sport History as Modes of Expression: Material Culture and Cultural Spaces in Sport and History," *Rethinking History: The Journal of Theory and Practice*, 16, no. 4 (2012): 465–477; Jeffrey Hill, *Sport and the Literary Imagination: Essays in History, Literature and Sport* (New York: Peter Lang, 2006); Kath Woodward, "The Culture of Boxing: Sensation and Affect," *Sport in History* 31, no. 4 (2011): 487–503; Gary Osmond, "Photographs, Materiality and Sport History: Peter Norman and the 1968 Mexico City Black Power Salute," *Journal of Sport History* 37, no. 1 (2010): 119–137; Colin Howell and Daryl Leeworthy, "Borderlands," in *Routledge Companion to Sports History*, ed. S.W. Pope and John Nauright (London: Routledge, 2010), 71–84; Nancy L. Struna, "Reframing the Direction of Change in the History of Sport," *The International Journal of the History of Sport* 18, no. 4 (2001): 1–15; Andrew Ritchie, "Seeing the Past as the Present That It Once Was: A Response to Nancy Struna's 'Reframing the Direction of Change in the History of Sport," *The International Journal of the History of Sport* 20, no. 3 (2003): 128–152.

2 S.W. Pope and John Nauright, "Introduction," in *Routledge Companion to Sports History*, ed. S.W. Pope and John Nauright (New York: Routledge, 2010), 4.

3 Matthew L. McDowell, "Sports History: Outside of the Mainstream? A Response to Ward's 'Last Man Picked,'" *The International Journal of the History of Sport* 30, no. 1 (2013): 16, emphasis in original; Malcolm Maclean, review of Pascal Delheye (ed.) *Making Sport History: Disciplines, Identities and the Historiography of Sport* (London: Routledge, 2014), *The International Journal of the History of Sport* 32, no. 5 (2015): 728–731.

4 Allen Guttmann, "Straw Men in Imaginary Boxes," *Journal of Sport History* 32, no. 3 (2005): 395–400. See also Jaime Schultz, "Sense and Sensibility: Pragmatic Postmodernism for Sport History," in *Critical Sport Histories: Paradigms, Power and the Postmodern Turn*, ed. Richard Pringle and Murray Phillips (Morgantown, WV: Fitness Information Technology, 2013), 59–76.

5 Because this volume focuses on (North) American sport history, I primarily attend to regionally specific issues.

6 Nancy L. Struna, "Beyond Mapping Experience: The Need for Understanding in the History of American Sporting Women," *Journal of Sport History* 11, no. 1 (1984): 121.
7 Rob Ruck, "The Field of Sports History at Critical Mass, *Journal of American History* 101, no. 1 (2014): 192.
8 Martin Johnes, "Putting the History Into Sport: On Sport History and Sport Studies in the U.K.," *Journal of Sport History* 31, no. 2 (2004): 146–147. On international sport history journals, see Thierry Terret, "Finding the Path: Academic Journals in the Field of Sport History," in *Making Sport History: Disciplines, Identities and the Historiography of Sport*, ed. Pascal Delheye (London: Routledge, 2014), 134–147.
9 Paul Ward, "Last Man Picked. Do Mainstream Historians Need to Play with Sports Historians?" *The International Journal of the History of Sport* 30, no. 1 (2013): 10.
10 Daniel A. Nathan, "Asking a Fish About Water: Three Notes Toward an Understanding of 'the Cultural Turn' and Sport History," *Sporting Traditions* 27, no. 2 (2010): 39. Emphasis in original.
11 Alan Tomlinson and Christopher Young, "Sport in History: Challenging the *Communis Opinio*," *Journal of Sport History* 37, no. 1 (2010): 7.
12 Booth, *The Field*, 221.
13 Mike Cronin, "Reflections on the Cultural Paradigm," *Sporting Traditions* 27, no. 2 (2010): 6–7.
14 Quoted in Jeffrey Hill, "British Sports History: A Post-Modern Future?" *Journal of Sport History* 23, no. 1 (1996): 2.
15 Adrian Burgos, Jr., "Wait Till Next Year: Sports History and the Quest for Respect," *Journal of American History* 101, no. 1 (2014): 179.
16 Carlo Rotella, "The Stepping Stone: Larry Holmes, Gerry Cooney, and *Rocky*," in *In the Game: Race, Identity, and Sports in the Twentieth Century*, ed. Amy Bass (New York: Palgrave MacMillan, 2005), 239.
17 Kimberle, Crenshaw, "Mapping the Margins: Intersectionality, Identity Politics, and Violence against Women of Color," *Stanford Law Review* 43, no. 6 (1991): 1241–1299.
18 Mike Huggins, "Second-Class Citizens? English Middle-Class Culture and Sport, 1850–1910: A Reconsideration," *The International Journal of the History of Sport* 17, no. 1 (2000): 2, 4. Emphasis in original.
19 John Lowerson, "Opiate of the People and Stimulant for the Historian?—Some Issues in Sports History," in *Historical Controversies and Historians*, ed. William Lamont (London: Routledge, 1998), 209.
20 Laura Nader, "Up the Anthropologist: Perspectives Gained By Studying Up," in *Reinventing Anthropology*, ed. Dell Hymes (New York: Vintage, 1974), 284–311.
21 Michael A. Messner, "Studying Up On Sex," *Sociology of Sport Journal* 13, no. 3 (1996): 222–223. In response, see Judy Davidson and Debra Shogan, "What's Queer About Studying Up? A Response to Messner," *Sociology of Sport Journal* 18, no. 2 (1998): 359–366.
22 Colin Howell, "Assessing Sport History and the Cultural and Linguistic Turn," *Journal of Sport History* 34, no. 3 (2007): 461–462.
23 Wray Vamplew, "The History of Sport in the International Scenery: An Overview," *Tiempo* 17, no. 35 (2013): 12.
24 Steven W. Pope, "Rethinking Sport, Empire, and American Exceptionalism," *Sport History Review* 38, no. 2 (2007): 93. Emphasis in original.
25 Mark Dyreson, *Making the American Team: Sport, Culture, and the Olympic Experience* (Urbana: University of Illinois Press, 1998); idem. "Globalizing the Nation-Making Process: Modern Sport in World History," *The International Journal of the History of Sport* 20, no. 1 (2003): 91–106; Barbara J. Keys, *Globalizing Sport: National Rivalry and International Community in the 1930s* (Cambridge, MA: Harvard University Press, 2006); Gerald R. Gems, *The Athletic Crusade: Sport and American Cultural Imperialism* (Lincoln: University of Nebraska Press, 2006).
26 Lynn Hunt, "The Future of the Discipline: The Prospects of the Present," *Perspectives on History*, December 2012. www.historians.org/publications-and-directories/perspectives-on-history/december-2012/the-future-of-the-discipline
27 Gabrielle Spiegel, "The Task of the Historian," *American Historical Review* 114, no. 1 (2009): 1–15.
28 John Horne, Alan Tomlinson, Garry Whannel, and Kath Woodward, *Understanding Sport: A Socio-Cultural Analysis* 2nd ed. (London: Routledge, 2013), 37.

29 Joan Wallach Scott, "Wishful Thinking," *Perspectives on History*, December 2012. www.historians.org/publications-and-directories/perspectives-on-history/december-2012/the-future-of-the-discipline/wishful-thinking
30 Sylvia Schafer, "Still Turning: Language, 'Theory,' and History's Fascination with the New," Differences: A Journal of Feminist Cultural Studies 23, no. 2 (2012): 168.
31 Spiegel, "The Task of the Historian"; Michael S. Roth, "Ebb Tide," *History and Theory* 46, no. 1 (2007): 66–37; Schafer, "Still Turning," 169.
32 Schafer, "Still Turning," 170–171. Emphasis in original.
33 Jeffrey Hill, "Introduction: Sport and Politics," *Journal of Contemporary History* 38, no. 3 (2003): 361.
34 Howell, "Assessing Sport History," 461.
35 Jeffrey Hill, *Sport, Leisure, and Culture in Twentieth Century Britain* (New York: Palgrave, 2002), 187.
36 Special thanks to Andrew D. Linden for his help identifying NASSH members' departmental affiliations.
37 NASSH, "Call for Entries: 2015 NASSH Book Awards." www.nassh.org/NASSH/content/nassh-2015-book-awards-submissions-invited
38 Kay Schiller and Christopher Young, "The History and Historiography of Sport in Germany: Social, Cultural and Political Perspectives," *German History* 27, no. 3 (2009): 313. In 2015 the American Historical Society announced its "taxonomy of areas of interest," which includes "Sports" as one of its "Thematic Categories." See American Historical Society, "Proposed New Taxonomy" (no date). www.historians.org/x15216.xml
39 Ward, "Last Man Picked," 11.
40 Tony Collins, "Work, Rest and Play: Recent Trends in the History of Sport and Leisure," *Journal of Contemporary History* 43, no. 2 (2007): 398. See also Jeffrey Hill, "Introduction," 360.
41 See, for example, Burgos Jr., "Wait Till Next Year."
42 Lisa Doris Alexander, "Sports History: What's Next," *Journal of American History* 101, no. 1 (2014): 173.
43 Stephen Hardy, "Where Did You Go, Jackie Robinson? Or, the End of History and the Age of Sport Infrastructure," *Sporting Traditions* 16 (1999): 93–95.
44 Nancy L. Struna, "Sport History," in *The History of Exercise and Sport Science*, ed. John D. Massengale and Richard A. Swanson (Champaign, IL: Human Kinetics, 1997), 169.
45 There are two indices in the ranking system: Faculty (66 percent) and Student (34 percent). The NAK determines faculty evaluations by productivity, funding, and visibility (i.e., editorial boards, National Academy members, and National Fellows). Student indices include items such as GRE scores, graduate assistant support, publications, and employment in the field. See "Frequently Asked Questions—Doctoral Program Review," National Academy of Kinesiology. www.nationalacademyofkinesiology.org/frequently-asked-questions
46 Pascal Delheye, "Prologue," in *Making Sport History: Disciplines, Identities and the Historiography of Sport*, ed. Pascal Delheye (London: Routledge, 2014), xvi.
47 Michel Vigneault, personal correspondence, April 28, 2015. The same is true in the United States, where administrators at Iowa State University, for example, eliminated its sport history courses from the kinesiology curriculum in the late 1990s. Susan Rayl, personal correspondence, May 5, 2015.
48 Fred Mason, "Losing Ground in the 'Run Toward Science': The Liberal Arts and Social Sciences in Kinesiology," *Presentation on the International Conference on the Liberal Arts*, September 30–October 1, 2010. Unpublished paper, 10. www.google.com/url?sa=t&rct=j&q=&esrc=s&source=web&cd=1&ved=0CB8QFjAA&url=http%3A%2F%2Fw3.stu.ca%2Fstu%2Facademic%2Fdepartments%2Fsocial_work%2Fpdfs%2FMason.pdf&ei=8R8oVcXQCPHmsASXwIK4CA&usg=AFQjCNFtk9Bs_nR8Itr9dsNCIwXBvYIl7w&sig2=FxiyLtFJ7ntaElu-I3a15Q&bvm=bv.90491159,d.cWc
49 Martin Polley, "History and Sport Studies: Some Methodological Reflections," in *Making Sport History: Disciplines, Identities and the Historiography of Sport*, ed. Pascal Delheye (London: Routledge, 2014), 66.
50 Diane L. Gill, "Integration: The Key to Sustaining Kinesiology in Higher Education," *Quest* 59, no. 3 (2007): 275, original emphasis.

51 David L. Andrews, "Kinesiology's Inconvenient Truth and the Physical Cultural Studies Imperative," *Quest* 60, no. 1 (2008): 49–50.
52 Patricia Vertinsky, "Mixed Fortunes in an Academic Environment: The Institutional Gendering of Sport History," in *Making Sport History: Disciplines, Identities and the Historiography of Sport*, ed. Pascal Delheye (London: Routledge, 2014), 163.
53 Douglas R. Hochstetler, "Handing Each Other Along: Developing Leadership in Kinesiology," *Quest* 60, no. 3 (2008): 337–338.
54 See Jerome Kagan, *The Three Cultures: Natural Sciences, Social Sciences and the Humanities* (New York: Cambridge University Press, 2009).
55 Schultz, "Sense and Sensibility," 59–76.
56 Allen Guttmann, *Women's Sport's: A History* (New York: Columbia University Press, 1991), 3; John Loy, "The Nature of Sport: A Definitional Effort," *Quest* 10 (1968): 6; David Sansone, *Greek Athletics and the Genesis of Sport* (Berkeley: University of California Press, 1988), 37; Peter Donnelly, "Prolympism: Sport Monoculture as Crisis and Opportunity," *Quest* 48 (1996): 25–42.
57 See George Eisen and David K., Wiggins, eds. *Ethnicity and Sport in North American History and Culture* (Westport, CT: Greenwood Press. 1994); Nancy L. Struna, " 'Good Wives' and 'Gardeners', Spinners and 'Fearless Riders': Middle- and Upper-Rank Women in the Early American Sporting Culture," in *From "Fair Sex" to Feminism: Sport and the Socialization of Women in the Industrial and Post-Industrial Eras*, ed. J.A. Mangan and Roberta J. Park (London: Frank Cass, 1988), 235–255; Catriona M. Parratt, "From the History of Women in Sport to Women's Sport History: A Research Agenda," in *Women and Sport: Interdisciplinary Perspectives*, ed. D. Margaret Costa and Sharon R. Guthrie (Champaign, IL: Human Kinetics, 1994), 5–14.
58 Roberta Park, "Sport History in the 1990s: Prospects and Problems," *American Academy of Physical Education Papers* 20 (1987): 96–108.
59 Jennifer Hargreaves and Patricia Vertinsky, *Physical Culture, Power, and the Body* (London: Routledge, 2007), 1. See also David Kirk, "Physical Culture, Physical Education, and Relational Analysis," *Sport, Education and Society* 4 (1999): 63–73.
60 Alan G. Ingham, "Toward a Department of Physical Cultural Studies and an End to Tribal Warfare," in *Critical Postmodernism in Human Movement, Physical Education, and Sport*, ed. Juan-Miguel Fernandez-Balboa (Albany: State University of New York Press, 1997), 157–182.
61 Andrews, "Kinesiology's Inconvenient Truth," 50. Emphasis in original.
62 Colin Tatz, "History Lessons," *Sporting Traditions* 16 (1999): 20.
63 Amy Bass, "The Last Word on the State of Sports History," *Journal of American History* 101, no. 1 (2014): 197.
64 Susan K. Cahn, "Turn, Turn, Turn: There Is a Reason (for Sports History)," *Journal of American History* 101, no. 1 (2014): 182.
65 Booth, *The Field*, 221.

3

THE WILD WEST OF PEDAGOGY

Thoughts on Teaching American Sport History

Ryan Swanson

Introduction

Tom Mix, the prolific cowboy movie star (he appeared in more than 250 films), helped create the image of the American West as a place of opportunity, daring exploits, and endless possibilities. If nothing else, the West in early Hollywood films was someplace very different than your place—wherever that might have been. "The Old West," Mix remarked, summing up his career, "is not a certain place or a certain time, it's a state of mind. It's whatever you want it to be." And beginning this assessment of sport history pedagogy in the United States, I assumed I would find something akin to the stories and ideals often associated with the American West: a teaching niche characterized by new opportunities, few entrenched traditions, rugged individualism, and perhaps even stories of daring experiments and nobly failed undertakings. But just as Frederick Jackson Turner and subsequent historians have demonstrated that myth and reality when it comes to the American frontier are intertwined, the reality of sport history teaching is something different than one might expect.[1] Although sport history courses are often trumpeted by those outside of academia as something completely novel and exciting (and indeed they are in some cases), sport history courses usually fit comfortably within the pedagogical traditions that rule most history offerings.

So how is sport history taught in American universities? What types of classes are being offered? This project considers a sampling of available course syllabi, the literature on teaching sport history, and the thoughts of 11 longtime instructors of sport history. In doing so, it reveals, among other ideas, three trends regarding the teaching of American sport history courses at the undergraduate level. First, sport history courses mostly use traditional lecture, exam, and paper-writing formats. Second, most of the sport history syllabi sampled identify investigations of "race, class, and gender" as primary learning objectives. And third, baseball history courses are the most well-established sport history courses in terms of their position as regularly offered undergraduate courses.

The geneses for this project were a couple of teaching opportunities. In the fall of 2012, I was given the opportunity to create four new courses focusing on sport history for George Mason University (GMU). A few years later, I undertook a similar task in my position in the Honors College at the University of New Mexico. At GMU, the courses were to be part of a new Sport and American Culture minor, a program that was conceived of in order to bring together the university's History Department and School of Recreation, Health and Tourism.[2]

The hope was that the interdisciplinary study of sport would attract students and allow for a unique assessment of U.S. culture. The curriculum would fit somewhere between the offerings typically associated with a Sport Management program, those offered by History departments, and those found in a Physical Education or Health and Kinesiology department. Do something new with sports, the thinking went, and certainly the students will show up and interdisciplinary collaboration would occur.

I had taught sport history before. As an advanced graduate student, and again as a new assistant professor, I taught the "History of the United States through Sports." The course covered sports and athletic activities in the United States from colonial times through the twentieth century. I had taught the course both as a seminar and as a larger, lecture-based class. The course emphasized sports as a lens, rather than as the topic of focus. In preparing these courses, I focused on what I believed to be the traditional pantheon of American sport history topics, including the rise of baseball, the significance of boxing, the implementation of the color line, the golden age of sports heroes, and Title IX. I highlighted the typical sports VIPs such as Jackie Robinson, Babe Didrikson, Red Grange, Jack Dempsey, and Muhammad Ali. The courses were mostly successful. They attracted full enrollment. Student evaluations credited the courses as rigorous and rewarding. But, I wondered, how did my sport history courses compare to those taught at other colleges and universities?

The acceptance of sport history courses has followed the broader acceptance of sport history itself. The *Journal of American History*'s 2014 "State of the Field: Sports in American History" issue made clear that most historians consider sport a viable subject. That Lisa Doris Alexander, Amy Bass, Adrian Burgos Jr., Susan Cahn, Daniel Nathan, and Rob Ruck were invited to debate the field's future in a *JAH* special issue signaled broad disciplinary acceptance.[3] Thus undergraduate sport history courses are offered at many American universities. The courses are often standalone, elective history courses. For the most part, the courses do not attract derision, as they once did, as "history-light" or covering topics not worthy of serious consideration. Since the 1970s, most courses offer students a one-semester examination of sport history. Then those students who did not intend to focus on the more applied study of sport—say, sport management or sport sociology—are left only with ESPN Classic to continue their investigation of sport history. Sport history courses are to an extent episodic, supplementing either a broader history or sport studies curriculum.

In creating the history department side of the American Sport and Culture minor, I settled on a rotation of four courses for students who wanted to focus more specifically on sport history. The courses I introduced were the History of American Sport, History of Collegiate Athletics, Baseball and American Society, and the History of Race, Gender, and Sport. For the most part, I felt good about my selections. A curriculum committee subsequently signed off on my choices, and students enrolled in the classes. But increasingly I wondered if I had chosen wisely. Who was to say that a football course, for example, should not be offered instead of the more traditional investigation of baseball history?[4]

I went looking for pedagogical data and best practices on the teaching of sport history. And by this I do mean sport *history*. Lines in the pedagogical sand were quickly drawn. In order to facilitate a fair set of comparisons, my investigation did not consider several possible avenues of inquiry, including sport sociology, sport psychology, or sport management courses that offered only a peripheral focus on sport history. Instead, I focused my investigation on those courses that paid particular attention to the history of sport and using sports to understand history. With that in mind, I looked, quite simply, for those courses that either had "sport history" or "the history of sport" in the title, or those that prominently declared that understanding sport history was a primary learning objective of the course. I focused on courses that emphasized U.S. sport history and courses that were taught in American universities. I analyzed only undergraduate courses, but after a brief foray into the nebulous world of course numbering systems at various universities, I did not limit courses by their standing in the curriculum (i.e., a perceived introductory course versus an upper-division one). I was not particularly concerned with the department in which such courses were housed, but in the end I primarily considered the syllabi of courses in American studies, history, sport management, kinesiology, physical education, and humanities departments.

What follows is a brief analysis of the available pedagogical scholarship on sport history, a statistical study of 55 separate sport history syllabi, and a recounting of 11 interviews conducted with well-established scholars who have taught sport history for at least 10 years.[5] This is, to be clear, much more a "thoughts on teaching sport history" project than an exhaustive analysis of best practices or a prescriptive argument.[6] Because insufficient data were available even on common practices and tendencies among instructors of sport history courses, I determined this to be a vital first step of a multistep process. After considering the existing pedagogical literature, interviewing experts and analyzing sport history syllabi, several conclusions emerged that I believe will not only provide some new information to teachers of sport history, but, just as importantly, stimulate further discussions on how sport history might be taught more effectively.

Certainly lumping together sport history courses, which are designed for various curricular levels, varying course enrollment caps, and for different purposes within several disciplinary departments, is one of the challenges of this project. Obviously each sport history course has its own goals. Additionally, some schools offer only a single sport history course, whereas others have several courses meant to gradually build a student's knowledge of sport history across the curriculum. This is an important difference. Western Michigan University, for example, offers a large introductory general education Sport in American Culture course, followed by a writing-intensive upper-division course on American Sport History. Then a capstone, research course, Race and Ethnicity in American Sport History, completes the WMU sequence.[7] This purposeful scaffolding provides WMU students with a very different experience than their counterparts at schools with only a single sport history offering. Relatedly, this structural difference makes analyzing courses under the broad banner of "Sport History" a complex, yet fascinating task.

The methodology of how syllabi were collected for analysis deserves some mention at the outset. The intention of this study was to sample the syllabi of sport history courses that are either currently or have recently been taught at the undergraduate level. Thus, the majority of the analyzed syllabi, 43 of the 55, are from courses that have been taught in the last seven years. A smaller sampling, nine, represented courses taught 2003 to 2007. And three syllabi from pre-2003 were included. I gathered these syllabi by requesting them from North American Society of Sport History (NASSH) members and by accessing them through online searches. Additionally, H-SPORT has recently begun a teaching initiative and posting syllabi.[8] I considered both American Sport History syllabi, as well as courses that approached sport history, by focusing on one particular sport (most often baseball) or subtopic. I limited my search to courses taught at American universities. This was done as a necessary study control; hopefully further research will place this American sampling in context with sport history courses taught outside of the United States.[9]

The Syllabi

The sampling of syllabi for this study was purposely diverse in a number of ways. First, the syllabi came from a wide variety of universities and colleges. The institutions ran the gamut: from Mercer Community College, to St. Johns University, to California State University, Los Angeles, to Yale University. Second, the syllabi reflected classes that were taught in a number of different academic departments. Sport history–focused courses from American studies, history, kinesiology, physical education, and sport management departments were examined. Third, the syllabi varied in their focus. About half outlined courses in "American Sport History" or "U.S. History through Sports." Others had more specific focuses. Baseball history; African American sports history; Olympic history; and the history of sports, race, and gender were among those considered.

Diversity was difficult to find, however, in one key area: less than 10 percent of the syllabi analyzed were for classes taught by female instructors. This does not, to be clear, suggest a hard statistical reality, that is, that less than 10 percent of all sport history classes are taught by women. But the general reality holds true. The vast majority of sport history courses are still taught by men. This is cause for concern.

The analysis of 55 sport history syllabi revealed several relevant trends. First, the vast majority of sport history courses follow a very traditional model. They feature lectures, exams, and essays. Second, "race, class, and gender" are specified as key focal points of a majority of sport history classes. Third, baseball has been nearly institutionalized as a suitable method by which to teach American history and culture.

A look at these syllabi from recently taught sport history courses reveals that more than 80 percent of sport history courses follow the very traditional model of classroom procedure: the professor lectures, the students take notes, periodic exams (usually including a midterm and a final) are given, and students write a series of short papers. About half of all sport history courses utilize textbooks. In short, although some administrators and students perceive the approach to be rather novel, the methods of sport history courses are nearly identical to most other history courses.[10]

This may not come as a surprise. Sport history courses reflect the broader trends of university teaching. Although new data continue to suggest that lecturing does not produce the best educational results, many professors still lecture. As Mel Adelman, recently retired from Ohio State University, quipped, tongue firmly in cheek, "I believe in Adelman University. Students should not speak until they are sophomores."[11] In part, this traditional structure is perhaps a result of the healthy enrollments in sport history courses. William Gienapp transitioned from teaching a discussion-based seminar to a larger lecture format at Harvard University, for example, simply to allow more students into the high-demand baseball history course he was offering.[12]

There is, of course, much disagreement over what works best. Sarah Fields of the University of Colorado-Denver reported trying "to lecture as little as possible" and using a modified Socratic method in the classroom.[13] On the other hand, Maureen Smith of California State University, Sacramento, lectures "every day" in her sport history course.[14] Regarding textbooks, sport history patriarchs Ronald Smith of Pennsylvania State University and Steven Riess of Northeastern Illinois University represent divergent opinions on the subject. Smith said he never used textbooks. Riess always did; "necessary to have structure," he explained.[15]

Despite these differences, sport history courses look remarkably similar as one flips from one syllabus to another. Midterms, final exams, and short papers represent the status quo. In analyzing 14 syllabi for History of Sport in America courses (rather than a focus on race and sport or baseball, etc.), conformity is the rule. The progression for each class goes something like: colonial sport, the rise of baseball, the golden age of sport, sport and Jim Crow, TV and sport, Title IX, and Tiger Woods. Although one might creditably point out that these are indeed the subjects in which sport history courses should focus, the uniformity suggests that most instructors are writing their course outlines while consulting a sport history textbook.[16]

The question of why sport history courses seem to follow similar benchmarks and have rather ubiquitous structures is a difficult one to address. Perhaps sport historians have fallen into conservative approaches in the classroom in order to demonstrate that sport history courses are serious and should be taken seriously by their colleagues. Perhaps a belief by professors in the intrinsic appeal of sport to students has undercut the perceived need for innovation. Or, and this would be my best guess, perhaps instructors of sport history courses, like most instructors, have simply followed the lead of those who taught similar courses before them. Regardless, the lack of diversity in course structure suggests there is room for experimentation and adaptation. Courses emphasizing a group project or visits to historical sites, when the class size allows, might provide new benefits to students.[17] Similarly, courses heavily utilizing digital repositories (such as the LA84 Foundation's sources or Retrosheet) could combine new technologies with a topic that is still perceived by many nonsport historians as something innovative.[18]

The tendency of sport history courses to emphasize that studying sport is a useful way to understand race, class, and gender stood out as the second trend when analyzing these 55 syllabi and interviewing long-time teachers of American sport history. More than half of the syllabi examined explicitly stated in their course description or learning outcomes (or the equivalent) that students would gain new insight about race, class, and gender divisions within U.S. history. After baseball history courses, sport history courses emphasizing race and racism emerged as the most common subemphasis for a sport history class.

Yale University's "Race and Sport in U.S. History" was representative of this particular focus. "Our course," Dr. Jeffrey Gonda explained in his course description, "will explore the terrain of American sport in the twentieth century as a way to understand the profound impact that the phenomenon of athletic competition has had in the development of American race relations."[19] Similar courses have been recently taught at Marshall University, the University of Pennsylvania, and West Virginia University.[20] Such courses, obviously, make sense. Historians remain very interested in issues of race. Sport offers the interested student a unique set of sources, stories, and circumstances by which to analyze the history of race and racism in the United States. Gerald Gems asked his students pointed questions about names they already knew, but in the context of race and civil rights. "Who is more important, Muhammad Ali or Michael Jordan?" Gems often asked his classes.[21] Such questions work on a number of levels.

The third pattern that emerges when considering the types of sport history courses that have been taught recently and are being taught regularly is baseball's preeminence. Baseball history as a means of explaining American history has been nearly institutionalized. Everybody does it. Or at least it seems that way. In gathering a sampling of baseball history syllabi, an interesting litmus test emerged regarding just how much the professor teaching the course planned to argue for baseball "explaining it all." "Baseball and American Society [or American History]" was a common title.[22] But slight changes to this title revealed something interesting. One class declared that the course would be "America *Through* Baseball." Another went further: the baseball history course at Mid-Plains Community College was "Baseball *IS* America."[23] Instructors' enthusiasm for baseball courses was noticeable in reading their syllabi and in interviews.

Baseball history courses in particular seem to catch the attention of university and college marketing and administration officials. The University of Connecticut and the University of Massachusetts are only two of the latest schools to publish laudatory articles about the innovative baseball classes being offered on their campuses. "A Swing and a Hit: Students Flock to New Class on Baseball and Society," *UCONN Today* reported in April 2012.[24] A University of Massachusetts article gushed in similar fashion about its own baseball history course.[25] George Kirsch, a noted sport historian and baseball scholar, remarked in an interview that he was always interested in teaching a baseball history course, but that he waited until he "was safely tenured" before actually beginning the class. There's not much danger of backlash anymore. "What they're getting from me is a social history course that uses sports . . . I don't know much trivia," Kirsch explained.[26] Baseball history courses have become institutions at many universities. San Francisco State University, for example, revived the late Dr. Jules Tygiel's popular baseball course shortly after Tygiel's death. "There's just something about baseball that demands to be taught," read the school's website announcing news of the class.[27]

Baseball history courses are not universally offered in higher education, but they are no longer anomalies either. Bentley University's Christopher Beneke voiced a popular chorus in a 2013 post on the Historical Society website entitled "Why I Teach Baseball History: A Brief, Self-Serving Manifesto."

> Very few people ask me why I teach baseball history. I love baseball. Lots of students love baseball. But let me offer another explanation, something out of left field: baseball history is also a really effective way of teaching American history. . . . Part of what makes baseball so appealing as a tool for teaching American history is the happy coincidence of professional baseball history with the chronology of the modern survey course.[28]

Community colleges, too, occasionally offer baseball history courses. Noted baseball scholar Charles Alexander long taught a *two-semester* baseball course at Ohio University. Given the footholds established by baseball history courses, there is a strange incongruity between the scholarly community's embracing of baseball as a viable tool for history courses and university promotional staffs' tendencies to hype the courses as something quite unheard of before. Baseball history courses, like baseball scholarship among sport history, are far ahead of the pack. Because of this lead, the teacher of baseball history has more resources available to him or her than the instructors of other sport history courses. Jules Tygiel's *Past Time: Baseball as History* provides foundational theories regarding why and how baseball works within the historical discipline.[29] More recently, Edward Rielly's *Baseball in the Classroom: Essays on Teaching the National Pastime* provides some thought-provoking strategies among its 25 chapters.[30]

Although "History of American Sports" courses are most popular, and baseball and race and sport courses appear in course registries as the most frequently offered subtopic of sport history, one can find a great variety of sport history courses if willing to dig deep enough. There is an episodic diversity of sport history courses, if not a substantial collection of courses offered widely. Among those sport history courses that have been offered recently for undergraduates are courses focusing on the history of soccer, collegiate sport, masculinity and sport, physical education, sports history through biographies, history and sports films, the Olympics, and American football.

Studies on Teaching Sport History

The pedagogical studies focused particularly on how best to teach sport history are few in number and mostly outdated.[31] And one might ask at this point, though, whether it is practical to expect that there would be any literature at all on teaching sport history specifically. Certainly the instructors of sport history courses can derive helpful information and techniques from a much broader variety of pedagogical studies than simply those focused on the teaching of sports' past. Studies addressing the teaching of history, sport management, American studies, and many other disciplines are relevant to professors of American sport history. But sport history courses are somewhat anomalous. They are taught in a multitude of different departments (including History, Kinesiology, and Sport Management), by scholars trained in a number of different fields, oftentimes with very different disciplinary goals.

As Steven Riess remarked pointedly in a 2015 letter to the editor of the *Journal of American History*, "Sport history classes are hardly rare today."[32] This is true, but sometimes sport history courses operate as outliers within their home departments. Some members of a sport management department might, for example, question the practicality of a sport history course, whereas some faculty in a history department might place sport history far behind religious or political history courses in their pecking order. In short, instructors of sport history courses face unique challenges as they cross disciplinary boundaries. Thus professors teaching sport history would benefit from pointed pedagogical studies.

None of this is to say that some excellent studies have not been undertaken. Rather the point to emphasize is that there is still much to be done, and much to be updated. The primary pedagogical journal for historians, *The History Teacher*, last featured a sport history article in, unfortunately, 1978. "Sport as History" delineated how and why a course on sport history might be offered. "The stuff of history is no more nor less than the sum total of human experience, and sport has increasingly occupied an important part of this experience in modern society," Robert Wheeler noted.[33] Sport history is real history; a sport history course is a real history course. These were the sentiments of the article. Although significant at the time, that argument—regarding whether sport history is legitimate and has a place in the classroom—has largely been settled. By 1986 even, Joseph Arbena declared, in the *Journal of Sport History*, "the academic study of sport no longer requires extended justifications or apologies."[34]

Professors teaching sport history in other parts of the world have published more extensively than their counterparts in the United States on the best practices of teaching sport history classes. There have been excellent studies published in academic journals on teaching sport history in Latin America, "in the European Context," in the United Kingdom, New Zealand, and Korea, among other places.[35] Although more studies have been focused on non-American sport history, similar disciplinary tensions seem to be present wherever the locale. Alvarez and Gorrono, for example, declared that "the teaching of History of Physical Education and Sport has reached a crisis in the European University."[36] They point to an emphasis on health, sport management techniques, kinesiology, and biology as a cause for sport history courses being pushed out of history departments.

Steve Pope's 1998 determination that, despite the growth of sport history and its presence in university classrooms, "there has been a conspicuous reticence for thorough, searching review and evaluation," still rings true 15 years later. Especially when considering pedagogy. One cannot help but wonder if the enormous popularity of sport history courses (William Gienapp at Harvard University: "Too many students wanted to take [Baseball and American Society: 1840-Present] . . . the ones who didn't get in were very unhappy.") has impeded the necessary discussion among instructors of course materials, class formats, and the role of technology and digital history as they specifically relate to teaching sport history.[37] Questions ripe for consideration include:

- How might an instructor effectively reorient students who enroll in a course as "fans" of sport without discouraging them from engaging in a scholarly investigation of the topic?
- Do students in a sport history course really benefit from a textbook?
- How can an instructor best combine historical sports topics with more modern manifestations?
- How might historical sporting places be utilized for educational purposes?
- How might a class structure effectively communicate that sport will be the lens, not just the topic?
- What digital repositories are best suited for students in sport history courses?[38]
- How, or does, an instructor of sport history consider not "over intellectualizing" sports, as Jules Tygiel warned?[39]

There are, of course, dozens of other questions that might be addressed. Book-length studies addressing such questions of sport history teaching have been virtually nonexistent. The commendable, but now badly outdated, Vanderwerken text (mentioned previously) was a useful effort. Similarly Douglas Noverr and Lawrence Ziewacz's *Sport History: Selected Reading Lists and Course Outlines from American Colleges and Universities* provides interesting foundational ideas, but harkens to the pre-Internet era in terms of its practical applications.[40]

Conclusion: Going Forward . . .

Mark Dyreson, a scholar and teacher of sport history who has worked in both history and kinesiology departments, raised the significant question of where the future home of sport history courses will be. "I don't know where [sport history] is going to end up," he remarked, pointing out that historians don't secure significant grants to make the fit in science-based departments an easy one.[41] The fact, however, that sport history courses typically draw large enrollments suggests that they will continue to have a place in many university catalogues. But where? Ron Smith predicted history departments would eventually seize upon sport history courses as a means of drawing in students. Drawing precisely the opposite conclusion, Maureen Smith suggested that sport management programs would continue to grow, and that's where sport history courses will eventually end up.[42] Will history departments come fully to terms with the use of sports; will sport management and kinesiology programs embrace the historical approach? What outcome would be best?

The key division stressed by most sport history teachers interviewed for this project, between themselves and those instructors who teach other aspects of sport, is one of focus. Sport historians tend to view sports (whether corporately or just baseball, just football, etc.) as the lens by which to examine broader cultural themes and institutions. Neither the sport, nor the athlete, is an end in and of itself. This focus can create tension in nonhistory departments, where subjects such as ticket sales or anterior cruciate ligament (ACL) injuries might matter more. The teachers of sport history are generally less interested in students knowing every detail about a sport or improving their performance in a sport than they are about students asking new questions and finding new cultural patterns through the investigation of sport.

With questions abounding about where sport history courses and their instructors fit into the broader university community, perhaps a conclusion by way of a few more practical questions is order. Having demonstrated that many sport history classes adhere rigidly to the exam and research paper model, are sport history instructors prepared to experiment with new grading formats? More than 20 years ago Ken Burns provided sport historians and sport history classes with his seemingly endless, but excellent, documentary on baseball's history. Given the availability of cost-effective technology, exploring the possibility of students creating documentaries as a final project seems viable. So, too, does an increased emphasis on group work. Students might be paired together to create a marketing campaign for football player Bronko Nagurski or golfer Lee Elder. Similarly, assignments to visit historic sporting landmarks might supplant one reading assignment or two. Hopefully, as sport history instructors conduct these types of experiments they will share their results. The annual conference of the North American Society for Sport History has traditionally included, but not emphasized, pedagogical panels. NASSH or some other group, perhaps one of the centers for the study of sport being created at American universities, might well take the lead in providing a website home and a database for materials on teaching sport history.[43]

The role of digital and technology resources also looms as an opportunity and challenge for those instructors teaching sport history courses.[44] Roy Rosenzweig, the late founder of the Center for History and New Media, challenged sport historians nearly a decade ago to get with the times and assess the tools available for the historical study of sport:

> What, then, is the overall breadth and depth of web-based materials related to the history of sports? How good is the web as a digital archive and library of sport history? The simple answer is that we do not know yet. . .[45]

And to a certain extent, we still do not know. Richard William Cox and Michael A. Salter provided a fantastic analysis of the possibilities—but 15 years ago.[46] Having interviewed 11 veteran teachers of sport history and analyzed dozens of sport history syllabi, digital history does not seem to be of particular concern to teachers of sport history. Sources such as the sport history pieces on Grantland.com, for example (see Brian Phillips' excellent Pedestrian article) do not appear often on sport history syllabi. At least not yet.[47]

Undoubtedly, teachers of sport history recognize the opportunities and challenges that come with technology. Certainly sport history syllabi will become increasingly digital and tech-savvy. One wonders too, if sport history students might not help with the spade work. Student assignments assessing the viability of certain sport history sites, blogs, and online commentaries could serve to provide them with analytical opportunities and sport history instructors with increased information about resources.

This project began due to a lack of pedagogical materials on the teaching of sport history. By interviewing long-time sport history instructors and reviewing dozens of syllabi, some conclusions have emerged. Among them: sport history courses are offered in a variety of departments, usually have very traditional structures, tend to emphasize race and gender, and baseball courses hold a very preeminent place in academia. From these conclusions, more questions than answers arise. Many scholars suggest that sport history courses will continue to be taught due to their large enrollments, but the question of which departments best facilitate sport history is yet to be answered. Similarly, the question of how the instructors of sport history courses might better utilize digital resources (beyond the basics: "YouTube is an amazing thing" declared one interviewee) deserves serious consideration. So, although sport history teaching may not be a veritable "Wild West," my hope is that future debates and discussions over what it should and could be will be mapped out and seriously explored.

Notes

1 The long and ongoing debate over the "correct" interpretation of the American West will not be covered here. But as an introduction, see Frederick Jackson Turner, "The Significance of the Frontier in American History," *American Historical Association Conference*, Chicago, July 12, 1893. http://nationalhumanitiescenter.org/pds/gilded/empire/text1/turner.pdf (accessed May 1, 2013); and Donald Worster, "New West, True West: Interpreting the Region's History, *The Western Historical Quarterly* 18 (April 1987): 141–156.
2 See "Sport and American Culture Program," George Mason University. http://sportculture.gmu.edu/ (accessed March 1, 2015).
3 Amy Bass, ed., "State of the Field: Sports in American History," *Journal of American History* 101, no. 1 (2014): 148–197.
4 The issue of "this sport versus that one" as a pedagogical question is addressed well by Vernon L. Andrews, albeit in a different context. See Vernon L. Andrews, "Baseball, Cricket, Gridiron and Rugby: Opposites Attract in Teaching American Sports Culture Abroad," *Australasian Journal of American Studies* 27 (July 2008): 104–114.
5 Interviews were conducted with Mel Adelman, Mark Dyreson, Sarah Fields, Gerald Gems, George Kirsch, Dan Nathan, Catriona Parratt, Sam Regalado, Steven Riess, Maureen Smith, and Ronald Smith.
6 Steve Pope's insightful "Sport History: Into the 21st Century," *Journal of Sport History* 25 (Summer 1998) i–x, provided a valuable model for this study.
7 Communication with Linda J. Borish, History Department, Western Michigan University, June 2015.
8 "H-Sport Teaching Initiative," *H-Net*. https://networks.h-net.org/node/2622/pages/27928/h-sport-teaching-initiative (accessed May 12, 2015).
9 See Juan L. Hernandez Alvarex and M. Eugina Martinez Gorrono, "The Teaching of History of Physical Education and Sport in the European Context: Status, Problems in Methodology, and Its Importance in the University Curriculum," *Journal of Sport History* 33 (Fall 2006): 387–403.
10 For an interesting assessment of the perseverance of lecture-based courses, see: Sara Dolnicar, "Should We Still Lecture or Just Post Examination Questions on the Web?: The Nature of the Shift Toward Pragmatism in Undergraduate Lecture Attendance," *Quality in Higher Education* 11, no. 2 (2005): 103–115.
11 Interview by Ryan Swanson, Mel Adelman, June 4, 2012.
12 Robert H. Giles, "An Historian Plays Ball: William Gienapp Highlights National Issues Through a Hard Sport," *Harvard Magazine*, May 2001, 3.
13 Interview by Ryan Swanson, Sarah Fields, June 3, 2012.
14 Interview by Ryan Swanson, Maureen Smith, June 4, 2012.
15 Interviews by Ryan Swanson, Ron Smith, and Steven Riess, June 4, 2012.
16 Benjamin G. Rader's *American Sports: From the Age of Folk Games to the Age of Televised Sports* (Lincoln: University of Nebraska, 2004) was cited most frequently in syllabi and by interviewees as their textbook of choice. Other popular sport history textbooks include Richard O. Davies, *Sports in American Life: A History* (Malden, MA: Wiley-Blackwell, 2007); Gerald R. Gems, Linda J. Borish, and Gertrud Pfister, *Sports in American History: From Colonization to Globalization* (Champaign, IL: Human Kinetics, 2008); and Elliott J. Gorn and Warren Goldstein, *A Brief History of American Sports* (Urbana: University of Illinois Press, 2013).
17 Linda J. Borish, Mitch Kachun, and Cheryl Lyon-Jenness "Rethinking a Curricular 'Muddle in the Middle': Revising the Undergraduate History Major at Western Michigan University," *Journal of American History* 95 (March 2009): 1102–1113.

18 See "Research," *LA84 Foundation*. www.la84.org/research/ (accessed April 3, 2013); *Retrosheet*. www.retrosheet.org/ (accessed April 8, 2013).

19 "Race and Sport in US History," Syllabus, Jeffrey Gonda, Yale University, Summer Session A, 2012.

20 "Race and Ethnicity in Sport," Syllabus, Neil Lanctot, University of Pennsylvania, Fall, 2013; "Race and Sport in American History," David Peavler, Marshall University, Fall, 2012; "African Americans in Sport," Syllabus, Dana Brooks, West Virginia University, Fall, 2012.

21 Interview by Ryan Swanson, Gerald Gems, June 4, 2012.

22 See "Baseball and American Culture, 1840–Present," Matthew M. Briones, University of Chicago, Spring, 2012; "Baseball Is America," Dr. Wolar, Mid-Plains Community College, Spring, 2009.

23 "America Through Baseball," Syllabus, Martin C. Babicz, University of Colorado, Spring, 2011.

24 Stephanie Reitz, "A Swing and a Hit: Students Flock to New Class on Baseball and Society," *UCONN Today*, April 13, 2012.

25 John Mael, "History Department Offers Course about Baseball's Past," *UMass Media*, February 7, 2013.

26 Interview by Ryan Swanson, George Kirsch, June 4, 2012.

27 "Baseball Class Goes Beyond Balls and Strikes," San Francisco State University. http://news.sfsu.edu/baseball-history-class-goes-beyond-balls-and-strikes (accessed April 2, 2015).

28 Chris Beneke, "Why I Teach Baseball History: A Brief, Self-Serving Manifesto," *The Historical Society* (blog). http://histsociety.blogspot.com/2013/01/why-i-teach-baseball-history-brief-self.html (accessed March 30, 2013).

29 Jules Tygiel, *Past Time: Baseball as History* (New York: Oxford University Press, 2000).

30 Edward J. Rielly, ed., *Baseball in the Classroom: Essays on Teaching the National Pastime* (Jefferson, NC: McFarland, 2006).

31 See David L. Vanderwerken, ed., *Sport in the Classroom: Teaching Sport-Related Courses in the Humanities* (Toronto: Associated University Presses, 1990). See particularly, Allen Guttmann, "Teaching 'Sport and Society,'" in Vanderwerken, ed., *Sport in the Classroom*, 237–247.

32 Steven Riess, "Letter to the Editor," *Journal of American History* 101, no. 4 (2015): 1363.

33 Robert Wheeler, "Sport as History," *The History Teacher* 11 (May 1978): 312.

34 Joseph L. Arbena, "Sport and the Study of Latin American History: An Overview," *Journal of Sport History* 13 (Summer 1986): 87.

35 Arbena, "Sport and the Study of Latin America"; Juan L. Hernandez Alvarex and M. Eugina Martinez Gorrono, "The Teaching of History of Physical Education and Sport in the European Context: Status, Problems in Methodology, and Its Importance in the University Curriculum," *Journal of Sport History* 33 (Fall 2006): 387–403; Vernon L. Andrews, "Baseball, Cricket, Gridiron and Rugby: Opposites Attract in Teaching American Sports Culture Abroad," *Australasian Journal of American Studies* 27 (July 2008): 104–114; Martin Jones, "Putting the History in Sport: On Sport History and Sport Studies in the United Kingdom," *Journal of Sport History* 31 (Summer 2004): 145–160; and Bang Chool-Kim, "State of the Field, Teaching and Writing Sport History in Korea: The Vision from America," *International Sports Studies* 24, no. 2 (2002): 45–61.

36 Alvarez and Gorrono, "The Teaching of History of Physical Education and Sport in the European Context," 387.

37 Robert H. Giles, "An Historian Plays Ball: William Gienapp Highlights National Issues Through a Hard Sport," *Harvard Magazine*, May 2001, 3.

38 See Gary Osmond and Murray G. Phillips, *Sport History in the Digital Era* (Urbana: University of Illinois Press, 2015).

39 Tygiel, *Pastime*, ix–x.

40 Douglas Noverr and Lawrence E. Ziewacz, eds., *Sport History: Selected Reading Lists and Course Outlines from American Colleges and Universities* (New York: Markus Wiener Publishing, Inc., 1987).

41 Interview by Ryan Swanson, Mark Dyreson, June 4, 2012.

42 Interview by Ryan Swanson, Ron Smith, June 4, 2012; Interview by Ryan Swanson, Maureen Smith, June 4, 2012.

43 Over the past few decades, the following centers, among others, have been established: the California State University, Fullerton Center for Sociocultural Sport and Olympic Research, the George

Mason University Center for the Study of Sport and Leisure in Society, and the Northeastern University Center for the Study of Sport in Society.

44 Osmond and Phillips, *Sport History in the Digital Era.*

45 Roy Rosenzweig, "Sport History on the Web: Towards a Critical Assessment," *Journal of Sport History* 31 (Fall 2004): 373.

46 Richard William Cox and Michael A. Salter, "The IT Revolution and the Practice of Sport History: An Overview and Reflection on Internet Research and Teaching Resources," *Journal of Sport History* 25 (Summer 1998): 283–302.

47 Brian Phillips, "Pedestrian Mania: How Edward Payson Weston Became the Most Well-Known Athlete in the World. . .in the 1870s," *Grantland.* www.grantland.com/story/_/id/8339692/brian-phillips-edward-payson-weston (accessed April 21, 2013).

Part II

SPORT AND EDUCATION

4

PROGRESSIVE-ERA SPORT, EDUCATION, AND REFORM

Brian M. Ingrassia

Introduction

America's Progressive Era dated roughly from the early 1890s to 1919, from the Panic of 1893 (and the subsequent depression) to the end of World War I. This three-decade period encompassed a time of reform, experimentation, and innovation spearheaded by politicians, writers, educators, and activists. Americans coped with changes wrought by the onset of widespread urban growth and industrialization, seeking reforms that would reshape modern life. In the latter decades of the 1800s, moreover, new understandings of human origins emerged in the writings of Charles Darwin, and researchers began to realize the significance of the central nervous system. As a consequence, thinkers and reformers began to stress the essential role of the properly developed mind and active body, especially the healthy male body. Subsequently, progressives—many of whom were guided by a desire to make society safe for a white, middle-class, self-consciously rational "public"—envisioned a significant societal role for sport and education. To ensure a positive impact on the body, mind, and public, concerned Americans crafted reforms that conveyed a long-lasting impact on sport, education, and society.

Progressive Era Overview

Historians often pair the Progressive Era with the Gilded Age—a time following the Civil War when the American economy grew quickly and so-called "robber barons" used new technologies, such as railroads, to create economies of scale, build monopolies, and amass substantial fortunes. By the early 1890s, however, many Americans pushed back against the inequality of intensely concentrated wealth. At the grassroots level, Southern and Western farmers crafted "Populist" movements that advocated monetary policies favorable to the poor. By the mid-1890s, white middle-class Americans in rapidly growing industrial cities spearheaded reforms. Reformers crafted voluntary organizations and promoted governmental intervention at local, state, and federal levels. Fearing the power of both wealthy tycoons and working-class "mobs," reformers hoped to find a middle course; some even formed alliances with wealthy philanthropists, working-class immigrants, or labor unions. Only through rational "public" discourse, progressives argued, could society shape moderate reforms that would help fix the era's significant problems and make urban-industrial society livable.[1]

Progressivism was a collection of movements that attacked modern problems from various angles. Reformers included politicians, writers, urban activists, intellectuals, and educators.

Many influential Progressive Era figures such as Jane Addams occupied multiple categories, and alliances did not always agree with each other. President Theodore Roosevelt, for example, was a progressive politician and writer, but he criticized so-called "muckraking" journalists whom he saw as exposing economic and urban problems without proposing solutions. This wide variety of reformers supported a diverse array of movements. Progressive causes included social settlements, women's rights, temperance, pure food and drugs, public transportation, safe tenements, public parks, and playgrounds. Reforming education—from the primary level to secondary and higher education—was also a major progressive cause.

Just one generation removed from the Civil War, Americans were joining together into a single nation. As historian Robert Wiebe famously put it, the United States was a nation of "island communities" that were becoming connected. Railroads and other transportation technologies, including automobiles and good roads, brought Americans closer together. Meanwhile, Progressive-Era Americans sought to impose "order" on their often chaotic society.[2] To craft reforms of national importance, though, people needed to use means of national scope. Reformers often banded together to create national organizations to fix problems ranging from child labor to race relations to intercollegiate football.

Progressivism was not an exclusively American phenomenon. Wherever people dealt with problematic issues of modernity (including Europe or Japan), similar movements emerged. Historians have made it clear that American progressivism was shaped by "Atlantic crossings" that served as a conduit for European influences—and Europeans also took note of American reforms. Urban space, economic theory, and educational reform were just a few of the progressive causes that drew on international influences.[3] Less widely studied are the Pacific Rim influences that shaped America's Progressive Era, the most prominent example being Australian ("secret") ballot electoral reform.[4] Indeed, different areas of the United States developed unique regional movements. Northeastern cities like Boston and New York were in the vanguard, but progressivism also found a special home in Midwestern industrial urban centers like Chicago, Cleveland, and Milwaukee, as well as smaller cities like Madison, Wisconsin, which pioneered a brand of progressivism (the "Madison Idea") that stressed cooperation between public universities and state government.[5] In the South, progressivism was often tied to racial issues. Many white Southerners portrayed Jim Crow segregation laws as "progressive," because they might prevent black-white violence. For many African Americans, though, eliminating segregation and ending the extralegal practice of lynching—one of the goals of the National Association for the Advancement of Colored People (NAACP), founded in 1909—would be a significant progressive reform.[6] On the West Coast, a distinct brand of California progressivism developed.[7]

Progressive-Era Education and Views of Sport

Education was an issue of particular importance for many Progressive-Era Americans. Schools were places that could shape young people for a lifetime of public service and economic contributions. Many reformers hoped to make public education mandatory, build better school facilities, increase education funding, and lengthen the amount of time children spent in school. Although not all Americans agreed with these goals, progressive reformers nevertheless implemented many changes. By 1918, every state in the Union had passed laws mandating compulsory school attendance. Throughout the United States, educational reformers built high schools, made them accessible to a broader segment of the public, took control of extracurricular activities, and generally increased the prominence of secondary education in American life. Educational reformers "banded together" to create national reform agencies, such as the Association of American Universities (AAU), the American Council on Education (ACE), and the Carnegie Foundation for the Advancement of Teaching.[8]

At many levels, sport and physical culture became an integral part of American education. Progressive-Era Americans understood physical activity as a way to develop physical, mental, and moral traits that young people—especially young men—would need to survive in and contribute to modern society. Some progressives even viewed sport programs in schools or social settlements as a way to Americanize immigrant children. One of the most prominent late nineteenth-century educational theorists who advanced the idea that mind and body should be educated in tandem was G. Stanley Hall. Hall, who earned America's first PhD in psychology studying under William James at Harvard, served as professor of philosophy and psychology at The Johns Hopkins University in the 1880s before becoming the first president of Clark University (and first president of the American Psychological Association). Throughout his career, Hall was a proponent of the "child study" movement, and in 1904 he published a famous study titled *Adolescence*. Hall's educational psychology stressed children's health and development, and he supported anthropometry, the science of measuring bodies and calculating ideal body types. Although Hall opposed strict gymnastics programs, he did view exercise as an instrumental part of education. Hall based his educational theory upon the idea of *biological recapitulation*, which posited that individuals of a particular species recapitulated the entire development of the species as they grew from conception to adulthood. As a result, Hall argued that (white) boys had to reenact primitive manners and behaviors before they could grow into moral adulthood, which might be traced through the types of games played—with simple chase games representing primitive hunters, and strategic team games exemplifying higher levels of civilization. Such atavistic behavior would also help to prevent *neurasthenia*, or "nervous exhaustion," later in life. As historian Gail Bederman has noted, Hall hoped turn-of-the-century application of his theories would help improve the "race" and strengthen young, white American men.[9]

Thinkers like Hall accelerated a trend that had been present in America's colleges and schools since the pre–Civil War era, when physical training first became an important part of education. Influential proponents of physical education and anthropometry included Dudley Allen Sargent, the director of Harvard's Hemenway Gymnasium from 1879 to 1919. Among Sargent's noteworthy students was Luther Halsey Gulick. Born to Christian missionaries in Hawaii in 1865, Gulick based his physical education advocacy on the beliefs of "Muscular Christianity," a movement that originated in mid-1800s Britain. Proponents of Muscular Christianity contended that modern Christian men needed physical exercise in order to maintain and develop their physical, mental, and spiritual attributes for gender roles. Through his extensive efforts with the Young Men's Christian Association (YMCA), Gulick promoted the idea that body, mind, and spirit were intrinsically linked. While working at the YMCA training school (founded in the 1880s) in Springfield, Massachusetts, Gulick influenced a generation of physical educators and helped develop indoor games appropriate for wintertime play. In 1891, Gulick assigned teacher James Naismith the task of creating a game that would keep an unruly class occupied. Naismith subsequently combined aspects of lacrosse, soccer, and football to create the new game of basketball. Soon, the game caught on in densely populated cities, because it did not require a large field. In urban centers, basketball was often played in educational settings or in settlement houses, where it was carefully supervised. It quickly became an important part of the progressive effort to guide and Americanize immigrant youth through sport and extracurricular activities.[10]

Although men's sport and education was the focus of many progressives, women's physical education also gained traction during this time. Opinions differed, though, regarding the type of physical education or sport to which girls should be exposed. In the 1870s, some physicians had contended that women should not participate in strenuous physical activity at all. For example, Harvard medical professor Edward Clarke, influenced by a new generation of Euro-American psychologists, published an influential book called *Sex in Education; or, A Fair Chance for the Girls* (1873), in which he claimed that sport would take away the vital physical energy that women needed for reproduction. He even went so far as to say that exercise would disrupt women's menstrual cycles, or "periodicity." His ideas shaped women's education for decades, as many schools did not allow women to participate in vigorous and highly organized physical activities. In the 1890s, though, some educators and women's rights leaders challenged Clarke's ideas, and by the early 1900s many Americans agreed that it was acceptable for women to play sports—as long as they were not too competitive or too strenuous, adhering to female gender lines.

Some also feared that girls would be "masculinized" by overly competitive sport. By the early 1900s, though, girls' basketball briefly caught on in some school districts. One of the key figures in challenging Clarke's ideas was Dr. Clelia Duel Mosher, who attended The Johns Hopkins Medical School in the 1890s before returning to her alma mater, Stanford University in California, as a professor. Mosher's research disproved the idea that women were more fragile or less physically capable than men, thus making her one of a number of voices who challenged "separate spheres" ideology and paved the way for widespread women's physical education.[11] The rise of women's athletics and Mosher's research reflected the appearance of the so-called "New Woman"—an independent, strong, and self-reliant figure—in the 1890s. Such women were most famously portrayed by illustrator Charles Dana Gibson, whose "Gibson Girl" was a strong and athletic woman who nevertheless remained feminine in figure and in dress.[12]

The increasing embrace of physical culture was part of a larger change in Progressive-Era modes of thinking about education and pedagogy. As cultural historian Donald J. Mrozek has argued, the late 1800s was a time when "philosophical pragmatism" emerged and was incorporated into daily life—including sport and education. Pragmatic philosophers contended that knowledge was created through everyday experience and observation rather than being derived from inherited wisdom. For pragmatists, ideas were tools, not absolute truths. Thus, the Progressive Era "was an age that placed special emphasis on 'physical learning'"—especially the idea that an individual learned via physical activity.[13] Indeed, the turn-of-the-century America era witnessed the rise of a new brand of pedagogue. By the early 1900s, G. Stanley Hall had been supplanted by one of his former students, John Dewey, as America's leading educational theorist. Dewey gained special prominence at the University of Chicago (1894–1904), where he established the famous Laboratory School—which tested new ideas about education in a practical setting—before moving to Columbia University in New York. A pragmatic philosopher, Dewey viewed education as a holistic process consisting of steps that advanced throughout a child's development. His ideas influenced generations of American educators.[14]

A hallmark of Dewey's famous 1916 treatise *Democracy and Education* consisted of his emphasis on pedagogies that would help children to develop knowledge via hands-on activities. Work and play, he argued, taught lessons organically, in a more effective manner than musty medieval-style scholasticism. Informed by late-1800s physiological psychology, Dewey emphasized that mind and body were connected via the central nervous system—"a specialized mechanism for keeping all bodily activities working together." For a human brain to learn about the outside world, he argued, knowledge had to be developed through stimuli gathered by all five senses. Individuals, therefore, needed to be active participants in their education.[15] Play—seen as a type of constructive and instructive work that fostered learning—was important, not frivolous. In addition to providing relief from tedious and mentally taxing schoolwork, play symbolically reproduced adult activities and thus taught children lessons they would need later in life. Dewey argued that schools had to create a setting where work and play would "be conducted with reference to facilitating desirable mental and moral growth."[16]

Dewey's ideas dovetailed with those of other significant progressives, including social settlement pioneer Jane Addams. In 1889, shortly after visiting Toynbee Hall in London, Addams established Hull House on Chicago's west side. At this iconic "settlement house," middle- and upper-class reformers hoped to assist and uplift the Windy City's diverse immigrant population. Influenced by the Social Gospel, Addams desired to use Christianity to improve everyday society. Like other social settlement proponents and social work pioneers, Addams developed a pragmatic and reciprocal approach, looking for ways to learn from the new arrivals at the same time they learned from her. Hull House and other urban settlement houses functioned essentially as community centers that developed innovative solutions for social problems. Among their many programs, settlements increasingly incorporated education—including kindergartens and manual training—into their mission. They also saw physical activity as a way to teach important lessons and foster interaction between community members. Settlement workers developed athletic clubs and built playgrounds for neighborhood residents. Through sports and play, immigrant men and women could come together and practice democratic behavior.[17]

Playgrounds were not just built at social settlements. They also appeared at schools and public parks, representing a larger Progressive-Era concern with physical development and urban populations. Historian Dominick Cavallo has written that turn-of-the-century playgrounds were supposed to provide a sense of fair play and "team spirit" intended "to foster immigrant acculturation and enhance democratic values." Playgrounds represented places where the children of a diverse urban society could come together on an equal ground. In theory, cooperation trumped individualism on playing fields, thus creating a clear sense of discipline and public spirit.[18]

Although many Progressive-Era thinkers stressed the importance of play for participants, some also addressed the issue of spectatorship. This topic was especially significant in an era when spectator sports were becoming an important part of American higher and secondary education—as well as urban society more generally. John Dewey, for one, did not have a positive view of athletic spectatorship in relationship to education. The prominent educator noted that whereas a spectator was largely "indifferent," a participant was "bound up with what is going on." Dewey thought that participants got more from their education than spectators.[19]

Not all early twentieth-century thinkers, however, saw such a clear line of demarcation between spectators and participants. Harvard's celebrated pragmatic philosopher Josiah Royce addressed this issue when fleshing out an idea that he called "loyalty to loyalty." Royce argued that instead of maintaining selfish individualism or unthinkingly devoting oneself to the groupthink of the mob, each individual needed to remain committed to his own values—as well as to the values of fellow human beings. To be a fully realized self, Royce argued, a person had to devote himself or herself to others while at the same time respecting those other individuals as fellow selves with their own distinct loyalties.[20] Like Addams, who tried to find a way for the peoples of a diverse and heterogeneous city to come together on common ground, Royce sought to re-establish community in an era when few shared common interests or goals.

Royce addressed sport and spectatorship in his 1908 book *Race Questions*. Because physical development was closely related to moral development, he said, it was not enough for one to *feel* loyal. The body also had to *express* loyalty. One way "to prepare a man for a loyal life" was "to give him a careful and extended motor training" that would help him harmonize actions "with his nobler sentiments."[21] Such training would help individuals learn how to relate to each other ethically within a democratic society. Royce argued that whereas an unorganized gang of youths might become "a menace to the general social order," a group "duly organized into athletic teams, in the service of the schools" would "become centres [*sic*] for training in certain types of loyalty." Such training, in turn, would "extend its influence to large bodies of boys who, as spectators of games or as schoolmates, are more or less influenced by the athletic spirit."[22] Athletic spectatorship, in other words, could help teach modern morality nearly as well as athletic participation. Nevertheless, Royce realized that sport could pose moral dangers. With recent controversies and scandals regarding intercollegiate athletics in mind, he asked whether school-sponsored sports invariably led to the development of loyalty. It seemed to Royce that the moral potential of physical culture had been squandered for the sake of spectatorship in modern America. No one, after all, could learn the philosophy of loyalty from a mob. Using his own institution as an example, Royce argued that Harvard Stadium (built in 1903) was an "admirable place" when it did not host too large of a crowd. But when full of spectators it was "a bad place for the moral education of our youth," because large crowds promoted "ideals" focused on personal gratification, rather than loyalty or commitment to the greater good.[23] For sport to be educational and progressive-minded, implied progressives like Royce, it would have to be carefully orchestrated and supervised—and spectators would have to be properly incorporated into the ritual of educational athletics.

Athletic Reform and Education in the Progressive Era

Progressive educators, reformers, and thinkers saw education as a cornerstone of the public-spirited society they hoped to build. In a pragmatic era when ideas were formed through action and pedagogy was based on physical experience, properly regulated sport needed to be placed squarely at the center of society. With institutions of higher education providing the foundation for so many of the era's reforms and innovations, not surprisingly, many progressives focused their attention on the reform of college athletics—especially intercollegiate football—in the 1890s and early 1900s.

By the turn of the century it was clear that football, the prototypical intercollegiate sport, had become tainted. Although intramural football games were played during the antebellum era, the first intercollegiate match was contested by Princeton and Rutgers a few years after the Civil War, in 1869. The rise of effective transportation technology (especially railroads) and Gilded-Age America's competitive spirit led to increased intercollegiate competition in the 1870s and 1880s. At this time, innovators at Northeastern colleges, especially Walter Camp at Yale, introduced new rules—including downs, timing, and yard measurements—that transformed rugby into American football. With the new rules, football was rationalized in a manner resembling the rational management techniques of late-1800s industrialists such as Frederick Winslow Taylor. This newly rationalized running and kicking game caught on and quickly spread throughout the country. By the 1890s football was played in the colleges and universities of the Midwest, the West Coast (especially the San Francisco Bay Area), and the industrializing and urbanizing New South. Even colleges for African Americans and Native American boarding schools embraced the game. With such rapid growth, though, came corruption and scandal at a wide range of institutions. Driven by a keen desire for victories and promotion, colleges and universities turned a blind eye as teams brought in semiprofessional ringers. Many purported collegiate athletes did not even bother attending classes. To make matters worse, a significant number of athletes were being injured or dying on the field. Spinal injuries were a major issue by the end of the century, especially with the death of Richard "Von" Gammon of the University of Georgia in October 1897. In the wake of this tragedy, the Georgia state legislature nearly outlawed college football. The game was only saved in that state when proponents touted it as a "manly" game that had a positive influence on college students and strengthened modern American society in an international context. Still, some physicians and critics feared that football might have long-lasting effects upon the players, including some negative effects that would not be visible for years or decades to come.[24]

Among college football's most outspoken critics was Charles William Eliot, who served as Harvard University's influential and innovative president from 1869 to 1909. Eliot himself had participated in athletics (especially rowing) while a mid-century student at Harvard, but by the late 1800s he was skeptical of the value of spectator-oriented sports. In 1894, Eliot even suggested in his annual report that Harvard should end or severely limit its participation in the intercollegiate game. Eliot's important critique inspired a loud response by proponents of football. Many Americans accused Harvard's president of being an unmanly coward. This reaction was not surprising, considering the then-prevailing notion that strenuous physical activities were necessary for proper masculine development. Other university presidents, including Stanford's David Starr Jordan and Chicago's William Rainey Harper, defended football; they cited the game's potentially positive impact on students, athletes, and society. Some academic psychologists even cited the work of G. Stanley Hall when they discussed the ways that atavistic physical activity could help replicate aspects of evolutionary development. Some claimed that football provided stress relief for men who faced a serious risk of nervous exhaustion as a result of being immersed in the modern economy.

Whereas elite Northeastern schools had collaborated to establish common rules and schedules as early as the 1870s and 1880s, by the 1890s some Midwestern universities consciously created a formal regional organization designed to regulate athletic relations. The first athletic conference was the Intercollegiate Conference of Faculty Representatives—later known as the "Western Conference" and, after 1910, the "Big Ten." In January 1896, delegates from seven Midwestern universities met at the Palmer House Hotel in Chicago at the suggestion of Purdue University President James Smart. As historian John Sayle Watterson has argued, Smart might have used as his template 1890s federal legislation banning the kind of corruption that had crept into interstate commerce via railroad monopolies. In addition to trying to curb "tramp athletes" and professionalism in college athletics, Smart and his fellow university presidents were interested in protecting football revenues—and enhancing their prestige by banding together with other prominent regional institutions of higher education.[25]

Despite some reforms, including the formation of regional regulatory associations, football's problems persisted. By 1905, many Americans started to see the need for a more widespread, nationally focused intercollegiate football reform. The 1905 season was particularly dangerous. That fall, approximately 18 college and high school men died on American gridirons. In October 1905, progressive Republican President Theodore Roosevelt, acting upon a proposal by educator Endicott Peabody, called athletic leaders from the so-called "Big Three"—Harvard, Yale, and Princeton—to the White House for a meeting. Roosevelt charged these universities with the task of reforming the game. Although Roosevelt certainly provided leadership on this issue, his role in implementing football reforms has become somewhat overstated in the last century. Arguably, the most significant impetus for progressive football reform came as much from the American public as from the president.

In 1905 several muckraking journalists published articles exposing football's moral and educational dangers in reform-oriented mainstream periodicals. Henry Beach Needham's two-part article on "The College Athlete" appeared in *McClure's* in the summer of 1905, and Edward S. Jordan's four-part "Buying Football Victories" (focused on Midwestern universities, including Chicago, Wisconsin, Michigan, and Minnesota) appeared in *Collier's* in November and December of that year. Many Americans were outraged, and two well-publicized on-field incidents only enlarged their anger. On a single day in November, a player was visibly injured by a late hit in the prominent Harvard-Yale rivalry game. In New York City, another player, Union College's Harold Moore, was mortally injured in a game against New York University (NYU). Immediately, NYU's Chancellor Henry MacCracken called for football's reform or abolition. MacCracken proclaimed that America's growing and progressive-minded universities—which aspired to prominent international status—could no longer sponsor such an apparently corrupt activity. He convened meetings of delegates from interested colleges and universities in New York in late December 1905 and early January 1906.[26]

Delegates from 13 institutions met and discussed the problem of intercollegiate athletics on December 8, 1905. Three weeks later, they reconvened with delegates representing additional universities and formed the Intercollegiate Athletic Association of the United States. By 1910, this organization changed its name to the National Collegiate Athletic Association (NCAA). As we have already seen, the formation of a national organization was not unique to intercollegiate athletic reform. Progressives typically realized the need to "band together" and craft national agencies to implement significant reforms. Among the NCAA's first acts as an advisory agency was to recommend new football rules. Soon, the organization supplanted the old rules committee led by Yale's Walter Camp, the person who had essentially invented American football 25 years earlier. The new committee recommended rules intended to make the game more "open." These rules included adding extra officials, establishing heavier penalties for rules infractions, creating a neutral zone between the two teams, preventing below-the-knees tackling, and legalizing the forward pass.[27]

The forward pass may have been the most representatively *progressive* of all of the 1906 reforms. Some proponents said that the new "open" style of play inaugurated by the forward pass would be safer for players' health, because it would reduce mass play and serious spinal or head injuries. This argument mirrored the larger Progressive-Era concern with public health, represented elsewhere by meatpacking reform or garbage removal.[28] Other proponents disagreed with this line of reasoning, saying that the forward pass and the new style of play would not necessarily be any safer than the old game of mass plays and crushing tackles. Nevertheless, they still supported a legalized forward pass because they thought the more open style of play that resulted would enhance student and public morality. Using an argument that echoed Royce's discussion of spectatorship and sport in education, these proponents of the forward pass argued that because both officials and spectators could see what was happening on the field, they could more easily punish rules infractions. In this way, the forward pass resembled progressive laws designed to implement transparency in the manufacture or packaging of consumer goods, such as the Pure Food and Drug Act of 1906. It also echoed progressives who advocated openness in international relations, such as Theodore Roosevelt, who negotiated the 1905 treaty ending the Russo-Japanese War, or Woodrow Wilson, who issued his famous Fourteen Points at the end of World War I.

The NCAA was created and the forward pass implemented at the height of the Progressive Era. Not all progressives, however, agreed that this was the best way to deal with football or to reform America's higher education institutions. Several prominent university professors called for football's suspension. One of the most famous of these voices was Frederick Jackson Turner, a famous historian at the University of Wisconsin, who contributed to "Madison Idea" progressivism. In January 1906 Turner proclaimed in a speech that the "public" had "pushed its influence inside the college walls," thus "making it impossible for faculties and for the clean and healthy masses of the students to keep athletics honest and rightly related to a sane university life." Like many progressives, Turner wanted to ensure that progressive institutions—especially universities—were maintained as pure spaces that could be sullied neither by the mob nor by plutocrats. When he suggested that the Midwestern "Big Nine" conference (Ohio State, the tenth member, had not yet joined) suspend football, students at Wisconsin burned Turner in effigy and threatened to toss him in a nearby lake.[29]

Clearly, not all Americans responded the same way to proposed football reforms. While reformers in the Northeast and Midwest were organizing the NCAA and creating a new game around the legalized forward pass, reformers on the West Coast spearheaded a different kind of reform. Many Californians thought that college football played in the West was purer and less violent than the Eastern game. When the 1905 scandals broke, some Bay Area educational leaders decided that they would rather replace football with a different game than try to reform the old one. They decided to switch to rugby, the game that Walter Camp had transformed into American football over two decades earlier. Stanford's President David Starr Jordan, along with psychology professor Frank Angell, declared that rugby would be a healthier game than American football. Even though rugby did pose a risk to the bodily extremities, they said, it was not as dangerous to the central nervous system, the physiological basis of manly energy and sensation. These two proponents were joined by President Benjamin Ide Wheeler of the University of California in Berkeley, who said that rugby would get more men involved in a healthy sport that could help make Anglo-Saxon (white) society the world's most dominant.

To implement their unique reform, Stanford and the University of California in Berkeley brought in professional players from Britain's Pacific Rim empire—especially New Zealand and Vancouver—to teach the new game to students. Although the reform was originally intended as a temporary experiment, its staying power was apparently increased by the San Francisco earthquake of April 1906. Many in the Bay Area saw this as a time of rebuilding and new beginnings. Rugby seemed a distinct, West Coast brand of progressive athletic reform. Jordan and Wheeler even waged a campaign to convince high schools and colleges throughout America to convert to rugby. However, they were only (temporarily) successful in the West. Stanford and California played their "Big Game" rivalry match under rugby rules for nearly a decade, and many schools in California, Nevada, and surrounding states followed suit. Not until World War I and the decline of progressivism did the last West Coast holdouts return to American-style football.[30]

Despite renegade reforms such as California's rugby experiment, mainstream progressive football reform continued apace in the East. Reformers implemented additional reforms around 1910 intended to continue to make the game safer and more appealing to spectators. The ball was elongated to facilitate passing. The forward pass was allowed anywhere on the field, rather than being restricted to the middle. End zones were created to accommodate receivers. Some universities even began to stitch numbers on players' jerseys, an innovation that was supposed to help both officials and spectators by making it easier to see the action on the field, punish players who broke the rules, and even keep referees honest. Although the NCAA at first resisted the idea of professional coaches, by the 1910s it was starting to come around to an idea proposed by reformers like Purdue economics professor Thomas Moran: make coaches professional members of the university staff, so that they would have a vested interest in maintaining the purity of the game and the institutions that played it. Coaches such as Michigan's Fielding Yost implicitly supported suggestions such as Moran's by publicly stating football coaches' ability to use spectator sports to teach *all* the people in the stadium—not just the players on the field—ethical and disciplined behavior. In this way they echoed Josiah Royce's arguments about the potential educational benefits of spectatorship. By the 1920s, it was increasingly common for college football coaches to have permanent positions—often serving as tenured faculty members or as directors of athletic departments. As in other aspects of American life, athletic reformers sought order and control, and they were able to implement both via bureaucratization.

Although the most celebrated arguments for progressive athletic reform centered on intercollegiate athletics, there was a similar movement to reform high school (or *interscholastic*) athletics at the turn of the century. Early 1900s reformers hoped to impose order on the competitive sports played by high school students, especially via greater faculty control. Progressive-Era physical educators "almost universally saw the value of high school sports in terms of social control, as being both an inhibitor toward schoolboy vices . . . and a force to guide the schoolboy into the norms of society under standards of good citizenship."[31] Educational sport, to put it more bluntly, was supposed to create good Americans who could contribute to a democratic society. States created high school athletic associations beginning in the 1890s, and major cities created their own athletic leagues after the turn of the century. Even though some students pushed back against such oversight and regulation, soon state and city athletic leagues became common across America.[32]

Many historians see the Progressive Era as ending around World War I, after which many Americans retreated to conservatism and isolationism. Nevertheless, there is a compelling case to be made that aspects of progressivism persisted well into the 1920s and 1930s.[33] Progressivism persisted after 1919 in the case of high school athletics. As more and more students attended comprehensive high schools in the early decades of the twentieth century, greater numbers of them participated in sports. These athletes included girls and African Americans, although in many areas high school athletic competition was limited to whites. By the 1920s, national governing bodies asserted greater control over interscholastic sports competition, and by the early 1930s, universities had been taken out of the business of sponsoring interscholastic sports, and the regulation thereof had been put in the hands of national agencies.[34]

Aspects of progressivism were also evident in college athletics after World War I. A good example is the many reinforced-concrete stadiums constructed on college campuses during the 1920s. Two decades earlier, some reformers had stressed that intercollegiate contests should be played on campus, safely under the watchful eye of university officials and away from the corrupting influence of cities and professional gamblers. Those early 1900s reformers had also wanted to replace rickety wooden grandstands with safer steel-and-concrete structures that were less prone to fire or collapse. The enormous stadiums built after World War I—often seating from 20,000 to 60,000 spectators—were the athletic equivalent of the sturdy "fireproof" buildings constructed in cities like New York or Chicago at the height of the Progressive Era. Yet even though these massive, permanent arenas fulfilled progressive desires by contributing to public assembly and health, they also served other purposes: they were monuments to manly combat, often built explicitly as memorials designed to reinforce nationalism and to prevent Americans from forgetting the recent global conflict.[35]

Conclusion

Ultimately, sport and education were closely intertwined with Progressive-Era reforms. As Americans realized the importance of the body for modern society, they crafted a new type of education that placed physicality front and center. Sport, in turn, became a significant part of education. Although not all educators agreed on the role of spectators in collegiate or scholastic sports, many members of the public gathered round to watch the contests. In turn, subsequent reforms reshaped American games—especially football—so that they would be safe and useful for a modern, democratic society. In so many ways, the terrain of American educational sport in the early twenty-first century was shaped in the early twentieth century, during America's complex and multifaceted Progressive Era.

Notes

1 See Michael McGerr, *A Fierce Discontent: The Rise and Fall of the Progressive Movement in America* (New York: Oxford University Press, 2003); Maureen A. Flanagan, *America Reformed: Progressives and Progressivisms, 1890s–1920s* (New York: Oxford University Press, 2006); Shelton Stromquist, *Reinventing "The People": The Progressive Movement, the Class Problem, and the Origins of Modern Liberalism* (Urbana: University of Illinois Press, 2005). On cross-class alliances, see Georg Leidenberger, *Chicago's Progressive Alliance: Labor and the Bid for Public Streetcars* (DeKalb: Northern Illinois University Press, 2006).

2 Robert H. Wiebe, *The Search for Order, 1877–1920* (New York: Hill and Wang, 1967); see also Alan Trachtenberg, *The Incorporation of America: Culture and Society in the Gilded Age* (New York: Hill and Wang, 1967). On the Civil War's long shadow over the Progressive Era, see Robert M. Crunden, *Ministers of Reform: The Progressives' Achievement in American Civilization, 1889–1920* (Urbana: University of Illinois Press, 1982), 4–6.

3 Daniel T. Rodgers, *Atlantic Crossings: Social Politics in a Progressive Age* (Cambridge, MA: Harvard University Press, 2000).

4 See Eldon Cobb Evans, *A History of the Australian Ballot System in the United States* (Chicago, IL: University of Chicago Press, 1917).

5 On Midwestern progressivism, see Stromquist, Reinventing 'the People," 61–63; Flanagan, *America Reformed*, 86–87; Robin F. Bachin, *Building the South Side: Urban Space and Civic Culture in Chicago, 1890–1919* (Chicago, IL: University of Chicago Press, 2004).

6 McGerr, *Fierce Discontent*, 182–202.

7 On California Progressivism, see George E. Mowry, *The California Progressives* (Berkeley: University of California Press, 1951); Tom Sitton and William Francis Deverall, eds., *California Progressivism Revisited* (Berkeley: University of California Press, 1994).

8 McGerr, *Fierce Discontent*, 109–110; Lawrence A. Cremin, *The Transformation of the School: Progressivism in American Education, 1876–1957* (New York: Vintage, 1961), 23; Robert Pruter, *The Rise of American High School Sports and the Search for Control, 1880–1930* (Syracuse, NY: Syracuse University Press, 2013), 46; Hugh Hawkins, *Banding Together: The Rise of National*

Associations in American Higher Education, 1887–1950 (Baltimore, MD: The Johns Hopkins University Press, 1992).

9 Dorothy Ross, *G. Stanley Hall: The Psychologist as Prophet* (Chicago, IL: University of Chicago Press, 1972), 293, 295; Gail Bederman, *Manliness and Civilization: A Cultural History of Gender and Race in the United States, 1880–1917* (Chicago, IL: University of Chicago Press, 1995), 99, 78, 109.

10 Clifford Putney, *Muscular Christianity: Manhood and Sports in Protestant America, 1880–1920* (Cambridge, MA: Harvard University Press, 2000), 70–71; Rob Rains, *James Naismith: The Man Who Invented Basketball* (Philadelphia: Temple University Press, 2009), 32–45; Steven A. Riess, *City Games: The Evolution of American Urban Society and the Rise of Sports* (Urbana: University of Illinois Press, 1989), 107–108; Linda J. Borish, "The Robust Woman and the Muscular Christian: Catharine Beecher, Thomas Higginson, and Their Vision of American Society, Health, and Physical Activities," *The International Journal of the History of Sport* 4 (September 1987): 139–154.

11 See Rosalind Rosenberg, *Beyond Separate Spheres: Intellectual Roots of Modern Feminism* (New Haven, CT: Yale University Press, 1982), 98–99, 105; Pruter, *Rise of American High School Sports*, 147–148.

12 On the Gibson Girl and the New Woman, see Patricia Marks, *Bicycles, Bangs, and Bloomers: The New Woman in the Popular Press* (Lexington: University Press of Kentucky, 1990); Michael Oriard, *Reading Football: How the Popular Press Created an American Spectacle* (Chapel Hill: University of North Carolina Press, 1993), 261–272.

13 Donald J. Mrozek, *Sport and American Mentality, 1880–1910* (Knoxville: University of Tennessee Press, 1983), 31.

14 Cremin, *Transformation of the School*, 135–136, 138–139, 172–173.

15 John Dewey, *Democracy and Education: An Introduction to the Philosophy of Education* (1916; New York: Free Press, 1944), 336.

16 Ibid., 196, 194, 203.

17 Mina Carson, *Settlement Folk: Social Thought and the American Settlement Movement, 1885–1930* (Chicago, IL: University of Chicago Press, 1990), 69, 173–174; Cremin, *Transformation of the School*, 60–62.

18 Dominick Cavallo, *Muscles and Morals: Organized Playgrounds and Urban Reform, 1880–1920* (Philadelphia: University of Pennsylvania Press, 1981), 149.

19 Dewey, *Democracy and Education*, 124 (quotations), 338.

20 John Clendenning, *The Life and Thought of Josiah Royce* (Madison: University of Wisconsin Press, 1985), 321.

21 Josiah Royce, *Race Questions, Provincialism, and Other American Problems* (New York: Macmillan, 1908), 241 (quotation), 229–230, 236, 239.

22 Ibid., 260–261.

23 Ibid., 285–286 (quotation), 271.

24 This and the following several paragraphs on intercollegiate football reform are taken primarily from the following sources: Brian M. Ingrassia, *The Rise of Gridiron University: Higher Education's Uneasy Alliance with Big-Time Football* (Lawrence: University Press of Kansas, 2012); John Sayle Watterson, *College Football: History, Spectacle, Controversy* (Baltimore: Johns Hopkins University Press, 2000).

25 Watterson, *College Football*, 49.

26 Ingrassia, *Rise of Gridiron University*, 56–59.

27 A good account of the NCAA's founding is Ronald A. Smith, *Pay for Play: A History of Big-Time College Athletic Reform* (Urbana: University of Illinois Press, 2010), 42–51.

28 On pure food and drugs, see James Harvey Young, *Pure Food: Securing the Federal Food and Drugs Act of 1906* (Princeton, NJ: Princeton University Press, 1989). On city streets and garbage removal, see Daniel Burnstein, *Next to Godliness: Confronting Dirt and Despair in Progressive-Era New York City* (Urbana: University of Illinois Press, 2006). Garbage removal was a major issue for Jane Addams in Chicago; see Addams, *Twenty Years at Hull-House, with Autobiographical Notes* (New York: Macmillan, 1910), 281–287.

29 See Brian M. Ingrassia, "Public Influence Inside the College Walls: Progressive Era Universities, Social Scientists, and Intercollegiate Football Reform," *The Journal of the Gilded Age and Progressive Era* 10, no. 1 (January 2011): 59–60, 76–77.

30 A standard account of the West Coast rugby experiment is Roberta J. Park, "From Football to Rugby—and Back, 1906–1919: The University of California-Stanford University Response to the 'Football Crisis of 1905,'" *Journal of Sport History* 11, no. 3 (1984): 5–40.

31 Pruter, *Rise of American High School Sports*, 58.

32 Ibid., 68, 69–83.

33 For instance, Southern progressivism picked up speed after World War I, especially regarding public education and the good roads movement. See, for example, Mary S. Hoffschwelle, *Rebuilding the Rural Southern Community: Reformers, Schools, and Homes in Tennessee, 1900–1930* (Knoxville: University of Tennessee Press, 1998); Tammy Ingram, *Dixie Highway: Road Building and the Making of the Modern South* (Chapel Hill: University of North Carolina Press, 2014). The New Deal of the 1930s also had Progressive-Era antecedents; see David M. Kennedy, *Freedom from Fear: The American People in Depression and War, 1929–1945* (New York: Oxford University Press, 1999), 120–121.

34 Pruter, *Rise of American High School Sports*, 292, 294–302.

35 See Ingrassia, *Rise of Gridiron University*, 165–166.

5

INTERCOLLEGIATE SPORTS

Ronald A. Smith

Introduction: The Beginnings

Intercollegiate athletics, like most aspects of American culture, followed the leadership coming from the British Isles, especially England. The idea of colleges or universities competing against each other athletically came from two elite universities in England: Oxford and Cambridge. The nineteenth-century Oxbridge universities were the early models for the Americans, particularly America's two most prestigious universities, Harvard and Yale. Eventually the rest of America imitated Harvard and Yale in their sporting pursuits, just as the two leading Eastern institutions looked across the ocean for their inspiration. Students in American institutions of higher education, who formed and controlled the first college sports, accepted the British conventions, such as written rules and the ideals of amateurism. However, because of cultural differences between the upper-class English universities and those in America, the manner in which intercollegiate athletics were conducted soon had marked distinctions from those in England. An emphasis on a commercial-professional model rather than the English elitist-amateur model developed quickly.[1]

The first intercollegiate sport in America came about as a commercially sponsored crew meet, wholly financed by a dominant corporate entity of the nineteenth century, a railroad. Following the lead of the first modern industrialized society in Britain, the rails created a rapid means of travel for the club sports that were developing in American colleges. In 1852, the Boston, Concord, and Montreal Railroad paid the expenses of the Harvard and Yale rowing clubs to travel to a vacation spot, Lake Winnipesaukee in the middle of New Hampshire, provided they would row against each other and offer entertainment for the vacationers.[2] Through the twentieth century and into the next, commercial enterprises continued to provide much of the finances for college athletics. Commercialism came first, but it was soon followed by a second trait of American intercollegiate athletics, professionalism. Whereas baseball became the second intercollegiate sport to be played in a game between Amherst and Williams' colleges in 1859, it was in crew that the first professional coach was hired. Yale, after losing to Harvard several times in the 1850s, decided in the midst of the American Civil War to engage a professional rower as its coach in an effort to beat their social superiors from Cambridge, Massachusetts.[3] Yale was successful, and professional coaching expanded nationally for the next century and a half, with the coach often becoming the highest-paid individual employed by a university.

The commercial-professional emphasis occurred first under student leadership, just as the extracurriculum in other areas, such as fraternities, bands, and newspapers, began in institutions of higher education in the nineteenth century. Students dominated, or as Walter

Camp, "Father of American Football," stated at the time, college athletics "is a structure which students unaided have builded [*sic*]."[4] Most sports played on college campuses by men and women in the twenty-first century were first developed under student control. For men, these include the first five intercollegiate sports, crew, baseball, cricket, track and field, and football, all contested in the first two decades following the first crew meet. Male students throughout America in the nineteenth century began playing a variety of sports, and at nearly every institution students would form an athletic association to provide financial and morale support for the sports they deemed most important. The initial support in Eastern colleges was principally for crew and baseball, but after track and field and especially football became prominent, athletic associations expanded their horizons. When a team was formed, irrespective of sport, a student captain would generally be chosen, and it was he, rather than a professional coach, who would determine the starting lineup and the strategy of the contest. Once a professional coach was hired, he would typically begin to dominate, but often it was the captain who would select the coach, and the captain would continue to direct much of the strategy and placement of players.

Under male student control, the tenets of amateurism, carried over from the elite institutions of the mother country, were soon lost. Professionalism increasingly emerged in the last half of the nineteenth century. It was revealed in competitions for cash and valuable, noncash prizes, contesting against professionals, charging money at the gate, paying for the athletes' training table and for athletic tutors by others than the athletes, recruiting and paying athletes to attend college, and hiring professional coaches.[5] The recruitment and payment of athletes and the hiring of professional coaches were the most blatant violations of amateurism. Prior to the twentieth century, professionalism had invaded college sports and had defeated amateurism, as it was then understood. Yet, colleges everywhere continued to call their form of athletics amateur. Thus, the amateur-professional athletic dilemma developed. If a college had truly amateur sport, it would lose contests and thus prestige. If a college acknowledged outright professionalism, it would lose respectability as a middle-class or higher-class institution. Be amateur and lose athletically to those who were less amateur; be outright professional and lose social esteem. The American solution was to claim amateurism while accepting professionalism. Such a practice has continued unabated, thus for men and eventually for women.

Athlete Eligibility and Conference Development

Operating under a professional model resulted in a dramatic increase in the recruiting of athletes and accompanying attempts to keep them scholastically eligible for athletic competition. A college faculty generally set eligibility rules, such as who was considered a bona fide student, whether an admitted "special" student or transfer student was eligible for athletic participation, what level of scholastic achievement was needed to remain eligible to play, whether freshman undergraduates or graduate students were eligible, and how many years of eligibility were allowed. Because each college set its own rules, there was no consistency, and there were, for example, athletes who participated at one school until graduation and then attended graduate school and played another three or four years. Obviously, an institution with graduate schools in such areas as law, medicine, or theology would be able to play athletes who were in their mid-20s or older. Conflicting eligibility rules led to problems and breaking of athletic relations in the late 1800s and early 1900s. Out of this chaos came the creation of athletic conferences in an attempt to create a level playing field for their members. In the Midwest, the Intercollegiate Conference of Faculty Representatives (Big Ten) was created in the mid-1890s. It drew up rules that established faculty, rather than student, control and demanded bona fide students doing full and successful academic work, prohibited competition against professional teams, and limited athletic eligibility to no more than four years.[6] The Big Ten was one of many conferences established during the Progressive Era. Other conferences that were organized included the Missouri Valley Conference (1907), Southwest Athletic Conference (1914), Pacific Coast Intercollegiate Athletic Conference (1915), and Southern Conference (1921). Some conferences that were formed later were the Missouri Valley Intercollegiate Athletic Association (Big 7) in 1928, the Southeastern Conference breaking away from the Southern Conference in 1932, the Ivy League in 1945, and the Atlantic Coast Conference in 1953.

In the East, where an early reluctance among colleges to form conferences because of the tradition of independence existed, the prominent Walter Camp of Yale was one example of the perennial athletic veteran at the Connecticut school, beginning in 1876, that created the need for conferences and a national organization. He played four years as an undergraduate and two more years while in medical school before being hurt, cutting his athletic career to six years. Camp was not an exception in the number of years of competition. No wonder other schools began to question athletic eligibility at Yale and most other institutions. As the number of conferences increased, there was pressure for a national conference to provide guidelines—if not rules—for eligibility and for setting common rules for the most important sports. Football became the dominant game by the turn of the century. When a crisis in football ethics and injuries came about during the 1905 football season, there were demands for a national organization for common game rules and a venue for discussion of eligibility rules and questions of amateurism.[7] Walter Camp, who had been on the Eastern-dominated football rules committee from 1877 until well into the twentieth century, was involved, though negatively, in the creation of what became known as the National Collegiate Athletic Association (NCAA) at the conclusion of the 1905 football season.

Camp had been the dominant individual in creating the rules of football, changing rugby football rules that he played under to American football in the early 1880s. Actually, intercollegiate football, soccer style, began in 1869 with a contest between Rutgers and Princeton, but soccer (or Association football) was dropped by the Eastern leaders in favor of rugby in 1876, Camp's first year at Yale. At that time, the Intercollegiate Football Association was formed by Columbia, Harvard, Princeton, and Yale for common rules of the game and for creating a national championship game that began with the Princeton-Yale Thanksgiving Day game played in metropolitan New York City. Within years of the rugby game introduction, Camp championed the creation of a clearly defined "scrimmage" line, with the possession of the ball by the team whose runner was tackled, rather than the indeterminate ball possession of the "scrummage" in the rugby game. He was instrumental in creating the number of yards to be gained in a certain number of attempts (downs) in the early 1880s. Clearly, he was the "father of American football." Camp was not, however, interested in seeing his game changed drastically when the NCAA was formed.[8]

Brutality in football, the most important college sport by the early twentieth century, was the impetus for a national conference, the NCAA, to be formed. Violence continued after the most brutal play ever developed in football, the flying wedge, was banned by the rules committee in 1894. As football mayhem persisted, a White House conference was called in 1905 and directed by President Teddy Roosevelt with Harvard, Yale, and Princeton delegates in attendance.[9] That season experienced several deaths and questionable ethics, leading to the creation of a national organization. This followed New York University Chancellor Henry MacCracken's meeting of Eastern colleges to either ban football or reform it. Shortly after that December 1905 gathering came a national conference to reform football. The National Collegiate Athletic Association was born. Out of the football chaos came a new set of football rules, including the introduction of the forward pass, a play that Camp opposed but one that eventually came to dominate the game and increase its popularity. While perceived evils in football necessitated the development of a national organization, the NCAA was originally given no power to legislate solutions, except for game rule changes. Thus "home rule" by individual institutions and conferences continued for the next half century. Only at mid-century and the conclusion of World War II was the NCAA granted the power by individual members of the organization to legislate and enforce the legislation for such activities as eligibility requirements and control over telecasting of events.

Commercialism and Stadium Building

Intercollegiate sport for men by the time of the NCAA included a number of sports in order of introduction: crew (1852), baseball (1859), cricket (1864), soccer football (1869), track and field (1873), rugby football (1874), rifle (1877), lacrosse (1877), bicycle (1880), tennis (1883), cross-country (1890), fencing (1894), ice hockey (1895), basketball (1895), golf (1896), trap shooting (1898), water polo (1899), swimming (1899), gymnastics (1899), wrestling (1905), and soccer—again (1905). No sport came close to challenging football for popularity, although both baseball, nationally, and crew, in the East, had early on been the major sports. Football, probably because it gave an appearance of virility and masculinity to institutions of higher education that lacked this image, attracted not only college students and graduates, but also the general public to what was considered a manly game. That it was considered so is of no small importance at the end of the nineteenth century. Americans questioned if there was a softening of society and lack of manliness due to urbanization and the closing of the Western frontier. Were Americans losing a rightful place in the world as the Social Darwinian "survival of the fittest" was a dominating thought? A number believed that football, not tennis, golf, or swimming, proved to be the standard for the strong surviving and prospering at the expense of the weak, languishing or perishing.[10] The expansion of football dominated college sport during the twentieth century—and it had an impact on the most important commercial activity, the construction of stadiums throughout America.

Building upon the professionalization and commercialization of college sport by procuring the players, producing rigid training schedules, eating the right foods, and hiring the best coaches, American colleges began erecting the finest facilities, especially in football. Pressed by an increasing number of spectators, and with the financial aid of alumni at each institution, colleges went beyond the construction of wooden bleachers to design facilities, found previously in the ancient Roman Empire to enhance their often bloody spectacles of chariot races and gladiatorial combats. Harvard was the first institution to construct a concrete stadium reinforced with steel in 1903. By then, alumni had come to dominate college athletics, because students did not have the financial resources to create what became known as big-time athletics. It is not ironic that the Harvard stadium construction began with an enormous $100,000 gift from the Harvard alums of 1879, the class as freshman who experienced the first Harvard-Yale football game. Harvard was the pace setter in higher education with such innovations as graduate education and raising admission and graduation standards for professional schools, requiring a bachelor's degree for admittance to its degree-granting medical school, freeing its divinity school from the trammels of sect, making attendance at religious services voluntary for its undergraduates, allowing multiple electives for undergraduates, creating a university student union, and innovating sabbatical leaves for its faculty. Not unexpectedly, Harvard would create the first reinforced concrete stadium in the world. The 33,000-seat stadium, which would eventually become a National Historic Landmark, began the rush for permanent stadiums to meet the needs of a growing spectator sport. The most significant edifices constructed were those of the other two members of the "Big Three" big-time schools, Yale and Princeton. Yale proposed a stadium in 1908 that would seat over 70,000, about 30 percent larger than the ancient Roman Coliseum, whereas Princeton decided upon one of about 40,000.[11]

The emulation of Harvard, Yale, and Princeton stadiums came to fruition following World War I, principally in the Midwest and the Far West. Every Big Ten institution built a stadium in the 1920s, led by Ohio State University and the University of Michigan with stadiums seating over 70,000. On the West Coast, the University of California at Berkeley and Stanford University competed to build the first nearly 70,000-seat college stadiums in the early 1920s. The commercialization of college athletics grew exponentially, but not without opposition, especially from faculty members. A good example was a Stanford professor, Frank Angell, educated at the University of Leipzig in Germany and one who favored the English, Oxford University system of athletics, patronized by gentlemen, purely amateur, and not commercialized. Angell had once played rugby at Oxford. Opposing the constructing of a commercialized stadium at Stanford as chair of the Board of Athletic Control, he resigned when athletic interests and local businessmen won control of "amateur" athletics at Stanford and construction of its stadium went ahead. At other universities across America, the likes of Frank Angell consistently lost the battle for less commercialized and professionalized sport. Critics such as Angell were muted by the cheers of those sitting in the "Roman coliseums" of the twentieth century.

The grand stadiums of leading institutions in the 1920s went a long way to promote the virile image of major universities and endear institutions of higher learning to the masses of Americans. Tying the masses to higher education and promoting universities through intercollegiate athletics in a country that provided almost no federal money to universities, a common funding source among European nations, was a major accomplishment. Although American universities survived in the 1920s without federal support, to provide for institutional growth the major universities felt the need for self-promotion through athletics as a major method of advertising and gaining financial backing from state and local governments, alumni, and the general public. The governing boards, which were increasingly dominated by business leaders and professional men, saw the benefits that football and large stadiums could provide their institutions. It was clear that the outstanding academic institutions in America were the same institutions that had built or were building giant stadiums. Harvard, the leading educational institution, had precipitated the movement that others soon followed.

The building of elaborate facilities came about in the twentieth century's second most important college sport, basketball. For basketball, only invented by James Naismith after football had become the number one college sport, it is not surprising that facilities to accommodate spectators did not generally come until basketball became a nationally prominent sport in the 1930s. However, there was some pressure in the 1920s to build indoor facilities, particularly for basketball. Two Big Ten institutions, Michigan and Wisconsin, built large facilities, with Michigan leading the way in 1923 when it built the Fielding H. Yost arena and Wisconsin constructing an arena that could accomodate 12,000 in 1930. Yet, basketball did not become the dominant winter sport until it was made popular by basketball contests held in New York City's Madison Square Garden during the Great Depression of the 1930s.[12] Journalist Ned Irish began sponsoring benefit basketball games in the Garden for the unemployed and soon realized the commercial possibilities of pitting the best New York teams against colleges across the country. By 1934 and the depth of the Depression, a collegiate double-header drew 16,000 fans. Games with distant teams such as Colorado, Kentucky, Notre Dame, and Stanford provided the window for basketball's popularity. By 1938, Madison Square Garden sponsored the first National Invitation Tournament, and with its popularity, the NCAA decided to hold its own tournament the following year. Enjoying its early success, the NCAA basketball tournament became the most profitable nationally sponsored championship for the NCAA following World War II. The NCAA tournament eventually created a wealthy organization, giving the NCAA a powerful place in controlling intercollegiate athletics after mid-century.

The Media and National NCAA Rules

By World War II several technological advances helped promote college sport on a national basis—travel by airplanes, broadcasts through radio, and a new invention, television. Because of rapid travel and communications, there was more regional and national competition, especially in the two dominating sports, football and basketball. Both sports were popularized by radio broadcasts beginning in the 1920s and 1930s and two decades later telecasts on a national level as leading teams from various sections of the country could be brought together. Intersectional games also created a greater need for recruitment and subsidization rules for a more level national playing field. In 1948, the NCAA finally decided to create national rules for both recruiting and paying players and to enforce the rules on a national rather than conference level. The new NCAA policy was called the "Sanity Code," for it was intended to bring a sane athletic policy to all college sports. To attempt to keep sports amateur, financial aid to an athlete was to be based on financial need and could not exceed the cost of tuition and fees. Further, there was to be no recruiting of athletes by athletic representatives of the colleges. Although the "Sanity Code" was passed in a near-unanimous action by NCAA representatives, the new legislation was violated by institutions across America.[13] The "Sanity Code" soon failed. Nevertheless, commercialization through radio and television continued to popularize college sport. "Home rule" was restored in the area of eligibility as the NCAA failed in its first attempt to control recruiting and subsidization nationally. However, that was not true relative to the NCAA's success in controlling television in the dominating sport, football.

Shortly after World War II as television grew exponentially, a major question arose as to the negative impact that TV might have on the number of spectators who would attend football games rather than watch at home on TV. Because big-time football paid the bills of most of the other sports sponsored by an institution, television was considered a major threat to all of intercollegiate sport. Whether or not television would ruin gate receipts dominated the thought of athletic leaders. After a three-year decline in football gate attendance, an NCAA television study committee in 1949 concluded that TV was a threat to the entire financial structure of college sport. In 1950, the NCAA voted overwhelmingly to restrict the telecasting of football by creating a policy limiting national telecasting. The policy of only one or two games being telecast weekly continued until the U.S. Supreme Court ruled in 1984 that the NCAA television plan violated the 1890 Sherman Antitrust Act constricting free trade.[14]

Within a week, Notre Dame, the most visible national institution in football, was offered $20 million for a national television contract. Notre Dame did not accept the offer at the time, but institutions and conferences were allowed to create their own TV contracts, and a national cartel of big-time institutions, known as the College Football Association, created its own television network. Television had not created big-time football, but it contributed to a growing commercial element in college athletics. The result was to increase pressure to recruit the best athletes, regardless of academic potential, to produce winners who would be shown on TV and bring in additional millions and prestige to the institutions. The already considerable pressure on coaches to produce both winners and revenue led to more firings and the breaking of rules by coaches in their quest for victories. While intercollegiate athletics for men were never seriously considered an important part of the educational endeavor, with the advent of television there was even a greater divide between athletics and the scholarly function of colleges.

The Question of Race and Gender

Intercollegiate athletics became the dominant extracurricular activity in most colleges by the end of the nineteenth century, and they did so with little participation of two significant segments of American society, African Americans and women. The lack of participation of these two groups was reflective of the absence of equality in the larger American society. Both, however, became important in the development of athletics in the period following World War II. If America fought with African Americans in World War II against Hitler and the Nazi ideology of Aryan racial superiority, it was hypocritical for Americans to carry out their own brand of racial superiority, known as "Jim Crow" segregation, from the period after the Civil War into the twentieth century. Not only were blacks segregated legally, but socially as well. Until the conclusion of World War II, few blacks had participated in either professional or amateur college sport since the 1800s.[15] At the close of the war, professional football and baseball, the two most important sports at the time, opened the doors to blacks' participation. Colleges, although never completely excluding black enrollment or participation in athletes, were reluctant to go against cultural bias until World War II and the following Cold War with the Soviet Union made the climate more acceptable to the African American.

The U.S. Supreme Court ruling in 1954 outlawed school segregation of whites from blacks in its *Brown v. Board of Education* decision. It was instrumental in breaking down segregation in schools, especially in the South where segregation remained the most ingrained in society. By the 1960s, segregated white colleges in the Southern United States began to admit black students. Within a generation, black athletes were a significant part of the enrollment in American colleges, and they made a big difference in the competitiveness of both Southern and Northern athletic teams, especially in football and basketball, the two dominant sports for college men.

The growth of women's intercollegiate sport came on the heels of progress for African Americans during the civil rights movement of the 1960s. During the first six decades of the twentieth century, intercollegiate athletics for women had been sporadic. With the women's movement by the 1960s, an increasing number of colleges began to participate in women's competitive athletics, replacing "play days" and "sports days" in which socialization dominated competition. Unlike men's competition that was generally outside an educational setting, women's athletics had been controlled by women physical educators who wanted athletics to be an integral part of the educational process. For decades, women physical educators opposed highly competitive athletics and had been the group most opposed to intercollegiate contests. But the women's movement strove for equality and that meant, among other changes, the right to participate in highly competitive intercollegiate athletics.[16]

An important federal government action in 1972 brought about greater women's equality with men in schools and colleges. That year Title IX, an amendment to a 1964 Civil Rights Act, became law. It stated that "No person in the United States shall, on the basis of sex, be excluded from participation in, be denied the benefits of, or be subjected to discrimination under any education program or activity receiving federal financial assistance." When passed, it became obvious that sport in educational institutions was not providing women equal opportunities and adequate resources and facilities, a blatant area of sex discrimination. Only about 1 percent of all athletic financial resources went to women's sport. The discrimination was clearly seen in the lack of college athletic scholarships for women, the traditional method in men's athletics of financing the cost of an athlete's education. Almost immediately, athletic scholarships for women were demanded. Title IX had pushed women closer to athletic equality with men at the same time it moved women toward the men's professional and commercial competitive model and away from the women's attempt at integrating athletics in an educational setting.[17]

Bringing women into increased intercollegiate athletic competition, like breaking down the barriers to African American participation, raised the level of performance in college athletics. The entrance of blacks and women into college athletics was most visibly seen in basketball. Although basketball had been the most popular women's college sport almost from its origin in the 1890s, Title IX helped raise performance in all women's competition, especially basketball. In a similar way, the influx of blacks on men's basketball teams raised the level of performance to such a height that it challenged football as the most dynamic sport on college campuses by the end of the twentieth century. Such popularity was best seen in the national championships in basketball for both men and women. "March Madness" in basketball created billion-dollar TV contracts for men, enriching the National Collegiate Athletic Association, and large crowds for women, though much less money from TV. Over 90 percent of the NCAA income came from the telecasting of the 60-some teams in the men's national playoff. This income was used for conducting many activities, including all of the national championships of the three divisions of the NCAA, small colleges with no athletic scholarships to big-time competition, and paying the high salary of the NCAA president, nearly as much as college football and basketball coaches and more than most college presidents.[18]

The Failed Quest to Reform Athletics

Critics of big-time intercollegiate sports demanded significant reforms to better ensure academic integrity even after institutional college presidents took over complete NCAA control from faculty representatives in 1990s. Reform efforts had existed before the NCAA was formed in 1905 (then called the Intercollegiate Athletic Association of the United States), but most were only partial successes. The Carnegie Foundation for the Advancement of Teaching's lengthy report on *American College Athletics* in 1929 was an unsuccessful effort to eliminate much of the commercialism and professionalism that had developed by the 1920s.[19] The reform attempts by the American Council on Education in the 1950s and two decades later and the Knight Foundation's Commission on Intercollegiate Athletics in the 1990s were failures. The Knight Foundation made attempts for several decades, but the commission, formed principally of college presidents or ex-college presidents, was no more successful than previous endeavors. In particular, the Knight Commission's presidents had fallen far short of recommending action to better ensure academic integrity.[20] An example of this was the commission's refusal to do anything about presidential "special admits," a device to allow university heads to admit athletically superior but academically inferior students. Because teams in the most commercialized sports were often composed of a high percentage of presidential admits (those who were not even close to the academic average of the rest of the student body), it was necessary to set up elaborate counseling units in each university to keep athletes eligible. These units were found guilty of improper services such as writing term papers for athletes and funneling athletes into courses and curriculums that were exploited specifically for the benefit of athletes. It became clear that presidents would not reform the intercollegiate athletic programs that they had been in charge of for generations at the institutional and national levels. They would not reduce the increased number of contests, reduce the number of hours devoted to athletics, reduce the number of contests dictated by TV in the middle of the school week, or attempt to reduce the multimillion-dollar head coaching contracts. Because college athletics was such a strong part of the culture of the nation, it was little wonder that college presidents, pressured to turn out winners, refused to reform the dominant part of the extracurriculum to conform to the rigors of academia.[21]

Faculty, who had once set academic standards to be met by athletes, had generally been removed from the academic-athletic equation as the twentieth century progressed. By the beginning of the twenty-first century, faculty had been eliminated from nearly all aspects of athletics, and the faculty representative to the NCAA, though a faculty member, was really the presidential representative, appointed by the president in nearly all institutions of higher education. A new organization of faculty, the Coalition on Intercollegiate Athletics (COIA), emerged from its 2002 beginnings by a faculty member of the University of Oregon, James Earl, a professor of medieval literature and president of his faculty senate. His idea of an "academics first" resolution was soon sent and accepted by a group of faculty senators of the PAC-10 athletic conference. The PAC-10 then asked the Big Ten faculty senates to become involved in athletic reform. The Big Ten then took the idea nationally, and a Coalition on Intercollegiate Athletics among university faculty senates was formed. The COIA raised questions about the need for higher eligibility and admission standards; improving the welfare of athletes; pointing out advising, gender, and race issues; limiting training time and length of playing seasons; and slowing the "arms race" for the best athletic facilities. The COIA sought shared governance, which would include faculty along with the athletic administration, governing boards, and presidents.[22] Those college faculties were again considering their place in governing the extracurriculum's most important activity was symbolic in showing that presidents and athletic administrations had been unsuccessful in eliminating the abuses in intercollegiate athletics.

While it was problematic that the COIA might be a force in athletic reform, a greater possibility existed that two outside agencies, branches of the federal government, might be more effective. The passage of federal laws and decisions of the judicial system could be keys to intercollegiate athletic reform. Federal laws, rather than actions by colleges or the NCAA, have been the most effective means of women and African Americans becoming more integral in intercollegiate athletics with the passage of civil rights legislation and a 1972 amendment to a civil rights law, Title IX. A major Supreme Court decision had broken up an NCAA television monopoly in the 1980s, and future Supreme Court decisions could help reform college athletics.

If the courts would decide that college athletic policies, especially those of the NCAA, conferences, or individual institutions, were unconstitutional, the impact upon college sports could be drastically changed in a variety of ways. For instance, the NCAA in the twenty-first century was demanding that athletes would not be eligible for competition if they did not sign away their rights to their personal images. If courts might find this to be illegal under the Sherman Antitrust Act of 1890, another NCAA monopolistic action would be corrected. If the courts would claim that intercollegiate athletics are not amateur but rather commercial and professional, athletes might well come under workers' compensation laws, and colleges would come under federal tax laws and relinquish their tax-exempt status as found in other professional sports. If courts found that athletes received head injuries because of inadequate safety rules, litigation could have a major impact on athletic income. If Congress amended the Family Educational Rights and Privacy Act (Buckley Amendment) so that institutions could not protect athletic interests under cover of the academic records disclosure FERPA law, it might have a major impact in countering the hiding of an athlete's academic records by individual institutions and raising the level of academic integrity of athletic programs. Federal legislation and court decisions could have a major impact on athletic reform.

Many of these issues revolve around the issue of whether college sports are both educational and amateur. Because the concept of amateurism was first developed in the nineteenth century, amateurism has lost nearly all of its meaning, but it remains an emphasized concept in the NCAA constitution. The NCAA claims amateur status whenever it is involved in either legislative or judicial actions. However, nearly all decisions engaged in by big-time athletic institutions, conferences, and the NCAA are professional in nature and not amateur, including the minimal payment of athletes to attend college.

Past precedent would indicate that in the future, athletics within the NCAA and its member institutions shall no longer be considered either amateur or educational. In the 1984 football telecasting case, *Oklahoma v. NCAA*, the U.S. Supreme Court ruled that the NCAA was a monopolist in violation of the Sherman Antitrust Act.[23] This was the first time the Supreme Court ever ruled that "amateur" sport was in violation of antitrust laws. If the Supreme Court were ever to rule that college sport is so commercialized and professionalized that it is no longer considered part of the educational function of institutions of higher learning, the nature of college sport will have a major transformation.

Conclusion

From the nineteenth century intercollegiate athletics in America have been dominated by the commercial and professional model. That model had first been introduced by the elite Eastern colleges such as Harvard and Yale, but it spread rapidly across America at an early time. This highly rationalized process of producing winning teams through commercialization and professionalization suited the American system of higher education. The prestige attained from winning teams helped promote the extraordinary number of American colleges and universities, all attempting to survive and prosper in the highly competitive nature of higher education. Big-time athletics in the twentieth and twenty-first centuries were a physically symbolic form of intense competition for prestige existing among the various independent institutions of higher learning. Winning athletic teams were simply the most visible signs of the larger contest for prestige in all areas of university life. Nearly all universities stood for and competed for increasing undergraduate enrollment, attracting superior graduate students, hiring "star" professors, maximizing faculty publications, obtaining research monies, and accumulating gifts and endowments. The construction of a huge stadium for football or an arena for basketball proved no less important to the prestige of an American college than the beautifying of the campus, constructing a large chapel, erecting a student union, hiring a star professor, or enlarging the library holdings. Intercollegiate athletics were to a great extent a reflection of the need in American higher education for self-promotion in an intense struggle to gain recognition and prosper. From that standpoint, intercollegiate athletics served well the needs of American higher education.

Notes

1 Ronald A. Smith, *Sports and Freedom: The Rise of Big-Time College Athletics* (New York: Oxford University Press, 1988). See specifically "Amateur College Sport: An Untenable Concept in a Free and Open Society," 165–174.
2 James Whiton, "The First Harvard-Yale Regatta (1852)," *Outlook* 68 (June 1901): 286–289.
3 R.M. Hurd, "The Yale Stroke," *Outing* 15 (December 1889): 230–231.
4 Walter Camp, "College Athletics," *New Englander* 44 (January 1885): 139.
5 Ronald A. Smith, *Pay for Play: A History of Big-Time College Athletic Reform* (Urbana: University of Illinois Press, 2011), 58.
6 Carl D. Voltmer, *A Brief History of the Intercollegiate Conference of Faculty Representatives with Special Consideration of Athletic Problems* (Menasha, WI: George Banta Publishing, 1935), 5–8.
7 John S. Watterson, *College Football: History, Spectacle, Controversy* (Baltimore, MD: The Johns Hopkins University Press, 2000), 64–98.
8 See Parke H. Davis, *Football the American Intercollegiate Game* (New York: Charles Scribner's Sons, 1911) for a fine early history of intercollegiate football.
9 For a description of the White House Conference by a participant see Ronald A. Smith, ed., *Big-Time Football at Harvard: The Diary of Coach Bill Reid* (Urbana: University of Illinois Press, 1994), 192–196.
10 For a discussion of manliness in institutions of higher education see "Football and Manliness: A Measure of the American College," in Smith, *Sports and Freedom*, 195–198.
11 Ronald A. Smith, "Far More than Commercialism: Stadium Building from Harvard's Innovations to Stanford's 'Dirt Bowl,'" *The International Journal of the History of Sport* 25 (September 2008): 1453–1474.
12 Joseph Durso, *Madison Square Garden: 100 Years of History* (New York: Simon & Schuster, 1979), 155–160.
13 Allen L. Sack and Ellen J. Staurowsky, *College Athletes for Hire: The Evolution and Legacy of the NCAA's Amateur Myth* (Westport, CT: Praeger, 1998), 43–46.
14 Ronald A. Smith, *Play-by-Play: Radio, Television, and Big-Time College Sport* (Baltimore, MD: The Johns Hopkins University Press, 2001), 72–78, 152–176.
15 Charles H. Martin, "White Supremacy and American College Sports," in his *Benching Jim Crow: The Rise and Fall of the Color Line in Southern College Sports, 1890–1980* (Urbana: University of Illinois Press, 2010), 1–26.
16 Susan K. Cahn, *Coming on Strong: Gender and Sexuality in Twentieth-Century Women's Sport* (New York: Free Press, 1994) is a strong account of women's place in American sport.
17 Sarah K. Fields, *Female Gladiators: Gender, Law, and Contact Sport in America* (Urbana: University of Illinois Press, 2005) offers a nice explanation of Title IX and the equal protection clause in the Fourteenth Amendment to the U.S. Constitution, 6–14.
18 Andrew Zimbalist in *Unpaid Professionals: Commercialism and Conflict in Big-Time College Sports* (Princeton, NJ: Princeton University Press, 1999) discusses the NCAA, basketball's final four and the economics of college sports.
19 Howard J. Savage, Howard W. Bentley, John T. McGovern, and Dean F. Smiley, MD, *American College Athletics* [Bulletin No. 23] (New York: Carnegie Foundation for the Advancement of Teaching, 1929).
20 A lengthy discussion of failures of reform are found in Ronald A. Smith, *Pay for Play: A History of Big-Time College Athletic Reform* (Urbana: University of Illinois Press, 2010), 109–120, 131–140, and 175–187.

21 There is an array of books on troubles and reform in college athletics, but one might start with Charles T. Clotfelter, *Big-Time Sports in American Universities* (New York: Cambridge University Press, 2011).

22 Smith, *Pay for Play*, 193–197.

23 Brian L. Porto in *The Supreme Court and the NCAA* (Ann Arbor: University of Michigan Press, 2012) looks specifically at two Supreme Court decisions and their impact on college sport: the TV monopoly decision and the Jerry Tarkanian due-process decisions of the 1980s.

6

HIGH SCHOOL SPORTS

Robert Pruter

Introduction

The secondary schools in the United States, in common with its colleges and universities, established sports as part of their educational program by gradually incorporating them from around 1880 to around 1930. Before that time sports and games in the private boarding schools of the New England and Mid-Atlantic states can be dated back to the eighteenth century. In these schools, boys under their own initiative and direction, at recess and after school hours, played bat and ball games and unruly football-like games, which evolved into baseball and football by the early 1830s. At the same time, headmasters and other school authorities introduced exercise programs (beginning with Round Hill School in the 1820s) and a surprising number of recreations, including swimming, archery, wrestling, boxing, and ice skating. In the late 1850s, sports competition in these private schools became more organized as students began forming athletic associations to sponsor and support intramural class competition in baseball, cricket, football, and boat racing. The next step, the emergence of interscholastic competition, was slowed by the Civil War. But by the late 1860s, in such sports as rowing and baseball, boarding schools had begun competing among each other, most notably Phillips Andover, Phillips Exeter, Lawrenceville, Hill, and St. Paul's.[1]

The term "interscholastic," meaning competition between or among high schools, was introduced in 1879, when the *New York Times* first described the inaugural track and field meet held by the city's private day schools. This event marked the debut of interscholastic sports competition in New York City.[2]

Public high schools in the United States emerged during the 1830s and 1840s, but were slower to develop formal sports than the private academies. Interscholastic sports, like those in prep schools, were managed by students who formed sponsoring athletic associations. Baseball teams, which emerged in the 1870s, and field days, which began in the 1880s, were two of the first sponsorships undertaken by such associations. Football in some high schools appeared in the late 1870s. Gradually in more and more schools, students introduced sports competitions in football, baseball, and track and field, so that by the end of the 1880s they were establishing some of the first student-directed leagues and tournaments.[3]

Full Emergence of Public High School Sports

During the 1890s, the secondary education system experienced dramatic growth, with the expansion of public school education that increased the number of public high schools dramatically—from 2,526 in 1890 to 6,005 in 1900. In 1890, one-third of all high schools were private, enrolling about one-third of the secondary school students, but by 1900 the public schools were enrolling more than 80 percent of the students, which by 1918 had increased to 91 percent. Thus, during the 1890s, public schools moved past private schools in the development of high school sports.[4]

Spurred by the huge growth in the number of secondary students, high school sports experienced an explosive increase during the 1890s as students began reaching each out to adult authorities for the use of facilities, for officiating, and for the awarding of trophies and prizes. The students also formed alliances with private athletic clubs and other groups that could provide these things, whose facilities were particularly needed in such sports as track, tennis, and football.[5]

During the 1890s, high schools began building indoor gymnasiums that were designed for physical education classes but led to the emergence of indoor baseball, basketball, and gymnastics competition. At this time, adult authorities were unaware, or if aware, indifferent to emerging problems of sportsmanship and other ethical abuses evident in incipient high school sports. The physical educators of the day were unconcerned about organized sport (not viewing the extracurriculum as something under their purview), focused instead on developing physical education as a requirement in the high schools.[6]

Establishment of Institutional Control

After 1900, physical educators began examining the state of sports in schools and were highly critical of the student-run organizations fostering many abuses, notably the use of ringers, unsportsmanlike conduct, and neglect of academics. Having developed physical education as a part of the curriculum, they then brought student athletics under their regulatory control, not only to end reputed abuses, but also to make it a part of the physical education program. This imposition of control was tied to the overall reform in American education and American society during the Progressive Era. Reformers of high school sports reflected the era's values in their vision that athletics and games for youth would help ameliorate some of the pathologies of modern industrial society, particularly in large urban centers.[7]

The reform of high school sports involved establishing school-sponsored athletic leagues to replace student-run leagues. This reform was led by New York's Public Schools Athletic League (PSAL), established in 1903 by Luther Gulick, bringing student athletics under control of adult authorities while expanding sports opportunities for students. The formation of the PSAL influenced the development of similar leagues across the country. In one report from 1917, 17 cities in the United States formed athletic leagues reportedly modeled after the PSAL. In metropolitan Chicago, school authorities took gradual control during 1898–1904, leading to the formation of separate city and suburban leagues in 1913. Philadelphia formed a school-administered league in 1901, followed by an all-public school league in 1912. Boston formed a public school league in 1905, and Los Angeles in 1911.[8]

Equally significant to the imposition of institutional control was the formation of statewide high school athletic associations. The formation of high school athletic associations originally occurred in the Midwestern states, first in Wisconsin (1895), Illinois (1900), Indiana (1903), and Ohio (1907). By World War I, state associations had been formed across the country, notably in Texas (1910), Virginia (1913), Pennsylvania (1913), and California (1914). Most state associations initially focused on only one or two sports—usually basketball and sometimes track and field—with little interest in regulating other sports.[9]

Most students acquiesced to the new faculty control and governance reform and accepted the new order of things. Some educators, however, faced persistent student resistance, stiffened by rebellious high school fraternities, and continued abuses in the decade leading up to World War I. High school sports were thus plagued by issues relating to eligibility, professionalism, fraternity membership, interstate travel, and student rowdiness.[10] The advent of faculty control in the first decade of the new century was accompanied by an expansion of the sports programs. In outdoor sports, golf, cross-country, and soccer emerged nationwide, whereas lacrosse and rowing flourished in the East. During the winter, basketball was extraordinarily popular, but swimming and rifle marksmanship also grew nationally in addition to a slew of regionally popular sports—indoor baseball (Chicago), water polo (California), ice hockey (East), speed skating (East), and handball (New York). There was no opposition on the part of educators to this crowding of the sports calendar. Indeed, the broadening of the athletic extracurriculum expanded the benefits of sports to more students, benefits that included physical and character development essential to the educational mission of high schools and the aspirations of progressives to uplift society as a whole.

The early 1900s also witnessed the development of high school sports for girls, particularly basketball, but also indoor baseball, tennis, and track and field. Initially not under any institutional control, educators viewed girls' sports through the lens of prevailing attitudes toward female athletics, particularly basketball. Interschool competition, much physical exertion, playing before crowds, and male direction were deemed unsuitable for girls by many physical educators. But in most sections of the country, girl basketball players traveled through their states, often coached by men, competing against other schools before unruly mixed crowds and playing a brand of basketball based on boys' rules that involved a degree of roughness and exertion that many educators considered inappropriate and even unhealthy for young ladies. Reformers increased their anticompetition campaign in earnest around 1907–1908, and within a few years they ended female interscholastic competition in all sports in most states. Some competition, mainly basketball, did persist in rural areas in some Midwest and Southern states, where the success of their girls' teams reflected community pride.[11]

High School Athletics and the Golden Age of Sports

During the 1920s, high school sports grew dramatically with regard to student participation, the spread of sports to more high schools, and the increasing number of sports being made available. Fueling the growth in the number of students participating in sport was the broadening of the student population beyond college preparatory, leading to development of the comprehensive high school. By 1918, such schools, with their variety of vocational, home making, and college prep courses designed to serve all kinds of students, were deemed the standard organization for secondary education. The growth in the number and variety of students was a result of compulsory attendance laws that after 1900 spread to the majority of states and, in many cases, increased the age of attendance up through high school. Antichild labor legislation also fueled this growth.[12]

The National Education Association in its policy-shaping 1918 report, *Cardinal Principles of Secondary Education*, viewed one of the roles of the comprehensive high school as instilling "ethical character" and common social values in its students. The educational establishment strongly believed high school sports brought students together in shared interests and kept the marginally engaged students in school and therefore encouraged their development.

Education historian Ellwood P. Cubberley typified their views in his remarks on faculty-directed sports:

> Few other things do so much to transform the yard bully into a useful school citizen, bring out the timid and backward pupils, limit accidents, create good feeling, reduce discipline, teach pupil self-control, train the muscles and eye to coordination in games involving learned skills, or awaken the best spirit of the pupils.

Cubberley and other educators throughout the 1920s extolled high school sports for their character-building impact on the secondary school student. In neighborhoods and towns, high school sports programs became a means of promoting community and pride.[13]

The number of sport offerings increased, mostly in the big cities, which had a large number of comprehensive schools with huge student populations. For example, New York City's PSAL offered 14 sports, many of them unknown in other parts of the country such as lacrosse, handball, and ice hockey. Philadelphia offered 11 sports, including the less common sports of bowling and gymnastics. The Chicago Public High School League offered more sports than any other major city—namely wrestling, gymnastics, indoor golf, ice skating (speed skating), rifle, and fencing—so that by the end of the decade it would sponsor 16 sports. The growth of wealthy suburban school districts with extensive athletic facilities and large campuses also encouraged the adoption of more sports.[14]

Intersectional and national competition exploded among high schools during the 1920s. Intersectional football games appeared very early in the century (c. 1900), and the crowning of national champions by the media came into vogue, along with a significant expansion in national tournaments in various sports sponsored by private clubs and universities. The University of Chicago, under famed football coach Amos Alonzo Stagg, sponsored two of the most notable competitions, the National Interscholastic Basketball Tournament and the National Interscholastic Track and Field Meet. Northwestern University sponsored national indoor track, swimming, and wrestling meets. The University of Pennsylvania sponsored national tournaments in swimming and cross-country, as well as a regional meet in gymnastics. Prep schools had their own national tournaments at the University of Wisconsin, and the prep schools sponsored major sectional tournaments in golf and rowing. The involvement by the universities and private clubs became increasingly commercialized and larger and more national in scope, which became a major concern of state high school associations. The growth in high school sports during the 1920s affected all sectors and elements of American society—notably Roman Catholics, African Americans, women, and devotees of military preparedness.[15]

Military sports in secondary schools emerged most fully after World War I, when the country awoke to the need for military preparedness. The high schools began to train students in drill (marching and handling rifles with precision) and review (standing at attention with precision) to instill discipline and obedience in future soldiers. Most high schools that developed such activities also included quasi-military sports such as fencing and rifle shooting, and in some private schools, polo. New York's PSAL developed the most robust rifle marksmanship program in the nation, but sizable high schools programs were developed in Washington, DC, which had the largest girls' rifle marksmanship program in the country, and in Chicago. Fencing programs were developed in both the New York and Chicago public schools, and a national championship was held in New York under the sponsorship of the Amateur Fencing League of America. Polo was limited to a half-dozen elite preparatory and military academies, and competition focused on an annual national interscholastic contest, began in 1929 and held in various New York City armories under sponsorship of the United States Indoor Polo Association.[16]

Catholic schools trailed behind the public and private secular schools in their offerings, but became more active in promoting sports during the 1920s. The Chicago Catholic League, formed in 1912, expanded its sports offerings during the decade to include golf, tennis, and swimming. Philadelphia Catholic high schools became sufficiently numerous to organize a league in 1920. In New York City, the Catholic high schools were slower to organize, competing in occasional contests against each other until forming their first league in 1927. Catholic schools also organized their own state athletic associations, and a number of Catholic universities began to sponsor high school tournaments, notably Loyola University of Chicago, which launched its national basketball tournament in 1924. By 1930, the Church could boast of supporting some 2,125 secondary schools nationally, serving 242,000 students. The average student body nearly doubled from 58 in 1915 to 114 in 1930. The increase meant sizable student populations that could support athletic programs. By the end of the decade, the Catholic Church, with its own leagues, state athletic associations, and array of tournaments sponsored by universities, had mirrored developments in the public school sector.[17]

During the 1920s, African Americans, living in segregated environments, created a world of parallel institutions and competitions in support of high school sports. This world began in 1906 in Washington, DC, with the formation of the Inter-Scholastic Athletic Association of the Middle Atlantic States in 1906. Much subsequent growth in African American high school sports, mostly in the 1920s, took place in the "border regions" between the North and South, notably West Virginia, Maryland, Kentucky, Southern Illinois, Missouri, and Kansas, with college-sponsored track and field and basketball tournaments, league formation, creation of state athletic association, and intersectional competition. In the Deep South, where black schools were more poorly supported, such developments did not begin in earnest until the early 1930s.[18]

The dramatic expansion of high school sports in the 1920s also resulted in a resurrection and growth in girls' high school sports after a decade in which interschool competition was successfully suppressed under the widespread belief that girls were physically and psychologically unable to handle highly intense and vigorous sports competitions. In 1919 West Virginia, South Carolina, and Oklahoma inaugurated state basketball championships, and by 1925 10 states were sponsoring such extravaganzas. In addition, a national high school girls' basketball tournament thrived from 1923 to 1928. Curbing interscholastic basketball during the 1920s, therefore, consumed much of the energies of women physical educators at this time, which had greater success in the universities and colleges than in the high schools in their crusade to ban interschool competition. Most regions of the country that sponsored interschool contests for girls were in rural areas, and largely in the Midwest and the South, where resistance to the noncompetitive ideology persisted. Yet in some big urban centers, notably Chicago, Detroit, and Philadelphia, girls' interscholastic competition in basketball, swimming, and track and field was considerable during the 1920s.[19]

The physical education establishment in the 1920s, while working to suppress competition, particularly between schools, brought many more girls into sports participation through its Girls Athletic Associations (GAA) program in the high schools, and across the country the number of girls engaged in intramural high school sports exploded. Near the end of the decade, the establishment succeeded in suppressing girls' interscholastic competition in most areas and introduced "play days" and telegraphic meets as substitutes. Play days, designed to lessen competitiveness, involved bringing several schools together and mixing all the schools' teams, often designated by color.[20]

Triumph of State Associations' Governance

The expansion of high school sports and their promotion through sectional and national tournaments during the 1920s, in turn, greatly increased their popular interest. But throughout the decade, opposition had been building among high school educators, who believed the increasing aggrandizement and commercialization of high school sports were eroding the educational and character-building mission of high schools. This opposition had coalesced around the National Federation of State High School Athletic Associations (National Federation), which emerged in 1923. The growth of state associations had been steady in the previous two decades, and by the end of World War I every Midwestern state had an organization that sponsored and governed high school athletics. This led five states in 1920 to form a Midwest federation. In 1923, membership had reached 15, with new members from the South and the East, and the group became the National Federation.[21]

From its inception, the National Federation was concerned about rising commercialism in collegiate and private club sponsorship of high school athletic contests and worked steadily to eliminate those competitions. By 1929, the federation had grown considerably more powerful and took a more forceful approach to the issue, particularly over the explosive growth in national tournaments. The group's ire was directed primarily toward the University of Chicago's national basketball interscholastic competition, and in 1929 the National Federation refused to sanction any "interstate basketball tournaments," targeting the Chicago competition.[22]

The decision of the National Federation severely crippled the Stagg tournament, as state associations responded by withdrawing support. Stagg terminated the event in 1930, which signaled the end of collegiate sponsorship of interstate meets, and one by one the other tournaments fell. In early 1931, the University of Michigan ended its sponsorship of indoor and outdoor track meets and a swimming meet. That year Northwestern also announced the abandonment of its national indoor track, swimming, and wrestling meets. In the East, Yale ended its interscholastic tennis and track meets back in 1928, and both Harvard and Pennsylvania ended their interscholastic track meets in the early 1930s. In 1934 the National Federation voted to end all national meets, thus terminating the Stagg track and field meet.[23]

High school sports declined during the Great Depression, as school districts came under ever greater budgeting constraints. The hardest hit were girls' programs, which in the states that still supported interschool competition (mostly in the South and the Midwest) experienced the termination of their state basketball championships. Two factors explained why reformers abolished girls' interschool competition in basketball—the exploding popularity of boys' basketball and the rise of state high school associations. The growth in boys' basketball found many schools adding a lightweight class or frosh-soph and junior varsity levels to their heavyweight or varsity program, and school authorities welcomed the freeing up of courts through the elimination of girls' programs which fell victim to reformers' restraints.[24]

Resurgence After World War II

At the close of the 1920s, high school sports were essentially put on hold for some 15 years. The Depression, which brought a halt to growth in the extracurriculum due to limited finances, followed by World War II, with gas rationing and other wartime restrictions, effectively curtailed many interschool athletic programs in the high schools. With the end of the war pent-up demands exploded into a prosperity boom that benefitted high school sports. Across the country, high schools added more levels of competition from freshmen to varsity, and more sports, so that wrestling, gymnastics, cross-country, golf, tennis, and swimming were added to the usual four of football, basketball, track and field, and baseball. Northern states added such winter sports as skiing, curling, and ice hockey. The trend toward creating more and more competition classes—a common designation being 1A, 2A, 3A, 4A—based on school enrollment accelerated in many states fueled by a long-established concern for ensuring that all schools participate on an equal competitive level.

At the same time, the big cities saw a decline in their high school sports programs, as deteriorating inner-city schools dropped sport offerings and the middle classes abandoned the cities for the suburbs. Whereas prior to the war many city schools were competitive in such "country club" sports as swimming, golf, and tennis, the postwar years saw both a gradual decline of city schools offering such sports and a growing lack of institutional support in coaching, equipment, uniforms, and transportation. For example, New York City's high school athletic program suffered from inadequate funding in the postwar years and was severely damaged by a teacher strike in 1951 that temporarily shut down extracurricular activities. Many New York high schools subsequently curtailed their sport offerings. By the 1960s, inner-city schools in most major cities were competitive only in basketball and track and field.[25]

In 1954 the Supreme Court's famous *Brown v. Board of Education* decision ended legal segregation in the country. While Southern school districts fought the ruling for more than a decade, school segregation greatly diminished during the 1950s and 1960s, and African Americans gradually were brought into the mainstream of high school sports competition. The South resisted integration by organizing private high schools, called "segregation academies" by detractors. During the 1960s these schools formed athletic leagues and state associations to conduct championship competition.[26]

In the South and Midwest areas that still supported girls' high school sports, there was some retrenchment in sports for girls in the immediate postwar years. A notable exception at this time was Iowa, which not only sponsored the most popular girls' basketball tournament in the nation, but also expanded opportunities—softball in 1955, tennis and golf in 1956, track and field in 1962, and cross-country in 1966.[27]

At the end of World War II Catholics still constituted a predominantly working-class immigrant group, but as postwar prosperity increased and the population moved from the city to the suburbs, Catholics grew faster in socioeconomic status than any other religious group except Jews. Catholics had emerged out of their "Catholic ghetto." They also saw the weakening of their parallel institutions, notably their high school athletic programs. Across the nation, Catholic high schools increasingly joined state athletic associations, many of which changed their public school–only policies so as to encompass private schools.[28]

In many communities outside major metropolitan areas, the bonds between citizens of local towns and their high school athletic teams that had represented a powerful cultural force in America for decades became even stronger during the postwar years as small colleges dropped football and amateur town teams disappeared. To sports fans in local towns, high school teams represented their community, a devotion that often led to excess, notably the building of huge basketball arenas. Basketball in Indiana, for instance, helped local farm communities find redemption and uplift during a time when their way of life and economy were disappearing. Similarly, high school football in Ohio and Texas produced the same kinds of community bonds with their athletic teams, and the same kind of excess.[29]

Wherever students competed during the 1950s and 1960s, the pervasive culture viewed sports as uplifting and character building, serving as an antidote to what was perceived as a wave of juvenile delinquency in the 1950s and social rebellion in the 1960s. It was universally understood that athletes received moral guidance from their coaches; were taught life lessons; developed good character; grasped how to accept rules and discipline; and learned teamwork, sportsmanship, and the value of hard work and effort.[30]

The most significant changes in high school sports took place in the 1970s, when state high school athletic associations across the nation introduced sports competition and greatly expanded opportunities for girls' participation. The women's movement of the 1960s and 1970s produced many changes in the country's laws and customs, including the sports world. In 1972, Title IX of the Education Amendments Act banned sexual discrimination by all school districts and institutions of higher learning that received federal money. Although unanticipated by the law's sponsors, Title IX had profound consequences for women in sport. This act impelled state athletic associations to make available interscholastic sports competition to women. The growth was dramatic. During the 1970–1971 school year, 294,015 girls participated in interscholastic sports, compared with 3,666,917 boys (these totals reflect multiple participation in sports by individuals). By the 2013–2014 school year female participants numbered 3,267,664, reaching 41.7 percent.[31]

Title IX's influence on boys' sports proved a mixed story. Some boys' sports, competing for resources and gymnasium space, went into decline, notably gymnastics. Rifle marksmanship had been in decline for decades, and the Columbine High shooting massacre of 1999 spurred educators nationwide to ban the sport. Only Georgia survived with a substantial rifle marksmanship program. Some boys' sports significantly increased in participation, notably lacrosse, soccer, and ice hockey, reflecting increasing popularity of those sports in the college and amateur ranks.[32]

High school sports during the 1980s began to repeat the excesses of the 1920s, creating highly competitive, pressurized sports environments, with increasingly commercialized programs that became national in scope. High school athletic programs, particularly in basketball, moved into alliances with corporate sponsors, with the companies typically supplying shoes, uniforms, and equipment for the athletic teams. Such support proved invaluable in helping impoverished school districts make athletics available to students.[33]

National rankings, beginning with the *USA Today* football poll in 1982, grew to include ever more sports and more ranking organizations, so that there are three or four national ranking services each in football, boys and girls basketball, baseball, and softball. These rankings fueled a boon in intersectional matches—particularly in football and basketball—along with attendant national television exposure. Although national tournaments continued to be opposed by the National Federation, such tournaments arose in wrestling, golf, and soccer, drawing private schools and some public schools. In the desire for college scholarships and an eventual professional career, students increasingly specialized in one sport, attending expensive sports camps during the summers and private clubs during the school year. Some students traveled hundreds of miles to attend special private secondary schools with fifth-year programs designed to hone sports skills.[34]

Television exposure on the national level for high school sports increased after the start of the twenty-first century, augmenting the various all-star games that had showcased individual talent for a couple of decades. Many state associations also expanded television coverage to more of their state tournaments. The expansion of competition to a national level, the coast-to-coast travel, and increased television coverage of high school sports led to growing concern for many educators. They perceived potential damage to their students because of the excess media coverage and star treatment of young immature players and teams, as well as the heightening pressure for them to perform and obtain scholarships.[35]

Conclusion

By the 2013–2014 school year, total participation in interscholastic sports in the United States was 7,795,658, which included 4,527,994 boys and 3,267,664 girls (totals reflect multiple participation in several sports by individuals). Boys' participation was greatest in 11-player football (1,093,234 participants), outdoor track and field (580,321), basketball (541,054), baseball (482,629), and soccer (417,419). Girls' participation was greatest in outdoor track and field (478,885), basketball (433,344), volleyball (429,634), soccer (374,564), and fast-pitch softball (364,297). The overall growth in student participation in interscholastic sports was also tempered by a growing trend of students leaving high school programs to participate in private club programs. Also, the lack of resources in many school districts kept numbers down, with inner-city and rural schools lagging behind suburban schools in the level and variety of sports offered to their students.[36]

Despite the problems and faults that educators found in high school sports as the country entered the second decade of the new century, they have become so thoroughly infused throughout secondary-school systems that it is unthinkable that they would ever dramatically be reformed, let alone removed. Providing the undergirding of support for high school sports is the broadly and long-held belief that they helped to build the American character and that the values taught through the inculcation of competitive sports have helped build this country's democracy and overall moral fiber. Above all, Americans of every race, religion, ethnicity, and social strata still value high school sports for their entertainment value, especially for those who are watching their son or daughter compete and participate for their local high school.

Notes

1 Axel Bundgaard, *Muscle and Manliness: The Rise of Sport in American Boarding Schools* (Syracuse, NY: Syracuse University Press, 2005), 6–16, 34–44, 52–53.

2 "School Boys as Athletics," *New York Times*, May 18, 1879.

3 Melvin I. Smith, *Evolvements of Early American Foot Ball; Through the 1890/91 Season* (Bloomington, IN: AuthorHouse [privately printed], 2008), 39–46, 57, 70; "Village Sports," *Evanston Index*, June 15, 1878; Tournament at Phillips," *Boston Globe*, October 21, 1878.

4 Elmer Ellsworth Brown, *The Making of the Middle Schools* (New York: Longmans, Green, and Co., 1907), 468–469; James Alfred Montgomery, "The Development of the Interscholastic Athletics Movement in the United States, 1890–1940" (Ed. D. Diss., George Peabody College for Teachers, 1960), 20.

5 "Eight Nines in the Interscholastic League," *Boston Globe*, March 17, 1889; "High-School Pupils in the Field," *Chicago Tribune*, June 25, 1890; "New-Jersey Interscholastic League," *New York Times*, February 9, 1896; "Long Island Schoolboys' Games," *New York Times*, March 1, 1896. "Indoor Meet a Success," *Chicago Tribune*, March 15, 1896; "William Dana Orcutt, "The Interscholastic Movement," *American Lawn Tennis* 1 (May 12, 1898): 65–66.

6 Robert Knight Barney, "Physical Education and Sport in North America," in *History of Physical Education and Sport*, ed. by Earle F. Zeigler (Englewood Cliffs, NJ: Prentice-Hall, 1979), 196; Roberta J. Park, "Science, Service, and the Professionalism of Physical Education: 1885–1905," *Research Quarterly for Exercise and Sport* Centennial Issue (April 1985): 7–20.

7 Dudley A. Sargent, "Athletics in Secondary Schools," *American Physical Education Review* 34 (1903): 57–69; Guy Lewis, "Adoption of the Sports Program, 1906–39: The Role of Accommodation in the Transformation of Physical Education," *Quest* 12 (May 1969): 36–37.

8 J. Thomas Jable, "The Public Schools Athletic League of New York City: Organized Athletics for City Schoolchildren, 1903–1914," in *The American Sporting Experience*, ed. by Steven A. Riess (Champaign, IL: Leisure Press, 1984), 217–238; "High School League Formed," *Chicago Tribune*, February 5, 1898; "New Rules Are Disliked: Rigid Regulations Confront High School Athletics," *Chicago Tribune*, March 13, 1904; "Government of Athletics in Philadelphia," *American School Board Journal* 45, no. 5 (November 1912): 47; "New School League," *Boston Globe*, February 14, 1905.

9 Lewis Hoch Wagenhorst, *The Administration and Cost of High School Interscholastic Athletics* (New York: Teachers College, Columbia University, 1926), 21–23.

10 "Fights a Menace to School Sport," *Chicago Tribune*, January 17, 1908; "Trip Stirs School Board," *Chicago Tribune*, December 19, 1908; Seward S. Travis, "High School Fraternities," *Education* 29 (April 1909): 515–527.

11 Scott Johnson, "The Girls Were First," in *Illinky: High School Basketball in Illinois, Indiana, and Kentucky*, ed., Nelson Campbell (New York: Stephen Greene/Pelham, 1990), 48–50; "Lynn 17, Cushing Academy 11," *Boston Globe*, March 3, 1899; Lynne Fauley Emery and Margaret Toohey-Costa, "Hoops and Skirts: Women's Basketball on the West Coast, 1892–1930s," in *A Century of Women's Basketball: From Frailty to Final Four*, ed., Joan S. Hult and Marianna Trekell (Reston, VA: American Alliance for Health, Physical Education, Recreation and Dance, 1991), 137–148; Milo S. Walker, "Indoor Base Ball for Women," *Spalding's Official Indoor Base Ball Guide: 1903* (New York: American Sports Publishing, 1903), 87; "Lake View High School Pupils Brave the Rain and Hold Their Field Day Exercises," *Chicago Tribune*, June 7, 1902; "Los Angeles Takes All Tennis Honors," *Los Angeles Times*, June 2, 1907.

12 *Cardinal Principles of Secondary Education, Bulletin 1918, No. 35* (Washington, DC: Government Printing Office, 1937 [reprint of 1918]), 8, 24; Ellwood P. Cubberley, revised by Walter Crosby Eels from 1925 edition, *An Introduction to the Study of Education* (Boston: Houghton Mifflin Company, 1933), 331–332.

13 *Cardinal Principles*, 21–23; Cubberley, 338.

14 "Interscholastic Athletic Championships," Chicago Public High School Athletic Association, July 1953, from Chicago Board of Education files; "High School Championships," New York City Public Schools, Public Schools Athletic League, Division of High Schools, [1960], from New York City Public Schools files; "Championships and Runners-Up Boys Sports," Philadelphia Public Schools. www.philsch.k12.pa.us/osess/athletics/athlhome6.htm (accessed January 27, 2005).

15 "Mercersburg Now Real Live Champs," *Philadelphia Inquirer*, December 1, 1916; "Newark Second in Penn Gym Meet" *New York Times*, April 6, 1924; "Froebel Takes Track Title in Northwestern Prep Meets," *Chicago Tribune*, March 24, 1929; Harland Rohm, "Morton Preps Win U.S. Basket Title," *Chicago Tribune*, April 3, 1927; "California Prep Tracksters Fail to Grab Championship," *Los Angeles Times*, May 27, 1923; "Mooseheart Wins Track," *Chicago Tribune*, March 23, 1930; "Culver Cops Swim Meet," *Milwaukee Journal*, March 23, 1930; "Columbia's Eight Scores in Henley," *New York Times*, May 27, 1928; "Scholastic Golf Body to Meet Here," *New York Times*, January 5, 1924.

16 Edward B. DeGroot, "Physical Education Versus Military Training in Secondary Schools," *American Physical Education Review* 22 (April 1917): 302–304; Jable, "The Public Schools Athletic League of New York City," 228–230; "Sellaro, New York Boy Wonder, Takes National Interscholastic Foils Title," *New York Times*, April 3, 1921; "Englewood Tops Rifle Tourney," *Chicago Tribune*, May 15, 1924; "Englewood, Senn Win in Prep Gym, Fencing Meet," *Chicago Tribune*, May 25, 1924; "Central's Girls Shots Have Enviable Record," *Washington Post*, January 17, 1924; "Optimists and Harvard Gain Class A Polo Final—Berkshire Wins School Title," *New York Times*, April 7, 1929.

17 "Catholic 'Prep' Leaguers Frame Charts at Meeting," *Chicago Tribune*, November 21, 1912; *Chicago Catholic High School Athletic League Champions* (Chicago, IL: Wisklander Printing, [1959]), 3; "National Catholic Cage Meet At Loyola," *Chicago Tribune*, January 21, 1924; "Catholic Schools Form Sports Body," *New York Times*, March 30, 1927; J.A. Burns and Bernard J. Kohlbrenner, *A History of Catholic Education in the United States* (New York: Benziger Brothers, 1937), 255.

18 Edwin Bancroft Henderson, *The Negro in Sports* rev. ed. (Washington, DC: Associated Publishers, 1939), 238, 273–275; Charles W. Whitten, *Interscholastics: A Discussion of Interscholastic Contests* (Chicago, IL: Illinois High School Association, 1950), 134–139; Charles Herbert Thompson, "The History of the National Basketball Tournaments for Black High Schools" (PhD. Diss., Louisiana State University, 1980), 10–12.

19 Paula Welch, "Interscholastic Basketball: Bane of Collegiate Physical Educators," in *Her Story in Sport: A Historical Anthology of Women in Sports*, ed. Reet Howell (West Point, NY: Leisure Press, 1982), 428–429; W.W. Mustaine, "Tabulation of Replies to Questionnaire on Girls' Basket Ball," *American Physical Education Review* 32 (January 1927): 41–45; E.C. Delaporte, "Physical Education High Schools," *Annual Report of the Superintendent of Schools for the Year Ending June 30, 1926* (Chicago, IL: Chicago Department of Education, 1926), 114; Keith McClellan, "Wilma Rudolph Spotlights Women's Sports," unpublished manuscript, 2007, 1–26; Catherine D'Ignazio, "The History of High School Girls' Sport in the City and Suburbs of Philadelphia, 1890–1990," (PhD. Diss., Temple University, 2010), 11–14; Bob Barnett, *Hillside Fields: A History of Sports in West Virginia* (Morgantown: West Virginia University Press, 2013), 258–268.

20 "31,778 High School Girls Play Inter-Class Games," *Chicago Evening American*, June 18, 1925; Ellen Mosbek, "Camp and Play Days," *The Illinois High School Athlete* 2 (September 1929): 6–7; Ellen Mosbek, "Telegraphic Basket Shooting Contest," *The Illinois High School Athlete* 2 (September 1929): 7; Sarah Jane Eikleberry, "More Than Milk and Cookies: Reconsidering the College Play Day," *Journal of Sport History* 41 (Fall 2014): 467–486.

21 Whitten, *Interscholastics*, 141–142.

22 *Minutes of the 1929 Annual Meeting of the National Council of the National Federation of S.H.S.A. Assoc., Cleveland Athletic Club, Cleveland, Ohio, February 25, 1929*, Amos Alonzo Stagg Papers, Special Collections, Joseph Regenstein Library, University of Chicago, Chicago.

23 "Abandon Prep Meets," *Chicago Tribune*, January 11, 1931; "N.U. Gives Up 18 Year Old Prep Meet," *Chicago Tribune*, January 21, 1931; "Abandon Court Tourneys," *New York Times*, December 9, 1930; "Penn Interscholastic Meet Abandoned in Economy Move," *New York Times*, February 25, 1932; "U.S. Prep Meet at U. of C. Is Discontinued," *Chicago Tribune*, April 14, 1934.

24 Susan K. Cahn, in her *Coming on Strong: Gender and Sexuality in Twentieth-Century Women's Sports, 1900–1960* (New York: Free Press, 1994), 89–90; Cindy L. Himes, "The Female Athlete in American Society: 1860–1940" (PhD. Diss., University of Pennsylvania, 1986), 186–188.

25 Charles G. Bennett, "Closing of Schools In Fund Cut Urged," *New York Times*, April 17, 1951; "Moss Group Weighs Unifying the Athletics of High Schools Under Single Director," *New York Times*, April 20, 1951; Leonard Buder, "City Urged to Aid School Sports by Annual Subsidy of $300,000," *New York Times*, October 6, 1954.

26 David K. Wiggins, "'With All Deliberate Speed': High School Sport, Race, and Brown v. Board of Education," *Journal of Sport History* 37 (Fall 2010): 335–337; Kenneth T. Andrews, "Movement-Countermovement Dynamics and the Emergence of New Institutions: The Case of 'White Flight' Schools in Mississippi," *Social Forces*, 80 (March 2002): 911–936; Anthony M. Champagne, "The Segregation Academy and the Law," *The Journal of Negro Education* 42 (Winter 1973): 58–66.

27 Pamela Grundy, "From Amazons to Glamazons: The Rise and Fall of North Carolina Women's Basketball, 1920–1960," *Journal of American History* 87 (June 2000): 112–146; Shelly Lucas, "Courting Controversy: Gender and Power in Iowa Girls' Basketball," *Journal of Sport History* 30 (Fall 2003): 286, 302; D'Ignazio, "The History of High School Girls'," 231–234, 239.

28 Charles R. Morris, *American Catholics: Saints and Sinners Who Built America's Most Powerful Church* (New York: Times Books, 1997), 223, 256; Jay P. Dolan, *The American Catholic Experience: A History from Colonial Times to the Present* (Notre Dame, IN: University of Notre Dame Press, 1992), 357–358; "Catholic League to Join IHSA; Cites Competition," *Chicago Tribune*, January 31, 1973; "New High School Sports Federation of New York," *New York Times*, October 14, 1973.

29 Greg Guffey, *The Greatest Basketball Story Ever Told* (Bloomington, IN: Indiana University Press, 1993); Luther Emery, "Massillon: A Rich and Glorious Tradition," *High School Football* 1, no. 1 (1963): 10–16, 80–81; Bill McMurray, "Texas: King Sized Football," *High School Football* 1, no. 1 (1963): 6–8.

30 Eldon E. Snyder, "Teaching the Sociology of Sport: Using a Comic Strip in the Classroom," *Teaching Sociology* 25 (July 1997): 239–243.

31 U.S. Commissioner on Civil Rights, "The Impact of Title IX: Participation in High School and College Competitive Athletics," in *The American Sporting Experience*, ed. Steven A. Riess (Champaign, IL: Leisure Press, 1984), 386–397; National Federation of State High School Associations, "2013–2014 High School Athletics Participation Survey." www.nfhs.org

32 "2013–2014 High School Athletics Participation Survey."

33 J. Thomas Jable, "Progress or Plight: The Growing Commercialism of High School Athletics in the United States," paper presented at the 2004 NASSH Convention, Asilomar, CA, May 30, 2004, unpublished; "NFHS Corporate Partners," National Federation of State High School Associations. www.nfhs.org/content.aspx?id=3250&terms=corporate + partners

34 Jable, "Progress or Plight;" Kelley King, "The Little School That Can't Be Beat," *Sports Illustrated* 101 (August 23, 2004): 78–85; "1999 NHSCA National Open High School All-Americans," National High School Coaches Association. www.nhsca.com/events_history_show.php?id=20127; "Event History—2001 Final Four of High School Wrestling," National High School Coaches Association. www.nhsca.com/events_history_show.php?id=20117

35 Jerry Sullivan, "Star High School Basketball Player Sure to Have the Last Laugh," *Buffalo News*, December 29, 2002; Taylor Bell, "Pressure's On Like Never Before: Retired Coaches Say Today's Game Has Become Too Big," *Chicago Sun-Times*, September 3, 2006; Douglas Lederman, "Use Sports to Lure Inner-City Youths to Education, Preaches a Coach Who Directs a University of Chicago Institute," *Chronicle of Higher Education*, September 19, 1990; H.G. Bissenger, *Friday Night Lights: A Town, a Team, and a Dream*, paperback ed. (Cambridge, MA: Da Capo Press, 2000), 128–152, 363–364.

36 "2013–2014 High School Athletics Participation Survey;" John Gehring, "Athletic Choice: Students Shun School Teams," *Education Week* 23 (October 8, 2003): 1, 15.

7

YOUTH SPORTS

Dennis Gildea

Introduction

It was an ideal New England autumn day, the sky a clear blue with just a hint of chill in the air, the leaves turning brilliant colors. A perfect day for a football game, so the suburban Connecticut couple decided to drive to a nearby town to watch their nephew play. They joined the other spectators at the field just in time to see the Jets, their nephew's team, line up against the Raiders. All the players were five years old.

"Their uniforms were exactly like their namesake NFL teams, except for the colors," the husband said. "The Jets colors were red and white. The coaches on the sidelines, adult men, of course, were decked out in team jackets; there were cheerleaders; there were concession stands where they sold team paraphernalia and all sorts of food. It was like they were emulating the NFL, and they were taking it very seriously."

The husband and wife looked at the scene around them and then exchanged quizzical glances. "Steve and I were looking at each other and thinking is this a joke," the wife remembered. "The coach was yelling at the kids like he was Rex Ryan. Were we the only weirdos who saw the absurdity of this?"[1]

Unlike the other adult spectators at the biddy football game, Steve Rushin and Rebecca Lobo were thoroughly acculturated to the world of big-time sports. Lobo played on an NCAA championship women's basketball team at the University of Connecticut and on a gold-medal winning team in the Olympic Games; she played in the Women's National Basketball Association for a number of years; and in her post-basketball career, she was an on-air analyst for women's basketball for ESPN-TV. Rushin, who was selected as the Sportswriter of the Year in 2005, had written for *Sports Illustrated* and a number of other sports-oriented publications. Their vast sports experiences notwithstanding, they had never seen anything like this.

The atmosphere surrounding the football game for five-year-olds that Rushin and Lobo experienced may have been a bit extreme, but it was not unusual.[2] Regulated sports programs aimed primarily at small boys and administered by adult authorities outside the school began cropping up in the United States in the 1920s. In 1952, highly organized competitive sports were defined as "any athletic activity, which involves a considerable amount of the leisure time of the youngster in formalized practice, which encourages extensive attendance by adult spectators, which is limited to the outstanding players, and which involves the selection of winners on a state, regional, or national basis."[3]

Youth Sports and the Rhetoric of the Sublime and Apocalypse

For virtually as long as they have existed, youth sports have drawn both praise and condemnation. "I don't want our reaction to this experience to sound overly critical of youth sports,"

Rushin said. "For both of us, sports have been a lifetime joy and even a meal ticket. And we'd rather have kids in youth sports than not. Rebecca is coaching our daughter's fifth-grade basketball team at school. But we get a bit leery about sports for kids being treated like miniaturized versions of organized, professional sports."[4]

In an article complimentary of Little League and his eight-year-old daughter's experience playing organized softball, Rushin wrote:

> Despite the countless distractions available to kids today, many are still obsessed with baseball. Solitary pursuits like playing video games and skateboarding can't compete with the thrill of mobbing a teammate as he scores the winning run—nor do they end with a post-game trip to Dairy Queen.[5]

To a great extent, Rushin is referencing the ideal, the underlying rationale for all athletic competition, especially team competition in youth sports. From the beginning and certainly in more recent history, the proponents and the opponents of organized youth sports have generated and persistently espoused two conflicting narratives: a rhetoric of the sublime promise and a rhetoric of the apocalyptic threat involved in the movement. Luther Halsey Gulick (1865–1918) was a pioneering advocate of the value of youth sports, and Gulick did more than anyone else at the time to establish and encourage competitive youth sports. Gulick, a champion of Muscular Christianity and a trailblazing instructor at the International Young Men's Christian Association Training School (now Springfield College), was one of the founders of the Public Schools Athletic League in New York City in 1903, a leader in the Playground Association of America, a leader in the American Boy Scout movement, and cofounder with his wife of the American Campfire Girls.[6] About fostering a sense of justice in young people, Gulick wrote, "There is a more comprehensive morality that comes in with the team games . . . the beginning of altruism on which a complex civilization must depend."[7] As an educator, Gulick fully intended for competitive youth sports to function as a breeding ground for his notion of civic morality.

Early Promoters and Promise of Youth Sports

Concurrent with Gulick's early attempts to popularize youth sports came an effort in fiction that was equally influential in planting the seed of honorable competition in the hearts of American children. Thomas Hughes's *Tom Brown's School Days* was published in England in 1857, and it was the first literary work to feature a young athlete in a school setting. The novel, an argument for the necessity of a Muscular Christianity, was "immensely successful throughout the English-speaking world."[8] Similar youth sports–oriented works soon appeared in both Great Britain and the United States.

As early as the antebellum period in America, Catharine Beecher argued in print for the development of robust and healthy American girls and women to counter what Beecher lamented as "a race of sickly and deformed pigmies."[9] Beecher's approach to improving the health and physical fitness of women was similar to Gulick's philosophy in the sense that it was infused with religious fervor and a staunch faith in the perfectibility of a person.[10]

Rural women, Beecher maintained, were physically fit and fully able to perform their domestic duties. Such was not the case, however, for the growing number of women and girls in cities. Poor health plagued wealthy women of leisure as well as poor working women in urban areas, and Beecher paid particular attention to the physical fitness of girls. In 1823 she founded the Hartford Female Seminary, an institution she used to promulgate her ideas on domestic and physical education. Her treatise titled *Calisthenic Exercises for Schools, Families, and Health Establishments* was published in 1856. As part of the curriculum at the Hartford Female Seminary, Beecher included a regimen of calisthenics taught by a female physical education instructor. To a great extent, the exercises amounted to a gender-based light weight training.[11]

The Male Hero in Youth Sports Fiction

Whereas Beecher urged girls to participate in healthful calisthenics, boys were urged to play games. The most popular and influential American contribution to the fiction of youth sports first appeared in 1896 when Gilbert Patten, writing under the pen name Burt L. Standish, launched his Merriwell stories in *Tip-Top Weekly*, a cheaply produced publication that sold for a nickel and was available by subscription and at newsstands throughout the United States. The publisher wanted Patten to write a series of stories based on "American school life" in which the protagonist, Frank Merriwell, would undertake a variety of dangerous adventures as well as excelling in sports while always upholding the highest moral values. As he began formulating ideas for his stories, Patten noted that he saw in them "an opportunity to feature all kinds of athletic sports, with baseball, of which I was best informed, predominating."[12] Before going to Yale, Merriwell preps at Fardale Academy where he becomes the star pitcher of the baseball team. As was the case with the athletic ideal of achieving confidence through sports that Steve Rushin and Rebecca Lobo cited, Frank Merriwell gains acceptance and becomes a leader at Fardale largely by virtue of his pitching prowess.[13]

For virtually all of the two decades between the appearance of Merriwell in 1896 to 1916, Patten churned out stories at the clip of 20,000 words per week. As he was writing the stories, Patten was struck with the thought that with "half-a-million kids reading [Merriwell] each week, I had about the biggest chance to influence the youth of this country that any man ever had."[14] The influence he wielded with American youth helped foster an interest in sports and clean living.

A similarly didactic impulse appeared in the sports fiction of Clair Bee, an enormously successful basketball coach at Long Island University from 1932 to 1951 and the author of the immensely popular (more than 2 million copies sold) Chip Hilton series. Published from 1948 through 1966, Bee's 23 Chip Hilton books taught a new generation of boys (and the majority of his readers were boys) the value of sportsmanship, honesty, and the sheer joy of sports. Ironically, Bee was ousted from his coaching position when in 1951 members of his Long Island University (LIU) team were arrested for cooperating with gamblers in a nationwide point-shaving scandal.[15]

Didactic fiction and the zeal of at least one Muscular Christian led to the formation of the Public School Athletic League (PSAL) of New York City in 1903. The ideals of the league reflected Gulick's sublime approach to youth sports. Athletes participating in the PSAL's many sports were urged to embody the organization's watchwords: "duty," "thoroughness," "patriotism," "honor," and "obedience." The PSAL stressed three separate forms of competition: an athletic badge test in which student performance was evaluated in several physical feats; class athletics, which involved pitting different school classes against each other in track and field competition; and district and city championships, which eventually would draw considerable media and spectator attention.[16] Because of its success, the idea of the

PSAL soon spread to education systems in other cities. But it also spawned the quest for national glory and interstate games among high school squads as early as the turn of the twentieth century.

As the lure of highly competitive interscholastic athletic leagues spread, so, too, did an apocalyptic fear of competitive sports—at least among many traditional educators. Citing the situation in Chicago schools in the late nineteenth century, Gerald R. Gems quotes a schoolboy journalist's concern that football players were hindered on their path to victory by academic demands. "Who can hope for success in Foot-Ball when most of the players are weighed down daily by a long Cicero lesson, or some other mark of tyranny of the 'powers that be?'"[17] Some of the educational "powers that be" reasoned that if you can't beat them, join them. In 1889, a Chicago-area high school hired Frank Percival as its physical education director, and Percival promptly launched a program of games and intramural competition for boys and girls.[18]

The Growth of Youth Sports in the Period between the World Wars

Following the armistice declaration that ended World War I, American citizens eagerly embraced virtually all forms of mass entertainment, a movement that most definitely included sports. The 1920s are widely regarded as the Golden Age of Sports, and youth sports were swept along in the same wave of athletic enthusiasm as were professional and intercollegiate sports. In addition to becoming more popular, sports were becoming more commercialized, a tendency that reflected most aspects of American culture. Not surprisingly, youth sports followed suit. Private citizens and organizations with no connection to educational institutions leaped eagerly into the establishment of elite competitive sports leagues for children, primarily for boys and most definitely for white children.[19] In 1924, the Cincinnati Community Service started a junior baseball tournament for boys younger than 13. The city of Denver organized a tackle football program for boys under 12 in 1927. A year later, Los Angeles organized a Junior Pentathlon program, and in 1930 Pop Warner football was launched in Philadelphia, and the Catholic Youth Organization (CYO) started a junior tennis program with the help of the Southern California Tennis Association.[20]

In general, religious and ethnic groups grasped the necessity of combining athletic and religious activities to keep the interest of their youthful members. "[E]thnic clubs, faced with the loss of youthful members to the athletic programs of the schools, parks, and playgrounds, turned to the wholesale adoption of American sports forms."[21] The CYO, founded in 1930 in Chicago, proved to be one of a group of religious organizations that sponsored youth programs. The B'Nai Brith Youth Organization (BBYO) sought to keep Jewish children active in both athletics and their religion. Such was the mission of the Young Men's Christian Association (YMCA), and both the Young Men's Hebrew Association and the Young Women's Hebrew Association (YWHA) were actively courting their young people to combine sport and their religion. As early as the 1920s, a bulletin produced by the YWHA implored young women to "combine health-building exercise with a good time."[22]

Sports, a good time, and a social agenda that sought to negate the temptations of American society in the morally liberated post–World War I era led to the formation of the CYO. Bishop Bernard J. Sheil, a former athlete and the driving force behind the CYO in Chicago, regarded participation in sports as a solution to social problems that were leading young boys to lives of crime. "We'll knock the hoodlum off his pedestal and we'll put another neighborhood boy in his place," Sheil wrote of the CYO's role in Chicago. "He'll be dressed in CYO boxing shorts and a pair of leather mitts, and he'll make a new hero."[23]

From its inception, the CYO in Chicago encouraged participation by African American Catholic boys. Despite the fact that Catholic parishes were almost completely racially segregated into the 1950s, "the citywide youth program provided numerous opportunities for black and white interaction."[24] Much of this "interaction" occurred in the boxing ring. The CYO's boxing tournaments were enormously popular, and "Race, color, ethnicity, or class" were not eligibility issues, although at least initially the CYO insisted that to be eligible, a boxer had to be a Catholic, a stipulation it eventually dropped.[25]

The Press and the Promotion of Youth Sports

Bishop Sheil's declaration that youth sports would provide a positive alternative for boys, in particular, was bolstered by Arch Ward, a conservative Catholic and the editor of the *Chicago Tribune*. Ward, a master promoter who conceived of the Major League All-Star game in the middle of the Great Depression in 1933, used his sports pages to support Sheil's efforts. Not coincidentally, publicity for the CYO and other such youth sports organizations also increased readership for Ward's paper. Noting that the "sports editor and the bishop helped one another," Thomas B. Littlewood wrote that Ward saw to it that his sports section "gave lavish publicity to Sheil and the activities of the CYO."[26] Moreover, Ward had a promotional counterpart in New York City where Paul Gallico, the sports editor of the *New York Daily News*, became the publicity and organizational force behind the Golden Gloves boxing tournament.[27]

Beginning in the 1920s and continuing into ensuing decades, mass media, particularly print media, played an enormous role in generating knowledge and enthusiasm for a variety of youth sports endeavors. An article and pictorial in *Life* magazine in 1939 functioned as a means to publicize and, more importantly, legitimize youth sports in American culture. The article was an account of the motivation behind the founding and the on-field operation of the Denver Young American League. The magazine piece extolled themes such as character, courage, nationalism, the disgrace of a boy's "turning yellow" during play, and most emphatically the need for launching similar programs throughout the nation.[28] The article made a convincing case. In 1944, the community of Scarsdale, New York, started a tackle football league for elementary school boys, which proved so successful that it was followed a year later by programs for baseball, basketball, and tennis.[29]

A plethora of summer sports camps for boys and girls, many of which are located on college campuses and almost all of which emphasize developing and improving technical skills within the sport, began to dot the American landscape in the final decades of the twentieth century. However, the more contemporary trend is simply a matter of quantity. Commercialized youth sports camps began as early as the 1920s, and no less a sports icon than Notre Dame football coach Knute Rockne was a pioneer in the field. "[Rockne] soon saw the potential of this untapped source of revenue and had the idea of coaching camps for young athletes long before the concept occurred to his colleagues. He experimented with [a sports camp] at Camp Rockne, his boys' summer camp in Wisconsin, and shortly before he died (in 1931), planned to develop it on a large scale."[30] Rockne also went into partnership with University of Wisconsin basketball coach W.E. "Doc" Meanwell to run joint football and basketball camps, ventures that proved profitable for both coaches.[31]

An irony of Rockne's youth sports camps is one that exists in many big-name coaches' summer camps today—the coach is present in name only. Rockne, "frantically busy during summers," found he could not "visit Camp Rockne for long, even when his sons attended."[32] Lured by a coach's reputation as a winner and the promise of genuine improvement in a sport, American children flocked to summer sports camps, which by mid-century proved plentiful and profitable. Long Island University basketball coach Clair Bee ran summer camps at the New York Military Academy in the mid–Hudson River Valley and at Kutsher's Resort in the Catskills, averaging 550 youthful campers each summer.[33] Summer sports camps for young athletes—primarily boys—became so popular that in 1975 the *New York Times* published a report on the burgeoning phenomenon, a story headlined "Where Fun and Games Are Taken Seriously."[34]

The Birth and Growth of Little League Baseball

Spawned by the intersection of such positive national publicity, the growth of school sports, and the work of civic and private organizations, the groundwork was established for the birth of what would become the most famous (or infamous, depending upon the rhetoric an observer preferred) youth sports organization in history. Legend has it that it was the summer of 1938 when Carl Stotz tripped over a root from a lilac bush while playing catch with his nephews in their backyard in Williamsport, Pennsylvania. What the boys needed, Stotz reasoned after he picked himself up and dusted himself off, was a better place to play, and teams to play against. He spent the winter months seeking minimal financial support from Williamsport area businesses. Fifty-six businesses rejected his idea before the Lycoming Dairy gave him 30 dollars, and Lundy Lumber and the Penn Pretzel Company added a few dollars more. Stotz had just enough money to purchase equipment and uniforms. The first Little League game was played on June 6, 1939, when Lundy Lumber defeated Lycoming Dairy, 23–8. At the museum in the Little League complex in South Williamsport, a gray flannel Lycoming Dairy uniform is displayed.[35]

Stotz thought of Little League baseball as a summer pastime for boys between the ages of 8 and 12. From its start in 1939 through 1944, growth was steady but hardly phenomenal. Just 16 teams in four leagues were playing in 1944, and all were located in the Williamsport area.[36] As suburban developments were built outside American cities in the post–World War II period, Little League baseball expanded. Between 1949 and 1958, 4,662 leagues consisting of 21,911 teams were franchised. As the 1960s began, Little League had spread to all 50 states and the Territory of Guam, as well as to Cuba, Mexico, England, France, Germany, Turkey, Korea, Japan, the Philippines, Morocco, Saudi Arabia, and Canada. By this time, more than 1 million boys were playing Little League baseball throughout the world.[37]

As was the case with youth football and publicity arising from the *Life* magazine piece, Little League baseball benefited from a 1949 article in *The Saturday Evening Post*, which served as a prime example of the rhetoric of the sublime in the sense that it emphasized the value of Little League for boys and went so far as to suggest that communities that sponsor such programs reap civic benefits, an idea all but ripped from Gulick's words written a half-century earlier.[38] In 1962, the annual Little League World Series championship game became a fixture on ABC's Wide World of Sports.[39]

Youth Sports and Physical Fitness in the Post–World War II Era

In the years following the end of World War II and with the onset of Cold War fears in the early 1950s, Americans, especially young Americans, were perceived to be physically inferior to their counterparts in other nations. In 1953, Hans Kraus, an American physician, and Ruth P. Hirschland gave Austrian and Italian children the same Kraus-Weber physical fitness test they had earlier administered to American children. A total of 56 percent of American children failed the test, as opposed to just 8 percent of the Europeans. The test entailed such minimal fitness measures as toe-touching, sit-ups, and leg lifts to measure abdominal strength. The dismal American results received widespread publicity in national media. *Newsweek*, for example, dealt with the issue of youth fitness in an article titled "Why the President Is Worried about Our Fitness."[40] Americans were "soft," a designation that appeared to be substantiated by the physical and psychological malleability of American prisoners of war (POWs) during the Korean conflict. Contrasted with prisoners taken during World War II, the men imprisoned in North Korea were too compliant with the orders and manipulations of their communist captors. Their willingness to collaborate was cast as a product of "American softness."[41]

A key response to counteract the decline of physical fitness in American children was the establishment in 1956 by President Dwight Eisenhower of the President's Council on Youth Fitness (PCYF, now known as the President's Council on Fitness, Sports, and Nutrition). Pennsylvania Senator James H. Duff and Philadelphian John B. Kelly, a former sculling champion, brought the test results to Eisenhower's attention and urged him to take action to improve the health and fitness of American children. Interestingly, the Eisenhower administration cast "fitness" into an idea that went beyond just physical fitness and instead encompassed "spiritual, mental, emotional, social, [and] cultural" health.[42] The broader definition of "fitness," of course, had much in common with the notion of fitness espoused by Catharine Beecher and Luther Gulick in the previous century.

A few weeks prior to John F. Kennedy's inauguration as president, an article appeared under his name in *Sports Illustrated.* In "The Soft American," Kennedy pointed out the lack of improvement in the physical fitness of American children in the years since Eisenhower started the PCYF. Once in office in 1961, Kennedy installed highly successful Oklahoma University football coach Bud Wilkinson as the director of the program.[43] In addition to Kennedy's article, *Sports Illustrated* published earlier in 1960 a lengthy two-part series on the emergence of Australia as a nation of fit, sports-minded people. "From the beginning, Australia was a land of hardy, outdoor men," Herbert Warren Wind wrote, implying that Australia in 1960 was what the United States used to be.[44] A year later in the same magazine, George Munger, the director of the physical education department and formerly the head football coach at the University of Pennsylvania, made similar observations about the physical superiority of European youth as contrasted with American children. He quoted President Kennedy as asking why Europeans "have moved ahead of younger people in this country in their ability to endure long physical hardships, in their physical fitness and in their strength."[45]

The decade of the 1960s also saw the beginnings of a cultural revolution in the United States that resulted in improved civil rights for African Americans and for women. For many years, Little League and most youth sports programs limited participation to white boys. An especially poignant example of racial discrimination occurred in 1955 when the Cannon Street YMCA Little League team of Charleston, South Carolina, an African American squad, missed its chance to play in the Little League World Series because all the white teams in South Carolina and the southern region refused to play against them in a qualifying tournament. The refusal, which most likely reflected the prejudice of the adults in charge rather than the feelings of most of the young players, led to forfeitures that in turn led to the National Little League office having to abide by a rule that prohibited teams who advance by forfeiture from competing for the World Championship. Sensitive to the injustice the Cannon Street team had suffered, Little League officials invited the team to come to Williamsport for the World Series as its guests. The players were housed with other teams in dorms at Lycoming College, and they were allowed to warm up on the Lamade Stadium field as people in the stands shouted, "Let them play; let them play."[46]

The plea to "let them play" did not apply to girls seeking to play baseball. In 1928 at the age of 14, Margaret Gisolo was a key player on the Blanford (Indiana) Cubs in American Legion baseball. Her participation as the only girl on the team "sent the world of youth athletics spinning and helped open the door for increased acceptance of women in sports."[47] The increased acceptance, limited though it may have been, did not come without a struggle. Gisolo had knocked in the winning run in extra innings, a clutch hit that gave her team the league championship in her Indiana county, but the losing team protested on the grounds that American Legion baseball was established exclusively for boys. A three-man commission that included Major League commissioner Kenesaw Mountain Landis ruled in favor of Gisolo's participation, and she and her team went on to compete in Chicago's Comiskey Park. "Because of her accomplishments and the high profile of the case, thousands of girls across the country wanted to sign up for American Legion baseball." For the next season, however, American Legion baseball changed the rules, specifying that girls were not eligible.[48]

Gender discrimination in youth baseball continued until well into the second half of the century. As the women's rights movement of the early 1970s became more prominent and vocal in American life, the demand for the inclusion of girls in youth sports previously restricted to boys became a rallying point for both adult women and young girls. A girl in California took her case clear to the White House. In May 1973, Jenny Fuller wrote to President Richard M. Nixon to inform him that she was not allowed to play on her local Little League team because of her gender. She received a response from the Office of Civil Rights, but no action was taken that would allow her to play with the boys.[49]

Also in 1973, the National Organization for Women (NOW) filed a discrimination claim that sought to admit 12-year-old Maria Pepe from Hoboken, New Jersey, as a participant in her local Little League. "The institution of Little League is as American as the hot dog and apple pie," said Sylvia Pressler, the hearing examiner for the New Jersey Civil Rights Division. "There is no reason why a part of Americana should be withheld from girls."[50] Regardless, legal representatives of the National Little League argued for the continuation of its exclusionary practices, using as a key witness Creighton Hale, an exercise physiologist and vice-president of the league. Citing what he considered to be physiological evidence that girls were not fit for highly competitive sports because of their weaker bone structure and slower reaction time, Hale argued in vain. Pressler ultimately ruled in favor of the inclusion of girls, noting that because Little League Baseball was provided public financial support and used public accommodations, "it was indeed subject to state and federal laws preventing discrimination."[51]

As the second half of the twentieth century progressed, virtually every sport—mainstream and otherwise—practiced in the United States developed a youth component. Biddy Basketball began as early as 1951 in Scranton, Pennsylvania; pee-wee hockey leagues sprang up in more temperate climes that earlier in the century would not have cared at all about the sport; and when Bill Koch became the first American to win an Olympic medal in the 30-kilometer cross-country ski race in the Innsbruck Winter Games in 1976, the Bill Koch Youth Ski League for boys and girls between the ages of 8 and 13 was launched.[52] The Special Olympics program for mentally challenged children achieved great popularity. Given impetus by Eunice Kennedy Shriver, the Special Olympics began with a summer camp in the early 1960s, and the first International Special Olympics Games were held in Soldier Field, Chicago, on July 19–20, 1968.[53] In 1997, as a result of joint sponsorship by the Professional Golfers Association, the Ladies Professional Golfers Association, the PGA Tour Master's Tournament, and the United States Golf Association, the First Tee program began. Besides introducing children to golf, the program, not surprisingly, stressed the positive values that go hand-in-hand with the rules of the game.[54]

In terms of popularity and participation, youth soccer now rivals Little League baseball, even introducing a term that has become part of the American lexicon, the soccer mom, the mother who drives her children to and from soccer practices and games. In 2015, the American Youth Soccer Organization, founded with nine teams in Los Angeles in 1964, boasted 50,000 teams and 500,000 players nationwide.[55] When the United States women's soccer team won the women's World Cup in July 2015, enthusiasm for the sport grew tremendously, especially among young girls and boys. When the team was honored with a ticker-tape parade in lower Manhattan, the parade route was "mobbed by young girls." Thirteen-year-old Ireland Giaquinto held a sign that read: "Thank you for letting me dream."[56]

The Quest for Victory and the Inevitable Apocalypse?

On rare occasions, youthful sports dreams have turned into nightmares. In the wake of the revelations that coaches and organizers of the Jackie Robinson West All-Star Little League team from Chicago used ineligible players while winning the American championship of the Little League World Series in 2014, *Boston Globe* sportswriter Christopher L. Gasper adopted a rhetoric of the apocalypse in a column headlined "Fun and Games Until Adults Get Involved." In writing this column, Gasper was adding his take on the subject to a lengthy list of physical educators and journalists who have made similar points.[57] Gasper noted that he has covered most of the major events in sports, including Super Bowls, National Basketball Association finals, and Major League World Series games. "All wonderful events," he wrote, "but none of them can bump the slice of baseball Eden that is South Williamsport, Pa., off the top spot. Waxing poetic on Williamsport is easy. It's like the sports version of Neverland."[58] The possibility of intrusion and exploitation of 12-year-olds by ESPN television coverage notwithstanding, Gasper stayed with fairy tale similes to describe the atmosphere of the Little League World Series. For the youthful players—and even some cynical sportswriters—the days at the Series are "like a baseball Magic Kingdom with Lamade Stadium as Cinderella's Castle."[59]

The walls of Cinderella's Castle, however, were assailed by scheming adults. The Jackie Robinson West team was stripped of its title when Little League authorities discovered that the team's organizers had submitted a falsified boundary map and had recruited players from beyond the team's boundaries in order to make a successful march to Williamsport. The boys on the team were forced to pay for the sins of their elders. "Little League scandal should be an oxymoron," Gasper wrote, burdened by the knowledge that it is anything but. "The lesson here is that there is nothing for kids that overzealous adults can't ruin with their misplaced aspirations."[60] When misguided adults scale the idealized castle walls, the apocalypse ensues.

Conclusion

As the twenty-first century dawned, opportunities for children to participate in organized sports grew. To some extent, that was both the good news and the bad news. Continuing and expanding a trend that began in the early decades of the twentieth century, youth sports organizations were becoming increasingly privatized and costly for participants. Writing of prospects for the future, sport sociologist Jay J. Coakley observed, "Organized youth sports will become increasingly privatized in most American communities. Publicly funded programs will be cut back or eliminated, and park and recreation departments will increasingly become brokers of public spaces and facilities."[61] Wealthier middle-class parents will pay participation fees to allow their children to pursue a sport. Families from lower socioeconomic classes will be hard-pressed to afford the cost of organized activities, a situation, Coakley argues, that has the potential to create an unfair imbalance in young athletes competing in and progressing through the ranks of organized sports.

A solution may lie in the rally cry "let them play"—that is, let them play more informal, genuinely fun, and free games. Coakley cites a *New York Times* article that extolls the value of urban street baseball.

> The neighborhoods of New York are a potpourri of makeshift baseball. Without the sterile accoutrements of organized ball, their games depend less on rain or shine than on an abandoned car at second base or the erratic mood of local residents.[62]

Who organizes such games? Who makes up the rules? Who plays? Children, without an adult on the scene.

A different and certainly serious problem plaguing America in the twenty-first century is childhood obesity. And for children participating in the rougher sports such as football, ice hockey, and wrestling, injuries have become a medical concern, stirring again the refrain of the rhetoric of the athletic apocalypse. "Though the spread of childhood obesity in the last decade has spurred health authorities to ramp up their efforts to promote youth activity," school physical education classes proved to be only a small part of a solution to the problem, a *New York Times* reporter wrote in 2012. Physical education classes "do not offer students the same level of regular, challenging exercise as competitive sports," researchers discovered. The *Times* story quoted Keith M. Drake, a research fellow at the Hood Center for Children and Families at the Geisel School of Medicine at Dartmouth College, as saying,

> I think being a part of some kind of team or organization gives kids the opportunity to have moderate to vigorous activity consistently. Kids are not in P.E. that often, and when they are, the physical activity is not that strenuous.[63]

The Catch-22 to increased strenuous physical activity for youth is that such activity can lead to overuse injuries and possibly concussions. Higher training volumes, overscheduling, poorly fitting equipment, and coaches and supervisors ignorant of the risks involved can result in serious injuries that can affect a child even into adulthood. The Centers for Disease Control and Prevention's Heads Up initiative offers a website that includes information on brain injuries, helmet safety, and advice for coaches and parents. In addition to basic information, the CDC website has as a regular feature with online training courses in sports safety measures for coaches, parents, and athletes.[64]

League rules, territorial boundaries, overemphasis, physical fitness, safety, and exuberant parents living their athletic lives vicariously through their children (as television reality shows such as *Friday Night Tykes* and *The Short Game* make clear) all notwithstanding, "Our job as parents and coaches is to let the kids have fun playing sports," Rebecca Lobo said. "That's what we should be all about."[65]

Notes

1 Author interview with Steve Rushin and Rebecca Lobo, March 5, 2015.

2 Much has been written on the role of adult coaches and organizers in youth sports. A partial list of such articles would include Jack W. Berryman, "From the Cradle to the Playing Field: America's Emphasis on Highly Competitive Sports for Pre-Adolescent Boys," *Journal of Sport History* 2 (1975): 112–131; Jay J. Coakley, "Burnout Among Adolescent Athletes: A Personal Failure or Social Problem," *Sociology of Sport Journal* 9, 3 (1992), 271–286; Joan Ryan, *Little Girls in Pretty Boxes: The Making and Breaking of Elite Gymnasts and Figure Skaters* (New York: Doubleday, 1995); and Bennett J. Lombardo, "The Behavior of Youth Sport Coaches: Crisis on the Bench," in *Fractured Focus: Sport as a Reflection of Society*, ed. Richard E. Lapchick (Lexington, MA: Lexington Book, 1986): 199–205.

3 The definition appears in "Are Highly Competitive Sports Desirable for Juniors? Conclusions from Committee on Highly Organized Sports and Athletics for Boys Twelve and Under, National Recreational Congress," *Recreation* 46 (December 1952): 423.

4 Author interview with Rushin and Lobo.

5 Rushin, "The Perfect Game," *Parade*, June 1, 2014, 7.

6 For a concise treatment of Gulick's career, seen Benjamin G. Rader, *American Sports: From the Age of Folk Games to the Age of Televised Sports* (Englewood Cliffs, NJ: Prentice Hall, 1990), 215–219.

7 Luther H. Gulick, *Philosophy of Play* (New York: Association Press, 1920), especially Chapter XIV, "Play and Moral Growth," 189–192. Gulick's papers are available in the Springfield College Archives and Special Collections, MS 503.

8 Rader, 214. Pioneering youth sports fiction is treated briefly in David K. Wiggins, "A Worthwhile Effort?: History of Organized Youth Sports in the United States," *Kinesiology Review* 2 (2013): 66. Also see Christian K. Messenger, *Sport and the Spirit of Play in American Fiction* (New York: Columbia University Press, 1981); Michael Oriard, *Sporting with the Gods: The Rhetoric of Play and Games in American Culture* (Cambridge and New York: Cambridge University Press, 1991); Timothy Morris, *Making the Team: The Cultural Work of Baseball Fiction* (Urbana and Chicago, IL: University of Illinois Press, 1997); and Michelle Nolan, *Ball Tales: A Study of Baseball, Basketball, and Football Fiction of the 1930s Through the 1960s* (Jefferson, NC: McFarland, 2010).

9 Catharine Beecher, quoted in Gerald R. Gems, Linda J. Borish, and Gertrud Pfister, *Sports in American History: From Colonization to Globalization* (Champaign, IL: Human Kinetics, 2008), 73.

10 Gems et al., *Sports in American History*, 73.

11 For illustrations of Beecher's calisthenics, see Ibid., 75.

12 Gilbert Patten, *Frank Merriwell's "Father"* (Norman: University of Oklahoma Press, 1964), 178.

13 Burt L. Standish (Patten), "By Fair Means or Foul." The story was originally a *Tip-Top Weekly* story reprinted in *Frank Merriwell's Schooldays* (New York: Smith Street Publications, 1971), 216.

14 Quoted in John Dinan, *Sports in the Pulp Magazines* (Jefferson, NC: McFarland, 1998), 67.

15 For a biography of Clair Bee and an analysis of his Chip Hilton books, see Dennis Gildea, *Hoop Crazy: The Lives of Clair Bee and Chip Hilton* (Fayetteville, AR: University of Arkansas Press, 2013).

16 Thomas Jable, "The Public School Athletic League of New York City School Children, 1903–1914," in *Sport in American Education: History and Perspectives*, ed. W.M. Ladd and A. Lumpkin (Washington, DC: American Alliance for Health, Physical Education, Recreation, and Dance, 1979), ix–18. Also see Wiggins, "A Worthwhile Effort?" 66.

17 Quoted in Gerald R. Gems, *Windy City Wars: Labor, Leisure, and Sport in the Making of Chicago* (Lanham, MD: Scarecrow, 1997), 67.
18 Ibid., 68.
19 See Wiggins, "A Worthwhile Effort?", 65.
20 Ibid., 67.
21 Gems, *Windy City Wars*, 175.
22 Quoted in Linda J. Borish, "Jewish American Women, Jewish Organizations, and Sports, 1880–1940," in *Sports and the American Jew*, ed. Steven A. Riess (Syracuse, NY: Syracuse University Press, 1998), 106–107.
23 Quoted in Gems, *Windy City Wars*, 182,
24 Timothy B. Neary, "'An Inalienable Right to Play': African American Participation in the Catholic Youth Organization," in *Sports in Chicago*, ed. Elliott J. Gorn (Urbana and Chicago, IL: University of Illinois Press, 2008), 165.
25 Ibid., 174.
26 Thomas B. Littlewood, *Arch: A Promoter, Not a Poet* (Ames, IA: Iowa State University Press, 1990), 52.
27 See Ibid., 52–56.
28 "*Life* Goes to a Kids' Football Game," *Life* 7 (October 9, 1939): 90–93.
29 See Harold T. Friermood, "Balance," *Journal of Health and Physical Education* 18 (June 1947): 382.
30 Murray Sperber, *Shake Down the Thunder: The Creation of Notre Dame Football* (New York: Henry Holt, 1993), 226.
31 Ibid., 226–227.
32 Ibid., 227.
33 For Clair Bee's camps, see Gildea, *Hoop Crazy*, 297–300.
34 George Vecsey, "Where Fun and Games Are Taken Seriously," *New York Times*, July 14, 1975, 18.
35 Rushin, "The Perfect Game," 7–8.
36 Michael H. Carriere, "'A Diamond Is a Boy's Best Friend': The Rise of Little League Baseball, 1939–1964," *Journal of Sport History* 32, no. 3 (Fall 2005): 352.
37 Ibid.
38 Harry T. Paxton, "Small Boy's Dream Come True," *The Saturday Evening Post* 221 (May 14, 1949): 26–27, 137–140.
39 See ESPN Media Zone, "ABC and ESPN2 Combine to Present Little League World Series from Williamsport." http://espnmediazone.com/05/press-release/2012/08 (accessed April 17, 2015).
40 Shelly McKenzie, *Getting Physical: The Rise of Fitness Culture in America* (Lawrence, KA: University Press of Kansas, 2013), 15.
41 Susan L. Carruthers, "*The Manchurian Candidate* and the Cold War Brainwashing Scare," *Historical Journal of Film, Radio, and Television* 18 (March 1, 1998): 76.
42 McKenzie, *Getting Physical*, 16.
43 See Ibid., 51–52. Kennedy's article, "The Soft American," appeared in *Sports Illustrated*, December 26, 1960, 15–17.
44 Herbert Warren Wind, "Visit to a Small Continent," *Sports Illustrated*, May 16, 1960, 92.
45 George Munger, "Challenge to Bud Wilkinson," *Sports Illustrated*, July 21, 1961, 38.
46 Wiggins, "A Worthwhile Effort?," 68. Also see Rushin, "The Perfect Game," 10.
47 "Margaret Gisolo Obituary," *The Arizona Republic*, November 8, 2009. www.legacy.com/obituary.aspx?n=margaretgisolo (accessed July 8, 2015). Gisolo had become the director of the dance program at Arizona State University.
48 Ibid.
49 Wiggins, "A Worthwhile Effort?," 68.
50 Quoted in Rushin, "The Perfect Game," 10.
51 Quoted in Wiggins, "A Worthwhile Effort?," 69.
52 On Biddy Basketball, see "Our History." www.Biddybb.com (accessed April 22, 2015). On the Bill Koch Youth Ski League, see *Nordic Skiing Competition Guide, 1984* (Colorado Springs, CO.: United States Ski Association, 1984), 14. Also see John Fry, *The Story of Modern Skiing* (Hanover, NH: University Press of New England, 2006), 197–201.
53 See www.specialolympics.org/history/aspx (accessed April 22, 2015).

54 Wiggins, "A Worthwhile Effort?," 71.
55 Statistics cited at www.AYSO.org (accessed July 8, 2015).
56 Jonathan Lemire, "Parade Honors US Women," *Boston Globe*, July 11, 2015, C8.
57 Christopher L. Gasper, "Fun and Games Until Adults Get Involved," *Boston Globe*, February 15, 2015, C-1.
58 Ibid.
59 Ibid.
60 Ibid.
61 Jay J. Coakley, *Sport in Society: Issues and Controversies* 5th ed. (St. Louis: Mosby, 1994), 455.
62 Marc Bloom, "Street Ball: Where Foul Is Fair and Fair Is Foul," *The New York Times*, 1976; reprinted in Coakley, *Sport in Society*, 126–127.
63 Anahad O'Connor, "Sports Promote Healthy Weight in Teenagers," *New York Times*, July 17, 2012. www.NewYorkTimes.com (accessed July 9, 2015).
64 See www.cdc.gov/headsup/youthsports/ (accessed July 9, 2015).
65 Lobo author interview.

Part III

RACE, ETHNICITY, AMERICAN SPORT, AND IDENTITY

8

NATIVE AMERICAN SPORTS

John D. Bloom

Introduction

Most sources of information on Native American history provide very limited information on sports.[1] In fact, most of what academics, journalists, or bloggers recently have written about Native Americans and sports has to do with demeaning images of Indigenous people that sports mascots often communicate. Much of the scholarship on this topic is excellent.[2] Indeed, teams such as the National Football League franchise in Washington, DC, defiantly continue to brand their products with extremely offensive nicknames and imagery, despite repeated objections and pleas by Native American activists to remove the monikers. As important as it is to critically examine demeaning appropriations of Native American imagery, an exclusive focus on this topic can tend to overshadow other, more complex and dynamic stories of Indigenous Americans as actors within their own sports histories. Native people of the Western Hemisphere have a sports heritage that dates back over the course of centuries, and is, in many respects, far older than that which European Americans "introduced" to Indigenous societies in the late nineteenth century. Indigenous sports cultures continue to thrive in the Americas in ways that are vibrant, creative, and sovereign.

The diversity and complexity of Indigenous languages and cultures make it impossible to provide a comprehensive overview of Indigenous American sports history in the space of a single book chapter. However, one can draw from case studies and examples that illustrate the deep roots of American Indian sports and some of the common threads that have connected different Indigenous sports cultures. Multiple American Indian groups have incorporated significantly contemporary popular sports, often learned at boarding schools, like basketball, boxing, football, and baseball. However, shared Indigenous sports cultures have a much deeper history. In the case of sports like long-distance running and lacrosse, it is a history that remains a part of Indigenous life today.

The Mesoamerican Ball Game

Indigenous people of the Western Hemisphere actually created perhaps the world's oldest team sport, the Mesoamerican *ullamalitzli*, or ball game. The ball game has its origins in the culture of the Olmec civilization. The term Olmec translated from Nahuatl means "rubber people," and, indeed, their complex societies emerged in the tropical forests of what is today southcentral Mexico where rubber plants grow abundantly. It is from these trees that the Olmecs first constructed the balls used in the ball game. Archeological discoveries of balls and ball courts suggest that Mesoamerican societies played the game at least 3,800 years ago.[3]

The Mayan creation story, *Popul Vuh*, recently translated from the Mayan script, tells the story of two brothers playing the ball game against an evil set of gods.[4] This source, along with the hundreds of ancient ball courts discovered in modern times and contemporary players of the game in northern Mexico, provide some of the best evidence of how people actually played this game. Although many versions seem to have existed, they all commonly matched two teams against one another. Each side would propel a solid rubber ball that might weigh as much as seven pounds and vary between 4 and 12 inches in diameter by striking it with their hip, thigh, or shoulder toward the other side. In some versions of the game, the object was to advance the ball past an end line.[5]

Given the sport's long history, it would be problematic to assume that all who played it in Mesoamerica did so in exactly the same way, for exactly the same reasons, at all times. Among the Maya, however, there is strong evidence that the ball game became tied to important religious ritual, political ideology, and public spectacle. Similarly designed, elaborately decorated rectangular ball courts are an almost universal feature of Mayan city centers. The rulers of Copan sponsored the construction of perhaps the largest ball court of the Mayan era, an arena containing detailed reliefs carved into the masonry.[6]

By the time of contact with Europeans, the Mexica (Aztecs) continued to play the game, often as an extension of ritualized forms of warfare and conquest. Spanish friar Diego Duran, who lived in Mexico 50 years after the Spanish conquest, described the game from interviews and demonstrations that elders provided for him. He noted that large teams played against one another, but occasionally the ball game featured a contest between individuals, such as territorial rulers who staked the fate of their cities upon the outcome of the match. Duran, coming from a society that did not have complex team sports, was not entirely clear about rules and scoring, but it appears that no matter the accumulated score of a game, if either side managed to shoot the ball through a small hoop protruding from the wall of the court (an extremely rare occurrence), it would be declared the winner. Players wore protective "yokes" around their hips, and gloves, yet a high-speed collision with the heavy ball sometimes resulted in a fatal injury.[7]

Beyond Mesoamerica, historians and archeologists have discovered ball courts in the southwest of the contemporary United States. The ruins of ancient Hohokam villages often contain oval shaped ball courts. The Hohokam sites date to 700 CE, and seem to have been active into the fourteenth century.[8] Similarly, archeologists have found ancient ball courts on the Caribbean Islands such as Puerto Rico.[9]

While a discussion of Native American sports inevitably leads to the introduction of games like basketball, football, soccer, and baseball to Indigenous communities throughout the Americas in the twentieth century, the example of the ball game provides a more complex reading of sports history itself, suggesting that team sports originated among Indigenous Americans long before they became popular in Europe or the United States.[10]

Archery

In 1963 and 1965, the United States won first place in the World Archery Championships. They did so thanks to the strong performance of Joe Tindle Thornton (Cherokee), a graduate of the Chilocco Indian School in Oklahoma and a 1978 inductee in the American Indian Athletic Hall of Fame. Thornton finished second place in each competition and might have won Olympic medals had archery been a part of the Olympics at that time. His success in the modern sport is, in many respects, a continuation of Indigenous competition and skill in archery that dates back to roughly 500 CE.[11]

Archery, as a sport, a part of warfare, and a tool for hunting has been a part of almost every human society. Using bows to launch projectiles has provided numerous peoples with the ability to shoot them with greater accuracy, with greater force, and at a longer distance than they might by simply throwing a spear. Native peoples had used throwing sticks, called atlatls, and spears for thousands of years before developing their own bows and arrows. According to early twentieth-century ethnographer Stewart Culin, simple archery games involving the shooting of an arrow at a stationary target were not common among Native Americans.[12] However, archery became a central component of Indigenous life across the Americas, used in warfare, hunting, ceremonies, and sports.

Games were sometimes organized around gambling; others developed skill in young archers. George Catlin famously described a speed shooting game among the Mandan in 1841 in which contestants competed to keep as many arrows in the air at one time. In some cases, archery also served as a designation of gender identity, as women were not allowed to touch bows that men used.[13] Like other individual sports and dances practiced globally, archers took part in a form of play that exhibited prowess in talents developed while working, so rules over gender provide a window into larger gender roles that might have existed within some Indigenous societies.

Indigenous archery is, in many respects, on the opposite side of the sports spectrum from the Mesoamerican ball game. Whereas players of the ball game pioneered in the creation of a team sport, archers were individual athletes. In fact, archery as both sport and practical skill existed almost everywhere in the world by the time Europeans and Indigenous Americans made contact.

Lacrosse

In the early decades of the twentieth century, many associated baseball with professionalism, corruption, and indecency. At the Carlisle Indian School, this reputation provoked Pop Warner and Superintendent Moses Friedman to discontinue the school's baseball team in 1910. As stated in the school newspaper, the *Arrow*,

> because of the evils of summer or professional base ball [sic] and the fact that many students have been lured away from school and into temptations and bad company by professional offers before they had finished school, it would be best not to develop, by encouraging base ball, an ambition in the students to become professional players, since so few have the strength of character or the ability to engage in such a calling successfully.[14]

To replace the three baseball teams that the school's leaders had decided to eliminate, Pop Warner chose lacrosse. For a school founded upon "killing the Indian," it is deeply ironic that Carlisle's Anglo leaders had decided to replace America's "national pastime" with perhaps the most popular, and historically established, team sport in the history of Indigenous North America.

Of course, by 1910, Canadian and American colleges and prep schools had appropriated the sport, along with others like football, to masculinize their elite students. In 1867, William

George Beers, a white dentist from Montreal who had learned lacrosse from Mohawk Indians, created the first rules for the modern game, seeking to develop a national sport for Canada, a country whose leaders were looking for a national identity after emerging from its first years of independence.[15] By the end of the 1920s, exclusive prep schools and colleges in New England and Maryland established a lacrosse tradition. Universities like Johns Hopkins in Baltimore and prep schools like Phillips Academy in Andover, Massachusetts, changed the profile of the sport from an ancient Indigenous ritual to an almost exclusively white, male, Anglo Saxon, Protestant pastime for the ruling classes.[16] Of course, a driven football coach like Pop Warner was likely less interested in using lacrosse as part of Carlisle's "civilizing mission" than he was in keeping his football players in shape during the off-season. Nevertheless, it is certainly an inescapable paradox that he reintroduced an Indigenous sport to Indigenous students being taught to leave their Indigenous cultures behind.

It is unclear where and when lacrosse began, but a wide range of Native American people from across the eastern portions of North America played the game at the time that Europeans came in contact with them in the seventeenth century. Ethnographer Stewart Culin describes variants of the sport, which he calls "racket" or "racket ball," as being practiced most frequently by Algonquian and Iroquoian peoples along the Atlantic coast and Great Lakes, the Dakota in the plains, and the Muskhogean people in the south. He also reports that the Chinook and Salish in the Pacific Northwest and some groups in California played the sport. According to Culin, among most Native American societies, men tended to play lacrosse, unlike other ball games like shinny, which women tended to play. Early Europeans who observed lacrosse describe it as a pastime, often connected to wagering, but also as something connected to religious ritual.[17]

Like the contemporary game, the ancient version generally involved two teams seeking to advance a small ball across a playing field toward a goal. Players carried the ball in a pouch woven into the end of a stick that varied in length. People who lived in the Mississippi Valley and southern coast of what is today the United States used two sticks, each with enclosed pockets. The size of teams and fields varied according to culture, custom, and tradition. Some teams competing against each other might have been small, whereas others might have numbered in the hundreds.[18]

When Beers modified lacrosse as a national sport for Canadians, he did so based upon a number of assumptions. For one, he disapproved of what he viewed as a propensity of Indigenous lacrosse players to run with the ball. Indeed, Indigenous players tended to emphasize carrying the ball while running against the opposition over passing the ball to teammates. Instead, Beers modified the rules to require and emphasize passing by shortening the field and regulating boundaries, establishing set positions for players, and limiting the number of players on the field to 12.[19] Most established lacrosse leagues follow these rules today.

However, Indigenous teams and players have figured prominently in the contemporary game. A number of Six Nations teams, composed of players from the confederacy of the Seneca, Cayuga, Onondaga, Oneida, Tuscarora, and Mohawk, excel at a version of the sport known as "box lacrosse" played inside the boarded confines of a hockey arena. Originally developed in the early 1930s as a way to market a professional game as an indoor sport during the winter, it failed initially as a commercial venture. However, Indigenous players have continued to play it, both indoors and outdoors. Since 2003, international teams have competed against one another every four years in the World Indoor Lacrosse Championship. As a sign of their prowess, the Iroquois Nationals, the team representing players from across the Six Nations (independent of the U.S. national team), has finished with a silver medal for each of the three Indoor Championships held so far. In 2007, they lost to Canada by a score of 15–14 in an overtime thriller. In the United States, scholastic and university governing bodies have not given Native American players a great deal of notice, but in Canada, a great many players who have excelled at both versions of lacrosse over the years have been given a great deal of attention, such as the father and son stars Ross and Gaylord Powless, who have been enshrined in the Canadian Lacrosse Hall of Fame.[20]

A few Indigenous factories still manufacture lacrosse sticks that a wide variety of players use in competition, providing perhaps the most direct connection between the ancient and contemporary games. Until the late 1960s, Saint Regis, Onondaga, and Six Nations craftsmen produced most lacrosse sticks, all made of wood, used in competition around the world. When the largest of these, the Chisholm Lacrosse Manufacturing Company, burned to the ground in 1968, however, consumers looked for alternative suppliers. By the 1980s, companies like STX successfully began to market lacrosse sticks made of synthetic materials. Mohawk International has been able to continue the tradition of Indigenous manufacturing for this market.[21]

Despite becoming involved in the competitive market to manufacture and sell lacrosse equipment, members of Iroquois nations still take the sport seriously as medicine. Because of its important religious significance, the Six Nations Confederacy Council in Ontario, Canada, long held to the tradition that only men should be allowed to play the game. This has created some debate within the Six Nations Confederacy. Some women, although admirers of the game, agree with the council that only men should play and that females should not even engage in the version of lacrosse modified for female players. Nevertheless, others have found their way onto women's teams in recent years. In May 2007, for example, Amber Hill (Tuscarora) helped Syracuse University defeat Georgetown for the Big East championship. As the first Iroquois woman to play in the women's NCAA lacrosse tournament, she made 13 crucial saves in goal. In 2006, the council granted a team of women the right to play internationally under the Haudenosaunee flag, which represents the Six Nations. Since then, women's teams have played in the 2009 World Cup in the Czech Republic and the 2011 Under-19 games in Germany. At the 2013 World Cup in Canada, the Haudenosaunee women finished seventh out of 19 teams, the most improved team in the tournament.[22]

After establishing the first World Games for lacrosse in 1960 be played between the United States, Canada, Australia, and the United Kingdom, the International Lacrosse Federation formally recognized the Iroquois Nationals in 1987.[23] A team that represented members of Iroquois nations across a territory that included several U.S. states and Canada, the Iroquois Nationals competed in their first World Games in 1990.[24] Yet even very recently, some nations involved in international lacrosse did not recognize the sovereignty of the Iroquois team. When the United Kingdom hosted the World Championship in 2010, their government refused to grant the Iroquois nationals entry if they used their tribal passports. As representatives of the Iroquois nations, the team refused and therefore was not allowed to compete.[25] Four years later in Denver, facing a field of 38 nations (the largest number of teams in the history of the FIL World Championships) the Iroquois Nationals finished in third place, earning a bronze medal with a 16–5 win over Australia. It was their best showing ever in the outdoor tournament.[26]

Running

Fans knowledgeable about the sport of distance running might recall the story of Billy Mills. The Oglala Lakota runner won a gold medal for the United States in the 10,000-meter run at the 1964 Tokyo Olympics. His victory surprised virtually the entire world track and field establishment and took place in a thrilling, come-from-behind fashion. In fact, Mills' qualifying time was almost a full minute behind that of the favorites that day, Australia's Ron Clarke and Tunisia's Mohammed Gammoudi. It took Mills 28 minutes and 24.4 seconds to finish, establishing an Olympic record.[27] This was the first time that a member of the U.S. Olympic team had ever won a gold medal in the men's 10,000-meter race. In fact, until Galen Rupp's silver medal in the 2012 London Games, only one other U.S. runner had ever even medaled in the event. Louis Tewanima,[28] the prolific Hopi runner who began his competitive track and field career at the Carlisle Indian School, took a silver medal in the 1912 games held in Stockholm.[29]

Mills and Tewanima represent only a small portion of the great Indigenous American runners who have competed in the United States and internationally over the past century and a half. Seneca Louis "Deerfoot" Bennet was considered the "world's best runner" in the middle of the nineteenth century, and Thomas Longboat (Onondaga) and Ellison Myers "Tarzan" Brown (Narragansett) each won the Boston Marathon in 1907 and 1940, respectively.[30] Despite the variety and diversity of Indigenous societies throughout the Americas, a wide range of Native Americans from across the entire hemisphere share strong distance-running traditions that, like the Mesoamerican ball game, extend into the ancient past.

Before the arrival of Europeans, most Native peoples of the Americas employed neither the wheel nor reliable beasts of burden, so messengers traveled exclusively on foot. Among the people of the Andes, Mesoamerica, and the contemporary Southwestern United States, running provided a major organized form of long-distance communication. By the time of Spanish contact in the sixteenth century, the Inca's stone-paved road system extended over 24,000 miles along the Pacific coast of South America. Runners carrying *khipus*, knotted string belts used to keep records, delivered messages between densely populated cities.[31] Yet the tradition of running in the Andes certainly dates back even further, to the existence of complex urban societies between 3000 and 200 BCE.[32]

In the southwest of what today is the United States, running couriers also served to connect small villages, labeled by Spanish explorers as pueblos, over hundreds of miles apart. These runners were central to the organization and planning of the 1680 rebellion that drove Spanish conquerors and missionaries from New Mexico until the recapturing of Santa Fe in 1698.[33] Indigenous people of the southwest also ran for play and ritual. Anglo anthropologists in the nineteenth century describe relay races among the Pima and Hopi in Arizona and the Pueblos in New Mexico.[34]

Of course, in the United States, runners like Louis Tewanima excelled in competition after enrolling at Indian boarding schools. This is especially ironic because Tewanima came from a band of Hopis who were arrested specifically because they resisted sending their children to boarding schools. After first attending the Fort Wingate federal boarding school in western New Mexico, in 1907, Tewanima left to enroll in the Carlisle Indian School in Carlisle, Pennsylvania. He joined the track team there, performing under the guidance of Pop Warner. Trained as a football coach, Warner, by his own admission, "knew less than nothing about track and field."[35] Tewanima ended up competing both in the 1908 and 1912 Olympics, the second being where he earned his silver medal in the 10,000-meter run. As Warner's recollections suggest, Tewanima brought a running tradition that he already knew well to Carlisle. While Indian boarding schools played a key role in promoting modern Native American athletics in the United States, distance runners like Tewanima illustrate that such schools served more to appropriate the traditions and talents of their students than to train them in the skills needed to win.

Modern Sports and the Influence of Boarding Schools

On October 8, 1904, the girls' basketball team from the Fort Shaw Indian School in Montana defeated a group of Missouri high school all-stars in St. Louis by a score of 17 to 6. The Fort Shaw girls had been part of the Model Indian School constructed for the 1904 St. Louis World's Fair, which was held in coordination with the 1904 St. Louis Olympics. With their victory, the Fort Shaw girls closed out a remarkably successful campaign in which they had defeated non-Indian high school teams, including the champions from the state of Illinois, over the course of the previous spring and summer. Their prowess in the newly invented sport of basketball impressed visitors to the fair, so much so that their final game attracted an overflow crowd. In the end, they earned the trophy that declared the Fort Shaw girls' basketball team to be the champions of the 1904 World's Fair.[36]

The Fort Shaw girls did, indeed, triumph, but they did so during a festival that illustrates the dangerous ground upon which Indigenous athletes competed in American society. As part of the 1904 World's Fair, the event's organizers had created an Anthropology Department that exhibited the world's "primitive" peoples for the elucidation and entertainment of largely white audiences. Along a tramway called The Pike, Indigenous peoples from around the world built "traditional" small exhibit compounds. The fair's Anthropology Department arranged these compounds so that visitors would see what they defined as the most primitive first (Mbuti or African Pygmies). Fair attendees would proceed up a hill through increasingly advanced examples of biocultural evolution. At the top they would encounter the Model Indian School where the Fort Shaw girls were among the residents. As part of this exhibition, the Louisiana Purchase Exposition staged a two-day "Special Olympics," called the "Anthropology Days," in which the Indigenous residents of the Pike competed in Olympic events such as the shot put, running, broad jumping, and weight lifting. Event organizers such as the head of the Department of Anthropology, W J McGee, a pre-academic anthropologist who at the time was president of the American Anthropological Association, compared the results from untrained Indigenous event participants to those of the highly trained European and American Olympians. The discrepancies in performance served to "prove" white racial superiority.[37]

Athletes like the Fort Shaw girls' basketball team might inspire Indigenous Americans, but potentially they also could be used for racist spectacle and amusement. One can see this paradox played out most intensely at Indian boarding schools like Fort Shaw. It was at such schools that large numbers of Native Americans first became involved in modern American sports on an institutional level. While boarding schools were created to destroy Native American identities, their athletic teams and athletes provided victories and pride during very difficult times for Indigenous Americans.[38]

No athlete emerged from Indian boarding schools with more fame and success than Jim Thorpe (Sac and Fox), arguably the nation's best athlete during the twentieth century. Thorpe not only starred on the Carlisle Indian School's track and football teams, but while there won gold medals in both the Olympic pentathlon and decathlon at the 1912 Stockholm games. Claiming that he violated his amateur status by playing semiprofessional baseball in the summer, the International Olympic Committee later stripped Thorpe of his medals. However, that decision never really undermined the depth of his athletic accomplishments or talent.

Thorpe's 1912 Carlisle football team lost only one game, finishing with a record of 12–1–1, and defeating Army. After leaving school, he went on to play major and minor league baseball for 15 years. He also became the first president of the organization that would later become the National Football League, recorded a stellar career as a professional football player, and was inducted into the Pro Football Hall of Fame in the town where he played his most successful seasons, Canton, Ohio.[39]

In his childhood and early teens, Thorpe ran away from agency school in Oklahoma, as well as Haskell in Lawrence, Kansas, and Carlisle in Pennsylvania. He was unhappy at these institutions and longed to return home after the deaths of his mother and father.[40] Yet, according to his daughter, Grace Thorpe, he had positive memories of life in boarding school. "Dad told me once that his happiest years were spent at Carlisle," she remembers. "That's where he first came to fame, was in Pennsylvania, at Carlisle."[41] Indeed, Thorpe illustrates one of the great ironies that emerged out of the use of sports to promote the civilizing mission of federal Indian boarding schools. Richard Henry Pratt had famously written that it was necessary for Indian boarding schools to completely eradicate Indigenous identities. As he wrote, "kill the Indian in him, and save the man."[42] Yet for those who know of the Carlisle Indian School, most first think of Jim Thorpe, a Native American student who never denied his Indigenous identity, and whose daughter, Grace, became an environmental activist who defended the sovereignty of reservations.

Of course, Thorpe's career at Carlisle came years after Pratt had been forced to retire in 1904 as the school's superintendent. Subsequent leadership at Carlisle paid less attention to Pratt's assimilationist ideals and allowed Warner to operate the football program with almost no oversight. As a result, the Carlisle Indians became famous across the nation and had a great influence upon other federally operated Indian boarding schools. The Haskell Institute in Lawrence, Kansas, also fielded nationally ranked football teams and drew support of enough Native American leaders to fund the construction of a 10,000-seat stadium on campus entirely through donations from Indigenous sources. Much to the chagrin of the Bureau of Indian Affairs, a collection of tribes celebrated the venue's opening with a great pow-wow in 1926.[43]

As much as Thorpe may have enjoyed his fame, he never could fully escape exhibiting a stereotype for white audiences. As scholar Phil Deloria recounts, in 1922 and 1923, he and other former players from Haskell and Carlisle joined the Oorang Indians, a professional football team that combined a barnstorming schedule with Buffalo Bill–style barnstorming. "Like the Globetrotters," Deloria writes, the Oorang team "fused athletic exhibition with a familiar minstrelsy tradition." With no home field, the Oorang squad was essentially a road show who would act out a "naïve Indian in the big city" shtick while on the road—this despite being far more educated and experienced in the world than most of their white audiences.[44]

In the 1930s, after the federal government began to withdraw support for the Indian boarding school system, and after the Bureau of Indian Affairs implemented stricter age requirements for students, Indian boarding schools could no longer compete athletically on the high-profile, collegiate level. However, schools such as Haskell, Chilocco in Oklahoma, Santa Fe and Albuquerque in New Mexico, and Phoenix in Arizona developed highly ranked boxing teams. Famed Navajo painter Narciso Abeyta/Ha So Da trained at the Santa Fe Indian School by its legendary art teacher Dorothy Dunn, was a New Mexico state champion, and was a regional Golden Gloves winner in the 1930s while still a student.[45]

Although better known for football, track, and boxing, the Indian schools also fielded baseball teams, and a number of former students eventually played professionally. Jacob

Jimeson (Seneca) was the first Carlisle player to enter into the professional ranks, but the most accomplished Carlisle alum, and one of the greatest baseball players in major league history, was Hall of Famer Charles Albert Bender (Ojibwe). Among the other major league players who emerged from Carlisle were Thorpe, Michael Balenti (Cheyenne), Frank Jude (Ojibwe), Charles Roy (Ojibwe), and George H. Johnson (Winnebago). There were also a number of players who went on to careers in the minor leagues or who played on a semiprofessional level. This is all the more remarkable because Carlisle always struggled to maintain its baseball team, losing players each spring to semiprofessional leagues and to the track team.[46]

Like most Indigenous professionals who played at the same time, baseball writers and fans tagged Bender with the moniker "Chief." Along with Bender, there was "Chief John Tortes Meyers, "Chief" Moses Yellowhorse, "Chief" George H. Johnson, and "Chief" Louis Leroy, among many others.[47] Most Native players found the tag offensive, a kind of sarcastic and demeaning way to call a player an Indian. As Powers-Beck has shown, Native American major leaguers, beginning in 1897 with Penobscot Louis Francis Sockalexis, faced racial taunts and humiliating stereotypes as they integrated baseball at the turn of the twentieth century.[48]

After enrolling and playing football and baseball for Carlisle between 1898 and 1901, Bender, whose father was German American and mother was of half-Ojibwe (White Earth) parentage, joined the Philadelphia Athletics in 1903. He became a pitcher known for precise control over his curveball and for his strategic use of his fastball. In 1910, he pitched to a 23–5 record, and in 1911 pitched three games in the World Series, winning two, and only losing to Christy Mathewson 2–1 in the opener. The Athletics went on to win the series in six games. Two years later, after completing the season with a record of 21–10, he once again won two World Series games against the Giants, guiding his team to another World Series championship. Manager Connie Mack famously said about him, "If everything depended on one game, I just used Albert—the greatest money pitcher of all time."[49]

Bender's loss in the opening game of the 1911 World Series, one of the few blemishes on his post-season record, came because he allowed another Indigenous player to score the winning run, John "Chief" Meyers (Cahuilla).[50] Meyers, a productive hitting catcher for the New York Giants, Brooklyn Dodgers, and Boston Braves compiled a .291 batting average during his nine-season career. He hit over .300 for three consecutive seasons between 1911 and 1913, leading the league with a .441 on base percentage in 1912, a year in which he finished third in voting for Most Valuable Player, behind winner Larry Doyle and runner-up Honus Wagner.[51] Meyers was born in a small, southern California Cahuilla town, but moved to Riverside, California, just before he became a teenager. As a major leaguer, Meyers became a favorite of the media, known for providing colorful quotes and for his interest in art and culture. Like Thorpe with the Oorang Indians, however, he also found himself performing stereotypes for audiences, in his case in 1910 as part of a vaudeville routine with Christy Mathewson. In the skit, Mathewson and Meyers learn how to act, going on to perform in a Wild West show where Mathewson served as a cowboy, and Meyers as what *Variety* called a "bad Indian." Meyers ended his baseball career in 1920 after fans booed him while he was playing for a semiprofessional team in San Diego. He returned to southern California where he worked for the Department of Interior, and often showed up for old-timers games with the Giants and Dodgers after the teams moved to California in 1958.[52]

The legacy of basketball introduced at boarding schools lives on as both women and men play what has become an extremely popular sport on reservations and among predominantly Native American high schools. Shoni Schimmel is a notable contemporary female star from the Confederated Tribes of the Umatilla Indian Reservation in Mission, Oregon. In the spring of 2013, she led the University of Louisville to a stunning upset of highly ranked Baylor University (featuring superstar Brittney Griner) in the regional semifinals of the NCAA basketball tournament. Louisville went all the way to the championship game where it lost to perennial powerhouse Connecticut. In 2014, the Atlanta Dream of the WNBA drafted Shimmel in the first round, and she went on to win the WNBA All Star Game Most Valuable Player award in her rookie season. Bronson Koenig (Ho-Chunk Nation) similarly helped to lead the University of Wisconsin to the finals of the men's NCAA basketball tournament in 2015, upsetting undefeated Kentucky in the national semifinals.[53]

Conclusion

Of course, the history of Indigenous American sports extends far beyond, and is much deeper than, a chronicle of those who have been successful in commercially mainstream athletics. Unlike many other nations of the Western Hemisphere, in the United States there exists a long history of demarcating a rigid line between "Indian" and "white." The Native American mascot controversy that dominates most discussion of Indigenous Americans and sports reinforces this idea. It can be seen as part of what Phil Deloria describes as "playing Indian," which has served to reinforce the concept of the Indian "other."[54] This line leaves Native athletes with a sense of having to choose between assimilation and Indigenous identity. Yet an expansive view of Native American sports provides a much more complex picture. As historian Allison Fuss Mellis illustrates, in sports like rodeo, Native Americans have selectively adapted particular sports in ways that have strengthened their tribal identities.[55] This is also true for the countless stories about basketball, hunting, powwow, baseball, and innumerable other sports that are part of Indigenous life on and off reservations. Stories of Indigenous sports, from the Mesoamerican ball game, to archery, to distance running, to lacrosse and into contemporary sports like basketball, football, boxing, and baseball illustrate enduring Indigenous identities that are remarkably independent, influential, and dynamic.

Notes

1 Over the past half-century, activists have grappled over the politics of the terminology used to describe and label the original inhabitants of the lands occupying the Western Hemisphere. In this chapter, I rely mostly upon the term "Indigenous American," but I also use the other terms interchangeably throughout.

2 See C. Richard King and Charles Fruehling Springwood, eds., *Team Spirits: The Native American Mascots Controversy* (Lincoln: University of Nebraska Press, 2001); C. Richard King and Charles Fruehling Springwood, *Beyond the Cheers: Race as Spectacle in College Sport* (Albany: SUNY Press, 2001).

3 David Drew, *Lost Chronicles of the Maya Kings* (Berkeley: University of California Press, 1999), 235; Warren D. Hill, Michael Blake, and John E. Clark, "Ball Court Design Dates Back 3,400 Years," *Nature* 392 (66679/1998): 878–879.

4 Dennis Tedlock, trans., *Popul Vuh: The Definitive Edition of the Mayan Book of the Dawn of Life and the Glories of Gods and Kings* (New York: Simon and Schuster, 1996), 119–122.

5 Nigel B. Crowther, *Sport in Ancient Times* (Westport, CT: Greenwood Publishing, 2007), 160–161; Vernon L. Scarborough and David R. Wilcox, eds., *The Mesoamerican Ballgame* (Tucson: University of Arizona Press, 1991), vii–ix.

6 Vernon L. Scharborough, "Courting the Southern Maya Lowlands: A Study in Pre-Hispanic Ballgame Architecture," and S. Jeffrey K. Wilkerson, "And Then They Were Sacrificed: The Ritual

Ballgame of Northeastern Mesoamerica Through Time and Space," in *The Mesoamerican Ballgame*, ed. Vernon L. Scarborough and David R. Wilcox, 45–71, 129–144.

7 Inga Clendinnen, *Aztecs: An Interpretation* (Cambridge: Cambridge University Press, 1991, 2014), 143–144.

8 David R. Wilcox, "The Mesoamerican Ballgame in the American Southwest," in *The Mesoamerican Ball Game*, ed. Vernon L. Scarborough and David R. Wilcox, 101–125.

9 Ricardo Alegria, "The Ball Game Played by Aborigines of the Antilles," *American Antiquity* 16, no. 4 (1951): 348–352.

10 Drew, *The Lost Chronicles of the Maya Kings*, 235.

11 "Joe Tindle Thornton," in *Native Americans in Sports Vol. 2*, ed. C. Richard King (Armonk, NY: M.E. Sharpe, 2004), 298–299.

12 Stuart Culin, *Games of the North American Indians* (New York: Dover, 1975/1907), 383.

13 "Archery," in King, ed., *Native Americans in Sports Vol. 1*, 19–23. Also see Reginald and Gladys Laubin, *American Indian Archery* (Norman: University of Oklahoma, 1980); Jim Hamm, *Bows & Arrows of the Native Americans: A Step-by-Step Guide to Wooden Bows, Sinew-Backed Bows, Composite Bows, Strings, Arrows & Quivers* (New York: The Lyons Press, 1989).

14 Donald M. Fisher, *Lacrosse: A History of the Game* (Baltimore, MD: Johns Hopkins University Press, 2002), 111–112.

15 "Lacrosse," in *Native Americans in Sports Vol. 1*, ed. C. Richard King,174.

16 Donald M. Fisher, *Lacrosse: A History of the Game* (Baltimore, MD: Johns Hopkins University Press, 2002), 81–84.

17 Culin, *Games of the North American Indians*, 562–563.

18 Ibid.

19 Ibid., 174.

20 "Lacrosse," in *Native Americans in Sports Vol. 1*, ed. C. Richard King, 176–177.

21 Ibid., 177; also see the website for Mohawk International Lacrosse, www.mohawklacrosse.net

22 Megan Schneider, "We Got Next: Rise of the Haudenosaunee." www.LaxMagazine.com (posted September 2, 2014; accessed May 26, 2015); Aimee Berg, "Cradle of a Sport Has Crossed the Gender Line," *New York Times*. www.nytimes.com (published May 13, 2007; accessed May 26, 2015).

23 Since 2008, the Federation of International Lacrosse (FIL) has governed international lacrosse after a merger with the International Federation of Women's Lacrosse Associations (IFWLA) that year. The FIL has become the sanctioning body for lacrosse World Championships. The size of the tournament has grown from its initial field of 4 in 1967 to a field of 38 teams for the Denver games in 2014.

24 "Lacrosse," in *Native Americans in Sports Vol 1.*, ed. C. Richard King, 178.

25 Thomas Kaplan, "Iroquois Defeated by Passport Dispute," *New York Times*, July 16, 2020; "No Trip for Iroquois Team," *New York Times*, July 17, 2010. www.nytimes.com (accessed May 27, 2015).

26 For information on World Lacrosse Championships, see the FIL website: www.worldlacrosse2014.com. Also see *Sacred Stick* (Vision Maker Media, 2013), a film that explores the history and significance of lacrosse, focusing upon its meanings to Indigenous societies.

27 "William Mervin 'Billy' Mills," in *Native Americans in Sports, Vol. 2*, ed. C. Richard King, 216–218. Also see Billy Mills with Nicholas Sparks, *Wokini: A Lakota Journey to Happiness and Understanding* (New York: Orion Books, 1990).

28 Tewanima's name is often misspelled as "Lewis Tewanima."

29 "Louis Tewanima," in *Native Americans in Sports, Vol.2*, ed. C. Richard King, 296.

30 "Louis 'Deerfoot' Bennett," in *Native Americans in Sports*, 47–48; "Ellison Myers 'Tarzan' Brown," in *Native Americans in Sports Vol. 1*, ed. C. Richard King, 61–63; and "Thomas Longboat," in *Native Americans in Sports Vol 2*, ed. C. Richard King, 192–194.

31 Terrence N. D'Altroy, *The Incas* (Malden, MA: Blackwell, 2002/3).

32 Peter Nabokov, *Indian Running: Native American History and Tradition* (Santa Fe, NM: Ancient City Press, 1981), 20.

33 Ibid., 10–35.

34 Culin, *Games of the North American Indians*, 806–807.

35 Glenn S. Warner, "Red Menaces," *Collier's*, October 31, 1931, 16.

36 Linda Peavy and Ursula Smith, "'Leav[ing] the White[s]. . .Far Behind Them': The Girls from Fort Shaw (Montana) Indian School, Basketball Champions of the 1904 World's Fair," in *The 1904 Anthropology Days and Olympic Games: Sport, Race, and American Imperialism*, ed. Susan Brownell (Lincoln: University of Nebraska Press, 2008), 243–277.
37 Nancy J. Parezo, "A 'Special Olympics': Testing Racial Strength and Endurance at the 1904 Louisiana Purchase Exposition," in *The 1904 Anthropology Days and Olympic Games*, ed. Susan Brownell, 59–126.
38 John Bloom, *To Show What an Indian Can Do: Sports at Native American Boarding Schools* (Minneapolis: University of Minnesota Press, 2001).
39 See Jack Newcombe, *The Best of the Athletic Boys: The White Man's Impact on Jim Thorpe* (New York: Doubleday, 1975).
40 In addition to Newcombe's biography, see Joseph Bruchac, *Jim Thorpe: Original All-American* (New York: Penguin, 2006); and Kate Buford, *Native American Son: The Life and Sporting Legend of Jim Thorpe* (New York: Knopf, ebook/www.aaknopf.com, 2010).
41 Grace Thorpe. Phone Interview with John Bloom, February 16, 2001.
42 *Official Report of the Nineteenth Annual Conference of Charities and Correction* (1892), 46–59.
43 Bloom, *To Show What an Indian Can Do*, 31–50.
44 Phillip J. Deloria, *Indians in Unexpected Places* (Lawrence: University Press of Kansas, 2004), 129–130.
45 "Narciso Platero 'Ciso' Abeyta," in *Native Americans in Sports Vol. 1*, ed. C. Richard King, 1–2.
46 See Jeffrey Powers-Beck, "'Chief,' The American Indian Integration of Baseball, 1897–1945," *American Indian Quarterly* 25, Autumn 2001, no. 4: 514–515. Also see his important book, *The American Indian Integration of Baseball* (Lincoln: University of Nebraska Press, 2004).
47 Jeffrey Powers-Beck compiled this list as part of his outstanding work on the history of Indigenous baseball. See Powers-Beck, "'Chief'."
48 Ellen Staurowsky, "An Act of Honor or Exploitation? The Cleveland Indians' Use of the Louis Francis Sockalexis Story," *Sociology of Sport Journal* 15 (1998): 299–316.
49 "Charles Albert 'Chief' Bender," in *Native Americans in Sports, Vol. I*, ed. C. Richard King, 44–45; Also see Powers-Beck, "'Chief'," and *The American Indian Integration of Baseball*; William C. Kashatus, *Money Pitcher: Chief Bender and the Tragedy of Indian Assimiliation* (State College: Penn State University Press, 2006); Stephen I. Thompson, "American Indians in the Major Leagues," *Baseball Research Journal* 13 (1983): 1–7.
50 Deloria, *Indians in Unexpected Places*, 227.
51 "Chief Meyers," Baseball Reference. www.baseball-reference.com/players/m/meyerch01.shtml
52 R.J. Lesch, "Chief Meyers," *Society for American Baseball Research*. http://sabr.org/bioproj/person/d090eef4; R.J. Lesch, "Chief Meyers," in *Deadball Stars of the National League*, ed. Tom Simon (Washington, DC: Brassey's, Inc. 2004), 29–86. Also see William A. Young, *John Tortes "Chief" Meyers: A Baseball Biography* (Jefferson, NC: McFarland, 2012).
53 For an account of Shoni Schimmel's rise from her Native roots in Oregon and the struggles of Native women seeking to achieve sports stardom, see *Off the Rez*, Produced and Directed by Jonathan Hock, 86 min. FilmBuff. 2010. Amazon Instant Video.
54 Philip J. Deloria, *Playing Indian* (New Haven: Yale, 1998). On the Native American mascot controversy, see Jennifer Guilano, *Indian Spectacle: College Mascots and the Anxiety of Modern America* (New Brunswick, NJ: Rutgers University Press, 2013).
55 Allison Fuss Mellis, *Riding Buffaloes and Broncos: Rodeo and Native Traditions in the Northern Great Plains* (Norman: University of Oklahoma Press, 2003).

9

AFRICAN AMERICANS AND SPORTS

Charles H. Martin

Introduction

Organized sports have played an important and highly visible role in African American life and culture since the late nineteenth century. For black men, much like their white counterparts, sporting activities provided a popular stage upon which to display their exceptional skills, experience the exhilaration and disappointment of competition, bask in adulation from adoring fans, and pursue fame and fortune. For spectators and fans, athletic events offered a welcome respite from the stress and disappointments of everyday life and afforded them the opportunity to form a collective identity around their favorite teams. At the same time, the sporting experiences of black athletes and their communities often differed in significant ways from those of the white mainstream. The widespread racism and discrimination that African Americans endured for over 100 years after emancipation affected virtually every aspect of their public life, including sports. Furthermore, racial restrictions in athletics exposed the glaring contradiction between the professed American values of liberty and equality and the harsh reality of discrimination and exclusion that existed on the playing fields. According to the prevailing egalitarian ideology of American athletics, sport was a democratic institution where individual success resulted from personal character and hard work on a level playing field, unaffected by external social and economic factors. As one idealistic black sportswriter remarked in 1957, "It doesn't matter whether your parents came over here on the Mayflower or a slave ship. If you've got guts, a competitive heart, lightning speed, and the will to compete, then brother you're in the game."[1]

In reality, however, a wide variety of factors severely affected athletic opportunity for African Americans until well after World War II. In their athletic endeavors, African Americans encountered the ideology of white supremacy, which emphatically maintained that they were mentally, physically, and socially inferior to whites. According to this racist ideology, excluding black athletes from integrated competition was imperative, because to accept such competition would imply the social and moral equivalency of all participants, thereby greatly lowering the status of whites. As one alarmed Georgia state senator warned in 1957 during his state's segregation crisis, "When Negroes and whites meet on the athletic fields on a basis of complete equality, it is only natural that this sense of equality carries into the daily living of these people."[2] African Americans responded to such discrimination and exclusion in a variety of ways. Some formed black sports clubs and college athletic programs in which African Americans could exercise control over their own activities, and athletic triumphs in this separate world could inspire collective racial pride. A separate athletic structure also permitted the development of distinctive styles of play and accompanying social customs.

At the same time, the black sporting world also served as a site of opposition and resistance to racial exclusion. For example, in those rare moments when individual black athletes were allowed to compete with whites and ultimately prevailed, their victories contradicted racist claims of physical inferiority and were widely reported in the black press. By emphasizing these triumphs, racial spokesmen attempted to leverage sports success as a first step toward the ultimate goal of racial equality in American society.[3]

From Slavery to Jim Crow, 1865–1910

The nature of the African American sporting experience varied over time and place, influenced by shifting internal and external forces. The extensive participation of African Americans in the national sporting culture was primarily a post-emancipation experience, as freedom opened up new possibilities in many areas of American life, including athletic competition. Before 1865, there were few opportunities for black sporting activities. On some occasions, slave owners might match their strongest male slaves against each other in a boxing match. Some enslaved men also served as jockeys in horse races, staged for the entertainment of their masters. After emancipation, African Americans actively participated in a variety of sporting activities over the next four decades, including horse racing, bicycle racing, baseball, college football, and especially boxing. Black prize fighters were sometimes accepted but never welcomed in the ring against white fighters. In the early 1800s, Tom Molineaux, reputedly a former slave, acquired some notoriety for his boxing skills before relocating to England in 1809, where he narrowly lost two bouts against the English champion Tom Crib. Towards the end of the century, several black boxers acquired national prominence, most notably West Indies native Peter Jackson. Many white contemporaries regarded Jackson, a heavyweight fighter, as one of the top pugilists of his era, but John L. Sullivan, the white world champion, refused to fight him on racial grounds. Another highly regarded black boxer, George Dixon, actually captured the U.S. bantamweight and world featherweight titles over white opponents, but by the time he lost the latter championship in 1900, white attitudes had hardened. One white Southerner crudely summed up the racist opposition to mixed prize fights in 1897 after he helped halt an interracial bout: "The idea of niggers fighting white men! Why, if that darned scoundrel would beat that white boy the niggers would never stop gloating about it, and, as it is, we have enough trouble with them."[4]

In horse racing, black jockeys were commonplace at race tracks by the 1850s, but by 1900 they had been mostly driven out of the sport. Their initial acceptance in the horse racing business reflected the low status of their job and the initial reluctance of whites to work in an occupation dominated by African Americans. Isaac Murphy emerged as the most talented black jockey of the period, guiding his mounts to three Kentucky Derby victories. In fact, most experts considered him to be the top jockey in the United States during the 1880s. But as his career declined in the 1890s, he found employment harder to obtain, as white jockeys and racehorse owners gradually conspired to exclude black jockeys from the sport.[5] In cycling, African Americans were often allowed to compete in major events against whites. Marshall "Major" Taylor won numerous prestigious bicycle races in the 1890s and the early twentieth century. By the end of his career, however, white competitors had succeeded in imposing a color line and eliminated African American riders from the sport.[6]

American interest in baseball grew rapidly in the late nineteenth century as the increasingly popular sport spread across the nation. African American males formed amateur baseball clubs and even some professional teams, as well as a few short-lived minor leagues. Black and white local teams occasionally played each other during this period, despite the stigma attached to whites who did so. The rise of white professional baseball leagues afforded a few talented African Americans an opportunity to display their skills on a wider stage. One source found that 73 African Americans had competed in white leagues during the late nineteenth century.[7] These players were forced to endure abuse from opponents and even their own teammates, who gave them incorrect signals, refused to defend them against violent tactics by rival teams, and ostracized them away from the field. The only two African Americans who advanced to what was then considered a "major league" were Moses Fleetwood Walker and his younger brother Weldy, who played for Toledo in the American Association during the 1884 season. Moses Fleetwood Walker then moved on to play in the International League, a high minor league, until team owners yielded to pressure from white players and began phasing out the league's few African Americans. Walker nonetheless hung on with the Syracuse franchise through the end of the 1889 season. With his departure, the purge of African Americans from the major and minor leagues of "organized baseball" was complete. "America's pastime" now became a racialized space from which whites deliberately excluded African Americans.[8]

In the 1890s, African American college students enthusiastically embraced the new athletic culture sweeping across American campuses, especially the manly sport of football. Most African American football players participated in athletic programs at segregated colleges in the Southern and border states, although a token few joined teams at Northern white schools. The first formal football game between historically black colleges and universities (HCBUs) took place in 1892 in North Carolina when Biddle University (later Johnson C. Smith College) defeated Livingstone College 4–0. In 1894 Howard University and Lincoln University clashed for the first time on Thanksgiving Day, inaugurating an annual classic that soon became the most important college rivalry in the black sports world. But because of rigid Jim Crow policies, black college teams were restricted to competition only on their side of the color line.[9] In the North, the small number of elite African American football players at predominantly white universities encountered a slightly more porous color line. In 1889 Thomas Fisher at Beloit College and the duo of William T.S. Jackson and William H. Lewis at Amherst College became the first African Americans to integrate Northern college teams. Lewis proved most successful, and Walter Camp later selected him for his prestigious All-America team in 1892 and 1893 when Lewis was attending the Harvard law school. After graduation he spent 12 years on the Harvard coaching staff, wrote one of the first football coaching manuals, and eventually served as assistant attorney general during the presidency of William Howard Taft.[10] Over the ensuing two decades a trickle of black athletes followed in these pioneers' footsteps. But white college teams from the South consistently refused to compete against these few integrated Northern teams. To avoid unexpected confrontations over racial policy in intersectional matchups, the major powers in college sports eventually reached an unofficial accord on the issue around 1910. This new national policy, labeled the "Gentleman's Agreement," decreed that Northern teams would automatically withhold any African American players on their roster when scheduling an opponent from a Southern or border state. Thus, in sports as in contemporary politics, sectional reconciliation had been achieved, but at the expense of African Americans.[11]

The Era of Segregation, 1910–1945

From the first part of the twentieth century through the end of World War II, systematic segregation and racial exclusion characterized most black–white relations in American sports.

Within their separate sphere, African Americans developed a vibrant athletic culture on both the collegiate and professional levels while continuing to struggle for inclusion into the larger sporting nation. In addition to Northern college football, another partial exception to the broader trend of racial exclusion could be found in the widely popular sport of boxing. Obtaining title bouts against white champions, however, remained a daunting challenge, especially in the higher weight divisions. The controversial career of Jack Johnson, the world heavyweight champion from 1908 to 1915, illustrated this difficulty. Johnson literally spent two years chasing champion Tommy Burns around the world before finally gaining a title match in Australia in 1908, which he won easily. Johnson's victory enraged many whites and eventually forced former champion Jim Jeffries, labeled "the great white hope," to come out of retirement in an unsuccessful attempt to reclaim the title for white America. Johnson's subsequent victory over Jeffries provoked antiblack violence across the United States, and the film of the black champion physically dominating his white challenger proved so inflammatory that it was banned by dozens of American cities, as well as several foreign countries. Johnson's flamboyant lifestyle, masculine bravado, and flagrant violation of racial taboos, including his open preference for white wives and girlfriends, further angered whites and embarrassed middle-class African Americans. Federal law enforcement officials eventually responded with a racially motivated indictment and conviction of Johnson in 1913 under the federal Mann Act (White-Slave Traffic Act).[12] Johnson fled the country, eventually lost his title to Jess Willard, and finally returned to the United States in 1920 to serve a one-year prison sentence.

Two decades later, the ascension of the next black heavyweight champion, Joe Louis (born Joseph Louis Barrow), revealed that racial bias in boxing had ebbed somewhat. Louis's humble and nonthreatening public persona, a sharp contrast to Jack Johnson's provocative image, helped make "the brown bomber" an enormously popular figure during the 1930s and 1940s. Louis defeated James Braddock for the heavyweight title in 1936 and then avenged an earlier defeat by knocking out German champion Max Schmeling in 1938. Louis's victories inspired great rejoicing and enhanced racial pride among African Americans. Moreover, his defeat of Schmeling, a Nazi favorite, and his patriotic activities during World War II made him a national hero to many white sports fans. Louis held the title until 1949, and boxing historians still regard him as one of the greatest heavyweight champions of all time.[13]

Although professional boxing allowed at least a few limited opportunities for African Americans, Major League Baseball offered none at all, as it continued its racist policy of barring black players. Excluded from baseball's mainstream, African Americans further expanded their own vibrant baseball culture within their separate athletic world. In 1920 former player and entrepreneur Andrew "Rube" Foster formed the Negro National League (NNL), composed of eight mostly black-owned, Midwestern teams. After Foster died in 1930, the loss of his leadership skills, as well as the Great Depression's economic devastation, forced the NNL to disband in 1931. Several black businessmen led by Gus Greenlee of Pittsburgh, an alleged gambling boss, revived the NNL in 1933, and a second league, the Negro American League, commenced operation in 1937. The champions of the two leagues met annually in the Colored World Series. The enormously popular interleague all-star game attracted even more attention, regularly drawing over 40,000 enthusiastic fans to Comiskey Park in Chicago. After World War II and the integration of Major League Baseball, though, attendance and revenue for the two Negro major leagues declined precipitously. The NNL disbanded in 1951, and the NAL limped on until 1960 as a shell of its former self.[14]

Foster strongly believed that black businessmen should own black teams, but the cost of financing professional clubs sometimes forced him and his successors to accept white ownership of a few teams, most notably the Kansas City Monarchs. Negro League teams were known for their wide-open style of play, featuring aggressive base stealing, trick plays, and occasional grandstanding. Some of this showmanship derived from the need to entertain fans, but part of it also reflected the expressive nature of African American popular culture. For financial reasons, most clubs barnstormed extensively across the country. Exhibition games against white major leaguers attracted widespread attention from black fans, and Negro League teams more than held their own against their more famous white counterparts. Arguably the three most outstanding players from the Negro Leagues were pitcher LeRoy "Satchel" Paige, who defeated major league star "Dizzy Dean" of the St. Louis Cardinals in several exhibitions, Joshua "Josh" Gibson, a power-hitting catcher whose home run prowess rivaled that of Babe Ruth, and speedy center fielder James T. "Cool Papa" Bell, who regularly led the Negro leagues in stolen bases.

Before the 1930s, African Americans achieved only modest success in track and field competition. John B. Taylor, a member of the victorious U.S. 1,600-meter relay team at the 1908 summer games, was the first African American competitor to win an Olympic gold medal. Nearly three decades later, it was sprinter Jesse Owens and several black teammates whose triumphs in the 1936 Olympics established African American men as a major force in international track and field competition. At the so-called Nazi Olympics in Berlin, Owens collected an unprecedented four gold medals, winning the 100- and 200-meter dashes, the long jump, and the 400-meter relay. Additional gold medals were won by Cornelius Johnson in the high jump, Ralph Metcalfe in the 400-meter relay, Archie Williams in the 400-meter run, and John Woodruff in the 800-meter race. Contrary to the often-repeated myth, Adolph Hitler did not deliberately snub Owens at the medal ceremonies. However, when Owens returned home, American businessmen were the ones who actually snubbed him by withholding the lucrative endorsements that undoubtedly would have been afforded him had he been white. Lacking a college degree and useful job skills, Owens struggled in his immediate post-Olympic employment career until the Cold War offered him new economic opportunities as a patriotic symbol of alleged American racial progress.[15]

Prior to World War II, there were limited opportunities for African Americans in professional football and basketball. A modest number of African Americans participated in the National Football League during the 1920s and early 1930s, including Frederick Douglass "Fritz" Pollard, Frederick "Duke" Slater, and Joseph Lillard. But in 1934, influenced by Washington Redskins' owner George Preston Marshall, NFL owners implemented an unofficial ban on African American players. Professional basketball was more fragmented than football, and the modern National Basketball Association was not formed until after World War II. The best known black professional teams of the era were the New York Renaissance, or "Rens," founded by black entrepreneur Robert J. Douglas in 1923, and the Harlem Globetrotters, formed in 1927 in Chicago and soon taken over by white entrepreneur Abe Saperstein. The Rens won the initial "world championship" professional tournament in 1939 over the all-white Oshkosh All-Stars but went into a slow decline during World War II. The Globetrotters also held their own against the top white professional teams before mostly abandoning orthodox basketball after 1949 and switching to an entertainment model that eventually made them the most widely recognized "basketball" organization in the world for many years.

In addition to professional sports, college athletics inspired great passion among African American fans, especially football games between HCBUs. Excluded from NCAA membership, black colleges created their own athletic conferences in order to organize and administer fair competition. A group of black colleges in the Upper South formed the first such group, the Colored (later Central) Intercollegiate Athletic Association (CIAA), in 1912, and other regional associations were established over the following decades. During the 1930s and early 1940s Morgan State College dominated the football scene and regularly captured first place in the CIAA standings. Some of the top players of the period included Tuskegee Institute halfback Benjamin F. Stevenson, the career-rushing record holder for HBCU teams; John "Big Train" Moody, a punishing runner for Morris Brown College; and Franz Alfred "Jazz" Byrd of Lincoln University, sometimes known as the "black Red Grange." Colorful rivalries were common, and by the mid-1930s the annual Morgan State College-Hampton Institute clash had eclipsed the Howard-Lincoln game as the biggest game of the season. The selection of the Negro College All-American team by the black press provided additional recognition for African American stars who were generally ignored by the white press.[16]

From World War I through the start of World War II, a few more black athletes succeeded in joining football teams at white universities in the North and West. Paul Robeson at Rutgers University (1916–1918) and Fritz Pollard at Brown (1915–1916) were such dominating players that Walter Camp selected them for his prestigious All-America team. In the late 1930s the Gentleman's Agreement finally began to be challenged. For example, the University of Maryland and Duke University both abandoned their "whites only" athletic policies in 1938 for away games against Syracuse University and its famous black quarterback Wilmeth Sidat-Singh. In order to audition for a lucrative Rose Bowl post-season invitation, Southern Methodist University scheduled two games with UCLA, competing against Bruin stars Kenny Washington and Woody Strode in 1937 and Jackie Robinson in 1940. This trend heartened racial liberals, who hoped that such a growing movement against discrimination in sports would lead to a broader rejection of discrimination in other areas of society. The NAACP's magazine *The Crisis* optimistically remarked in 1939, "Fair play in sports leads the way to fair play in life."[17] Developments during World War II further inspired racial reformers, as the color line in sports continued to weaken. Nonetheless, when MLB and the NFL ran short of skilled players due to military service, both leagues called up retired and marginally talented white athletes rather than sign African American athletes.

The Age of Integration, 1945–1980

After World War II, the sports world gradually underwent a racial revolution that profoundly altered the course of American race relations. One immediate breakthrough came when Major League Baseball and professional football abandoned their policies banning African American players. In baseball the two men most responsible for the sport's racial transformation were Branch Rickey and Jackie Robinson. A far-sighted businessman with an idealistic core, Rickey stunned the sports world when his Brooklyn Dodgers organization signed Robinson to a contract in October 1945 and assigned him to the Dodgers' affiliate in Montreal for the 1946 season. Robinson thus became the first African American to participate in "organized" baseball since Moses Fleetwood Walker in 1889. In the spring of 1947 Robinson joined the Brooklyn squad, continuing "baseball's great experiment." Subjected to oppressive press coverage, indifference if not outright hostility from many of his teammates, and extensive verbal abuse and dirty play from opposing players, Robinson nonetheless persevered, demonstrating that "Rickey had uncovered not only an outstanding baseball player, but a person of charisma and leadership."[18] Three months after Robinson debuted with the Dodgers, the Cleveland Indians added outfielder Larry Doby to their roster, making him the second African American to play in the major leagues in the twentieth century. Despite the outstanding performances of Robinson and Doby, as well as those athletes who soon followed, several clubs still resisted integrating their rosters. Not until 1959 did the last holdout, the Boston Red Sox, finally add an African American player, Elijah "Pumpsie" Green, to their squad.

Professional football also dropped its racial barriers after World War II, but with much less press coverage. In 1946 the newly formed All-America Football League (AAFL) announced that it would allow its franchises to sign African Americans. Before any of the AAFL teams could act, however, the Los Angeles Rams of the NFL unexpectedly signed former UCLA stars Kenny Washington and Woody Strode to contracts in the spring of 1946. The Rams acted after protests by local civil rights activists and black sportswriters endangered their right to use the publicly funded Los Angeles Coliseum. Several months later, the Cleveland Browns of the AAFL added Marion Motley and Bill Willis to their squad. Subsequently these four African Americans officially integrated professional football during the fall 1946 season. In 1947 five additional AAFL squads signed African Americans, whereas no NFL team took similar action until a year later. Eventually the AAFL disbanded, with several teams then joining the NFL. Full league integration was not complete until 1962, when George Preston Marshall's Washington Redskins finally signed several black players.[19] The National Basketball Association, formed in 1946, did not initially accept black athletes but dropped its color line in 1950. Charles Cooper, Nat "Sweetwater" Clifton, Earl Lloyd, and Hank DeZonie all joined NBA teams for the 1950–1951 season. The number of African Americans in the NBA grew slowly but steadily for the rest of the 1950s, with black players privately complaining that there were unofficial racial quotas for each team and that they were used primarily for defense and rebounding. During the 1960s, though, the league featured numerous African American stars, including Bill Russell, Wilt Chamberlain, Oscar Robertson, and Elgin Baylor, who literally changed the face and the style of professional basketball.

The growing integration of professional sports and the emergence of more African American stars in college sports and amateur track and field in the 1950s provided valuable ammunition to the U.S. government for the cultural side of the Cold War. Because the Soviet Union repeatedly emphasized racial discrimination in the United States as part of its worldwide propaganda campaign, the success stories of black American athletes offered powerful counternarratives to Soviet accusations. According to one scholar, "African American athletes were employed as the embodiment and personification of freedom and democracy."[20] Among the star athletes, almost exclusively male, who were selected for these overseas cultural missions included Olympic track and field sensations Jesse Owens, Mal Whitfield, and Rafer Johnson, as well as the 1956 NCAA champion University of San Francisco basketball team led by center Bill Russell. Even the Harlem Globetrotters received assistance from the State Department in arranging international goodwill trips. Althea Gibson, the first black woman to win the U.S. Open tennis championship tournament, was one of the few women invited on such international tours in the 1950s. Black women in track and field also played an expanding role in Cold War athletic competition against the Soviet Union. Sprinters Wilma Rudolph and Wyomia Tyus, as well as others from Tennessee State University's famous "Tigerbelles" program, dominated the Olympic sprint competition throughout the 1960s.[21]

College sports also underwent a social revolution after World War II. Under pressure from African Americans, liberal white students, and veterans, the old Gentleman's Agreement in sports soon collapsed. In the early 1960s, as the federal government forced the last Southern universities to admit black undergraduates, attention then turned to when these schools would integrate their athletic teams. Basketball players Charles and Cecil Brown at Texas Western College in the 1956–1957 season and football players Abner Haynes and Leon King at North Texas State College in the fall of 1957 were apparently the first African Americans to play at the varsity level for a major college in an ex-Confederate state. But outside of western and northern Texas, athletic integration did not gain much ground until the late 1960s. In the Southeastern Conference (SEC), the "final citadel of segregation," Nathaniel "Nat" Northington of the University of Kentucky became the first African American football player in the fall of 1967, and Perry Wallace of Vanderbilt integrated SEC basketball later that year. As their numbers slowly grew, black football players voiced concern about the "stacking" of African Americans at certain "instinctive" positions like halfback and wide receiver, whereas central, so-called "thinking" positions such as quarterback and offensive center, were reserved for whites. Despite the start of athletic integration in the South, black college football continued to enjoy great popularity among African Americans in the 1960s and 1970s. Florida A&M College, coached by Alonzo "Jake" Gaither, and Grambling College, led by Edward G. "Eddie" Robinson, who eventually became the all-time winningest coach in Division I football, dominated competition after World War II, along with Tennessee A&I (later Tennessee State University), and Prairie View A&M. One important milestone occurred in 1949 when Grambling's Paul "Tank" Younger, a powerful halfback and linebacker, became the first black college veteran to make an NFL team roster, thereby opening the door for other athletes from these colleges. Unfortunately, the integration of white college teams in the South had a long-term negative impact on black college sports, because white universities eventually succeeded in recruiting the most talented African American prospects away from black schools. This development was one of several negative side effects that educational integration inflicted on black institutions across the South.

The latter half of the 1960s and early 1970s witnessed widespread racial conflict and upheavals across the United States. In sports, the so-called "Revolt of the Black Athlete" offered an unprecedented challenge to white coaches and administrators and temporarily disrupted the triumphalist narrative of American racial progress through athletic integration. Despite the passage of landmark civil rights legislation in the mid-1960s, African Americans became increasingly frustrated with the slow pace of racial change. Displaying a new assertiveness, African American athletes at all levels challenged specific discriminatory practices in their individual sports. Some athletes went further and attempted to turn athletics into a broader vehicle through which to attack systemic racism in American society. One early example of this new assertiveness occurred in January 1965, when black players selected for the American Football League's all-star game forced the league to hastily move the contest to Houston after they encountered widespread discrimination in restaurants and bars in New Orleans, the original venue. On the college level, African American athletes at virtually every major university outside the South eventually staged some kind of demonstration against discrimination in athletics. One study identified 37 such protests during the 1967–1968 academic year alone.[22]

The two best-known examples of the "Revolt of the Black Athlete" involved an unprecedented action at the 1968 Mexico City Olympics and the controversial political stand of heavyweight boxing champion Muhammad Ali. In the fall of 1967, Harry Edwards proposed that black athletes boycott the 1968 Olympics to protest continuing racism both in the United States and in global sports, as well as to "reassert the basic masculinity of black men." Edwards formed the Olympic Project for Human Rights (OPHR) and convinced several male athletes to refrain from trying out for the U.S. Olympic team, but his campaign eventually faltered. Influenced by the OPHR movement, however, sprinters Tommie Smith and John Carlos staged a dramatic protest in Mexico City at the awards ceremony for the medalists in the 200-meter sprint, when each athlete lowered his head during the playing of the American national anthem and raised one clenched fist inside a black glove while standing barefooted in black socks. In response, Smith and Carlos were promptly suspended from the U.S. team and kicked out of the Olympic village, but their dramatic gesture, captured in an iconic photograph, reverberated worldwide as a symbol of profound black dissatisfaction with racial conditions in the United States.[23]

The African American athlete who had the greatest impact on American society during the 1960s and 1970s was Muhammad Ali. Born Cassius Marcellus Clay, the brash young fighter stunned the boxing world by knocking out Sonny Liston in 1964 to claim the world heavyweight title and then revealing that he had joined the Nation of Islam (NOI)—the so-called Black Muslims—and had abandoned his "slave name" in favor of Muhammad Ali. Ali's outspoken comments praising the NOI, condemning racism in the United States, criticizing the Vietnam War, and verbally belittling his opponents made him a highly controversial figure in the United States for the next several years. After he refused induction into the U.S. Army in 1967, a federal jury found him guilty of draft evasion. While his conviction was under appeal, Ali was unable to fight professionally and became to many a symbol of government repression of black militancy. His willingness, at considerable personal cost, to take an unpopular stand in defense of his religion and his political views endeared him to millions around the world but infuriated many conservative Americans. In 1971 the U.S. Supreme Court overturned his conviction on a technicality, and Ali returned to the ring, eventually reclaiming his heavyweight title. His epic fights against Joe Frazier and George Foreman solidified his reputation as one of the greatest heavyweight boxers of all times. Yet even more enduring was his stature as a symbol of the new, proud black manhood of the 1960s.[24]

The Post-Integration Era, 1980–Present

By the 1980s African American athletes had achieved a significant presence in all the major American team sports except hockey, and the most talented had earned superstar status. The earlier black activism had forced a new racial equilibrium upon the sports world, one which included greater racial sensitivity but preserved white control of administrative positions, coaching, and ownership. During the subsequent decades, the focus of racial advancement in sports now shifted from guaranteeing African Americans full access to individual sports to broader questions concerning their collective power, economic exploitation, and civic responsibility.

The numbers of African Americans participating in professional basketball and football grew steadily into the early twenty-first century before leveling off. Participation in track and field remained high, whereas the number of black players in MLB declined sharply. Black Americans especially dominated the NBA, representing 74 percent of all players in the 2014–2015 season. Virtually all of the top stars in the league since the retirement of Larry Bird in 1992 have been African Americans, including such remarkable athletes as

Michael Jordan, Shaquille O'Neal, Kobe Bryant, and LeBron James. Benefitting from a brilliant marketing campaign by the Nike Corporation, Jordan became the first superstar to be turned into an international "brand," revealing the increasing globalization and commercialization of sports.[25] Although the percentage of African American head coaches dipped slightly to 30 percent during the 2014–2015 season, the NBA's record on racial diversity easily surpassed those of other professional sports. In international track and field competition, black Americans contributed disproportionately to the success of U.S. teams. Sprinters Carl Lewis, Florence Griffith Joyner, and Michael Johnson, as well as heptathlon champion Jackie Joyner-Kersee, were just a few of the black stars who won multiple Olympic gold medals for the United States.

On the college level, African Americans consistently dominated the All-America teams in men's basketball. After the passage of Title IX of the U.S. Education Amendments Act of 1972, which prohibited gender discrimination at education institutions, American colleges greatly expanded their women's sports programs. African American women eventually came to play an extremely influential role in basketball, the most prominent women's sport. The ability of talented players like Candace Parker of Tennessee and Brittney Griner of Baylor University to dunk the basketball also revealed a new level of physical skill by female athletes. Nonetheless, some critics pointed out that white women appear to have benefitted more than black women from Title IX, because they participated in a far wider range of athletic activities and therefore received far more total scholarships.[26]

In the NFL, African American participation grew steadily, and by the 2014 season black players represented about two-thirds of team rosters. Although black superstars like Thurman Thomas, Barry Sanders, and Emmitt Smith dominated the important running back position, whites continued to outnumber blacks at the high-profile quarterback position and thereby claimed a major share of the media spotlight. The NFL was much slower than the NBA to accept black head coaches. By 2014 African Americans held only15 percent of head coaching positions, despite the so-called Rooney Rule that required teams to interview at least one African American for every open head coaching position. Black athletes also initiated a cultural transformation of traditional football culture, introducing new styles of handshakes, choreographed touchdown celebrations, and verbal jousting with opponents, reflecting the expressive aesthetics of black popular culture. In MLB the number of black Americans reached a peak of 19 percent in 1986 but had declined to only 7.8 percent in 2015, despite various outreach programs. African Americans also occasionally left their mark in selected "elite" sports. In golf, Tiger Woods controlled the fairways from 1997 to 2013, and in tennis sisters Venus and Serena Williams dominated their sport for the first decade and a half of the twenty-first century.[27]

The extent to which African American athletes on the professional and collegiate levels continued to be exploited despite their seeming success became a controversial issue. In his provocative 2006 book, *Forty Million Dollar Slaves*, sportswriter William C. Rhoden argued that multimillion dollar contracts and free agency had not allowed professional black athletes, especially NBA players, to escape an updated plantation system. According to Rhoden, this seeming contradiction existed because true power still rested in the hands of white team owners and white-run media corporations. Some critics found the plantation metaphor exaggerated, and many sports fans, especially whites, expressed little sympathy for wealthy but "exploited" athletes. On the college level, a continuing debate focused on whether male athletes in football and men's basketball were exploited because colleges increasingly reaped tens of millions of dollars from their highly commercialized sports, whereas the players received only a four-year scholarship. Colleges were also chastised for not doing a better job of educating these athletes, as evidenced by their low graduation rates. The NCAA first responded by slightly tightening academic eligibility requirements. Then in 2015 the association made another concession by reluctantly allowing universities to provide athletes in the major sports with limited financial subsidies beyond their scholarships, but this conciliatory gesture failed to silence its critics.[28]

Another perennial topic of debate revolved around whether African American communities overemphasized sports, diverting limited community resources into young men's athletic activities rather than their educational development. Sociologist Harry Edwards once voiced grave concerns over this "single-minded pursuit of sports," but in the early 2000s he reversed his position, now arguing that the sheer lack of other opportunities for black youth in depressed inner-city neighborhoods made pursuing sports success a desperate but rational choice.[29] Success in athletics also had mixed results in changing outsiders' views concerning black abilities beyond the athletic arena. The integration of high school, college, and professional sports clearly played a pivotal role in reducing whites' negative attitudes toward African Americans. For example, individual black athletes often enjoyed widespread admiration from white fans, especially young men. On the other hand, the disproportionate black success in major sports reinforced for some whites the traditional racist stereotype that African Americans were physically gifted but intellectually limited. African American athletes also found themselves criticized for a lack of social responsibility, especially for abandoning their original communities. Earvin "Magic" Johnson, the former Los Angeles Laker superstar, proved to be a notable exception to this trend and was frequently lauded for his financial investments in urban locations. Unfortunately, many black former professional athletes were not in any financial position to assist their old neighborhoods. For example, one study reported by *Sports Illustrated* in 2009 found that "within five years of retirement, an estimated 60 percent of former NBA players are broke."[30]

Conclusion

Despite remarkable achievements by individual athletes, the broader cultural meaning of black athletic success in the United States remains somewhat unclear. Racial barriers preventing individual access to major sports have been demolished. Many talented black athletes have been able to demonstrate their athletic merit and be generously compensated in return. Some have even achieved worldwide recognition. Black athletes have helped facilitate the spread of black popular culture into mainstream American culture, and African American broadcasters and commentators are now widely featured on television. Attitudes of nonblacks toward African Americans have also clearly improved. Yet all of this remarkable change has not completely fulfilled the idealistic dream of racial liberals that the demonstration of black athletic merit would facilitate African Americans' full inclusion as a group into the mainstream of American social and economic life. Despite remarkable individual achievement, African Americans collectively continued to lag behind other groups in employment, income, health care, educational levels, and many other fundamental categories. Individual black athletes may have indeed marched far down what Arthur Ashe Jr. termed the "hard road to glory," but their individual success had not yet led to the collective transformation that black leaders and white racial liberals once dreamed of. The ability of sports to modify the fundamental social and economic structure of American society appears to be a limited one.

Notes

1 Marion E. Jackson, "Sports of the World," *Atlanta Daily World*, January 1, 1957.
2 *New York Times*, February 15, 1957, 1.
3 For a recent sweeping overview of the black sporting experience, see David K. Wiggins, "'Black Athletes in White Men's Games': Race, Sport, and American National Pastimes," *The International Journal of the History of Sport* 31 (2014): 181–202.
4 Arthur R. Ashe, Jr., *A Hard Road to Glory, Vol. I* (New York: Warner Books, 1988), 19–27; David K. Wiggins, *Glory Bound: Black Athletes in a White America* (Syracuse, NY: Syracuse University Press, 1997), 34–57; Dale A. Somers, *The Rise of Sports in New Orleans, 1850–1900* (Baton Rouge: Louisiana State University Press, 1972), 183 (quotation).
5 For African Americans and horse racing, see Katherine C. Mooney, *Race Horse Men: How Slavery and Freedom Were Made at the Racetrack* (Cambridge, MA: Harvard University Press, 2014).
6 Ashe, Jr., *A Hard Road to Glory, Vol. I*, 47–48; Wiggins, *Glory Bound*, 21–33.
7 Steven A. Riess and Donn Rogosin, "Baseball," in *The Encyclopedia of African American Culture and History*, ed. Charles V. Hamilton and Jack Salzman (New York: Macmillan, 1996), 270.
8 David W. Zang, *Fleet Walker's Divided Heart: The Life of Baseball's First Black Major Leaguer* (Lincoln, NE: University of Nebraska Press, 1995), 47, 62–63. William Edward White, an African American of biracial ancestry who "passed" for white as an adult and was regarded as a white player, participated in one game for the Providence Grays of the National League on June 21, 1879. Peter Morris and Stefan Fatsis, "Baseball's Secret Pioneer," *Slate*, February 4, 2014 (accessed May 17, 2015).
9 Ocania Chalk, *Black College Sport* (New York: Dodd, Mead, 1976), 40–42.
10 Evan J. Albright, "William Henry Lewis: Brief Life of a Football Pioneer, 1860–1949," *Harvard Magazine*, November–December, 2005 (accessed May 17, 2015).
11 Charles H. Martin, *Benching Jim Crow: The Rise and Fall of the Color Line in Southern College Sports, 1890–1980* (Urbana: University of Illinois Press, 2010), 8–18.
12 Recent books on Johnson include Geoffrey C. Ward, *Unforgivable Blackness: The Rise and Fall of Jack Johnson* (New York: Vintage, 2006), and Theresa Runstedtler, *Jack Johnson, Rebel Sojourner: Boxing in the Shadow of the Global Color Line* (Berkeley: University of California Press, 2012).
13 Chris Mead, *Champion—Joe Louis: Black Hero in White America* (New York: Scribner's, 1985), x–xii, 211–215, 259–274, 291–297; Jeffrey T. Sammons, *Beyond the Ring: The Role of Boxing in American Society* (Urbana: University of Illinois Press, 1988), 98–129.
14 Michael Lomax, *Black Baseball Entrepreneurs, 1902–1931: The Negro National and Eastern Colored Leagues* (Syracuse, NY: Syracuse University Press, 2014).
15 The classic biography of Owens is William J. Baker, *Jesse Owens: An American Life* (New York: Free Press, 1986).
16 Ashe, Jr., *A Hard Road to Glory, 1919–1945*, 99–106, 468.
17 *The Crisis* 46 (November 1939): 337.
18 Jules Tygiel, *Baseball's Great Experiment: Jackie Robinson and His Legacy* (New York: Vintage Books, 1983), 208.
19 On Marshall's racial policies, see Thomas G. Smith's *Showdown: JFK and the Integration of the Washington Redskins* (Boston: Beacon press, 2011).
20 Damion L. Thomas, *Globetrotting: African American Athletes and Cold War Politics* (Urbana: University of Illinois Press, 2012), 91.
21 Jennifer H. Lansbury, *A Spectacular Leap: Black Women Athletes in Twentieth-Century America* (Fayetteville: University of Arkansas Press, 2014).
22 Harry Edwards, *The Revolt of the Black Athlete* (New York: The Free Press, 1969), 80–88.
23 Douglas Hartmann, *Race, Culture, and the Revolt of the Black Athlete: The 1968 Olympic Protests and Their Aftermath* (Chicago: University of Chicago Press, 2003), 93–169 (quotation at page 134).
24 The literature on Ali is voluminous, but a good start is David Remnick, *King of the World: Muhammad Ali and the Rise of an American Hero* (New York: Random House, 1998).
25 Walter LaFeber, *Michael Jordan and the New Global Capitalism* (New York: W.W. Norton, 1999).
26 Especially critical of Title IX's impact is Billy Hawkins, *The New Plantation: Black Athletes, College Sports, and Predominantly White NCAA Institutions* (New York: Palgrave Macmillan, 2010).

27 On African Americans and tennis, see Cecil Harris and Larryette Kyle-DeBose, *Charging the Net: A History of Blacks in Tennis* (Chicago: Ivan Dee, 2007), and Sundiata Djata, *Blacks at the Net: Black Achievement in the History of Tennis, Vol. I* (Syracuse, NY: Syracuse University Press, 2006).

28 William C. Rhoden, *Forty Million Dollar Slaves: The Rise, Fall, and Redemption of the Black Athlete* (New York: Crown Publishers, 2006).

29 www.sportsbusinesssims.com/dr-harry-edwards-interview-decline-of-blacks-in-sports.htm (accessed September 23, 2015).

30 "How (and Why) Athletes Go Broke," *Sports Illustrated*, March 23, 2009.

10

LATINOS AND SPORT

Adrian Burgos, Jr.

Euphoria reigned in the Pittsburgh Pirates locker room as its players celebrated capturing the 1971 World Series. Prior to being interviewed about the team's triumph by NBC broadcaster Bob Prince, Pirates Roberto Clemente asked to address his family. Before the live international audience, Clemente spoke in Spanish: "On this the greatest day of my life, for my sons I send my blessing, and from my parents I ask for their blessing."[1]

Clemente's commandeering of the postgame interview to engage in the cultural practice of the blessing (*la bendicíon*) indelibly marked the presence of Latinos in U.S. sports. His honoring of tradition, openly exhibiting pride in his cultural heritage, along with his insistence on being treated with basic human dignity, bespoke a man fully aware how his Latino-ness, blackness, and foreignness too often shaped perceptions and actions. That 1971 moment also captures much of the tensions surrounding Latino participation in U.S. sports: recruited for their athletic talents, Latinos had to make efforts to overcome an imposed invisibility and carefully navigate expectations of assimilation and of their cultural difference, all the while seeking to make their presence in U.S. sports ordinary and respected.

The Latino presence in U.S. sports disturbs familiar narratives about race, place, and belonging in organized sports as much as in the wider U.S. society. Latinos not only have been participants in the major sports much longer than most realize, but perhaps equally significant, Latinos disrupted the clarity some desired in determining inclusion and exclusion within the color line system that dominated U.S. sports from the late nineteenth century into the mid-twentieth century. Given the brevity of this chapter, I focus on Latino/a participation in major team sports (baseball, basketball, football, and soccer) along with highlighting several Latina and Latino athletes in individual sports whose experience illuminate issues about identity along the intersecting lines of race, gender, and class.[2]

Roberto Clemente's playing career and his tragic death in December 1972 while attempting to transport relief supplies to earthquake-stricken Nicaragua elevated the Puerto Rican into the most well-known Latino in U.S. sports.[3] Recognition of Clemente belies the complex history of inclusion of Latinos in U.S. professional baseball, the impact of its color line, and of Latinos as integration pioneers. Moreover, as a native of Puerto Rico whose residents were granted U.S. citizenship through the 1917 Jones Act, Clemente helps illuminate the complicated line between inclusion and exclusion regarding Latinos in U.S. sports and society. After all, Mexican Americans who likewise held U.S. citizenship often encountered discrimination and hostilities even when included in sports. Such treatment of Mexican Americans was typically driven by perceptions of their racial and social standing as lower than that of white Americans. This issue was all the more intense in California, Texas, and much of the Southwest where Mexicans were more numerous. Different groups attached their own meaning to the sporting breakthroughs those of Mexican descent achieved. To those hostile toward Mexicans (or other Latinos), the achievements were the exceptions that proved the rule. To Mexicans, the success of Richard "Pancho" González on the tennis court, of Nancy López and Lee Trevino on the golf course, of Fernando Valenzuela on the baseball diamond, or of Anthony Muñoz on the gridiron, among others, were a testament to the resiliency, determination, and excellence that characterized their people.

Transnational migration bonded Latino athletes and communities regardless of their national citizenship status as they increasingly moved throughout the Americas in search of new opportunities. Early in the twentieth century, fans could follow the success of baseball players, boxers, and other athletes through print media, radio, and word of mouth. The advent of television and the Internet later in the century made such fandom even easier. Importantly, transnational migrants were incorporated into U.S. sports as much for their affordability as their athletic talent. The racialization of Latino labor became particularly evident in professional baseball where Latino prospects (especially the foreign born) were acquired at relatively lower signing bonuses by franchises looking to secure outstanding talent during its color line era. When Major League Baseball (MLB) instituted its amateur draft in 1965, MLB maintained the practice of signing Latin American prospects as amateur free agents eligible to be signed at the age of 16. Conversely, MLB established rules that U.S. (and Canadian) citizens must be at least 18 years old and initially go through the amateur draft before being signed. The difference in eligibility status and higher signing bonus drafted players received translated into greater legal protections for drafted prospects versus Latinos signed as amateur free agents. The larger initial investment in the form of a signing bonus also resulted in an institutional mind-set granting greater attention and patience with those drafted versus those signed as free agents.[4]

They Came Before Clemente

By the 1860s one could find groups of Cubans, Mexicans, and Californians playing baseball, and the game's multidirectional spread within the Americas meant baseball arrived in parts of Mexico and the Caribbean about the same time it did in California. Migrants, laborers, students, and military personnel who transported the sport to these lands continually infused baseball with particular meaning about nation, race, and social belonging. Indeed, many in the United States viewed baseball in an imperial manner, that the sport be used as a tool of socialization and in discerning who could be assimilated wherever the U.S. flag was flown.

Baseball's arrival in Cuba occurred largely as a by-product of the children of Cuban elites attending educational institutions in the United States.[5] In the early 1860s Cuban students transported the game to the island as part of their accrued cultural knowledge. Cuban native Esteban Bellán was a key figure in that cultural exchange. Bellán learned baseball as a student at Rose Hill College before leaving his studies to pursue a professional playing career. He would earn the distinction as the first Latino major leaguer when he joined the Troy Haymakers in 1871. Much like what would occur to later generations of Latino players, Bellán's first name would be Anglicized to "Steve" in U.S. sporting circles. Equally significant, after his playing days stateside ended, Bellán participated in the formal organization of Cuban baseball as a founding member of the Havana Baseball Club and as a player in the inaugural Cuban professional league in 1878. Bellán's activities took place during a 30-year period (1868–1898) when Cubans linked baseball to their nationalist struggle for independence against colonial Spain. Extended periods of armed conflict between *independistas* and

Spanish colonial forces also marked this period in Cuban history, spurring waves of emigration from Cuba. Everywhere Cuban émigrés went throughout the Caribbean region they brought the sport, established clubs, formed leagues, and preached the gospel of baseball.[6] This facilitated baseball's prominent place in the cultures of Dominicans, Puerto Ricans, and Venezuelans. As a result, Caribbean Latinos would be the first group of immigrants that arrived in the United States as baseball enthusiasts.

Touted as the best catcher "produced on the Pacific Slope," Vincent "Sandy" Nava pioneered a different path when he entered the National League in 1882. Introduced as the "Spanish catcher of the Providence Club," Nava was in fact U.S. born and of Mexican parentage. Providence Grays management attempted to use ethnicity to make Nava a "strong advertising card" and draw fans. Quite importantly, their labeling of Nava also reflected the era's racial hierarchy where Spanish people were held in higher esteem than Mexicans. The intentional misidentification as Spanish fit into a wider set of practices within baseball and a sporting world increasingly divided by a color line as the nineteenth century drew to a close.[7]

Baseball's color line had a profound impact on Latino ballplayers. Fifty-four U.S. and foreign-born Latinos performed in MLB between the setting of its color line in 1884 and its dismantling in 1947; over four times as many participated in the black baseball circuit during that same period. Whereas MLB selected its Latino talent based more on skin color than talent and on-field performance, the Negro Leagues welcomed Latinos of all shades, drawing players initially from Cuba then Panama, the Dominican Republic, Puerto Rico, and Venezuela.[8] Latinos enjoyed opportunities in the black circuit that they would wait decades for in the MLB, serving as team's managers, as Cuban José Méndez did for the Kansas City Monarchs from 1923–1928, or owning a franchise as did Alejandro "Alex" Pompez from 1923 through 1950. MLB's first Latino franchise owner came in 2003 when Mexican American Arte Moreno purchased the Anaheim Angels. Determining the first Latino hired as a MLB manager exposes the complexities of Latino identity. Some credit Al Lopez as MLB's first Latino manager; the Lopez family, however, was from Spain and not Latin America. Others hail Ted Williams as the first Latino due to his Mexican-American mother May Venzer—this despite Williams not openly identifying as Latino throughout a big-league career that spanned 1939 to 1972 as a player then manager. As a result, most credit Dominican Felipe Alou as MLB's first Latino manager with the Montreal Expos hiring him in 1992.[9]

The dismantling of baseball's color line initiated by Jackie Robinson's 1945 signing and his 1947 debut with the Brooklyn Dodgers opened up organized baseball to all Latinos. Over the next several decades, black Latinos joined African Americans as central actors in the desegregation of minor and major league squads. Four Latinos pioneered the racial integration of major league teams: Orestes "Minnie" Miñoso (White Sox, 1951), Nino Escalera (Reds, 1954), Carlos Paula (Senators, 1954), and Ozzie Virgil (Tigers, 1958). Wider participation of Latinos did not end practices that racialized them within baseball circles: rather, the sporting press continued to poke fun at their accents and often relied on stereotypes to describe their personalities or explain their actions. Team and league officials likewise still looked to Latin America for securing "talent on the cheap" and signing teenage Latino prospects from Caribbean countries with a "boatload mentality,"[10] that is, signing handfuls of Dominican prospects for the price of one drafted U.S. player. Eventually MLB organizations developed the Dominican baseball academy system, which refined the preparation of Dominican prospects for performing in organized baseball while also engaging in practices that some contend verges on exploitation.[11]

"Quarterbacking While Mexican"

Whereas baseball was hailed as the national pastime during the early twentieth century, football had surpassed baseball in mass popularity by the 1960s. The timing and geographic spread of the two sports influenced their popularity among Latinos. Football evolved into an established sport in Texas and the U.S. Southwest where Mexican-origin people were numerous in the early twentieth century while never truly becoming part of the sporting culture in the Spanish-speaking Caribbean. As a result, players and coaches of Mexican descent figure more prominently in football, whereas Caribbean Latinos predominate in baseball. Yet, quite similarly to professional baseball, Latinos were present in football but often rendered barely visible in press coverage through the first half of the century. The English-language press gave little notice to the ethnic background of Latino football players. Cuban-born Ignacio "Lou" Molinet, as well as U.S.-born Jesse Rodríguez, Kelly Rodríguez, and Waldo Don Carlos, thus played in relative obscurity in the first incarnation of the National Football League (NFL). Little would change for Joe Aguirre, Peter Perez, Eddie Saenz, and the dozen other Latinos who performed in the NFL during the 1940s and 1950s.[12] Assimilation, whether individually realized or assumed, perhaps influenced how sportswriters ignored their ethnic identity.

Mexican American athletes often encountered resistance to their participation in high school and collegiate football during the first half of the twentieth century. Those who viewed Mexican Americans as racially inferior to whites attempted to impose a color line against them. The association of football with a particular version of "American" masculinity was used to diminish their accomplishments or deride their desire to be on the field. Opponents persisted in proclaiming stereotypical beliefs about Mexican Americans, insisting they lacked the requisite size, stamina, or intelligence to succeed in football, regardless of their actual on-field performance. Due to these lingering ideas and hostilities, Mexican Americans reveled in the sporting feats of their players, viewing their sporting successes as their own ability to overcome the obstacles they faced in U.S. society.[13]

The diminished view many held about people of Mexican descent made the success of Mexican Americans in the high-profile position of quarterback all the more celebrated in their communities. Although he was not the first Latino to play quarterback in either college football or the NFL, Jim Plunkett proved a pivotal figure in Latinos, finally garnering national attention and respect for their gridiron success. Plunkett, a Mexican American, first gained acclaim as a quarterback at Stanford University, winning the 1970 Heisman Trophy, college football's highest honor. The first pick in the 1971 NFL draft, injuries derailed his professional career early on before he led the Oakland Raiders to two Super Bowl championships (1981, 1984). Plunkett's greatest NFL success came under Raiders' head coach Tom Flores, himself a trailblazing figure in professional football. Flores, also Mexican American, overcame failure in the Canadian Football League (CFL) and the NFL in 1958 and 1959 to become the starting quarterback with the Oakland Raiders of the American Football League (AFL) in 1960. In addition to becoming the first Latino starting quarterback in professional football, Flores made history when the Raiders named him head coach in 1979. In his nine years as Raiders head coach, Flores' team won two Super Bowl championships. In so doing, Flores, like Latino coaches at the high school and collegiate levels, shattered stereotypes about leadership and men of color in sports. Their success as head coaches, according to sport historian Jorge Iber, "worked to change perceptions" of Latinos just as the "increased participation by [Latino] athletes on football fields challenged stereotypes."[14]

Attention to the Latino presence in football increased in the 1990s. Latinos such as offensive lineman Anthony Muñoz and tight end Tony González emerged during the last three decades among the sport's elite. Significantly, the NFL began to more actively market the sport to Latino fans by hosting Hispanic Heritage Month celebrations and the occasional preseason and regular season game in Mexico. Indeed, the NFL has proven more successful at attracting Latinos as fans than participants, as Latinos represented only 0.6 percent of NFL players in 2013.[15]

Greater presence of Latinos as football fans has not necessarily alleviated tensions about Latinos as athletes, such as the wariness about their potential emotional volatility or of their possible unassimilability. These tensions came to the fore during a 2007 nationally televised football game between Notre Dame and University of Southern California. During the game, USC quarterback Mark Sánchez wore a mouthguard with the colors of the Mexican flag. Angry fans used social media and sports radio to deride Sánchez for sporting the colors of his Mexican forebears—although he had led USC to a 38–0 victory. The reaction hinted at larger issues in U.S. society, a particular unease with the prominent place of Latinos in sport—Sánchez was quarterback as USC was enjoying an extended run atop collegiate football. Sánchez's proud display of his Mexican heritage was what roiled some. The toll of such fan reaction affects not just how individual players share their Latino identity but also how NFL teams market their Latino stars. The carefully crafted image of Dallas Cowboys quarterback Tony Romo is one particular case where the visible invisibility of Latino identity occurs; most NFL fans are not quite sure whether Romo is "white." In fact, in a 2013 interview Cowboys owner Jerry Jones confessed he assumed Romo was Italian before learning he was Mexican American. But, upon discovering this, Jones thought it wise to market Romo to the Dallas Cowboys' significant Latino following. Success leading one of the NFL premier franchises in conjunction with his racial and ethnic ambiguity perhaps contributes to Romo being named one of the most-disliked NFL players according to a 2013 Forbes.com story.[16] In either case, whether Mark Sánchez's proud display of his Mexican heritage or of the more muted Latino identity of Tony Romo, football remains a sport where the significance and the reception of open display of Latino cultural identity remains mixed.

Fighting for Respect

Media attention Latinos received in team sports came decades after a number of Latino boxers had gained international acclaim. From the 1930s through 1950s, the print media detailed the boxing feats of Puerto Ricans Sixto Escobar, Pedro Montañez, and Primo Flores; of Cubans Kid Chocolate (Eligio Sardinias) and Kid Gavilan (Gerardo González); and of Mexicans Rodolfo "Baby" Casanova and Bert Colima. Equally significant, these Latino boxers were celebrated within their communities as disproving Social Darwinian assumptions of their racial inferiority as men and as a people.

The Latino heritage of earlier boxers often remained hidden, however. The world featherweight champion after defeating black Canadian George Dixon in 1897, Solomon "Solly" García Smith's mixed background as the son of an Irish father and Mexican mother was unbeknownst to most boxing aficionados.[17] Name changes to make boxers more palatable to wider audiences likewise attempted to obscure Latino identity. Jose Ybarra fought under the name Joe Rivers; sportswriters nonetheless continued to refer to him as "Mexican Joe" despite his claims of having three-quarters Spanish ancestry and one-quarter California mission Indian.[18]

Boxing exposed fissures within as much as across Latino groups. Boxers from differing Latino backgrounds fought nationalistic rivalries in the ring. There were other divides. Two versions of Mexican masculinity were at stake in the rivalry that pitted Mexican great Julio Cesar Chavez versus Mexican American Oscar De La Hoya. Chavez's unrelenting fighting style embodied a rugged masculinity that gained him the admiration of ethnic Mexicans. Many Chavez backers, however, derided De la Hoya's more scientific, less brawling style, seeing it as performing a weakened masculinity that was indicative of the dangers of assimilation to American culture. The radical challenge to traditional gender conventions about Latinas and sport the advent of Latina boxers, such as U.S. Olympic bronze medalist Marlen Esparza in the late twentieth century, raised similar questions about the impact of embracing American culture. Seen as a vehicle of social mobility for working-class Latina/os, boxing meant breaking away from the strictures typically placed on Latinas about competition, physicality, and aggressiveness. Even still, Latinas, just like other women boxers, continue to endure gender-based practices within boxing culture with its male-dominated gyms and bikini-clad ring girls.[19]

Where Futból Is Soccer

Unlike American football, Mexican and transnational migrants from Latin America typically enter U.S. society with a passion for *futból* (soccer). The most popular sport in Latin America, soccer is a transnational practice for Latinos, one that connects them to their national identity, to fellow Latinos as a shared experience, and that distinguishes them from *Americanos*. On the other hand, "the marginalization of soccer [in the US] has been attributed to its "foreign" image compared to the more American connotations of baseball, basketball, and football," notes sport historian Jorge Iber.[20] This enduring association of soccer with foreignness has been interpreted by some as an indication of the refusal of Latinos to assimilate to "American" culture.

Soccer occupies a peculiar place within the U.S. sporting landscape, particularly when viewed from a Latino perspective. Whereas in Latin America, *futból* is primarily played by the working class and poor, soccer is more closely associated with the middle class in the United States. The pay-to-play model of U.S. youth soccer where travel and elite clubs serve as the predominant means of youth talent development proves prohibitive for most working-class families. This, in turn, affects the sport's racial and class diversity at the grassroots level and all along the talent pipeline. A culture clash arises for Latino soccer enthusiasts who are used to a certain style of play, organization, and fandom in their countries of origin and with which they often engage through television, social media, and the occasional friendly match. This clash becomes particularly evident in the multiple efforts to institutionalize men's professional soccer in the United States.

Organizers of the North American Soccer League (NASL), formed in 1967, attempted to grow the game through the importation of foreign players while developing home-grown "American" talent they hoped would enhance the league's appeal in the United States. Attempts to attract a Latino fan base included franchises with names such as Toros and Aztecs. The Los Angeles–based Aztecs, founded in 1974, engaged in a direct appeal to Mexican fans by "appropriat[ing] the Aztec name attributed to the Pre-Columbian Indians of Mexico" and "actively recruit[ing] players from Mexico and local Mexican Americans."[21] The NASL short-circuited this effort with requirements that attempted to "Americanize" the circuit, mandating teams have a U.S.-born player on the field at all times (1979) and that active rosters of all franchises have at least four "American" players. The impact of the rule changes for the LA Aztecs was that the "New Aztecs" team had "no Latin touch," upsetting Mexican and Mexican American fans and journalists. The critique of Mexican American sportswriter Horacio "Ric" Fonseca was particularly biting, "accus[ing] the NASL of trying to "Americanize" the game by discriminating against Latinos, both the U.S.-born and foreign players." Specifically, in his article entitled "Pro-Soccer's Anti-Latino Game Plan," Fonseca complained U.S. Latinos were treated as if they were not Americans in being traded away from the Aztecs.[22] Fonseca typified the criticism among Latinos that league organizers did not treat Latino footballers, whether U.S. or foreign-born, as desirable as European nationals or white Americans.

Organized in 1996, Major League Soccer (MLS) has likewise developed a complicated relationship with Latinos. Like its NASL predecessor, MLS has attempted to appeal to a Latino fan base through franchises that make connections to Mexican soccer and Latino culture. After all, Latinos represent the largest minority group of soccer enthusiasts in the United States. Predominantly of Mexican descent, Latinos' passion for *futból* remains, as does their ambivalence about how MLS seeks fan loyalty. The founding and folding of Chivas USA illuminates these tensions. Based in southern California and owned by Mexican businessmen Antonio Cue and Jorge Vergara, Chivas USA entered MLS in 2004 as a subsidiary of the Mexican League's Chivas Deportivo Guadalajara. Yet, after assuming sole ownership in 2013, Vergara's efforts to build a more clearly Mexican-identified team through an emphasis on players of Mexican descent and requiring all coaching staff members to have Spanish-speaking ability led to multiple lawsuits by coaches who claimed discrimination after being dismissed.[23] The turmoil resulted in Vergara selling the franchise to MLS; the league folded the team after the 2014 season. In the aftermath of the MLS's failed experiment with Chivas USA, MLS president Don Garber claimed that targeting the Latino market with Chivas USA "was more a bad idea than bad execution."[24]

Misgivings persist about MLS executives' understanding of the Latino market. Latinos complain MLS officials have focused on elevating the circuit's status by signing European football stars such as David Beckham as opposed to building their brand through greater recruitment of Latin American stars such as Ronaldinho or Neymar in addition to Mexican stars such as Cuauhtémoc Blanco. The selection of a team name for the Houston franchise in 2006 rekindled such misgivings. Owners initially chose Houston 1836, this in keeping with European tradition of naming a soccer club after a key moment in the home city's history. Houston 1836 recognized the year of Houston's founding as part of the newly independent Republic of Texas. Featuring a profile of Sam Houston riding a horse into battle, the team logo furthered the association with a particular version of Texas' past that offended a host of Tejanos, Mexicanos, and other area Latinos. Many asked how does honoring the legacy of the war against Mexico by white settlers such as Sam Houston serve to attract Mexican Americans to the franchise. As one Latino marketing specialist noted: "Clearly, not enough homework was put into this. Historically speaking, 1836 was not something [Hispanics] celebrate."[25]

The ambivalence Latinos often feel toward organized soccer in the United States takes on a different tenor when it comes to Latinas. Whereas Latino participation in soccer is often read as a means to maintain their cultural practices and, for some, as a sign they are not assimilating, Latinas playing soccer is viewed as an indication of assimilation and embracing of "American" culture. Greater emphasis on women sports in the United States means women's soccer is more formally organized than in Latin American countries, resulting in the perception of women soccer as more part of American culture than Latino culture.

Participating in soccer, like boxing, provides Latinas a means to challenge gender norms about women and sport within their own families, among fellow Latinos, and in their local communities. Latinas encounter resistance to their desire to play soccer, especially from family members with traditional gender views and, just as often, due to family financial concerns that pushes Latinas into the formal and informal labor market. Nonetheless, as illuminated by anthropologist Paul Cuadros' study of Latinas (primarily Mexican and Central Americans, many undocumented) in rural North Carolina communities, Latinas create new gender norms in forming their own women soccer leagues, competing on local high school teams, and performing on university soccer teams. For these Latinas soccer fueled empowerment about their status within their families and in U.S. society. Equally important, soccer evolves into a shared cultural practice with other Latinas, the broader Latino community, and also non-Latinos.[26]

Latina soccer players have made breakthroughs from the local to the national and transnational level, including performing on national teams in the Women's World Cup (WWC). Cuban-American Amy Rodríguez has twice participated on the United States Women's National Team (USWNT) in the WWC (2011, 2015). However, the Mexican National Team (MNT) has featured many more U.S. Latinas since its debut in the 1999 WWC. The MNT's inclusion of Mexican Americans was not without its own controversy. On occasions Mexican-born players have expressed displeasure competing with teammates who hardly spoke Spanish. Yet, half of the Mexican roster in the 2015 WWC consisted of U.S.-born players of Mexican descent.[27] For players such as Californian Teresa Noyala, playing for MNT means an opportunity to compete on the grandest stage for women's soccer, the WWC, as much as, if not more, than representing the country of their Mexican ancestors. That opportunity is also a reflection of the transnational practices that not just athletes but everyday Latinos engage in while in pursuit of economic prosperity.

Be Like Mike or Manu?

Following soccer in popularity in Latin America, the globalization of basketball has opened the NBA to Latinos in an unprecedented manner. Headlined by Argentine Manu Ginobili, the number of Latinos in the NBA increased markedly in the early twenty-first century. This is the product of basketball's increased popularity and NBA franchises widening search for talent. However, the invisibility that often cloaks the presence of Latinos in U.S. sports is also quite evident in professional basketball. This proves particularly striking in the case of black Latinos who participated in the days before the full bloom of the NBA's globalization.[28]

Although Mark Aguirre and Cedric Ceballos enjoyed lengthy NBA careers, the fact they are part of the history of Latinos in the NBA remains unbeknownst to most fans. Widely perceived as African American, the fathers of Aguirre and Ceballos were actually Mexican. Butch Lee had a similar experience as the NBA's Latino pioneer. The first-round draft pick of the Atlanta Hawks in 1978 following a stellar collegiate career at Marquette, Lee was initially perceived as African American and not recognized as Latino. Born in Puerto Rico in 1956, Lee was raised in Harlem after his parents participated in the great migration from Puerto Rico to New York City that took place from the mid-1950s through the late 1960s.[29] There Lee developed his playing skills, earning a scholarship to Marquette before performing in the NBA. The family history of NBA All-Star Gilbert Arenas provides a powerful example of an Afro-Latino family that assimilated into the African American community. Arenas' family roots dated back to the 1890s in the Cuban community of Ybor City (Tampa).

A talented athlete, Hipolito Arenas, Gilbert's grandfather, played professionally for black baseball teams in Tampa and on the Cuban Stars in the Negro Leagues. Together, these cases illustrate the significance of migration in shaping Latino experience, as well as the different permutations that experience had for black Latinos in the United States. Indeed, there was more than one path for assimilation and identification for Latino athletes. Where some assimilated into a broader black community in the United States, others would also embrace a pan-ethnic Latino identity, whereas another contingent would associate most closely with their compatriots of their ancestral community.

Breaking Barriers

Latinas have not been as numerous in the WNBA or in college basketball compared with Latinos in the NBA, although there have been a few prominent Latina players. Raised in the United States to a Cuban father and Polish mother, Rebecca Lobo had an all-too-brief WNBA playing career after being an illustrious collegian. Her story, along with that of Diana Taurasi (whose parents emigrated from Argentina), reveals a different pattern when it comes to the participation of Latino/as in elite basketball in the United States. Most U.S. Latinos who have performed in the NBA have tended to be darker skinned such as the aforementioned Lee, Arenas, Aguirre, and Ceballos (or currently Charles Villanueva and Carmelo Anthony). By comparison, most Latinas who have played for elite college programs or in the WNBA have been lighter skinned and are typically from middle-class backgrounds. This difference may be partly attributable to the expansion of athletic scholarship opportunities created by Title IX, which prohibited discrimination on the basis of sex in any federally funded education program or activity. However, the pay-to-play system of U.S. youth sports limits the full impact of Title XI as it privileges middle- and upper-class families able to afford the high costs of elite amateur sports and suppresses participation of girls from working-class and economically disadvantaged backgrounds. This holds particularly true for Latinas, especially those from families that adhere to traditional views on gender matters and place prohibitions on Latinas playing sports. This contributes to fewer Latinas entering youth sports that serve as a talent development system that feeds college athletics.

The limited opportunities to pursue sports before Title IX made Nancy López's ascent to the top of women's golf all the more incredible. The California-born and New Mexico–raised López won New Mexico Women's Amateur Tournament at the age of 12 in 1969, but still had to threaten a lawsuit in order to play on her high school's golf team (which only had a boys' team). López claimed her first LPGA title at age 21 and would win a total of 48 LPGA titles during her career. Success in her first year on the LPGA tour led to many accolades, with López being named the tour's Rookie of the Year and Player of the Year as well as the Associated Press Female Athlete of the Year. Despite her achievements and a carefully crafted image, some complained, including the Chicano press, that her media image failed to promote a more Chicano self-identification. One critic, noting that the assorted commercial endorsements she had were likely to pay the then 21-year-old López nearly $500,000, wrote "Someone who means that much to that many advertisers can hardly be permitted . . . to water down in any way her all-American, apple pie image—certainly not by playing up her latinidad."[30] López's success elevated her among women's golf all-time greats, resulting in her induction into the LPGA Hall of Fame in 1987.

No other U.S. Latina has enjoyed a similar impactful career on the LPGA tour since Lopez. Economics certainly play a major role. Equipment, green fees, and travel costs limit who is able to afford participating in youth golf with the intermediate goal of securing a college golf scholarship or the ultimate goal of earning a LPGA tour card. The association of golf with white middle-class and upper-class men likewise affects Latino/as who might be interested in pursuing the sport; peers questioning them whether their sporting choices are indicative of a desire to assimilate into white America. The significance of gender is revealed in how the pathway to playing on golf has been different for young boys and girls. There have been a few success stories of Latinos such as Mexican American Lee Trevino and Puerto Rican Juan Antonio "Chi Chi" Rodríguez going from youths caddying at local golf courses and learning the game to achieving success on the PGA tour. However, the same pathway is not as readily available to young girls aspiring to perform in the LPGA.

Like golf, access has proven a significant hurdle in the development of U.S. Latino/as in tennis. Prior to the mid-twentieth century, most urban areas lacked significant numbers of public tennis courts, particularly in areas adjacent to African American or Latino neighborhoods. Securing access to country clubs and their well-maintained tennis courts proved a substantial hurdle. After all, many country clubs barred Mexican Americans in addition to African Americans from membership. Los Angeles-born Richard "Pancho" González started playing tennis in Exposition Park in south LA, one of the few places that he could play the sport. His play drew the notice of a country club member who invited González to play at the club. The country club scene was quite alienating for González, who poignantly described his experience: "I found not one familiar face as I started for the locker room. No one smiled at me. No one even talked to me."[31] Despite the sense of isolation, González won U.S. national titles in 1948 and 1949 and was a dominant force on the professional tennis circuit until 1969.

The racialization of González persisted in spite of his elevation into a national symbol of Cold War democracy and racial progress. González had numerous encounters with racism and the global color line, including being barred from entering apartheid South Africa when officials there only viewed him as Mexican and not as a U.S. citizen who was Mexican American.[32] Yet, it was being given the Pancho nickname that was a most telling indication of how race mattered in his life on and off the tennis court. Usually reserved for those named Francisco, historian José Alamillo notes that both Richard and his mother viewed the Pancho nickname as offensive, especially given its post–World War II usage when it was "often used in a derogatory manner toward Mexican males. They were considered rebellious and combative, like the legendary Mexican Revolution general Pancho Villa." González, according to Alamillo, "reluctantly tolerated it for promotional and publicity purposes."[33] The unease caused by González's physical appearance prompted attempts to whiten his image, figuratively and literally. This was vividly illustrated in González's appearance on the 1959 program cover for *Jack Kramer Presents World Championship Tennis* where he was "given blond hair, lighter skin, a smaller nose, and smaller lips."[34] Alteration of González's appearance worked to present him as a more palatable Mexican American, even as his nickname marked him as a potentially dangerous Mexican foreigner.

Becoming Brown in the Sporting Arena

Participation in U.S. professional sports provides the setting for the articulation of new identities, affirmation of ethnic and racial bonds, and forging of transnational ties for Latinos. Self-identification mattered to a degree. Experience on and off the playing fields reveals a dynamic wherein most Latinos were marked as neither white nor black in the U.S. sense. The racialization of their labor, talent, and culture placed them into a "brown" category within the U.S. racial system. Collectively, Latino athletes were not treated like whites, even when individually a few were upheld as success stories of assimilation and even perceived as white by some in the sporting public.

Once in these sporting spaces, Latinos often served as a counterpoint to whiteness. Moreover, the specific racialization of Latino cultures, whether practices such as speaking Spanish or of personal behavior seen in lingering stereotypes of the hot-blooded Latino or Latina spitfire, distinguished them from African Americans. Of course, black Latinos such as Roberto Clemente, boxer Kid Chocolate, or football player Victor Cruz complicate this reality, both for white Americans and African Americans as well as among Latinos themselves. They reveal that many Latinos are part of the (continuing) African diaspora in the Americas. Yet, the struggle of black Latinos like Clemente was not fully applicable to all Latinos, as demonstrated in the policing of the color line during the Jim Crow era. There was certainly a variant of racial segregation that scholars and journalists aptly label *Juan* Crow in Texas, California, and parts of the South and Southwest that prevented Mexicans, Tejanos, and other Latinos from enjoying the same access to spaces, services, and opportunities that white Americans more fully enjoyed. However, Clemente and other black Latinos endured two strikes in the words of Puerto Rican Orlando Cepeda: one for being Latino, another for being black.

Notes

1 NBC Broadcast, September 1971. www.youtube.com/watch?v=sVf13pJ_TqE (accessed June 11, 2015).

2 For the sake of this chapter, Latino/as are defined as individuals with origins from the Spanish-speaking Americas who were racialized as an ethnoracial group that was alternately foreign, non-white, and, in the minds of some, inassimilable.

3 David Maraniss, *Clemente: The Passion and Grace of Baseball's Last Great Hero* (New York: Simon & Schuster, 2007), and Kal Wagenheim, *Clemente!: The Enduring Legacy*, 3rd ed. (Princeton, NJ: Markus Wiener Publishing Inc 2011).

4 Rob Ruck, *Raceball: How the Major Leagues Colonized the Black and Latin Game* (Boston: Beacon Press, 2012), Adrian Burgos, Jr., *Playing America's Game: Baseball, Latinos, and the Color Line* (Berkeley: University of California Press, 2007), and Alan Klein, *Growing the Game: The Globalization of Major League Baseball* (New Haven, CT: Yale University Press, 2011), and *Dominican Baseball: New Pride, Old Prejudice* (Philadelphia: Temple University Press, 2014).

5 Louis A. Pérez, "Between Baseball and Bullfighting: The Quest for Nationality in Cuba, 1868–1898," *Journal of American History*, 81: 2 (September 1994): 493–517; Burgos, *Playing America's Game*; and Roberto Gonzalez Echevarria, *Pride of Havana: A History of Cuban Baseball* (New York: Oxford University Press, 1999).

6 Ruck discusses how Cubans became viewed as spreading "the gospel of baseball," see chapter 1, *Raceball*.

7 Burgos, *Playing America's Game*, 34–46.

8 For analysis of the incorporation of Latinos while the Major Leagues' color line stood in place, see Part Two, "Latinos and the Racial Divide," *Playing America's Game*, 71–176.

9 A number of Latinos briefly served in the managerial role while filling in for the regular manager serving a suspension or as an interim manager for a fired manager. Alou was the first self-identifying and publicly received Latino hired to serve as a regular season manager.

10 Regalado, *Viva Baseball: Latin Major Leaguers and Their Special Hunger* (Urbana: University of Illinois Press, 2008); and Marcos Bretón, *Away Games: The Life and Times of a Latin Ball Player* (Albuquerque: University of New Mexico Press, 2000).

11 For discussion of issues about the Dominican academy system, see Klein, *Dominican Baseball*; Arturo Marcano and David P. Fidler, *Stealing Lives: The Globalization of Baseball and the Tragic Story of Alexis Quiroz* (Bloomington: Indiana University Press, 2002); and Ruck, *Raceball*.

12 These numbers are drawn from Mario Longoria's work on Latinos in football, see "History: Latin-Americans in Pro Football." www.profootballhof.com/history/general/latin-americans.aspx (accessed July 3, 2015). For more on Mexican American football players and coaches, see Mario Longoria, *Athletes Remembered: Mexicano/Latino Professional Football Players, 1929–1970* (Tempe: Bilingual Press, 1997), and also chapters 7 and 8, Jorge Iber, ed., *More Than Peloteros: Sport and U.S. Latino Communities* (Lubbock: Texas Tech University Press, 2015), 184–231.

13 Iber, Samuel Regalado, José Alamillo, and Arnoldo DeLeón, *Latinos in U.S. Sports: A History of Isolation, Cultural Identity, and Acceptance* (Champaign: Human Kinetics Publishing, 2011), 130.

14 Ibid., 170.

15 Percentage cited in Richard Lapchick, "The 2014 NFL Racial and Gender Report Card," (accessed July 3, 2015). http://nebula.wsimg.com/1e912077d1fd5c5c7ee7c4633806cfb5?AccessKeyId=DAC3A56D8FB782449D2A&disposition=0&alloworigin=1

16 Jon Machota, "Survey: Dallas Cowboys QB Tony Romo is the seventh most-disliked NFL player," *Dallas Morning News*, posted October 21, 2013. http://cowboysblog.dallasnews.com/2013/10/survey-dallas-cowboys-qb-tony-romo-is-the-seventh-most-disliked-nfl-player.html/. Jerry Jones' quote drawn from a 2013 radio interview on 105.3 The Fan [KRLD-FM], cited in Jon Machota, "Jerry Jones: Tony Romo's Hispanic Heritage makes him best possible QB for the Dallas Cowboys," *Dallas Morning News*, posted October 22, 2013. http://sportsday.dallasnews.com/dallas-cowboys/cowboysheadlines/2013/10/21/survey-dallas-cowboys-qb-tony-romo-is-the-seventh-most-disliked-nfl-player

17 Iber et al., *Latinos in U.S. Sports*, 101.

18 Ibid., 102.

19 Gerald Gems, *Boxing: A Concise History of the Sweet Science* (New York: Rowman & Littlefield, 2014), 227–238.

20 Iber et al., *Latinos in U.S. Sports*, 94.

21 Ibid., 212–213. The Toros franchise moved multiple times, starting in Los Angeles and moving to San Diego before landing in Miami.

22 Ibid., 213, 214.

23 Kevin Baxter, "When Will MLS Save Chivas USA from Itself?" *Los Angeles Times*, May 20, 2013. http://articles.latimes.com/2013/may/30/sports/la-sp-sn-mls-chivas-usa-20130530 (accessed July 5, 2015); Brian Straus, "Life Comes Next Moment: Chivas USA folds, MLB Will Relaunch a Second Team in LA in 2017," *SI.com*, October 27, 2014. www.si.com/soccer/planet-futbol/2014/10/27/chivas-usa-contraction-folds-mls-los-angeles-realignment (accessed July 6, 2015).

24 Jeff Carlisle, "MLS Shuts Down Chivas USA; New Club, Ownership to Return in 2017," *ESPNfc.us*, October 27, 2014. www.espnfc.us/chivas-usa/story/2112968/mls-shuts-down-chivas-usa-new-club-ownership-to-return-in-2017 (accessed July 6, 2015).

25 Ric Jensen and Jason Sosa, "Major League Soccer Scores an Own Goal in Houston: How Branding a Team Alienated Hispanic and Latino Fans," in Iber, ed., *More Than Just Peloteros*, 265, 266.

26 Paul Caudros, "Latina Integration Through Soccer in the 'New South,'" *Southeastern Geographer* 51, no. 2 (Summer 2011): 233.

27 Doug McIntyre, "Red, White, and Green: Dual Citizens Suit for Mexico's National Team." *ESPNW*, June 6, 2015. http://espn.go.com/espnw/news-commentary/2015worldcup/article/12962975/dual-citizens-help-comprise-mexico-women-world-cup-roster (accessed July 6, 2015).

28 For a list of Latin American players who have performed in the NBA, see www.nba.com/enebea/hispanos/alltime_nba_latino_players.html. Note this listing includes players from Spain, which most Latino Studies scholars do not consider Latinos given their European origin.

29 *Chicago Tribune*, March 19, 1992. On the Puerto Rican migration to stateside communities, see Gina Pérez, *A Near Northwest Side Story* (Berkeley: University of California Press, 2004); Lorrin Thomas, *Puerto Rican Citizen* (Chicago: University of Chicago Press, 2012).

30 Iber et al., *Latinos in U.S. Sports*, 219.

31 González quoted in Ibid., 146.

32 Jose Alamillo, "'Bad Boy' of Tennis: Richard 'Pancho' González, Racialized Masculinity, and the Print Media in Postwar America," in Iber, ed., *More Than Just Peloteros*, 122, 124.

33 Ibid., 125.

34 Ibid., 139.

11

IRISH AMERICANS AND SPORT

Ralph C. Wilcox

Introduction

Over time, the names "Fighting Irish," "Celtics," and other symbolic remnants of Gaelic influence have become deeply embedded in the popular imagination of American sporting culture. Although often viewed as colorful amusements practiced within immigrant neighborhoods of the city, athletic pursuits represent a significant yet complex chapter in the story of Irish America. It is a tale that spans the rude and all too frequently brutal world of the nineteenth-century prize ring; the continuing practice of traditional sports within the urban remnants of Gaelic ethnic enclaves; and the outstanding accomplishments by Irish Americans at the pinnacles of sporting endeavor: the Olympic Games, the practice, ownership and business of the professional sports arena, and intercollegiate athletics.[1]

As Irish men, women, and children departed from their homeland for America during the nineteenth century, they left behind a system of sport patterned on that found in England. Although field sports such as fishing, shooting, and hunting were popular among Ireland's landed gentry, the vast majority of the Irish devoted what little recreational time they had to the pursuit of simple athletic traditions practiced in the fields, along the rural lanes, and at country fairs. For the most part, organized sport was controlled by the Amateur Athletic Association of England. It was not until 1884 that the Gaelic Athletic Association was founded, primarily as a response to this absentee control. In the years that followed, Ireland witnessed a resurgence in popularity of the traditional and ancient Tailtean Games, which evidence suggests predated the ancient Greek Olympic festivals. Above all, this late nineteenth-century Gaelic athletic revival brought increased structure and codification to the traditional team sports of hurling and Gaelic football and provided the framework for the County Societies in America to compete against one another.[2]

In search of both identity and status in their new home, Irish immigrants soon discovered that their participation in fishing, billiards, cockfighting, pugilism, pedestrianism (the predecessor of track and field), swimming, rowing, cricket, and, eventually, baseball pleased America's civic leaders who saw their fundamental responsibility as forging a new and unified nation out of the thousands of culturally diverse immigrants who were landing on their shores daily. Beyond the search for acceptance, and excluded from the prestigious athletic clubs of the day, experience showed Irish Americans that these sports could become a ladder for socioeconomic advancement, an important motivation for many immigrants.[3]

The Irish American Prizefighting Tradition

It is likely that more has been written about Irish American success in the prize ring over the past 150 years than about any other ethnic group in sport. Indeed, a veritable library of biographies, novels, films, manuals, and newspaper and magazine accounts has, over time, built a reputation of mythical proportions for the Irish American prizefighter.[4] At the same time, it is regrettable that so many commentators have found it necessary to dwell on Irish Americans' pugilistic endeavors at the expense of their other athletic pursuits and cultural contributions. It has long been argued by scholarly proponents of "ethnic succession" that throughout history boxing has witnessed its greatest appeal among oppressed minorities, promising them a rapid escape from poverty and discrimination. The Irish American has surely done his best to affirm this belief. Such colorful characters as Sam O'Rourke, Cornelius Horrigan, John C. "Benecia Boy" Heenan, James "Yankee" Sullivan, and John Morrissey graced the antebellum American prize ring. James Ambrose "Yankee" Sullivan was born in Ireland in 1807. He earned his nickname from the American flag that he proudly wore around his waist in the ring. In 1853, Sullivan lost his American heavyweight title to fellow Irishman John Morrissey who had earlier settled in New York City. Morrissey went on to be elected to the U.S. Congress in 1866, and again in 1868, lending support to the notion that Irish Americans treated boxing and politics with comparable passion.[5]

Nor would the story change in the years following the Civil War, as the nation's foremost heavyweight fighters remained of Irish American stock. Paddy Ryan, Jake Kilrain, John L. Sullivan, and "Gentleman Jim" Corbett each attest to the Gaels' affinity for the sport. The most prominent of America's late nineteenth century athletes was John L. Sullivan, better known as "the Boston Strong Boy." Born in 1858, the son of Irish immigrants, Sullivan was the link between the London Prize Ring and the Marquis of Queensbury Rules, pioneering the transition from bareknuckle boxing to the gloved era. World heavyweight champion from 1882 to 1892, Sullivan has been credited with anywhere between 75 and 200 victories in the ring. The subject of at least 10 autobiographical and biographical works, "John L" became the first modern sporting superstar. His career purse exceeded 1 million dollars, an enormous amount of money at the time. Roughhewn and fond of the bachelor subculture of the saloon, Sullivan pioneered sporting celebrity status like never before as his name recognition reached outside the prize ring and extended far beyond America's shores. Among the personal, entrepreneurial ventures he used to supplement purses from prizefights was a token appointment as sports editor of the New York–based *Illustrated News*, his endorsement of a Lipton Beef Company product, numerous and varied stage roles, and even an attempt to launch his own "John L. Sullivan Motion Picture Company." Having met with royalty, Pope Leo, and every president since James Garfield, Sullivan's decision to pursue the favored Irish career path of politics might have been expected, but proved to be unsuccessful.[6]

Irish American domination of the prize ring continued into the twentieth century. Jack Dempsey, "the Manassa Mauler," hailing from humble roots in Colorado on the western frontier, personified the pugnacious and ruthless style of pugilism that had become expected of those of Irish lineage. His classic rags-to-riches story stood in marked contrast to Gene Tunney, who, born in New York City, the son of immigrants from County Mayo, Ireland, adopted a more scientific approach to the sport. Having risen through the weight classes, Tunney retired as world champion in 1928 ending, perhaps, what had been a long domination of "the ring" by Irish Americans. Succeeded for the most part by newer immigrant groups, first Italians and later African Americans and Latinos, Irish fighters, proudly wearing the green, occasionally re-emerge most recently through the popularity of MMA (mixed martial arts).[7]

Professionalism and Irish American Pedestrians and Rowers

Pedestrian meets also offered poor Irish immigrants the opportunity to fill their pockets with prize money. Although Edward Payson Weston is most often remembered as America's nineteenth century "Champion Pedestrian of the World," the comparable achievements of Daniel O'Leary have frequently gone unnoticed. Born in County Cork, Ireland, in 1846, O'Leary arrived in New York City at the age of 20. Moving on to Chicago, his career as a professional pedestrian began with the defeat of Weston in a 200-mile race in October 1874. One year later O'Leary won the $1,000 stake by beating Weston in a six-day walking match held in Chicago. Weston's complaints of foul play were largely responsible for a long-awaited rematch in London, England, in 1877. Billed as "the greatest athletic feat on record," the $5,000 stake generated enormous interest and the spectacle attracted upward of 20,000 spectators. Once again, the Irish American was victorious covering a record 520 miles in six days. The London match might be considered to be the most important event in the relatively short-lived history of pedestrianism because it prompted Sir John Astley, eager to promote the sport further, to establish the Astley Belt Championship.[8]

O'Leary beat his English challengers handily, winning the Astley Belt and $3,750 in prize money and gate receipts. Promised the opportunity to win the belt outright, the world champion O'Leary took on all comers in New York in 1879. Among his challengers were John Ennis, who arrived in Chicago from Ireland in 1869, and Patrick Fitzgerald, another Irish American resident of New York. O'Leary was expected to win, but an Englishman, Charles Rowell, took the belt and $20,398 in prize money. Accused of having "thrown" the race, O'Leary went on to establish the O'Leary Belt Race for the Championship of America. The first running of this race took place in Madison Square Garden in 1879.[9]

In addition to the prize ring and the pedestrianism, rowing presented early Irish immigrants with the opportunity to earn fame and fortune in a familiar sporting milieu. Although the professional rowing community of northeastern stevedores was a world apart from the fraternal life of America's most prestigious colleges, it appears that professional boat races gained some legitimacy in mainstream American society. Fully entrenched in the labor and longshore traditions of northeastern U.S. ports, Irish Americans took to rowing with great vigor, forming several prominent boat clubs. Challenges frequently appeared in the Irish American press of the day as stakes, set between $250 and $1,000 a side, regularly attracted crowds of 30,000 spectators or more. Irish Americans champions dominated professional rowing throughout the last three decades of the nineteenth century.[10]

Emerald Diamonds: Irish Americans and the National Pastime

By 1870, baseball had emerged as America's uncontested "national pastime," and Irishmen flocked to the diamond in droves.[11] Some claimed that baseball had its origin in the ancient Gaelic games of *Iomain*, so feeding an appetite for ethnic identity and pride. Irish teams sprang up across North America in the years following the Civil War.

Although the national pastime found broad grassroots appeal among immigrants, it was the professional players who won baseball laurels for Irish Americans. The reputation of Irish ballplayers soon became so great that others began to take Irish names to purportedly help them in their baseball careers. In 1872, a correspondent to the *Sporting News* claimed that one-third of major league players were of Irish extraction. By the turn of the century another observer noted that "all the prominent clubs of last year were captained by Irish Americans."

Indeed, a stroll through the Baseball Hall of Fame, in Cooperstown, New York, reminds the visitor of the deep presence of professional Irish baseball players in the nineteenth century.

The "king" of baseball, Michael Joseph Kelly, was the son of an Irish immigrant paper-maker, born in Troy, New York, in 1857. Making his debut with the Olympic Club of Patterson, New Jersey, in 1887, he went on to record a superlative professional career as a catcher, outfielder, and shortstop with the Buckeye Club of Columbus, Ohio; the Cincinnati Red Stockings; and the Chicago White Stockings. His subsequent "sale" to the Boston Red Stockings in 1887 remained unprecedented in the sport and, while causing a furor in baseball circles, brought the "Ten Thousand Dollar Beauty" immediate renown. Best remembered for his base running and sliding abilities, his name was immortalized in the popular song "Slide, Kelly, Slide," celebrating his 84 stolen bases during his first season in Boston. Later, in a stage adaptation of Ernest Thayer's *Casey at the Bat*, Kelly was cast in the title role alongside the London Gaiety Girls. Appearing in 1888, Thayer's musical featured lyrics about mythical baseball players, all with typical Gaelic names such as Blake, Flynn and, of course, Casey.[12]

The powerful Irish American presence on the diamond continued into the twentieth century as evidenced by the election of Joe Cronin, Jimmy Collins, Tim Keefe, and Ted Lyons to membership in the Hall of Fame. Cronin, who was voted MVP of the American League in 1930, and was a seven time All Star, went on to serve two terms as president of the American League. Connie Mack, who served as manager of the Philadelphia Athletics (1901–1951) until he retired at age 88; Joe McCarthy, who managed the New York Yankees through the 1930s and into the following decade; and John McGraw, who managed the New York Giants (1902–1932), were inducted into the Hall of Fame for their management prowess. Yet it was Walter O'Malley who perhaps showed the greatest sustained impact of any Irish American on professional baseball. Starting out as general counsel to the Brooklyn Dodgers, he later transitioned into ownership and is likely best remembered for his role in breaking the color barrier, as Jackie Robinson joined the Dodgers in 1947, and for moving the club to Los Angeles in 1958.

Remembering the Shamrock: Irish Americans Athletic Clubs and the Olympics

Although Irish American interest in track and field might be viewed as a logical extension of their affinity for pedestrianism, the two sports possessed separate and unique pedigrees. Footraces, hurdling, jumping, and throwing events, which had long been part of native celebrations in rural Ireland, were soon included in Gaelic events in America. Many Irish immigrants used their athletic prowess for monetary gain as North American clubs sponsored an annual professional circuit of traditional Caledonian and Hibernian games. Yet the most significant contribution of Irish Americans to the sport was reserved for the highly respected, organized, and socially prestigious amateur track and field competitions of the 1890s.[13] Modeled after its London counterpart, the New York Athletic Club had opened its doors in 1868. Frequented by the Astors, Belmonts, Roosevelts, Vanderbilts, and others of New York Knickerbocker Society, it was to be the better part of three decades before the first Irish American athletes were to be found competing for "the Winged Footers." Due in large part to the exclusionary policies and practices of the New York Athletic Club, the Boston Athletic Association, and similar elitist organizations, Irish athletic clubs were formed in New York City and Boston during 1879. Later changing their names to Irish American athletic clubs, they became powerful forces in international track and field by the turn of the century.

At its inaugural track and field meet with the London Athletic Club in September 1895, the New York Athletic Club was represented by at least three Irish American athletes; among them was J.T. Coneff, who was born in County Kildare in 1866. Running for the New York club, he won both the mile and three-mile events, and Thomas E. Burke, "the Lowell Mercury," won the 440-yard race. The following year, while representing the Boston Athletic Association, Burke ran to victory in the 100-meter and 400-meter events at the first modern Olympiad in Athens. Increasing Irish American representation in Greece, Tom Curtis won the 110-meter hurdles race. At the Paris Olympics in 1900, Irish-born Mike F. Sweeney (high jump champion of the world from 1892 to 1895) took home 750 francs for winning the 100-meter race, the high jump, and long jump events for professional athletes. John F. Flanagan, a New York City policeman who was born in Limerick in 1868, won the Olympic hammer event for the New York Athletic Club. After winning the Metropolitan and Junior National Championships of the Amateur Athletic Union in 1904, the Greater New York Irish American Athletic Association was represented at the St. Louis Olympics by Flanagan, who retained his Olympic title in hammer throwing; Martin Sheridan, who won the discus event; and Jim Mitchell who had come to America with the Gaelic Athletic Association's "invasion" of 1888.

The story of early Irish American Olympic success continued in 1908 when Flanagan became the first modern Olympic athlete to win three successive titles in a standard event. Once again, Flanagan found ample Celtic company in Sheridan, who won his second gold medal, and another New York City policeman, Matt McGrath, who finished in second place in the hammer throw. Later joined by Pat McDonald and Pat Ryan, these athletic behemoths became known collectively as "the Irish Whales," each one a son or grandson of Ireland. Most of "the Whales" were members of the New York City police department.

Perhaps the most accomplished Irish American athlete at the turn of the century was James Brendan Connolly. Born in South Boston in 1868, the son of Irish immigrants, Connolly became the first modern Olympic victor with the revival of the games in 1896, when he won the first event, the triple jump. He is now much better remembered as the author of 25 best-selling maritime novels and 200 short stories than for his exceptional athletic accomplishments. After passing the entrance examination in October 1895, Connolly enrolled at the Lawrence Scientific School of Harvard University to study engineering. His hopes of playing football for "the crimson" were dashed when he broke his collarbone in the first scrimmage. Joining the university's track team, Connolly won the amateur hop, step, and jump championship of the United States in his first attempt. After the Harvard University administration turned down his request for an eight-week leave of absence, Connolly chose to forsake a collegiate education in favor of paying his own way to the Olympic Games in Athens. Representing the South Boston Athletic Club, Connolly recorded a first place in the triple jump, second place in the high jump, and third place in the broad (long) jump.[14]

By the turn of the century, Irish American athletes had begun to wrest the track and field laurels from Scottish pioneers and members of the exclusive athletic clubs as members of New York's Irish American Athletic Club (IAAC), proudly displayed its emblem: a green fist set against a background of green shamrock inserts and traversed by a diagonal band of red, white and blue, on the winner's podium the world over.[15]

Preserving Cultural Identity in America: Irish American Sport

It is important to note that the Irish immigrants' ready acceptance of, and participation in, the popular American sports of the day rarely constituted total assimilation. The Irish American athlete's insistence on Gaelic names for their rowing, baseball, track and field, and lacrosse teams, while taking every opportunity "to parade the green" in the sporting arena, helped satisfy the group's need to maintain a strong sense of cultural identity. Yet Irish American sport also provided an abundance of evidence to support the existence of intracultural and intercultural conflict. Although it is generally believed that the unparalleled success of nineteenth-century Irish prizefighters did much to change the self-esteem of their fellow countrymen, others saw it differently. As early as 1871, the *Irish World* cautioned:

> The Irish, from their connection with the English, have unfortunately acquired some of the barbarous habits and customs of the Saxons, as they did their language. But Irishmen even in the prize ring are not wholly lost to honor. The genuine Celt fights, not for money, but for fame—such poor fame as it is—and he could never forget his manhood so far as to make himself, like the Saxon villain, a bull-terrier gladiator for the sport of a blackleg nobility.[16]

To set the blame on English soil was not unexpected, but still questions surrounding the moral virtue and worthwhile qualities of prizefighting could not be denied. As one observer pointed out, "the rugged young men who survived [bareknuckle fights] did their share to give the Irish a bad name by being usually Irish or of second generation Irish stock."[17] Moreover, at the same time as "the Boston Strong Boy" received honors as a civic hero upon ascending the throne of world heavyweight champion, one local newspaper reported that "blue blooded Boston is disgusted with the notoriety the Hub has gained through the brutal victory of its hard hitting son, Sullivan."[18] Soon the middle-class, literary, lace-curtain Irish joined the fray, denouncing the Gaelic domination of the American prize ring as "human butchery," promoted by a "worthless, gambling class of lodgers" who frequented saloons, poolroom, and other "gilded haunts."[19] Such perceptions did much to fuel the common stereotype of the ignorant, drunken, belligerent, and pugnacious Irish buffoon so actively ridiculed by "polite" American society.

Indeed, while the Gaelic immigrant's physical proficiency often confirmed the Anglo-American Protestant stereotype that painted the Irish as having strong backs but weak minds, it also furnished an opportunity to advance the process of assimilation. As the nineteenth century wore on, the playing field increasingly became the pit in which cultural and political squabbles between immigrants and the Yankee establishment were settled. The annual encounter between the Maid of Erin and Harvard rowing crews on the Charles River reflected a fundamental cleavage between Boston's Irish Catholic neighborhoods and New England's Puritan families. The words of a ballad written by the Reverend William R. Huntingdon, of the Harvard class of 1859, suggest a disguised satisfaction at his boat's triumph over the Irish-crewed Fort Hill Boy. Mocking all that was Irish, the accent, the dialect, and open self-confidence, the author questions the trustworthiness of the losing crew whose payment of bets was dependent upon victory, an indication of their poverty and professional status. Reversing Irish ridicule of the Harvard "lady pets," "fops," and "Beacon Street swells," Huntington paints a picture of the social and athletic superiority of the university shell over the flat-bottomed ferry scow as beyond all doubt. Yet, perhaps such contests served as a cathartic outlet, replacing outright conflict with regularly scheduled and socially sanctioned clashes.[20]

If Irish American athletes found increased pleasure in waging war with other ethnic groups in the sports arena, the English became their favored adversary, and John L. Sullivan their leading warrior. "The Boston Strong Boy" made a point of wearing green breeches in the ring and readily exhibited the contempt for Englishmen so common among his oppressed forbears. On one occasion, in Canada, he publicly declined to toast "her Majesty" adding that "A true Irishman never drinks the health of a British ruler, King or Queen."[21] If such ethnocentric taunting angered anglophiles in the New World, he would commonly follow-up with a calm and diplomatic appeal to their patriotism. Later, at the 1908 Olympics in London, the Irish American disdain for the English resurfaced. That year, the American team included at least 10 members of the Irish Athletic Club. Indeed, so prominent was Irish American representation on the national team that a *Times* editorial went so far as to suggest that "owing to the number of Irish Americans among their members, it might almost be said that the British athletes . . . competed with Irishmen, not Americans."[22] The most memorable event at these games was Ralph Rose's refusal, at the urging of his "Irish Whale" teammates, to lower the Stars and Stripes before King Edward VII. His teammate Martin Sheridan later famously explained that the American flag "dips to no earthly king."[23]

Viewed as an instrument of assimilation, sport could also strengthen the search for ethnic independence and resistance to American nationalist attempts at cultural homogenization. Following the 1873 Irish National Games in Philadelphia, the *Irish World* posited: "Few, if any, who either participated in, or were spectators of, those manly games, were not forcibly reminded of home and fatherland . . . The Germans, Scotch, English, and others have their national games, and why not we?"[24] Eventually, an increasing number of Irish American militia, religious, political, benevolent, and cultural organizations included "Irish Games" on the program at their annual picnics and excursions. From the Fenian Brotherhood to the Ancient Order of Hibernians, St. Patrick's Mutual Alliance Association, Catholic Total Abstinence and Benevolent Society, and Young Men's Catholic Abstinence Society, members thronged to sites across the country to compete in footraces, hurdling, jumping events, throwing the light and heavy stone, boat races, and target shoots. By 1871, members of the Clan Na Gael Association of New York were joined at their second annual picnic by representatives from Troy, New York; Wilmington, Delaware; and Philadelphia, Pennsylvania. Including Gaelic football and hurling matches on the program, a reporter explained that:

> The object of these associations is not dissimilar to that of the German Turnverein. It aims at the physical, social, and intellectual elevation of the Irish in America. It promotes a love of literature and social life in its clubrooms and in its gymnastic exercises it helps develop the Irish muscle.[25]

Advertisements appeared in the local press urging Irish Americans to join native excursions to Spy Pond, outside of Boston, and Jones' Wood in New York. By 1878, the Clan Na Gael picnic in New York attracted 13,000 participants. As purses grew, the festivals began to attract professional athletes. At the Emerald and Hamilton Rowan Clubs' picnic at Jones' Wood in 1878 "a leading feature of the occasion was the Irish national games and an athletic match between Duncan O. Ross, the Scottish champion, and James Lynch, the Irish athlete for $500 a side and the championship of the world."[26]

Irish American militia groups had appeared in New York City by mid-century and soon spread across the country. The Irish rifle clubs and companies left little doubt as to their Gaelic affiliation. Other associations were named after Irish nationalist heroes.[27]

Although some might argue that the establishment of these organizations was a response to the exclusionary policies of "native" companies, the Fenian agitation of 1866 and the deeply held belief that one day they would return to liberate Ireland from the grip of England's "John

Bull" suggested an alternative motive. Moreover, an article in the *Irish World* suggested that newfound democracy might have played a part in the rapid growth of Irish American militia groups. As the author explained: "In Ireland the people are denied by law the right to bear arms; [whereas] in the United States it is deemed a patriotic duty in citizens to enroll themselves in military organizations."[28] Nevertheless, many Americans continued to condemn foreign-born militia for fostering divided loyalties and standing in the way of assimilation. By the turn of the twentieth century, most groups underwent undergone a metamorphosis with the once active militia becoming competitive rifle clubs.

In 1881, a reporter for the *Boston Pilot* noted that "a large number of the Irish people in Boston are becoming interested in the exhibition of the games and pastimes of their ancestors."[29] Traditional Irish sports were not new to America. In New York, Irish Americans practiced handball throughout the city's neighborhoods from their earliest arrival, and organized hurling teams first began to appear in the 1850s. Considered to be the most ancient of Irish sports, the earliest reference to organized hurling (*Caman* in Celtic, and *Iomain* in Gaelic) in the United States was the formation of a club in San Francisco in 1853. It was to be another four years before the Irish Hurling and Football Club was established in New York to revive that "truly Irish national sport." However, it could never be said that the sport flourished during these years. As one observer explained:

> When men are selected who understand the scientific way to play the national game. When men will play for the sake of the sport and not for the winning of a certain amount of money. When men will endeavor to strike the ball and not the man. When suitable grounds are secured and when the players will endeavor to imitate the game as played in ancient times . . . then indeed Ireland's national game, hurling, will become popular in every state in this great country.[30]

The Gaelic Athletic Association's tour of North America in 1888 had a noticeable impact on the growth of hurling by the turn of the century. One correspondent optimistically reported:

> Since the Gaelic Invasion of America . . . hurling has taken a firm root on American soil, and the present series of games at the magnificent grounds at Celtic Park for the James R. Keane Cup are certain to arouse an amount of interest and enthusiasm, and to make the Irish national pastime extremely popular with the exiled Gaels of Greater New York.[31]

The Greater New York Irish American Athletic Association awarded the Kean Gaelic Hurling Trophy to the city's champion team, while in New England clubs competed for the John Boyle O'Reilly Hurling Cup.

Gaelic football does not appear to have shared the widespread following that hurling claimed. The earliest account of an organized team appeared in New Orleans, in 1859, where the game, first promoted by Irish fire companies and later by clubs, featured such nationalistic appellations as Erin Go Bragh and Faugh a Ballagh. In Philadelphia the leasing teams were the Red Branch Knights and the Irish Nationalists, while San Francisco could boast the Emmets, Parnells, and Geraldines. In New York, the names of Irish national heroes were also favored, as the Sarsfield and Geraldines became the city's leading clubs. By 1899, the Dunn trophy was donated to the Greater New York Irish American Athletic Association, "intended for the encouragement of the Gaelic football game and amateur sports for which Ireland was noted."[32] That season, the Association's 20 affiliated clubs competed for the trophy. The ancient sports of Ireland received an impetus in 1884, with the establishment of the Gaelic Athletic Association (GAA) in Ireland.

Although Gaelic football never found popular appeal across the American sporting landscape, Irish American influence on the gridiron is undeniable.[33] Notre Dame's "Fighting Irish" stand among the true icons of intercollegiate football teams. Chartered by the Indiana legislature in 1844, it was 1887 before the university fielded its first football team leading to a remarkable story of success. Occasionally returning to Ireland to play, the team has over time been led by such colorful Irish American coaches as Leahy, Brennan, Devine, and, most recently, Kelly. Not surprisingly, the professional game has had its fair share of Irish American superstars, with Art Donovan, John "Paddy" Driscoll, Ray Flaherty, Ed Healey, Jim Kelly, Mike McCormack, Tommy McDonald, Hugh McElhenny, and John "Blood" McNally each being inducted into the Professional Football Hall of Fame. Yet it is left to two family dynasties, the Mara family owners of the New York Giants (since 1925), and the Rooney family owners of the Pittsburgh Steelers (since 1933) to fully appreciate the impact of Irish Americans on their franchises and the National Football League. Both families have both father and son enshrined in the Hall of Fame.

Conclusion

Today, there are nearly 40 million Americans who claim Irish heritage, or seven times the entire population of Ireland. From the annual St. Patrick's Day celebrations, to the ubiquity of the Irish pub across the nation, the mystique of Irish American identity and affiliation has clearly sustained itself over time. The pervasive contribution of Irish immigrants to the construction of modern America, through organized labor, law enforcement, literature, political, religious and temperance organizations, dance, and music, has been widely documented and analyzed. So, too, has sport played a significant role. From serving as a catalyst for community identity among early immigrants, to providing an arena for sanctioned conflict among competing immigrant groups and Anglophiles, to offering a pathway to cultural assimilation and eventual upward social mobility, the impact of the prize ring, baseball diamond, football field, Olympic arena, and sporting clubs cannot be underestimated.

Notes

1 Among the most useful sources for sport and the Irish Americans are: Sara Brady, "Irish Sport and Culture at New York's Gaelic Park" (PhD. Diss., New York University, 2005); Arthur Daley, "The American Irish in Sports," *Recorder* 34 (1973): 43–100; Paul Darby, "Gaelic Sport and the Irish Diaspora in Boston, 1879–90," *Irish Historical Studies* XXXIII (November 2003): 132; Paul Darby, *Gaelic Games, Nationalism, and the Irish Diaspora in the United States* (Dublin: University College Dublin Press, 2009); George Eisen and David K. Wiggins, eds., *Ethnicity and Sport in North American History and Culture* (Westport, CT: Greenwood Press, 1995); Larry McCarthy, "Irish-Americans in Sports: The Twentieth Century," in *Making the Irish American: The History and Heritage of the Irish in the United States*, ed. J.J. Lee and Marion R. Casey (New York: New York University Press, 2006), 457–471; Patrick R. Redmond, *The Irish and the Making of American Sport, 1835–1920* (Jefferson, NC: McFarland and Company, 2014); Ralph C. Wilcox, "Irish-Americans in Sports: The Nineteenth Century," in Lee and Casey, eds., *Making the Irish American: The History and Heritage of the Irish in the United States*, 443–456; Ralph C. Wilcox, "The Shamrock and the Eagle: Irish Americans and Sport in the Nineteenth Century," in *Ethnicity and Sport in North American History and Culture*, ed. George Eisen and David K. Wiggins (Westport,

CT: Praeger, 1994), 55–74; Ralph C. Wilcox, "Sport and the Nineteenth Century Immigrant Experience," in *Immigration and Ethnicity. American Society—"Melting Pot" or "Salad Bowl,"* ed. Michael D'Innocenzo and Josef P. Sirefman (Westport, CT: Greenwood Press, 1992), 177–189.

2 County Societies were formed based upon the immigrants' place of origin in one of the 32 counties in Ireland. They provided Irish Americans with a sense of community identity and pride in their new home. By the beginning of the twentieth century they exerted a growing influence in the life of Irish Americans, replacing the once powerful and older fraternal organizations such as the Ancient Order of Hibernians. In New York, they became the catalyst for organizing Gaelic football and hurling teams after 1900, eventually replacing the team names of Irish patriots with their county affiliation. By 1904, they led to the formation of the Irish Counties Athletic Union, which later became known as the United Irish Counties.

3 One of New York City's earliest sporting clubs, the East River Fishing Club, was formed by Irishmen in 1833, Robert Ernst, *Immigrant Life in New York City, 1825–1863* (Port Washington, NY: Ira J. Friedman, 1965), 127.

4 Elliott J. Gorn, *The Manly Art: The Lives and Times of the Great Bare Knuckle Champions* (London: Robson Books, 1986); also, see S. Kirson Weinberg and Henry Aroun, "The Occupational Culture off the Boxer," *American Journal of Sociology*, 57: 5 (March 1952), 460–469, for a useful discussion on race and ethnicity in American boxing.

5 William Edgar Harding, *John Morrissey: His Life, Battles and Wrangles, from His Birth in Ireland* (New York: Richard K. Fox, 1881).

6 Michael T. Isenberg, *John L. Sullivan and His America* (Urbana, IL: University of Illinois Press, 1994).

7 Randy Roberts, *Jack Dempsey: The Manassa Mauler* (Urbana, IL: University of Illinois Press, 2003). Conor McGregor, born in Dublin, has risen to become featherweight champion of the Ultimate Fighting Championship (UFC) and, along with fellow Irishmen Tom Egan, Joseph Duffy, Patrick Holohan, and a woman fighter, Aisling Duffy, has done much to perpetuate the braggadocious and colorful reputation of the Irish prizefighter in America.

8 John R. Tansey, *Life of Daniel O'Leary* (Chicago: n.p., 1878); *Irish World*, October 24, 1874, 8; May 12, 1877, 3, 8; May 26, 1877, 3; June 30, 1877, 5; July 7, 1877, 8; July 14, 1877, 5; March 30, 1878, 8; and March 22, 1879, 5.

9 P.S. Marshall, King of the Peds. www.kingofthepeds.com (accessed March 15, 2016).

10 Robert F. Kelley, *American Rowing. Its Background and Traditions* (New York: Putnams, 1932); Thomas Corwin Mendenhall, *A Sports History of American Rowing* (Boston: Charles River Books, 1980), 16–17, 60–70; *Irish World*, April 8, 1871, 7; March 2, 1872, 8; May 3, 1873, 8; September 6, 1873, 8; April 11, 1874, 8; June 27, 1874, 8; September 12, 1874, 6; September 19, 1874, 8; October 3, 1874, 8; June 12, 1875, 8; July 24, 1875, 3, 8; September 4, 1875, 8; January 13, 1877, 8; July 7, 1877, 8; July 28, 1877, 8; August 25, 1877, 8; June 8, 1878, 8; and September 7, 1878, 8; *Newport Daily News* May 19, 1902; July 5, 1902; September 20, 1902; and September 8, 1903.

11 Baseball, perhaps more than any other sport, offered Irish Americans a pathway to celebrity and even heroism, socioeconomic advancement, and acceptance in their new home: Marty Appel, *Slide, Kelly, Slide: The Wild Life and Times of Mike "King" Kelly, Baseball's First Superstar* (Lanham, MD: Scarecrow Press, 1999); Jerrold Casway, *Ed Delehanty in the Emerald Age of Baseball* (Notre Dame, IN; University of Notre Dame Press, 2004); David L. Fleitz, *The Irish in Baseball: An Early History* (Jefferson, NC: McFarland and Company, 2009); Norman L. Macht, *Connie Mack and the Early Years of Baseball* (Lincoln, NE; University of Nebraska Press, 2007); Richard F. Peterson, "'Slide, Kelly, Slide': The Irish in American Baseball," in *The American Game*, ed. Lawrence Baldassaro and Richard A. Johnson (Carbondale, IL: Southern Illinois University Press, 2002); Charley Rosen, *The Emerald Diamond: How the Irish Transformed America's Greatest Pastime* (New York: Harper Collins, 2012).

12 The most useful study of immigrants' affinity for the national pastime is Steven A. Riess, "Race and Ethnicity in American Baseball, 1900–1919," *Journal of Ethnic Studies* 4, no. 4 (Winter 1977): 39–55. Also, James S. Mitchel, "The Celt as a Baseball Player," *The Gael*, May 1902, 151–155; *Irish World*, October 31, 1874, 8; June 5, 1875, 8; July 17, 1875, 8; July 24, 1875, 8; August 14, 1875, 8; June 3, 1876, 8; June 10, 1876, 8; June 17, 1876, 8; June 24, 1876, 8; November 11, 1876, 8; May 26, 1877, 8; and July 28, 1877, 8; Ernest L. Thayer, "Casey At The Bat (A Ballad of the Republic. Sung in the Year, 1888)," *San Francisco Examiner*, June 3, 1888.

13 With the primitive stereotype of the Irish perpetuated by blueblood Protestant elites and the door to athletic club membership frequently slammed in the face of Irish American sportsmen, Clan Na Gael picnics, Irish American Athletic Clubs, the Gaelic Athletic Association, and even the Olympic stage fueled the Irish Americans' pride in their cultural roots: John A. Lucas, "Pat 'Babe' McDonald: Olympic Champion and Paragon of the Irish-American Whales," *Journal of Olympic History* 5, no. 3 (Fall 1997): 8–9; Kevin McCarthy, *Gold, Silver and Green: The Irish Olympic Journey 1896–1924* (Cork: Cork University Press, 2010); John Schaefer, *The Irish American Athletic Club: Redefining Americanism at the 1908 Olympic Games* (New York: Archives of Irish America, 2001); Ralph C. Wilcox, "'The English as Poor Losers' and Other Thoughts on the Modernization of Sport. The Works of James Brendan Connolly, First Modern Olympic Victor and Literator," *The Sports Historian. The Journal of the British Society of Sports History* 17, no. 1 (May 1997): 63–92.

14 Wilcox, "'The English as Poor Losers.'"

15 *Irish World*, June 7, 1899, 8; *New York Times*, July 18, 1900; August 21, 1904; Bob Considine and Fred G. Jarvis, *A Portrait of the N.Y.A.C. The First 100 Years* (London: The Macmillan Company, 1969), 98–105; James Brendan Connolly, "Oh How They Ran!" *Colliers*, Vol. 104 (September 16, 1939): 27, 75–76; Ernest Cummings Mariner, *Jim Connolly and the Fishermen of Gloucester* (Waterville, ME: Colby College Press, 1949); James Brendan Connolly, *An Olympic Victor. A Story of the Modern Games* (New York: Charles Scribner's Sons, 1908); James Brendan Connolly, "The Spirit of the Olympian Games," *Outing Magazine* 48 (April 1906): 101–104; James Brendan Connolly, "How Cronan Went to Athens," *Everybody's Magazine* 22 (April 1910): 466–475; James Brendan Connolly, "The Capitalization of Amateur Athletics," *Metropolitan Magazine* (July 1910): 443–445; James Brendan Connolly, "Record Breaking", *Colliers* 100 (November 13, 1937): 17, 68–69, and James Brendan Connolly, "Oh, How They Ran!," Vol. 104, the author reminisces about growing up in South Boston and examines changes in the world of athletics.

16 *Irish World*, June 3, 1871, 5.

17 J.C. Furnas, *The Americans. Social History of the United States, 1687–1914* (New York: G.P. Putnam's Sons, 1969), 659, cited in John Rickards Betts, *America's Sporting Heritage: 1850–1950* (Reading, MA: Addison-Wesley Publishing Company, 1974), 222.

18 *Donahoe's Magazine* 9 (May 1883): 466–477; 14 (November 1885): 44–46; 20 (July–August 1888): 24–31.

19 John Boyle O'Reilly, *The Ethics of Boxing and Manly Sports* (Boston: Ticknor and Company, 1888). O'Reilly was born in Ireland in 1844. An Irish Nationalist, ardent Democrat, and editor of the Pilot (organ of the Boston Catholics), he strongly supported the rights of immigrant workers and, as an avid sportsman, relished the active, outdoor life as he reportedly refereed at Harvard, sparred with John L. Sullivan, and canoed New England's waterways.

20 Reverend William R. Huntingdon, "Songs of the Harvard versus Fort Hill Boy Rowing Match of 1858," *Harvard Magazine*, July 1858.

21 Quoted in Nathaniel S. Fleischer, *The Boston Strong Boy: The Story of John L. Sullivan. The Champion of Champions* (New York: O'Brian, 1941), 35.

22 Bill Mallon, "To No Earthly King," *Sport Heritage. The Journal of Our Sporting Past* 1, no. 3 (May–June 1987): 27–28.

23 Bill Mallon, "To No Earthly King. . . .," *Journal of Olympic History* Vol. 7: 3 (September 1999): 21–28.

24 *Irish World*, September 6, 1873, 7; August 19, 1871, 7; May 18, 1872, 8; August 10, 1872, 8; September 6, 1873, 5; August 8, 1874, 8; August 15, 1874, 8.

25 *Irish World*, August 29, 1874, 8; August 14, 1875, 8; May 27, 1876, 8.

26 *Irish World*, June 16, 1877, 8; June 30, 1877, 2; July 14, 1877, 8; July 28, 1877, 8; August 11, 1877, 8; August 25, 1877, 8; June 22, 1878, 8; July 20, 1878, 8; July 27, 1878, 8; August 10, 1878, 8; and June 7, 1879, 8.

27 *Irish World*, February 21, 1874, 8; April 25, 1874, 8; September 19, 1874, 8; September 26, 1874, 4; May 8, 1875, 6; August 14, 1875, 8; August 25, 1875, 8; June 24, 1876, 8.

28 *Irish World*, September 8, 1877, 8; June 29, 1878, 8; August 17, 1878, 8; September 7, 1878, 8.

29 *Boston Pilot* 4 (June 25, 1881), cited in Stephen Hardy, *How Boston Played. Sport, Recreation, and Community, 1865–1915* (Boston, MA: Northeastern University Press, 1982), 138; *Irish World*, July 27, 1878, 8; August 31, 1878, 8; Also, Robert P. Smith, "Heroes and Hurrahs: Sports in Brooklyn, 1890–1898," *Journal of Long Island History* XV, no. 1 (Fall 1978): 11.

30 *Irish News*, December 12, 1857; January 2, 1858; *Irish World*, August 19, 1871, 7; August 14, 1875, 8; July 14, 1877, 8.

31 Maurice Dinneen, "The Game of Hurling," *The Gael*, September 1901, 291–292. The failure of the 1888 GAA tour did not deter the organization, which returned to the United States in 1926, 1927, and finally in 1947, for the All Ireland Football Final played before 35,000 spectators at the Polo Grounds in New York.

32 *Irish World*, August 19, 1871, 7; September 6, 1873, 7; June 17, 1876, 8; June 24, 1876, 8; *The Gael*, October 1899, 196; March 1901, 102.

33 Marcus DeBurca, *The GAA: A History of the Gaelic Athletic Association* (Dublin: Cumann Luthchleas Gael, 1980); Jack Mahon, *A History of Gaelic Football* (Dublin: Gill and Macmillan, 2000). Robert Peterson, *Pigskin: The Early Years of Pro Football* (New York: Oxford University Press, 1997); Murray Sperber, *Shake Down the Thunder: The Creation of Notre Dame Football* (New York: Henry Holt, 1993).

12

GERMAN AMERICANS AND SPORT

Annette R. Hofmann

Introduction

The Germans represent a forceful current in the stream of immigration to the United States. Over 7 million Germans have settled in the United States, and as such represent one of the largest immigrant groups to come to this country. According to the 1990 census, about 23 percent of Americans—or 58 million adults—identified themselves as having German ancestry, making them the largest ethnic group in that decade.[1] In the eighteenth and nineteenth centuries the majority of these Germans immigrants were an independent group within American society, assimilated to the American way of life and employment, but simultaneously cultivating German culture in their leisure time. This lasted until the American government developed anti-German policies during World Wars I and II. Thus, the Americanization process was forced upon them. This demanded a new definition of ethnic boundaries and symbols. Although many German American institutions and organizations became victims of anti-German campaigns and German Americans as an ethnic group fragmented, their group identity did not disappear completely. Instead, it evolved into a more personal form and became limited to individuals' less visible private lives. Today, ethnic Germans are fully integrated and assimilated into American society.

The culture and traditions that the German immigrants brought to America took on new forms of expression in the new environment: German American ones. Many have become part of the American mainstream culture and are not recognizable as German in origin. Still, there are traces that show German roots. For instance, German names and terms are part of the American vocabulary, such as kindergarten, dachshund, delicatessen, and gesundheit. In a variety of American towns the influence of German architecture is recognizable, and the foods "hamburger," "sauerkraut," and "wieners" are known to almost every American. To honor the influence the German immigrants had on American educational institutions, trade unions, social laws, but also on music, art, and science, the American government officially declared October 6 as "German Day" in 1987.

Many American cities still celebrate German festivities, such as an annual Oktoberfest, or a German Day. These events mostly take place in the Midwestern cities with once large German settlements such as Chicago, Cincinnati, Indianapolis, or Milwaukee, formerly known as the German belt. At the end of the twentieth century in Chicago alone, there were still 80 German clubs in existence.[2] In these societies, called "*vereine*," with their democratic structures, German customs, rituals, and cultural practices were perpetuated in an adapted form to fulfill the new needs of the host society.[3] Especially in the nineteenth and early twentieth centuries these German American clubs functioned as "nurseries of ethnicities."[4] Today through such groups, German culture is preserved in the United States to a certain degree. One can talk of a symbolic ethnicity which Gans defines as "ethnicity of last resort." According to him, it is characterized by ". . . nostalgic allegiance to the culture of the immigrant generation, or that of the old country, a love and pride in tradition that can be felt without having to be incorporated into everyday behaviour."[5] This includes the acceptance of symbols or activities from the ethnic heritage that an individual chooses as a sign of ethnic consciousness, although these do not further influence one's daily life.[6]

There still exist *vereine* (clubs) for physical culture and sport. The so-called *turnvereine* or *turner* movement, which in the United States goes back to the mid-nineteenth century, was the most prominent one. The *turnvereine* were "havens for ethnicity."[7] They were more than an ethnic movement for German-style physical culture called *turnen.* Due to the turners' political background, the turner movement also contributed to American politics and education. In many American cities the turners were the first to establish physical education in public schools. Their institute for the education of turner instructors (*Turnlehrer*) and later on also physical education teachers influenced them in the last third of the 1800s. Today, their former Normal School is part of the Indiana University-Purdue University.

The turner societies were not the only opportunities for German Americans to engage in physical activities and sport. An unknown number of clubs with German heritage had such activities, mainly in the big cities. For instance, in New York City the German-American Athletic Club, founded in 1884, was quite famous. Together with the German-American Football Association, it organized an annual German Sport and Athletic Day on Randall's Island, New York, from the late 1930s to the 1960s.

German Americans were also engaged in American sports. During the nineteenth century, some German baseball teams existed, such as the Rosing's baseball club from Kenosha, Wisconsin.[8] In Buffalo, New York, the Buffalo Germans, a nationally successful basketball team, was established at the turn of the century. From the 1910s on, it was soccer that often attracted German immigrants, who founded not only teams but leagues as well, especially along the East Coast.[9] Other Germans participated on mainstream American teams. Among them were baseball players George Herman "Babe" Ruth (1895–1948) and Henry Louis Gehrig (1903–1941), both second-generation Germans.[10] The majority of the 1936 Olympic soccer team was German American.[11]

Other athletes of German heritage became national heroes and were inducted into the International Swimming Hall of Fame in Fort Lauderdale, Florida. These include, for instance, the outstanding swimmers of the 1920s and early 1930s, Peter Jonas (Johnny) Weissmueller (1904–1984) and Gertrude Ederle (1907–2003). Weissmueller, who became famous as an actor for his roles as Tarzan, won a total of five Olympic Gold medals, in both the 1924 and 1928 Olympic Games, and he officially broke 52 American and 38 world records. In 1926, Gertrude Ederle, a second-generation New York–born German, became the first woman to swim the English Channel.[12] Gretchen Fraser (1919–1994), who had a German mother and a Norwegian father, was the first American ever to win an Olympic Gold medal in alpine skiing in 1948. The extraordinary swimmers Mark Spitz and Michael Phelps, along with the golfer Jack Nicklaus, known as the "Golden Bear," belong to the younger generation of successful American athletes with German roots. Hardly anyone is aware of the ethnic background of these outstanding athletes. The list could include many more names and sports.

Today it is no longer important whether athletes are German Americans or not, but in former decades, often unaware, these athletes played a special role for members of their own ethnic groups. On the one hand, they proved that they could make it to the top in their "new" country—even in sports—thus becoming heroes for their own ethnicity. On the other hand, by joining American teams and sports organizations, these athletes, who were often second-generation German Americans, demonstrated their willingness to become "true" Americans who no longer considered themselves immigrants.

Of all the German American sport and physical activity clubs, the turners had the most lasting influence on American society and made their movement quite visible until World War I. Other groups also prospered, such as the Buffalo Germans, a successful basketball team in the beginning of the twentieth century. The German American soccer clubs were quite influential in spreading soccer in the United States from the 1920s on. The German American Athletic Club in New York was a well-known institution among wrestlers and weight lifters as well as runners.

The American Turnverein Movement

The American Turners, as the umbrella organization of the *turnvereine* in the United States is called, go back to nineteenth-century German immigrants. Their members, the turners, founded about 700 *turnvereine.* In 1998 the first American Turner societies celebrated their 150th anniversary, and in 2015 the 55th National *Turnfest* was organized. This event is the longest-running national sport competition in the United States and has been organized continuously on a four-year cycle. Until the 1960s, a number of turners also belonged to the American National Gymnastic teams who participated in the Olympic Games. Especially at the 1904 Olympic Games in St. Louis, the German American turners dominated.[13]

The turner movement originated in eighteenth- and nineteenth-century Germany, a time closely connected to intellectual, political, social and economic changes, and technical advancement. In this context, new educational ideas and concepts arose in which national unity and patriotism played a special role. One was the concept of German *turnen*, largely developed by the so-called *Turnfather* Friedrich Ludwig Jahn (1778–1852). Initially, the goals of the turners were the liberation from French occupation, which followed a defeat in the Napoleonic Wars, the overthrow of the feudal order, and an end to the division of Germany into many small states in favour of a one-nation state.[14]

The Hasenheide, a park in Berlin, is considered to be the cradle of *turnen.* Here Jahn established the first gymnastic ground (*Turnplatz*) in 1811. The movement spread throughout the German Confederation states, and *turnvereine* were founded from 1815 onwards. The gymnastic grounds and *turnvereine* became meeting points for young men for political discussions, but also for participating in games, tumbling, exercises on apparatus, and so-called *volkstümliche Übungen* (popular exercises) like running, jumping, lifting and climbing as well as fencing, swimming and wrestling. Over the years, turner festivals (*Turnfests*), trips and social gatherings became popular aspects of the movement.[15]

From 1819 to 1942, Prussia and some other German states banned *turnen* because the turners, along with nationalistic student associations (*Burschenschaften*), were classified as forces of opposition. After the lifting of the ban, many Turner societies were founded. They became centers of political discussion and physical activities. Many turners were involved during the Revolution of 1848–1849 that strove for freedom, equality, and fraternity of the united German people. Some *turnvereine* established a militia to maintain law and order and uphold republican ideals and the constitution of the German *Reich.* After the revolution failed, many turners who had defended the constitution with weapons left their home country because imprisonment or the death penalty awaited them. Some immigrated to Switzerland and some left for England or the United States.[16]

Beginning of *Turnen* in the United States

The political refugees of the 1848 revolution in Germany were not the first to transfer *turnen* to the United States. *Turnen* had already been introduced to educational institutions in New England in the early 1820s by German political exiles Karl Beck (1789–1866), Karl Follen (1796–1840), and Franz Lieber (1800–1872), who had all been followers of Jahn.[17] Although *turnen* had an enthusiastic start on the American continent, its initial success lasted only a few years. It was a quarter of a century later—in 1848—that the first turner societies were founded in the United States by those turners who had been among the thousands of individuals who left Germany for the United States in the wake of the 1848 revolution.[18]

From the very beginning, *turnen* in the United States experienced a different fate than in Germany. On the one hand, it is important to note that it was a German movement of physical culture transported to a country in which other immigrant groups also had brought their own systems of exercises and sport. On the other hand, it should not be forgotten that it was the democratically and socialistically oriented turners that emigrated. This is reflected in the political goals of the first American turner societies and their umbrella organization, the "Socialistische Turnerbund," officially founded in 1851. The Turner movement saw itself as a "nursery for all revolutionary ideas" that had their origins in a rational world view.[19] The turners promoted a socialism that concentrated on the rights and freedom of the individual[20] and opposed monarchy and religious indoctrination. This meant that in terms of the socio-political circumstances prevailing in the United States, they fought American "nativism," the system of slavery, and the temperance and Sabbath-day laws.[21] Until the outbreak of the Civil War turner societies maintained a strong political orientation. Their political attitudes reflected the opinions of freethinkers, an antireligious movement that advocated rationalism, science, and history. Although the turners possessed German roots, they considered themselves to be in the tradition of American intellectuals who embodied political and religious freedom in an enlightened America. A close connection between the turners and the freethinkers remained until the twentieth century.

According to Conzen, the *turnvereine* were places where German or rather German American culture and traditions were fostered through their social and cultural activities. Following their motto "mens sana in corpore sano"—sound mind in a sound body—the *turnvereine* not only offered classes in gymnastics (*turnen*) from the very beginning, but also provided intellectual offerings. The turner halls were places in which not only German language but also German customs and celebrations were preserved. They provided a social center for political debates, lectures, Sunday schools, and libraries for the further education of German immigrants. The affiliated restaurants or bars were popular places for German *Gemütlichkeit* or social affairs.[22] Besides fostering German culture and nationalism, the turners tried to establish a bridge between the old culture and the new by offering English-language classes, and strongly supported American citizenship among their members in order to accelerate their integration into American mainstream society.[23] In 1851, the first National Gymnastic Festival (*Turnfest*) was organized as both a competitive and social event.[24]

Like other ethnic groups, the Germans faced the hostility of native-born Americans who did not approve of the high rate of immigration. Especially in the Midwest, turners were physically attacked on several occasions. To defend themselves they were urged by the

Turnerbund to include shooting and other military exercises in their physical program. Later, during the American Civil War, they benefited from these exercises in their military service.[25] In the 1850s and 1860s the *Turnerbund* supported the Republican Party. This resulted in the establishment of a bodyguard for Abraham Lincoln´s first inauguration, the defense of abolitionist meetings, and the formation of different turner regiments at the beginning of the Civil War in 1861. Some thousands of turners fought in different military units for the North. The turners in the Southern states—some decided to defend the Confederacy, others left to fight for the Union army.[26]

After the Civil War, the turner union took on the name *Nordamerikanischer Turnerbund,* to signal its depoliticization and to express its new identity, which now strongly focused on educational goals. These goals were related to society in general, such as the prohibition of children's work or the introduction of compulsory school attendance. The turners also strongly promoted the introduction of physical education in public schools. In some American cities the German system was adopted from the 1860s on.[27] In 1866, a *Turnlehrerseminar* was opened, which later became the *Normal School of the American Gymnastic Union.* Today it is integrated into the *School of Physical Education and Tourism Management* of the Indiana University-Purdue University in Indianapolis. This institution became important for the education of physical education teachers and *turnlehrer*, not only of German heritage.[28]

However, despite the apolitical name, political topics continued to be discussed in the umbrella organization, and some societies were active in the American workers' riots during the 1870s and 1880s in the Midwest, especially in Chicago, the center of labor unrest. At a bomb explosion during a demonstration on May 4, 1886, in the Chicago Haymarket, several people were killed. Among the people who were found guilty and sentenced to death was August Spies, the publisher of the *Chicagoer Arbeiterzeitung* and a member of the *Aurora Turnverein.*[29] Furthermore, turners often discussed the rights of women in American society; this did not apply to the turner movement itself until the end of the century. Nevertheless, classes in *turnen* for women were introduced in the 1860s, and many societies established a "Ladies Auxiliary" during that time.[30] Not until the 1990s did all the American turner societies change their statutes so that women could become regular members.[31]

During the postbellum years, the number of German immigrants increased; thus in many American cities new turner societies were founded, and others enlarged their membership. The development of the German American Turner movement climaxed shortly after the peak of German immigration to the United States in the 1890s. In 1894, there were 317 societies comprising approximately 40,000 members, with more than 25,000 children and 3,000 women participating in the activity classes.[32] This boom had ceased by the beginning of World War I, a time when the radical and socialistic tendencies in the turner movement had declined. Most "Forty-Eighters," the pioneers of social reforms, were no longer living.

Assimilation and Americanization

Over the years an assimilation process among the German immigrant population became apparent, especially with the growth of the American-born generations. These newer generations were no longer fluent in German and to a certain extent had lost their cultural affinity to, and interest in, the land of their ancestors. This trend toward Americanization was also intensified by the anti-German politics of the American government in the years between 1914 and 1918. Many Americans with a German background were accused of disloyalty to the nation. This anti-German hysteria objected to everything that was German, especially to language and culture: "Kultur of the Kaiser's kind not to be promoted . . ." and "The German tongue has no place in America. . . ." were slogans appearing in a Cincinnati newspaper.[33] This resulted in vandalism, a prohibition of the German language in schools and universities, the elimination of German journals and newspapers, the ban of German composers from concert halls, the closing of German theaters, and the Americanization of German names—persons, streets, towns, organizations, or societies.[34]

In the years after World War I, the Turner movement became more and more Americanized, as seen by the loss of German as the official language in the minutes of turner society meetings and in the *Amerikanische Turnzeitung*. Gradually, Turner societies adopted English as their language and even Americanized their names, which always included a "Turners," but dropped the German *Turngemeinde* or *Turnverein*. In 1936 the *American Turner Topics* became the official turner organ. The *Nordamerikanischer Turnerbund* kept its name until 1938, and then changed it to *American Turners*. In 1935 the new slogan of the turners became "Turnerism is Americanism."[35]

The statistical reports of the turner union show that the number of societies and membership remained constant during World War I. The union had around 200 societies with approximately 38,000 members. The decline started after the war in 1918 until 1943, when fewer than 100 societies with only 16,000 turners were affiliated with the American Turners. After World War II, new members were recruited from the latest wave of German immigration. The membership numbers of the turner societies reached 25,000 again, organized in approximately 80 societies.

American Turners at the End of the Twentieth Century

Unlike in Germany where the *Deutsche Turner-Bund* (DTB), the umbrella organization of turners today, counts almost 20,000 *turnvereine* with about 5 million members, and as such is a leading sport body for elite sport as well as for sports for all, *Turnen* never was able to develop into a national movement in the United States. In 2014, 54 clubs belonged to the *American Turners* with about 13,000 members.[36] Today, a typical American turner society no longer exists. Each association presents an individual picture, resulting from the wide range of membership numbers, the members' ethnic backgrounds, and the different activities. And it is these characteristics that account for the transition from what were once ethnic German societies to the European American organizations that the *turnvereine* have become today, although members of German descent still make up the largest share of the membership. As a result of the modification and broadening of the activities available in the Turner societies of today and due to their ethnically mixed membership, a discrepancy between tradition and Americanization is evident. It expresses itself, on the one hand, in the adherence to certain German traditions and Turner symbols, and, on the other hand, in the adoption of American values and acculturation to American society.[37]

Although *turnen* never developed in the United States into a national movement, the turners have contributed to American culture and history and to the American sporting heritage. Today, the *American Turners* are a member of the sport federations USA Gymnastics and USA Volleyball. A group of American Turners regularly visits the *turnfests* in Germany, a huge sports-for-all event with up to 100,000 participants, and they still celebrate their own national Turnfest every four years, which counts a few hundred participants.

Basketball: The Buffalo Germans

Not all German Americans joined a turner society; there was also interest in American sports. In some cases they founded ethnic German sports teams. One very successful example is the Buffalo Germans, a basketball team from the German YMCA in Buffalo, New York. At the beginning of the twentieth century, the Buffalo Germans became not only one of the most successful basketball teams, but they also won the Olympic Basketball tournament in 1904.

The Buffalo Germans were coached by Fred Burkhardt, the physical director of the Buffalo YMCA and a former student of James Naismith.[38] The team members of the Buffalo Germans consisted of Americans with a German or Dutch background. Until 1898 the 16- to 18-year-olds played against other junior teams. Due to their skill they soon competed against men. They realized their first success in 1901 when the AAU organized the first national basketball tournament during the Pan-American Exposition in Buffalo. The Buffalo Germans won the tournament without a single loss.[39] Three years later at the Olympic Games in St. Louis the first Olympic basketball tournament was played. Only six American teams entered this competition. The Buffalo Germans[40] did not lose a single game and won the tournament. After their two outstanding titles of 1901 and 1904 they called themselves World Champions.[41]

In the aftermath of their Olympic victory, they won 111 games in a row between 1908 and 1911. At this time—supposedly due to some arguments with management—the Buffalo Germans no longer belonged to the YMCA; they separated in 1904 or 1905.[42] According to Peterson, they then were an independent "barnstorming team" that travelled through the northeast and sometimes as far as Ohio to play against local teams. Because the Buffalo Germans dominated their opponents, they attracted many spectators.[43] In 1915 the team officially changed its name to "Orioles," borrowed from the sponsor, Nest No. 1 of the Fraternal Order of Orioles. However, within the basketball community they remained known under their original name.[44] One possible explanation for this name change might also be that during the years of World War I when many Americans directed feelings of hatred against everything that was German, they were forced to change their name to make their German background less obvious.

The Buffalo Germans existed for 29 years in different configurations, and for the first 9 years of their existence they remained amateurs. In 1904, after the Olympic Games, they became professionals, winning 762 of 847 games in the three decades of their existence. Thus, not surprisingly historian Don Sayenga calls them "the Original Dream Team." As a consequence of their extraordinary success, they were admitted to the Basketball Hall of Fame in 1961.[45]

The Buffalo Germans athletes, unlike many of the Turners, played the sport for itself and not for the sake of social or political engagement. Although bearing a German name, they did not seem to contribute much to German American identity. Today, only basketball insiders know about them.

Soccer, the Game for German Americans after World War I

Unlike nineteenth-century German immigrants, later immigrants from Germany often had contact with other sports besides *turnen* in their home country. In the 1870s and 1880s, various English sports were introduced to Germany, among them soccer. Konrad Koch, a teacher who had spent some time in England, introduced soccer after his return in 1870 to a school in Braunschweig. Besides Koch, English sailors, businessmen, and students spread soccer to various German cities. Soccer had to face many difficulties to become an established sport in Germany because the turners were against the introduction of English games and sports. They criticized them for their emphasis on records, specialization, hard training, and violation of aesthetics. Regarding soccer, for instance, Karl Planck, a "Turnlehrer" and "gymnasial professor," published a book called "Fußlümmelei" (slump footing), a term of disgrace for soccer. In his book, he writes deprecatingly about "Stauchballspiel" (butt ball).[46] Despite such criticism, soccer became very popular for men and boys and in 1900 the German Soccer Federation (*Deutscher Fußball-Bund, DFB*) was founded.[47] Many immigrants to the United States must have had contact with this game before they left their home country.

The spread of soccer in the United States, especially along the East Coast and the Chicago area, where a number of ethnic soccer clubs could be found, was influenced by German immigrants. One of the first known German American soccer clubs was Football Club Germania, founded in Hoboken in 1912. Due to the difficulties that German Americans faced within the greater American society during the time of World War I, it changed its name in 1917 to the Hoboken Football Club (Hoboken F. C.), and still exists under this name. In 1923 the German-American Soccer League was put together by the S.C. New York, Wiener Sports Club, D.S.C. Brooklyn, Hoboken F.C. and Newark S.C. This league was reorganized in 1927 as the German-American Football Association (G.A.F.A).[48] In 1977 it became the Cosmopolitan Soccer League to erase its ethnic image. The league is still active in the New York City area.

It is the oldest continuous soccer league in the United States.[49] Although predominantly German, the league was dominated by teams with various ethnic connections, such as Austrian, Czechoslovakian, and Hungarian.[50] One of the most famous teams was the Philadelphia Germans, organized in the 1920s. In 1942 they changed their name to the Philadelphia Americans because of World War II. It was the best American Soccer League team from the mid-1930s to the mid-1950s. It won the National Amateur Cup in 1933 and 1934, and five of its players participated on the 1934 American World Cup team.[51] The high skill level of German American soccer players is also reflected in the fact that 10 players of German American background were on the 1936 American Olympic Soccer Team.[52]

Together with the German-American Athletic Club, the G.A.F.A. was responsible for organizing the German Sports and Athletic Day also known as the German-American Sport Festival, held at Downing Stadium on Randall's Island, New York. In addition to various German American sport clubs, Italian clubs participated. In retrospect, this event dating back to the late 1930s and beginning of the 1940s has to be viewed rather critically. It was a time when followers of the German Nazi movement tried to influence German American life and their clubs, so the number of Nazi sympathizers grew in the States. At the German Sport and Athletic Day, the swastika banner could be seen aside the American flag, and some of the participating athletes proudly wore a swastika on their clothing. The president of the German-American Athletic Club, Eugene E. W. Rieflin, described himself as the "US Representative of Hans von Tschammer und Osten, *Reichssportführer*" (head of sports for the Third Reich).[53] However, in the end, the Nazi engagement within the German American population and sport was not successful and disappeared after the Americans entered World War II in 1941. The German Sports Day continued to take place until the late 1960s as an event that mostly concentrated on sports competitions, especially soccer. In the 1950s and 1960s, the G.A.F.A. invited German soccer teams to play in the United States.[54] There was usually one game at the German-American Sports Festival and then the German teams played various other American teams around the country. Among them were such well-known teams as the HSV Hamburg, Stuttgarter Kickers, FC Schalke, and 1860 München.[55] Just as in the 1930s and 1940s, the German Sports Day continued to honor German as well as American culture. Some of the programs of the 1950s printed the first verse of the American national anthem as well as of the "Deutschlandlied," the German national anthem. It was also a popular event with the American population, as the annual programs of the 1960s showed, which included appreciative greetings by the mayor of New York City.[56]

German-American Athletic Club (GAAC)

As stated earlier for a period the German-American Athletic Club (GAAC), originally founded in 1884 for wrestling and weightlifting, collaborated with G.A.F.A in the organization of the annual German Sports Day. German born Dietrich Wortmann an Olympic wrestler at the 1904 Games in St. Louis became its president in 1910. Because of the club's strong ethnic identity under his lead it was disbanded due to anti-German sentiments during the World War I. In 1928 Wortmann revived the Athletic Club again, which until the mid-1930s became important for long-distance running. Among the active members was Paul de Bruyn, winner of the Boston Marathon in 1932. Until the mid-1930s Jewish members could also be found. Due to the club´s closeness to Nazi ideology through Wortmann, who had contacts with Josef Goebbels, the Minister of Propaganda in the German Reich, many of them left it. Wortmann's Nazi affiliation played no role in the American world of sport before or after the war. He was, however, a friend of Avery Brundage and became an important sport official. He served as head of the German-American Olympic Fund-Raising Committee for the 1936 Olympic Games in Berlin and in 1948 was elected president of the Metropolitan Association of the AAU. In 1951 he became president of the Fédération Internationale de Halterophile (FIH).[57] The GAAC ceased to exist in the 1950s.Why it ended is not known.

Conclusion

Participation in American sports and physical culture can be viewed from two aspects: ethnic separation or assimilation. This means that an individual participates either in ethnic sport organizations on ethnic teams or in mixed American teams. According to historian Ralph Wilcox, sport contributed to the decline of cultural barriers and thus supported assimilation into American society. In this process, English-speaking groups had it easier than, for instance, Germans and Italians.[58]

Especially in the nineteenth century, many German immigrants preferred their own physical culture: *turnen* was part of their ethnicity. Until the mid-twentieth century, the Turner movement was a typical example of an ethnic sport organization. Despite the fact that the Turners were always engaged in American politics, most of its members were of German heritage, and the cultural background of the *Vereinsleben* was basically German with some affiliation with American culture and tradition. In the course of time, the Turners had to welcome other ethnic groups in order to survive, because they had lost members and no longer served as an "ethnic harbour" for new German immigrants. Not only did English become the main language in the 1930s, but early in the twentieth century some *Turnvereins* already tried to establish baseball or basketball teams. The orientation toward the American world of sports is also seen in the fact that the umbrella federation, American Turners, are members of American sports federations such as USA Gymnastics and USA Volleyball. National conventions with large Turner Union events are held under the American flag and according to a distinctly American ritual. Today, at many of these events, the American national anthem is played and the Pledge of Allegiance is recited.[59] Such a fusion of American and German symbols could also be seen at the annual German-American Sports Day in New York City between the 1930s and 1960s.

Although the *turnvereine* have Americanized their rituals as well as their athletic and social programs, they still remember their German origins and certain parts of their history, such as the celebrating of the *Turnfest* every four years. This is of importance for those members who use these places to symbolically demonstrate their ethnicity. However, many turners are unaware of their organization's German roots. Although members continue to call themselves "turners" they often do not know the meaning of this term. With the exception of a few ethnic societies, the turners have adopted a new identity—one that is European American.[60]

As elaborated, the German Americans were successful not only in *turnen*. In the past, examples can be found illustrating their engagement on various sport teams. The example of the Buffalo Germans shows that in some cases they did this quite successfully. With their participation in an identifiable American sport and in an American organization like the YMCA, the Buffalo Germans demonstrated a certain degree of assimilation into American culture and identification with the American nation while also showing their "German-ness"—at least in their name. The American nation recognized their successes by inducting them into the Basketball Hall of Fame.

A quote from *USA Today* cited by Markovits and Hellerman reads: "If you were a fan who loved baseball, then you were American," which can also be applied to basketball, football, and boxing, according to the authors. Furthermore, they contend that in the past a soccer fan "was viewed as at least resisting—if not outrightly rejecting—integration into America and its general ethos."[61] This cannot generally be said about the German American soccer clubs. Compared to the turners, they showed less traces of "Germanism" and tried to Americanize by changing their club names much earlier than the turner clubs did. Relating to German Americans, ethnic assimilation has taken place in sports just as it has in other institutions.

Today, very few German immigrants come to the United States. German teams or leagues no longer appear in American sports. Only a few *turnvereine* are left. However, now and then there are German athletes, such as the basketball player Dirk Nowitzki, who come over to play sports, but not to immigrate to the United States. Another example is "Kaiser Franz" (Franz Beckenbauer), probably the most famous German soccer player of the late twentieth century, who played in 1983 for the New York Cosmos. Jürgen Klinsmann has been the head coach of the American national men´s soccer team since 2011. This indicates that some Germans are still part of American sports, and vice versa, as American coaches and players can be found in German hockey and basketball leagues, but this does not involve any more German Americans in a continued transnational flow.

Notes

1 Willi Paul Adams, *The German-Americans. An Ethnic Experience. American Edition* (Indianapolis: Max Kade German-American Center, 1993), 1–3.

2 Frankfurter Allgemeine Zeitung, March 18, 1998.

3 Eric Hobsbawm, "Introduction. Inventing Traditions," in *The Invention of Tradition*, ed. Eric Hobsbawm and Terence Ranger (New York: Cambridge University Press, 1985), 1–15, especially 12; Richard D. Alba, *Ethnic Identity. The Transformation of White America* (New Haven, CT: Yale University, 1990), 20, 25, 75.

4 Kathleen N. Conzen, "Ethnicity as Festive Culture: Nineteenth-Century German-Americans on Parade," in *The Invention of Ethnicity*, ed. Werner Sollors (New York: Oxford University Press, 1989), 44–76, especially 58; LaVern Rippley, "Germans," in *Encyclopedia of Ethnicity and Sports in the United States*, ed. George B. Kirsch, Othello Harris and Claire E. Nolte (Westport, CT: Greenwood Press, 2000), 179–186.

5 Herbert J. Gans, "Symbolic Ethnicity. The Future of Ethnic Groups and Cultures in America," in *On the Making of Americans: Essays in the Honor of David Riesmann*, ed. Herbert J. Gans, Nathan Glazer, Joseph B. Gusfield, and Christopher Jencks (Philadelphia: University of Pennsylvania Press, 1979), especially 193–220 and 204–206.

6 Ibid., 205–206.

7 Alba, *Ethnic Identity*, 239.

8 Kathleen N. Conzen, "Pattern of German-American History," in *German in America: Retrospect and Prospect*, ed. Randall M. Miller (Philadelphia: Science Press, 1984), 14–36, 32.

9 Roger Allaway, Collin Jose, and David Litterer, *The Encyclopedia of American Soccer History* (Lanham: Scarecrow Press, 2001).

10 Conzen, "Pattern of German-American History," 32; Annette R. Hofmann, "Ruth, George Herman 'Babe' (1895–1948)," in *Encyclopedia of German-American Relations*, ed. Thomas Adam (Santa Barbara, CA: ABC-Clio, 2005), 931–932.

11 See, the homepage of the National Soccer Hall of Fame: "90-Year Anniversary Articles: Soccer Wire Decades (1930–39)," *U.S. Soccer*. www.ussoccer.com/stories/2014/03/17/11/18/90-year-anniversary-articles-soccer-wire-decades-1930–39 (accessed January 2, 2014).

12 Christiane Job and Patricia Vertinsky, "Gertrude Ederle, First Woman to Swim the Channel in 1926," in Thomas, ed., *Encyclopedia of German-American Relations* (Santa Barbara, CA: ABC-Clio, 2005), 291–292; Annette R. Hofmann, "Weissmueller, Peter Jonas (1904–1984)," in Thomas, ed., *Encyclopedia of German-American Relations*, 1124–1125; see Linda J. Borish, on Gertrude Ederle and her swimming career, "'The Cradle of American Champions, Women Champions . . . Swim Champions': Charlotte Epstein, Gender and Jewish Identity, and the Physical Emancipation of Women in Aquatic Sports," *The International Journal of the History of Sport* 21 (March 2004): 197–235.

13 The current membership numbers were given by the National Office of the American Turners. See also Annette R. Hofmann, *Aufstieg und Niedergang des deutschen Turnens in den USA* (Schorndorf: Hofmann, 2001). For the Turner Olympians see Heinrich Metzner, *History of the American Turners* 4th rev. ed. (Rochester, NY: National Council of the American Turners, 1989).

14 Annette R. Hofmann and Gertrud Pfister, "Turnen—A Forgotten Movement Culture. Its Beginnings in Germany and Diffusion in the United States," in *Turnen and Sport: Transatlantic Transfer*, ed. Annette R. Hofmann (Münster: Waxmann, 2004), 11–24.

15 Ibid., 12.

16 Ibid., 13–16.

17 Erich Geldbach, "Die Verpflanzung des deutschen Turnens nach Amerika: Beck, Follen, Lieber," *Stadion* Vol. 1 (1975): 331–376, see 360–370.

18 It is almost impossible to arrive at an exact number of all the "Forty-Eighters" who emigrated to the United States. Sources estimate that no more than 3,000 to 4,000 persons emigrated for purely political reasons between 1847 and 1856. See Joachim Reppmann, *'Freiheit, Bildung und Wohlstand für Alle!' Schleswig-Holsteinsche 'Achtundvierziger' in den USA 1847–1860* (Wyk auf Föhr: Verlag für Amerikanistik, 1994), 12–13.

19 See the Convention Protokoll of the Socialistische Turnerbund from 1859/60.

20 The Turn-Zeitung (December 1, 1851) printed the article *'Sozialismus und die Turnerei.'*

21 Socialist Turnerbund of North America, Constitutions adopted at their convention at Buffalo September 24–27 (Buffalo, 1855).

22 For further details, see also Betty Spears and Richard Swanson, *History of Sport and Physical Education in the United States* (Dubuque, IA: Wm. C. Brown Publishers, 1988), 128–129.

23 Even today American Turners demand American or Canadian citizenship of their members. See Metzner, *History of the American Turners*, 51.

24 Hofmann, *Aufstieg und Niedergang*, 135.

25 Ibid., 140.

26 Ibid., 148–163.

27 Annette R. Hofmann, *The American Turner Movement: A History from Its Beginning to 2000* (Indianapolis: Max Kade, 2010), 139–141.
28 Hofmann, *Aufstieg und Niedergang*, 164–166, 196–202.
29 Hofmann, *The American Turner Movement*, 131–133. For a more detailed description of the turmoil leading to the Haymarket Affair and its consequences, see Ralf Wagner, *Zwischen Tradition und Fortschritt: Zur gesellschaftspolitischen Entwicklung der deutschamerikanischen Turnbewegung am Beispiel Milwaukees und Chicagos, 1850–1920*. (PhD. Diss., München University, 1988), 182–206.
30 Hofmann, *Aufstieg und Niedergang*, 191–193; Hofmann, *The American Turner Movement*, 154–158.
31 Hofmann, *The American Turner Movement*.
32 See Nordamerikanischer Turnerbund, *Jahresbericht* (1896) or Robert K. Barney, "German Turners in American Domestic Crisis," *Stadion* 4 (1978): 344–357; and Eric Pumroy and Katja Rampelmann, *Research Guide to the Turner Movement in the United States* (Westport, CT: Greenwood Press, 1996), 289.
33 Franziska Ott and Don Heinrich Tolzmann, *The Anti-German Hysteria. German-American Life on the Home Front*. An exhibit on the commemoration of the 1994 Prager Memorial Day, April 5. University of Cincinnati, Blegan Library, March 15–April 15, 1994.
34 Frederick C. Luebke, *Bounds of Loyalty. German-Americans and World War I* (De Kalb: Northern Illinois University Press, 1974), 248–250.
35 Hofmann, *Aufstieg und Niedergang*, 244–256.
36 Information given by the National Office of the American Turners.
37 Hofmann, *Aufstieg und Niedergang*, 300–316,
38 Benjamin G. Rader, *American Sports. From the Age of Folk Games to the Age of Televised Sports* 4th ed. (Englewood Cliffs: Prentice Hall, 1998), 103.
39 Hofmann, "The Buffalo Germans," 19–22.
40 For the members of the Olympic team, see Bill Mallon, *The 1904 Olympic Games: Results for All Competitors* (Jefferson, NC: McFarland & Company, 1999), 216.
41 Peterson, *Cages to Jump Shots*, 58–59.
42 Hausauer, 'The Second Fifty Years," 25.
43 Redecker, Basketball in den USA, 21–22; Peterson, *Cages to Jump Shots*, 59.
44 Peterson, *Cages to Jump Shots*, 60–61.
45 Donald Sayenga, "The 1904 Basketball Championship or Were the 'Buffalo Germans' the Original Dream Team?" *Citius, Altius, Fortius* 4, no. 3 (1996): 7–8.
46 Karl Planck, *Fusslümmelei. Über Stauchball und englische Krankheit* (Stuttgart: Kohlhammer, 1898); Michael Krüger, "Vom 'Stauchballspiel' zum Frauenfußball—zur Geschichte des populärsten deutschen Sports," in *Rund um den Frauenfußball. Pädagogisches und sozialwissenschaftliche Perspektiven*, ed. Annette R. Hofmann and Michael Krüger (Münster: Waxmann, 2014), 11–36, especially 22–23; Gertrud Pfister, "Frauen-Fußball-Geschichten(n)," in *Auf den Spuren des Frauen- und Mädchenfußballs*, ed. Silke Sinning (Weinheim: Beltz, 2012), 14–47, especially 18–19. For the conflict of the Turners and football see Krüger, "Vom Stauchballspiel."
47 Krüger, "Vom Stauchballspiel," 24–25.
48 The German name is Deutsch Amerikanischer Fussballbund (DAFB). The yearbooks only mention the name on its cover, although they are written in English.
49 Eastern New York State Soccer Association. 100th Anniversary, July 13, 2013, n.p.
50 Allaway et al., *The Encyclopedia on American Soccer*, 109.
51 Ibid., 232–233.
52 "90-Year Anniversary Articles."
53 Carolyn Marvin, "Avery Brundage and American Participation in the 1936 Olympic Games," *American Studies* 16 (1980): 81–106, especially 95.
54 See the *38th Yearbook DAFB*, Sunday, May 14, 1961, n.p.
55 All German soccer teams that came over to play at the German-American Sports Festival between 1950 and 1965 can be found in the yearbook of the 43rd Anniversary. German-American Football Association, 1966, n.p.
56 See the various yearbooks of the Deutsch Amerikanischer Fussballbund in the 1960s.

57 Annette R. Hofmann, "Die deutsch-amerikanische Turnbewegung und ihr Umgang mit nationalsozialistischen Einflüssen," in *Sport, Geschichte, Pädagogik. Festschrift zum 60. Geburtstag von Michael Krüger*, ed. Emanuel Hübner and Kai Reinhart (Hildesheim: Arete, 2015), 169–189.

58 Ralph C. Wilcox, "Sport and the Nineteenth Century Immigrant Experience," in *Immigration and Ethnicity: American Society—'Melting Pot' or 'Salad Bowl'?*, ed. Michael D'Incenzo and Joseph P. Shireman (Westport, CT: Greenwood Press, 1992), 177–189, 184–185.

59 Hofmann, *Aufstieg und Niedergang*, 311–312.

60 Ibid., 314–316.

61 Andrei S. Marcovits and Steven L. Hellerman, *Offside, Soccer and American Exceptionalism.* (Princeton, NJ: Princeton University Press, 2001), 52.

13

SPORT AND ITALIAN AMERICAN IDENTITY

Gerald R. Gems

Introduction: Lack of Identity

In 1877 Cesare Orsini brought 14 professional players from Italy to New York to demonstrate "*pallone*," a game similar to *jai alai* that he proclaimed to be the Italian national sport. The Italians expected a measure of wealth from their venture; but their efforts proved a dismal failure and left the players stranded until a series of fundraising events earned enough to send them home. That same year Lewis Pessano "Buttercup" Dickerson joined the Cincinnati baseball team in the National League. Although Dickerson's Italian heritage is debated, the incidents present some historical questions as to the nature of sport and Italian identity.[1] Orsini's claim of *pallone* as the Italian national sport assumes an Italian national identity at that time, and the debate relative to Dickerson questions the role of sport in the transition to an American identity among Italians who had migrated to the United States.

Benedict Anderson has stated,

> [I]dentity is a socially constructed sense of being, both personal and communal in nature. It is a fluid process in which one perceives him- or herself as an individual and as a member of a larger social group, with whom solidarity is shared as well as a sense of difference from other groups.

Anderson has termed this an "imagined community."[2] History plays a primary role in the construction of identity because individual or group identity is learned over time due to interactions with new ideas, new environments, and new allegiances. Italian history is characterized by centuries of conflict between warring city-states and occupation by foreign powers. Italy did not win its independence until 1861 when the army of Giuseppe Garibaldi liberated the peninsula and Sicily from foreign domination in the name of King Victor Emmanuel II. It took another decade of civil war for the king to exert his dominion over southern Italy and Sicily, whose inhabitants perceived him as just one more oppressor. Geographical, political, and economic divisions lingered, and there was, as yet, no national language to bind Italians together. Local residents remained wedded to their regional dialects. Their allegiance rested only with family and with their communal *paesani*.[3]

Life in the territory south of Rome offered brutal conditions for the peasantry: poor soil, overpopulation, long hours of manual labor, low wages, and continual hunger. Peasants, exploited by their absentee landlords, expressed a sense of despair and fatalism known as *la miseria*, with little hope for the future. Life expectancy for a laborer in Cosenza Province (in the toe of the peninsula) in 1900 amounted to only 29 years.[4] It is little wonder that more than 4,000,000 Italians, mostly illiterate southern peasants, migrated to the United States between 1880 and 1924.[5]

The Italians faced greater obstacles than many other ethnic groups in the assimilation process in America. The Irish spoke English. The Germans arrived with the Irish in the 1840s, and many of them were skilled craftsmen and tradesmen who found ready employment. The Jews, although poor and oppressed, were educated and enjoyed the benevolence of the German Jews, who had fled Europe earlier in the face of anti-Semitism and fared well in their half-century of residence in the United States. The Italians sought asylum in Little Italies, ghetto colonies within urban centers. There they tried to replicate the only culture familiar to them, but unlike Italy, they could not exclude non-Italians or Italians from other regions of the homeland.[6] Residents of such neighborhoods faced limited opportunities for assimilation. Nor were they wanted by the mainstream society. "Few argued on behalf of the assimilability of the Italians at the time of their arrival, for they entered as one of the most despised of European immigrant groups."[7] In 1902 Woodrow Wilson, then a professor at Princeton, derided the "alteration of stock" potentially caused by the "multitudes of men of the lowest class from the south of Italy."[8]

Developing an Italian Identity

For those Italians who lived outside of the Little Italies, their leisure led them to sporting activities and a greater measure of assimilation. Some Italian players reached the professional baseball ranks by the 1880s, and Ed Abbaticchio, the son of immigrants, gained national renown as a professional football and baseball player in the 1890s, indicating an early level of integration. In 1899 Lawrence Brignoli(a), the son of an immigrant peddler, won the Boston Marathon, a prelude to his successful life as a runner, rower, baseball player, owner of a stable of trotting horses, and a boxing promoter.[9]

The distance-running fad of the era brought Dorando Pietri to the United States in 1908. Earlier that year Pietri had collapsed before the finish line at the Olympic marathon in London, enabling the American Johnny Hayes to claim a disputed victory. Pietri sojourned to America for a rematch, which the Italian not only won before 10,000 spectators in Madison Square Garden, but set a new world record by almost 12 minutes. Pietri continued his competitions with other ethnic rivals on the running circuit in America, performing before crowds of cheering Italians who feted him and showered him with gifts wherever he appeared. Fans took pride in Pietri's accomplishments and in their own growing identity as Italians.[10]

A public transition to an American identity became evident when Gaston Strobino, an Italian immigrant who chose to become a naturalized American citizen, won a bronze medal in the 1912 Olympic marathon in Sweden. Upon his return to Paterson, New Jersey, he was feted as an American hero.[11] Such accolades proved temporary, however. American newspapers made continual references to an Italian Mafia and a Black Hand Society that painted all Italians as sinister gangsters.[12]

The Question of Whiteness

In the media, popular culture, and in the labor force, Italians were ascribed a nonwhite status. The term "guineas," a reference to African slaves, was used by white Americans to describe Italians by the 1890s. The Louisiana legislature equated Italians with blacks, sending their children to segregated schools; banned both groups from the New Orleans police force; and disenfranchised Italians with poll taxes, literacy tests, and residency requirements. In the North and the mining towns of the West, Italians were the lowest paid of all workers.[13]

The Italians had to compete with members of the dominant culture for positions above them on the social, economic, and labor scale, but also with the other ethnic groups for the same jobs, status, or resources among the immigrant working class. Other ethnics accosted Italian children in the urban playgrounds, and Italian newsboys had to fight to hold their territories. Even within the confines of the American Catholic Church, Italians faced discrimination. Until their numbers reached a critical mass that enabled them to request their own parish church, they attended religious services at German and Irish churches and were assigned seats with black Catholics in the rear of the building.[14]

In 1914 Edward Alsworth Ross, an influential sociologist, published *The Old World in the New*, which provided a presumably scientific basis for racism, in which he claimed the southern Italians in particular to be physically, intellectually, emotionally, and morally inferior to northern Europeans. Ross's work was buttressed by Madison Grant's *The Passing of the Great Race or the Racial Basis of European History* in 1916, which proposed a hierarchy of racial types and maintained that the Nordics were the only pure race. Southern Italians were presumably descended from slaves, and Grant feared their negative characteristics would be transmitted across generations. Prescott Hall of the Immigration Restriction League proclaimed that the southern Italians derived from African Negroes. In their minds, Italians could never obtain whiteness and could only dilute the stock of the white Anglo Saxon Protestants (WASPs) who composed mainstream American society. Not only skin color, but also adoption of middle-class norms, values, and standards, as well as proficiency in the English language and fervent Protestantism, constituted acceptable whiteness.[15] Among the nativists, a resurgent Ku Klux Klan meant to reinforce such dictums in the nascent twentieth century, and the federal government embarked on a program of eugenics, sterilization, and immigration quotas.[16]

Yet Italian boxers had already begun to challenge the notions of physical debility as they competed with other ethnic fighters of the pre–World War I years. A New Jersey newspaper article of 1915 acknowledged the Italians' success.

> The sons of sunny Italy have taken a prominent part in the boxing game. Although boxing has never been popular in Italy itself . . . the Italian expatriates . . . have long been among the most enthusiastic devotees of the game. . . . Little Casper Leon, the Sicilian, was a bear in the bantamweight division some twenty years ago. . . . Of all the Italian boxers since the beginning of the game the ring now has the best in the person of Joseph Carrora. . . . Joe and his people migrated to New York and in the Italian quarter of the metropolis he developed into a little bundle of energy. . . . [H]is destinies were taken charge of by Scotty Monteith. The first thing Scotty did was to pull off a christening party, and Joe emerged duly tagged as Johnny Dundee. Since then he has traveled under that monaker (sic), and is known from coast to coast as the Scotch Wop.[17]

The article indicates that Leon's designation as a Sicilian marks him as something other than an Italian, and the references to "his people" and "Italian quarter" provide a sense that Dundee is not considered to be American, but is designated as an "other." The prescribed alias denotes the affecting of pseudoidentities to gain acceptance within the boxing hierarchy, and the denigrating nickname of the Scotch Wop is just another example of Italians' disparagement within the mainstream press.[18]

The *Washington Post* credited any success to American influences, stating that "[I]t would seem that the sons of Italy are not of a boxing race; that they are ill fitted to the sport. . . . [E]very Italian pugilist gained practically all his knowledge of the game after coming to the United States."[19] The contention that Italian fighters had learned their craft in the United States was accurate, and the media's designation of nationality helped to fix an Italian identity among the Italians themselves.

Americanization Efforts

The social reformers of the Progressive Era instituted a systematic approach to Americanize the children of ethnic immigrants by first enacting child labor laws to remove children from the industrial workforce and to then require education, which provided teachers with a captive audience with which to teach the prescribed values. Many of their captive students could not speak English, and physical education became a required course. The addition of intramural and interscholastic athletics instilled competition, the basis for the capitalist economy (in opposition to the radical sympathies of many Italian workers involved in the labor movement). Team sports taught teamwork, self-sacrifice, and leadership, desired qualities in a democracy. Athletes also learned that arguing with a referee could get them expelled from a game, a lesson cherished by employers who had to face striking workers. The national game of baseball even helped immigrant children make sense of the sometimes confusing American society. When on defense, all nine players had to operate like their communal families if they were to succeed, but on offense each batted separately and gained recognition and even profit based on their individual production, as in the workplace. Municipalities built playgrounds in the immigrant neighborhoods and field houses in the larger public parks, staffed by male and female supervisors, who taught the children to play in the prescribed manner.

Francesco Pizzolo, the son of immigrants, learned his baseball lessons so well that he dropped out of high school to pursue a career under the pseudonym of Ping Bodie. The powerful slugger became a star and a fan favorite in the American League. His success brought financial rewards and a measure of celebrity, but dishonor to his family, as his father disowned him for Anglicizing his name. Many other Italian youths who were drawn to American games faced admonishment from their parents, who found the games to be a waste of effort when their time could be better spent working and contributing to the family coffers.[20]

Conflicting Identities

Despite the adoption of American sports by some Italian youth, their allegiance to the United States remained doubtful. Italian immigrants and their offspring in the United States were deemed to be citizens of the Italian government and subject to its military draft when World War I erupted in Europe. Tens of thousands returned to Italy to serve, and Italian-language newspapers in the United States raised funds for the war effort. Others, such as Jerry Da Prato, who led the nation in scoring at Michigan Agricultural (now Michigan State) during the 1915 college football season, joined the American military along with an estimated 300,000 other Italian Americans as young men were forced to make choices as to their national identity.[21]

Such difficult choices continued for many Italians during the interwar years. Benito Mussolini made concerted efforts to retain the loyalty of Italians in the United States with

Italian-language schools in America and international exchange programs. Italians suffered another blow to Americanization efforts when their character was assailed in the clearly biased trial of Nicola Sacco and Bartolomeo Vanzetti that dragged on throughout the 1920s. The anarchists were eventually convicted of murder and robbery based on largely circumstantial evidence in a verdict that drew international protests, yet tarred Italians' image in the United States.[22]

Developing an American Identity

Such negative perceptions were countered by a growing Italian presence in Major League Baseball and by their contributions to the American Olympic teams. Tony Lazzeri starred as a second baseman for the New York Yankees during the 1920s. Although Italians feted him throughout the cities of the American League, he endured ethnic slurs and insults from fans and fellow players, some of whom held membership in the KKK. So many Italians appeared in MLB by the 1930s that Italian newspapers started naming all-Italian all-star teams.[23]

Italians also made a conspicuous appearance on the Olympic teams of the decade. Frankie Genaro (Di Gennaro) and Fidel LaBarba garnered gold medals as boxers in 1920 and 1924, respectively. Ray Barbuti, a football star at Syracuse University, won the only individual gold medal among Americans as a 400-meter runner in 1928 and ran a leg on the world record 1,600-meter relay team, cheered by both Italian and American fans at the Games. Upon his return to New York he announced that "I am an American of Italian origin, and I am proud of it."[24] Eleanor Garatti-Saville won fame as a national swimming champion, setting a world record in the 100-meter freestyle event, and won two gold medals as a member of the 1928 and 1932 Olympic teams. In the following decade, Italians competed as boxers, weight lifters, runners, and women's gymnasts on the American Olympic teams, further espousing an American identity.[25]

The participation of Italian girls in sport, who were typically shielded within the family until married, further distanced them from their Italian mothers. Clementine Brida (aka Maud Nelson) became not only a fan, but also an ardent practitioner of baseball. She began pitching for the Boston Bloomer Girls in 1897 as a sixteen-year-old. By 1911, she managed her own barnstorming team. When Margaret Gisolo won the Indiana state baseball championship for her American Legion team with a timely hit in the 1928 championship game, the male administrators of the league banned girls from further play. Nelson promptly hired Gisolo for her professional squad. Italian American women such as Nelson, Garatti-Saville, and Ada Lunardoni Cumiskey, a gymnast on the 1936 Olympic team, continued to compete even after their marriages. Their entrepreneurial and competitive ventures represented a distinct departure from the domestic lives of their female ancestors.[26]

The culture of working-class Italians revolved around physicality and a strong body, capable of manual labor, which mattered more than a sharp brain. A few young men translated that physical prowess into an education in the form of athletic scholarships, despite the warnings of nativists as to their inaptitude for sport or academic proficiency. Lou Little (Luigi Piccolo), a World War I veteran, managed to assume the reins of the football team at Georgetown University in 1924, and two other Italians, Joe Savoldi and Frank Carideo, starred at Notre Dame. Savoldi, a bruising fullback born in Italy, had only been in the United States since 1920. Carideo, an All-American quarterback, teamed with Savoldi to lead Notre Dame to two undefeated seasons and national championships in 1929 and 1930.[27] John Billi, a sportswriter for the *Il Progresso Italo-American*, began naming college all-star teams composed entirely of Italian football players in the 1930s, indicating the depth of Italian integration in the collegiate game.[28]

Hank Luisetti, the son of Italian immigrants, won national renown as a basketball player who revolutionized the game with his leaping, one-handed set shots. He accepted a basketball scholarship to Stanford University, where he became a national phenomenon as a three time All-American and the first college player to score 50 points in one game.[29]

Such college athletes won greater recognition for Italians and helped to dismiss the charges of intellectual deficiencies, but Italian youth were still attracted to contact sports more suitable to working-class physicality. Whereas many Italian boxers of earlier eras assumed Irish names as a camouflage, by the 1930s Italians reveled in their own surnames, and the number of Italian champions during the interwar years gives an indication of their success in that field. From 1924 to 1939 Italian Americans accounted for at least 21 champions and 185 top 10 contenders.[30] Boxing proved more acceptable to Italian parents as well. When Willie Pep (Papaleo) began fighting in 1937 as a 15-year-old he Anglicized his name, which drew a protest from his father, who earned 15 dollars per week as an employee of the Works Progress Administration. When the son gave his father 40 of the 50 dollars he had earned for two bouts in one night, his father told him to "see if you can fight twice a week from now on."[31] Other working-class sports, such as billiards and bowling, also drew interest. When Willie Mosconi lost his job that helped support his sick parents and seven siblings in 1931, he turned to pool and won a local tournament. He gave the $75 prize money to his father, who told him "Now go out and find yourself another tournament." He soon bought his father a tavern, where he could become his own boss.[32] Several Italians channeled their knowledge of bocce ball into the American form of bowling, gaining world championships in the 1920s and 1930s. Among them, Andy Varipappa arrived from Italy at the age of 11 and plied his athletic talents as a semipro baseball player, a boxer, and billiards player before realizing that he could make the most money as a bowler after losing a machinist's job in 1921.[33]

The Transition from Race to Ethnicity

It was baseball that marked one as truly American, and Italian players proliferated on the diamond during the 1930s. Joe DiMaggio epitomized the public transition to Americanization as he became widely acknowledged as the best player in the national game. The timing of DiMaggio's rise to stardom is important, as it coincided with an ideological transition during the interwar years. Anthropologist Franz Boas at Columbia University and sociologists Ernest Burgess and Robert E. Park at the University of Chicago led the way in separating the concepts of race and ethnicity, which had previously been conflated. Rather than the biologically determined categorization of races promoted earlier by Edward Alsworth Ross and Madison Grant, they argued for a greater recognition of cultural differences based on common ancestry, place of origin, belief systems, language, religion, or a shared history. Such new paradigms held great repercussions for the Italians and other groups on the margins of mainstream society; for if categorized by ethnicity rather than race Italians might aspire to the status of whiteness and its privileges. That was particularly true for second generation Italians like DiMaggio, who were born and raised in the United States under different historical, social, economic, and political circumstances than their parents and saw themselves as Americans rather than Italians.[34]

At that time, however, many Italians still lived an insular existence in the United States. A 1929 survey in Boston determined that more than 88 percent of Italians married others from the same province in Italy. A 1937 Chicago study found that 23 percent of Italian women still spoke no English, and by 1941 42.5 percent of the Italians had not yet become citizens.[35]

The Power of Sport

DiMaggio turned many of the recalcitrant Italians into baseball fans, including his own father who opposed the game until Joe and his older brother, Vince, earned pro contracts that paid much more than he earned as an immigrant Sicilian fisherman.[36] Italians took great pride in the public display of DiMaggio's physical prowess, and Italian boys aspired to his stature and relative wealth. He was offered $225 a month as a teenager at the height of the Depression when that figure approximated the annual wage for an Italian construction worker.[37]

After a brief but stellar minor league career, Joe DiMaggio joined the New York Yankees in 1936 and immediately attracted hosts of Italian fans to the game, who brought their Italian flags to the stadium and inundated the clubhouse with mail thanking him for the way he represented Italians.[38] He adhered to Italian custom by sending most of his salary to his parents, buying them a house, and purchasing a fishing boat for one of his nine siblings. The Yankees won four World Series titles in a row, and DiMaggio won acclaim as the Most Valuable Player in the American League in 1939. An article in the popular *Life* magazine that year acknowledged him as the most sensational player in the game, but characterized him as a freak, shy, inarticulate, and a paragon of laziness, who slicked his hair with water rather than olive oil or bear grease, ate chicken chow mein rather than spaghetti, and did not reek of garlic, a measure of his Americanization.[39] DiMaggio's greatness and his humility would eventually win over the American media as he confronted stereotypes. After his 56 consecutive game hitting streak during the 1941 season, the schoolchildren of Cincinnati voted him "the greatest American of all time." During the dire years of the Great Depression and the onset of World War II Americans needed a hero, and many attested to the inspiration provided by DiMaggio.[40] During his 13 years as a Yankee, the team won ten American League pennants and nine World Series, while he garnered three Most Valuable Player awards, but that tenure was interrupted by World War II, which resurrected doubt as to Italian loyalty.

The Impact of World War II

Italians in America had supported Mussolini's imperial ambitions in Africa during the 1930s, as more than 100,000 sent their gold wedding bands and money to Italy to help finance his invasion of Ethiopia.[41] When Mussolini sided with Hitler at the onset of World War II, even DiMaggio came into question. Nativists encouraged him to "go back to Italy with the rest of the coward wops."[42] In the aftermath of the Japanese attack on Pearl Harbor, Italian noncitizens as well as Japanese residing in the United States were declared enemy aliens. Those living along the California coast, including DiMaggio's parents and even those whose sons were serving in the U.S. military, were removed inland as potential threats. The war forced difficult choices on Italians, many of whom had relatives in Italy and were themselves still considered to be Italian citizens. If the Axis powers won the war they would be considered traitors. If they joined the American army they might be sent to fight against their Italian relatives. An estimated half-million Italians joined the U.S. military, many opting for the Marine Corps which meant assignment to the Pacific rather than in Europe. DiMaggio enlisted reluctantly in the Army Air Corps in 1943; he had a wife and child by that time, but volunteering enhanced his status as a patriotic and thankful American.[43] His brief second marriage to the Hollywood goddess, Marilyn Monroe, substantiated the Italian claim to whiteness and a greater measure of acceptance in mainstream American society.

Foreign language broadcasts declined by 40 percent from 1942 to 1948, pushing Italians closer to the mainstream. Having chosen an American identity during the war, many Italians assumed greater trust in American democracy. By 1950, nearly 80 percent of foreign-born Italians had opted for citizenship, greatly accelerating fuller Americanization.[44]

Boxing as a Measure of Whiteness

Rocky Graziano (Thomas Rocco Barbella) took a longer path to acceptance. Dishonorably discharged from the army in World War II after knocking out a captain in an altercation, Graziano spent 10 months in Leavenworth prison. Both he and Jake La Motta had spent considerable time in juvenile reformatories for their criminal offenses, but channeled their street-fighting skills into professional boxing careers during and after the war. Graziano obtained the world middleweight title by 1947, which allowed for social mobility, but not the relinquishment of his Italian culture. Jake La Motta captured the middleweight championship in 1949, but lost it in 1951 in his sixth bout with the great Sugar Ray Robinson. La Motta had been the first to ever defeat Robinson in 1943. Carmen Basilio managed to take the middleweight crown from Robinson in 1957. Graziano, La Motta, and Basilio still exemplified their Italian ancestry in their speech, food, friendships, and physicality, but they carried the torch for whiteness in the face of the rising number of black and Hispanic champions. African Americans had held the heavyweight title, symbolic of boxing and presumably racial superiority, since Joe Louis defeated Jim Braddock in 1937. Rocky Marciano (Marchegiano) represented the "Great White Hope" in a sea of black heavyweights. Louis had knocked out five Italian fighters until Marciano restored Italian pride in a 1951 knockout of his own idol. The next year he dethroned Jersey Joe Walcott for the title, retiring undefeated in 1955. His biographer attributed his ascendance and popularity at least partly to the racial connotations attached to his fights, and Marciano reveled in his ethnic identity. He desired to bring his family back to Italy to meet relatives and the Pope. Italian boxers would continue to challenge blacks and Hispanics throughout the remainder of the century, long after other ethnics had abandoned the ring for middle-class aspirations.[45]

Popular Culture as a Road to Mainstream Acceptance

The rise and acceptance of Italian athletes was accompanied by similar gains by performers within the popular culture. By mid-century Frank Sinatra stood atop the pantheon of musical and screen stars, and "through the power of his art and his personality, he became one of a very small group that would permanently shift the image of Italian Americans."[46] That cultural capital coincided with the athletic prowess of DiMaggio and Marciano, and by the 1960s Green Bay Packers Coach Vince Lombardi also reached iconic status as football surpassed baseball as the American national game. Lombardi preached discipline, work ethic, order, organization, religious devotion, and family values, which coincided with conservative American ideals of mainstream whites during a period of cultural upheaval. Such cultural capital gained by Italians translated into political and economic power. Bart Giamatti, the grandson of an immigrant laborer, served as president of Yale University and then as commissioner of the MLB before his untimely death. He represented a symbol of the Italian odyssey for respect, acceptance, and success within American culture.

A Resurgence of Ethnicity

For some Italians ethnic identity remained an incomplete journey. In the 1980s, third- and fourth-generation Italians experienced a resurgence of ethnic pride. Few could still speak their ancestral tongue, but a Dallas survey revealed that 80 percent still relished Italian foods, and 84 percent remained Catholics. Bocce ball clubs appeared across America and Italian festivals proliferated throughout the nation extolling Italian pride, a phenomenon that continues today and still marks a degree of ethnicity.[47]

Sociologists refer to such a process as segmented assimilation, which produces an amalgamated culture, something less than the full acculturation predicted by the melting pot theorists, and more like a salad bowl in which the ingredients retain their distinctive features while encompassing part of a greater whole. Although many Italian Americans have risen to the pinnacle of the American sports world as owners of professional franchises, critics claim that the continued portrayal of Italians as gangsters in literature, cinema, and art or the glorification of the hedonistic and materialistic guido culture featured on television series still stereotype Italians in a negative image. Although Italian American youth have altered and remade their American Italian identity to meet their own psychic needs, they have retained some of the traditional values of their ancestors.[48]

A large number of Italian American athletes have chosen to represent Italy, their ancestral homeland, on its Olympic teams. Although that phenomenon has much to do with the opportunities presented to athletes, it also gives an indication of a still somewhat conflicted identity. Nine of the 20 players on the 1984 Italian Olympic baseball team were born in America. Since then the numbers have escalated. Thirteen of the players and four of the coaches on the Italian national team in 2009 were American citizens. Identity has even been reversed in the case of Giuseppe Rossi, born in New Jersey, who chose to return to Italy to play for its national soccer team rather than the United States. He was the leading scorer for Italy at the 2008 Olympic Games, but he retains dual citizenship. In that sense the cultural flow of the previous century has now been reversed.[49]

Conclusion

Whereas Italian immigrants traveled to the United States in the late nineteenth century without a national identity of their own, they developed multiple identities in the United States. That transition from the local or regional identity of the homeland to a recognition of themselves as Italians, to a decidedly hyphenated Italian-American and a more thoroughly, but incomplete (for some), American identity in later generations took place in the United States. Al Dinon, born in Philadelphia, learned American sports and played soccer in college before a successful career in the United States as a businessman. Yet he travels to Italy regularly and maintains that it is "the best place in the world."[50]

Despite Italian gains in social, economic, and political capital over more than a century of acculturation, Italian American memorials to their collective past no longer honor Christopher Columbus, or the multitude of national leaders, or military heroes as unifying figures from whom they might choose. Many memorials reflect athletic memories that are ritually recycled with each generation. Sport historians have stated that "Monuments dedicated to sportspeople celebrate moments, events, or deeds that are purported to have cultural significance. In celebrating such deeds monuments tailor the past to satiate the psychic needs of the community." The numerous memorials to Joe DiMaggio erected long after his playing career attest to his continued significance as a bridge across generations. As grandparents and parents relate the meanings of such edifices to their progeny, they will continue to recast their identity and the role of sport with each new interpretation, indicating that the process of identity formation is a continually evolving one.[51]

Notes

1 See www.baseball-reference.com/bullpen/Buttercup_Dickerson; Lawrence Baldassaro, *Beyond DiMaggio: Italian Americans in Baseball* (Lincoln, NE: University of Nebraska Press, 2011), 424 n.3, and Joseph Dorinson, "'Poosh 'Em Up, Tony!': Italian Americans in Baseball," in *Horsehide, Pigskin, Oval Tracks, and Apple Pie: Essays on Sport and American Culture*, ed. James Vlasich (Jefferson, NC: McFarland, 2005), 38–51, on debates regarding the first Italian to play in MLB.

2 Gerald R. Gems, *Sport and the Shaping of Italian-American Identity* (Syracuse, NY: Syracuse University Press, 2013), xii (quote); Benedict Anderson, *Imagined Communities: Reflections on the Origin and Spread of Nationalism* (New York: Verso, 1991 [1983]).

3 Frances M. Malpezzi and William M. Clements, *Italian-American Folklore* (Little Rock, AR: August House, 1992), 33.

4 David A. Richards, *Italian American: The Racializing of an Ethnic Identity* (New York: New York University Press, 1999), 104–112; George A. Dorsey, "Sicilian Immigrant Brings Ideas Strange to America," *Chicago Tribune*, June 2, 1910, 10.

5 Chuck Wills, *Destination America: The People and Cultures That Created a Nation* (New York: DK, 2005), 164.

6 See Gems, *Sport and the Shaping of Italian-American Identity*, 13–17, for life within the Little Italy settlements.

7 Richard D. Alba, *Ethnicity and Race in the U.S.A.: Toward the Twenty-First Century* (New York: Routledge, 1989), 136.

8 Wilson cited in Vincent J. Cannato, *American Passage: The History of Ellis Island* (New York: Harper, 2009), 230–231; see the belated protest in *La Paroli dei Socialisti*, March 23, 1912, Foreign Language Press Survey, at Chicago Historical Museum.

9 The surname is reported variously. See Gems, *Sport and the Shaping of Italian American Identity*, 55–56.

10 *Chicago Tribune*, November 26, 1908, 14; *New York Times*, November 26, 1908, 1, November 28, 1908, 6, December 7, 1908, 7. See Matthew P. Llewellyn, "Viva Italia! Viva Italia! Dorando Pietri and the North American Professional Marathon Craze, 1908–1910," *The International Journal of the History of Sport* 25, no. 6 (2008): 710–736.

11 David E. Martin and Roger W.H. Gynn, *The Olympic Marathon* (Champaign, IL: Human Kinetics, 2000), 94; *Janesville, (WI) Daily Gazette*, August 8, 1912, 3; *Waterloo (IA) Times-Tribune*, July 30, 1912, 2.

12 American Citizen, "Sicilian Immigrants," *New York Times*, May 25, 1909; Robert M. Lombardo, *The Black Hand: Terror by Letter in Chicago* (Urbana, IL: University of Illinois Press, 2010).

13 Lee D. Baker, *From Savage to Negro: Anthropology and the Construction of Race, 1896–1954* (Berkeley: University of California Press, 1998), 73–80, 83; Richard Gambino, *Vendetta: The True Story of the Largest Lynching in U.S. History* (Toronto: Guernica, 1998), 64, 133; James R. Barrett and David Roediger, "Inbetween Peoples: Race, Nationality, and the 'New Immigrant' Working Class," *Journal of American Ethnic History* 16, no. 3 (1997): 3–44; David Roediger, *Working Toward Whiteness: How America's Immigrants Became White; The Strange Journey from Ellis Island to the Suburbs* (New York: Basic Books, 2005), 37–39, 47, 74, 76–7; Richard Gambino, *Blood of My Blood: The Dilemma of Italian-Americans* (Garden City, NY: Anchor Books, 1975), 77; Donna R. Gabaccia, "Race, Nation, Hyphen: Italian-Americans and American Multiculturalism in Comparative Perspective," in *Are Italians White? How Race Is Made in America*, ed. Jennifer Guglielmo and Salvatore Salerno (New York: Routledge, 2003), 44–59; Alexander

De Conde, *Half Bitter, Half Sweet: An Excursion into Italian-American History* (New York: Charles Scribner's Sons, 1971), 91; *Outlook*, November 16, 1907, 556, clipping, Box Immigration Studies Articles, Report of Commissioner-General of Immigration, 1903 folder, Schiavo Papers, Italian American Renaissance Foundation, New Orleans; Patrick J. Gallo, *Old Bread, New Wine: A Portrait of the Italian-Americans* (Chicago: Nelson-Hall, 1981), 118; Jerre Mangione and Ben Morreale, *La Storia: Five Centuries of the Italian American Experience* (New York: Harper Collins, 1992), 212.

14 Pierre Bourdieu, *Outline of a Theory of Practice* (Cambridge: Cambridge University Press, 1977); Salvatore La Gumina, *Wop! A Documentary History of Anti-Italian Discrimination* (Toronto: Guernica, 1999), 221, 328; Di Liberto interview, 21–22, Italians in Chicago Oral History Project, University of Illinois at Chicago, Special Collections; Riha interview, Villa St. Ben Oral History Project, North Central College Archives.

15 Edward Alsworth Ross, *The Old World in the New: The Significance of Past and Present Immigration to the American People* (New York: Century, 1914); Madison Grant, *The Passing of the Great Race: or, the Racial Basis of European History* (New York: Charles Scribner's Sons, 1916, De Conde, *Half Bitter, Half Sweet*, 119.

16 Karen Brodkin, *How Jews Became White Folks: And What That Says About Race in America* (New Brunswick, NJ: Rutgers University Press, 1998), 95.

17 "John Dundee One of the Best Boxers from Sunny Italy's Shores," *Trenton Evening Times*, November 22, 1915, 8.

18 Gems, *Sport and the Shaping of Italian-American Identity*, 22–23.

19 "Not a Single Italian Fighter Has Been a Titleholder," *Washington Post*, October 19, 1913, 53.

20 Gems, *Sport and the Shaping of Italian-American Identity*, 47–49.

21 *L'Italia*, March 18, 1917, Jeffrey E. Mirel, *Patriotic Pluralism: Americanization Education and European Immigrants* (Cambridge, MA: Harvard University Press, 2010). Joseph Salituro, "Italian Americans and Nationalism: A Case of Mixed Loyalties," in *To See the Past More Clearly: The Enrichment of the Italian Heritage, 1890–1990*, ed. Harral E. Landry (Staten Island, NY: American Italian Historical Association, 1994), 256–257 cites a 1916 study of 60,000 to 70,000 returnees to Italy at that time. Mangione and Morreale, *La Storia*, 340, claim that Italians made up 12 percent of U.S. Army personnel. The National Italian American Foundation claims a figure of 300,000 and another 87,000 Italian nationals that joined the U.S. military services.

22 Paul Avrich, *Sacco and Vanzetti: The Anarchist Background* (Princeton, NJ: Princeton University Press, 1991), La Gumina, *Wop!*, 239–242, Nancy C. Carnevale, *A New Language, a New World: Italian Immigrants in the United States, 1890–1945* (Urbana, IL: University of Illinois Press, 2009), 87–91.

23 Baldassaro, *Beyond DiMaggio*, 65–74, Lawrence Baldassaro, "Go East Paesani: Early Italian Major Leaguers from the West Coast," in *Italian Immigrants Go West: The Impact of Locale on Ethnicity*, ed. Janet E. Worall, Carol Bonomo Albright, and Elvira G. Di Fabio (Cambridge, MA: Italian American Historical Assn., 2003), 100–108; *Corriere de America*, December 21, 1933, 7, October 4, 1936, 11.

24 International Boxing Hall of Fame files; Frank J. Cavaioli, "Ray Barbuti," in *The Italian American Experience: An Encyclopedia*, ed. Salvatore J. La Gumina, Frank Cavaioli, Salvatore Primeggia, and Joseph Varacalli (New York: Garland, 2000), 54–55.

25 Gems, *Sport and the Shaping of Italian-American Identity*, 122, 148.

26 Ibid., 80–81, 122.

27 Rob Ruck, Maggie Jones Patterson, and Michael P. Weber, *Rooney: A Sporting Life* (Lincoln, NE: University of Nebraska Press, 2010), 54–55. www.hickoksports.com/biograph/littlelou.shtml

28 John Billi, "U.S. Sports Firmament Is Dotted with Many First Magnitude Stars of Italian Origin;" G. Billi, "Per l'All-Italian, 1937;" *Corriere D'America*, November 1, 1932, 7, November 3, 1932, 7; November 4, 1932, 7; November 5, 1932, 7; November 8, 1932, 7; November 10, 1932, 7, November 11, 1932, 7; November 13, 1932, 13; November 17, 1932, 17, November 22, 1932, 7; November 26, 1932, 7; November 27, 1932, 9; November 29, 1932, 7.

29 https://alumni.stanford.edu/get/page/magazine/article/?article_id=36959 (accessed March 26, 2014).

30 Gems, *Sport and the Shaping of Italian-American Identity*, 221. The number is likely higher due to the use of aliases and incomplete biographical information.

31 Willie Pep with Robert Sachi, *Willie Pep Remembers. . . Friday's Heroes* (New York: Friday's Heroes, 1973), 5.
32 Willie Mosconi and Stanley Cohen, *Willie's Game: An Autobiography* (New York: Macmillan, 1993), 22.
33 "Andy Varipappa: Bowling's Greatest Showman." www.bowl.com/articleView.aspx?i=11475&f=1
34 Stow Persons, *Ethnic Studies at Chicago, 1905–1945* (Urbana, IL: University of Illinois Press, 1987), Patricia Boscia-Mule, *Authentic Ethnicities: The Interaction of Ideology, Gender Power, and Class in the Italian-American Experience* (Westport, CT: Greenwood, 1997); Richard W. Rees, *Shades of Difference: A History of Ethnicity in America* (Lanham, MD: Rowman & Littlefield, 2007), 5–31.
35 On adherence to Italian lifestyles, see Anna Zaloha, "A Study of the Persistence of Italian Customs among 143 Families of Italian Descent Members of Social Clubs at Chicago Commons" (Masters' Thesis, Northwestern University, 1937); William M. De Marco, *Ethnics and Enclaves: Boston's Italian North End* (Ann Arbor, MI: UMI Research Press, 1981), 38; Carnevale, *New Language, New World*, 21–42; 72, 117, 136–156; Stefano Luconi, *From Paesani to White Ethnics: The Italian Experience in Philadelphia* (Albany: State University of New York Press, 2001), 55; Gaetano De Fillipis, "Social Life in an Immigrant Community," Box 130, folder 2, Burgess Papers, University of Chicago, Special Collections; La Gumina, *Wop!*, 249–264, Talese; *Unto the Sons*, 15, 41, 585.
36 Baldassaro, *Beyond DiMaggio*, xi–xii. Younger brother, Dom, also became an all-star for the Boston Red Sox.
37 Gems, *Sport and the Shaping of Italian-American Identity*, 83; Richard Ben Cramer, *Joe DiMaggio: The Hero's Life* (New York: Simon & Schuster, 2000), 44.
38 David Jones, *Joe DiMaggio* (Westport, CT: Greenwood, 2004), 26.
39 Noel F. Busch, "Joe DiMaggio: Baseball's Most Sensational Big League Star Starts What Should Be His Best Year So Far," *Life*, May 1, 1939, 62–69.
40 Jones, *Joe DiMaggio*, 68; see Gems, *Sport and the Shaping of Italian-American Identity*, 133–137, on testimonials.
41 Luconi, *From Paesani to White Ethnics*, 84–94; Stefano Luconi, "Forging an Ethnic Identity: The Case of Italian Americans," Revue Francais d'Etudes Americaines 96 (2003): 1–33; Sebastian Fichera, *Italy on the Pacific: San Francisco's Italian Americans* (New York: Palgrave Macmillan, 2011), 136; Dominic L. Candeloro, *Italians in Chicago* (Chicago: Arcadia, 1999), 71–76; Thomas A. Guglielmo, *White on Arrival: Italians, Race, Color, and Power in Chicago, 1890–1945* (New York: Oxford, 2003), 45–58, 113–125.
42 Cramer, *Joe DiMaggio*, 202.
43 Gems, *Sport and the Shaping of Italian-American Identity*, 144–149.
44 Carnevale, *New Language, New World*, 139, 151–152; Mirel, *Patriotic Pluralism*, 138.
45 Gems, *Sport and the Shaping of Italian-American Identity*, 152–166; Arch Ward, "In the Wake of the News," *Chicago Tribune*, September 25, 1953, pt. 4:2; Russell Sullivan, *Rocky Marciano: The Rock of His Times* (Urbana, IL: University of Illinois Press, 2002), 86–95, 115–130.
46 Pete Hamill, *Why Sinatra Matters* (Boston: Little, Brown 1998), 37.
47 Marcelo M. Saurez-Orozco, "Everything You Ever Wanted to Know About Assimilation But Were Afraid to Ask," in *Life in America: Identity and Everyday Experience*, ed. Lee D. Baker (Malden, MA: Blackwell, 2004), 45–62; Valentine J. Belfiglio, "Cultural Traits of Italian Americans Which Transcend Generational Differences," in *The Italian Americans Through the Generations*, ed. Rocco Caporale (New York: American Italian Historical Association, 1986), 126–142; Rudolph J. Vecoli, *Italian Immigrants in Rural and Small Town America* (New York: Italian Historical Association, 1987), 132, 188; Mary Elaine Lora, "The Roman Bowl," *Dixie*, August 30, 1978), 24, 33, 36; Anthony La Ruffa, *Monte Carmelo: An Italian-American Community in the Bronx* (New York: Gordon and Breach, 1988), 72, 83, 108; Luconi, *From Paesani to White Ethnics*, 138–139; A.V. Margavio and Jerome J. Salomone, *Bread and Respect: The Italians of Louisiana* (Gretna, LA: Pelican, 2002), 242.
48 Gems, *Sport and the Shaping of Italian-American Identity*, 210–214.
49 Josh Chetwynd, *Baseball in Europe* (Jefferson, NC: McFarland, 2008), 54, 56; Gems, *Sport and the Shaping of Italian American Identity*, 202–206.

50 Dinon interview, May 5, 2009, Villa St. Ben Oral History Project, in North Central College Archives.

51 Gems, *Sport and the Shaping of Italian-American Identity*, 196–217; David Paul Nord, "The Uses of Memory: An Introduction," *Journal of American History* 85, no. 2 (1998): 409–410, Murray G. Phillips, Mark E. O'Neill, and Gary Osmond, "Broadening Horizons in Sport History. Films, Photographs, and Monuments," *Journal of Sport History* 34, no. 2 (2007): 271–293, 285 (quote).

14

JEWS AND AMERICAN SPORTS

Steven A. Riess

Introduction

Jews have fared well in the United States, producing about one-third of American Nobel Prize winners and laureates and amassing a median household net worth 4.5 times the national average. One area where they purportedly did not succeed was in sports. This chapter argues that Jewish participation in sports, connected mainly to socioeconomic factors, surpassed their 2 percent of the national population. The population of Jews in the United States ranged from 1.97 in 1900 to 2.2 percent today.[1]

Jews were a small minority in antebellum America. The first notable Jewish athletes were boxers from London's impoverished West End. Pugilism was a major English sport in late eighteenth- and early nineteenth-century England, highlighted by boxing champion Daniel Mendoza (1792–1795). Many outstanding boxers migrated to the United States at mid-century, including Young Barney Aaron, the American lightweight champion in 1857.

The German Jewish Experience in the Nineteenth Century

The Jewish population in the United States rose from about 50,000 in 1850 to 240,000 in 1880 with the migration of German-speaking Jews who came mainly for economic opportunities. These emancipated Ashkenazi Jews were literate; mainly settled in cities; and often became artisans, shopkeepers and merchants. They believed, like other Germans, that to be German meant being physically active, and by 1821, Jews belonged to the Hamburg turner society in Germany. Jewish immigrants joined turner societies in the United States that promoted German culture, political activism, gymnastics, support for working-class issues, and the promotion of physical education. In the late 1860s there were Jewish presidents in Chicago and Milwaukee turner societies. Printer and journalist Philo Jacoby was the most prominent immigrant athlete, who won the Berlin Shooting Championship in 1868, making him one of the first American international sports title holders.[2]

German Jews and American Sports Clubs

Membership in voluntary sports clubs reflected personal interests and social class. The highest status clubs participated in expensive sports and strictly limited membership by blacklisting undesirable applicants. A few rich Jews belonged to thoroughbred racing clubs, including Ben Cohen, treasurer of the Maryland Jockey Clubs in the 1830s. New York's prestigious American Jockey Club had at least six Jewish members when founded in 1865, including president August Belmont, an immigrant from Alzey, Germany. The financier had no interest in Jewish commercial affairs, married outside the faith, and was disowned by the Jewish community. Jacob Pincus, who worked for Belmont, was the top trainer in 1869. Belmont's Nursery Stud produced the top money winners in 1889 and 1890. Other leading horsemen were Cincinnati yeast manufacturer Charles Fleischmann, and Julius C. Cahn, whose Typhoon II won the 1897 Kentucky Derby.[3]

Jews also made important contributions to track and field. Daniel Stern was one of four founders of the New York Athletic Club. He won the first American amateur walking championship in 1876, but in the 1880s anti-Semitism became a notable factor in the sport. The NYAC eventually barred Jews, a custom that continued for nearly 100 years. Such prejudice caused well-to-do young Jews, including Bernard Baruch, to form their own sports clubs, like New York's City Athletic Club in New York, founded in 1906.

The preeminent American track star was Lon Meyers, son of a Richmond, Virginia clerk, whose family came to New York in the seventeenth century. Meyers held every national record from 50 yards to the mile, set 11 world records, and won 15 American championships. In 1884, the National Amateur Athletic Association of America (NAAAA) investigated his amateur status because he was paid by the Manhattan Athletic Club as their secretary. The NAAAA accepted his amateur status, but in 1888 the Amateur Athletic Union was established to tighten amateur rules. By that time, Myers had become an overtly professional runner.[4]

The Young Men's Hebrew Association

The Young Men's Hebrew Association (YMHA) was the premier Jewish athletic organization, a counterpart to the YMCA. The YMHA was founded in 1854, mainly by reform Jews for middle-class young men to enjoy uplifting rational recreations. There were over 20 Y's by the mid-1870s, including New York's outstanding 92nd Street YMHA established in 1874, which added a gymnasium three years later. Twenty cities in the 1890s had YMHA gymnasiums with swimming pools and trained physical educators, intended to make members healthier and better Jews. Women's programs were introduced at the Philadelphia Y in 1874, and by the 1880s facilities were often made available for women, who became auxiliary members of the YMHA before Young Women's Hebrew Associations became formed in the early twentieth century. Societies then also offered night classes to help Eastern Europe newcomers assimilate. The 100 YMHAs in 1900 had 20,000 members. They promoted "muscular Judaism," Dr. Max Nordau's concept to destroy negative stereotypes by creating manly Jews with the mental and physical capabilities to promote Zionism.[5]

Football and Baseball in the Late Nineteenth Century

Football and baseball attracted few Jews. Among the handful of Jews in early college football was Lucious Littauer, son of a wealthy glove manufacturer, who played at Harvard (1875, 1877) and served as its first coach. Phil King, a four-year All American Princeton quarterback and halfback (1890–1893), later coached at Princeton and the University of Wisconsin.

Only six Jews played major league baseball in the nineteenth century. Lip Pike, son of a Dutch haberdasher, learned to play baseball in Brooklyn and was one of the first paid players in the late 1860s. Pike joined the Troy Haymakers of the National Association of Professional Baseball Players in 1871, the first professional league, as a player/manager, and led the league in home runs three straight years. In 1876 he played in the new National League with the St. Louis Brown Stockings, and the Cincinnati Reds in 1877, leading the league in home runs, while also managing.[6]

Jews achieved considerable success in the business of baseball, which reflected the strong entrepreneurial tradition the immigrant generation brought to the United States. Like the Jews who went into the early movie industry, Jews invested in baseball franchises at a time when they were lower-status businesses that did not appeal to men of old wealth who preferred more prestigious and less risky options. Early Jewish owners also saw ownership as a means to show their civic-mindedness and gain acceptance in the community. Cincinnati major league teams had four Jewish owners, including clothier Aaron Stern, who owned the Red Stockings of the American Association (1882; 1886–1890), and Julius Fleischmann of the Cincinnati Reds (NL) (1902–1915). Tammanyite Andrew Freedman, a realtor, owned the New York Giants (1895–1902), but he was the most hated owner of his day, fighting with fans, players, umpires, and sportswriters. Barney Dreyfuss migrated from Germany to Louisville where he worked for relatives who manufactured bourbon. In 1889 he became a partner in the Louisville Colonels of the American Association, which joined the 12-team National League (NL) in 1892. When the NL contracted after the 1899 season, and Louisville lost its franchise, Barney bought the Pittsburgh Pirates, which he owned until his death in 1932.[7]

Nineteenth-century Jewish entrepreneurs looked to sports as an opportunity to make money by breaking into a new, undeveloped enterprise and to demonstrate civic pride and gain status. The first notable Jewish sports entrepreneur was John M. Brunswick, a Swiss teenager who came to the United States in 1834 to become a carpenter. In 1845 he designed the billiard table that became the standard in the industry and made his fortune in what became the Brunswick Billiard Manufacturing Company.[8]

The Eastern European Jew and American Sport in the Early 1900s

Jewish American life changed dramatically in the late nineteenth century with the migration of about 2 million eastern European Jews. These Orthodox Yiddish speakers came from a premodern world with limited skills. They encountered a lot of prejudice, mainly settling in impoverished inner-city neighborhoods in New York and Chicago where they tried to recreate their Old World culture. They had no familiarity with sports, which they considered a waste of time, if not immoral, and pulled sons away from the community.[9]

Inner-City Sports

Second-generation youth first learned the pleasures of sports on the street where they played stoopball, punch ball, and stickball. They had limited opportunities to gain proficiency in sports like baseball, which needed a lot of open space, and were more successful at inexpensive and accessible sports like basketball, billiards, boxing, and track. They believed in the dominant sport ideology that depicted athletics as meritocratic and democratic, and expected that achievement would secure them recognition and acceptance, proof of their manliness, respect for the ethnic group from the broader society, and possibly social mobility.

Settlement houses in tough inner-city neighborhoods were important places for boys and girls to first learn sports. Boys' workers promoted organized sports programs to draw local youths into their institutions where they could teach them good American values like teamwork, improve their fitness, and disprove negative stereotypes about Jewish manliness.

German Jews were heavily involved in establishing facilities like New York's Educational Alliance (1889) and the Henry Street Settlement (1893) to help fellow Jewish immigrants adjust to American life, even though they were uncomfortable with their Old World behavior and Orthodox religious beliefs. By 1910 there were at least 75 Jewish settlements and community centers and another 50 that mainly catered to a Jewish clientele, which usually had a gymnasium and education programs. The Educational Alliance pioneered in promoting physical training and sport for girls, and by 1895 engaged instructors for females as well as males to promote fitness and Americanization. The reformers also supported the park movement as a way to provide children access to fresh air and space to play, although that space often became the scene of ethnic turf wars. Girls participated in sport at such settlements like Chicago's Hull House, the Chicago Hebrew Institute, and Pittsburgh's Irene Kaufmann Settlement.[10]

Urban Jewish youth also turned to YMHAs and YWHAs, which in the 1900s began devoting more attention to second-generation Russian Jews. The Y's began merging in 1917 with the newly established Jewish Community Centers (JCC) that promoted religious and cultural programs, including sports, under the aegis of the National Jewish Welfare Board. Some 350 JCCs currently exist in North America.[11]

Immigrant parents opposed sports for their daughters as unfeminine, but such views were contested by daughters who exercised and played basketball at settlement houses and YWHAs, which considered the physical training of Jewish females an important part of their mission. These programs emphasized gymnastics, exercise, basketball, and swimming, advocating a play spirit rather than competitiveness. Some American Jewish young women, however, desired to compete in appropriate sports for women. In basketball, women used rules adapted by Lithuanian immigrant Senda Berenson, a director of physical education at Smith College in 1892, to fit the prevailing stereotypes of women's limited physicality. Charlotte Epstein is considered to be the mother of American women's swimming, a sport that promoted femininity as well as competition. She founded the Women's Swimming Association of New York in 1917 that produced many future Olympic champions.[12]

Boxing

Jews first gained national recognition in boxing, an inner-city sport that required little space or equipment and fit well with the lifestyles of slum youth, though it was detested by parents as inappropriate for good Jewish boys. Boxing was useful to master at a settlement house or boxing gym because Jewish boys were often attacked by Irish, Polish, or Italian boys and needed to defend themselves or their pals. Tough Jews who stood up for fellow Jews became neighborhood heroes. Boxing icons at the turn of the century included featherweight Joe Bernstein, "the pride of the ghetto" and especially heavyweight Joe Choynski, who fought four future champions, including Gentleman Jim Corbett. Choynski did not fit the model of the Jewish fighter because his father, a German-speaking Polish immigrant, was a Yale graduate and prominent San Francisco journalist.

Early Jewish boxers were generally small in stature and started out in amateur matches at stags or local boxing gyms for prizes or badges convertible into cash. Top amateurs became professionals who could make money, gain fame, and date beautiful women. The first Jewish world champion was Chicago bantamweight Harry Harris, the "Human Hairpin," in 1901. Abe Attell of San Francisco, an all-time great featherweight who gained universal recognition as champion in 1906, defended his crown 21 times until losing in 1912. The "Little

Champion" earned about $100,000 during a career marred by crooked bouts. In the 1910s there were four Jewish world champions, most notably lightweight Benny Leonard, perhaps the greatest ring general of all time, who won 69 of 70 lightweight fights while champion (1917–1925) Like many Jewish fighters, he fought under a pseudonym in an effort to hide his identity from his parents and the general public. Benny was a great attraction, whose 1923 defense of his lightweight title at Yankee Stadium drew nearly 60,000 spectators. Leonard was seen in the Jewish American media as a hero who fought anti-Semitism and negative Jewish stereotypes.[13]

Track and Field

Track was a third sport that fit inner-city requirements. Boys in the early 1900s participated in running contests at settlement houses, YMHAs, and public school associations, especially New York's Public Schools' Athletic League (PSAL) established in 1903. The Yiddish press praised the PSAL for giving boys a chance to compete, improve their health, and gain the respect of the broader community.

A few Jewish track stars achieved international renown, most notably Myer Prinstein, world record holder in the long jump, who won four gold medals and one silver medal in the long and triple jumps in the 1900, 1904, and 1906 Olympic Games. (He was hired by Germany to coach their 1916 Olympic team, which never took place due to World War I.) Abel Kiviat, 1,500-meter world record holder, and Alvah Meyer both captured silver, respectively, in the 1,500-meter and 100-meter in 1912. They all competed for the Irish-American A.C. because more prestigious clubs barred Jews.

The National Pastime and the Inner City

The absence of Jews from working-class sport was most evident in baseball—a sport described by an immigrant letter writer in 1903 as "a crazy game," dangerous, and purposeless. Abraham Cahan of the Yiddish *Forward* recommended forbearance: "Let us not so raise the children that they should grow up foreigners in their own birthplace." Four years later it printed an article in Yiddish, translated as "The Fundamentals of Baseball Explained to Those Unfamiliar with Sports"[14]

Jewish boys in the early 1900s seldom played highly organized baseball because of insufficient space for diamonds and fields to develop their skills. They did become ardent fans who read and talked about their heroes, but rarely attended games because of the cost and inaccessibility. There were only 5 Jews in the major leagues in the 1900s and 13 in the 1910s. These pioneers encountered a great deal of discrimination from teammates, owners, fans, and even the media. Some Jewish players protected themselves against anti-Semitism by changing their names. The first five major leaguers whose surname was Cohen all played under pseudonyms.

Jewish Sport in the Interwar Years

Opportunities to participate in sport increased after World War I, as assimilated second-generation Russian Jews benefited from the improved standard of living with shorter working hours and more discretionary time, increased attendance at high schools, and new sports programs for the working class sponsored by corporate welfare capitalism programs and unions like the International Ladies Garment Workers Union that tried to improve the quality of life of members by promoting summer outings and athletic competitions. During the Depression, men and women also benefited from New Deal programs which built parks, athletic fields, beaches, and swimming pools.

The growing number of Jews in high schools provided opportunities to participate in sport. Historian Paula Fass found that in the 1930s and 1940s, when Jews comprised 44.9 percent of male students in New York City high schools, they made up 41.3 percent of track athletes and 51.5 percent of basketball players, but just 37.8 percent of football players, including quarterback Sid Luckman of Erasmus Hall, an All-American in 1938 at Columbia University, which reflected parental opposition to the game and their physical stature. Jewish girls, who constituted 44.8 percent of a similar cohort of female high school students, were underrepresented in basketball at just 33.7 percent, of the basketball players, but made up 45.3 percent of the players in other sports.[15]

Boxing in the Interwar Years

There were 11 Jewish boxing champions in the 1920s and 11 in the 1930s, and their Jewish fans were legion. The most imposing was heavyweight champion Max Baer (1934–1935), who had 52 knockouts, and killed two men in the ring. Baer was not widely accepted as Jewish then because he had a gentile mother and did not observe the faith. However, he identified ethnically as Jewish, and in his 1933 fight with Germany's Max Schmeling, he wore a Star of David on his trunks. The biggest Jewish boxing hero in the decade was welterweight Barney Ross, an Orthodox Jew and Zionist. The first pugilist to simultaneously hold three world championships, Ross was a product of Chicago's impoverished Near West Side. He had a record of 74–4–3 and was never knocked down.[16]

Jews also achieved enormous prominence in all aspects of the sport. Top referees including Ruby Goldstein, who refereed 39 championship fights, and Davey Miller, who adjudicated about 5,000 pro bouts. They were extremely important as trainers, particularly Ray Arcel, who trained 22 champions. Prominent managers included Al Weill, who worked with Rocky Marciano, and Joe "Yussel the Muscle" Jacobs, who handled Max Schmeling despite Nazi bans on Jewish managers. There were over 20 Jewish boxing promoters by the 1930s, most notably Mike Jacobs, who sponsored 61 world championship bouts from 1937 to 1947. The premier manufacturer of boxing equipment was tailor Jacob Golomb who created the Everlast Company in 1910.[17]

Basketball

Jews were a dominant force in basketball at all levels, from B'nai B'rith boys youth leagues, which featured Jewish and non-Jewish quintets to high school, college, and professional competition. Basketball became a favorite of the Jewish press because it required toughness, agility, and sharp thinking. Women, too, played basketball in Hebrew Athletic Leagues and in JCC leagues and played against YMCA teams for this popular sport.[18]

By the 1910s and 1920s, a disproportionate number of star high school players in cities with large Jewish populations were Jewish. They were recruited by colleges across the nation into the mid-1960s. In New York City, the mecca of college basketball until the early 1950s, New York University, Long Island University, and St. John's all had at least seven Jewish All Americans, and CCNY had nine.

Jews were very visible in the early eastern professional leagues. In the 1920s, Barney Sedran in the 1920s made $12,000 in one season when most players got under $75 a game. These teams barnstormed frequently, and Jewish players encountered considerable prejudice, including signs in gyms like "Kill the Christ-Killers." One of the top teams in the late 1920s was the SPHAs (South Philadelphia Hebrew All-Stars) who won six American Basketball League championships in 13 seasons. Young Jewish couples went to their games, which would be followed by a dance. As late as 1945–1946, the ABA's rosters were nearly 45 percent Jewish, though thereafter, the Jewish prominence in pro basketball declined sharply.[19]

Football

Middle-class Jewish periodicals followed the exploits of Jewish collegian athletes in individual and team sports, proud of both their athletic and scholarly accomplishments that countered negative stereotypes and provided greater acceptance in the broader society. Historian Dan Oren claims that the first Jewish athletes at the most selective colleges like Yale were most visible in individualistic sports. Jewish football players were far more visible than in the past, and in 1929, over 500 played intercollegiate football. The first nationally known Jewish star was Benny Friedman, son of a Russian immigrant tailor, All-American quarterback at Michigan in 1926, and future pro star. In 1936, 25 Jews played in the National Football League (NFL), and by 1950, 111 had played in the NFL. Just 40 appeared in the next 40 years. Jews remain highly underrepresented in pro football, with only nine in the NFL in 2014.[20]

Second-Generation Jews Make Their Mark in the Major Leagues

Jewish names were still rare in MLB, and there was a lot of anti-Semitism in the game, but their representation rose considerably, with 14 in the 1920s 24 in the 1930s (12 in 1936 alone), and 22 in the 1940s. One-third were New Yorkers at a time when 42.6 percent of American Jews lived in the metropolis, in localities where they were more assimilated. The Dodgers and Giants actively sought Jewish players to bolster interest with Jewish fans. Second baseman Andy Cohen was brought up by the Giants for a "cup of coffee" in 1926 as a ghetto kid making good, although he was actually from Waco, Texas. Then in 1928, he came back full time to replace future Hall of Famer Rogers Hornsby, but did not measure up.[21]

Hank Greenberg of the Detroit Tigers was the preeminent Jewish athlete in the first half century. At 6' 4," 215 pounds, the Bronx boy did not fit the effete Jewish stereotype. He batted .313 during his career, set an American League record for RBIs with 183 in 1937, 58 homers in 1938, and had the sixth highest slugging percentage of all time. He led the Tigers to four pennants and two world championships. In 1934, Greenberg played on Rosh Hashanah, the Jewish New Year, stroking two home runs to win the game 2–1. However, he did not play on Yom Kippur, the Day of Atonement, instead going to synagogue, for which he was widely praised. Greenberg fought anti-Semitism on the diamond and served longer in the military than any major leaguer during World War II, which further enhanced his stature and popularity.

The number of Jewish owners in MLB rose in the 1920s. Besides Dreyfuss, there was Judge Emil Fuchs of the Boston Braves (1923–1936), Sydney Weil in Cincinnati (1929–1933), and advertising giant Albert D. Lasker, a principal owner of the Cubs (1917–1925). He was the person primarily responsible for the creation of the commissioner system. However, as team ownership became more prestigious, Jewish presence among owners declined. The only Jewish owner from 1936–1946, was Deyfuss's son-in-law, William Benswanger. There were no Jewish owners in the American League from 1901 when Sydney Frank owned the Baltimore Orioles, until Greenberg became a minority partner and general manager of the Cleveland Indians in 1949.[22]

Anti-Semitism popped up in the press following the Black Sox scandal. *Sporting News* noted that, "There are no lengths to which the crop of lean-faced and long-nosed gamblers of these degenerate days will go." Henry Ford, a notorious anti-Semite, blamed the scandal on underworld Jews through his mouthpiece, the Dearborn *Independent* which published two articles in September 1921 entitled "Jewish Gamblers Corrupt American Baseball" and "The Jewish Degradation of American Baseball." He saw the scandal as evidence of how Jews were destroying the inner fabric of American society. In *The Great Gatsby* (1925) F. Scott Fitzgerald gave voice to the conventional wisdom that the notorious Arnold Rothstein had orchestrated the fix. Although not true, Rothstein did help finance it.[23]

Handball, Table Tennis, and Weight Lifting

Handball was dominated in this era by working-class Jewish New Yorkers, where playing surfaces and walls were very accessible in parks and beaches. Victor Hershkowitz, a New York fireman won 40 national and international titles in the 1940s and 1950s. The greatest player in history was probably Jimmy Jacobs, an all-around athlete from Los Angeles who went undefeated from 1955 through 1969.[24]

European Jews dominated table tennis from the 1920s until the 1950s, and Jews were the finest players in the United States. New Yorker Marcus Schussheim, who learned to play in the East Side Boys Club, won the first national championship in 1930, when 7 Jews finished in the top 20, and he repeated this one year later. Dick Miles dominated after World War II, taking 10 national championships between 1945 and 1962, followed by Marty Reisman, a renowned hustler, who won the 1958 and 1960 singles titles and the 1997 U.S. hard bat championship when he was 67. The top woman was Leslie Thall-Neuberger, number three in the world in 1951, who won 29 national championships.

Jews also had success in weightlifting, a heavily ethnic and working-class sport. In 1948, middleweight Frank Spellman, a machinist, won Olympic gold. Isaac Berger, a featherweight, held 23 world records and won a gold and two silver medals (1956–1964).

Upper Middle Class and Elite Sports: The Country Club

The country club, modeled after the English gentry lifestyle, emerged in the late nineteenth century and typically barred Jews from tournaments and membership. Elaine Rosenthal Reinhart was a three-time winner of the Western Open (1917–1918, 1925), but Jewish women were often barred from tournaments. Wealthy Jews, who wanted to play golf or tennis, or just socialize, organized their own suburban resorts. In 1910, elite German Jews in Chicago opened the Lake Shore Country Club with such members as President Julius Rosenwald of Sears, Roebuck, shoe manufacturer Leonard Florsheim, and Modie Spiegel of the eponymous catalogue company. Jewish clubs separated German Jews from eastern European Jews who founded their own facilities like Los Angeles' Hillcrest Country Club in 1920, where self-made immigrants who became Hollywood moguls, movie stars, and other entertainers could relax and enjoy the tumult of *landsman* and *yiddishkeit* at their clubs.[25]

Thoroughbred Racing

Despite the prejudice among elite horsemen, upwardly mobile Jewish immigrants played a significant role in horse racing. Chicagoan John D. Hertz, a self-made man who established the Yellow Cab Company in 1915 and Hertz-Rent-A-Car in 1923, and his wife raced horses. In 1928 her Reigh Count won the Kentucky Derby, and his Count Fleet captured the Triple Crown in 1943. Jews became even more prominent after World War II, notably second-generation entrepreneur Louis Wolfson, whose Affirmed won the Triple Crown in 1978. Yet Jews were barred from the prestigious Jockey Club, formed in 1894 to supervise American thoroughbred racing, until 1951 when Harry F. Guggenheim, of the ore smelting family, was elected.[26]

Wealthy Jews were also very active in establishing and managing racetracks. Hertz's syndicate bought the two-year old Arlington Park in 1929 to keep it out of the hands of the underworld. Hollywood Jews, unwelcomed at Santa Anita's turf club, established Hollywood Park, led by movie mogul Harry M. Warner and director/producer Mervyn LeRoy. On the other hand, Arnold Rothstein was involved in Maryland's Havre de Grace Racetrack, and underworld kingpin Meyer Lansky invested in Florida's Tropical Park and Gulfstream Park.[27]

Working-class Jews were also heavily involved in racing as jockeys, trainers, bookmakers, and gamblers. Trainer Hirsch Jacobs won $15,340,534 and 3,596 races, at one time the most in history. Two of the top American jockeys were Walter Miller, who at 16 in 1906 won 388 races, a rational record, unmatched until 1950. Walter Blum, national champion in 1963 and 1964, rode 4,382 winners in 22 years.[28]

Dr. Robert Underwood, a veterinarian, was the "founding father of American bookies." He first sold auction pools in New Orleans in 1855. Bookmaking was originally dominated by Irishmen, but Sol Lichtenstein, Abe Levy, and Kid Weller were prominent at the turn of the century, and later Rothstein laid off bets for smaller bookies. In the interwar years, off-track betting became an important venue for Jewish crime syndicates. Max "Boo Hoo" Hoff of South Philadelphia started off as a bookie before becoming a bootlegger, and Meyer Lansky was one of the leading gambling entrepreneurs in the United States. They got their information from Moses Annenberg who ran the racing wire from 1927 to 1940 and published the *Racing Form* and the *Morning Telegraph*, racing's papers of record.[29]

Working-class Jews were active bettors on and off the tracks where they frequented neighborhood Jewish bookies who gave credit and were more accessible than the race courses. They saw betting as the poor man's version of the stock market. After World War II middle-class Jews went to the races and bet more heavily than their peers.

The 1936 Olympics

American Jews earned 11 Olympic gold medals before 1936, including 5 in track and 3 in boxing. Irving Jaffee's two gold medals in speed skating at the 1932 Winter Olympics in Lake Placid, New York, was an important breakthrough because Jews were underrepresented in winter sports because of geographic and class reasons. There was also a lot of anti-Semitism in small resort towns like Lake Placid, where Jews were often barred from the premises.[30]

A broad-based movement began in 1933 to boycott the 1936 Summer Games in Berlin to protest Nazi discrimination, encompassing Jews, Catholics, the AFL, the AAU, and such liberal magazines and newspapers as the *Christian Century* and the *New York Times.* A Gallup

Poll reported that 43 percent of the American people supported the proposed ban. However, the movement was defeated by the anti-Semitic Avery Brundage.[31]

Several Jewish athletes from around the world boycotted the Games, including Americans Lillian Copeland, who won silver in the 1928 Olympics and gold in the 1932 Olympics in the javelin, and Sybil Koff, who qualified in the broad and high jump events. Swimmers like Janice Lifson and American Olympic coach Charlotte Epstein boycotted the Nazi Olympics, too. However, one Jewish American participated in the winter games at Garmisch-Partenkirchen, and six at the summer games in Berlin. Marty Glickman and Sam Stoller, scheduled to run the 400-meter relay, were dropped at the last minute, and replaced by African Americans Jesse Owens and Ralph Metcalfe. Glickman believed that anti-Semitism was the root cause.[32]

The Jewish American Sporting Experience Since 1945

Jewish participation in sport has dramatically changed, most markedly in the near total absence of boxers and the sharp drop in basketball players. There has been an increased presence in individual sports, including tennis, swimming, fencing, and gymnastics. These developments were the product of Jewish economic success, the accompanying migration to suburbia, and structural assimilation among third-generation Jewish Americans. The need for Jewish athletic heroes to prove Jewish prowess or fight anti-Semitism ended by the 1960s. Orthodox Jewish participation remains largely limited to recreational participation, more because of time constraints in high school than theological reasons except for the ultra-orthodox, like the residents of the town of Kiryas Joel, a village in Orange County, New York, primarily Satmar Hasids, who frown on any physical culture as a distraction from piety.[33]

Boxing in the Post-1945 Years

Jewish American fighters virtually disappeared after World War II because they found other, safer opportunities to get ahead. The next Jewish American champion was light heavyweight Mike Rossman (1978–1979), who had an Italian father and a Jewish mother, followed by Jewish-reared African Americans Saoul Mamby, the WBC junior welterweight champion (1980–1982), and Zab Judah, who held five titles (2000–2007). Jews continued to be prominent as coaches, trainers and managers. One of the top promoters, especially since the 1980s, was Bob Arum.

Elite Sport

Jews did not have a lot of success in golf. Amy Alcott won 33 tournaments, and is a member of the World Golf Hall of Fame. However, they enjoyed considerable success in tennis with Dick Savitt, Vic Seixis, Brad Gilbert, Brian Gottfried, and Julie Heldman. Gladys Medalie Heldman edited and published of *World Tennis Magazine* (est. 1953) and founded the Virginia Slims professional tour in 1971.

Olympic Sport

Central European Jews had a rich gymnastics tradition, but American Jews lagged well behind. The first Jewish American Olympic medalists were George Gulack (gold in flying rings) and Phil Erenberg (silver in clubs) at the 1932 Games, but the next was not until the achievements of Mitch Gaylord in 1980, with four medals (including gold in team competition). Kerri Strug took gold in team gymnastics in 1996, and Aly Raisman captured three medals in 2012, including two gold. Central European Jews were a dominant force for years in fencing, with 13 gold medals by 1912. The United States had little success in fencing. The first Jewish American medalist was Albert Axelrod's bronze in foil in 1964. American Jews have recently become a major force in saber, led by Sada Jacobson with three medals in 2004 and 2008 and Tim Morrison's silver in 2008. Jews have also done very well in figure skating and ice dancing, with five medals since 2002, including gold by Sarah Hughes in 2002.[34]

Jews have been extremely successful in swimming with 35 Olympic medals since 1972. Mark Spitz won 11 medals, including 7 gold in 1972 at the tragic Munich Olympics, scene of the Palestinian terrorist attack on the Israeli athletes. Lennie Krayzelburg captured four gold medals, including three in 2000, and Jason Lezak captured a total of seven medals, including four gold in three Olympics. Dana Torres swam in five Olympics, and won 12 medals, including 4 gold.

Basketball

The basketball decline has been sharp. There were 42 Jewish players in the NBA through 1965, but few since, including currently just one Jewish American. The best Jewish player in the NBA was Dolph Schayes, a 12-year all-star, who established records for most games, points, rebounds, and consecutive games (764). This reflects the post–World War II migration of Jewish families out of inner cities, where athletes historically developed the level of skills required for the NBA, to suburbia where sons had other options for success.

The most outstanding Jewish women's basketball players in the 1972 post–Title IX era were Nancy Lieberman, a three-time All American at Old Dominion University (1978–1980), and pioneer pro basketball player Sue Bird, whose Connecticut team went 114–4 during her years at the school. She has been an eight-time WNBA All-Star and won three Olympic and three FIBA (Federation of International Basketball Associations) gold medals.

Jews were also associated with the seamier side of basketball. Leo Hirshfield in the 1940s set the betting line based on the point spread that helped popularize gambling on basketball. This led to the college betting scandals of 1951 when many of the gamblers involved were Jewish, as were 8 of the 15 New York City collegians convicted of taking bribes. Jack Molinas, a Jewish All-American at Columbia and former NBA player, orchestrated a second national scandal which occurred a decade later.[35]

The historic Jewish prominence in basketball continued off the court, to include referees like Mendy Rudolph and Norm Drucker, and coaches Red Auerbach, Red Holzman, and Larry Brown. Jews were prominent as team owners since the early 1900s, starting with Frank Basloe, a basketball promoter in the early 1900s, and Abe Saperstein, who managed the Harlem Globetrotters in 1927. Many of the first NBA owners were Jewish, including Ben Kerner (St. Louis Hawks), Max Winter (Minneapolis Lakers), Eddie Gottlieb (Philadelphia Warriors), and Walter Harrison (Rochester Royals).[36] Currently, 13 of the 30 NBA teams have Jewish owners, more than any other sport. The three Jewish NBA commissioners were Maurice Podoloff (1949–1963), David Stern (1984–2014), and Larry Silver (2014–).[37]

Changing Patterns in Major League Baseball

There were 20 Jews in MLB in the 1950s and 23 in the 1960s, when Sandy Koufax was the preeminent pitcher. He won three Cy Young Awards (1963, 1965–1966) and led the MLB in ERA, wins, and strikeouts. He retired prematurely in 1966 because of traumatic arthritis in his elbow, with a record of 165–87, and an ERA of 2.76. Koufax was a hero to Jews because of his on-field accomplishments and decision not to pitch Game 1 of the 1965 World Series because it fell on Yom Kippur. He was the last Jewish athlete who was an ethnic hero. The number of Jewish players declined to just 9 in the 1980s, but picked up thereafter. In 2014, there were 15 players in MLB, often sons of intermarriage. The increased numbers reflect the attractiveness of multimillion dollar salaries to Jewish youth living in suburban California and Florida where they can play year-round.[38]

The Business of Sport

A large number of Jews own and operate sports franchises. The Jewish presence in baseball reached its nadir with no majority owners in 1946, following Benswanger's sale of the Pittsburgh Pirates. Hank Greenberg was a minority owner of Bill Veeck's Cleveland Indians in 1949, but encountered significant anti-Semitism from the other owners. The first team to have majority Jewish control was the Baltimore Orioles under Jerry Hoffberger in 1954. Currently, 8 of 30 MLB teams are Jewish owned.[39]

There were no Jewish owners in the NFL until 1940, when Fred Levy, Jr., became co-owner of the Cleveland Rams and Fred Mandel, Jr., took over the Detroit Lions. The formation of the rival All-America Football Conference in 1946 provided new opportunities for Jewish investors, notably Benjamin Lindheimer, who owned the Los Angeles franchise and was league commissioner. Currently, 9 of 32 NFL franchises have Jewish owners.[40]

A recent study of 60 senior executives in major sports leagues, talent agencies, and media outlets found that 43 were Jews (72 percent), reflecting declining anti-Semitism in the business world. Because Jews are about 2 percent of the national population, Jews are overrepresented by about 3600 percent.[41]

Sport Communication

The fascination of American Jews with sports in postwar America was indicated by their eminence in sports communications, including sports writing, radio and television, and literature. Writing on sports was a way for them to concretely demonstrate their assimilation into the broader culture. The first noted Jewish sportswriter was Jacob C. Morse, baseball editor of the *Boston Globe* in 1885 and author of *Sphere and Ash: A History of Baseball* (1888). He was followed by Nat Fleischer, founder of *Ring* Magazine in 1922, and Shirley Povich, who covered sports for the *Washington Post* from 1923 until 1998. After World War II prominent Jewish boxing writers included Barney Nagler and Lester Bromberg, and the top baseball writers included Roger Kahn, Dick Young, Milt Gross, Leonard Koppett, and Jerome Holtzman.[42]

Jewish prominence in broadcasting dates back to radio reporter Bill Stern in the 1930s, and later Marty Glickman and Mel Allen. The tradition has been maintained by such notable television personalities as Marv Albert, Howard Cosell, Al Michaels, and Dick Schapp.[43]

Conclusion

Jewish participation in American sport was historically underrecognized because of their underrepresentation in two of the biggest sports, baseball and football, and because their absence fit in well with negative stereotypes of Jewish manliness. The actual degree of participation by Jewish men and women was partly influenced by religious factors among Orthodox observers, but more importantly, anti-Semitism, which limited access in both elite and plebeian sports, as well as urbanization, assimilation, and social class, which provided opportunities in certain sports, but curtailed options in other sports. Thus in the nineteenth century, assimilated German Jews participated in German as well as American sports, except elite sports like yachting, golf, and tennis because upper-class sports clubs discriminated against them. In the early twentieth century working-class sons of Eastern European immigrants dominated inner-city sports, and as subsequent generations moved up the social ladder, their sons became highly visible in swimming and tennis, and even produced national stars in baseball and football. Furthermore, since the late nineteenth century, Jews played a major role in sports as entrepreneurs and communicators, a strong reflection of their interest in sport and growing prominence in business and communications.

Notes

1 From "Statistics," *Jewish Encyclopedia* (1906). www.jewishencyclopedia.com/articles/13992-statistics; "Vital Statistics: Jewish Population in the United States, by State (1899 – Present) www.jewishvirtuallibrary.org/jsource/US-Israel/usjewpop.html (accessed May 4, 2015).

2 Steven A. Riess, "Sports and the American Jew: An Introduction," in *Sports and the American Jew*, ed. Steven A. Riess (Syracuse, NY: Syracuse University Press, 1998), 6–9; "Jacoby, Philo," in *Encyclopedia of Jews in Sports*, ed. Bernard Postal, Jesse Silver, and Roy Silver (New York: Bloch Publishing, 1965), 411–412. Hereafter cited as *EJS.*

3 Riess, 'Sports and the American Jew," 10–11; "Belmont, August," *American National Biography; EJS*, 309–311, 322–323.

4 Willis, Joe D., and Richard G. Wettan, "L.E. Myers, 'World's Greatest Runner,'" *Journal of Sport History* 2 (Summer 1975): 93–111; *EJS*, 475–478.

5 Jeffrey S. Gurock, *Judaism's Encounter with American Sports* (Bloomington, IN: Indiana University Press, 2005), 37–39; Riess, "Sports and the American Jew," 9; Linda J. Borish, "Women, Sport and American Jewish Identity in the Late Nineteenth and Early Twentieth Centuries," in *With God on Their Side: Sport in the Service of Religion*, ed. Tara Magdalinski and Timothy J.L. Chandler (London: Routledge, 2002), 71–98.

6 Burton A. Boxerman and Benita W. Boxerman, *Jews and Baseball: Volume I: Entering the American Mainstream, 1871–1948* (Jefferson City, NC: McFarland, 2007), 71–98.

7 Steven A. Riess, "From Pike to Green with Greenberg in Between: Jewish Americans and the National Pastime, in *The American Game: Baseball and Ethnicity*, ed. Lawrence Baldassaro and Richard A. Johnson (Carbondale: Southern Illinois University Press, 2002), 117–119.

8 "Brunswick, John M," *EJS*; Rick Kogan, *Brunswick: The Story of an American Company From 1845 to 1985* (Skokie, IL: Brunswick, 1985), 4–10, 14–20.

9 Riess, "Sports and the American Jew," 14–18.

10 Ibid., 14, 16, 18; Linda J. Borish, "'Athletic Activities of Various Kinds': Physical Health and Sport Programs for Jewish American Women," *Journal of Sport History* 26 (Summer 1999): 240–270.

11 Gurock, *Judaism's Encounter with American Sports*, 91–107.

12 Ralph Melnick, *Senda Berenson: The Unlikely Founder of Women's Basketball* (Amherst: University of Massachusetts Press, 2007), 4–29; Linda J. Borish, "'The Cradle of American Champions, Women Champions . . . Swim Champions': Charlotte Epstein, Gender and Jewish Identity, and the Physical Emancipation of Women in Aquatic Sports," *The International Journal of the History of Sport* 21 (March 2004): 197–235.

13 Steven A. Riess, "Tough Jews: The Jewish American Boxing Experience, 1880–1940," in Riess, ed., *Sports and the American Jew*, 75–79; Peter Levine, *Ellis Island to Ebbets Field: Sport and the American Jewish Experience* (New York: Oxford University Press, 1992), 162; "Benny Leonard," *BoxRec.* http://boxrec.com/list_bouts.php?human_id=9001&cat=boxer&pageID=1 (accessed May 4, 2015).
14 Ande Manners, *Poor Cousins* (New York: Coward, McCann & Geoghegan 1972), 278.
15 Paula S. Fass, *Outside In: Minorities and the Transformation of American Education* (New York: Oxford University Press, 1989), 240–241.
16 Riess, "Tough Jews," 84–91; Douglas Century, *Barney Ross* (New York: Nextbook, 2006); "Max Baer." www.jewishvirtuallibrary.org/jsource/biography/Max_Baer.html (accessed April 15, 2015).
17 Dave Anderson, *In This Corner: Great Boxing Trainers Talk About Their Art* (New York: William Morrow, 1991), 119–150.
18 Riess, "Sports and the American Jew," 23–27; Linda J. Borish, "Jewish Women in the American Gym: Basketball, Ethnicity and Gender in the Early Twentieth Century," in *Jews in the Gym: Judaism, Sports, and Athletics*, ed. Leonard J. Greenspoon (West Lafayette, IN: Purdue University Press, 2012), 213–237.
19 Riess, "Sport and the American Jew," 26–28.
20 Dan A. Oren, *Joining the Club: A History of Jews at Yale* (New Haven, CT: Yale University Press, 1985), 36.
21 Riess, "From Pike to Green," 122–127.
22 Ibid., 119, 133–134.
23 *The Sporting News* (October 9, 1919): 4; Daniel Nathan, "Anti-Semitism and the Black Sox Scandal," *Nine* 4 (December 1995): 94–100.
24 *EJS*, 301–302; Richard Hoffer, "Fight Manager, Collector Jimmy Jacobs Dies at 58," *Los Angeles Times*, March 24, 1988.
25 Peter Levine, "'Our Crowd' at Play: The Elite Jewish Country Club in the 1920s," in Riess, ed., *Sports and the American Jew*, 160–184.
26 Riess, "Sports and the American Jew," 11, 46–48.
27 Ibid., 47–50.
28 Ibid., 119; "Jacobs, Hirsch," *Jewish Virtual Library*. www.jewishvirtuallibrary.org/jsource/judaica/ejud_0002_0011_0_09900.html (accessed April 16, 2015).
29 Michael Alexander, "The Jewish Bookmaker: Gambling, Legitimacy, and the American Political Economy," in *Jews and the Sporting Life*, ed. Ezra Mendelsohn (Oxford: Oxford University Press, 2008), 54–69.
30 Riess, "Sports and the American Jew," 31; Peter Hopsicker, "'No Hebrews Allowed': How the 1932 Lake Placid Winter Olympic Games Survived the 'Restricted' Adirondack Culture, 1877–1932," *Journal of Sport History* 36 (Summer 2009): 205–222.
31 Riess, "Sports and the American Jew," 31–34; Richard Mandell, *The Nazi Olympics* (New York: Macmillan, 1971), 68–82.
32 Borish, "Women, Sport and American Jewish Identity," 89; Riess, "Sports and the American Jews, 32–33.
33 Gurock, *Judaism's Encounter with American Sports*, 154–187; David Berger, "At a Camp for Hasidic Boys, Studying Faith Is Their Daily Exercise," *New York Times*, July 14, 2014, A19.
34 For a list of Jewish Olympic medalists, see George Eisen, "Jewish Olympic Medalists," *International Jewish Sports Hall of Fame*. www.jewishsports.net/medalists.htm (accessed November 2, 2014).
35 Richard O. Davies, and Richard G. Abrams, *Betting the Line: Sports Wagering in American Life* (Columbus: Ohio State University Press, 2001), 131–132; Charles Rosen, *The Wizard of Odds: How Jack Molinas Almost Destroyed the Game of Basketball* (New York: Seven Stories Press, 2001).
36 David Vyhorst, prod., "The First Basket: A Jewish Basketball Documentary," JEJ Media (2008). On the Globetrotters original owners, see Ben Green, *Spinning the Globe: The Rise, Fall, and Return to Greatness of the Harlem Globetrotters* (New York: Armistad, 2005), 34–50.
37 Josh Nathan-Kazis, "Why Are So Many Pro Basketball Owners Jewish (Like Donald Sterling)?: Tribe Lured to Hoops by Economics, History, and Love of Game," *Jewish Daily Forward*, May 6, 2014.

38 Riess, "From Pike to Greenberg," 130–133; Jane Leavy, *Sandy Koufax: A Lefty's Legacy* (New York: HarperCollins, 2002).

39 "Jews in Sports: Major League Baseball (MLB)," *Jewish Virtual Library*. www.jewishvirtuallibrary.org/jsource/History/baseballtoc.html (accessed May 11, 2015).

40 "Jews in Sports: National Football League (NFL)," *Jewish Virtual Library*. www.jewishvirtuallibrary.org/jsource/History/footballtoc.html (accessed May 12, 2015).

41 "Who Controls Professional Sports? | Who Controls America?." http://thezog.wordpress.com/who-controls-professional-sports/ (accessed November 10, 2014).

42 Jacob C. Morse, *"Sphere and Ash:" History of Baseball* (San Francisco: Norman, 1999); Charlie Bevis, "Jake Morse." http://sabr.org/bioproj/person/3d3c9efa (accessed April 19, 2015); Nat Fleischer, *50 Years at Ringside* (New York: Fleet, 1958); Ralph Berger, "Shirley Povich." http://sabr.org/bioproj/person/b0dbc9e9 (accessed April 19, 2015); Barney Nagler, *James Norris and the Decline of Boxing* (Indianapolis, IN: Bobbs-Merrill, 1964); "Barney Nagler, 78, Writer of the Ring and the Race Track," *New York Times*, October 24, 1990, B6; Roger Kahn, *The Boys of Summer* (New York: Harper & Row, 1972); Leonard Koppett, *The Thinking Fan's Guide to Baseball* (New York: Simon & Schuster, 1991); Bruce Weber, "Jerome Holtzman, 82, 'Dean' of Sportswriters, Dies," *New York Times*, July 22, 2008, B6.

43 Marty Glickman with Stan Isaacs, *The Fastest Kid on the Block: The Marty Glickman Story* (Syracuse, NY: Syracuse University Press, 1996); Steven Borelli, *How About That! The Life of Mel Allen* (Champaign, IL: Sports Publ., 2005); Mark Ribowsky, *Howard Cosell: The Man, the Myth, and the Transformation of American Sports* (New York: W.W. Norton, 2012); Al Michaels, *You Can't Make This Up: Miracles, Memories, and the Perfect Marriage of Sports and Television* (New York: William Morrow, 2014); Mike Penner "Dick Schaap, 67; Sports Journalist," *Los Angeles Times*, December 22, 2001.

15

ASIAN AMERICANS AND SPORT

Joel S. Franks

Introduction

For decades, Asian immigrants came to the United States hoping to aid economically beleaguered families in their homelands and build futures for themselves. Greeted as "strangers from a different shore," they and their offspring often experienced labor exploitation, restrictive immigration laws, racial discrimination, and, in the case of West Coast Japanese Americans, World War II internment camps. At the same time, Asian Americans represented a small number of America's population outside of Hawaii and the West Coast before 1965. Primarily working and lower middle class, they represented Chinese, Japanese, Filipino, Korean, and Indo American descent.[1]

As a result of the civil rights movement and Cold War politics, the United States liberalized immigration laws in the 1960s. Subsequently, refugee status was granted to thousands of struggling Southeast Asians making the often harsh journeys to the United States to escape the turmoil of postwar Southeast Asia in the late 1970s and early 1980s. Thus, although Asian Americans represented less than 1 percent of the U.S. population in 1965, nearly 6 percent of Americans in 2010 were of Asian descent. In the process, Asian Americans have become more diverse in terms of ethnicity, class, and region of residence.[2]

Asian Americans have also become more evident in sport. Not only have very visible American athletes of Asian descent such as Tiger Woods, Kristi Yamaguchi, Michelle Wie, and now Jeremy Lin realized fame and fortune in American sport, but relatively anonymous Asian Americans are now participating in increasing numbers in college sport. Moreover, in places like California's Silicon Valley Asian Americans are found on high school basketball and Little League teams. Significantly, some of these athletes, famous and not so famous, possess non-Asian ancestry. They are often referred to in Asian Pacific Islander communities as *hapas*.[3]

To be sure, finding their way onto playing fields and courts in the United States has not been easy for Asian Americans. Racially based immigration restriction legislation limited the Asian ethnic groups compared to European counterparts until the late twentieth century. Thus, although millions of German and Irish Americans faced bigotry and discrimination, they encountered little in the way of immigration restriction and proved relatively adept at nurturing world-class athletes. Eastern and Southern European immigrants were not so fortunate. More likely than the Irish or the Germans to be perceived as insufficiently "white" in America, they confronted substantial immigration restriction during the second third of the twentieth century. Yet for decades, Eastern and Southern European immigration went unrestricted, although hardly unnoticed. Meanwhile, from Eastern and Southern European immigrant communities emerged the likes of Joe DiMaggio, Hank Luisetti, and Hank Greenberg. Asian American athletic achievements, however, derived from a much smaller population base.

Socioeconomic class played a role in diminishing Asian American athletes. Far from economically privileged, Asian American families often needed "all hands on deck" when it came to work. If not at school, families expected their children to help out on the family's farm or business. If there was no family farm or business, children were required to get paid jobs once they were capable of such work. The burden was intensified for females because they were frequently expected to take care of younger siblings and perform housework in addition to wage work. This was, of course, not unique to Asian immigrants and their offspring. Hard-pressed immigrant parents, regardless of nativity, often considered sport a wasteful diversion.[4]

The combination of racial and gender ideology has generally worked against prospective Asian American athletes. When male Asian immigrants initially arrived in the United States in significant numbers in the late 1800s and early 1900s, European Americans racialized and gendered them. Asian males were, therefore, perceived and represented in America as unmanly. Feeding into the gendered racial ideology regarding Asians were the dietary practices of many Asian societies, dietary practices rendering Asian men shorter and slimmer than white men, Because early Chinese immigrant men, in particular, wore queues in the United States, upon penalty of death mandated by the Chinese government, they and other Asian males were widely gendered as unmanly by racist nativists. Accordingly, the idea of Asians competing with non-Asians in the rough and tumble world of masculine sport seemed absurd to many European Americans. Because of their martial reputation and their embrace of baseball, Japanese athletes gained some respect interlaced with condescension. In the meantime, Asian females struggled with the stereotypes of either sly, immoral Dragon Ladies or dainty China Dolls, neither of which encouraged esteem for Asian female athletes.[5]

Despite the obstacles, Asian Americans engaged in a variety of sports for decades and not just sports stereotypically associated with them such as the martial arts, but sports such as American football, soccer, baseball, basketball, prize fighting, wrestling, golf, tennis, and volleyball. They have found through sport a way to reinforce a sense of community with people who share their ethnicity. They have also found through sport the means to build cultural bridges with people who do not share their ethnicity. Some have become elite athletes and even famous and wealthy celebrities. However, as Asian Americans have made their way into sport, their journeys have been marked by personal and structural efforts to dismissively "bench" them—to label them as "strangers," culturally unfit for inclusion in American society.[6]

Community and Sport to 1965

Similar to other racial and ethnic groups in the United States, Asian Americans created durable community institutions to sustain themselves in a land that for years proved institutionally biased against them. Many of these community institutions furnished meaningful spiritual, economic, political, and cultural supports to beleaguered Asian Americans. Moreover, across ethnic lines Asian Americans have sought ways to sustain a sense of community through sport.

By the early to mid-twentieth century, Asian Americans created sport organizations to link mainly young men frequently cut off from their loved ones by thousands of miles.

Community leaders often supported these efforts, hoping that sport could divert young men from disreputable recreational activities such as gambling, substance abuse, and prostitution as well as violent criminal activity and radical political militancy. Some of these community sport organizations had roots in the native lands of Asian immigrants, whereas other community sport organizations reflected the globalization of more modern athletic competition. Japanese immigrants in Hawaii, as well as on the American mainland, engaged in sumo but also rapidly formed baseball teams. In part, this was because baseball had been introduced to Japan by the 1870s and proved popular among college-educated males. (Sumo, by the way, had a working-class and peasant following in Japan.) An *Issei*, or first-generation, Christian preacher named Takie Okumura founded the first Japanese Hawaiian baseball team before the turn-of-the-twentieth century. Reflecting a transethnic concern for how young working-class people spent their free time from New York City to Honolulu, Okumura assembled a club named the Excelsiors to lure young male Japanese immigrants or *Issei* away from trouble.[7]

Historically, Asian American communities have embraced many sports, but none more so than basketball. Because basketball before World War II relied more heavily on speed, ball handling, and guile than on size, many Asian American teams were able to compete effectively against non-Asian American teams. The sport, moreover, allowed Asian American communities to foster female participation.

Chinese Americans organized basketball teams as early as the 1910s. In the late 1920s and early 1930s, Chinese American young women played on a highly competitive squad sponsored by the Dennison Settlement House in Boston. In the 1930s, Portland, Oregon's Chinese community nurtured a powerful contingent of young women playing for the Chung Wah Club. And by 1940, sports-minded Chinese Americans, of which more than a few existed, called San Francisco's Chinatown a mecca of community basketball. Indeed, out of San Francisco's Chinatown emerged a tough, male traveling professional team known as Hong Wah Kues.[8]

In the 1940s, St. Mary's Catholic Church in San Francisco's Chinatown served as a major sponsor of community basketball. Called the San Francisco Chinese Saints, the male squad competed effectively against community and commercial fives in the San Francisco Bay Area. The team star was five-foot, three-inch Willie "Woo Woo" Wong, an excellent shooter and ball handler. The Saints' five was chosen by the U.S. government to travel to Asia in the mid-1950s to persuade Asians that contrary to communist propaganda, racial democracy was alive and well in the United States. St. Mary's also sponsored female teams. Led by Helen Wong, a great all-around athlete and Willie Wong's sister, these teams ranked among the best Asian American female fives in the nation.[9]

Japanese American and Filipino Americans also embraced community basketball. Stockton's Busy Bees, a female Japanese American squad, proved difficult to beat by opponents, regardless of ethnicity, in the late 1930s. The San Jose Zebras comprised a talented male squad before and after World War II. Meanwhile, the 1940s witnessed the growth of Filipino American basketball. Led by Frank "Babe" Samson, the San Francisco Mangoes surfaced as one of the best known Filipino American fives on the West Coast. The Mangoettes were also organized for Filipino American women.[10]

Crossing Cultures to 1965

Asian Americans have crossed cultural borderlands to compete with and against non-Asian Americans. This has been truer of Hawaii than the American mainland, because social stigmas were more associated with class on the islands than they were on the more race-conscious mainland. Yet wherever Asian Americans have lived in significant numbers on the mainland, one can find their presence in a variety of high school and youth sports.

Through baseball and softball, Asian Americans encountered non-Asian Americans. Hawaiian baseball has long been multiethnic. Hawaiian Filipino Crispin Mancao well exemplified this. A clever southpaw, he pitched for the Chinese Tigers and the predominantly Japanese American Rural Red Sox in the Hawaii Baseball League during the mid-twentieth century. Mancao even took the rubber for the Hawaiian Islanders of the Pacific Coast League when Triple A minor league baseball arrived in Honolulu in the early 1960s.[11]

As early as the 1910s, mainland Asian Americans played ball with non-Asian Americans. In the 1930s, Russ Hinaga captained the predominantly European American Milpitas nine in California's Santa Clara County and played as well with the Japanese American San Jose Asahi. His sister, Alice Hinaga, starred as a pitcher in San Jose's Night Ball League, which operated for both men and women and featured a ball that was larger than the traditional hard ball but smaller than a softball. Starting her athletic career in Denver in the 1940s, Nancy Ito became one of the most prominent softball players in the country. She also competed in the National Girls Baseball League in the early 1950s along with Californian Gwen Wong.[12]

Bill Kajikawa, Buck Lai, Jr., and Les Murakami merit mention as college baseball coaches. Kajikawa was a true trailblazer as an Asian American coach. Born in California but raised in Arizona, in the mid-1930s, Kajikawa starred as an all-around athlete at Arizona State Teachers' College, now Arizona State University. Upon graduation, he coached the school's baseball team until World War II and after serving, resumed the position for many years. He also coached basketball and assisted the football team. Buck Lai, Jr., coached baseball and basketball at Long Island University after World War II. And Les Murakami coached the University of Hawaii's baseball team for 29 years, leading that program to national respectability.[13]

Asian Americans crossed racial and ethnic barriers in other sports as well. In the early 1930s, Japanese American Ted Ohashi stood out at the University of California in basketball. Nancy Ito excelled in American Athletic Union basketball in Denver in the late 1940s. Around the same time, Helen Wong starred on her Star of the Sea high school basketball team before becoming one of the best tennis players in California. In football, the swift halfback Taro Kishi excited fans of Texas A&M in the mid-1920s. The 1930s witnessed the emergence of Tommy Kaulukukui, a Hawaiian of indigenous and Chinese ancestry. The speedy, versatile Kaulukukui became a small college All-American for the University of Hawaii. Just after World War II, George Fong and Babe Nomura shined for Cal and San Jose State, respectively. In the 1960s, Danny Wong was a solid fullback for Navy.[14]

Trailblazers and Stars to 1965

Asian Americans traversed difficult cultural terrain to achieve recognition in amateur and professional sport. Some of these athletes became major national and international celebrities. Yet other, not so well known or forgotten athletes of Asia ancestry also deserve attention as trailblazers in American sport history.

Prize fighting is a sport that historically attracted working-class young men of color as participants and supporters. In the 1920s, the Philippine Islands, colonized by the United States since the dawn of the twentieth century, dispatched dozens of Filipino young men to box professionally in America. Meanwhile Filipino immigrants performed low-paid but necessary labor on the Pacific Coast of the United States and Hawaii. Historian Linda España-Maran claims that supporting *Pinoy* prize fighters helped give Filipinos "dignity and self-definition." No one was more honored by Filipino communities in the United States than a prize fighter who performed as Young Pancho Villa. Coming to the United States in the early 1920s, he fought his way to the world flyweight championship and held the title until his premature death in 1924. Other *Pinoy* prize fighters boxed their way to fame during the middle decades of the twentieth century. In the 1930s, few were anxious to get into the ring with Ceferino Garcia, a fearsome middleweight. During the 1940s, flyweight Filipino American Dado Marino became the first Hawaiian to win a world championship.[15]

Teammates on a famed Hawaiian Traveler barnstorming team in the 1910s, Vernon Ayau, Andy Yamashiro, and Buck Lai were Asian American groundbreakers in professional baseball. A slick fielding shortstop, Ayau became the first ballplayer of Chinese ancestry to play professional organized baseball when he scooped grounders in the Pacific Northwest League for Seattle, Tacoma, and Vancouver in 1917, arousing considerable opposition in a region well known for anti-Chinese fervor. *Nikkei* Andy Yamashiro joined a minor league team in Gettysburg, Pennsylvania, in 1917 and then moved up the minor league ladder to perform for Bridgeport of the Eastern League in 1918.[16]

Early in 1915, Buck Lai and a Hawaiian Traveler teammate, Lang Akana, were set for tryouts with the major league Chicago White Sox and the Pacific Coast League Portland Beavers, respectively. Neither played elite professional baseball on the American mainland. The Hawaiian Chinese Akana clearly was victimized by racial opposition. Lai was rumored to be targeted by racism as well. In 1918, the Philadelphia Phillies gave Lai a tryout. By this time, Lai had fallen in love with a white woman on the East Coast. He eventually married her and stayed in the Philadelphia area for most of the rest of his life. Unfortunately, Lai did not make the Phillies and he subsequently joined Andy Yamashiro on the Bridgeport nine. For four years, Lai patrolled third base for Bridgeport and then left the Eastern League to excel in independent baseball clubs such as the then famed Brooklyn Bushwicks. In 1928, Lai tried out for the illustrious New York Giants. Once again, Lai was cut and had his full-time professional baseball career ended at 32. For the next several years, Lai played for the Bushwicks and operated a barnstorming basketball team called the Hawaiian or Aloha All-Stars, although most of the players were not Hawaiian. The short-lived basketball team might have given Lai the idea to organize a truly Hawaiian baseball team, which toured North America from 1935 through 1937.[17]

Buck Lai's son, William T. Lai, Jr., performed on his father's Hawaiian touring team. In the late 1930s, he went to Long Island University, where he played first base and outfield for the varsity nine. After serving in World War II, Buck Lai, Jr., returned to Long Island University where he became an assistant basketball and head baseball coach. He then took over the basketball program, reviving it from possible extinction after its involvement in the infamous point-shaving scandal in the early 1950s. Lai also served as the university's athletic director and provost. Meanwhile, he worked for the Brooklyn Dodgers as a scout and instructor and wrote two highly popular instructional books on baseball and basketball.[18]

Southern Californian Bobby Balcena was the first Asian American to play Major League Baseball. A son of Filipino immigrants, he signed with the St. Louis Browns after World War II. He then lingered in the minor leagues for years, playing in places such as Mexicali, Wichita, San Antonio, Kansas City, Buffalo, Vancouver, and Honolulu. Balcena became a fan favorite in Seattle in the mid-1950s, particularly among that city's relatively large Filipino population. He also attracted the attention of the Cincinnati Redlegs' franchise, which called him up at the end of the 1956 season. Balcena got what ballplayers call a "cup of coffee" in the big leagues. After a few at bats and insertions as a pinch runner, Balcena's brief big league career was over.[19]

Hawaiian Nisei Wally Yonamine pioneered the difficult terrain of post–World War II Japanese big-league ball. Indeed, Yonamine stands out as a double pioneer. A son of plantation workers, Yonamine's gained notoriety first as a marvelous high school football player on the islands. Touring the mainland with a Hawaiian all-star football team, Yonamine's dazzling skills as a ball carrier attracted a scholarship offer from Ohio State and bids from the New York Yankees and the San Francisco 49ers of the All American Football Conference. In 1947, Yonamine joined the 49ers.[20]

Yonamine's stay with the 49ers proved neither long nor seemingly all that happy. Some say it was because he was not used to playing in front of big crowds, Yonamine became too nervous to do well. Yonamine himself contended that he was concerned about anti-Japanese hostility in the post–World War II San Francisco Bay Area. Moreover, Yonamine injured an arm while playing baseball on the islands, hampering his ability to excel as a ball carrier.[21]

Not discouraged, Yonamine played minor league professional football in the Pacific Coast Football League, but he was lured by the money that could be made in professional baseball. He tried out for the San Francisco Seals in 1950. Although he did not make the Pacific Coast League team, manager Lefty O'Doul was impressed enough to sign him to a Seals contract and farm him out to Salt Lake City, where he batted well over .300.[22]

However, O'Doul, convinced that Yonamine could not make it to the American big leagues, persuaded him to consider a career in the Japanese major leagues. The Tokyo Giants, the most prestigious franchise in the Japanese major leagues, wanted Yonamine, offering him a signing bonus to play in Japan in 1951. Yonamine accepted the Giants' proposal and became the first prominent American to play professionally in Japan since the end of World War II. He subsequently won over Japanese fans who considered him a foreigner—a *gaishin*. In the process, he batted consistently over .300, taught Japanese ballplayers to play more aggressively, and gained a spot in Japan's Baseball Hall of Fame. Yonamine was the best of Japanese Americans to play in the Japanese big leagues, but he was not the only one. Hawaiian "Bozo" Wakabayashi was a successful pitcher in Japan before World War II. In the 1950s, Hawaiian Jyun Hirota and Californian Fibber Hirayama also shined for the Tokyo Giants and the Hiroshima Carp, respectively.[23]

Gridders of Asian ancestry have broken into the ranks of professional football. Possessing Chinese and indigenous Hawaiian ancestry, Walter Achiu played for the Dayton Triangles of the young NFL after starring in the backfield for University of Dayton in the mid-1920s. Around the same time, *Nikkei* Art Matsu also suited up for the Triangles after he gained fame as a quarterback for William and Mary.[24]

Wat Misaka was the first Asian American to play big league professional basketball. A native of Utah, Misaka gained fame as a defensive wizard for the University of Utah when it copped the NCAA and National Invitational Tournament (NIT) titles in the mid-1940s. The NIT tournament, held at Madison Square Garden, was at the time more prestigious than its NCAA counterpart. When Misaka took the court with the University of Utah five against well-established basketball powers such as the University of Kentucky, he immediately became a fan favorite, due to his hustle and intensity. Thus, it was not all that surprising that the New York Knicks, playing out of the Garden, signed Misaka for their inaugural 1947–1948 season. Misaka managed to get into a few games for the New York five. However, he was eventually released—perhaps because he was too short to be useful to the Knicks or perhaps he was too Asian.[25]

Asian Americans have won more than their share of Olympic medals. In 1948, Korean American Sammy Lee became the first Asian American to win the Olympic gold medal. A diver, Lee won both the platform and the springboard championships. Lee's skills as a diver were so widely admired that South Korea's leader Syngman Rhee asked him to represent South Korea in the 1952 Olympiad. Lee thought about it but decided to dive for the United States again and was able to take home two more gold medals. In 1953, Lee became the first Asian American to win the prestigious Sullivan Award as America's best amateur athlete. After retiring from competitive diving, Lee, who became a physician, continued in the sport by coaching.[26]

Lee has few peers as an American patriot. However, he has always acknowledged how American racism shadowed his life. He recalled that when living in Pasadena in the 1930s, he found it hard to practice at the local Brookside Pool. Only on a once-weekly basis could people of color swim in the pool—that day was called "International Day." When International Day was completed, Brookside's director was ordered by the city to drain the pool and provide its white clientele with clean water the next day. The pool director confided in Lee that he did no such thing—that it was too costly and time consuming to obey the city order. But the point is that Sammy Lee, as did many other Asian Americans at the time, lived under the shadow of racial exclusion.[27]

Vicki Manalo was born in San Francisco in 1924. Her father was a Filipino immigrant and her mother was an English immigrant. Growing up in a "South of Market," working-class neighborhood, the athletic Manalo wanted to take up diving on a serious basis. However, San Francisco's leading swimming and diving teams typically practiced in pools that excluded nonwhites. She, therefore, changed her last name to Taylor, her mother's maiden name, and launched her career in competitive diving. As a teenager, Manalo blossomed into one of the best divers in the nation. Moreover, by the mid-1940s, she began to dive using her real last name. Heading into the 1948 Summer Olympiad, Manalo's coach was her husband Lyle Draves, and with his help she dived past other more famous American competitors to win the Olympic gold in platform and springboard diving. As a consequence, Vicki Manalo became the first Asian American woman to win Olympic gold.[28]

In swimming, Japanese Hawaiians did well in the post–World War II Olympics. Ford Konno and Yosh Oyakawa won Olympic gold medals in the 1950s. And Evelyn Kawamoto was another world-class swimmer. Sadly, one of the greatest Japanese Hawaiian swimmers of all, Keo Nakama, was never able to medal in the Olympics mainly because his peak years occurred in the midst of World War II.[29]

Several Asian Americans performed well in weightlifting after World War II. One was Tommy Kono, who took up weightlifting while in a World War II concentration camp. Weightlifting proved more than merely a way to pass time, as Kono became arguably the most versatile weightlifter of the 1950s, winning world and Olympic titles in more than one weight division.[30]

Asian Americans and Sport Since 1965

Before 1965, the Asian American population, limited by immigration restriction, largely consisted of people of Japanese, Chinese, Filipino, and to a lesser extent Korean and South Asian descent. With immigration liberalization of the mid-1960s and the influx of refugees from Southeastern Asia in the late 1970s and 1980s, the Asian American population has grown more abundant and more diverse. The sons and daughters of these "new immigrants" and refugees have made their way into every walk of American life, including sport. Meanwhile, institutional barriers to interracial marriage collapsed after the war on the U.S. mainland encouraging biracial and multiracial athletes of Asian descent to gain more visibility in American sport.

Asian Americans continue to assemble community teams and leagues in the late twentieth century and into the twenty-first century. In recent years South Asian American males in Chicago have competed in an annual hoops tournament. Hmong fives have been assembled in Minnesota. And in Los Angeles County, Filipino and other Asian Americans organize leagues and stage basketball clinics for youthful hoopsters.[31]

In more recent years, Asian American women have excelled in soccer, ice hockey, volleyball, and softball. Raised in Silicon Valley, Lorrie and Ronnie Fair are of Chinese ancestry. Lorrie starred for the powerful University of North Carolina soccer team and subsequently became a defender for the U.S. World Cup team in the late 1990s. Ronnie was good, too, as she sparked Stanford's soccer team. Being of Filipino descent, Tiffany Roberts also stood out for North Carolina and U.S. soccer teams represented in international competitions. In recent years, Hawaiian Natasha Kai starred first for the University of Hawaii soccer team before helping the U.S. women's team capture the gold medal in the 2008 Olympiad. Kai later played rugby internationally. In ice hockey, New Englander Julie Chu became an All-American at Harvard in the early 2000s. Since high school, she has been a key member of the U.S. women's ice hockey team, competing in four Olympics. The University of Hawaii Rainbow Wahines have been a perennial power in Division I women's volleyball. Coached by Dave Shoji, the team has been sparked by talented Asian Americans such as Robyn Ah Mow, a clever setter who also played for the U.S. Olympic team. Logan Tom, who possesses Hawaiian and Chinese ancestry, emerged as a commanding spiker for another perennial power in women's college volleyball—Stanford. Tom, too, played for the U.S. Olympic team. Meanwhile, Vietnamese immigrant Kim Maher Ly played for the 1996 U.S. Olympic champion softball team.[32]

Aside from the Asian American college coaches already listed, Colleen Matsuhara has been a pioneering women's basketball coach at Nebraska and the University of California, Irvine. Hawaiian David Nakama served as an assistant baseball coach at Stanford before becoming the head coach at San Jose State. In football, Hawaiian Norm Chow was a successful offensive coordinator at Brigham Young University, North Carolina State, USC, and UCLA before he finally landed a head coaching job at the University of Hawaii in 2012, becoming in the process the first Asian American head coach of a Division 1 NCAA football team.[33]

By the late twentieth century, a few American professional ballplayers of Asian ancestry carved out solid American major league careers. Mike Lum was a hard-hitting Hawaiian of Japanese ancestry and Chinese Hawaiian stepparents, playing for teams such as the Atlanta Braves and Cincinnati Redlegs. After starring for the University of Nebraska baseball team, Japanese Hawaiian pitcher Ryan Kurosaki got into a few games for the St. Louis Cardinals, becoming the first Japanese American major leaguer in 1975. In the 1980s, Lenn Sakata became the first *Nikkei* to play in the American World Series as a valuable utility infielder for the Baltimore Orioles. Part-Japanese Atlee Hammaker had a few good seasons pitching for the San Francisco Giants in the 1980s. Possessing Chinese ancestry, Ron Darling was a fine pitcher in the 1980s and 1990s for the New York Mets and Oakland Athletics. And Benny

Agbayani, a Hawaiian of Filipino and Samoan background, proved a dependable hitter for the New York Mets in the early 2000s.[34]

In the last few years, Johnny Damon, Tim Lincecum, and Kurt Suzuki have stood out. A son of an American military father and Thai mother, Damon helped the Boston Red Sox achieve their first World Series victory since 1916. A dynamic lead-off hitter and outfielder, Damon was for a while one of baseball's most charismatic and popular players. A son of a Filipino mother, San Francisco Giant pitcher Tim Lincicum was awarded the prestigious Cy Young award in his second and third years of big league ball. Across from the San Francisco Bay, Kurt Suzuki was handed the Oakland Athletics' regular catching job in 2007. With the Athletics, Washington Nationals, and Minnesota Twins, Suzuki gained a reputation as a fine handler of pitchers and an adequate hitter.[35]

A former coach for the Athletics and marginal major leaguer, Don Wakamatsu achieved trailblazing status in 2009 when he became the first big league manager of Asian ancestry. Possessing Japanese descent, Wakamatsu was named manager of the Seattle Mariners. However, a bad 2011 season for the Mariners led to Wakamatsu's firing. He subsequently joined the Toronto Blue Jays and then the Kansas City Royals as a bench coach.[36]

Asian Americans in the NFL have been breaking down stereotypes. A son of a Filipino immigrant worker, Roman Gabriel was an All-American quarterback at North Carolina State before enjoying several fine seasons in the NFL with the Los Angeles Rams and Philadelphia Eagles in the 1960s and early 1970s. Possessing Chinese ancestry, Kailee Wong was an All-American linebacker at Stanford before turning in a solid career in the NFL. Dat Nguyen, a son of Vietnamese refugees, was also an All-American linebacker at Texas A&M and then became a hard-hitting regular linebacker for the Dallas Cowboys in the early 2000s. Starring at linebacker for the powerful New England Patriots in the early 2000s was Teddy Bruschi, son of a Filipino mother. UCLA graduate Brandon Chillar was an outstanding linebacker for years in the NFL. Along with Bobby Singh and Sanjay Beach, Chillar became one of the few NFL players of Asian Indian ancestry. Meanwhile, University of Georgia star Hines Ward, who has a Korean-born mother, developed into a solid NFL receiver. In international football, Major League Soccer (MLS) has included Asian American professionals such as Brian Ching, Kyle Nakazawa, and Anthony Ampaipitakwong.[37]

Since the 1960s, a few American basketball players of Asian ancestry competed professionally in the United States. Hailing from San Jose, Raymond Townsend starred as a guard for the UCLA five in the late 1970s. Townsend's mother, a Filipino American, was also quite active as a community basketball player in the 1950s. After leaving UCLA, Townsend was drafted by the Golden State Warriors and pursued a short-lived NBA career. *Hapa* Corey Gaines played for various NBA teams after his hoops career at Pepperdine ended in the late 1980s. Gaines subsequently became head coach of the Phoenix Mercury of the Women's National Basketball Association. Another *hapa*, Rex Walters, learned his basketball while playing for the San Jose Zebras. He became a top contributor to the University of Kansas' success in the early 1990s. From Kansas, Walters headed to the NBA, where he played several seasons, generally in a utility role. Walters, as of this writing, is head coach of the University of San Francisco. After the turn of the century, Stanford's Lindsey Yamasaki played for teams such as the Miami Sol and New York Liberty in the Women's National Basketball Association. Possessing a multiethnic Asian background, Leilani Mitchell has had her share of fine games in the WNBA. In terms of coaching, the Miami Heat named part-Filipino Erik Spoelstra to succeed the legendary Pat Riley in 2008. Although some have doubted the former Portland State point guard's ability to handle high-priced superstars such as LeBron

James and Dwayne Wade, the Heat managed to win the NBA championships in 2012 and 2013.[38]

Of course, one can hardly forget about Jeremy Lin. After graduating from Harvard, Lin went undrafted by the NBA. Lin's strong showing in the NBA summer league for prospective players piqued interest from NBA teams. In 2010, the Bay Area native signed a contract with the Golden State Warriors. Lin played little and often poorly for the Warriors. Relatively rich in backcourt talent, the Warriors cut Lin before the 2011–2012 season. The Houston Rockets tried out Lin, but wound up cutting him as well. However, the New York Knicks signed Lin, but it looked like he would again linger on the bench. A number of injuries forced the Knicks to use Lin as a regular, and he responded with a sensational a set of games. Followers of the NBA were stunned, partly because Lin went to Harvard, partly because he failed to impress the Warriors and the Rockets, and partly, of course, because he was Asian American. "Linsanity" also erupted because Lin played for a team in the media capital of the United States. Although many across racial and ethnic lines cheered Lin on, bigotry shadowed him as media personalities, other athletes, and regular Americans seemed to find it necessary to use race and ethnicity to demean his accomplishments.[39]

Professional golf has inspired the participation of marvelously talented Asian American stars. Before his personal life took a hit late in 2009, Tiger Woods was celebrated as an icon of multicultural America. Possessing African, Native American, Thai, and Chinese descent Woods has arguably played better golf in the late 1990s and early 2000s than anyone has before and anyone might in the near future. Unfortunately, injuries have perhaps kept him from being the dominant male golfer of the 2010s. Female professional golfers Jean Park, Christine Kim, and *Pinay* Dorothy Delasin have, meanwhile, emerged from America's Korean and Filipino American communities, respectively, to win their share of Ladies Professional Golf Association (LPGA) tournaments. Possessing Japanese ancestry, Pat Hurst has also done well on the LPGA tour. Hawaiian-born Michelle Wie has perhaps disappointed those who considered her a potentially dominant golfer along Woods' line. However, she has done well as both an amateur and a professional player of the game.[40]

In professional tennis, Michael Chang stands out. At 17, Chang won the prestigious French Open in 1989. And throughout the 1990s, he was considered one of the best tennis players in the world. However, before Chang shined on international courts, Ann Kiyomura was a top-flight women's professional tennis player in the 1970s and 1980s. Indo American Laxmi Poururi also played professionally in the 1990s and 2000s.[41]

In more recent years, Asian American ice skaters have gained attention as prominent Olympic competitors. In 1992, Kristi Yamaguchi skated to Olympic gold. For many years after, America's greatest ice skater was Southern California's Nancy Kwan. However, although she had won many international titles, Olympic gold escaped her. Once she took second to Tara Lipinsky. MSNBC's website consequently announced that an "American" had defeated Kwan, prompting protests from Asian Americans and a belated and not very satisfactory response from the network.[42]

Apollo Ono and Bryan Clay have shined as well in Olympic competition. Ono, a son of a Japanese father, has won several medals, including gold, in speed skating. Bryan Clay, interestingly, has received less publicity than the charismatic Ono. Historically, the winner of the Olympic decathlon, composed of 10 track and field events, has been considered the world's greatest athlete. Magnificent and well-publicized track and field performers such as Jim Thorpe, Bob Mathias, and Rafer Johnson have won the Olympic gold in the decathlon. In 2008, *hapa* Bryan Clay won the event to much less acclaim.[43]

Conclusion

Through sport Asian Americans could assert a sense of community and agency under often harsh conditions and cross cultural boundaries to play with and against non-Asian Americans. Through sport, they could achieve at least a semblance of fame and, in the case of Tiger Woods and now, Jeremy Lin, a large amount of money and media attention. Through sport they could express a conviction that they were not "strangers from a different shore"—that they, too, belonged on America's playing fields and gym floors, as well as in American civic life. Perhaps most important of all, they could have fun, when, at times, fun was often too hard to find. However, "racism's traveling eye," to quote scholar Elaine Kim, shadowed Asian American athletes, reducing their numbers by way of immigration restriction, segregating them from nonwhites in Chinatowns and Little Tokyos, making it harder for some to make teams, and making it harder for others such as Michelle Kwan and Jeremy Lin to get the respect their athletic prowess deserved.[44]

Notes

1 Ronald Takaki, *Strangers from a Different Shore: A History of Asian Americans* (Boston: Back Bay, 1998).
2 Ibid.; Shelley Sang-Hee Lee, *A New History of Asian America* (New York: Routledge, 2013); "The Rise of Asian Americans," *Pew Social Trends*, August 18, 2004. www.pewsocialtrends.org/2012/06/19/the-rise-of-asian-americans (accessed March 3, 2015).
3 David Kiefer, "The Changing Face of Basketball," San Jose Mercury News. www.mercurynews.com/sports/ci_5030270/the-changing-face-of-basketball (accessed July 16, 2015).
4 Valerie J. Matsumoto, *Farming the Home Place: A Japanese Community in California, 1919–1942* (Ithaca, NY: Cornell University Press, 1993), 63.
5 Yen Le Espiritu, *Asian American Men and Women: Labor, Laws, and Love* (Lanham, MD: Rowman & Littlefield, 2008).
6 Takaki, *Strangers*, 3–21.
7 Joel S. Franks, *Crossing Sidelines: Crossing Cultures: Sport and Asian Pacific American Cultural Citizenship* 2nd ed. (Lanham, MD: University Press of America, 2009), 43–47; Samuel O. Regalado, *Nikkei Baseball: Japanese American Players from Immigration and Internment to the Major Leagues* (Urbana: University of Illinois Press, 2013), 20.
8 *Boston Herald*, February 21, 1935, 21; *Portland Oregonian*, December 23, 1934, sports, 2; Kathleen S. Yep, *Outside the Paint: When Basketball Ruled at the Chinese Playground* (Philadelphia: Temple University Press, 2009), 37–63.
9 Yep, *Outside the Paint*, 81–117; Ellen D. Wu, *Color of Success: Asian Americans and the Origins of the Model Minority* (Princeton, NJ: Princeton University Press, 2013), 126.
10 "Yoshi Grace Hattori," *Legacy.com*. www.legacy.com/obituaries/montereyherald/obituary-print.aspx?pid=142512798 (accessed November 30, 2013); *San Jose Mercury*, January 14, 1937, 15, January 16, 1946, 8; *San Francisco Examiner*, January 21, 1949, 15; Juanita Tamayo Lott, *Common Destiny, Filipino American Generations* (Lanham, MD: Rowman & Littlefield, 2006), 44.
11 Joel S. Franks, *Asian Pacific Americans and Baseball: A History* (Jefferson, NC: McFarland & Company, Inc., 2008), 91–92.
12 Ibid., 74; Franks, *Crossing*, 100; Chris Lambert, "Filmmaker Adam Chu and the National Girls Baseball League." http://www.chicagosportandsociety.com/2013/06/28/adam-chu-and-national-girls-baseball-league/ (accessed September 8, 2014).
13 Franks, *Asian Pacific Americans*, 82–83, 85, 96.
14 *Berkeley Daily Gazette*, December 29, 1932; *Pacific Citizen*, April 5, 1952, 7; *Monitor* (San Francisco), April 12, 1947, 6; *Dallas Morning News*, October 29, 1925, 16; Franks, *Crossing*, 116–117, 125, 126, 131, 142; *Silver City Daily Press*, November 2, 1965, sec. 2, 1.
15 Linda España-Maran, *Creating Masculinity in Los Angeles's Little Manila: Working-Class Filipinos and Popular Culture, 1920s–1950s* (New York: Columbia University Press, 2006), 73–105; Franks, *Crossing*, 34.

16 Joel S. Franks, *The Barnstorming Hawaiian Travelers: A Multi-Ethnic Baseball Team Tours the Mainland, 1912–1916* (Jefferson, NC: McFarland & Company, 2012), 174–188.
17 Ibid., 196–223.
18 Ibid.
19 Franks, *Asian Pacific Americans*, 166–172.
20 Franks, *Crossing*, 128–130.
21 Ibid.
22 Ibid; Franks, *Asian Pacific Americans*, 181–187; Robert Fitts, *Wally Yonamine: The Man Who Changed Japanese Baseball* (Lincoln: University of Nebraska Press, 2008).
23 Ibid.
24 Franks, *Crossing*, 115–116, 125.
25 Ibid., 171–172.
26 Ibid., 205–207.
27 Ibid., 13.
28 Ibid., 207–208.
29 Ibid., 201–203.
30 Ibid., 241–242.
31 Stanley Thangaraj, "Ballin' Indo-Pak Style: Pleasures, Desires, and Expressive Practices of 'South Asian American' Masculinity," *International Review for the Sociology of Sport* 45 (2010) 372–389. http://events.hmoodle.com/event/all-hmong-j4-basketball-tournament/ (accessed October 4, 2013); Sahaeli, "Sikhs in Basketball—Singh Sensations," *The Langar Hall* (blog), March 24, 2010. http://thelangarhall.com/sikhi/sikhs-in-basketball-singh-sensations/ (accessed May 25, 2013); "Hooptown International Youth Basketball," *Hooptown Basketball*. www.hooptown-bball.com/about-us/ (accessed December 1, 2012).
32 Franks, *Crossing*, 139–140, 146, 30, 231; Mikaela Conley, "Hockey Player Julie Chu to Be Flag Bearer in Olympic Closing Ceremony," *Yahoo! Sports* (blog), February 21, 2014. http://sports.yahoo.com/blogs/fourth-place-medal/hockey-player-julie-chu-to-be-flag-bearer-at-closing-ceremony-111401162.html (accessed July 28, 2014).
33 Alexander J. Ige, "Coach Matsuhara Is an Inspiration to Young Women," *Culver City News*, July 29, 2012 http://www.culvercitynews.org/printable/coach-matsuhara-is-an-inspiration-to-young-women/ (accessed July 25, 2013); Franks, *Crossing*, 139–140; "Norm Chow," Hawaii Athletics. http://hawaiiathletics.com/coaches.aspx?rc=1366 (accessed October 2, 2014).
34 Franks, *Asian Pacific Americans*, 196–223.
35 Ibid.
36 Regalado, *Nikkei Baseball*, 135–143.
37 Franks, *Crossing*, 113–155.
38 Ibid., 174, 185; "WNBA Player Profile: Leilani Mitchell," *She's a Baller*. www.shesaballer.com/index.php?option=com_content&view=article&id=195:wnba-player-profile-leilani-mitchell&catid=42:wnba-profiles (accessed January 13, 2013); Lydia Lin, "The Heat Is on for NBA's 1st APA Head Coach," *Pacific Citizen*, May 6, 2008. http://pacificcitizen.org/news/sports/heat-nbas-1st-apa-head-coach?page=show#sthash.mRaBn9Un.dpu (accessed June 29, 2013).
39 Scott Kurashige, "Dear America, Please Don't Ruin Jeremy Lin's Story," *Huffington Post.com*, February 21, 2012. www.huffingtonpost.com/scott-kurashige/jeremy-lin_b_1286428.html (accessed July 16, 2015); David Zirin, "Jeremy Lin Inspires a Nation," *Nation.com*, February 19, 2012. www.thenation.com/article/jeremy-lin-inspires-nation/ (accessed July 16, 2015).
40 Franks, *Crossing*, 211, 217–224.
41 Ibid., 215–216.
42 Ibid., 232–234, 261.
43 Ibid., 234, 239; "Brian Clay," *USA Track & Field*. www.usatf.org/Athlete-Bios/Archive-Bios/Bryan-Clay.aspx (accessed September 24, 2014).
44 Elaine Kim, preface to, Jessica Hagedorn, ed., *Charlie Chan Is Dead: An Anthology of Contemporary Asian American Fiction* (New York: Penguin Books, 1993), vii.

Part IV

GENDER AND AMERICAN SPORT

16

THE HISTORICAL INFLUENCE OF SPORT IN THE LIVES OF AMERICAN FEMALES

Roberta J. Park

Introduction

Subsumed within the lengthy 1900 Exposition Universelle, the 1900 Olympic Games were disorganized and lasted for more than four months. This troubled Pierre de Coubertin, who was even more perturbed that 22 women had taken part in five sports (tennis, golf, croquet, boating, equestrianism). Among the small number of pioneers seven were from the United States. Three of them won a gold, a silver, or a bronze medal in golf (nine holes) and a fourth won two bronze medals in tennis (women's singles and mixed doubles).[1] Things would be remarkably different at the 2012 London Olympics, where for the first time the United States was represented by more female (269) than male (261) athletes; they also won more medals (29 gold, 14 silver, and 15 bronze) than did the men. Moreover, for the first time all of the participating countries had sent at least one female athlete, offering powerful illustrations of what females now have achieved.[2]

It was also in 2012 that United Nations Educational, Scientific and Cultural Organization (UNESCO) published *Empowering Girls and Women Through Physical Education and Sport*—an advocacy brief that called for quality programs for all girls and women not just for the most athletically talented. Although the growth of opportunities that has occurred in the United States since the late 1970s for those females who have the desire (and abilities) to become athletic "high achievers" is commendable, the decline of opportunities for millions of others to enjoy and benefit from participation is too often overlooked.

Games Engaged in by Indigenous and Colonial Females

It is postulated that Paleo-Indian populations had begun migrating across the Bering Land Bridge (Siberia to Alaska) to the Americas at least 20,000 years ago. Parts of the North American land mass had considerable populations by the time that Columbus purportedly discovered America in 1492. Stewart Culin's *Games of the North American Indians* (1907), which replicates the *Twenty-Fourth Annual Report of the Bureau of American Ethnology (1902–1903)*, offers valuable information about of the extent of the games that once were engaged in by indigenous peoples of North America. Although many were deemed inappropriate for females, "double ball" (using sticks to toss small buckskin bags) was considered to be "especially a woman's game." In some regions they also played their own versions of stickball and other games.[3]

Colonists from Britain, the Netherlands, and elsewhere often brought with them games and sports (as "sports" were then defined) from the countries they had left; they also would create new ones. Although in many instances females were expected to be spectators, not participants, in the South they might sometimes ride horses, run races, paddle canoes, or swim (provided they were appropriately attired). In the middle colonies (New York, Pennsylvania, Delaware, New Jersey) such activities as walks in the countryside, sleigh rides, and skating could be enjoyed.[4] Although in perpetual servitude, black females on Southern plantations also sometimes found opportunities to swim.[5]

Becoming a Nation: The Revolutionary Period

In 1775 the *Pennsylvania Magazine* had published an article that encouraged greater acknowledgement of the "rights" of women even if their duties in life might differ from those of men.[6] However, the Declaration of Independence, enacted on July 4, 1776, stipulated only "All men are created equal." It would not be until the Nineteenth Amendment to the United States Constitution in 1920 that females got the right to vote in national elections. In 1790 the *Massachusetts Magazine* began a series of articles titled "On the Equality of the Sexes" in which Judith Sargent Murray (an early advocate of women's rights) declared that the limited education, employment, and recreation that was permitted to women was enervating their bodies and debilitating their minds. This, she insisted, must change. Her contemporary, Charles Brockden Brown, also advocated greater rights for women, stating in his 1798 book *Alciun* that men and women both needed adequate exercise. Two decades later Hannah Mather Crocker (another early advocate of rights for women) maintained that the relationship between a sound body and a sound mind was no different for women than it was for men.[7] She was by no means alone!

More forceful when setting forth such views would be Elizabeth Cady Stanton, who devoted much of her long life to advancing women's rights. Reflecting sentiments similar to those that the English writer Mary Wollstonecraft had set forth in her book *A Vindication of the Rights of Woman* (1792), Stanton declared in 1850:

> We cannot say what the woman might be physically, if the girl were allowed all the freedom of the boy in romping, swimming, climbing, and playing hoop and ball. . . . Physically as well as intellectually, it is use that produces growth and development.

As a youth she had enjoyed joining with boys as well as girls in running races and playing games. To put her beliefs into practice Stanton had climbing ladders and other apparatus installed near her home for her children to use. Deeming it important that girls also "grow up strong, well-developed, and free," she brought them to the gymnasium that she opened in Seneca Falls, New York, were they as well as boys could be given exercises.[8]

Catharine Beecher, one of Stanton's contemporaries, adhered to traditional views regarding what was appropriate for females. Nonetheless, she was in several ways ahead of the times. Although the focus of the school that she opened for females at Hartford, Connecticut, in 1823 was domestic education and preparing them to be good mothers, the curriculum included instruction in algebra, rhetoric, philosophy, Latin, and also daily exercise by means of calisthenics. Beecher would do similarly at the Western Female Institute, which she opened in Cincinnati, Ohio, in 1832. Her book *Course of Calisthenics for Young Ladies* (1831) was followed by *Physiology and Calisthenics for Schools and Families* (1856) and other publications in which she described numerous exercises, often accompanied with illustrations of girls (and some of boys) performing them. Beecher also encouraged schools to make exercise a part of the curriculum.[9] Others had been doing this for several years.

Scottish-born William Russell had initiated the *American Journal of Education* in 1826. From the outset it gave considerable attention to active recreations, physical education, and more opportunities for females. The initial issue had included a five-page article titled "Physical Education" that stated:

> Several of the recent institutions in our country have introduced arrangements for corporal exercise. . . . The time we hope is near when there will be no literary institution unprovided with proper means of healthful exercise and innocent recreation.[10]

The November 1826 issue of the *American Journal of Education* included an article titled, "Gymnastic Exercises for Females" (which recently had appeared in the *Boston Medical Intelligencer*). Events that occurred within the broader society helped to increase opportunities for growing numbers of females to enjoy at least a modicum of exercise and even recreational sports.

Agricultural fairs, which had arisen in New England before 1800, would grow considerably in number and location. Before long they would be providing opportunities for women to participate (in a controlled manner) in several things, not just as spectators but also as competitors. Although matters involving domestic skills such as producing dairy products predominated competing in equestrian events and similar things began to appear. In 1854 the Harford County Agricultural Society would arrange to include "the first trial of 'horsemanship' by the ladies." Although some individuals undoubtedly were opposed to such an occurrence, the *Hartford Courant* reported that thousands of spectators gathered to observe this novel event.[11] Opportunities for females to engage in sporting events, although still limited, continued to grow. In his 1907 book *Harford Fair* (including a brief history of the Harford, Pennsylvania Agricultural Society) Wallace Thacher stated: "Boys and girls, young men and maidens, play . . . games of skill and sports of various kinds on the grass and under the shade of trees."[12]

Women's Sports in the Progressive Era and Gilded Age: Challenges and Prospects

When Stanton had been writing about allowing a girl "all the freedom of the Boy," the types of sports that are popular today had barely emerged. In 1845 Alexander Cartwright had set down rules for the evolving game of baseball; contests between the *Knickerbockers* and the *New York Nine* soon launched what became America's "national game."[13] Young women at Vassar College played "baseball" on their campus as early as 1866. At Mount Holyoke, Wellesley, and other all-female colleges they soon were doing likewise. What often is said to have been the first "public" baseball game to be played by females (purportedly largely for entertainment) took place in September 1875 between the Blonds and the Brunettes at Springfield, Illinois; however, two years before the Cincinnati Red Stockings became the first professional men's baseball team (1869) there had been opportunities to watch the Dolly

Vardens (young African American women) playing the game. The St. Louis Black Broncos was another early African American female team. Many other women's teams would be formed before World War I; among these the Young Ladies Baseball Club played against several men's teams during the early 1890s.[14]

The urbanization that followed the Civil War (1861–1865) brought about many changes in society. A surge of sports and organized recreation was one of the more pronounced. By the 1880s wealthy Americans created venues like country clubs to enjoy their extensive free time separated from the lower and middle classes. An 1894 article titled "The American Sportswoman," written by Elizabeth Cynthia Barney, noted that many country and tennis clubs now had ladies' departments or offered affiliated memberships, which introduced females to certain sports.[15] The U.S. National Tennis Championship had been inaugurated in1881; competitions for women began in 1887; the first winners were Ellen Hansell (1887), Bertha Townsend (1888 and 1889), Ellen Crosby Roosevelt (1890).[16] Country clubs proved to be especially significant in introducing American women to the game of golf. In 1891 the Shinnecock Hills Golf Club (Long Island, New York) made its nine-hole course available to them. The first women's golf tournament in the United States was held in 1894 at New Jersey's Morris Country Club.[17] At the same time the new "safety bicycle" was offering an increasing number of females both recreational and competitive opportunities that helped promote an image that many were striving to achieve—the more independent "New Woman." In 1896 the indefatigable women's rights advocate Susan B. Anthony would declare of the bicycle: "I think this has done more to emancipate women . . . than anything else in the world."[18]

As growing numbers of American women were beginning to play tennis and golf or ride bicycles recreationally, others were embracing a more professional approach to sport. Several already had engaged in rowing races before *Sporting Life* reported in 1884 that two "muscular" women had contested on New York's Staten Island Sound; considerable money had been wagered on the outcome. Among numerous other late nineteenth-century women's rowing contests, Rosa Mosenthein won the "ladies" mile-and-a-half single scull race at Austin, Texas, in 1895. America's interest in pedestrianism (long-distance walking) had been reignited by Edward Payson Weston's trek from Boston to Washington, DC, to celebrate Abraham Lincoln's presidential inauguration. Cities and towns from Maine to Oregon soon reported that women as well as men became contestants. The most noted to appear would be the English champion Ada Anderson, who undertook her first race in the United States (2,700 quarter miles in 2,700 consecutive quarter hours) at Brooklyn's Mozart Gardens in December 1878. Exilda La Chapelle soon would do likewise at Chicago's Foley Theater; there would be many others. During the 1880s professional female bicyclists like Louise Armaindo engaged in numerous competitions, sometimes against male cyclists.[19] Although such events usually received at least a modicum of attention in the public press, they tended to be ignored by periodicals directed to a more "elite" audience such as *The North American Review*. For a short time female wrestlers and boxers also enjoyed some popularity. Hattie Stewart was said to have a right cross similar to that of the noted heavyweight John L. Sullivan.[20] The *National Police Gazette* offered most of the information about female wrestlers and boxers and occasionally wrote about women playing baseball.

Senda Berenson, a Jewish immigrant from Lithuania, had been hired to teach gymnastics (calisthenics) to young women attending all-female Smith College. She quickly acquired knowledge of the new game of basketball and introduced it to her students in 1892. To dispel any argument that basketball might be inappropriate for females, she divided the court into sections and prohibited snatching the ball. This, Berenson maintained, encouraged teamwork rather than "star playing."[21] These matters reflected a tendency that would last for decades—making sports for girls and women separate—from the sports played by boys and men, often with their own rules and values. Interest in playing the game of basketball rapidly expanded among the country's females. Young women enrolled at the University of California played against a girls' team from nearby Miss Head's School in November 1892. The first intercollegiate game on the West Coast took place in San Francisco on April 4, 1896, between female, not male, students from Stanford and the University of California. Several hundred spectators watched, but the only male allowed to be present was the referee.[22] In Iowa basketball rapidly attained popularity after it was introduced in 1893. Many girls' as well as boys' teams were formed, and sometimes played against each other. First played in 1920, the Iowa Girls' State Tournament soon was attracting more spectators than the Iowa Boys' State Tournament.[23] Similar developments would occur in Texas, Kentucky, and elsewhere.[24]

Basketball had been introduced to girls at Fort Shaw Indian Boarding School in Montana in 1896 by their physical culture instructor Josephine Langley. This school (like others similarly created) had been designed largely to assimilate indigenous people into the dominant culture; basketball would have an especially powerful role. The Fort Shaw girls' basketball team played its first public game in 1897, and the young women's accomplishments soon began to alter what were referred to as the public's "anti-Indian" attitudes. Before long the school's superintendent received an invitation to send the girls' basketball team to the 1904 St. Louis World's Fair. Their exhibition games proved to be so popular that they were asked to perform again during the 1904 Olympic Games (which were subsumed within the St. Louis World's Fair).[25]

The first YWCA (then called Ladies Christian Association) in the United States had been established in New York City in 1858. By the early 1900s it was being acknowledged that exercise, basketball, and other sports should be an important part of the programs that it was providing in many cities and towns. A November 1906 article in the *American Gymnasia and Athletic Record* stated that when a new YWCA building was being planned, the gymnasium now received considerable attention. The primary reasons were (1) what occurs in the gymnasium can bring about better health and physical condition and (2) provide opportunities for positive social interactions that can help young women better understand that "the development of the spiritual life must go hand in hand with the physical."[26] Such goals were similar to those held by Jane Addams, who in 1889 had co-founded Chicago's Hull House, which became the model for many other turn-of-the-century settlement houses. Hull House and its offerings were so popular that it soon grew to more than 10 buildings and a summer camp at Waukegan, Illinois (about 35 miles away). Chicago's Hull House provided the community with classes in naturalization and citizenship, sewing, cooking, mechanical drawing, sports, and much more. Gymnastics classes rapidly became available for girls and women as well as for boys and men. The first Hull House men's basketball team was formed in 1896; the first women's basketball team in 1902.[27]

Another major figure in the turn-of-the-century settlement movement, Lillian Wald, founded the Henry Street Settlement in 1893. Born in Cincinnati, Ohio, to German Jewish parents, Wald graduated from the New York Hospital Training School for Nurses in 1891. She then turned her attention to creating a home nursing plan to assist poor immigrant families who lived on New York City's Lower East Side. After moving into the neighborhood she became convinced that more needed to be done to improve conditions. To help achieve this she opened the Henry Street Settlement, a gymnasium, one of New York City's earliest playgrounds, then a summer camp for boys and one for girls. In her 1915 book *The House on*

Henry Street, Wald noted that such things as prejudice against ball playing on a Sunday had largely vanished and that more attention now was being given to the needs and interests of females.[28] The many other settlement houses that were established to help serve the needs of Jewish immigrants would include sports and similar activities.[29]

The first of many Young Women's Hebrew Associations had opened in New York City in 1888. They offered opportunities for girls and women to engage in basketball, volleyball, swimming, and other sports and became increasingly popular. Charlotte Epstein, who would found the Women's Swimming Association (WSA) in 1920, maintained that in addition to being good for health, swimming offered a graphic way for females to demonstrate their abilities. Among her many accomplishments "Eppie" served as manager of the U.S. women's swimming teams that participated in the 1920, 1924, and 1932 Olympic Games. At the 1924 Paris Olympics Gertrude Ederle (who had learned to swim in the WSA) won a gold medal in the 400-meter relay and two bronze medals. Two years later she became the first woman to successfully swim the English Channel.[30]

Sports also served an important role in bringing Chinese Americans into contact with American culture. San Francisco's Chinese YWCA, which opened in 1916 (five years after that city's Chinese YMCA was established), soon began offering opportunities for girls and young women to play table tennis and badminton—then basketball and other sports. St. Mary's School (part of San Francisco's Catholic Diocese), Hip Wo Academy, and other groups created similar opportunities. Built on only a half-acre of land in the midst of San Francisco's densely populated Chinatown, the Chinese Playground opened in 1927; by 1930 it was accommodating the fifth largest number of participants of all that city's 29 playgrounds. Girls' basketball teams called the Mei Wahs ("Chinese in America") soon formed in both Los Angeles and San Francisco; the latter won the City of San Francisco Recreation League's 1935 tournament. Chinese Girl Scout Troop 14 played its first basketball game in 1936 (against the Chung Wah School) and hoped that contests soon would be arranged with teams in the Pacific Northwest, where sports involving Chinese American females also were rapidly growing. Founded in 1935 Chitena (Chinese Tennis Association of San Francisco) attracted a growing number of women as well as men. Helen Wong, recognized as one of the best Chinese American athletes of the 1940s and 1950s, had developed her basketball skills while playing as a forward with the Saint Mary's Saints. She also became an accomplished tennis player. In 1949 she won the *San Francisco Examiner's* Amateur Tennis Tournament.[31]

Many *Nisei* (second-generation Japanese American) children and youth gladly adopted American sports. Softball was especially popular with young women and girls. By 1935 13 Japanese clubs were participating in southern California's Women's Athletic Union. There also were a number of teams in the Pacific Northwest. Such sports served as important morale builders for many of the Japanese Americans who were sent to Manzanar and other internment camps during World War II.[32]

Many black community leaders, likewise, believed that games and sports were important for fostering health and proper social development. In 1924 more than 160 YMCAs and YWCAs were providing opportunities for African American youths. Washington, DC's Phyllis Wheatley YWCA (founded in 1905 and named for the noted young eighteenth-century African American poet) had a membership of more than 2,500 by 1924; gymnastics, basketball, and tennis were among the many activities that it offered. The woman's sport most frequently played at Tuskegee Institute and similar institutions of higher learning is said to have been basketball. Lucy Diggs Slowe, valedictorian at Howard University in 1908, was an accomplished tennis player whose victories at the American Tennis Association's 1917 and 1921 national championships demolished unwarranted assertions that the game was "too sophisticated" for an African American. (The American Tennis Association, one of the oldest African American sports organization in the United States, had been created in 1916.) Anita Gant, who had captained a YWCA basketball team and won medals in swimming, would win the ATA's national singles championships in 1925 and 1926 and mixed doubles titles in 1928 and 1930. Inez Patterson (who attended Temple University) was an accomplished swimmer and track athlete as well as a field hockey player.[33]

Although field hockey had been played by young women at Goucher College as early as 1897, credit for making it popular belongs to Constance M. K. Applebee, who arrived in the United States in 1901 and soon introduced the game at Vassar and several other colleges. A 1905 article in *Outing Magazine*, which gave considerable attention to women engaging in sports and recreation, stated: "there is no game to test the endurance, wind and agility of womankind that can be compared with hockey as they play it in England."[34] The writer wondered if this also might occur in America, which it did. In the United States field hockey would remain a game played and controlled almost exclusively by females. It became an important part of many of the extracurricular sports programs for female students that existed at institutions of higher learning from the early 1900s through the 1960s. Following graduation many who had played while in college would join a local women's field hockey club, which played against each other for 10 or more weekends during the fall, then against more distant teams at the end-of-season "sectional" tournament where first- and second-place teams were selected to enter the annual tournaments of The United States Field Hockey Association (established in 1921). Although playing well and winning certainly were valued, the defining "philosophy" of the USFHA throughout its more than half-century of existence was inclusiveness and "the game for its own sake."[35]

Contributions by Health Reformers, Physicians, Psychologists, and Others

The urbanization that followed the Civil War had intensified concerns about public health and increased desires to know more about how to attain and maintain good personal health.[36] New findings regarding the nervous system, circulation, and other research were improving the medical curriculum; they also gave support to the founding of the American Association for the Advancement of Physical Education (AAAPE) in 1885. At the 1889 Boston Conference on Physical Training, Edward M. Hartwell (who possessed both a medical degree and a PhD in biology) declared that the importance of physical education was being increasingly confirmed by these discoveries. Other physicians would do likewise.[37] Psychologist G. Stanley Hall and others soon would be conducting research studies that found that play and games could be especially important for mental and social development as well for many aspects of physical health. Reporting favorably about the creation of the AAAPE, in 1887 the *Boston Medical and Surgical Journal* (today *New England Journal of Medicine*) urged the Massachusetts State Board of Education to include physical education in all the schools of the state.[38]

Physical education classes (divided by sex) soon became a requirement at most universities and colleges. Propriety held that those for female students be taught by women, who also would provide them with educationally oriented extracurricular sporting activities. The first Field Day, which took place at Vassar College in 1895 (and featured track and basketball), was an important model for the many that emerged elsewhere. The prevailing attitude that underscored these programs was reflected in a 1901 *Cosmopolitan* article titled "A Girl's College Life": although the "triumph of their class colors" might be just as dear to them, young women did not "riot over an athletic victory" as male students often did.[39] By 1901 concerns about the growing "professionalism" of men's intercollegiate athletics (particularly football) had become extensive, and important educational leaders such as Harvard's President Charles William Eliot were calling for reforms.[40] Well aware of these criticisms female physical educators realized that if they tried to emulate what was occurring in men's intercollegiate athletics this could have a negative impact upon what they were creating. Moreover, most believed that their primary responsibilities were a student's health and moral development; therefore, accommodating as many participants as possible must be their focus. As part of the means to do this they already had started an extracurricular approach that was quite similar to what the National Collegiate Athletic Association's Committee on the Encouragement of Intra-Collegiate and Recreative Sports would recommend for male students in 1913—"intramural sports."[41] To this the women would add "interclass" competitions and end-of-semester "field days" that included competitions in several sports. They also instituted a modest number of "playdays" that involved playing with local colleges. However, a "playday" team was composed of students from more than one school, and these soon fell from favor. Before long "playdays" were replaced by "sportsdays" at which the young women played only on their own school's teams. Nonetheless, their faculty advisors (the term "coach" was then rarely used for women's school teams) insisted that "comradeship," not just winning, must remain a major emphasis. Intramural sports and "playdays" also became the focus of most of the extracurricular sports programs for girls that emerged at high schools across the nation.[42]

At the same time that such opportunities were occurring at educational institutions the Playground Association of America (PAA), established in 1906, provided an increasing number of community-based sporting opportunities for thousands of girls and women as well as boys and men. By 1919 423 cities administered nearly 4,000 supervised playgrounds and other recreational facilities. The PAA deemed maintaining good health to be an important goal; so was helping to teach children and youth, whatever their family origins, to be good citizens.[43]

Manufacturing and other business enterprises also began to provide many sporting and recreational activities for their employees, women as well as men. By 1916 more than 230 companies were offering opportunities in baseball, bowling, paddle tennis, shuffleboard, fishing, and much more. The sports that attracted the greatest number of female employees usually were bowling, basketball, and softball. World War II would bring forth more opportunities. As men left for military service shipbuilding and similar industries turned to hiring ever larger numbers of women. Many joined the growing sports programs that their companies offered. In early 1945 the *Industrial Sports Journal* stated that females were engaging in "vigorous sports with enthusiasm."[44] The Arizona Brewing Company Queens were winners of the National Softball Congress (Women's Division) in 1947. It was estimated that businesses soon would be spending more than $160, 000,000 on employee recreation.[45]

As more baseball players entered military service their absence began to have deleterious effects upon attendance at major league games. In 1943 Philip Wrigley (owner of the Chicago Cubs) decided to establish what would become the All American Girls' Professional Baseball League (which started as a softball league). From 1943 to 1954 an estimated 583 women played in the league. Athletic skill was quite important, but players also were held to conveying a strong sense of decorum and "femininity." Although the number of teams, the years that a team existed, and their "home locations" had varied, the AAGPBL has been credited with bringing forth 14 franchises in five Midwestern states.[46] Several efforts (some successful, many not) to establish professional women's leagues in a number of sports would ensue. A Women's Professional Football League (tackle football) was established in 1999. It was short-lived; however, in 2014 more than 40 teams across the United States comprised the Women's Football Alliance (established in 2009).[47] The short-lived Women's Professional Basketball League (1978–1981) would be followed by the more successful Women's National Basketball Association, which first played in 1997. The most successful efforts to create women's leagues in recent decades have centered around the game of basketball. In fact, basketball is more likely to be seen on national television than is any other women's team sport. However, it is not always a professional female player's athletic skills that the media choose to focus upon.[48]

Conclusion: Accomplishments by American Women in High-Level Sports Before and After Title IX

Comparatively few opportunities existed for women to engage in intercollegiate athletics before Title IX of the Education Amendment Act, enacted in 1972, ushered in major changes. Nevertheless, females already had attained many more athletic accomplishments than often is realized. For example, at the 1924 Paris Olympic Games (where they accounted for only 24 of their country's 299 contestants) America's women won six gold medals in swimming and diving, and Helen Wills and Hazel Wightman dominated the women's tennis events. Mildred "Babe" Didrikson (proclaimed "Woman Athlete of the Twentieth Century" in 1999) had launched her talents playing basketball at Beaumont High School (Texas). The Employers Casualty Company then hired her to be a secretary (actually, to play on its women's basketball team, the Golden Cyclones). Before long the company arranged for her to compete for a place on the women's track team that would represent the United States at the forthcoming Olympics Games. At the 1932 AAU Championships Didrikson won six events (shot put, javelin throw, long jump, 80-meter hurdles, baseball throw, and high jump). At the 1932 Los Angeles Olympics she won gold medals in the 80-meter hurdles and the javelin throw, and a silver medal in the high jump. She also became an outstanding golfer, winning the U.S. Women's Open Championship three times and British Ladies Amateur Golf Championship in 1947. At the 1960 Rome Olympics, where the United States was represented by 241 men but only 51 women, Wilma Rudolph (who had played intercollegiate sports while a student at Tennessee State University) won gold medals in three track events (100-meter, 200-meters, and 400-meter relay); the other three members of the relay team also had had been students at Tennessee State. At the same Olympics Chris von Saltza, who had developed her skills at the Santa Clara Swim Club, won three gold medals in swimming (400-meter freestyle, 400-meter freestyle relay, and 400-meter medley relay).[49]

Stimulated by books like Betty Friedan's *The Feminine Mystique* (1963) and the formation in 1966 of NOW (the National Organization of Women), what often has been described as "Second Wave Feminism" rose rapidly. When the Association for Intercollegiate Athletics for Women (AIAW) was formed in 1971, its primary goal was expanding opportunities for females to engage in sports at the intercollegiate level—something that the NCAA had been doing for a small percentage of male students for more than six decades. The AIAW soon was administrating regional and national competitions in 19 sports (e.g., badminton, basketball, field hockey, gymnastics, swimming, tennis, volleyball). Upon realizing that intercollegiate competitions between female athletes might become profitable, the NCAA soon decided to organize women's tournaments in its Divisions II and III, and then an institution could choose to compete in either the AIAW or NCAA championships. Because the NCAA seemed to offer the greatest advantages, 17 of the country's 20 best women's teams chose to enter the NCAA's Division I Basketball Tournament in 1982; by 1983 the AIAW had ceased to exist. Subsequently, women's intercollegiate athletics would increasingly emulate men's intercollegiate athletics.[50] After Title IX's implementation, college soccer became the third most popular sport for women after basketball and volleyball. In winning the 1999 World Cup in soccer, several U.S. women's team members benefitted from Title IX scholarships and coaching in their soccer careers.[51]

Although the growth of women's varsity teams may be considered impressive, these accommodate only a small percentage of females who attend institutions of higher learning. A recent report by the National Center for Educational Statistics put that number at 11,723,732 for the year 2012.[52] Many institutions of higher learning now provide considerably fewer opportunities in sports for the thousands of students who do not have the skills to be (or do not want to be) members of intercollegiate teams.

In 1996 (the year that the Centennial Olympic Games took place at Atlanta, Georgia) the Centers for Disease Control and Prevention (CDC) issued *Physical Activity and Health: A Report of the Surgeon General*, which discussed at considerable length the importance of physical activity for all Americans. In the forward to the *Report* the Olympic Games were referred to as "the summit of athletic achievement." Interestingly, that same forward ended with the statement: "Increasing physical activity is a formidable public health challenge that we must hasten to meet."[53] At the same time an increasing number of physiologists, physicians, psychologists, sociologists, and others have been producing what is now a monumental amount of scientific and clinical evidence that supports the importance of physical education, games, sports, dance, and other physical activities for many aspects of health as well as developing positive social interactions. Nevertheless, in spite of continuing publications such as the CDC's *School-Based Physical Education: Working With Schools to Increase Physical Activity Among Children and Adolescents in Physical Education Classes* (2008) and others, the quality physical education classes that once existed at public schools have too seldom been returned to the curriculum. The CDC recently reported that according to a 2013 study only 24 percent of high school girls had attended daily physical education classes.[54] Moreover, the CDC's recent *Guide to Strategies for Increasing Physical Activity in the Community* (2010) shows that too few towns and cities are providing the broad-based recreational and sports programs that once existed.[55] Research, reports, and proclamations will be of little value unless put into proper action.

Notes

1 John Horne and Garry Whannel, *Understanding the Olympics* (New York: Routledge, 2012), 169; International Olympic Committee, "Factsheet: Women in the Olympic Movement." www.olympic.org/Documents/Reference_documents_Factsheets/Women_in_Olympic_Movement.pdf (accessed July 12, 2015).

2 "Jacques Rogge speech at London Olympics opening ceremony," *Xinhua*. http://news.xinhuanet.com/english/sports/2012–07/28/c_131744127.htm (accessed July 12, 2015); Jack Rapp, "Olympic Medal Count 2012: US Women Stole the Show in London," bleacher report, August 13, 2012.

http://bleacherreport.com/articles/1294747-olympic-medal-count-2012-us-women-stole-the-show-in-london (accessed July 12, 2015).

3 Stewart Cullin, *Games of the North American Indians* (New York: Dover Publications, 1975), 647–665; Gerald R. Gems, Linda J. Borish, and Gertrud Pfister, *Sports in American History: From Colonization to Globalization* (Champaign, IL: Human Kinetics, 2008), 3–11.

4 Nancy L. Struna, *People of Prowess: Sport, Leisure, and Labor in Early Anglo-America* (Urbana: University of Illinois Press, 1996), 76; Benjamin G. Rader, *American Sports: From the Age of Folk Games to the Age of Spectators* (Englewood Cliffs, NJ: Prentice-Hall, 1983), 6–21.

5 Gems et al., *Sports in American History*, 23–28.

6 "An Occasional Letter on the Female Sex," *The Pennsylvania Magazine* (1775): 363–365.

7 Judith Sargent Murray, "On the Equality of the Sexes," *The Pennsylvania Magazine* (1775): 132–135, 223–226; Charles Brockden Brown and Lee R. Edwards, *Alcuin: A Dialogue* (New York: Grossman, 1971), 23–26, 56–60, 92–93; Hannah Mather Crocker, *Observations on the Real Rights of Women* (Boston: Printed for the Author, 1818), 18–20, 56–58.

8 Roberta J. Park, "All the Freedom of the Boy: Elizabeth Cady Stanton, Nineteenth Century Architect of Women's Rights," *The International Journal of The History of Sport* 18, no. 1 (2001): 7–26. Stanton's message had appeared in *The Lily* (April 1, 1850), on page 31.

9 See, for example, Roberta J. Park, "'Embodied Selves': The Rise and Development of Concerns for Physical Education, Active Games and Recreation for American Women, 1776–1865," *Journal of Sport History* 5, no. 2 (1978): 5–41; Linda J. Borish, "The Robust Woman and Muscular Christian: Catharine Beecher, Thomas Higginson, and Their Vision of American Society, Health, and Physical Activities," *The International Journal of the History of Sport* 4, no. 2 (1987): 139–154.

10 "Progress of Physical Education," *American Journal of Education* 1 (1826): 19–23. See also, Park, "Embodied Selves."

11 Linda J. Borish, "'A Fair, Without the Fair, Is No Fair at All': Women at the New England Agricultural Fair in the Mid-Nineteenth Century," *Journal of Sport History* 24, no. 2 (1997): 55–176.

12 Wallace L. Thacher, *Harford Fair: Embracing Pioneer History, Industries and Enterprises of Earlier Years . . .* (Binghamton, NY: Barnes, Smith & Co., 1907), 210.

13 Rader, *American Sports*, 108–122.

14 Gai Ingham Berlage, *Women in Baseball: The Forgotten History* (Westport, CT: Praeger, 1994), 6–7, 28–33; Leslie Heaphy, "Ladies of the Negro Leagues," *Black Sports: The Magazine*, October 2008, 20–23.

15 Elizabeth C. Barney, "The American Sportswoman," *Fortnightly Review* 62 (August 1894): 363–377. See also, Allen Guttmann, *A Whole New Ball Game: An Interpretation of American Sports* (Chapel Hill, NC: University of North Carolina Press, 1988), 145–146.

16 Steven J. Overman and Kelly Boyer Sagert, *Icons of Women's Sport: From Tomboys to Title IX and Beyond* (Santa Barbara, CA: Greenwood, 2012), 292; Joseph J. Cook, *Famous Firsts in Tennis* (New York: Putnam, 1978), 14; Janet Woolum, *Outstanding Women Athletes: Who They Are and How They Influenced Sports in America* 2nd ed. (Phoenix, AZ: Oryx Press, 1998), 5; "Ellen Roosevelt," International Tennis Hall of Fame. www.tennisfame.com/hall-of-famers/inductees/ellen-roosevelt/ (accessed July 12, 2015).

17 Richard J. Moss, *Golf and the American Country Club* (Champaign: University of Illinois Press, 2001), 25, 70–72; David L. Hudson, *Women in Golf: The Players, the History, and the Future of the Sport* (Westport, CT: Praeger, 2008), 6; "History of Women's Golf," *Women's Golf & Travel Concierge*. http://womensgolfandtravel.com/history-womens-golf/ (accessed July 12, 2015).

18 Ida Husted Harper, *The Life and Work of Susan B. Anthony, Vol. 3* (Indianapolis, IN: The Hollenbeck Press, 1908), 1293.

19 See Roberta J. Park, "Contesting the Norm: Women and Professional Sports in Late Nineteenth-Century America," *The International Journal of the History of Sport* 29, no. 5 (2012): 730–749.

20 "Hattie Stewart," *National Police Gazette*, May 17, 1884; "Women in the Prize Ring," *National Police Gazette*, September 14, 1892.

21 Senda Berenson, "The Significance of Basketball for Women," *Basketball for Women, Spalding's Athletic Library* (New York: American Sports Publishing Co., 1901), 20–27.

22 "Used Baskets for Goals," *San Francisco Examiner*, November 19, 1892; "Waterloo for Berkeley Girls," *San Francisco Examiner*, April 5, 1896.

23 Considerable information about these matters may be found in Janice A. Beran, *From Six-On-Six to Full Court Press: A Century of Iowa Girls' Basketball* (Iowa City: Iowa State University Press, 1993).

24 For an overview of the years from 1892 to 1990, see Joan S. Hult and Marianna Trekell, eds., *A Century of Women's Basketball: From Frailty to Final Four* (Reston, VA: American Alliance for Health, Physical Education, Recreation and Dance, 1991).

25 Considerable information about these matters may be found in Linda Peavy and Ursula Smith, *Full-Court Quest: The Girls from Fort Shaw Indian School, Basketball Champions of the World* (Norman: University of Oklahoma Press, 2008).

26 Mabelle M. Ford, "Physical Training in the Y.W.C.A. Gymnasiums," *American Gymnasia and Athletic Record: A Monthly Journal of Rational Physical Training* 3, no. 3 (1906): 62, 64.

27 See Roberta J. Park, "'Boys' Clubs Are Better Than Policemen's Clubs': Endeavors by Philanthropists, Social Reformers, and Others to Prevent Juvenile Crime, the Late 1800s to 1917," *The International Journal of the History of Sport* 24, no. 6 (2007): 749–775.

28 Lillian D. Wald, *The House on Henry Street* (New York: Henry Holt and Co., 1915).

29 Linda J. Borish, "Settlement Houses to Olympic Stadiums: Jewish American Women, Sports and Social Change, 1880s–1930s," *International Sports Studies* 21, no. 1 (2001): 5–24.

30 Valuable information about growing opportunities for, and achievements by, Jewish American females in sports and related activities, can be found in other articles by Linda J. Borish, "'Athletic Activities of Various Kinds': Physical Health and Sport Programs for Jewish American Women," *Journal of Sport History* 26, no. 2 (1999): 240–270 and "'The Cradle of American Champions, Women Champions Swim Champions': Charlotte Epstein, Gender and Jewish Identity, and the Physical Emancipation of Women in Aquatic Sports," *The International Journal of the History of Sport* 21, no. 2 (2004): 197–235.

31 Susan G. Zieff, "From Basketball to Bolero: Sport and Recreation in San Francisco's Chinatown, 1895–1950," *Journal of Sport History* 27, no. 1 (2000): 1–29; Roberta Park, "Sport and Recreation Among Chinese American Communities of the Pacific Coast From 'Time of Arrival' to the 'Quiet Decade' of the 1950s," *Journal of Sport History* 27, no. 3 (2000): 445–480. See also, Kathleen S. Yep, *Outside the Paint: When Basketball Ruled at the Chinese Playground* (Philadelphia: Temple University Press, 2009).

32 Samuel O. Regalado, "Sport and Community in California's Japanese American 'Yamato Colony', 1930–1945," *Journal of Sport History* 19, no. 2 (1992): 130–143; Samuel O. Regalado, "Incarcerated Sport: Nisei Women's Softball and Athletics During Japanese American Internment," *Journal of Sport History* 27, no. 3 (2000): 431–444.

33 Gwendolyn Captain, "Enter Ladies and Gentlemen of Color: Gender, Sport, and the Ideal of African American Manhood and Womanhood During the Late Nineteenth and Early Twentieth Centuries," *Journal of Sport History* 18, no. 1 (1991): 81–102; Linda D. Williams, "Before Althea and Wilma: African-American Women in Sports, 1924–1948," in *Black Women in America*, ed. Kim Marie Vaz (Thousand Oaks, CA: Sage, 1995), 276–297.

34 "Field Hockey as a Woman's Sport," *Outing Magazine* 45 (1905): 475–479.

35 Roberta J. Park, "From 'Hockey World' to World Hockey," in *Local Identity and Sport: Historical Study of Integration and Differentiation*, ed. Hideaki Okubo, *International Society for the History of Physical Education and Sport* 11 (2002): 381–385.

36 See, for example, Richard R. Means, *A History of Health Education in the United States* (Philadelphia: Lea & Febiger, 1962).

37 The informative (and lengthy) introduction of William D. McArdle, Frank I. Katch, and Victor L. Katch, *Exercise Physiology, Nutrition, Energy, and Human Performance* (Alphen aan den Rijn, Netherlands: Wolters Kluwer, 2015) provides an overview of late nineteenth- and early twentieth-century physiological and related research. See also Roberta J. Park, "Physiologists, Physicians, and Physical Educators: Nineteenth Century Biology and Exercise (Hygienic and Educative)," *The International Journal of the History of Sport* 24, no. 12 (2007): 1637–1673; Park, "Health, Exercise and the Biomedical Impulse, 1870–1914," *Research Quarterly for Exercise and Sport* 61, no. 2 (1990): 126–140. (Eleven of the first 12 AAAPE presidents—years 1885 to 1926—possessed a medical degree.)

38 Roberta J. Park, "Play, Games and Cognitive Development: Late Nineteenth-Century and Early Twentieth-Century Physicians, Neurologists, Psychologists and Others Already Knew What

Researchers Are Proclaiming Today," *The International Journal of the History of Sport* 31, no. 9 (2014): 1012–1032.

39 Lavinia Hart, "A Girl's College Life," *Cosmopolitan*, Vol. 39 (1901): 188–195.

40 "Football and Its Distorted Values," *The World's Work*, Vol. 11 (February 1906): 7147–7148. See also, Ronald A. Smith, "Preludes to the NCAA: Early Failures of Faculty Intercollegiate Athletic Control," *Research Quarterly for Exercise and Sport* 54 (1983): 372–382.

41 "Report of the [NCAA's] Committee on the Encouragement of Intra-Collegiate and Recreative Sports," *American Physical Education Review* 19, no. 5 (1914): 352–369.

42 See, for example, Ellen W. Gerber, Jan Felshin, Pearl Berlin, and Waneen Wyrick, *The American Woman in Sport* (Don Mills, ON: Addison-Wesley Publishing Co., 1974), 48–85.

43 "Three Years Work of the Playground Association of America," *The Playground* 14 (April 1920): 13–28.

44 Roberta J. Park, "'Blending Business and Basketball': Industrial Sports and Recreation in the United States from the Late 1800s to 1960," *Stadion* 31, no. 1 (2005): 35–49.

45 "Industrial Recreation: A $160 Million Activity Impacting 20 Million People," *American Industrial Management* 6 (April 1947): 10–11, 39.

46 Gai Berlage, *Women in Baseball: The Forgotten History* (Westport, CT: Praeger, 1994), 133–176.

47 "Standings," *Women's Football Alliance*. www.wfafootball.net/standings.html (accessed July 12, 2015).

48 For how the media sometimes depict players, see Zack Pumerantz, "The 20 Hottest WNBA Players," *bleacher report*. http://bleacherreport.com/articles/1193548-the-20-hottest-wnba-players (accessed July 12, 2015).

49 See Susan E. Cayleff, *Babe: The Life and Legend of Babe Didrikson Zaharias* (Urbana: University of Illinois Press, 1995); Jennifer Lansbury, *A Spectacular Leap: Black Women Athletes in Twentieth-Century America* (Fayetville: University of Arkansas Press, 2014); David Maraniss, *Rome 1960: The Olympics That Changed the World* (New York: Simon & Schuster, 2008), 195, 273–274, 351.

50 Jill Hutchison, "Women's Intercollegiate Basketball: AIAW/NCAA," in *A Century of Women's Basketball*, Joan S. Hult and Marianna Trekell, eds., A Century of Women's Basketball: From Frailty to Final Four (American Alliance for Health, Physical, Education, and Dance, 1991, chapter 17). For changes in women's intercollegiate sport, see R.V. Acosta and Linda Jean Carpenter, "Women in Intercollegiate Sport: A Longitudinal Study Twenty Three Year Update 1977–2000," *Women in Sport & Physical Activity Journal* 9 (September 30, 2000): 141. http://search.proquest.com/docview/230666429?accountid=15099

51 Gems, Borish, and Pfister, *Sports in American History*, 328–330.

52 "Digest of Education Statistics," National Center for Education Statistics, *Institute of Education Sciences*. https://nces.ed.gov/programs/digest/ (accessed July 12, 2015).

53 David Satcher, Philip R. Lee, Florence Griffith Joyner, and Tom McMillen, foreword to U.S. Department of Health and Human Services, *Physical Activity and Health: A Report of the Surgeon General* (Atlanta, GA: U.S. Department of Health and Human Services, Centers for Disease Control and Prevention, National Center for Chronic Disease Prevention and Health Promotion, 1996).

54 Laura Kann, Steve Kinchen, Shari L. Shanklin, Katherine H. Flint, Joseph Hawkins, William A. Harris, "Youth Risk Behavior Surveillance—United States, 2013," *Morbidity and Mortality Weekly Report, Surveillance Summaries* (Washington, DC, 2014): 63.

55 Centers for Disease Control and Prevention, *Strategies to Prevent Obesity and Other Chronic Diseases: The CDC Guide to Strategies to Increase Physical Activity in the Community* (Atlanta, GA: U.S. Department of Health and Human Services, 2011).

17

TITLE IX, RACE, AND RECENT SPORT

Sarah K. Fields

Introduction

Born during the storm and fury surrounding the Education Amendments Act of 1972, Title IX was enacted on June 23, 1972, with little fanfare. Although the 37-word Title IX section seemed unimportant at the time of its passage, it is arguably the most important gender equity law in education in the history of the United States. The law has also embodied a tension between race and gender that has haunted the application of the law throughout its history, a history that has been mostly about sport, despite the absence of the word sport from the law itself.

Title IX is a civil rights law prohibiting gender discrimination in federally funded educational settings. It reads, in its entirety:

> No person in the United States shall, on the basis of sex, be excluded from participation in, be denied the benefits of, or be subjected to discrimination under any education program or activity receiving Federal financial assistance.[1]

The language of the law says nothing about race, and on its face it appears to be racially neutral. In fact, the language of the Title IX was directly modeled after the language of Title VI of the 1964 Civil Rights Act which reads:

> No person in the United States shall on the grounds of race, color, or national origin, be excluded from participation in, be denied the benefits of, or be subjected to discrimination under any program or activity receiving Federal financial assistance.[2]

Despite the similarities between the language and the apparently racially neutral language of Title IX, race and gender have seemingly been pitted against each other throughout the history of Title IX.

This opposition is, of course, illogical and presumes that sexism and racism can never work simultaneously. It also presumes that somehow women of color live their lives as either women or people of color. It also falsely presumes that women of all races did not participate in or benefit from the civil rights movement and that the second wave feminist movement of the 1960s was not interconnected with the civil rights movement of that same era. None of these presumptions is true. bell hooks, among others, has written extensively on the intersection of race and gender and the challenges black women specifically have faced in civil rights struggles.[3] Mary King and Casey Hayden, two white women involved in the Student

Nonviolent Coordinating Committee (one of the most powerful civil rights organizations in the 1960s), drafted a memo in 1964 describing the parallels between the treatment of African Americans and women in the United States of the 1960s and calling for action.[4] Title IX was born during a time when the civil rights movement and the women's movement worked, sometimes in parallel and sometimes in tandem, to attain equality under the law.

The Origins of Title IX

From the moment of inception to the moment it was signed, no one seemed to think that Title IX's most public application would be a focus on sport. Like most matters, however, the story of Title IX began with personal stories and personal frustrations. In 1969 Bernice Sandler, a white woman who was a lecturer at the University of Maryland, was unable to find a tenure-track faculty position. After not getting an interview for one of the seven openings at Maryland, Sandler asked a faculty member and friend, why she had not been in the final pool of applicants. He told her "you come on too strong for a woman."[5] Frustrated, she went home, and her husband told her that the department was engaging in sex discrimination. Sandler gave her husband's opinion more credence when she was informed during another interview outside the university that she could not be hired because when her children got sick it would interfere with her duties. Sandler's indignation grew and she began to look into whether the treatment she received was legal. After much research, she discovered Executive Order 11246, signed by President Lyndon B. Johnson in 1968, which prohibited federal contractors (including universities) from employment discrimination on the basis of gender. Working with the Women's Equity Action League (WEAL), a national organization dedicated to improving the status of women, Sandler helped develop a class action complaint against universities, including Maryland, for their discrimination against women. She also began compiling evidence of gender discrimination in universities.[6]

Various women in the House of Representatives worked with Sandler, and WEAL Representative Martha Griffiths (D-MI) used Sandler's research as the foundation for the first speech on the floor of Congress in March 1970 about the discrimination against women in education. Representative Edith Green (D-OR) was chair of the Subcommittee on Higher Education, and like Griffiths, an advisory board member of WEAL. Green held hearings on gender discrimination in June 1970 and began working on legislative language to ban gender discrimination in higher education.[7]

Although Sandler's goal was always to prevent gender discrimination, the link between gender and race was present early on. Originally, Green intended to amend Title VI of the Civil Rights Act, which prohibited racial discrimination in any program receiving federal money, to include gender. According to Sandler, however, African American civil rights leaders asked that the gender bill be separated from Title VI so as not to weaken the existing law.[8] But as reported in a speech on the floor of the House in 2002, Assistant Attorney General for Civil Rights Jerris Leonard had testified before Green's subcommittee and made clear that the Justice Department did not support amending the Civil Rights Act, suggesting instead that the committee focus on education and gender discrimination, a more narrow casting of Green's original goal.[9] Green respected these wishes, and the bill became Title IX of the Educational Amendments Act. The tension between race and gender, the idea that one could not necessarily be affected by both racism and sexism, drew criticism. At Green's subcommittee hearings Rep. Shirley Chisholm (D-NY), the first African American woman elected to Congress, testified that she found her gender to be more of a handicap than her race.[10] In 1982 Chisholm reiterated this, telling the Associated Press, "I've always met more discrimination being a woman than being black."[11]

Title IX was included as part of a huge omnibus law entitled the "Education Amendments Act of 1972." Sandler and others went to Green to lobby for the gender equity portion of the bill, but Green discouraged them on the grounds that the language was much more likely to survive if no one noticed.[12] Title IX stayed under the radar for much of the debate over the Education Amendments Act. Senator Birch Bayh (D-IN), a white man whose wife had been repeatedly rejected by the University of Virginia School of Law (which only admitted men), shepherded a version of Title IX through the Senate.[13] The Senate version of the bill that came out of the Committee on Labor and Public Welfare had removed the language about gender discrimination, so Bayh successfully added the amendment on the floor after a voice vote.[14] Representative Patsy Mink (D-HI), the first Asian American woman in the House, handled the management of the bill on the House side.[15] Mink expressed a personal stake in the law; as a student, multiple medical schools had rejected her application because of her gender. Eventually, both the House and the Senate passed different versions of the Education Acts, and a conference committee was formed to find a compromise bill.

The final conference report, which became the version of the bill that both the House and the Senate would approve, was vast. In addition to Title IX, it created a National Institute of Higher Education, increased grants and student loans by $2 billion, improved college access for military veterans, and encouraged and funded Indian and Ethnic Studies programs. It also included a temporary stay of court-ordered busing to remedy desegregation: no federal money could be used to pay for busing until all court appeals were exhausted or 18 months had passed since the court order. Given that public school racial desegregation in 1972 made gains largely because of federally funded busing, this was a very large sticking point for many Congress members.[16]

For many women, the juxtaposition of Title IX with the antibusing provision meant choosing to support gender equity or supporting funding racial desegregation. Of the nine women voting in the House of Representatives, five of them voted yes, including Patsy Mink for whom the law would later be renamed, and four women voted no, including Edith Green and Shirley Chisholm. The law passed the House by a vote of 232–195.[17] Tragically, because of the politics of the bill, some of these congresswomen needed to vote against Title IX in order to protect federal funding of busing; race and gender issues were indeed pitted against each other.

The Senate featured only one woman in 1972: Margaret Smith (R-ME). Although Smith did not take an active role in promoting Title IX, she did vote in favor of the bill, as did Birch Bayh. Senator Edward Brooke (R-MA), the only African American senator at the time (and the first ever to be voted into the Senate), voted against it. The bill passed the Senate by a vote of 65 to 17.[18] Interestingly, on the day of the vote, the *Congressional Record* had 33 pages of discussion on the bill in the Senate as a whole. Nothing of note was said about Title IX specifically or gender equity generally; Senator John Beall Jr. (R-MD) mentioned that the Title IX language, along with other provisions, existed and was important.[19] Although she did not vote in favor of it, Edith Green was correct: the best way to pass Title IX was to hope that no one noticed. Although both the *Washington Post* and the *New York Times* reported on the passage of the Education Act, neither gave much space to Title IX.

Title IX and Sports

Title IX was not intended to open the doors of sport to women and girls; that was an unexpected byproduct. Congresswoman Mink explained in 2002 that

> Since its passage [in 1972] most people have come to associate Title IX with gains made by girls and women in athletics. Certainly, this is the most visible, spectacular, and recognized outcome of Title IX. However, many are surprised to learn that the topic of athletics did not even come up in the original discussions about Title IX. Our primary goal was to open up educational opportunities for girls and women in academics, and the most controversial issue at that time was the application of Title IX to institutional admissions policies.[20]

The impact of Title IX on higher education is undeniable. The gender of colleges and universities and their graduates changed radically over 40 years (Table 17.1).

Despite being an unintended consequence, the impact of Title IX on the gender of athletics was equally pronounced. In 1971–1972, girls comprised less than 8 percent of all high school athletes (fewer than 300,000 girls played organized high school sport) and in 2013–2014, over 3.2 million girls comprised almost 42 percent of high school athletes, reflecting 24 straight years of record female participation.[21] Female collegiate athletes' participation increased hugely, too. Although the National Collegiate Athletic Association (NCAA) did not sponsor women's sport prior to Title IX's enactment, other agencies did. The federal government estimated that fewer than 32,000 women were varsity collegiate athletes in 1971–1972, whereas just over 170,000 men played in NCAA-sanctioned events.[22] By 2012–2013, the NCAA was, by far, the largest administrative body for college sport for both men and women, and participation numbers for both men (265,645) and women (203,565) had skyrocketed.[23]

Table 17.1 Percentage of Women Earning Higher Education Degrees[i]

Degree	*1966*	*2010*
BA	40%	57%
MA	34%	63%
PhD	12%	53%
MBA	5%	46%
JD	2%	47%
MD	2%	48%
DVM	2%	78%

i Data in table compiled from House of Representatives Special Subcommittee on Education of the Committee on Education and Labor, "Discrimination Against Women," June 17, 1970, http://babel.hathitrust.org/cgi/pt?id=mdp.39015063177110;view=1up;seq=9; U.S. Census, "Education: Higher Education: Degrees," accessed June 17, 2015, www.census.gov/compendia/statab/cats/education/higher_education_degrees.html; Stephanie J. Monroe, U.S. Department of Education, Office of Civil Rights, "Dear Colleague Letter," last modified June 22, 2007, www2.ed.gov/about/offices/list/ocr/letters/colleague-20070622.pdf and Kay Koplovitz, "Today is the 40th Anniversary of Title IX," Huffpost Business, last modified July 7, 2013, www.huffingtonpost.com/kay-koplovitz/today-is-the-40th-anniver_b_3535190.html?view=print&comm_ref=false. Some estimate up to 90% of DVMs were awarded to women by 2013.

The process, however, of increasing female participation in high school and college sport was in no way a simple one. Soon after enacting Title IX, some members of Congress unsuccessfully attempted to exempt sport generally and certain college sports specifically from the law. At the same time, the Department of Health, Education, and Welfare struggled to draft enforcement regulations with regard to sport and gender. In 1975, Congress passed those enforcement regulations and gave schools until 1978 to comply with the law. Those enforcement regulations, however, limited the scope of Title IX to noncontact sport and allowed for the creation of segregated sports teams. In other words, under Title IX, schools had no obligation either to create female football teams or allow females to try out for the all-male football teams, but if a school offered golf for males, they had to offer a female golf team or allow females to try out for the male golf team.[24] In 1984 the United States Supreme Court further narrowed Title IX and concluded that the law only applied to the specific unit in a school that received federal financial assistance. Consequently, a medical school that received federal research grants had to comply with the law, but an athletic department that received no direct federal money did not.[25] In 1988 Congress negated that ruling when it overrode President Ronald Reagan's veto and amended the Civil Rights Restoration Act of 1987 to specifically state that if any unit in a school received any federal money, then the entire institution was required to comply with Title IX. Only in 1988 did Title IX clearly and unequivocally apply to noncontact sports in educational institutions.[26] Although Title IX applies to all levels of education, kindergarten through postgraduate education, most of the public discussion and court cases about the law and sport has focused on collegiate-level sports.[27]

In December 1979, the Office of Civil Rights, charged with enforcing Title IX, issued its first policy interpretation explaining how, on a practical level, a school should comply with Title IX when it came to sports. Those policy interpretations required that the experiences and benefits of male and female athletes be comparable (e.g., if the male team gets new uniforms every other year, the female team must get new uniforms every other year), and they also discussed how to measure if the opportunities for male and female athletes were in compliance with Title IX. A school is in compliance if it meets one of three criteria: (1) it has a history of expanding sporting opportunities for female athletes; (2) it meets the interests and abilities of its student enrollment; or (3) the proportion of female athletes is equal to the proportion of full-time female students.[28] The U.S. courts and a 1996 policy clarification from the OCR have given deference to the third proportionality criteria.[29] Failure to comply with Title IX and its companion policies and regulations might mean the possible loss of federal funding; however, no school in the history of the law has lost a penny of federal money because of Title IX violations.

Expansion of Female Sport and Possible Racial Impact

As a practical matter, schools had been told they needed to add women's sports to comply with the law, but they were faced with a challenging financial quandary. The spirit of Title IX suggested that the school essentially double its athletic department and its athletic budget by adding women's sports; however, the reality of funding made that difficult, if not impossible, for most colleges and universities. This meant that many schools chose to cut men's sports teams in order to add or retain women's sports teams. Several institutions eliminated some of their men's teams in the late 1990s through the early 2000s and blamed those cuts on Title IX and the need to offer more women's sports.[30] Men whose teams had been terminated turned to the courts hoping for reinstatement, but the courts generally concluded that the schools had an obligation to comply with Title IX and that their choice to cut men's teams was not a violation of the students' rights.[31] Although some scholars argued that the elimination of men's programs, although sad for the men's teams, were not in fact required by Title IX,[32] some in the media blamed the law and further suggested that the cuts had a disparate impact on African American male athletes.

The rhetoric in the black popular press of the era was particularly concerned about how the cuts of men's college sports would potentially harm African American men.[33] Eric St. John, a columnist with *Black Issues in Higher Education,* argued in 1999 that because men's basketball and football were revenue-producing sports, black men financed the athletic opportunities for white women in collegiate sport.[34] Alex Woods, the head football coach at James Madison University and vice-president of the Black Coaches Association in the late 1990s, repeatedly warned that black men would suffer from Title IX, arguing that "playing football is the only way that a lot of black players get to go to college at all."[35] Although his rhetoric matched fears that football would be cut, few (if any) football programs were eliminated in the late 1990s and early 2000s. Craig T. Greenlee, an African American columnist, consistently found Title IX at fault for what he perceived as dwindling opportunities for black male athletes. In 2002, he blamed Title IX for Howard University's choice to drop baseball as a varsity sport, despite the school's contention that its decision was based solely on a lack of facilities, and he claimed that South Carolina State University dropped men's baseball in 1993 in order to add women's softball. He argued that "because of budget limitations and the need to adhere to Title IX, [baseball] could face possible extinction at many schools."[36] The bonds of gender seem to trump the bond of race, at least in the sporting world. "The race versus gender issue is very real," said Alex Woods, president of the Black Coaches Association in 1999.[37]

The perception of race versus gender might have been real, but in the late 1990s through early 2000s the men's sports most often eliminated were wrestling, tennis, gymnastics, golf, and indoor track. Except for indoor track, these were not the sports that the black press worried would be eliminated and, therefore, hinder opportunities for black male athletes. In truth, some 400 men's teams were eliminated, but schools simultaneously added over 100 men's soccer programs and almost 40 men's football teams.[38] Overall numbers of male intercollegiate athletes actually increased after the enactment of Title IX.[39]

Furthermore, concerns existed in that same era (late 1990s and early 2000s), that Title IX failed to provide enough athletic opportunities for young female African American athletes. For example, in 1997 Craig T. Greenlee emphasized that black female athletes needed to broaden their sporting base beyond basketball and track and field in order to take advantage of the increased scholarship prospects in the emerging sports for women.[40] The *Chronicle of Higher Education* ran an article in 2001, "Title IX Has Done Little for Minority Female Athletes," arguing, in part, that women of color were shunted into traditionally "black" sports like basketball and track and field. Ironically, the few black women and girls who did participate in so-called "white" sports often found it difficult being a single minority on the team; sometimes they quit the team because of their sense of isolation.[41]

Black Issues in Higher Education reported in 2003 that minority women's groups wanted the Department of Education and the NCAA to increase minority women's participation in sport rather than modifying Title IX in such a way that might decrease women's opportunities in general.[42] The Northern California *Sun-Reporter* noted that "Title IX was designed to meet the needs of girls, but it appears white girls have cashed in." The rest of the article argued that more urban youth centers needed financial support so that more black girls could earn scholarships.[43] Similarly, Tina Sloane Green, director of the Black Women in Sport Foundation and a professor at Temple University, stated in 2001 that "Title IX was for white women. I'm not going to say black women haven't benefited, but they have been left out."[44] She argued that urban black girls needed to have greater opportunities in sports other than basketball and track and field, and her own organization sponsored golf and tennis clinics in various urban centers.[45]

Similarly, some suggested the problem was not the language of the law, but the will of the people. An anonymous black coach was quoted in the *Sun-Reporter* as saying "the problem stems from institutional racism and the increased privatization of sports in America," and the coach added that only black coaches commented on the problems and "they are seen as trouble makers. But if white girls were being shortchanged this would be Topic A."[46] Patricia V. Viverito, then-chair of the NCAA's Committee on Women's Athletics, argued in 1998 that the issue was in part about fathers: "mad dads are the ones making the difference in the white community. They are encouraging, even pushing their daughters into sports. We need more mad black dads."[47]

In fact, the press as a whole in the early 2000s reasonably questioned the impact of Title IX on female athletes of color. The Women's Sports Foundation (WSF) released a report concluding that women of color were underrepresented in college athletics when compared to their enrollment rates at colleges. Further, even when the underrepresentation of female athletes in college generally was acknowledged, female athletes of color remained underrepresented. Plus, the report warned of women of color. For example, women of color were only 7 percent of the participants in soccer, the fastest-growing female college sport at the time.[48] From 1997 to 2003, the NCAA added women's championships in rowing, ice hockey, water polo, and bowling. Except for bowling, the WSF found that less than 10 percent of the participants of these sports during that time were women of color.

Reconsidering Title IX

In 2001, George W. Bush became president and Dennis Hastert, a former wrestler, became speaker of the House. Their arrival, in conjunction with the backlash against the perceived negative impact of Title IX and fear that the expansion of women's sport infringed upon men's sporting opportunities, caused the Secretary of Education to establish a Commission on Opportunities in Athletics in 2002. The commission was charged with evaluating the impact and effectiveness of Title IX. After multiple public hearings held across the country, the commission released a report which 13 of the 15 commissioners supported. The other two members (soccer star Julie Foudy and WSF past president and Olympic swimmer Donna de Varona) released a minority report. The commission's report concluded that opportunities for female athletes vastly increased because of the law but that more opportunities for females needed to be created while still protecting the existing opportunities for male athletes. The majority offered a number of recommendations for clarifying the policies surrounding the law and for promoting sport for both men and women. The minority report argued that the law needed to be strengthened and that schools needed to be educated about the law and how it applied.[49] No mention of racial impact appeared in either the commission's report or the minority report.

Public response to the existence of the commission was mixed. A 2002 *USA Today* article suggested that the premise of the commission was to determine whether the implementation of Title IX was unfair to men.[50] Sports columnist Sally Jenkins mocked the entire proceedings of the commission, noting that the author of the policy interpretations under scrutiny was never asked to testify; she noted that the commission's "main mission, it seems, is to forward ill-informed, baseless and biased opinion."[51] After the release of the commission's reports, no one seemed particularly happy. Those who believed the implementation of the law harmed men's sport were disappointed that the commission had not recommended eliminating the proportionality test.[52] Advocates of women's sport were also angry; Marcia Greenberger, co-president of the National Women's Law Center, warned that the changes recommended by the majority could "devastate women's and girls' opportunities to participate in athletics and receive scholarships."[53] Despite, or perhaps because of, the hoopla and uproar surrounding the commission and its reports, the Bush administration announced six months later that it would make no changes to Title IX or its policies.[54]

Forty Years of Title IX

The 40 years since the passage of Title IX have without doubt seen a huge increase in opportunities for women and girls in sport. However, even in the second decade of the twenty-first century, the opportunities for white women in college sport seem to be greater than opportunities for women of color, particularly black women. The U.S. government estimated that in 2012 about 18 percent of all undergraduates were African American women,[55] and the NCAA reported in 2009–2010, the percentage of African American female athletes had increased to 11.6 percent.[56] Noteworthy though is the focus on black and white women in college sport; other women of color do participate but in smaller numbers: in 2009–2010, the NCAA estimated that of the 186,460 women who played collegiate sport 0.3 percent were Native American, 1.9 percent were Asian American, almost 4.0 percent were Hispanic, 0.2 percent were Hawaiian/Pacific Islander, 3.75 percent were other, and almost 1.0 percent were biracial. Black women constituted 11.6 percent of all collegiate athletes, whereas white women were about 77 percent of all participants.[57] The sports being promoted by the NCAA seem to continue the trend of expanding opportunities primarily for white women. In 2015 the NCAA emerging sports for women included equestrian, rugby, sand volleyball, and triathlon,[58] none of which is particularly popular among women of color. The WSF estimated in 2002 that about 2 percent of female collegiate equestrian participants were of color, and USA Triathlon in 2009 reported that about 11 percent of all their participants (regardless of age and gender) were of color.[59] Of note though, in 2009–2010 the NCAA estimated that about 11.5 percent of all Division III female rugby players were African American, but that data are limited because the total number of Division III female rugby players actually reported was 87.[60]

The discourse in the press surrounding the fortieth anniversary of the law consisted of a mixture of exaltation and a more restrained praise which recognized both the strengths and weaknesses of the law. The enthusiasm was sometimes fair and sometimes overblown. Sports columnist Christine Brennan wrote that the law's "success has been staggering."[61] However, the success of women in sport is due not just to the law but also to the cultural changes which resulted in the law.[62] Alana Glass, an attorney and woman of color, described the Coca-Cola–sponsored NCAA gala in 2012 which celebrated the anniversary of the law as well as the release of the ESPN film about the law, *Sporting Chance*. She attributed (but did not quote) the following language to Sharon Byers, senior vice-president of sport and entertainment marketing for Coke: "Sports transcend cultural barriers. It [sic] teaches us life lessons, from the young to the old. It is blind to color, disability, and thanks to Title IX it is blind to gender." Scholars have proven that sport is not blind to color, disability, or gender.

In contrast to the overenthusiasm of some coverage, other accounts in the press during the anniversary pointed out the weaknesses of the law, weaknesses about racial disparity that had been acknowledged for decades. The *Washington Post* reported "Title IX has made a big, and very positive, change in how female athletes are treated," while subsequently noting the limitations of unequal funding and limited opportunities for poorer children, particularly African American and Hispanic girls.[63] Zerlina Maxwell, who self-identified as "a Title IX baby," acknowledged that "Title IX fundamentally transformed our society from a world where sports was just for boys to a much more even playing field." Her article, however, also noted the limitations of the law, particularly relating to females of color and poorer women and girls. She pointed out that a "2007 Department of Education study concluded that, while 51 percent of white sophomore girls participated in sports, only 40 percent of black girls, 34 percent of Asian Pacific Islanders and 32 percent of Hispanics did."[64] These accurate critiques reflect the concerns of generations, while adding Asian and Hispanic females to those who failed to benefit to the same extent.

Angela Hattery's op-ed column in *USA Today* argued that it was "important to celebrate all the law has done, but we must not lose sight of all the work that remains." She noted the lack of female coaching opportunities, particularly for African American women, as well as the more limited impact of the law on minority female athletes.[65] In 2012, African American women were the head coaches of college teams at less than 8 percent of Division I teams, just over 5 percent of Division II teams, and just under 4 percent of Division III teams.[66] A brief law review article lauded the positive effects; it concluded, however, by calling for improvements in issues of financial equality between male and female sports, increased opportunities for female coaches and minority female athletes, and addressing issues of transgender athletes.[67]

One of the more critical celebrations of Title IX was William Rhoden's column for the *New York Times*. Rhoden noted that the law was "monumental in women's and girls' sports participation," but the rest of his column discussed the racial inequalities in a law designed to end gender inequality. He reported on two different panels held in June 2012 to discuss the issue of race and Title IX and how to address inequalities. He argued that the Aspen Institute Sports and Society Program concluded that the inequalities were unintentional and "could be corrected with good will." The Conference at the Schomberg Center for Research in Black Culture, however, took a different perspective. Rhoden maintained that there was a sense among some participants that "the gap was in some ways a moat designed to protect white privilege, opportunity and power."[68] The problems with Title IX from a racial perspective are accurate; the attribution of intent for that disparity, although interesting, is challenging to ascertain. The disappointment of Title IX is not the intent of unequal treatment, but a failure of the founders to anticipate the differing impact on women of color: a disparate impact that might be more closely tied to issues of class than to race and ethnicity.

Conclusion: Title IX in the Future

From the earliest conception of Title IX, race and gender were placed in opposition to each other, suggesting that racism and sexism could not co-exist (likely news to most women of color). African American civil rights leaders did not want the Civil Rights Acts amended to include gender, because they saw the inclusion as weakening the law. The vote on the bill forced members to vote for either gender inclusion or for racial integration—no vote could do both. The law seems to have benefitted white women in college sport more than women of color, and it has greatly advanced opportunities for female athletes in general. There have been recurrent concerns that Title IX has or would affect men's sport generally and that African American male athletes specifically would be harmed. The numbers do not support this concern, but the problem with suggesting, as has happened throughout the history of Title IX, that one can either combat sexism or racism is that it both pits men against women and ignores the multiple identities of women of color. Neither is acceptable, and both threaten to undermine the goals of the law, which calls for gender equity in educational settings.

For the world of sport, Title IX's role in helping women gain access to athletics in schools seems, at least momentarily, secure. From a sporting perspective, courts and schools are being asked to address broader questions, such as what is a sport? A federal district court in Connecticut concluded that cheerleading was not a sport under Title IX despite national championships in the activity.[69] This battle will likely continue about other physical activities as sports under Title IX. The fact that the court found that Quinnipiac University had manipulated rosters to the detriment of female athletes indicates that female athletes still need the law. Further, the National Women's Law Center (NWLC) and other activists have recognized that many high schools have failed to comply with Title IX, and the WNLC has pushed more public school districts to obey the law.[70]

But Title IX was never intended to be about sports; that was an unintended but remarkably successful consequence. Title IX was about getting women equal educational opportunities—eliminating gender-based quotas in colleges, giving women equal access to financial aid, and getting them into the classroom. Successful in this way, yet sport was the most public face of the law. That is changing. In 2011 a Dear Colleague letter from the Office of Civil Rights to colleges and universities indicated that "sexual harassment of students, which includes acts of sexual violence, is a form of sex discrimination prohibited by Title IX."[71] Subsequently, the OCR announced that Title IX required that campuses more effectively address issues of sexual harassment and sexual assault in public institutions of higher education. If the first 40 years of Title IX were about sport, the next few years may be about sexual violence.

Notes

1 Title IX of the Education Amendments Act of 1972, P.L. 92–318, 20 U.S.C. section 1681, hereafter Title IX.
2 Title VI of the 1964 Civil Rights Act, 42 U.S.C. section 2000d, hereafter Title VI.
3 bell hooks, *Ain't I a Woman: Black Women and Feminism* (Boston: South End Press, 1981).
4 See Mary King, *Freedom Song: A Personal Story of the Civil Rights Movement* (New York: Morrow, 1987), 571–574 and Susan Brownmiller, *In Our Time: Memoir of a Revolution* (New York: Dial Press, 2000).
5 Bernice R. Sandler, " 'Too Strong for a Woman': The Five Words that Created Title IX," in *Title IX: A Brief History with Documents*, ed. Susan Ware (Boston: Bedford/St. Martin's, 2007), 36.
6 Ibid, 35–39.
7 Ibid, 39–41.
8 Ibid, 41–42.
9 Patsy Mink, "In Celebration of the 30th Anniversary of Title IX of the Education Amendments of 1972, *Congressional Record*, July 17, 2002, H4861.
10 Sandler, " 'Too Strong for a Woman'," 40.
11 James Barron, "Shirley Chisholm, 'Unbossed' Pioneer in Congress, Is Dead at 80," *New York Times*, last modified January 3, 2005. www.nytimes.com/2005/01/03/obituaries/03chisholm.html?_r=0
12 Sandler, " 'Too Strong for a Woman'."

13 Welch Suggs, *A Place on the Team: The Triumph and Tragedy of Title IX* (Princeton, NJ: Princeton University Press, 2005).
14 Mink, "In Celebration," H4861.
15 Brian L. Porto, *A New Season: Using Title IX to Reform College Sports* (Westport, CT: Praeger, 2003).
16 Richard Nixon: "Statement on Signing the Education Amendments of 1972," June 23, 1972, posted in Gerhard Peters and John T. Woolley, *The American Presidency Project*. www.presidency.ucsb.edu/ws/?pid=3473 (accessed December 30, 2014). Numerous studies of busing and desegregation exist, see, e.g, J. Anthony Lukas, *Common Ground: A Turbulent Decade in the Lives of Three American Families* (New York: Vintage, 1986) and Bernard Schwartz, *Swann's Way: The School Busing Case and the Supreme Court* (New York: Oxford University Press, 1986).
17 See June 8, 1972, House vote on Conference Report on S. 659 Authorization of Higher Education Act of 1972. www.govtrack.us/congress/votes/92–1972/h451 (accessed June 17, 2015).
18 See May 24, 1972, Senate vote on Conference Report on S. 659. www.govtrack.us/congress/votes/92–1972/s589 (accessed June 17, 2015).
19 *Congressional Record*, May 24, 1972, S8395.
20 Mink, "In Celebration," H4861–H462.
21 National Federation of State High School Associations, "2013–2014 High School Athletic Participation Survey Results." www.nfhs.org/ParticipationStatics/ParticipationStatics.aspx/ (accessed June 17, 2015).
22 Ware, *Title IX*, 9.
23 National Collegiate Athletic Association, "Student Athlete Participation, 1981–1982–2012–2013." www.ncaapublications.com/p-4334–1981–82–2012–13-ncaa-sports-sponsorship-and-participation-rates-report.aspx (accessed June 17, 2015).
24 See Sarah K. Fields, *Female Gladiators: Gender, Law, and Contact Sport in America* (Champaign: University of Illinois Press, 2005), 10–13. The enforcement regulations can be found in Sections 106.33, 37, and 41 of Title IX.
25 *Grove City College v. Bell*, 465 U.S. 555 (1984).
26 Fields, *Female Gladiators*, 13.
27 See Ware, *Title IX*.
28 Policy Interpretations: Title IX and Intercollegiate Athletics, Federal Register, vol. 44, no. 239 at 71413, December 11, 1979. See Linda Jean Carpenter and R. Vivian Acosta, *Title IX* (Champaign, IL: Human Kinetics, 2005) for a complete discussion of the application of the law and copies of the policy interpretation.
29 *Cohen v. Brown University*, 101 F.3d 155 (1st Cir. 1996) and "1996 Clarification of Intercollegiate Athletics Policy Guidance: The Three Part Test," in *Equal Play: Title IX and Social Change*, ed. Nancy Hogshead-Makar and Andrew Zimbalist (Philadelphia: Temple University Press, 2007), 152–162.
30 Hal Bock, "Title IX: Leveling the Playing Field or Tilting It for 30 Years?," *[Dubuque, IA] Herald-Telegraph*, June 23, 2002, C5. See Jessica Gavora, *Tilting the Playing Field: Schools, Sports, Sex, and Title IX* (San Francisco: Encounter Books, 2002).
31 See *Kelley v. Board of Trustees University of Illinois*, 832 F. Supp. 237 (C.D. Ill. 1993), *Miami University Wrestling Club v. Miami University*, 302 F.3d 608 (6th Cir. 2002), and *Neal v. Board of Trustees California State Universities*, 198 F.3d 763 (9th Cir. 1999).
32 See Rich Haglund, "Counterpoint: Staring Down the Elephant: College Football and Title IX Compliance," *Journal of Law and Education* 34 (2005): 439–451 and Brian Porto, *A New Season: Using Title IX to Reform College Sports* (New York: Praeger, 2003).
33 See Sarah K. Fields, "Title IX and African American Female Athletes," in *Sports and the Racial Divide: African American and Latino Experience in an Era of Change*, ed. Michael E. Lomax (Oxford: University of Mississippi Press, 2008), 126–145.
34 Eric St. John, "Collegiate Athletics Highlights," *Black Issues in Higher Education*, August 19, 1999, 80.
35 Craig T. Greenlee, "Title IX: Does Help for Women Come at the Expense of African Americans?," *Black Issues in Higher Education*, April 17, 1997, 24–26.
36 Craig T. Greenlee, "Black College Baseball's Uncertain Future," *Black Issues in Higher Education*, August 1, 2002, 18.

37 St. John, "Collegiate Athletics Highlights," 80.
38 Greg Garber, "Landmark Law Faces New Challenges Even Now, *espn.com*. http://espn.go.com/gen/womenandsports/020619title9.html (accessed June 22, 2002).
39 The Women's Sports Foundation Report, "Title IX and Race in Intercollegiate Sport," 2003, 12.
40 Greenlee, "Title IX," 24–26.
41 Welch Suggs, "Title IX Has Done Little for Minority Female Athletes—Because of Socioeconomic and Cultural Factors, and Indifference," *Chronicle of Higher Education*, November 30, 2001, 14.
42 Ben Hammer, "Reconsidering the Status of Title IX," *Black Issues in Higher Education*, April 10, 2003, 20.
43 "Title IX: Black Girls Not Served," [San Francisco] *Sun Reporter*, January 4, 2001, 1.
44 Suggs, "Title IX Has Done Little," 14.
45 Debra E. Blum, "Competing Equities?" *Chronicle of Higher Education*, May 26, 1995, A37.
46 "Title IX: Black Girls Not Served," 1.
47 Jim Naughton, "Title IX Poses a Particular Challenge at Predominantly Black Institutions," *Chronicle of Higher Education*, February 20, 1998, A55.
48 The Women's Sports Foundation Report, "Title IX and Race in Intercollegiate Sport," 2003, 12–14.
49 For a full copy of the commission's and the minority reports as well as other testimony and responses, see Rita J. Simon, ed., *Sporting Equality: Title IX Thirty Years Later* (New Brunswick, NJ: Transaction Publishers, 2005).
50 Erik Brady, "Panel Eager to Assess 'Where We Are,'" *USA Today*, July 1, 2002, 10C.
51 Sally Jenkins, "With Panel, a Number of Concerns, "*Washington Post*, January 30, 2003, D1.
52 Erik Brady, "Critics Unhappy with Commission's Recommendations for Title IX," *USA Today*, January 31, 2003, 6C.
53 Diana Jean Schemo, "Title IX Plans Assailed as Broad and Harmful," *New York Times*, February 1, 2003, D4.
54 Frank Litsky, "Colleges: Bush Administration Says Title IX Should Stay as It Is," *New York Times*, July 12, 2003, D1.
55 "Table 306.10: Total Fall Enrollment in Degree-Granting Post-Secondary Institutions by Level of Enrollment, Sex, Attendance Status, and Race/Ethnicty of Student: Selected Years, 1976 Through 2012," *Digest of Education Statistics*. http://nces.ed.gov/programs/digest/d13/tables/dt13_306.10.asp (accessed January 1, 2015).
56 "Student Athlete Ethnicity, 1999–2000–2009–10," *NCAA*. www.ncaapublications.com/p-4214-student-athlete-ethnicity-2009–10-ncaa-student-athlete-ethnicity-report.aspx (accessed January 1, 2015), 7.
57 "Student Athlete Ethnicity, 1999–2000–2009–10," *NCAA*. www.ncaapublications.com/p-4214-student-athlete-ethnicity-2009–10-ncaa-student-athlete-ethnicity-report.aspx (accessed January 1, 2015), 104.
58 "Emerging Sports for Women," *nccaa.org*. www.ncaa.org/about/resources/inclusion/emerging-sports-women (accessed January 1, 2015).
59 "The Mind of the Triathlete—2009 Study," *USA Triathlon.org*. www.usatriathlon.org/about-multi sport/demographics.aspx (accessed January 1, 2015).
60 "Student Athlete Ethnicity, 1999–2000–2009–10," *NCAA*. www.ncaapublications.com/p-4214-student-athlete-ethnicity-2009–10-ncaa-student-athlete-ethnicity-report.aspx (accessed January 1, 2015), 10, 233.
61 Christine Brennan, "Title IX Needed Now More than Ever," *USA Today*. http://usatoday30.usa today.com/sports/columnist/brennan/story/2012–06–20/brennan-title-IX-needed-now-more-than-ever/55715430/1 (accessed June 20, 2012).
62 Sarah K. Fields, "A Brief Legal History of Women in Sport," in *Women, Sport, and Physical Activity: Challenges and Triumphs* 2nd ed., ed., Sharon R. Guthrie, T. Michelle Magyar, Ann Fran Maliszewski, and Alison M. Wrynn (Dubuque, IA: Kendall/Hunt Publishing Co., 2009), 85–98.
63 Fred Bowen, "Title IX Has Encouraged Girls to Play Sports," *Washington Post*. www.washington post.com/lifestyle/kidspost/title-ix-has-helped-encourage-many-girls-to-play-sports/2012/06/20/gJQARxx3qV_print.html (accessed June 20, 2012).
64 Zerlina Maxwell, "Title IX Turns 40, Flaws and All," *The Root.com*. www.theroot.com/print/63797 (accessed June 21, 2012).
65 Angela Hattery, "Title IX at 40: More Work Needs to Be Done," *USA Today*, June 21, 2012, 7A.

66 Richard Lapchick, "The 2012 Race and Gender Report Card: College Sport." www.tidesport.org/RGRC/2012/2012_College_RGRC.pdf (accessed July 10, 2013).

67 Maggie Jo Poertner Buchanan, "Title IX Turns 40: A Brief History and Look Forward," *Texas Review of Entertainment and Sports Law* 14, no. 1 (2012): 93.

68 William Rhoden, "Black and White Women Far from Equal Under Title IX," *New York Times*, June 11, 2012, D5.

69 See *Biediger v. Quinnipiac University*, 728 F. Supp. 2d 62 (D. Conn. 2010) and Jaime Schultz, *Qualifying Times: Points of Change in Women's Sport* (Champaign: University of Illinois Press, 2014).

70 National Women's Law Center, "Athletics." www.nwlc.org/our-issues/education-%2526-title-ix/athletics (accessed January 2, 2014).

71 "Dear Colleague Letter." www2.ed.gov/about/offices/list/ocr/letters/colleague-201104.html (accessed April 4, 2011).

18

SPORT AND MASCULINITY

Kevin B. Wamsley and Macintosh Ross

Introduction

Sport has historically been a cultural location where American manhood has been defined, promoted, and celebrated. For centuries, competing social, political, and economic meanings about the body in American history have defined what is valued, celebrated, and abhorred in the behaviors, attitudes, dress, and appearances of men and women. Religion, war, politics, nationalism, international relations, commercialization, education, racism, sexism, compulsory heterosexuality, entertainment, and business have all influenced the contested ideas about what it meant to be a man—whether a husband, a father, a brother, a leader, a worker, or athlete. Even presidents of the United States have occasionally weighed in on the value of sport in developing the consummate American man who could serve his country and lead in the development of his nation. In turn, those contested ideas have created and sustained institutional practices over long periods. Celebrations of iconic masculinity through sporting achievements have mobilized millions of Americans, while derogations of perceived inappropriate representations of manhood through sport have inspired citizens to violence and murder.

Masculinity is not a point of departure, or an endpoint, or simply an identity. Masculinity is a constantly changing process of social engagement and participation, within gender relations, which men and women experience and reproduce on a daily basis. Masculinity informs daily habits, relationships with others; it informs choices about physical activity, entertainment, clothing, and language. Dominant cultural forces in American history have privileged particular forms of masculinity in sport over others and, consequently, certain sports, athletes, and teams emerged as important signifiers in American cultural life. When integrated within broader, important social and political movements or events such as war, attitudes toward American manhood played out through sport have captured the attention of millions of people. Masculinity, in its many forms, is deeply embedded in our historical and current understandings of sport. This chapter provides an overview of some of the dominant ideas about sport and masculinity in American life.

Masculinity and Physical Activity in Early America

The arrival of Europeans to America obliterated the gender regimes of American Indians, forcing a constant reshaping of masculine identities among Native men for centuries.[1] Colonists, laborers, and settlers faced monumental tasks surviving in the Virginia Colony of the 1600s, for example; yet, to the dismay of colonial officials, they were reluctant to discard the English pastimes which they preferred over labor.[2] In colonial Virginia "sports were the prerogative of patriarchy, but not all patriarchs were equal."[3] The "pastimes and merry exercises" typical in early Jamestown (1607) were stamped out throughout the Virginian plantations, where a hierarchical master–servant system took root, fueled predominantly by white, indentured laborers. New settlers also turned their attention to more pressing concerns than the sports and recreations of the Old Country. Before long, however, the texture of Virginia social life was dramatically transformed. Indentured servants completed their work terms, additional immigrants arrived from England, and plantation owners enjoyed more consistent crops and profits. Furthermore, "as mortality rates dropped," "the possibility of permanent investment in labor—slavery—became feasible."[4]

For Pilgrims who fled England to practice their own versions of Christianity and founded Plymouth Colony in 1620, sport and leisure presented religious and practical challenges. Sport played no small role in the Pilgrims' decision to cross the Atlantic Ocean. In 1618, King James I issued the *Declaration on Lawful Sports*, outlining which activities were permissible on the Sabbath and holidays like Easter and Christmas. The Pilgrims, however, abhorred idleness of all sorts. Thus, the Pilgrims discouraged sport and recreations, used the Sabbath for prayer, and ignored most of the holidays celebrated by the Church of England. Upholding these religious beliefs, however, proved difficult. On Christmas Day, 1621, for example, Plymouth Governor William Bradford left several men with work orders. When he returned, Bradford found them "in the street at play openly; some pitching the bar, and some at stool-ball and such like sports."[5] The "rough" masculinities of laborers often expressed in undesirable activities such as alcohol consumption ran counter to religious values and the order of labor demanded by colonial officials.

Since the arrival of the Pilgrims in 1620, sport had remained a matter of fierce religious and political debate in England. In June 1630, Puritan religious dissenters arrived in present-day Massachusetts to settle the Massachusetts Bay Colony. Like the Pilgrims before them, the Puritans staunchly opposed James I's views on Sabbath sport. Thus, when Charles I reissued the *Declaration on Lawful Sports* in 1633, reaffirming the place of Sabbath sports in English society, a flood of Puritan opponents set sail to Massachusetts Bay to join like-minded colonists across the sea. In Puritan New England, a man's worth was tied primarily to his piety, family, and community. The obligations of "communal manhood" required men to exercise caution toward leisure, sport, and recreation, lest they succumb to morally corrosive idleness and its bedfellows, gambling and drunkenness.[6] Yet, Puritan officials stopped short of discouraging recreation entirely. As long as recreation benefited the community, proving useful and productive, Puritan officials saw no reason to curtail it. Not surprisingly, therefore, ideal recreations were "to be labor-like, to be productive, or at least to be beneficial to workers."[7]

In the Virginia Colony, the rhythms of work and leisure were very different from those in Plymouth and Massachusetts Bay. As black slaves became more common, white colonists increasingly derived their masculine worth from sport and recreation, rather than a hard day's work. "If enslaved blacks had to work," write historians Elliott Gorn and Warren Goldstein, "play was proof of freedom and of elevated social status. Labor was a burden of blackness; leisure, the prerogative of whiteness."[8] Yet, all white men were not equal in Virginia. Poor white males could derive manly dividends from gambling on blood sports or competing in lifting and fighting against their social equals. Competition between workers, or even small land owners, and the colony's social and economic elites, however, was virtually unheard of at the time.[9] Indeed, in most cases, wealthy plantation owners avoided anything that smacked of disorder, including fistfights and cudgeling, popular among artisans, general laborers, and indentured servants.[10] Yet, more often than not, the sports and recreations of wealthy Virginians were also available to other colonists, but conducted in a manner that promoted exclusivity and a higher degree of order, moderation, and fairness.[11] Horse racing, in particular, was common ground for most land-owning Virginians. Races between plantation owners and nonlanded Virginians were illegal—few colonists owned horses anyway—but all colonists were welcomed as spectators.[12] For wealthy plantation owners, lacking the hereditary titles of England, races were an opportunity to display their wealth and status to society, while demonstrating fair and orderly competition to the masses.[13] Public expressions and displays of masculinity and social class were not only inextricably linked for wealthy landowners; such articulations became fundamental in reproducing the social order.[14]

Sport, Identity, and Social Class

In the Puritan northeast, sport continued to be viewed with suspicion well into the eighteenth century. Militia training often represented a Puritan colonist's primary interaction with sport and recreation, providing opportunities for competition in wrestling, foot racing, shooting, and other activities deemed beneficial to soldiers.[15] During the early eighteenth century, however, New England was a region in transition. New immigrants, with little concern for Puritan values, arrived from England with their cultural traditions in tow and colonists set out in search of new opportunities, establishing new communities in the New England wilderness.[16] Undermined in part by this cultural and geographical diversification, the old Puritan order, predicated on communal cooperation, began to erode. By the mid-1700s, the Puritan penchant for moderation was giving way to old English sporting traditions, more common in the South. Horse racing was openly advertised in newspapers. Taverns offered games and sport for the average colonist.[17] Men gathered and competed to prove their masculine worth through sport, emphasizing individuality over community, if only for the duration of a contest or game.

During the eighteenth century, sport and recreation were well-established components of masculine identities formed in British North America. Some groups, however, did mount opposition to the average colonist's propensity for play and leisure. The Quakers, for example, founded Pennsylvania in hopes of securing a homeland free of excess and frivolity. To them, an ideal man acted with the utmost self-restraint, avoiding sport and recreation. His identity, like those of the earliest Puritans, was derived from his value to the group. Settlement, however, was not limited to Quakers alone. In Philadelphia, a growing German and English non-Quaker community pursued masculine prowess through a combination of work and leisure, partaking in blood sports and other traditional, typically rural, pastimes. Although the old Quaker order attempted to mold newcomers through laws and regulations, Pennsylvania's decidedly non-Quaker colonial administration, consisting of sport-loving gentry, worked against the Quaker's grand designs. Deriving their own masculine self-worth from leisure—particularly in horse racing, fishing, and hunting—the Pennsylvania gentry saw little reason to repress leisurely play and competition on a colonial scale, tacitly supporting the sporting traditions of the average, non-Quaker colonist.

By the mid-eighteenth century, particularly in more Southern colonies like Maryland, Virginia, Georgia, and the Carolinas, the gentry further distinguished themselves from the average colonist by importing English thoroughbreds for their horse races. The Southern gentry, ever concerned for their social standing, used thoroughbred racing to illustrate their wealth and masculine prowess through victory and successful gambling, permitting colonists of all social ranks to watch their races, but not to compete.[18] A man's knowledge of horse racing was a function of his available leisure time and, thus, his social and economic standing in the community. Southern male colonists of lesser means also used sport to forge masculine identities, particularly through blood sports like gander-pulling and cockfighting where they garnered praise and adulation from other men. Taverns games, likewise, provided opportunities for manly competition and camaraderie, allowing artisans, laborers, and others outside the gentry class to distinguish themselves from their neighbors through sport. The typical Southern male likely needed to "engage in raucous sports" to gain "full acceptance among his peers."[19]

In the Southern backwoods, far from the region's largest communities, sport and masculinity intertwined in very different ways, producing particularly violent displays of sporting prowess. Gouging or rough-and-tumble fighting, in which competitors attempted to remove noses, ears, fingers, eyes, and/or genitals flourished in the backwoods, reflecting the harsh realities of life on the margins of colonial society. "Above all," writes Gorn, "brutal recreations toughened men for a violent social life in which the exploitation of labor, the specter of poverty, and a fierce struggle for status were daily realities."[20] Thus, unlike in the Puritan and Quaker enclaves of the rural North, the best or most distinguished man throughout the Southern backwoods was "not the most moral, prosperous, or pious but the local champion who had whipped all the rest, the man most dexterous at extracting eyes."[21] An affront to one's honor was a challenge to one's sense of masculine identity. Southern men of different classes preserved honor through various physical activities, which related directly to their status. The winning man in any event, therefore, preserved and reinforced, if only temporarily, a rather fragile sense of class-based masculinity.

Toward the Self-Made Man

By the second half of the eighteenth century, sport-inclined colonists faced a series of new obstacles. Although "new modes of thought supported individual action," these emerging ideologies pushed back against the spread of numerous sporting pursuits. During the 1730s, the First Great Awakening of Evangelical Protestantism "advanced the idea of personal independence and undermined hierarchy as a social principle."[22] At the same time, however, Evangelicals attacked popular sports, both North and South, admonishing followers to focus their entire lives on piety and prayer. The realm of politics also produced ideological challenges to the colonies' growing sporting culture. "Republicanism, the fighting faith of the American Revolution (1775–1783)," writes Rader, "also tended to inhibit sports."[23] In 1774, the thirteen colonies formed the Continental Congress to protect their rights and interests from the excesses of the British government. To do so, however, Republicans believed that the sporting, gambling, and drinking of the English aristocracy needed to be stamped out in the thirteen colonies. Like the Puritans, however, Republican idealists feared idleness more so than sport. Thus, it is hardly surprising that the attendees at the First Continental Congress could discourage practices like bull baiting, horse racing, and cock fighting, while George Washington—the Republican Commander-in-Chief—openly encouraged "games of exercise for amusement."[24] To Republicans, useful recreations, producing strong, athletic men, could overthrow the extravagant British regime that was accustomed to leisure and excess.

Following the American victory in 1783, appropriate manhood was deeply entangled in broader debates around national identity. The American Revolution was a revolt against patriarchal authority, "a revolution in the understanding of the nature of authority that affected all aspects of eighteenth-century culture."[25] Symbolically, England was the 'father' of the thirteen colonies and the domineering patriarch that sparked the American Revolution. The attainment of American independence can therefore be regarded as an act of "symbolic patricide."[26] With their independence secured, social commentators and political leaders emphasized the importance of nurturing a republican, American manhood. Writing in 1785, Samuel Adams encouraged American men to pursue "frugality and simplicity of manners" while avoiding "effeminate refinements" associated with the English aristocracy.[27] Central to avoiding so-called refinements was the use of appropriate, useful sport. Promoters of horseracing, cockfighting, and bear baiting faced opposition, not, however, only because their sports of choice encouraged idleness and effeminacy, but because they smacked of Englishness.[28]

Following the Revolutionary War, American men facilitated a gradual shift away from communal masculinities, emphasizing submission and hierarchy, toward a more individualistic, accomplishment-based, self-made manhood.[29] By the dawn of the nineteenth century, men increasingly sought to define themselves by their actions, rather than their birth or community, carving out their own identities through "self-improvement, self-control, self-interest, and self-advancement."[30] With the emergence of the market economy, many of these men found themselves in a middling social position, managing labor rather than laboring themselves, earning comfortable incomes in the process. Some of these men were university educated, but a number were master artisans, adapting their shops to the realities of the growing market economy.[31]

In the 1840s and 1850s, white middle-class men, working largely in sedentary positions as managers, clerks, lawyers, accountants, and doctors, started formulating new ideas about order and respectability and appropriate physical activity to fortify their bodies outside of the workplace. "Sedentary students and workers who were worried about their fitness and unmanly nature of their work," explains historian Steven Riess, "were drawn to sports to improve their health and gain respect for their manliness."[32] Initially, cricket proved the most popular sport for middle-class men, who organized numerous teams after 1840, New York, New Jersey, and Pennsylvania in the North and, Georgia in the South.[33] According to Henry Chadwick, an English immigrant and journalist, cricket was an ideal sport because it nurtured "sobriety, self-denial, fortitude, discipline, fair play, and obedience."[34] It allowed young men to enjoy competition, and camaraderie, without promoting the idleness and vice associated with cockfights, prizefights, and other predominantly working-class sports.

For other middle-class men, fulfillment came beyond the workplace and local playing fields, throughout America's Western frontier. Many middle-class men, reacting to the growing urbanization of their localities, believed in the "tonic virtue of wilderness" and consumed it through hiking, fishing, and hunting. For others, more drastic measures were required. The frontier, brimming with danger and new opportunities, enticed numerous middle-class men to set out in search of adventure. Beginning in 1849, the California gold rush proved particularly attractive. The 1849ers found "a world of 'rude freedom' outside the traditional bounds of civilization." They attended prizefights, drank constantly, and gambled compulsively.[35] Alongside all of the rollicking scenes of violence and excess, men honed their ingenuity, resilience, and resolve, finding the necessary self-discipline to survive, if not thrive, in their new surroundings.[36] They routinely hunted, fished, fought, rode, and camped. More so than their Eastern counterparts, a 49er's masculinity was measured in displays of physical prowess and endurance. Similar scenes played out throughout the West in American territories like Nevada, Colorado, and Montana.

Not all American men were enamoured with self-restraint. Men in the artisanal trades, for example, often engaged in lifestyles in which work and leisure time were fluid, the one flowing into the other in the shop. Many artisans played just as hard, if not harder, than they worked. Artisans "engaged in a wide spectrum of leisure-time activities, ranging from competitive sport to lounging on street corners."[37] Often setting their own hours, artisans attended cockfights, dogfights, prizefights, and bear-baits; drank in the shop and the tavern; and, defended their honor with fists and boasts. Some reform-minded artisans practiced self-control and pious self-improvement,[38] but many more clung to traditional leisure practices, playing and competing, drinking and fighting, as they saw fit. The expansion and solidification of the market economy, driven primarily by improvements in transportation, challenged this way of life. Under the watchful eye of profit-minded entrepreneurs, some of them former artisans, work time was cleaved from leisure time. Men, increasingly paid hourly wages, placed a premium on productive labor. During the 1840s, immigration from Europe boomed, providing employers with a large pool of unskilled and semiskilled workers, most of whom would work for a fraction of the wages earned by their native-born counterparts. In the wake of shrinking incomes, limited workplace independence, and increased competition in the labor force, artisans forged highly competitive masculine identities, centered upon displays of physical prowess. The Irish and native-born workers, in particular, engaged in furious competitions, often ending in violent, sometimes fatal altercations. Such brawls and events "fostered a distinct working-class male identity that was centered on the boisterous public assertion of physical courage, independence, class pride, and American patriotism."[39] In this context, prizefighters like Tom Hyer, Yankee Sullivan, John Morrissey, and John C. Heenan became the earliest working-class sporting heroes, representing the numerous tensions—Catholic versus Protestant, skilled versus unskilled, Irish versus native-born—evident in the day-to-day working-class experience.

Black athletes, in particular, were largely excluded from the sports and games played by white men, working class or otherwise. In the South, slavery continued unabated until the mid-1860s. It took a bloody Civil War to finally break the cycle of servitude employed by white Southerners. Yet slaves constructed their own unique cultures.[40] In his *Life and Times*, leading abolitionist and escaped slave Frederick Douglass, provides a sketch of sports conducted by slaves. From Christmas to New Year's Day, slaves were typically granted a holiday by their masters, during which all "regular work was suspended." According to Douglass, "the majority spent the holidays in sports, ball-playing, wrestling, boxing, running, foot-races, dancing, and drinking whisky."[41] In this manner, slaves competed and earned accolades within their enclosed, enslaved community, demonstrating their physical prowess and athletic skill for their own entertainment. In the North, slavery slowly lost its hold on the African American population. Derogatory assumptions about race and manhood, however, continued to persist. Black men were considered atavistic, dangerous, and unintelligent. Under the law, African Americans, regardless if they were free or slave, could not attain American citizenship, forbidding black men from attaining 'American' manhood, in a very literal way, under the law. The notion of white men competing against black men in sport was largely unheard of. Yet, a small number of African Americans boxers did manage to test their physical prowess and skill against white opposition, albeit in England. In America, the heavyweight championship was reserved for white competitors only. Black fighters Bill Richmond and, later, Tom Molineaux both fought white boxers in England and effectively challenged prevailing notions about race and manhood.[42]

Muscular Christianity, War, and the Emergence of Consumption

With the outbreak of the Civil War in 1861, American men of all social backgrounds joined either the Union or Confederate armies, carrying their sporting abilities into service as soldiers. On both sides of the conflict, "men boxed, played baseball, and raced horses, often for the first time in their lives."[43] At the same time, war forced American men to adapt to new, often gruesome realities. According to historian Larry Fielding, "the cult of physical heroism, the kind of mental set that applauded men who died with their face to the enemy, demanded that skill and courage be displayed."[44] By the end of the war, the relationship between masculinity and sport was reinvented and re-entrenched, producing a rapid increase in the frequency and variety of sporting events across the nation.

During the last quarter of the nineteenth century, social commentators increasingly suggested that white middle-class American men were becoming feminized. They cited the abundance of women in young boy's lives, particularly mothers and teachers; the monotonous grind of the middle-class workplace; the increased presence of immigrants, with different cultural norms; and the feminizing influence of the church as the common forces plaguing American's young men.[45] Accurate or not, many middle-class men believed they were becoming more feminine and, as a consequence, sought new ways of displaying their masculinities. These men increasingly pursued a sort of "passionate manhood," celebrating man's primal, "animal instincts."[46] For many middle-class men, baseball and football became the antidote to what they perceived as the feminization of American males.

In the mid-1850s, "Muscular Christianity" crept into the American consciousness following the publication of the novels *Tom Brown's School Days* (1856), by Thomas Hughes, and *Two Years Ago* (1857), by Charles Kingsley. Unitarian minister and noted social reformer Thomas Wentworth Higginson, encouraged Protestant men to embrace sport, arguing that "physical health is the necessary condition of all permanent success," spiritual or otherwise.[47] Like the middle-class quest for rational recreation earlier in the century, Muscular Christianity championed vigorous, useful sports, while opposing the idle pastimes offered by urban halls and taverns. In the 1860s, American Muscular Christianity was institutionalized via the Young Men's Christian Association (YMCA). Initially intended as centers for bible study and education, YMCAs in Washington, New York, and San Francisco added gymnasiums that provided structure and organization for adherents of Muscular Christianity. By 1900, 455 YMCA gyms existed across America, encouraging a physically robust form of Christian masculinity.[48] According to Riess, "a respectable, gambling-free sporting culture was evolving, based on behaviors and attitudes consonant with Victorian values that stressed the functionalism of competitive athletics."[49]

During the American Civil War, baseball spread like wildfire as working- and middle-class men, from rural and urban backgrounds kept busy and bonded with bat and ball. Following the war, baseball quickly became the most popular team sport in most towns and cities. "With opportunities for exhibitions of physical manliness limited by radical changes in the nineteenth century work places and the prevailing Victorian restraints on self-expression," writes sport historian Benjamin Rader, "baseball offered an exciting arena for the display of physical prowess and aggressiveness in a controlled setting."[50] Not all men could compete on equal terms, however. The sport required leisure time, something many unskilled and even semiskilled laborers struggled to obtain. Thus, the baseball teams of late nineteenth-century America consisted of largely middle-class men—clerks, managers, proprietors—and skilled artisans, who maintained some control over the length of their workdays.[51]

The evolution and spread of professional baseball attracted considerable attention to the sport, while rumors of fixed games inspired criticism from those who promoted the gentleman amateur approach to the sport. An honorable man played for the love of the game, displaying physical prowess and athletic superiority. A man who sold such vaunted attributes for a quick buck was no man at all. Theodore Roosevelt railed against professional baseball but was nonetheless the de facto leader of a shift toward more aggressive, physical, even dangerous reformation of American masculine ideals. America, in Roosevelt's opinion, was quickly becoming a nation of flabby, overcivilized bookworms, lacking the strength and endurance of America's founders.[52] Roosevelt became "the manly advocate of virile imperialism."[53]

In 1899, hailed as an expert on all things militant and manly, Roosevelt addressed Chicago's Hamilton Club, outlining his "doctrine of the strenuous life," imploring his fellow men to embrace

> the life of toil and effort, of labor and strife; to preach that highest form of success which comes, not to the man who desires mere easy peace, but to the man who does not shrink from danger, from hardship, or from bitter toil, and who out of these wins the splendid ultimate triumph.

Roosevelt's theories, however, promoted a "violent, imperialistic manhood," emphasizing white, American supremacy. Formulating his theories of manhood upon prevailing, Social Darwinist ideas, Roosevelt insisted that only white citizens—not black, Asian, or aboriginal—constituted the superior "American Race."[54] Furthermore, Roosevelt believed it was the responsibility of American men to overcome other "uncivilized" races abroad, who would be "far happier after the white man had conquered them."[55]

To build and preserve the "American Race," Roosevelt encouraged white young middle- and upper-class men to engage in rugged, violent sports to preserve the frontier manhood that overcame the "savages" of the frontier. Roosevelt believed participation in rugged sports ensured a "hardy masculinity" for American men, capable of maintaining the nation's growing Imperial possessions.[56] By vehemently endorsing sport, Roosevelt believed he could "revitalize commercial America and build a new Anglo-Saxon super-race."[57] As the training ground for America's future politicians, doctors, ministers, lawyers, and entrepreneurs, America's universities were ideal environments for Roosevelt's vigorous brand of masculinity to take root. College football, more so than any other sport, exhibited Roosevelt's athletic doctrine. Under the watchful eye of Yale's Walter Camp, American football promptly surpassed all other college sports in popularity, becoming the leading symbol of "manliness and virility" on college campuses.[58] This was "passionate manhood" stretched to the extreme. Displaying violence surpassed by only the most brutal of prize fights, college football existed in a perilous grey area between respectable sport and brutality. Unlike baseball, for example, college football was plagued by on-field deaths. To Roosevelt, the dangers of football were part and parcel of its allure. What better prepared the nation's middle- and upper-class men for life's daunting challenges than a dangerous sport, where one's very life hung in the balance? When universities started discussing a ban on football, Roosevelt was flabbergasted, insisting he would "a hundred fold rather keep the game as it is now, with the brutality, than give it up."[59] Others, however, considered football little more than a large-scale prizefight. It was the game's tendency to expose "a person to every kind of violence," argued the editor of *The Nation* in 1893, "which puts football, under the present rules, into the same category with the prizefight, and makes it unlike all other games played by civilized man."[60]

Ironically, in 1905, Roosevelt called a White House meeting with delegates from Harvard, Princeton, and Yale to discourage foul tactics in football.

The same call to "passionate manhood" that fervently endorsed football opened the door to upper- and middle-class boxing, conducted with gloves and rounds, sterilized by athletic club decorum. In his study of Boston, historian Stephen Hardy argues that "restrictive membership policies and the exclusive nature of their activities ensured that many . . . sporting clubs occupied prominent positions as symbols of elite social and economic status."[61] If boxing was to exist in such a context, it needed to be distinct from its working-class, bare-knuckle counterpart. By the late nineteenth century, athletic clubs were already rallying against sporting professionalism by upholding amateur ideals of "sport for sports sake."

While Roosevelt railed against idle spectatorship and professionalism, others were turning tidy profits. In late nineteenth-century American cities, the consumption of manhood was starting to rival personal displays of prowess in popularity. The popularization of bodybuilding in the 1890s vividly illustrates this shift. Championed by Prussian-born Eugen Sandow, bodybuilding emphasized the development of large and defined muscles, displayed for paying onlookers. Sandow occupied a comfortable grey area between the practice and consumption of athleticism and physicality. He was, in a sense, the ideal compromise between idle entertainment and passionate manhood. As historian John Kasson explains, "spectators viewed Sandow's body as both an attraction and a challenge, a model of strength and an object of desire, an inspiration, a rebuke, and a seduction."[62] Sandow marked a subtle shift in American society, illustrating the growing "ethic of pleasure and consumption" evolving within the middle class. Bored with their lot in life, urban bourgeois men increasingly sought to "break out of old Victorian restraints" and revel in taverns, theaters, and museums after work.

Several men identified and exploited this "cultural thaw," offering up various sporting products for consumption.[63] In journalistic circles, no man seized upon the growing thirst for entertainment quite like Richard K. Fox, editor of the *National Police Gazette.* Fox championed the revival of prizefighting, providing detailed illustrations of muscular, bare-chested men battling with their fists. For working-class men and a growing number of consumption-oriented bourgeois urbanites, the heavyweight champion of America was the finest, most manly athlete in the nation.

When world heavyweight champion John L. Sullivan was matched to face a bank clerk turned prizefighter named "Gentleman" Jim Corbett in 1892, boxing appeared on the brink of mass appeal. On July 9, 1892, Corbett used the boxing skills of a refined athletic club regular to pummel Sullivan into submission and win the World Heavyweight Championship.[64] Corbett ushered in a new era of professional boxing, uniting the amateur and bare-knuckle forms of boxing on the sport's grandest stage. More so than ever before, the heavyweight champion was "the acknowledged physical superior of any living man," in all corners of society.[65] A strict color line remained in force atop the heavyweight division, preventing African American pugilists from challenging for the world championship. Sensational black boxers like George Godfrey and Peter Jackson, for example, tried and failed to arrange fights with reigning heavyweight champion John L. Sullivan. Jack Johnson defeated Canadian Tommy Burns to win the world championship in 1908, but it was not until 1937 that a black boxer was permitted to challenge for the title on American soil. After Johnson won the heavyweight title, a quest for a "great white hope" began immediately. As champion, Johnson promptly defeated a string of white opponents, driving racist, white anxieties to a fever pitch. After much discussion, Jim Jeffries, who retired while still heavyweight champion, was lured back to the ring to redeem the masculinity of white men everywhere. It was, to quote historian Randy Roberts, "for all the racial marbles."[66] Johnson's victory not only created a crisis in white masculinity; it inspired race riots, the murder of black citizens, and provided a voice for critics who viewed boxing as an uncivilized expression of manhood.

In the years leading up to World War I, the nation embraced professional sport on a grand scale, fostering a thoroughly consumption-oriented sporting culture. When athletes marched off to war, the homo-social confines of military life proved a breeding ground for passionate, even atavistic, displays of masculine prowess. Much like their Civil War–era brothers in arms, World War I soldiers incorporated a wide range of sports into their identities and sought to replicate these practices at home when they returned. It was during this time of postwar sporting enthusiasm that sporting celebrities entrenched themselves in the American psyche. The gruesome realities of trench warfare made virtually all sport—even boxing and football—appear tame recreations. "The barbarism of real war," writes historian Jeffrey Sammons, "made boxing seem dignified, if not dainty."[67] Under these circumstances, heavyweight champion Jack "The Mannasa Mauler" Dempsey emerged as America's most-popular sporting celebrity. He was the most spectacularly violent boxer in American history. During the 1920s, people from all corners of society, regardless of race, class, or gender, followed boxing as thoroughly as their ancestors followed labor trends and politics. The advent of radio sports coverage placed a physical, geographic barrier between consumers and the pandemonium at ringside. As a string of hopeful boxers fell at Dempsey's feet, American society reveled in the slaughter. America had become "a boxer's paradise."[68]

Sport and Masculinity Through the Twentieth-Century and Beyond

Despite the success of heavyweight champion Joe Louis, black American men continued to struggle for equal treatment in sport and society in general, leading a number of athletes to use sport as a platform for racial protest. Tommie Smith and John Carlos, for example, displayed the black power salute on the podium at the 1968 Olympic Games. Most famously, heavyweight boxing champion Muhammad Ali fought vigorously against racism in America for the balance of his career and beyond. Due to the intense racial divide still evident in much of America, the mere act of competing against and defeating white men, remains a powerful display of black masculine pride and prowess. As sociologist Ben Carrington explains,

> [S]ports provide an arena whereby black men can lay claim to a masculine identity as a means of restoring a unified sense of racial identity, freed, if only momentarily, from the emasculating discourses imposed by the ideologies and practices of White racism.[69]

Throughout the twentieth century and beyond, America never looked back. Violent sports such as boxing, football, hockey and much later, mixed martial arts celebrated American manhood; the power of the home run in baseball fascinated and thrilled spectators; and the drive to the Olympic podium epitomized the march of American athletes against the rest of the world. Even NASCAR drivers and promoters rationalized the role of violence and aggression in automobile racing. NASCAR emerged from the decades-long traditions of Southern stock car racing, and was closely linked in popularity and promotion to normalized versions of Southern masculinity. The "good ole boys" of the 1980s advertised oil, fried chicken, and beer on their cars to frenzied fans. The sport posed significant risks for its drivers, however, as fans were treated to narratives about aggressive driving, exciting crashes, even deaths on the track. NASCAR promotions traded on the intense rivalries between competitors and sometimes fights broke out between drivers following track altercations.[70] Ironically, the commercial influence of television directed NASCAR away from the promotion of Southern masculinities and Southern themes, as the sport sought out the larger market of American families as its audience.

Within an international context, the Olympic Games have reproduced a gender order through sport dictating who participates in what sport and how throughout the twentieth century. Domestically, however, the professional tele-sports of football, baseball, and basketball have structured patterns of spectatorship, consumption, spending, and language while creating and sustaining American dreams of athletic achievement or athletic manhood that inspire boys from elementary school through college.

Conclusion

The enduring power of such narratives and common understandings of the role of sport in men's lives has contributed significantly to the inequities between men and women in sport and society, more broadly. The sporting masculinity narrative has been so powerful in shaping everyday lives that U.S. presidents frequently invoke such relations and direct references in their political language to effectively resonate with their audiences.[71] John F. Kennedy, George W. Bush, and Barack Obama[72] frequently used sport references to represent their masculine leadership capacities as Roosevelt, the Muscular Christians, and Southern gentry had done long before them. For centuries, men in America have linked sporting prowess and the value of sport to manhood and social capacity to great advantage.

Notes

1 R.W. Connell, "The Big Picture: Masculinities in Recent World History," *Theory and Society* 22 (1993): 606.
2 Nancy Struna, *People of Prowess: Sport, Leisure, and Labor in Early Anglo-America* (Urbana and Chicago: University of Illinois Press, 1996), 42.
3 Elliott J. Gorn and Warren Goldstein, *A Brief History of American Sports* (New York: Hill and Wang, 1993), 23.
4 Ibid., 20.
5 William Bradford, *On Plymouth Plantation, 1620–1643*, ed. Samuel E. Morison (New York: Alfred A. Knopf, 1952), 97, as cited by Struna, *People of Prowess*, 47.
6 For "communal manhood" see, E. Anthony Rotundo, *American Manhood: Transformations in Masculinity from the Revolution to the Modern Era* (New York: Basic Books, 1993), 13; for caution towards recreations, see Bruce C. Daniels, *Puritans at Play: Leisure and Recreation in Colonial New England* (New York: St. Martin's Press, 1995), 18.
7 Struna, *People of Prowess*, 67.
8 Gorn and Goldstein, *A Brief History of American Sports*, 21.
9 See Gerald R. Gems, Linda J. Borish, and Gertrud Pfister, *Sports in American History: From Colonization to Globalization* (Champaign, IL: Human Kinetics, 2008), p. 20 for one such example.
10 Struna, *People of Prowess*, 105; and see also Gems et al., *Sports in American History*, Chapter 1 and Chapter 2 for examples.
11 Struna, *People of Prowess*, 114.
12 Gorn and Goldstein, *A Brief History of American Sports*, 22–23.
13 Ibid., 23. For the importance of honor as a surrogate for hereditary title, see Kathleen M. Brown, *Good Wives, Nasty Wenches, and Anxious Patriarchs: Gender, Race, and Power in Colonial Virginia* (Chapel Hill: University of North Carolina Press, 1996), 139.

14 See T.H. Breen, "Horses and Gentlemen: The Cultural Significance of Gambling among the Gentry of Virginia," *The William and Mary Quarterly* 34, no. 2 (April 1977): 239–257.
15 Benjamin G. Rader, *American Sports: From the Age of Folk Games to the Age of Televised Sports* (Upper Saddle River, NJ: Prentice Hall, 2004), 8.
16 Rotundo, *American Manhood*, 15.
17 Gorn and Goldstein, *A Brief History of American Sports*, 36.
18 Ibid., and see Breen in particular with respect to horseracing.
19 Rader, *American Sports*, 11.
20 Elliott J. Gorn, "'Gouge and Bite, Pull Hair and Scratch': The Social Significance of Fighting in the Southern Backcountry," *American Historical Review* 90, no. 1 (1985): 22.
21 Gorn, "Gouge and Bite," 23.
22 Rotundo, *American Manhood*, 15.
23 Rader, *American Sports*, 15.
24 George Washington, as quoted by Gorn and Goldstein, *A Brief History of American Sports*, 43.
25 Jay Fliegelman, *Prodigals and Pilgrims: The American Revolution Against Patriarchal Authority, 1750–1800* (Cambridge: Cambridge University Press, 1982), 5.
26 Michael S. Kimmel, *Manhood in America: A Cultural History* (Oxford: Oxford University Press, 2006), 15.
27 Samuel Adams, *Writings, Vol. 4*, 236–238, as quoted in Kimmel, *Manhood in America*, 16.
28 Gorn and Goldstein, *A Brief History of American Sports*, 50.
29 Rotundo, *American Manhood*, 18.
30 Ibid., 20.
31 Kimmel, *Manhood in America*, 27.
32 Steven A. Riess, "Sport and the Redefinition of Middle-Class Masculinity in Victorian America," in *The New American Sport History*, ed. S.W. Pope (Urbana and Chicago, IL: University of Illinois Press, 1997), 191.
33 Riess, "Sport and the Redefinition of Middle-Class Masculinity," 182–183; J. Thomas Jable, "Social Class and the Sport of Cricket in Philadelphia, 1850–1880," *Journal of Sport History* (*JSH*) 18, no. 2 (1991): 205–223; Timothy Lockley, "'The Manly Game': Cricket and Masculinity in Savannah, Georgia in 1859," *The International Journal of the History of Sport* (*IJHS*) 20, no. 3 (2003): 77–98.
34 Riess, "Sport and the Redefinition of Middle-Class Masculinity," 183; see also Jable, "Social Class and the Sport of Cricket in Philadelphia," 220.
35 Kimmel, *Manhood in America*, 42.
36 Rotundo suggests that time spent in the gold rush could provide men with "the self-discipline needed for the active life of the marketplace." Rotundo, *American Manhood*, 21.
37 Bruce Laurie, "Nothing on Compulsion: Lifestyles of Philadelphia Artisans, 1820–1850," *Labor History* 15, no. 3 (1974): 344.
38 Gorn and Goldstein, *A Brief History of American Sports*, 51.
39 Michael Kaplan, "New York City Tavern Violence and the Creation of a Working-Class Male Identity," *Journal of the Early Republic* 15, no. 4 (1995): 592.
40 See David K. Wiggins, "The Play of Slave Children in the Plantation Communities of the Old South, 1820–1860," in *Glory Bound: Black Athletes in a White America* (Syracuse, New York: Syracuse University Press, 1997), 3–20; "Sport and Popular Pastimes: Shadow of the Slavequarter," in *Sport in America: From Wicked Amusement National Obsession*, ed. David K. Wiggins (Champaign, IL: Human Kinetics, 1995), 51–68.
41 Frederick Douglass, *The Life and Times of Frederick Douglass: His Early Life as a Slave, His Escape from Bondage, and His Complete History to the Present Time* (Hartford, CT: Park Publishing Company, 1883), 180.
42 Tracey M. Salisbury, "Bill Richmond," in *African Americans in Sport*, ed. David K. Wiggins (New York: Routledge, 2015), 302.
43 Elliott J. Gorn, "Sports through the Nineteenth Century," in *The New American Sport History: Recent Approaches and Perspectives*, ed. S.W. Pope (Urbana and Chicago, IL: University of Illinois Press, 1997), 51.
44 Lawrence W. Fielding, "Sport: The Meter Stick of the Civil War Soldier," *Sport History Review* (*SHR*) 9, no. 1 (1978): 18.

45 Michael S. Kimmel, "Consuming Manhood: The Feminization of American Culture and the Recreation of the Male Body, 1832–1920," *The History of Men: Essays on the History of American and British Masculinities* (Albany, NY: State University of New York Press, 2006), 46–47.
46 Rotundo, *American Manhood*, 227.
47 Thomas Wentworth Higginson, "Saints and Their Bodies," *Atlantic Monthly* 1, no. 5 (1858): 585–586. For Higginson's views on Christianity and the body, see Stephen Hardy, *How Boston Played: Sport, Recreation, and Community, 1865–1915* (Boston: Northeastern University Press, 1982), 52–53.
48 Clifford Putney, *Muscular Christianity: Manhood and Sports in Protestant America, 1880–1920* (Cambridge, MA: Harvard University Press, 2001), 67.
49 Riess, "Sport and the Redefinition of Middle-Class Masculinity," 184.
50 Rader, *American Sports*, 57.
51 Warren Goldstein, *Playing for Keeps: A History of Early Baseball* (Ithaca, NY: Cornell University Press, 1989), 24–25. See also Steven A. Riess, *City Games: The Evolution of American Urban Society and the Rise of Sports* (Urbana and Chicago, IL: University of Illinois Press, 1989), 70.
52 Kimmel, *Manhood in America*, 123.
53 Gail Bederman, *Manliness and Civilization: A Cultural History of Gender and Race in the United States, 1880–1917* (Chicago: University of Chicago Press, 1995).
54 Ibid., 179.
55 Ibid., 189.
56 Kimmel, *Manhood in America*, 123.
57 Gorn and Goldstein, *A Brief History of American Sports*, 147.
58 Ronald A. Smith, *Sports and Freedom: The Rise of Big-Time College Athletics* (Oxford: Oxford University Press, 1988), 84.
59 Roosevelt, as quoted by Ronald A. Smith, *Sports and Freedom*, 95.
60 *The Nation [New York]*, November 30, 1893; see also Michael Oriard, *Reading Football: How the Popular Press Created an American Spectacle* (Chapel Hill, NC: University of North Carolina Press, 1993), 217.
61 Hardy, *How Boston Played*, 142.
62 John F. Kasson, *Houdini, Tarzan, and the Perfect Man: The White Male Body and the Challenge of Modernity in America* (New York: Hill and Wang, 2001), 29.
63 Gorn and Goldstein, *A Brief History of American Sports*, 118.
64 Elliott J. Gorn, *The Manly Art: Bare-Knuckle Prize Fighting in America* (Ithaca, New York: Cornell University Press, 1986), 239–241.
65 Mike Donovan, *The Roosevelt That I Knew: Ten Years of Boxing with the President—and Other Memories of Famous Fighting Men* (New York: B.W. Dodge and Company, 1909), 187.
66 Randy Roberts, *Papa Jack: Jack Johnson and the Era of White Hopes* (New York: The Free Press, 1983), 85.
67 Jeffrey T. Sammons, *Beyond the Ring: The Role of Boxing in American Society* (Urbana and Chicago, IL: University of Illinois Press, 1990), 50.
68 Christopher David Thrasher, *Fight Sports and American Masculinity: Salvation in Violence from 1607 to the Present* (Jefferson, NC: McFarland, 2015), 148.
69 Ben Carrington, "Sport, Masculinity, and Black Cultural Resistance," *Journal of Sport and Social Issues* 22, no. 3 (1998): 290–291.
70 See Jared Walters, "The South, Television, and Death at 200 mph. An Examination Into the Influence of Southern Masculinity, Honour, and Technological Changes on Violence and Safety in 1980s NASCAR," a paper presented to the North American Society for Sport History in Miami, Florida, 2015.
71 Jackson Katz, "Politics Is a Contact Sport," in *Media/Cultural Studies, Critical Approaches*, ed. Rhonda Hammer and Douglas Kellner (New York: Peter Lang Publishing, 2009), 537–556.
72 Aaron J. Moore and David Dewberry, "The Masculine Image of Presidents as Sporting Figures: A Public Relations Perspective," SAGE *Open* 2, no. 3 (2012): 1–11.

19

QUEERING FIELDS AND COURTS

Considerations on LGBT Sport History

Rita Liberti

Introduction

In February 2014 Michael Sam, University of Missouri football player "came out," proclaiming, "I am an openly, proud gay man."[1] At least one observer, a National League Football player, attempted to frame the moment's historical significance asserting that Sam's actions placed him in the company of Jackie Robinson, Martin Luther King, and Rosa Parks.[2] The chorus of responses that followed varied widely—though generally positive, they ranged from support to disgust. Various media outlets from television to social media rushed to cover and comment on the news of an out gay football player. The media frenzy around Sam continued through May, and his selection by the St. Louis Rams as a seventh-round NFL draft pick, made him the first out gay man to be chosen in the league's history.[3] An NFL film crew captured the moment, broadcasted live as the selection was made, as Sam and his boyfriend, in a very gay public display of affection, embraced in a "kiss seen around the world."[4] Responding to the event's significance, Rams' General Manager Les Snead concluded "I could feel the pivot in history at that moment."[5]

Beginning the chapter with this particular event is not meant to imply that homophobia and heterosexism in sport ceases to exist, with Sam's "coming out" as some declaration of its end. I am cautious to characterize any moment in time as a watershed event in sport history. However, Sam's actions and the somewhat favorable media coverage that followed spoke loudly against the silences regarding a gay male presence in professional football. In addition, we cannot know what analytical tools future historians will bring to bear on this moment or its ultimate historical significance, but what is certain is there will be ample evidence with which to examine it.[6]

Sam's "coming out" and the volume of evidence that followed is in stark contrast to twentieth-century histories of LGBT (lesbian, gay, bisexual, transgendered) people in sport and the broader society, where homophobia and heterosexism's legacy has been silence and invisibility. Indeed, the conundrum for those interested in interpreting LGBT pasts is to find them first, as it involves a "group of people" who faced with the realities of homo-hatred have "tried to cover their tracks, who spoke or wrote in code [and] who burned letters and diaries."[7] Evidence, or the lack thereof, on which to construct historical narratives of LGBT subjects and experiences is not the only obstacle, however.

Issues and Identity in LGBT History and Sport

The other issue that complicates LGBT narratives involves language, identity, and the politics of naming, within and across specific historical moments. For much of the twentieth century, for example, definitional boundaries of same-sex relationships, as well as the labels attached to homosexuality within public discourses were formulated and circulated by those not of the identity.[8] Needless to say these narratives were often less than complimentary, casting individuals as perverted. Scholars' interpretations of LGBT histories face other complications as well. What does it mean, for example, to affix a "lesbian" label to an early twentieth-century subject who may not have claimed that identity or in a culture or time for which "lesbian" or "gay" or "transgender" does/did not exist in the lexicon? Unlike other minority histories that tend to be more stable over time, LGBT categories are not. In relation to LGBT issues Bronski concludes, "language is both an entryway and a dead end."[9] Identities and the meanings attached to them are historically and culturally specific, oftentimes spilling over the limited designations at our disposal. When combined with questions around invisibility and evidence, the inadequacies of language make inquiry that much more difficult.

Beyond these obstacles, however, lies a potentially rich historical field of LGBT histories, experiences, and stories in sport. Thus, scholars are served by making histories of marginalized sexualities more central to, and a much more vigorous part of, sport history. Far from simply adding LGBT individuals to the historical mix, this work, at its core, has far more to offer our understanding of the past and our present. The important ties that bind LGBT communities are their challenge to heteronormativity and the dominant gender order.[10] Indeed, these histories force us to rethink and reconceptualize binary gender systems that can all too often seem entrenched and immovable, especially in the context of sport.

As the title of this chapter suggests, LGBT histories *queer* sport spaces in that they disrupt and challenge neatly defined gender categories, as they resist the tendency to essentialize classifications of difference.[11] Though in its infancy, there is a tremendous amount of insight to be gained from examining some of the subject matter in LGBT history of sport. With that stated, it is crucial that I highlight the fact that this is not meant to be a "status of the field" chapter. I was not eager to write from that frame, nor did the co-editors ask me to do so. Rather, as a sport historian, I seek to bring a handful of LGBT "episodes" from sport's past to the fore, namely, to explore the ways in which scholars have engaged the subject matter. I have chosen four examples: the first two include studies of lesbian softball culture in the middle decades of the twentieth century by Susan Cahn and Anne Enke, respectively.[12] The third illustration is very recent scholarship on 1920s tennis star Bill Tilden by Nathan Titman.[13] The final example is my own critical reading of the documentary *Out: The Glenn Burke Story* about 1970s Major League Baseball player Glenn Burke's experiences as an African American gay athlete.[14] The chapter, with the four aforementioned examples as a foundation, considers issues of method and theoretical approach; thus it trends toward a historiographical piece versus an analysis of LGBT sport history.

Borrowing from Thomas Piontek, I make use of the term *queer* not in reference to an identity per se, but to a "questioning stance" around gender and sexual identity, one that encourages us to "explore the taken for granted and the familiar from new vantage points."[15] Each example, and in total, throws into sharp relief the historical specificity on which constructions of sexuality and gender rest. Moreover, each scholarly approach uses different source material, which includes autobiography, oral history, and film and asks that we engage multiple subjectivities of the historical actors in question. Sexuality is thus a key identity marker upon which the analyses rest, but it is not the only one. Arguably, when we are mindful of the myriad subjective spaces occupied by historical actors, there is even more to be learned from those whose embodied presence in sport challenged heteronormativity and traditional gender arrangements.

Writing in support of analyses that engage multiple subjectivities, including sexuality, Samantha King argues that scholarship on LGBTQ issues in sport studies has been inadequate to date. According to King, "erasure of racializing forces," for example, at the intersection of marginalized sexualities reaffirms whiteness. Thus, "we must adopt a more robust queer sensibility if we are to avoid contributing to the drive toward normalization and instead effectively interrogate its premises and assumptions."[16] The section of scholarship I highlight in this chapter brings a bit of LGBT sport history to center stage, moving it in the direction advocated by King. More importantly, it exposes the power and potential of an intersectional analysis that, according to Catherine Mackinnon, "fills out the Venn diagram at points of overlap where convergence has been neglected, training its sights where vectors of inequality intersect at crossroads that have previously been at best sped through."[17] Thus, the following four examples chosen are selective, but not arbitrary, as each urges an intersectional understanding of marginal sexualities within the context of sport history.

Reclaiming Foul Territory: Lesbian Sport History

Though written over two decades ago, Susan Cahn's analysis of lesbianism and sport in *Coming on Strong: Gender and Sexuality in Twentieth-Century Women's Sport*, provides a very strong, early example of the directional path King and MacKinnon espouse.[18] Cahn, in "refusing to impose preexisting, ahistorical, or unitary identity categories (lesbian, woman) on her archive . . . is able" according to King, "to trace how sport is implicated in the constitution of inherently unstable identity categories and as such represents a key site for challenges to, and reaffirmations of, normativity, sexual and otherwise."[19] Utilizing extensive oral histories from women who played softball from the 1930s to the early 1960s, Cahn examines the experiences of participants at the junction of gender, sexual, and class identities.

In addition to rendering an analysis at the confluence of the multiple subjective spaces occupied by participants, Cahn attends to the fluidity of definitions associated with female intimacy over the first few decades of the twentieth century. By the mid-century, displays of physical and emotional closeness between women "signaled an 'improper' intimacy,"[20] in contrast to late nineteenth- and early twentieth-century conceptualizations of similar relationships as normal and even encouraged. What was deemed deviant or normal in relation to same-sex behavior remained far from static and was instead culturally and historically specific. This, of course, proves crucial in understanding more deeply how athletes and the broader society attached meaning to female athleticism in a largely homosocial context within this mid-century moment.

The supposed stability of the heterosexual/homosexual binary is problematic, as well, through the ways in which female athletes with whom Cahn spoke defined themselves and others. These examples speak to both the historical specificity and limits of language, in addition to underscoring the idea of sexuality as a social construction. "One of the unwritten rules [among the athletes]," Cahn asserts "was the avoidance of sexual labeling. The terms 'lesbian' or 'gay' were rarely used. Instead, through phrases like 'this one is going with that one,' sexuality was referred to as a relation, not a personal identity."[21] What may seem on one level silencing as a result of homophobia can be read in other ways that fortify rather than deny agency. Not laying public or private claim to a particular identity allowed many women, Cahn argues, a space within which to experiment and explore same-sex attraction.

Far from a simplistic reading of lesbian sport history, one grounded in repression and invisibility, Cahn presents us with a site that held both repressive and liberating elements for participants. Her analysis negotiates these tensions as she offers even more nuanced insights on the dynamics of class standing as they played themselves out within lesbian softball culture. The various athletic spaces were of enormous significance for working-class women for whom "sport was a lifeline, offering the chance to develop talents, win public acclaim, travel, and socialize with other lesbians."[22] Rather than undermining the oppressive realities of mid-century working-class lesbians, this work however, enables us to explore the potential of agency within these sites despite, or because of, the broader repressive space in which it was held. Cahn concludes that lesbian athletes at mid-century "found that athletic life facilitated the individual process of coming to terms with homosexual desires as well as the collective process of forging community ties among gay women."[23]

Queering Space, Politicizing Place: Women's Softball

Many of the core themes that run through Cahn's work are evident in Anne Enke's discussion of lesbian athletes and softball culture in Detroit and Minneapolis during the 1960s and 1970s in her *Finding the Movement: Sexuality, Contested Space, and Feminist Activism.*[24] Similar to Cahn, Enke moves her analysis along multiple lines of identity, beyond sexuality, to include class and race. In addition, Enke's examination connects queer athletic spaces with the larger political economy and in doing so LGBT histories become "less ghettoized . . . more connected to, and more essential for understanding broader narratives of US history."[25] Similar to Cahn, oral history is the foundation on which Enke's analysis rests. It is as a result of these life histories that the author begins to see the "collective politicization of place."[26] As Enke asserts, women athletes, many of whom identified as feminist or lesbian, moved in and took up space in public parks and on softball diamonds—areas historically defined by/through expressions of masculinity and heteronormativity. In the process, these spaces became *very public* locations around which normative understandings of gender, sexuality, class, and race were contested.

The experiences of the Motown Soul Sisters, one of the most successful Detroit area softball teams formed in the mid-1960s, helps to illustrate the ideological and structural challenges faced by African American women, many of whom were lesbians. Amid these constraints, team members unapologetically moved into the male preserve of public recreation and elite athletic space, filling "highly public roles as visible transgressor and trespassers of gender, sexual, and racist norms and boundaries."[27] In claiming a right to occupy public spaces such as parks and ball fields, the Soul Sisters enacted a decidedly political stance.

In still other ways the team's presence makes central the politicized position of the participants, but also of the space itself. Through the 1960s bars constituted the primary place in which LGBT individuals, including the Soul Sisters, gathered. Though technically defined as "public," the clubs were often far from it as they were removed from gazes of outsiders. Athletic fields and municipal parks presented an entirely different, new, and intensely public arena in which lesbians moved through their worlds. Softball diamonds were indeed, "as queer as [they were] athletic."[28] As embodied subjects, the female athletes in Cahn and

Enke's research, with every throw, slide, pitch, and catch, upset dominant norms. And in doing so anchored even more firmly the connection between a queer subculture and sport.

Courting Controversy: Bill Tilden and the Limits of Masculine Expression

Recent focus on 1920s white tennis star Bill Tilden marks the third of four scholarly contributions on LGBT sport history I explore in this chapter. In particular, Nathan Titman's article about Tilden makes an incredibly strong contribution to the nascent inquiry on marginalized sexualities and U.S. sport history.[29] Much like Cahn and Enke, Titman's examination of Tilden's experiences on and off the tennis court attends to the notion of intersectionality, as well as sport's uniqueness in carving out spaces of agency with potential for its gay and lesbian participants, despite the incredibly rigid heteronormative boundaries. For both of these reasons, Titman's work warrants our attention.

"Big" Bill Tilden was among the nation's athletic best during American sport's Golden Age, winning, among other contests, seven national singles titles and three Wimbledon titles by 1930. His superlative skills on the court earned him the Associated Press honor in 1950 as the best tennis player over the first half of the twentieth century. The athlete's physical dominance was so complete through the 1920s it earned him the moniker, "Tilden the Invincible."[30] His unassailability on the court, however, could not withstand Tilden's actions away from the game, as his arrests in the 1940s for soliciting sex with underage boys led to prison terms and ostracism from tennis and from his own family for the remaining years of his life.[31] Although these historical realities are indeed a part of Tilden's experiences, Titman is less concerned about verifying the tennis star's sexual identity and practices. Instead, his interest rests with examining Tilden's nonheteronormative expressions of agency as articulated on the court and off.

Relying on a range of primary and secondary sources, including Tilden's autobiography, Titman explores the ways in which the tennis great both embodied and expressed masculinities beyond normative expectations during the 1920s and 1930s, known as the "Golden Age of Sport." The author argues that Tilden's involvement in tennis cannot be conceived as purely a repressive space in which his nonheterosexual expressions and behaviors were contained. Rather, tennis "offered Tilden an opportunity to express a gender and sexual identity that constituted an alternative to contemporary expectations regarding male bodies and movement."[32] In a very literal sense, Tilden's unique display of physicality on the court moved tennis competition into the "realm of the theatrical," according to Titman. Tilden's athleticism, a combination of traditional expressions of masculinity such as speed and quickness were combined with the traditionally conceived feminine traits of "elegance and delicacy," prompting observers to make comparisons to the arts and dance.[33]

Significantly, Titman reads Tilden's performances on the tennis court at the intersection of the athlete's multiple identity markers—moving beyond sexuality as the single axis point of analysis. Class and Tilden's whiteness are the other subjective spaces around which Titman's interrogation of the 1920s tennis star revolves. In bringing Tilden's racial identity, his whiteness, to the fore Titman engages an intersectional analysis, but also one that upsets the preferred notion that race and sexuality are points of discussion only when people of color are the subjects.[34] Titman not only acknowledges Tilden's whiteness, but also argues that it is of consequence in more deeply understanding the very specific cultural and historical contexts in which power operates and is contested. Stating of Tilden, "On the level of movement and physicality, he wished to maintain the aesthetic value of male tennis athleticism—one that allowed spectators to witness the supposed refinement and control of white male bodies."[35] The author adds, "Male tennis players could perform the supposed aesthetic and physical superiority of the white body through dress, control, and easeful motion."[36] Tilden simultaneously reinscribed and challenged white normative constructions of gender through performance of a nonheteronormative brand of masculinity, which he displayed on courts across the nation and the world. In this way, Tilden's sexual identity cannot and should not be extricated from that athlete's racial white identity in making sense of his experiences.

Reading at the Intersections of Out: The Glenn Burke Story

The final episode of LGBT sport history I highlight in this chapter is a critical reading of the 2010 documentary *Out: The Glenn Burke Story*.[37] Arguably, one of the few ways contemporary audiences will come to *know* 1970s Major League Baseball player, Glenn Burke, is through this film. Thus, in general, it is incumbent upon us as sport historians to thoughtfully interrogate documentary film and other "sites of remembering" beyond the written word, as the past in all its forms is brought to the present.[38] The documentary's focus on Burke, a gay African American professional baseball player, offers up a unique and rarely told story in sport history: elite athletic experience at the intersections of gender, race, and sexuality. My aim is, thus, to explore the ways the film engages the multiple marginal subjectivities of its protagonist with the hope that it helps to expose the complexity and richness of life lived at this intersection.

Out follows filmic convention typical of documentaries as Glenn Burke's life is chronicled for viewers in linear fashion beginning with his teenage years as a high school athlete. Interviews with well over two dozen former players, coaches, journalists, friends, and family constitute the bulk of material used in *Out* as the documentary moves from one "talking head" to another in piecing together Burke's story. Notable major league players such as Davey Lopes, Dusty Baker, Tito Fuentes, and Rickey Henderson, among others, reflect on Burke's life and legacy in baseball. However, despite the many different voices throughout the documentary, viewers hear and see very little of Glenn Burke. Audio clips of the former athlete collected 16 years earlier in the final months of Burke's life are, however, spread across the film. Far from the bold, outspoken, and flamboyant figure described by others, Burke's presence in the film is reduced to a few sporadic, frail, and sometimes inaudible comments.[39]

In addition to the explicitness of the documentary's title, from its introduction forward to its conclusion, *Out* turns solely around the singular pivot point of Burke's identity as a gay man. As a result, issues related to gender and sexuality permeate the documentary, as filmmakers utilize the many "talking heads" to illuminate baseball's homophobic culture and Burke's struggles within it. The film makes clear Burke did not go to great lengths to hide his homosexuality, and as a result, many of the game's insiders, including players, coaches, and team management, knew of his sexual identity, especially near the end of his career. The sport's homophobic culture shortened his playing career, as Burke's tenure in baseball's top league lasted less than five years. For producers and consumers, Burke's identity as a gay man shapes and informs the documentary and the various new media materials that surround the film. What remains absent, however, is Burke's identity as African American. Burke's racial identity appears "invisible" and thus the ways in which he (and others) understood his gendered and sexual self, as a black gay man, are left unattended. This omission is a missed opportunity as much as a major criticism of the film. Neglected is an important and much-needed exploration of how athletic masculinities have been and continue to be constructed and lived at the intersectional axis of gendered, racial, and sexual subjectivities. To be clear, interrogating experiences at the juncture of multiple elements of identity involves not simply "uncovering" and exposing, in this case, Glenn Burke's history in baseball. The significance of the process also rests in examining and unpacking relationships of power, as well as how and where hegemony is contested.[40]

The documentary's glaring omission of race and its relationship to Burke's sexuality is especially puzzling given the athlete's inclusion of the topic in the co-authored text with Eric Sherman written years earlier. Whereas *Out* could afford and thus choose to ignore issues of race and racial identity, Glenn Burke could not, as his "othered" status was a permanent, far from optional, part of his being. In a discussion of playing minor league baseball in Ogden, Utah, Burke comments that the city "never was and never will be a hotbed for young gay blacks."[41] The racism he and his fellow African American teammates faced was not, unfortunately, confined to the boundaries of Ogden. Burke took note of inequalities in the majors as well. He noted that his friend and teammate Marvin Webb had superior skills and statistics on the field, yet was never called up to the majors. "I'm sure there was some racism involved in keeping Marvin down," Burke acknowledged, adding Webb was "robbed."[42] Burke was keenly aware, even as a young man, of others' perceptions of him and the broader racial politics that swirled around his actions and decisions. As a 19-year-old, Burke possessed the athletic skills to play baseball or basketball, and potential scouts from both sports came calling. Baseball's L.A. Dodgers won out over basketball offers, not only because of the cash-in-hand signing bonus they paid. Burke noted that if he turned down the contract, "I could get labeled as a black with a bad attitude."[43]

E. Patrick Johnson's work is especially instructive to this critical reading of *Out* as he argues for theoretical tools that provide more nuanced understandings of queer identity—understandings that include (rather than exclude) black gay men. For Johnson, queer theory,

> while [it] has opened up new possibilities for theorizing gender and sexuality, like a pot of gumbo cooked too quickly it has failed to live up to its critical potential by refusing *all* the queer ingredients contained inside its theoretical pot.[44]

Thus, Johnson borrows the term "quare"—his grandmother's black dialect inflected pronunciation of "queer"—to underscore the point that "sexual and gender identities always already intersect with racial subjectivity."[45] With that said, I employ a "quare" lens through which to view and make sense of *Out* that emerge as a result of the documentary.

Comments, assessments, and questions about Burke's gendered identity, as it related to his athleticism, circulate at numerous points and on various levels throughout the film and new media, though as stated, there remains a complete silence regarding race. Moreover, although gender issues are raised, they are not acknowledged as such or critically interrogated in the film. At the documentary's start, memories of Burke's superior physical skills and powerful body are recalled by former teammates. Burke's talents as a high school student on the fields and courts of San Francisco's East Bay were legendary, as peers remembered his strength and dominant presence. Jim Skeels, former Connie Mack baseball coach, recalls a specific incident that epitomized Burke's brawn. Burke, he claimed, "hit a line shot that probably did not get more than 15 feet off the ground. He hit it to dead center and this ball stuck, it was hit so hard, it stuck in the cyclone fence in centerfield!"[46]

Glenn Burke's body was also the location upon which straight male peers directed their gaze. Burke was a "top physical specimen," according to Shooty Babbitt, Berkeley High athlete and major leaguer. "I remember after games he would pull off his shirt," recalled journalist Nick Peters, "he was built like a Greek god." Another Berkeley High athlete, Claudell Washington, notes Burke was, "built like Adonis," adding he was like "no other man that I had seen." Within the many athletic spaces occupied by young men and boys in Berkeley in the late 1960s and early 1970s, Glen Burke embodied what it meant to be masculine. High school opponent to Burke and major leaguer Rickey Henderson concluded of the young men in the area, "[W]e always wanted to be like Glenn Burke."[47]

The brand of hypermasculinity on display by Burke, across the various fields and courts of the East Bay community in which he lived, did not constitute, however, the full range of the athlete's gender expression. Claudell Washington remembers the celebrations following the many Berkeley High basketball wins, in which Burke played an enormous role, "Glenn would get on top of the football lockers with a towel around him and his shower shoes [acting as a microphone] in his hands. He'd be sashaying around [singing]." His teammates' fascination with Glenn Burke's range of masculinities carried through to his years in professional baseball. On the field, teammate Manny Mota marveled at Burke's sporting talents. "I love to watch Glenn" during warm-ups, said Mota, who was awed by his powerful throws from all of the outfield positions. Burke, said Mota, "put up a show." As a Los Angeles Dodger during the 1977 season, Burke's "shows," like those of his high school years, did not begin and end on the diamond but extended to the locker room. Dodger teammate Joe Simpson remembered that even John Travolta's performance in the 1977 blockbuster film *Saturday Night Fever* could not compete with Burke's skills as he could "dance circles" around the movie's brightest star. Mota recalled, "everybody got around Glenn Burke to watch him dance." Glenn Burke stretched peers' assumptions about athletic masculinity and homosexuality, thereby confounding players and coaches by his actions. Bewildered, Shooty Babitt noted, "you look over at his locker and you know he had this red jock in his locker . . . *nobody* wore a red jock! Glenn wore a red jock and he'd be dancing around in the clubhouse [mimics dancing]."[48]

Although the documentary is replete with missed opportunities to recognize and critically engage the complexities of athletic masculinity, as lived by Glenn Burke, at least one instance is not. In the days just after the documentary's debut, KGO (810 AM) sports talk radio show in the Bay Area, hosted by Rich Walcoff, invited Abdul Jalil, Shooty Babitt, and Burke's friend John Lambert to discuss the issue of gay athletes in professional sport. *Out* producer Doug Harris videotaped the segment and then uploaded it to YouTube. In the clip, Jalil offers up an emphatic pronouncement of Burke's significance as a gay athlete:

> Whatever measure of a man you find to be pertinent, Glenn will exceed the criteria in every way. Whether it was physically as an athlete, it didn't matter. You set the bar [and] Glenn would exceed that and then come back and redefine what you classify a man to be, saying 'I'm gay, I'm Glenn, this is me.' So it wasn't just about breaking down barriers it was about redefining what a man was.[49]

Jalil's observations move us to think more deeply and analytically about the documentary and the gendered spaces Burke occupied as an athlete. He was, according to Jalil, far more than a gay pioneer whose history was no longer hidden. Rather, Burke's lived experiences disrupted notions of hegemonic masculinity and the narrow conceptualizations of manhood often associated with professional sport.

Dodger players in the 1970s did not share Jalil's enthusiasm of Burke's gender transgressions, however, as responses to the novelty and range of Burke's masculine performances were not always affirmed by teammates. This was especially so beginning in the season after the team's trip to the World Series in 1977. Burke's teammates had their limits within a harshly homophobic environment where players were expected to be "macho and manly" according to Dusty Baker. Teammates began to take note and be scornful of the ways in which Burke moved through his world in Major League Baseball. Shifting from one intensely homophobic clubhouse to another, Burke was traded in 1978 from the LA Dodgers to the Oakland A's. Burke, by this time, had become "a little bit more obvious about his preferences and a lot of guys [including A's manager Billy Martin] were turned off about it," according to sports agent Abdul Jalil. Teammates paid attention to and were made uneasy by the groups of unknown men in pink Cadillacs who picked Burke up after games. Just a couple of years earlier, Burke's performances in the clubhouse made the athlete a likeable attraction, now players were uncomfortable being in the same space with him. Not surprisingly, amid these conditions, Burke decided to leave baseball in 1980. He conceded to Eric Sherman over a decade later, "I could live my own life now [with] nobody looking over my shoulder. I was relieved . . ."[50]

Glenn Burke lived 15 years beyond his retirement from Major League Baseball and, in that time, life was not especially sweet. Burke's crack addiction, which began years earlier, continued, resulting in a prison term for the former Major Leaguer. In addition, he contracted HIV, leading to a painful death of AIDS-related complications in 1995. E. Patrick Johnson, in discussing Marlon Riggs' documentary, *Black Is . . . Black Ain't* notes that the film " 'quares' 'queer' by suggesting that identity, although highly contested, manifests itself in the flesh and, therefore, has social and political consequences for those who live in that flesh."[51] Crack and AIDS ravaged communities of color, including many black gay men in the 1980s and early 1990s. Throughout the film and into its final minutes, *Out* fails to make any connections, let alone critical ones, between Burke's racial and sexual identity, thus silencing not only the material reality of his life but the "consequences of his embodied blackness."[52]

Reception to the documentary and Burke's unapologetic embrace of his homosexuality was overwhelmingly positive. Glenn Burke's experiences in professional baseball over the second half of the 1970s, although pushed to the margins of history, nonetheless carried messages that were received favorably by many consumers of the film. Even Dave Zirin's usually fault-filled comments were suspended in his appraisal of the documentary. *Out* was a "brilliant" and "remarkable" film, said Zirin, one that "has the power to change lives."[53] Peter Hartlaub of the *San Francisco Chronicle*, was so taken with the film he suggested, "*Out* should be required viewing for rookies who are entering professional sports."[54]

Much like the documentary on which these reviews are based, none of them take note of the silences around Burke's racial identity, save for one that I have located thus far. In Pat Griffin's LGBT sport blog she notes, "I found it interesting that the documentary did not address race at all. The fact that Glenn Burke was a black man must have affected his experience as a gay baseball player."[55] Griffin's innocuous blog posting elicited a quick response from Jerry Pritikin who asserted "race had nothing to do with it."[56] Pritikin, one of the many "talking heads" in the documentary, played softball with Burke in the Castro's gay leagues of the 1980s. He inserts himself into a number of blog responses about the documentary, usually in rambling chronicles, which end up offering us little about Burke and more about

Pritikin. Mirroring a pattern found in *Out*, Pritikin's rejoinder to Griffin privileges a "single-variable"[57] understanding of Glenn Burke's life, as it dismisses his blackness. Participating in what Allen Berube calls, "gay whitening practices,"[58] these discourses, in and around the documentary, erode rather than further, the charge of gay politics by leaving behind men and women of color.

Despite the criticisms of the film, I do believe *Out* remains a provocative and important documentary in its attention to gay men's presence in sports' past despite (because of) homophobia's ceaseless intensity. Glenn Burke's story as described in this film would have been much more compelling, however, had it explored the various subjective spaces he occupied. Given Burke's life and experiences, what was lost was an opportunity to disrupt assumptions around stereotypical (and essentialized) notions of black and gay masculinity.

Conclusion

In 2006, sport historian Gary Osmond commented, "Gay sport histories are sadly lacking . . . due to the locked nature of the "closet."[59] To be sure, the study of queer pasts in sport history has barely begun. Unfortunate on one hand, it also presents exciting possibilities to explore dominant tropes, which have long circulated around sexuality, identity, and athleticism, as well as explore relationships of power within these spaces. As the glimpse into the four episodes presented here illustrate, sport is "invested in boundary maintenance" it likewise "operates as a complex site of pleasure and desire."[60] In many ways, the study of marginalized sexualities in sport, at its core, unpacks those two seemingly contradictory positions. As I have advocated in this chapter, the histories we seek to interpret are best served when we focus analytic lenses on the multiple subjectivities, including sexuality that people inhabit. It is then that the closet door is unlocked and fully open.

Notes

1 Chris Connelly, "Mizzou's Michael Sam Say's He's Gay." http://espn.go.com/espn/otl/story/_/id/10429030/michael-sam-missouri-tigers-says-gay (accessed December 1, 2014).

2 Brendon Ayanbadejo quoted in Aaron Wilson, "Brendon Ayanbadejo Calls Michael Sam a Pioneer in Tradition of Jackie Robinson," *The Baltimore Sun*, February 12, 2014. www.baltimoresun.com/sports/ravens/ravens-insider/bal-brendon-ayanbadejo-calls-michael-sam-a-pioneer-in-tradition-of-jackie-robinson-rosa-parks-martin-lut-20140212-story.html#page=1 (accessed November 29, 2014).

3 www.nfl.com/videos/nfl-draft/0ap2000000349399/Sam-reacts-to-getting-drafted (accessed November 29, 2014).

4 Rheana Murray, "Meet Vito Cammisano, Michael Sam's Boyfriend." http://abcnews.go.com/Sports/meet-vito-cammisano-michael-sams-boyfriend/story?id=23680199 (accessed December 1, 2014).

5 Caitlan Macneal, "Rams GM on Michael Sam: 'I Could Feel the Pivot Point in History.'" http://talkingpointsmemo.com/livewire/rams-general-manager-snead-michael-sam-history (accessed December 2, 2014).

6 Michael Sam was cut from the St. Louis Rams' squad after the 2014 pre-season games. The Dallas Cowboys added Sam to their practice team in September 2014, but waived him six weeks later. In May 2015, Sam signed with the Montreal Alouettes of the Canadian Football League.

7 John D'Emilio, *In a New Century: Essay on Queer History, Politics, and Community Life* (Madison: University of Wisconsin, 2014), 123. For an excellent example of how homophobia and internalized homophobia magnified silences and shaped the narratives of celebrity athletes, see Susan Ware, *Game, Set, Match: Billie Jean King and the Revolution in Women's Sports* (Chapel Hill: University of North Carolina Press, 2011), 179–206.

8 D'Emilio, *In a New Century*, 212.

9 Michael Bronski, *A Queer History of the United States* (Boston: Beacon Press, 2011), xviii. On issues of language and LGBT history, see Robert A. Schanke and Kim Marra, *Passing Performances: Queer Readings of Leading Players in American Theater History* (Ann Arbor: University of Michigan, 1998), 4–7; Leila J. Rupp, *A Desired Past: A Short History of Same-Sex Love in America* (Chicago: University of Chicago Press, 1999), 5–9; Genny Beemyn, "A Presence in the Past: A Transgender Historiography," *Journal of Women's History* 25, no. 3 (2013): 113–114.

10 Caroline Symons and Dennis Hemphill, "Transgendering Sex and Sport in the Gay Games," in *Sport, Sexualities and Queer/Theory*, ed. Jayne Caudwell (New York: Routledge, 2006), 124.

11 John D'Emilio and Estelle B. Freedman, *Intimate Matters: A History of Sexuality in America* (Chicago: University of Chicago Press, 2012), xiii.

12 Susan Cahn, *Coming on Strong: Gender and Sexuality in Twentieth-Century Women's Sport* (New York: The Free Press, 1994); Anne Enke, *Finding the Movement: Sexuality, Contested Space, and Feminist Activism* (Durham, NC: Duke University Press, 2007).

13 Nathan Titman, "Taking Punishment Gladly: Bill Tilden's Performances of the Unruly Male Body," *Journal of Sport History* 41, no. 3 (2014): 447–466.

14 Rita Liberti, "Reading at the Intersections of *Out: The Glenn Burke Story*" (paper presented at the annual meeting of the North American Society for Sport History, Halifax, Nova Scotia, Canada, May 24–27, 2013).

15 Thomas Piontek, *Queering Gay and Lesbian Studies* (Champaign: University of Illinois, 2006).

16 Samantha King, "What's Queer About (Queer) Sport Sociology Now? A Review Essay," *Sport Sociology Journal* 25 (2009): 420.

17 Catherine A. MacKinnon, "Intersectionality as Method: A Note," *Signs* 38, no. 4 (2013): 1020.

18 Cahn, *Coming on Strong*. See especially, 164–206.

19 King, "What's Queer About (Queer) Sport Sociology Now," 423.

20 Cahn, *Coming on Strong*, 193.

21 Ibid., 203.

22 Ibid., 204.

23 Ibid., 185.

24 Enke, *Finding the Movement.* See especially, 105–173.

25 D'Emilio, *In a New Century*, 218.

26 Enke, *Finding the Movement*, 4.

27 Ibid., 109.

28 Ibid., 132.

29 Titman, "Taking Punishment Gladly." For additional recent scholarship on Tilden see, John Carvalho and Mike Milford, " 'One Knows That This Condition Exists': An Analysis of Tennis Champion Bill Tilden's Apology for His Homosexuality," *Sport in History* 33, no. 4 (2013): 554–567.

30 Karen Crouse, "Bill Tilden: A Tennis Star Defeated Only by Himself," *New York Times*, August 31, 2009, F5.

31 Frank Deford, *Big Bill Tilden: The Triumphs and the Tragedy* (New York: Simon and Schuster, 1975); Arthur Voss, *Tilden and Tennis in the Twenties* (Troy, NY: The Whitston Publishing Company, 1985).

32 Titman, "Taking Punishment Gladly," 448.

33 Ibid., 460.

34 Mary G. McDonald, "The Whites of Sport Studies and Queer Scholarship," in *Sport, Sexualities and Queer/Theory*, ed., Jayne Caudwell (New York: Routledge, 2006), 151. See also, Mary G. McDonald, "Mapping Intersectionality and Whiteness: Troubling Gender and Sexuality in Sport Studies," in *Routledge Handbook of Sport, Gender and Sexuality*, ed. Jennifer Hargreaves and Eric Anderson (London: Routledge, 2014), 33.

35 Titman, "Taking Punishment Gladly," 448.

36 Ibid., 452.

37 *Out: The Glenn Burke Story*, TV, produced by Doug Harris and Sean Maddison (San Francisco, CA: Comcast SportsNet Bay Area, 2010).

38 Murray G. Phillips, Mark E. O'Neill, and Gary Osmond, "Broadening Horizons in Sport History: Films, Photographs, and Monuments," *Journal of Sport History* 34, no. 2 (2007): 288. On arguments in support of the "visual turn" in sport history, see Gary Osmond and Murray G. Phillips,

"Reading *Salute*: Filmic Representations of Sports History," *The International Journal of the History of Sport* 28, no. 10 (July 2011): 1463–1477; Mike Huggins and Mike O'Mahony, "Prologue: Extending Study of the Visual in the History of Sport," *The International Journal of the History of Sport* 28, nos. 8–9 (May–June 2011): 1089–1104; Linda J. Borish and Murray G. Phillips, "Introductory Essay: Sport History as Modes of Expression: Material Culture and Cultural Spaces in Sport and History," *Rethinking History: The Journal of Theory and Practice* 16, no. 4 (December 2012): 465–477.

39 The audio clips are recordings by Eric Sherman of interviews with Burke for use in Glenn Burke and Eric Sherman, *Out at Home: The Glenn Burke Story* (New York: Excel Publishers, 1995). Unless otherwise noted, quoted material in this section of the essay is taken from Harris and Maddison's, *Out: The Glenn Burke Story.*

40 Adia Harvey Wingfield, "Bringing Minority Men Back In: Comment on Anderson," *Gender & Society* 22, no. 1 (February 2008): 89.

41 Burke and Sherman, *Out at Home*, 29.

42 Ibid., 30–31.

43 Ibid., 63.

44 E. Patrick Johnson, "'Quare' Studies, or (Almost) Everything I Know About Queer Studies I Learned From My Grandmother," in *Black Queer Studies: A Critical Anthology*, ed. E. Patrick Johnson and Mae G. Anderson (Durham: Duke University Press, 2005), 147, original emphasis.

45 Ibid., 125–126. See also, Arthur Flannigan-Stint-Aubin, "'Black Gay Male' Discourse: Reading Race and Sexuality Between the Lines," *Journal of the History of Sexuality* 3, no. 3 (January 1993): 468–490; Jennifer Devere Brody, "'Boyz Do Cry: Screening History's White Lies," *Screen* 43, no. 1 (Spring 2002): 91–96.

46 *Out: The Glenn Burke Story*, TV, produced by Doug Harris and Sean Maddison (San Francisco, CA: Comcast SportsNet Bay Area, 2010).

47 Ibid.

48 Ibid.

49 Abdul Jalil, "Out Conversation," uploaded June 12, 2011, video clip. YouTube. www.youtube.com/watch?v=pV7V2rA5RnQ (accessed February 10, 2013).

50 Burke and Sherman, *Out at Home*, 51.

51 Johnson, "'Quare' Studies," 141. See also, E. Patrick Johnson, *Appropriating Blackness: Performance and the Politics of Authenticity* (Durham, NC: Duke University Press, 2003), 17–47.

52 Ibid., 144.

53 Dave Zirin, "Reviewing OUT: The Glenn Burke Story," *The Nation*, 9 November 2010. www.thenation.com/blog/155946/reviewing-out-glenn-burke-story#

54 Peter Hartlaub, "'Out: Glenn Burke Story': Tragedy Hits Home," *San Francisco Chronicle*, 9 November 2010. www.sfgate.com/news/article/Out-Glenn-Burke-Story-review-Tragedy-hits-home-3166647.php

55 Pat Griffin, "Out: The Glenn Burke Story," *Pat Griffin's LGBT Sport Blog*, 13 February 2011. http://ittakesateam.blogspot.com/2011/02/out-glenn-burke-story.html

56 Ibid.

57 Johnson, "'Quare' Studies," 5.

58 Allen Berube, "How Gay Stays White and What Kind of White It Stays," in *The Making and Unmaking of Whiteness*, ed., Birgit Brander Rasmussen, Eric Klinenberg, Irene J. Nexica, and Matt Wray (Durham: Duke University Press, 2001), 236.

59 Gary Osmond, Review of *In the Game: Gay Athletes and the Cult of Masculinity* by Eric Anderson. *Journal of Sport History* 33, no. 1 (2006): 95. For a brief discussion on the dearth of material on LGBT sport history, see Mary Louise Adams, *Artistic Impressions: Figure Skating, Masculinity, and the Limits of Sport* (Toronto: University of Toronto Press, 2011), 6–9.

60 Heather Sykes, "Queering Theories of Sexuality in Sport Studies," in *Sport, Sexualities and Queer/Theory*, ed. Jayne Caudwell (New York: Routledge, 2006), 126.

Part V

THE BUSINESS OF SPORT

20

SPORT, TELEVISION, AND THE MEDIA

Richard C. Crepeau

Introduction

At this point it is more than self-evident that television has affected sport. The development of the technologies of electronic media brought with it new layers of impact on sport, and indeed these media have all affected one another. No doubt there is considerable debate as to whether or not the impact on sport has been positive or negative.

There were isolated experiments with television and sport prior to World War II, but after the end of the war television quickly assumed a central place in the American home, and the search for programming by national networks and local stations began. In 1946 there were 12,000 television sets in the United States. By 1950 there were 4 million sets with the potential to reach an audience of 30 million people, or 20 percent of the population.[1]

The television broadcasting day grew quickly. From a few hours in the late afternoon and early evening, television moved to fill most of the waking hours of Americans and network television grew beyond the evening hours.

Early Television and Sport

Programming was needed at all levels, and sport presented television with program content that had a built in popularity and drama. In addition, production costs were relatively low and sport filled large blocks of time. Sports leagues and owners, however, approached the new technology with caution. They feared that giving the public free access to sports events would have a negative impact on attendance. The National Football League moved first among the major team sports to experiment with television, and it was wrestling that took the first major plunge into the medium on an experimental local station in Los Angeles.

Starting in a sound stage at Paramount wrestling became so popular that it was moved into the 10,000-seat Olympic Auditorium. This was the beginning of a 30-year run promoted by Dick Lane who had moved from vaudeville to fight promotion. The melodrama was provided by the likes of Mr. Moto, the Destroyer, and the Black Panther, and the first superstar of televised sport, Gorgeous George. Four years after bringing wrestling to television Dick Lane introduced roller derby to the small screen.[2]

The first sport to attract a national audience on television was boxing. In the late 1940s and through the 1950s boxing entered a golden age, brief as it may have been. In 1944 the Gillette Safety Razor Company signed a deal with Madison Square Garden to sponsor weekly telecasts of the fights, and quickly the Friday Night Fights became a must-see event on the viewing schedule of many sports fans across the country.

However, overexposure quickly became a problem. As televised boxing spread to other nights of the week the demand for more boxers who were winners increased beyond the capacity of the sport. When the corruption of boxing was exposed in televised Senate hearings, the public reacted. In addition as television itself developed attractive prime-time programming, boxing began to suffer in the ratings. In 1952 boxing was seen by 31 percent of all households watching television, but by 1959 that number had dropped to 10.9 percent.[3] As for the networks they showed little interest in sports after an initial boomlet in 1948. Sports seemed to have limited appeal to men only, sports for the most part did not fit into a finite time slot, and finally the upper-class executives at the networks tended to look down on sports fans among the masses. Neither NBC nor CBS had a sports division, and ABC was not yet a player. Sports were housed and often neglected within the news divisions.[4]

In the first five years of television there were no ground rules as the business had no experience to guide it.

> There were no television ratings, no demographic breakdowns of the audience. In this time of uncertainty and experimentation, prime-time programmers found themselves drawn to sport as a way to attract an audience to their new medium. For a short time this strategy worked as televised sport lured many people to watch television, first in taverns and restaurants, and then in their own homes.[5]

New Relationships Between Television and Sport

The Chicago Bears, Baltimore Colts, and Cleveland Browns dabbled in television in the late 1940s. The first major experiment with television came in Los Angeles where the Rams allowed local broadcasts of all their 1950 home games. To allay fears of the potential consequences, Admiral Television sponsored the telecasts with the arrangement that they would make up any losses in ticket sales from the previous year. When attendance dropped 110,000 Admiral Television had to produce $307,000. The following year the Rams televised only road games and home attendance bounced back to 1949 levels.

The first network telecasts occurred in 1951. The Bears had a 10-city network that spread from Nashville to Minneapolis and from Columbus to Omaha. Local stations sold advertising, and the Bears picked up production and distribution costs. They lost money. On the national level Dumont was the only network interested in televising NFL football. Beginning in 1951 Dumont paid $95,000 per year to televise five games as well as the NFL Championship. This arrangement lasted until 1955. Most teams began to develop television networks in the early 1950s and the revenues they were able to generate varied widely. In 1953 the Rams received $100,000, whereas Green Bay generated only $5,000. That was the year that Commissioner Bert Bell got a rule passed in the NFL that no home games would be televised and no game could be telecast in a market where a home game was being played. This rule was challenged in court but Judge Allan Grim of the U.S. District Court in Philadelphia ruled on the side of the NFL in November of 1953.

By 1954 there were 24 million television sets in the country and approximately two-thirds of the population had access to television. One of the areas of greatest programming need for television was the Sunday afternoon "ghetto." The National Football League filled that need. By 1956 all teams had some network arrangements with CBS, and NBC owned the rights to the Championship Game. Bert Bell sent out a memo to all league members urging them to present the best possible teams for television. The networks in turn were prohibited from showing fights and injuries because as Bell put it, "We don't want the kids sitting in their living rooms to see their heroes trading punches. That doesn't teach good sportsmanship." Bell held the right of approval over all television contracts even though individual teams were doing the contracting of their games.[6]

All of this was merely prologue. The advertising community was in the process of discovering the potency of sports on television, and they soon moved into professional football, which turned out to be more potent than anyone imagined. Still the television network executives had to be dragged into it. Fortunately there was a serendipitous factor at work as the advertising industry was centered in New York City where the New York Giants were becoming a force in the National Football League. When the executives at the agencies got a whiff of success from the men of the gridiron they found it intoxicating. From that point it was a reasonably simple matter to take television along into this new world.

Ed Scherick of the advertising agency, Dancer Fitzgerald, had put together Baseball's Game of the Week for Falstaff Beer in 1953. He then began to look at football and started by buying up half of the spots on the Bears and Cardinals football network at $2,000 per game, a number Scherick called the "greatest media buy in the history of television." When the beer people wanted more spots he went to CBS and sold them on it. He too then moved to CBS. The pieces were falling in place and money seemed to be falling from the sky. And it was only the beginning.[7]

Unlike the National Football League, Major League Baseball did not warm to television, as they had not warmed to radio. They feared that it would cut into attendance, and there was some empirical evidence to suggest that was the case. Attendance did drop in the early 1950s after a boomlet in the immediate postwar years. In fact baseball attendance in the late 1940s would not be matched again until the 1970s. Historians have attributed this to a wide range of factors, including the decay of the inner city and the lack of parking at the existing stadiums. It was surmised by many owners that television was the culprit, and the decline of minor league attendance and the collapse of many minor leagues offered confirmation of this view.[8] In addition television ratings for baseball ran well behind those for the NFL.

Unlike the NFL, Major League Baseball found it could not package its games for joint sale to the networks, as the NFL had done. In 1954 MLB submitted a plan to the Justice Department seeking the right to allow the commissioner to sell a "Game of the Week" package to the networks. The Justice Department ruled that this would violate antitrust law and MLB backed away from the plan. Given MLB's antitrust exemption it was an odd decision. So the networks negotiated individual contracts with each team, although not all teams were approached by the networks.[9]

On the intercollegiate front television developed slowly as universities were learning how to deal with this new phenomenon. The University of Notre Dame and the University of Pennsylvania were the first to televise their football games. By 1950 Penn was the leader in football telecasts. Notre Dame moved cautiously until it discovered that there was a significant demand for the product of Notre Dame football. The university then signed with the Dumont Television Network with no impact on game attendance. There was, however, a positive impact on Notre Dame's budget.

In 1951 the NCAA moved to gain control of television, convincing its membership to set aside home rule and create an experimental television plan. Notre Dame and Penn resisted but in the end came into line as 96 percent of the NCAA members accepted the idea, although the members resisted the NCAA's proposal to keep 60 percent of the revenues generated by television. There was considerable unhappiness over many aspects of the NCAA limitations on television but there was no unified alternative. With no clear evidence of the impact of the plan, the NCAA membership went forward with a plan for national control.[10]

In 1952, according to historian Benjamin Rader, the NCAA was at a turning point in solidifying itself as a cartel controlling intercollegiate athletics. At the 1952 convention the organization decided to permit full scholarships based solely on athletic ability; it then acquired power by adopting a system that allowed the NCAA to impose sanctions on those schools violating NCAA rules. This also allowed the NCAA to grasp control of the televising of games. Once it had control over television contracts the power of the NCAA was secured.[11]

The NFL and Television

In her analysis of the attractiveness of the NFL and football on television Joan Chandler argues that much of what made the game popular had been in place before television. The game had been opened up and speeded up offensively, attempts were made to equalize team strength, and it was marketed as a game representing honest and manly virtues. Television turned out to be a friendly medium for football as the ball was large enough to be seen on the TV screen and the action had a degree of predictability starting at the center/quarterback nexus and always moving out from there. The game on the black-and-white TV seemed to be able to hold the fans' attention.[12]

Part of football's TV appeal, writes Chandler, is that viewers "know that what they are watching is important." The stakes involved in one game in 16 are much greater than one in 162 as in baseball. "Football is a game of continual crisis" and was structured in that way.[13] Each crisis can be savored between the plays. Each play requires a series of important decisions by the coaches and quarterback. The routines of the games translate well visually, with players shuttling in and out, there is a variety of type of plays, and each play has one starting point from which the camera can follow the action. There is deceit and surprise also in play. There are plots and subplots to be followed, and there are just enough statistics to make it interesting.

"In translating football for viewers, TV executives have determined to make it intelligible and attractive. To watch a football game is therefore to be deluged with information." First, the players are personalized. Second, spectators are informed about the progress of the game. Third, there is an ongoing attempt to educate the audience with replay and other devices. Analysis of plays and strategy are ongoing. Fourth, spectators are expected and encouraged to be enthusiastic about the game with the best plays shown over and over again. Nonetheless Chandler claims that television did not change the game. It simply brought the game to more people and focused on its traditional elements.[14]

According to Benjamin Rader the impact of television was felt from the mid-1950s when major advertisers and the big networks began paying attention to the NFL. In 1954 Dumont's rating on Sunday afternoon rose to a 37 percent share and by then pro football was on television across a large segment of the country. In 1956 NBC got the title game away from Dumont and CBS began televising regular season games for which they paid just over a million dollars. The result was the creation of millions of new fans for the pro game: armchair fans, armchair coaches, armchair quarterbacks, all attuned to the drama of the game. When instant replay and slow motion became common in the 1960s the TV game became a totally different experience than the game in the stadium. This was followed by color television and artificial surfaces which "altered the appearance of the games." Teams added to the show by wearing more colorful uniforms and helmets and putting names on the backs of jerseys.[15]

The 1958 NFL Championship game between the New York Giants and the Baltimore Colts, televised by NBC, is considered a turning point for the NFL. The game was seen by 45 million people, even though blacked out for a 75-mile radius of New York City. The game went into sudden-death overtime after a dramatic finish in regulation time. A winning touchdown drive by the Colts in overtime added to the excitement. If not a turning point, the game did indeed create new fans and considerable excitement over the NFL across the world of television.[16]

The Roone Revolution

By 1960 American fans expressed a significant demand for the game, and a number of entrepreneurs sought franchises in the NFL. Failing to get them, Lamar Hunt and others organized the new American Football League (AFL). Its survival depended on securing a television contract, which they were able to do, first with ABC and then NBC. Competition between the NFL and AFL increased the popularity of professional football and led to a merger. It in turn produced the Super Bowl, the highest-rated televised sporting event in the United States, which has become a major midwinter holiday and cultural event.

Executives Tom Moore and Ed Scherick of ABC believed that sports would be a key element in challenging the dominance of NBC and CBS. It was Scherick who hired Roone Arledge at ABC, where college football came under his spell. He believed that sport must be approached as television programming first and then as sport. This meant it must entertain.

In a now-legendary 1960 memo, Arledge laid out his plan for televising NCAA football. He would put handheld cameras on the sidelines to show close-ups of players, coaches, and the pretty cheerleaders, capturing their range of emotions during the game. He used sideline microphones to capture the sounds of the game, particularly the bone-crunching sounds of a good solid hit and crowd noise. He wanted to capture all the "color and pageantry of college football." He put his cameras on jeeps, in helicopters, and on board blimps to show the games from every possible angle. Fans came to the games hoping to attract the cameras by their antics or costumes, or on a particularly cold day by bearing their bodies to the elements. In the process the game in the stadium changed becoming only a part of the action rather than its focus.[17]

It was Arledge who developed the replay in all its forms from "slo-mo" to "iso" shots following one player throughout the course of one play. He used the split screen to capture both ends of passing plays. He developed pre-recorded interviews and profiles of players and coaches, which evolved into the "up close and personal" segment used so effectively at the Olympics.

Wide World of Sports began in April of 1961. Moore and Scherick believed that they could "make people interested in events *because they were on television* (original emphasis)." It was Arledge who looked beyond the major sports in North America, "spanning the globe" to bring the "glory of victory and agony of defeat" into American living rooms.

In 1964 Arledge brought the Winter Olympics to American television for the bargain price of $200,000, and in 1968 Americans saw the summer games from Mexico City in prime time. Some even came to think of Arledge as the man who invented the Olympics.

According to Ron Powers,

> The hallmarks of Arledge's style were a high respect for the power of *story* over the human imagination, a probing visual intimacy with the subject matter, a relentless, even obsessive preoccupation with the smallest detail, and—most mystical of all—an abiding sense of ABC itself as an unseen but always involved character in whatever event it is transmitting (original emphasis).

As a result ABC and television became "an active agenda-setting force in America's relationship with athletics—and with the styles, economics, political dynamics and moral values that devolved from that relationship as well."[18]

By the end of the 1960s the marriage of television and sport had been consummated via professional football, college football, and increasingly college basketball. Two other sports found new popularity and spectacular growth via television during this decade of political and social turmoil.

In 1970 following the merger of the AFL and NFL Roone Arledge led another major innovation with the creation of *Monday Night Football* (MNF). It quickly proved to be a major success and changed television viewing habits in prime time. It is credited with expanding the number of women watching the game and in many households MNF became a family event.[19]

Outside the Main Stream

Golf and tennis emerged as major weekend sports featured on television. Both were attractive for television because of the economic demographic of their followers. Both appealed to upper-middle-class viewers who had considerable disposable income, particularly for higher-end luxury items. Attracted by the ability to reach this demographic, investment brokers and insurance companies bought advertising time on golf and tennis telecasts. In addition celebrities took up the game and then lent their names to golf tournaments, with the Bob Hope Buick Open one of the first to do so.

Simultaneously golf learned to market both its product and its stars for television, while tennis moved quickly to the open era and set itself up for television. The golf rivalry of Arnold Palmer, the people's choice, and Jack Nicklaus made for dramatic television. In 1956 the networks carried a total of five and one-half hours of golf. By 1970 that was available on a weekend.

Between 1947 and 1973 the number of tournaments more than doubled, increasing from 31 to 76. Television ratings and prize money jumped correspondingly, while the new money flowing into golf from television created divisions between the tour players and the PGA club pros. This ultimately led to the creation of the Tournament Players Division within the PGA, later renamed the PGA Tour. Women's Golf and the LPGA also benefited from the arrival of television and sponsorship although the growth of prize money and number of tournaments in the 1970s did not match that of the men's game.

Tennis followed a similar pattern as top players were turned into media stars and rivalries, real and imagined, were featured and promoted. Television forced changes in tennis lengthening the changeover time to allow commercials and eliminating the five- to six-hour matches. The "tie-breaker" was adopted for television networks, not for players, and soon the requirement that a set could be won only by a two-game margin, no matter how long it took, was a distant memory in all but a few cases.

In the early 1970s television tripled its coverage of tennis. Changes in playing surfaces were introduced to curb the serve and volley game that was seen as less attractive for television. World Championship Tennis (WCT) was created by Lamar Hunt in 1970. Stars were signed and they played in tournaments around the world. The WCT tour ended with a grand finale championship at the end of the season. NBC paid $100,000 for the rights to eight of these tournaments. The Grand Prix circuit sponsored first by Nabisco was created in the 1970s, and Bill Riordan's TV challenge matches arrived in the 1970s. In 1975 there were 50 tournament matches televised, and CBS paid $600,000 for a challenge match between Jimmy Connors and John Newcombe.

As the popularity of these two sports grew, so too did the number of and demand for tennis courts and golf courses. The number of people playing tennis in the first half of the 1970s tripled. The sport was being played by so many people that a tennis ball shortage developed despite the manufacturers running to full plant capacity. If you wanted a private court in Chicago in the winter and were lucky enough to get one, it could very well be at 3 a.m. despite the increase of indoor facilities in the city from 1 in the early 1960s to 43 in the mid-1970s. For golfers tee times for the most desirable courses were being booked weeks and months in advance.[20]

Television, Profits, and Change

What television brought to every sport it touched was money, and then more money. Television ratings produced higher advertising rates, and that in turn led to higher fees for the product itself. This in turn increased incomes for promoters, owners, and players. Battles over the money could and did in many cases produce work stoppages in the form of lockouts and strikes. And as the money increased, the battles intensified as everyone wanted "their fair share" of the TV windfall.

In 1969 *Sports Illustrated* (SI), in a series of articles written by William Johnson, looked back on the decade to assess the impact of television on sport. According to SI television "produced more revolutionary-and irrevocable-changes in sport than anything since mankind began to play organized games." Certainly this was an overstatement, or was it? [21]

SI pointed to the proliferation and elaboration of sports venues across the landscape, the new wealth showered on athletes, and the profits flowing into the pockets of owners. The geography of major sports was transformed as sport became a national obsession. Bear Bryant, the demi-god of Alabama football, most notably declared that if television wanted its games to start at midnight, then midnight it would be.[22]

The size of television markets helped determine the placement and movement of sports franchises. The bigger the TV market, the more likely a city was to have a professional sports franchise or even multifranchises. The move of the Dodgers to Los Angeles is often attributed to Walter O'Malley's search for television dollars, as was the transfer of the Braves from Boston to Milwaukee, and then to Atlanta.

SI pointed out the tremendous fees being paid by the networks for sporting events stressing the flood of money into the Olympics and college football. Televised games were getting longer as more commercials were needed to offset the fees that owners charged for rights to the games. Overall, however, SI concluded that television was more of a force for good than evil, and the overall impact of television had been positive.[23]

Historian Benjamin Rader found many troubling developments arising from the growth of televised sport. There was, of course, the flood of money and the commercialization of sport, but indeed sports were brought to more people than ever before. However, the way in which sports were experienced changed. According to Rader, television diminished the role of the athlete as hero and diminished the experience of the live game. "Television has essentially trivialized the experience of spectator sports." The drama of sport has been sacrificed to the requirements of entertainment. The "sporting experience has been contaminated with a plethora of external intrusions," Rader decried.

> [T]oo many seasons, too many games, too many teams, and too many big plays. Such a flood of sensations has diluted the poignancy and potency of the sporting experience. It has diminished the capacity of sports to furnish heroes, to bind communities, and to enact the rituals that contain, and exalt, society's traditional values.[24]

Furthermore the coming of instant replay, slow motion replay, color television, and artificial surfaces all altered the appearance of the games and threatened the "authenticity of the traditional sporting experience." To maximize and sustain the audience, the temptation was to constantly stress the excitement and drama of games, even if it had to be created by the producers. This led to "spectacle or simply entertainment." The nuances of sport were lost and sensationalism reigned.[25]

Did any of this matter to a nation drinking deeply of sport, especially professional football, in the turbulent decade of the 1960s? For John Powers, the answer to that question was a resounding "no" as he found the appeal more in the constructed drama of televised sport than in the essence of sport.

> TV sports became a kind of psychic refuge for millions of Americans, a way of numbing themselves to the horrible convulsions that threatened to disintegrate society as they understood it. At the same time TV sports provided Americans the pretext of engaging their hopes in something real, something vital, something collective and large . . . and emblematic of the status quo.[26]

The Satellite and Sport

The changes ahead in television dwarfed those already in place. The major networks were about to be challenged for the rights to televise sport by a new technology spinning out of the space program and innovations from other sources. Perhaps of all of these, the satellite was the most significant.

The beginning of the end for broadcast television's monopoly of sports came with the development of the Super stations, TBS, WGN, and WOR. Then in 1979 came ESPN, which in turn was purchased by ABC in 1984. These developments offered new choices in viewing, advertising, and advertising rates. The growing popularity of sports and the skills employed by those negotiating fees for the networks drove those fees skyward. To recoup those fees the networks made changes in the programming strategies. One choice was to concentrate on the major events, although this was not possible with the NFL. CBS separated some of their biggest events from packages such as separating the Masters tournament from the rest of its golf package. Another option that ABC used in World Cup coverage was to offer sponsor exclusivity to a package or an event. Logos were displayed during play with no commercials during the games, just before and after.[27]

The Super stations were the nose of the camel in the tent, whereas ESPN was a herd of camels filling and then overrunning the tent. The first growth and development of ESPN came with the rights to replay televised football games on tape delay. This was followed by the emergence of ESPN into the live market, which grew steadily through the late 1980s and the 1990s.

ESPN was one key factor in the expansion of the college football season. From there ESPN set its sights on bowl games, as it was ready to televise even the most obscure of bowls. This led to the growth of bowls designed for television, and ultimately ESPN developed and promoted new bowls, finally taking ownership of all of them. In the world of 24-hour sports channels, programming that filled time slots was needed, and the cost of developing bowls was considerably less expensive than developing original programming.

As the big conferences looked to add revenue streams and were able to break away from the NCAA via the courtroom, more games appeared on TV and more bowls developed tie-ins with conferences. These struggles were played out first between ABC and the NCAA, and between Roone Arledge and Walter Byers. As revenues increased, the major football powers banded together to remove themselves from NCAA restrictions while keeping the revenues in their own pockets. Penn State, Notre Dame, and seven conferences formed the College Football Association (CFA) to secure control of their television destiny.

The CFA formally organized in 1976 and over the next five years battled with the NCAA over television rights. In 1981 the CFA signed a separate but tentative TV deal with NBC that was rejected by CFA members in December 1981. A compromise was achieved and it led to the creation of Division I, which was committed to big-time college sport and giving the CFA institutions control over their television policies.

In 1981 the NCAA signed a deal with ABC, CBS, and TBS for the Saturday package increasing the number of games on television and limiting the number of appearances by one team to six in a season. The deal netted $74.3 million, which was double the previous contract. The resolution of the conflict with the CFA would take place in court. The package was voided by the U.S. Supreme Court in 1984, and the NCAA lost control of football policy. Each college and university was free to negotiate its own contracts. By the mid-1990s this led to conference reorganization and realignments designed to create more attractive television packages. In 1998 the Division I football power conferences and Notre Dame formed the Bowl Championship Series (BCS) to diminish the power of the bowls and create a "national championship."

The BCS and then the National Football Championship was nurtured by ESPN/ABC as it became the biggest player in the world of college football. Meanwhile ESPN's "College Game Day" made its national tour appearing on Saturday morning on the campus of one of the nation's football powers. Games started when TV wanted them aired, whereas fans holding tickets were often unsure as to the start times until less than a week before the games. This was one of those developments by which ESPN transformed itself from an arm of sports journalism to being a promoter of its own programming.

It is fair to say that ESPN/ABC ripped the control of college football out of the hands of everyone. It is also safe to say that ESPN fed the NCAA its lifeblood in the form of revenues generated from college basketball. ESPN played an enormous role in the creation of March Madness and essentially forced one of the big networks, in this case CBS, to get on board the money train. Again college athletic directors were more than happy to play on any night of the week, in virtually any locale, whether in conference or in made-for-TV matchups across conferences.

There was a growth of pre-season tournaments, conference challenges, and other made-for-TV events. Ultimately conferences began to realign and reconfigure in search of more and more dollars. The NCAA basketball tournament, which once had 8 teams, grew to 16, and rose gradually to 68, all in service to television and revenue streams. The NCAA generated the majority of its operating budget from March Madness, a term it put under trademark and aggressively enforced.[28]

This led to a widening financial gap between the haves and have-nots of college athletics. It also led to what has been termed the arms race, with more and more money spent on improved facilities that became a recruiting tool. With each incremental increase in revenue the pressure to win grew, and the demand for big-time coaches drove coaches' salaries ever upward. It was once a minor scandal if the football coach was paid more than the college president. (Public records show that the highest-paid public employees in 44 of 50 states are coaches.)

Colleges and universities lost control of athletics, and the tail was now wagging the dog. The pursuit of revenue became intense and between 2010 and 2014 led to a major realignment of conference membership. Conferences were seeking to create the most attractive package possible for sale to the television networks at maximum prices. Locations within television markets rather than geographic regions set the new boundaries for conferences. This led to the end of century-long rivalries. Conferences were spread over halfway across the country and travel expenses mounted, but television revenues more than compensated for those increased expenses. If this meant student athletes would spend more time on the road and away from class, no one seemed to be concerned.[29]

The result was that the rich got richer, and to guarantee that they would continue to get even richer, the NCAA in early August 2014 granted autonomy to the Power Five Conferences in terms of how they could reward their student athletes.

Television and the NBA

The other professional sport that has been deeply affected by television is the National Basketball Association (NBA). From its founding in the postwar world the NBA never enjoyed the attention of television that others were given. The NBA grew slowly through the 1950s but failed to develop a national audience. In 1962 NBC dropped its coverage of regular season games, and in 1964 ABC paid only $750,000 for coverage of the league.[30]

In the early 1970s when the ABC contract was due to end, the NBA negotiated a new deal with CBS. Angered by the NBA actions Roone Arledge created programming to counter the NBA on CBS. On Saturdays ABC challenged CBS with college football and undertook other programming moves. In what became known as Roone's Revenge, ABC killed CBS and the NBA in the ratings. By the time it was over CBS was reduced to offering playoff games on tape delay at 11:30 p.m. in the East.

The American Basketball Association (ABA) founded in 1967 based its strategy for success on obtaining a lucrative television contract. None came, lucrative or otherwise, and the league folded in 1976. By the late 1970s there were dire predictions about the demise of the NBA centering on the nation that the league was "too black" to attract a predominant white fan base. All of that would change in the next decade, and television would play a key role in that development.

Then between 1979 and 1992 two players, Ervin "Magic" Johnson of the LA Lakers and Larry Bird of the Boston Celtics, became the most popular players in the fastest growing of the professional sports. This process began when these two players were featured in the 1979 finals of March Madness in a made-by-TV rivalry. It was a marketers' dream, made for television. As these two exited the stage Michael Jordan moved in to the spotlight, and together with Nike he rivaled Muhammad Ali for popularity across the world.

The NBA, led by Commissioner David Stern, took their product around the world via television, then in live tours, and most notably by sending the "Dream Team" to the Olympics. All of this was duly reported and promoted by television. The NBA also became the first professional sports league to develop a television presence that was aired primarily on national cable networks with little concern for over the air broadcast television.[31]

New Trends in Media and Television

In 1990 there were 7,500 hours of sports programming on all television, which comes to 20.5 hours of sports every day, 365 days per year. The average household in 1992 received approximately 33 broadcast and cable channels, and at times there are as many as 10 events on at the same time.[32]

The number of sport-specific and league-specific dedicated channels continued to develop, regional sports channels multiplied, and intercollegiate conferences and individual intercollegiate teams created their own channels. Although it would seem that saturation would eventually become a problem, that point does not seem to have arrived as advertisers, sponsors, and institutions continue to fund these operations. Take all of this and throw much of it onto the Internet through streaming technology and the multiplier affect seems to approach infinity.

Indeed the coming of the Internet has produced yet another space for sport to thrive, and it has facilitated the growth of fantasy sport. According to the Fantasy Sports Trade Association there were 41.5 million people playing fantasy sports in the United States in 2014, or 14 percent of the U.S. population. The earliest available statistics from 1988 showed 500,000 people playing fantasy sports that year. From 2007 to 2014 the number of fantasy players doubled. The typical player is Caucasian, single, male, aged 34, with a college degree, over $50,000 annual income, and is likely playing fantasy football. Fantasy players also tend to play more than one sport and in more than one league simultaneously.[33]

The NFL has the largest presence online of any of the sports. Each team has a website, several fan groups of each team have websites and blogs, merchandise sales are ubiquitous on these platforms, and the fantasy player is a major target. The league, the players' association, and the Super Bowl have their own sites with the amount of traffic at these sites increasing yearly.

MLB adapted slowly to this new world of sport. Rather than seeing fantasy baseball, the first of the fantasy sports, as a marketing opportunity, MLB reacted defensively at first, suing fantasy sports operations over the use of baseball statistics for the games. As with radio and then television, the folks at MLB reacted in fear and resisted the new technology.

The streaming of sports events now is also quite common, and this is usually done as part of a pay-for-view operation. The leagues offer total access to out-of-market games for a fee, and each league has created considerable revenue in this way. MLB, the NFL, and the NHL have likewise created satellite television and radio broadcasting outlets offered variously by cable and satellite companies. These services are fully conscious of the fantasy player and provide information to them, often in real time. These have not necessarily affected the conduct of the game on the field, but have considerably affected the ways in which fans experience the games and the reasons why they consume these products. Mobile devices now allow for all of this information and service to be carried by the fan wherever they may be.

The Internet and mobile world has also been affected by the coming of Facebook and Twitter. Both of these platforms allow fans to interact nearly directly with players, coaches, owners, broadcasters, or most anyone associated with sports or sports teams. In turn these platforms have allowed players and teams to communicate directly with the fans without the interpretive mediation of the press. This has necessitated the creation of large communications operation within each team and league, and for the individual sports, a communications manager for each athlete.

Television technology has changed considerably over the past decade. It is generally accepted that of all the major sports football displays best on television. However, with the new HD technology, wide-screen televisions, and camera technology and more sophisticated production and direction, the gap between football and other sports has narrowed considerably. Indeed the technological advances in television often render the stadium experience inferior to the television experience of a given sport. Clearly the best seat for a football game is in front of a television.

Conclusion

Never before in the history of sport has there been so much information and access available to fans. Yet, this does not mean that fans have any more knowledge of the players—only more knowledge of game strategy. Information abounds, but knowledge does not necessarily follow. Today's fan probably knows as much about their favorite players as they ever did. It is what allows heroes to continue to exist, even if it means that disillusionment is more likely to become part of the sports reality, especially in the world of tell-all journalism.

This raises the issue of what constitutes journalism and the impact of the electronic age on sports journalism. We know that by virtue of all of the platforms dispensing sports news and information that the old journalism has changed correspondingly. If a sports network pays for the rights to televise a particular sport, league or team, can it be expected to offer objective reporting? Probably not, but the proliferation of sports media outlets has counteracted these tendencies as they compete with one another for news. A lack of objectivity by CBS is sure to be countered by reporting at a multitude of other outlets. So perhaps in the end objectivity is in no more jeopardy today than it was in the 1920s, and maybe even less.

Notes

1 Richard Crepeau, *NFL Football: The Rise of America's New National Pastime* (Urbana: The University of Illinois Press, 2014), 46.
2 Ron Powers, *Supertube; The Rise of Televised Sport* (New York: Coward-McCann, Inc., 1984), 47–48.
3 Benjamin G. Rader, *American Sports: From the Age of Folk Games to the Age of Televised Sports* 5th ed. (Upper Saddle River, NJ: Pearson Prentice Hall, 2004), 250–251.
4 Powers, *Supertube*, 52–54.
5 Jeff Neal-Lundsford, "Sport in the Land of Television: The Use of Sport in Network Prime-Time Schedules, 1946–50," *Journal of Sport History* 19, no. 1 (Spring 1992): 57.
6 Michael MacCambridge, *America's Game: The Epic Story of How Pro Football Captured a Nation* (New York: Anchor Books, 2004), 73, 103–104; Robert W. Peterson, *Pigskin: The Early Years of Pro Football* (New York: Oxford University Press, 1997), 196–199; Powers, *Supertube*, 80–81; Mark Yost, *Tailgating, Sacks, and Salary Caps: How the NFL Became the Most Successful Sports League in History* (Chicago: Kaplan Publishing, 2006), 66–69.
7 Yost, *Tailgating, Sacks, and Salary Caps*, 68; Powers, *Supertube*, 17, 80–81.

8 Benjamin G. Rader, *Baseball: A History of America's Game* 3rd ed. (Urbana: The University of Illinois Press, 2008), 188–194.
9 Rader, *American Sports*, 260–261.
10 Ronald A. Smith, *Play-By-Play: Radio, Television and Big-Time College Sport* (Baltimore: The Johns Hopkins University Press, 2001), 54–78.
11 Rader, *American Sports*, 281–282.
12 Joan Chandler, *Television and National Sport* (Champaign: The University of Illinois Press, 1998), 56.
13 Ibid., 68.
14 Ibid., 68–69.
15 Benjamin G. Rader, *In Its Own Image: How Television Transformed Sports* (New York: The Free Press, 1984), 87–88.
16 Crepeau, *NFL Football*, 48–50.
17 Powers, *Supertube*, 144–147.
18 Ibid., 14, 18, 22, 67–68, 96–98, 152; Rader, *American Sports*, 252–254; Richard C. Crepeau, "Remembering Roone and the Revolution," *Journal of Sport History* 29, no. 2 (Summer 2002): 357–359. Direct quotes from Powers, *Supertube*, 152.
19 Crepeau, *NFL Football*, 96–100.
20 Benjamin Rader, *American Sports: From the Age of Folk Games to the Age of Televised Sport* 2nd ed. (Englewood Cliffs, NJ: Prentice-Hall, 1983), 305.
21 William Johnson, "TV Made It All a New Game," Part I of a Series. http://vault.sportsillustrated.cnn.com/vault/article/magazine/MAG1083192/index.htm (accessed April 2, 2009).
22 Ibid.
23 Ibid.
24 Rader, *In It's Own Image*, 5–6, 88.
25 Ibid., 116.
26 Powers, *Supertube*, 67–68.
27 Jerry Gorman, Kirk Calhoun, with Skip Rozen, *The Name of the Game; The Business of Sports* (New York: John Wiley & Sons, Inc., 1994), 79–82.
28 Ron Smith, *Play-by-Play: Radio, Television, and Big-Time College Sport* (Baltimore: The John's Hopkins University Press, 2001) offers the best history and analysis of these developments.
29 Chris DuFresne "College Football's Game of Conference Realignment Is Finally Ending," *The Los Angeles Times*, August 16, 2014. www.latimes.com/sports/la-sp-college-football-realignment-20140817-column.html#page=1
30 Rader, *American Sports*, 277.
31 Ibid., 275–278; Bill Simmons, *The Book of Basketball: The NBA According to the Sports Guy*, (New York: Ballantine/ESPN Books, 2010), 110–111.
32 Gorman et al., *The Name of the Game*, 78.
33 www.fsta.org/?page=Demographics (accessed December 27, 2014).

21

COMMERCIALIZED SPORT, ENTREPRENEURS, AND UNIONS IN MAJOR LEAGUE BASEBALL

Braham Dabscheck[1]

Introduction

It would be reasonable to hypothesize that bosses, employers, call them what you will, would rather have nothing to do with unions, those organizations that pursue the collective interests of workers. Employers would prefer to negotiate wages and other employment conditions on an individual basis, maintaining that the involvement of unions in such matters adversely affects their 'special' relationship with their workforce. Workers form unions because of the belief, or hope, that by acting collectively they will gain improvements to their working lives not available to them under individual bargaining. Such suppositions apply as much to the world of professional team sports as other areas of commercial life.

The playing out of this labor relations dynamic varies across different sectors of the economy. The major determinant of labor relations in professional team sports centers on its "peculiar economics." The general norm of commercial life is for firms to compete vigorously with each other, to the point of driving each other to extinction, in enhancing their own economic welfare. Such exercises, in Schumpeterian "creative destruction," would be anathema for sporting clubs, in that they need each other to produce a product, namely a game, or a series of games to make up a season.[2] A club cannot play against itself! Leagues are natural cartels. Member clubs need to cooperate with each other to generate revenue. Revenue generation will be enhanced by clubs providing an exciting and uncertain competition on the field. What economists refer to as competitive balance is enhanced, not by business competition, but by "economic collusion" between the various clubs constituting a league.[3]

This need to collude does not mean that there will be an end to commercial competition between clubs. William Fellner maintains that

> Economic behavior under fewness is *imperfectly co-ordinated*... The competitive element stays significant; it applies mainly in the dynamic aspects of the problem which are connected with ingenuity and inventiveness and on the discounting of which it is difficult to reach agreement (emphasis in original).[4]

Imperfect coordination lies at the heart of the operation of the cartels that are sporting leagues. This is a problem that has cruelled their operation since time immemorial. Despite the need to be collusive, clubs nonetheless compete vigorously with each other in trying to enhance their own welfare.

Early Professional Baseball Owners

In the mid-1940s, Alva Bradley, the owner of Major League Baseball's (MLB) Cleveland Indians, in talking about his relationship with other owners, said "We all cheat if we have to . . . This fellow cheats, that fellow cheats, I cheat, too. We all cheat."[5] Ingenuity and inventiveness take many forms. Some clubs are more adept in their relationships with supporters, suppliers, government, and regulatory bodies. Like everywhere else, a bell curve of talent exists among the ranks of club managers. Branch Rickey, one of MLB's legendary general managers, used his ingenuity to outwit his rivals not once, but twice. The first instance occurred when he invented the farm system during his time with the St. Louis Cardinals, where clubs stockpiled players in lower-division clubs away from the clutches of rivals. The second instance was after World War II, when he cashed in on the bigotry of the times. In 1947, the Brooklyn Dodgers employed the African American Jackie Robinson and broke the color bar that had operated in MLB since the latter part of the nineteenth century.[6]

A major problem that has confronted sporting cartels is differences in the financial strength of member clubs. Clubs will vary in terms of their market success, whether they are in larger (smaller) cities or catchment areas, the strength of support, or lack thereof of fans, sponsors, and business partners and the ingenuity and inventiveness of their managerial staff. Such differences in financial strength directly affect the ability of clubs to compete (equally) for skilled players and the attainment of competitive balance.

Historically, most leagues across the globe have found it difficult to confront the problem of differences in the financial strength of clubs. It is the elephant in the room. Rather, they have instituted a series of labor market controls that have shifted the problem onto players, which has severely affected their economic freedom and income-earning potential. The mainstay of MLB's system of controls was the reserve, or option, system, which operated from 1879 to 1976. Players signed what ostensibly looked like a one-year contract. It contained an option clause, to be exercised by the club if it so desired, to renew that contract for another year (it was in effect a two-year contract). By signing a new contract each year, players found themselves bound to their club for as long as their club desired to employ them. Clubs traded players and/or assigned them to teams in their farm system.

The reserve system denied players the ability to test the market and left them at the mercy of their respective clubs. Clubs forced players to pay for the costs of their uniforms, travelling, and medical expenses and would impose fines for not playing well, swearing, and other misdemeanors on and off the field.[7] Possibly the best or worst example of how the reserve system could be wielded against players occurred when Ralph Kiner (who subsequently found his way into Baseball's Hall of Fame) negotiated a new contract with Branch Rickey, who in the 1950s was managing the Pittsburgh Pirates. Kiner tied the National League's home run record in 1952. The Pirates had had a bad year and finished at the bottom of the league. Rickey offered him a new contract with a 25 percent pay cut, the maximum then allowed under MLB's employment rules. Kiner objected and maintained that his skills with the bat drove fans through the turnstiles. Rickey trumped him when he said, "We can finish last without you."[8]

Early Attempts to Unionize

For almost a century, the owners held sway in their relationship with players. There were five unsuccessful attempts by players to form unions to counter the power of owners. They were the National Brotherhood of Professional Baseball Players (1885–1890), the first attempt to form a player union in the history of world sport; the League Protective Players' Association (1900–1902); the Baseball Players' Fraternity (1912–1918); the National Baseball Players' Association of the United States (1922–1923); and the American Baseball Guild (1946). Four of these five attempts coincided with organized baseball being involved in trade wars with rival leagues seeking to find a place in baseball's sun.

Once such challenges were resolved, by either a merger between the leagues or the destruction of the rival, the embryonic unions quickly folded. The National Brotherhood attempted to establish a Players' League in 1890. Both the Brotherhood and the League quickly disintegrated after the league's financial backers pulled out. The Protective Association coincided with the battle between the stalwart National League and the upstart American League, which resulted in the merger/creation of MLB's two-league structure and the World Series. The Fraternity emerged prior to MLB's battle and subsequent merger with the Federal League. Finally, the Baseball Guild coincided with the operation of a Mexican League, which attracted a number of major league players after World War II.[9] All of these attempts failed because of the concerted opposition of the owners, lukewarm support from players, and an inability to find leaders with the skills to build the internal cohesiveness necessary for the successful operation of a players' organization, and the competitive edge to take on owners in collective bargaining negotiations.

In 1946, Boston-based lawyer and labor organizer Robert F. Murphy failed in his attempt to garner support from players for the Baseball Guild. Despite this failure, his attempt began the slow and gradual process, which would fundamentally transform industrial relations in MLB. The owners were somewhat worried by this development and turned to a tried and trusted method that had been used by American employers to keep unions at bay—the representative system. Owners began the practice of meeting with representatives of players to discuss various employment issues and provide some "minor" concessions to ward off the evils of unionism. At these meetings, in 1946, owners agreed to payments for spring training, which became known as "Murphy money," and more importantly the establishment of a pension plan for players. Concern over the funding of the pension plan resulted in players forming the Major League Baseball Players' Association (MLBPA) in 1953. Player associations were also formed in basketball in 1954, football in 1956, and hockey in 1957.[10]

Challenges Confronting the Major League Baseball Players' Association

Having formed in 1953, the MLBPA struggled to find a leader with both the will and capacity to forge it into a viable organization. In 1959 it appointed Judge Robert C. Cannon of the Circuit Court of Wisconsin as part-time legal counsel to represent players. He was the son of Raymond Cannon who had been unsuccessful in attempting to establish the National Baseball Players' Association in the early 1920s. The younger Cannon was anything but a players' man. He believed players were lucky to be employed in America's "national pastime" and that they should do nothing to "jeopardize the fine relationship existing between the players and club owners."[11] Korr says of Cannon that his "view of how far the owners *could* go coincided with how far they were willing to go. He consistently put himself in their position, never seeing himself as the independent voice of players who had justified grievances"[12] (emphasis in original).

In 1965, the MLBPA decided it needed to appoint a full-time executive director to improve its effectiveness as an organization. The position was initially offered to Judge Cannon, who turned it down over issues associated with his remuneration. MLBPA leaders then turned to Marvin Miller, a 48-year-old industrial relations professional. He had worked for the National War Labor Board during World War II and a number of unions. Since 1950, he had worked as the chief economist and a negotiator for the Steelworkers Union of America. His appointment was dependent on endorsement by members of the MLPBA. He went on a tour of spring training camps in 1966 and told the players something that they had never heard before:

> I want you to understand that this is going to be an adversarial relationship. A union is not a social club. A union is a restraint on what an employer can otherwise do. If you expect the owners to like me, to praise me, you'll be disappointed. In fact, if I'm elected and you find the owners telling you what a great guy I am, fire me! Don't hesitate, because it can't be that way if your director is doing his job. The owners loved Judge Cannon. Don't make the same mistake with your new executive director.

He was endorsed by a vote of 489 to 136.[13]

Miller taught players their worth, provided them with information about the economic and business operation of baseball and their status as employees, and provided options and strategies for going forward, which would be decided democratically by a majority vote. Author John Helyar said of Miller's relationship with players that "he listened to them. He educated them. And slowly he radicalized them."[14] Former players and associates who spoke at the memorial celebration held for him at New York University in January 2013, following his death at age 95 in November 2012, refer to Miller's quiet and courtly demeanor. They said he was:

> Mild mannered, quiet, like a professor . . . An educator, a teacher, a mentor . . . A true friend, never talked down to you, helped you understand . . . I admired the way he explained the most complicated things simply . . . he educated the players to understand what they were fighting for . . . he explained issues and let [players] decide . . . Marvin taught us what we needed to know.[15]

Korr refers to Miller harnessing the natural competitiveness of players on the field to take on owners off the field. Similarly, the players saw in Miller someone who was as competitive and driven as them in his preparedness and skill in jousting with owners across the bargaining table.[16]

Marvin Miller is the most significant person in the last half-century of American baseball. Nonetheless, it took him almost a decade to work his magic and bring down the reserve system and develop an alternative industrial relations model for baseball. Following his appointment, Miller proceeded cautiously as he began educating players about their rights. He was wary of pursuing an action that was not endorsed by the players. His first major achievement was to negotiate a collective bargaining agreement with the owners in 1968. It provided an increase in the minimum wage and some "minor" concessions for players. Its most important feature was to remove the hitherto power of the commissioner of MLB to resolve grievances between players and owners. Grievances would be determined by an independent arbitrator, per arrangements under the National Labor Relations Act (1935).

In the Basic Agreement of 1973, the parties agreed to a system of salary arbitration to resolve wage disputes between players and clubs, to begin in 1974. Any player with a total of two years of Major League service, or in at least three different seasons, was eligible to submit a claim to a final and binding arbitration. Under this system, independent arbitrators jointly appointed by MLB and the MLBPA were required to choose either the offer of the club or the demand of the player. It was a system of either/or, with no room for splitting the difference. Moreover, the arbitrator was not required to provide any reasons for his decision. The object of this system was to "encourage" the club and the player to reach a compromise during negotiations, in fear of a "worse" determination being handed down by the arbitrator.[17]

Taking on the Reserve System

Miller's target remained the reserve system. His first attempt to bring it down proved to be unsuccessful. In 1922, the Supreme Court, in a decision involving the resolution of a trade war between MLB and the Federal League, exempted baseball from the reach of the Sherman Antitrust Act (1890). It found, despite clubs and players crossing state borders to play games, that such activities were "purely state affairs," and exchanges of money connected with their playing "would not be called trade or commerce in the commonly accepted use of these words."[18] The Supreme Court upheld this decision, in 1953, in *Toolson* following the application of *stare decisis* (precedent).[19] It did not, however, afford such protection from antitrust actions to other American sports.[20]

In 1969, star St. Louis Cardinals' center fielder, Curt Flood, was traded to the Philadelphia Phillies. He refused to go, objecting to being treated as a piece of property. After consulting with Marvin Miller and the MLBPA he decided to challenge his trade and the reserve system as a breach of the Sherman Antitrust Act. The Supreme Court ruled against Flood and, on *stare decisis*, again upheld baseball's exemption. In noting the special privilege afforded to baseball over other sports it said it "is, in a very distinct sense, an exception and an anomaly . . . an aberration confined to baseball."[21]

Paragraph 10 (a) of the Uniform Player Contract stated "[T]he club shall have the right . . . to renew this contract for a period of one year."[22] Miller believed that if a club exercised this option and the player did not sign a new contract he would be a free agent after having played out the second year of his contract. The trick was to find a player, or players, who were prepared not to sign a new contract once their club had exercised its option. Eventually, two players, pitchers Andy Messersmith and Dave McNally, agreed to go down this route. When they had played out their option (or second year of their contract) they claimed they were free agents. MLB said they were not. It claimed they were still the property of their clubs per arrangements that had operated in baseball since 1879. The matter led to the grievance procedure, which Marvin Miller had first convinced MLB to include in the Basic Agreement of 1968. The private arbitrator, Peter Seitz, two days prior to Christmas 1975, sided with the players.[23] He found they were free agents and thereby brought about an end to the reserve system.

During the hearing of the grievance, Seitz had urged the parties to resolve their differences over the reserve system via collective bargaining, but to no avail. The owners, anticipating a favorable decision, saw no reason to move from the status quo. Seitz's decision reduced the power of owners. All players now had the prospect of becoming free agents. Miller, who it should be remembered had trained as an economist, did not look forward to such a development. He "did not believe that free agency rights after one year were in the best interest of the players—that large a supply of free agents every year would hold salaries down."[24] He wanted to restrict the supply of free agents and, thereby, drive up salaries.

The parties eventually entered into a new Basic Agreement in July 1976 which included free agency after six years. It also incorporated the final offer salary arbitration provisions of the 1973 Basic Agreement. Players with two years' service could use this provision to link their salaries to the performances of players who had become free agents. This became known within the MLBPA, and among players, as "a rising tide lifting all boats."[25] In 1985, the owners managed to convince the MLBPA to alter the availability of salary arbitration from two to three years. In 1990, the MLBPA were able to re-establish access to salary arbitration for "super" players who had two years of service with their clubs.[26] Other than for these changes concerning salary arbitration (and some additions which will be examined later), this model of free agency after six years and salary arbitration after two/three years has been the mainstay of baseball's industrial relations for almost four decades, though, as will be shown, not without a fight or two.

The monopsonistic reserve system restricted the ability of players in salary negotiations with owners. Its abolition, and the new arrangements that prevailed after 1976, turned this situation on its head. Both absolute and relative shares of income obtained by players increased substantially (Table 21.1).

Table 21.1 provides data on minimum and average salaries in MLB for selected years in the period 1966 to 2014. In 1966, the year Marvin Miller assumed his stewardship of the MLBPA, minimum and average salaries were $6,000 and $19,000, respectively. By 1976, the year of the first Basic Agreement, after the overturning of the reserve system, the minimum salary had increased to $19,000 and the average salary to over $51,000. Thereafter, both the minimum and average salaries took off. The minimum salary reached $100,000 in

Table 21.1 Minimum and Average Salaries in MLB: 1966 to 2014

Year	*Minimum Salary ($)*	*Average Salary ($)*
1966	6,000	19,000
1976	19,000	51,501
1980	30,000	143,756
1990	100,000	578,930
1992	109,000	1,084,408
1999	200,000	1,572,329
2001	200,000	2,089,065
2007	380,000	2,824,751
2010	400,000	3,014,572
2012	480,000	3,213,479
2013	490,000	3,390,000
2014	500,000	Not Available

Source: Dabscheck, *Reading Baseball*, 16; The Statistical Portal, Minimum Salary of Players in Major League Baseball, accessed 30 July 2014; ESPN MLB, MLB average salary, accessed 30 July 2014.

Table 21.2 Industrial Stoppages in MLB: 1972–1975

Year	*Nature*	*Length*	*Regular Season Games Lost*
1972	Strike	14 days	86
1973	Lockout	12 days	0
1976	Lockout	17 days	0
1980	Strike	8 days	0
1981	Strike	50 days	712
1985	Strike	2 days	0
1990	Lockout	32 days	0
1994/95	Strike	232 days	938

Source: Zimbalist, *May The Best Team Win*: 78.

1990, $200,000 in 1999, $400,000 in 2010 and $500,000 in 2014. By 1990, the average salary had increased to almost $580,000, to over $1 million two years later, more than $2 million in 2001, $3 million in 2010 and $3.39 million in 2013.

In 1974, prior to the end of the reserve system, players received 20.5 percent of baseball revenue. In 1977, a year after the negotiation of the 1976 Basic Agreement, it had jumped to 25.1 percent. It increased to 39.1 percent in 1980,[27] to 54 percent in 1992, 56 percent in 2000, 67 percent in 2002, and back to 51 percent in 2007.[28] The Batting Leadoff website reports, that in recent years, the players' share of revenue has fallen further, to 40 percent.[29]

Owners were alarmed by the escalation in salaries that occurred after 1976. In the negotiation of subsequent collective bargaining agreements they sought to wrest back the control they had hitherto exercised over players. Except for the 1985 Basic Agreement, where the exemption from salary arbitration was increased from two to three years, the MLBPA strenuously resisted these attempts. The negotiation of every collective bargaining deal, in the quarter of a century beginning after 1970, involved a strike or a lockout.[30]

Table 21.2 provides a brief summary of the major dimensions of these disputes. The stoppages resulting in no regular season games lost occurred in spring training or were made up by alterations to the playing schedule. There are three disputes that resulted in the "cancellation" of regular season games. The 1972 strike was over a failed attempt by owners to not increase contributions to the pension plan during the "high" inflation years that gripped America and most of the Western world in the first half of the 1970s. The 1981 strike thwarted an attempt by owners to introduce compensation for clubs following the movement of a free agent to another club.

Between the 1981 and 1994/95 disputes, the owners sought another way to escape the escalating increases in salaries that players enjoyed under free agency. An anticollusion clause, banning both owners and players from banding together in salary negotiations, was included in the 1968 Basic Agreement. In the mid-1980s, owners agreed not to bid for players from other clubs who became free agents. The MLBPA filed grievances on three occasions, each of which was upheld by two private arbitrators. The owners were ordered to pay $280 million in collusion damages.[31]

The Disunity of Owners

A problem that negatively affected owners in their dealings with the MLBPA was their lack of internal cohesiveness. They fought among themselves. In 2005 Bud Selig, who was

MLB's acting commissioner from 1992 to 1998, and official commissioner from 1998 until his retirement in 2014, reminisced on the first owners' meeting he attended as a principal of the Milwaukee Brewers. He said

> I was stunned when I left there because of the hatred and anger . . . It never got better until two or three years ago . . . The anger and the mistrust—it was really quite sad, and the sport itself suffered.[32]

There were two dimensions to the owners' diffidence toward each other. First, there was the problem of the clashing egos. Helyar quotes a leading negotiator from the steel industry who said:

> The owners were a loose amalgam of highly individualistic entrepreneurs, who were the worst people in the world to deal with labor. They're impatient, eccentric and exasperating to represent. Most of them had never worked inside structures where cooperation with other strong personalities was required. They were thus very poor at cooperating in the face of unified opposition.[33]

Second, differences existed in the financial strength of the respective franchises, differences between big, medium, and small city-based clubs. This problem was particularly acute when the issue of revenue sharing was raised as a possible means to resolve the economic and industrial relations problems that confronted baseball. Self-interest, or what was described earlier by Fellner as "the competitive element," rather than the "economic collusion" advocated by Neale, ruled supreme. In 1994 a report was released by a Major League Baseball Study Committee. Henry J. Aaron, an independent member of the committee and health economist with the Brookings Institution, was highly critical of the inability of the owners to embrace revenue sharing. He said "Unless that problem is addressed and solved, labor-management peace will never come to baseball."[34]

Bud Selig turned the disunity in owner ranks around. He is the only MLB commissioner in history who had experience as an owner. He was an insider who understood the problems that owners experienced. He was a consummate "diplomat" with "uncommonly effective interpersonal skills."[35] Under his leadership, MLB had a more consistent and direct focus, was more innovative, and ushered in a new period of growth for the sport.

In 1994, the owners agreed to a system of revenue sharing where $58 million would be redistributed to low-revenue teams. However, the proposal was dependent on the MLBPA agreeing, among other things, to the implementation of a salary cap. The MLPBA demurred. While negotiations over a new Basic Agreement were proceeding, with neither side having declared an impasse, MLB unilaterally imposed its desired set of arrangements: a salary cap, changes to free agency, salary arbitration, and elimination of anticollusion. The MLBPA called a strike and initiated proceedings before the National Labor Relations Board (NLRB) that MLB had breached "the good faith bargaining" provisions of the National Labor Relations Act (1935). Under the act, a party cannot initiate action until an impasse (breakdown) in bargaining has been declared. The NLRB found for the players, a decision that was subsequently upheld by Judge Sonia Sotomayor of the District Court in 1995.[36] In August 2009 she was appointed by President Obama to the Supreme Court.[37] The owners had jumped the gun. Their action resulted in a strike of 232 days and cancellation of the 1994 World Series.

Following Judge Sotomayor's decision, the parties recommenced negotiations of a new collective bargaining agreement. MLB dropped its plan for a salary cap. The organization realized it was a plan that the MLBPA would not accept. A new Basic Agreement was hammered out in 1996, effective from January 1, 1997. It returned to the key innovations of the Miller years: free agency, salary arbitration, and the no-collusion clause. It included three new developments: revenue sharing, a luxury tax on clubs spending over a threshold limit on wages, and an industry growth fund.[38] This "détente" has been modified and adopted in all of the subsequent Basic Agreements negotiated between MLB and the MLBPA.[39]

Current Issues Confronting Owners and Players

Before considering the major issues associated with baseball's new regime, it is necessary to first examine an aspect of MLB's relationship with antitrust law and the reserve system. In 1996, the Supreme Court ruled that a union could not sue an employer in an antitrust action if it was involved in collective bargaining.[40] If a union wished to pursue an antitrust action it would first need to decertify under the National Labor Relations Act (1935). In 1998, Congress passed the Curt Flood Act, which removed baseball's antitrust exemption from (only) labor issues. Signed into law by President Clinton it is a change to the legal landscape of baseball that will probably never be acted upon.

The major issues associated with the revenue sharing and luxury tax of the new "détente" are whether the former has perverse effects in discouraging owners to bid for "high" priced players and/or to "low ball" salaries and enhance profits by relying on income from revenue sharing pools, and whether the latter acts as a disincentive for clubs who's salary scale is close to the "taxing" threshold to bid for "quality" players.[41] In July 2000, a Blue Ribbon Panel appointed by MLB's commissioner reported on the results of the 1996 "détente." It stated that

> The goal of a well-designed league is to produce competitive balance. By this standard, the MLB is not well-designed . . . to reform baseball's structure to produce reasonable competitive balance, substantially more of the industry's revenues . . . should be distributed in ways that cause all clubs to operate within a much narrower band of unequal economic performance. The band should be broad enough to allow baseball entrepreneurship to be rewarded, but narrow enough that intractable differences between local markets do not produce a baseball underclass of chronically uncompetitive clubs.[42]

Problems with the "appropriate" designing of both may be the cause in the declining shares of revenue being obtained by players in recent years (see earlier).

Conclusion

For almost a century owners used the reserve system to dominate players in negotiations concerning their income and working conditions. Denied the chance to go elsewhere, except when owners were involved in a trade war with a rival league, players found themselves compelled to be thankful for whatever "concessions" they received. On five occasions, players formed unions in seeking redress from their weakened bargaining position. They all failed. In 1953, players initiated a sixth attempt and formed the MLBPA. Initially, it was little more than a company union.

In 1966, players turned to Marvin Miller, a seasoned union negotiator, to become their leader. It took him almost a decade to educate the membership of their rights and to use a grievance procedure to bring about abolition of the reserve system. Free agency after six years and salary arbitration for players with two/three years' service became the new model for industrial relations in baseball. The owners resented the loss of power brought about by these new arrangements. Subsequent negotiations over new Basic Agreements where characterized by strikes and lockouts, the best or worst example being the 232-day strike of 1994/95. This forced a change in the behavior of owners who looked to variants of revenue sharing to solve differences in the financial strength of clubs.

There has not been an industrial dispute in baseball in the last two decades. This is in direct contrast to the previous three decades. Recent declines in the players' share of revenue may put strains on the relationship between the parties; or maybe it won't. There have been, or are about to be changes to the leadership of both the MLBPA and MLB. Former player Tony Clark became the new executive director of the MLBPA in December 2013, following the death of Michael Weiner. Bud Selig stepped down as the commissioner of MLB at the end of 2014. The actions of his replacement, Rob Manfred, and the approach of Tony Clark will determine the contours of the next era of industrial relations in baseball.

The 1996 changes and subsequent Basic Agreements have included provisions for joint ventures between the parties, one of which is player tours or international play.[43] In recent years, the start of a new season has begun with games being played, on a rotation basis, in Japan, Korea, and Taiwan. On March 22 and 23, 2014, the opening series found a new home with the Diamondbacks entertaining the Dodgers in Sydney, Australia. London has been scheduled as another location for an opening series. The surpluses from these ventures are evenly split between MLB and MLBPA. The MLBPA allocates its share between the participating players and a fund to sustain its operation, for two years, in the event of a lockout.[44] The future direction of the relationship between owners and the MLBPA is in transition. The MLBPA has an insurance policy it can fall back on if it heads in a direction not to its liking.

Notes

1 Parts of this chapter draw on Braham Dabscheck, *Reading Baseball: Books, Biographies and the Business of the Game* (Morgantown, WV: Fitness Information Technology, 2011).

2 Joseph Schumpeter, *Capitalism, Socialism and Democracy* (London: Unwin University Press, 1965, first published 1943).

3 Walter Neale, "The Peculiar Economics of Professional Team Sports: A Contribution to the Theory of the Firm in Market Competition and Sporting Competition," *Quarterly Journal of Economics* LXXVIII, no. 1 (1964): 2.

4 William Fellner, *Competition Among the Few: Oligopoly and Similar Market Structures* (New York: Augustus M. Kelly, 1965, first published 1949), 35.

5 Quoted in Jerome Holtzman, *The Commissioners: Baseball's Midlife Crisis* (New York: Total Sports, 1998), 45.

6 Jules Tygiel, *Baseball's Great Experiment: Jackie Robinson and His Legacy* (New York: Vintage Books, 1983); Jules Tygiel, ed., *The Jackie Robinson Reader: Perspectives on an American Hero* (New York: Dutton Books, 1997); Scott Simon, *Jackie Robinson and the Integration of Baseball* (Hoboken, NJ: John Wiley & Sons, 2002); Lee Lowenfish, *Branch Rickey: Baseball's Ferocious Gentleman* (Lincoln: University of Nebraska Press, 2007).

7 Robert Burk, *Much More Than a Game: Players, Owners and American Baseball Since 1921* (Chapel Hill and London: The University of North Carolina Press, 2001), 51–90.

8 Quoted in Charles Korr, *The End Of Baseball As We Know It: The Players Union, 1960–1981* (Urbana and Chicago: University of Illinois Press, 2002), 18.

9 Bryan Di Salavatore, *A Clever Base-Ballist: The Life and Times of John Montgomery Ward* (New York: Pantheon Books, 1999); Robert Burk, *Never Just a Game: Players, Owners and American Baseball to 1920* (Chapel Hill: The University of North Carolina Press, 1994); Lee Lowenfish, *The Imperfect Diamond: A History of Baseball's Labor Wars* (New York: Da Capo, 1991, first published 1980); James Dworkin, *Owners versus Players: Baseball and Collective Bargaining* (Boston: Auburn House, 1981), 8–21. David Voigt, "Serfs versus Magnates: A Century of Labor Strife in Major League Baseball," in *The Business of Professional Sports*, ed. Paul Staudohar and James Mangan (Urbana and Chicago: University of Illinois Press, 1991), 95–114.

10 Korr, *The End of Baseball*, 14–16; Paul Staudohar, *Playing for Dollars: Labor Relations and the Sports Business* (Ithaca and London: ILR Press, 1996), 65, 105, 148.

11 Quoted in Korr, *The End of Baseball*, 23.

12 Korr, *The End of Baseball*, 33. Also see Charles Korr, "From Judge Cannon to Marvin Miller: From Players' Group to Players' Union," in *Diamond Mines: Baseball and Labor*, ed. Paul Staudohar (Syracuse: Syracuse University Press, 2000), 1–20.

13 Marvin Miller, *A Whole Different Ball Game: The Sport and Business of Baseball* (New York: Birch Lane Press, 1991), 47, 61.

14 John Helyar, *Lords of the Realm: The Real History of Baseball* (New York: Ballantine Books, 1995, first published 1994), 27.

15 DVD, Marvin Miller Memorial Celebration, January 21, 2013, Tishman Auditorium, New York University, School of Law, Major League Baseball Players' Association.

16 Korr, *The End of Baseball*; and Charles Korr, "Marvin Miller and the New Unionism in Baseball," in Staudohar and Mangan, eds., *The Business of Professional Sports*, 115–134.

17 Dworkin, *Owners versus Players*, 136–173.

18 *Federal Baseball Club of Baltimore v. National League of Professional Baseball Clubs*, 259 US 200 (1922), 208, 209; Daniel Levitt, *The Battle That Forged Modern Baseball: The Federal League Challenge and Its Legacy* (Lanham, MD: Ivan R. Dee, 2012); Nathaniel Grow, *Baseball On Trial: The Origin of Baseball's Antitrust Exemption* (Urbana: Illinois University Press, 2014).

19 *Toolson v. New York Yankees*, 346 US 356 (1953).

20 *Hart v. BP Keith Vaudeville Exchange*, 262 US 271 (1925); *United States v. Shubert*, 348 US 222 (1955); *United States v. International Club of New York*, 348 US 236 (1955); *Radovich v. National Football League*, 352 US 445 (1957); *Heywood v. National Basketball Association*, 401 US 1204 (1971); Roger Abrams, *Legal Bases: Baseball and the Law* (Philadelphia: Temple University Press, 1998); Stuart Banner, *The Baseball Trust: A History of Baseball's Antitrust Exemption* (Oxford: Oxford University Press, 2103).

21 *Flood v. Kuhn*, 407 US 258 (1972), 282; Brad Snyder, *A Well Paid Slave: Curt Flood's Fight for Free Agency in Professional Sports* (New York: Viking, 2006).

22 For a full text of the clause see Dworkin, *Owners versus Players*, 63.

23 In the Matter of the Arbitration between The Twelve Clubs Comprising The National League of Professional Baseball Clubs and the Twelve Clubs Comprising The American League of Professional Baseball Clubs (Los Angeles Club and Montreal Club) and Major League Baseball Players Association (John A. Messersmith and David A. McNally), Peter Seitz, Chairman, Decision No. 29, Grievance Nos. 75–27, 75–28, 23 December 1975; *Kansas City Royals Baseball Corporation v. Major League Baseball Player Association* 532 F.2d 615 (1976), MLB's unsuccessful appeal of Seitz's decision.

24 Miller, *A Whole Different Ball Game*, 255.

25 DVD, Marvin Miller Memorial Celebration.

26 Miller, *A Whole Different Ball Game*, 336–338, 356–361.

27 Michael Haupert, "The Economic History of Major League Baseball," *EH.net* (accessed October 14, 2014).

28 Andrew Zimbalist, "Reflections on Salary Shares and Salary Caps," *Journal of Sports Economics*, 11, no. 1 (2010): 24.

29 Max Fogle, "MLB Players' Salaries as a Share of Revenues: Laying Out the Issues," *Batting Leadoff.com*, April 16, 2014.

30 Helyar, *Lords of the Realm*; Miller, *A Whole Different Ball Game*; Burk, *Much More Than a Game*, 145–304; Kenneth Jennings, *Swings And Misses: Moribund Labor Relations in Professional Baseball* (Westport, CT and London: Praeger, 1997): Andrew Zimbalist, *May The Best Team Win: Baseball Economics And Public Policy* (Washington, DC: Brookings Institution, 2003), 75–122; William Gould, *Bargaining With Baseball: Labor Relations in an Age of Prosperous Turmoil* (Jefferson, NC: McFarland & Co, 2011), 53–154.

31 Gould, *Bargaining With Baseball*, 90–91.

32 Quoted in Andrew Zimbalist, *In The Best Interests Of Baseball? Governing the National Pastime* (Lincoln: University of Nebraska Press, 2013, first published 2006), 126.

33 Helyar, *Lords of the Realm*, 33.

34 Quoted in Helyar, *Lords of the Realm*, 556.

35 Zimbalist, *In the Best Interests*, xiii.

36 *Silverman v. Major League Baseball Player Relations Committee*, 880 F. Supp, 246 (1995); Gould, *Bargaining With Baseball*, 97–112; Daniel Marburger, ed., *Stee-rike Four!: What's Wrong with the Business of Baseball* (Westport, CT: Praeger, 1997).

37 Biographies of Current Justices of the Supreme Court, Supreme Court of the United States. www.supremecourt/gov/about/biographies.aspx (accessed April 22, 2015).

38 Basic Agreement Between the American League of Professional Baseball Clubs and the National League of Professional Baseball Clubs and Major League Baseball Players Association, Effective January 1, 1997.

39 For example, see Basic Agreement Between the 30 Major League Clubs and Major League Baseball Players Association, Effective December 12, 2011.

40 *Brown v. Pro Football*, 518 US 231 (1996).

41 Zimbalist, *May the Best Team Win*, 90–115; Zimbalist, *In the Best Interests*, 158–170: Gould, *Bargaining with Baseball*, 113–154.

42 The Report of the Independent Members of the Commissioner's Blue Ribbon Panel on Baseball Economics, July 2000, 5, 6.

43 Basic Agreement, Effective 2011, Article XV (K), Article XXV, Attachment 30.

44 Personal communication, March 23, 2014.

22

PLAY FOR PAY

Professional Sports and American Culture

Richard O. Davies

Introduction

The persistent growth in the value of sports franchises since 1945 is indicative of the growth in popularity of professional sports. In 1989, Jerry Jones, the president of a small oil and gas exploration firm in Arkansas, purchased the Dallas Cowboys of the National Football League (NFL) for $140 million. A quarter century later, according to *Forbes Magazine*, the franchise was worth an estimated $3.2 billion. The other 31 teams in the NFL had also enjoyed substantial increases in value, the average pegged at $1.5 billion.[1]

Although the enormously popular NFL leads the other major sports leagues in team valuations, Major League Baseball Franchises have also enjoyed rapid growth in value. The New York Yankees have the highest valuation at $2.5 billion, but when shipping magnate George Steinbrenner headed a group of investors that purchased the Yankees in 1973, the sale price was just $8.8 million. Estimated worth of franchises in 2015 in the National Basketball League were slightly lower, with the New York Knicks priced at $1.4 billion, but closely followed in valuation by the Los Angeles Lakers, Chicago Bulls, and Boston Celtics. The average value of an NBA franchise, according to *Forbes*, was $635 million, but that figure was likely to increase substantially when in 2014 retired software executive Steve Ballmer purchased the Los Angeles Clippers for the staggering sum of $2 billion. In 1981, Los Angeles real estate developer Donald Sterling had purchased the (then) San Diego Clippers for $12.5 million. Despite the inflated purchase price—Ballmer reportedly paid $1.4 billion over the estimated value—economists confidently projected that in 10 years he would be able to sell his franchise for a sizeable capital gain.[2]

Economists believe that the value of professional sports franchises will continue to escalate because of their history of rising valuations, beneficial tax advantages, generous public subsidies, and especially, lucrative television revenues. However, such was not always the case. Not until after World War II did the values of franchises began to escalate consistently, becoming for the first time a significant component of the American economy, driven by a surging postwar economic expansion that produced heretofore unheard-of amounts of discretionary income and leisure time for a rapidly expanding middle class.[3]

Various league histories are replete with examples of struggling owners fighting off creditors, sometimes being forced into bankruptcy. As but one example, Connie Mack repeatedly faced serious financial problems throughout his 50 years as owner (and field manager) of the Philadelphia Athletics. On two separate occasions, with creditors demanding payment on delinquent loans, he had no option other than to part with high-salaried star players who had won him pennants and World Series titles.

At age 92 in 1954, with his last-place team attracting a paltry 300,000 spectators for the season and facing imminent bankruptcy, Mack had no option but to sell his team to Chicago businessman Arnold Johnson for $1.5 million. The new owner promptly moved the team to Kansas City. In 1960 after Johnson's death, the ball club was sold to insurance entrepreneur Charles O. Finley, who, failing to make money in Kansas City, moved the A's to Oakland in 1968. Still considered a "small city" club in 2015 and burdened with a dreary outmoded stadium, the team was nonetheless valued at $500 million. Such an increase in value is testimony to the growth of professional sports in the 60 years since a disconsolate Connie Mack was forced to sell-off his lifetime's work for just $1.5 million.[4]

The Formative Years, 1865–1920

Professional sports began with the decision by a few city boosters in Cincinnati in 1868 to establish a baseball club in which each player would be compensated. The team president hired the acclaimed English cricket player turned baseball standout, Harry Wright, at a substantial salary of $1,200 to recruit the best talent available and authorized him to offer salaries that were roughly double what skilled factory workers earned annually. The concept of a professional team defied the popular belief of the time that athletes should play solely for the satisfaction derived from participation in a sporting event; the idea of paying grown men to play a game defied conventional thinking. In 1858, the National Association of Base Ball Players (NABBP) had been established with the primary intent of standardizing the rules of the popular new game, but the organization also embraced a strong code of amateurism. When Wright's Red Stockings won 56 games in 1869 without a single loss, however, the opponents of professionalism lost the battle. Large crowds paid good money to watch the talented team perform on its national barnstorming tour. The result was a rapid increase in the number of professional teams, but there did not yet exist a strong controlling organizational structure.[5]

Chicago businessman William Hulbert, owner of the Chicago White Stockings, saw a promising business opportunity and in 1876 established a new eight-team professional league—the National League of Professional Base Ball Clubs. Franchise owners would operate their club as any other business, and players were barred from participation in the ownership or operation of the team. Players were now considered to be employees, rather than members of a cooperative as existed during the short-lived and loosely organized National Association of Professional Base Ball Players that had begun play in 1871.[6]

Although the National League encountered many difficulties, including initial financial losses, Hulbert steadfastly persevered. By the time of his death in 1882, the National League had become a reasonably stable entity, and the financial potential it demonstrated sparked the creation of a rival, the American Association. In order to attract spectators and establish credibility, the new league began to raid the National League of leading players with offers of higher pay. In an attempt to prevent salaries from escalating too high, management of the two leagues agreed upon a policy whereby players could not be induced to switch teams or leagues. They signed off on a "National Agreement" that assured each team would respect the contracts of players that other teams had identified as "reserved," thereby ending the practice of players "revolving" from one team to another in search of higher pay. In 1885, the two leagues agreed to cap players' salaries at $2,000 a season and inserted a "reserve clause" into player contracts that created a modern-day form of serfdom. Once a contract was signed, a player was bound to that team until the team traded or sold him to another team. The reserve clause would constrain players' salaries until it was jettisoned in the mid-1970s. In 1892, a deep recession doomed the American Association and the National League became a 12-team league.[7]

Until the second decade of the twentieth century, games were played in rickety wood-constructed ballparks that seated upwards of 10,000. The game grew in popularity despite the difficult economic times of the 1890s, and in 1901 former Cincinnati newspaperman turned baseball executive, Ban Johnson, orchestrated the creation of a rival "major" league, the American. In 1903, after considerable acrimony, the two leagues agreed to a three-man commission to operate the two leagues, and the Pittsburgh Pirates and the Boston Americans met in the first World Series. As historian Charles Alexander observes, "Modern baseball had begun."[8]

Such star players as Honus Wagner, Cy Young, Christy Mathewson, and Ty Cobb stimulated rising attendance, prompting owners to invest in double-decked ballparks that utilized structural steel beams and reinforced concrete. Tangible evidence of the financial future envisioned by club owners, the new ballparks seated upwards of 30,000 spectators. The first of the new structures, Philadelphia's Shibe Park, opened in 1909, and was soon emulated across the two leagues. Two such ballparks, Fenway Park in Boston (1912) and Wrigley Field in Chicago (1914), remain in use yet today and are considered national treasures. Baseball, widely proclaimed as "Our Game" and "America's Pastime," was clearly the most popular sport in America. Even the scandal that stunned the nation when the Chicago White Sox were exposed for throwing the 1919 World Series did not permanently harm the game's popularity.[9]

Baseball's dominance as a professional sport was unquestioned. One potential rival, bare-knuckle prizefighting, had existed along the margins of American life since before the Civil War, but the blood sport was illegal everywhere. So-called "championship" bouts, held secretly in clandestine locations beyond the reach of law enforcement, nonetheless received considerable newspaper coverage. In the 1880s, prizefighting became a major story line in the *National Police Gazette* as well as daily newspapers. As a result, popular heavyweight John L. Sullivan became the nation's first sports "star." In 1892 the city of New Orleans legalized the sport if it were conducted under the new Marquis of Queensbury rules that required the use of padded five-ounce gloves, three-minute rounds, and other rules designed to reduce the violent image of the sport. In 1897 the Nevada legislature legalized prizefighting so that a championship bout between Jim Corbett and Bob Fitzsimmons could be held in Carson City.[10]

Progressive reformers, however, continued to condemn prizefighting because of its brutal nature, but also because it encouraged gambling. They also took due notice of prizefighting's close ties with saloon owners and corrupt urban political machines. Nonetheless, when a major championship fight was held, such as the "Fight of the Century" between the black champion Jack Johnson and the "Great White Hope" Jim Jeffries in Reno in 1910, the attention of the nation was intently focused upon the event. In the hours after Johnson knocked out his white challenger, angry mobs of young white men roamed the streets of major cities attacking both jubilant young black men and innocent citizens. Boxing, as its many critics claimed, had the potential of producing abhorrent behaviors. However, the brutal sport that its adherents called the "sweet science" gained widespread popularity because it was used in training doughboys for the Great War. Pioneer promoter George "Tex" Rickard had proven that big money could be made promoting fights, and with the decline of the progressive impulse following the Armistice, prizefighting was quickly assimilated into the mainstream of American professional sports.[11]

Horse racing also suffered from staunch opposition by progressives because gambling was its primary appeal. The sport had become entrenched in American society well before the American Revolution, especially in the mid-Atlantic region of Maryland and Virginia, and it enjoyed popularity in Tennessee and Kentucky during the early nineteenth century. Following the Civil War the sport grew rapidly with the construction of enclosed oval tracks and grandstands operated by jockey clubs or investors. By the end of the nineteenth century, operators owned some 300 tracks across the United States, with major races attracting crowds of 20,000 or more. Illegal betting parlors flourished by offering off-track wagering with race results at distant racetracks being transmitted across telegraph wires. Although prominent friends of the turf came from families of high social standing, the sport fell on hard times due to widespread allegations of fixed races, doped horses, crooked jockeys, undue influence by state and local politicians in cahoots with organized crime, and even the abuse of horses. Horse racing, even more than prizefighting, became a favorite target of progressive reformers. In many states, legislatures passed laws outlawing the sport, and by 1910, only 25 tracks remained in operation. Significantly, New York's progressive Republican governor Charles Evans Hughes persuaded the legislature to close all of the racetracks in the Empire State. Racing remained viable in only two states, Kentucky and Maryland, enabling the Kentucky Derby and Preakness to become the most prestigious of all races.[12]

Professional Sports in an Age of Prosperity, Depression, and War, 1920–1950

Baseball dominated American sports well into the 1950s with only boxing, college football, and horse racing giving it competition. Baseball's overwhelming popularity was driven by extensive newspaper coverage. Live radio broadcasts of games began in the mid-1930s and further enhanced baseball's appeal. The new "live ball era," highlighted by Babe Ruth's prodigious home run production, spurred the game's growth during the 1920s. In 1923, the magnificent three-deck 63,000-seat Yankee Stadium opened before a capacity crowd, towering proudly over the lower Bronx, a tangible symbol of the economic vitality and vast popularity of the national pastime.

Ruth's popularity was enhanced by the image his publicist Christy Walsh constructed. Walsh astutely molded Ruth's public persona, creating a template for future sports stars that included product endorsement and carefully crafted coverage of the player and his positive attributes.[13] Black professional baseball players, however, were forced to ply their trade with little attention provided by the mainstream press. Organized baseball's nefarious "Gentlemen's Agreement" established in the mid-1880s to ban blacks remained in full force. Such mega-talents as pitcher Satchel Paige, slugging catcher Josh Gibson, and a host of others were forced to compete in the undercapitalized Negro National League that was founded in 1920. In 1938, with the American economy showing signs of emerging from the Great Depression, the Negro American League was established. Both leagues enjoyed a brief period of rising attendance as a result of the booming wartime economy, but after the Brooklyn Dodgers signed Jackie Robinson away from the Kansas City Monarchs in 1945, the Negro Leagues suffered a major exodus by their top players. By the early 1950s the Negro Leagues had disbanded.[14]

It was during this so-called "Golden Age" of sports that intensive media coverage produced a galaxy of sports "stars." Historian Randy Roberts persuasively argues that Ruth's popularity was most closely approximated by heavyweight champion Jack Dempsey, who's powerful knockout punches enabled Tex Rickard, having moved from Nevada to become president of Madison Square Garden, to promote five outdoor fights that produced boxing's first million-dollar gates.[15] In his effort to keep the seats of Madison Square Garden filled, Rickard scheduled frequent fight cards and acquired a franchise in the National Hockey League, prompting appreciative New York journalists to dub the team Tex's "Rangers." Boxing's appeal extended to many cities across the country where promoters offered fight cards, and private gymnasiums provided training facilities and instruction for prospective pugilists. Almost overnight, boxing moved from being a moral outlier to the center of American sports.[16]

A similar turnabout in public sentiment in the 1920s also thrust horse racing back into the national spotlight as legislatures, no longer pressured by antigambling groups, sought new sources of tax revenue. All across the land, once shuttered tracks were reopened. Large crowds flocked to watch the thoroughbreds run, and even the Great Depression did not produce a noticeable decline in attendance. Legalization by state legislatures of parimutuel betting helped draw record crowds, leading to the opening of such notable upscale tracks as Hialeah and Gulfstream in Florida and Del Mar and Santa Anita in California.[17]

The prospects of professional football, however, were not nearly as bright. The sport gained a tenuous foothold with the establishment of the National Football League in 1920. Well into the 1930s, a lack of operating capital and low attendance led to constant franchise turnover. Teams were located at various times in numerous small cities. The NFL survived because of the dedication of such owners as George Halas of the Chicago Bears, whose signing of famed Illinois halfback Harold "Red" Grange in 1924 gave the league a modicum of credibility and its first major attraction other than aging Jim Thorpe.[18]

The NFL's popularity paled in comparison with college football, which attracted large crowds to recently constructed college stadiums that seated upwards of 60,000. Although college football's masters strongly argued that their enterprise was pristinely amateur, in reality it was a professional sport in all but one important respect. Affluent alumni boosters wrote large checks to support programs, athletic departments sold tickets, and prominent coaches such as Notre Dame's Knute Rockne or Michigan's Fielding "Hurry Up" Yost were paid lofty salaries. Although the Carnegie Commission released a blistering critique of the widespread ethical shortcomings of college football in 1929, the nascent reform movement it stimulated was soon thereafter lost in a fog of fawning media coverage. Cleverly structured as a near-perfect cartel, college football was professional in every way except that the workers, that is, the athletes, were not compensated beyond tuition waivers. The game's supporters succeeded in convincing the American public that football was the epitome of the amateur ideal and should be an integral part of higher education. This resulted in the creation of one of the biggest myths in the history of American sports.[19]

The Great Depression of the 1930s seriously threatened professional baseball and football, but attendance at college football games remained steady and horse racing actually increased attendance, presumably by offering to Depression-burdened spectators the possibility of picking a long-shot winner at the $2 dollar window. Boxing found a new star in Joe Louis, who won the heavyweight championship at age 21 and thrilled a nation in 1938 when he avenged a rare loss by knocking out German Max Schmeling in the first round as 45,000 fans looked on at Yankee Stadium while an estimated 100 million Americans, including President

Franklin Roosevelt, gathered by radios.[20] Led by example of the St. Louis Cardinals, baseball established a new (initially very modest) revenue source by selling broadcasting rights, and the Cincinnati Reds demonstrated that attendance, even during hard times, could be boosted by playing games at night under the glare of electric lighting.[21] In 1941, as the winds of war swirled around the globe, the NFL championship game was broadcast on a national network for the first time; how many listeners stayed tuned for long, however, is questionable as the Chicago Bears defeated the Washington Redskins 73–0. With the economy on the rebound and the new medium of television being tested, the prospects for professional sports seemed bright. The anticipated new era for American sport, however, had to be postponed following the bombing of Pearl Harbor.

Sports in the Age of Television and the Internet: 1950–2015

Professional sports assumed a significantly expanded role in American popular culture in the decades following World War II. Fears that the postwar economy would be thrust into a deep recession were soon forgotten as the economy rapidly gained momentum after 15 years of depression and wartime rationing. The economy hummed with activity as rising wages thrust millions of Americans into a rapidly expanding middle class, and sociologists contemplated the significance of America's new "affluent society." By 1960, 90 percent of American homes contained a television set, which provided families with a new and compelling form of entertainment. Although only dimly perceived as the postwar era began to unfold, the new medium of television held the key to the future of professional sports.[22]

The surge in popularity of professional sports resulted from several interrelated socioeconomic factors. By the 1960s, a pivotal decade of expansion and growth for American professional sports, the national network of major cities and their rapidly expanding suburbs contained 74 percent of the nation's population. The Census of 2000 revealed that the percentage or metropolitan dwellers stood at 83 percent. Professional sports can only succeed in a metropolitan environment where a critical mass of potential ticket buyers exists. Affluent urbanites had both the leisure time and financial wherewithal to attend sporting events. The American economy had generated sufficient capital, both private and public, with which to build and operate new and larger football stadiums, baseball parks, and indoor arenas. Business and political leaders viewed the presence of professional teams to be essential for a city to be recognized as "major league," and taxpayers were repeatedly tapped to provide funding to erect facilities to accommodate professional teams. Nearly all of the venues for professional sports built since 1960 were publicly funded. Team owners repeatedly followed the same game plan: pressure local government to build a new home for a team with the threat of moving to a city that would. Critics complained in vain while multimillionaire owners happily accepted public welfare. As but one recent example: in 2010 fears that the Minnesota Vikings, owned by New Jersey real estate mogul Zygi Wilf, would decamp to Los Angeles if the outdated 30-year-old Hubert Humphrey Metrodome was not replaced by a new indoor stadium, prompted Minnesota's political leaders to agree to pay approximately $500 million dollars toward the construction of a new $1.1 billion indoor football stadium in downtown Minneapolis.[23]

Changes in the structure of professional sports were dramatic. Where ticket sales had once been almost exclusively the source of income for a professional team, management now tapped into multiple streams of revenue that seemed to grow with each passing year. Teams benefitted from a multiplicity of government subsidies and tax loopholes, revenue from parking fees, food and beverage concessions, sale of expensive seat licenses (which permitted the purchaser to buy a limited number of season tickets), fees generated by the leasing of luxury boxes (considered a major public relations opportunity for corporations that wrote off the cost as a business expense), "naming" rights to the stadium or arena (e.g., Lincoln Financial Field, home of the Philadelphia Eagles; AT&T Park, home of the San Francisco Giants; United [Airlines] Center in Chicago, home of the Bulls and Blackhawks), and the sale of merchandise emblazoned with the copyright-protected team logo (hats, jackets, coffee cups, key rings, automobile license plate holders, beer mugs, tee-shirts, etc.). But far more important were the fees generated from network and cable television companies.[24]

Television initially posed major challenges for all professional sports. Team and league executives were uncertain as to the best way to exploit the new medium without hurting ticket sales, but by the 1960s, as advances in technology improved the viewing experience—color, instant replay, graphics—audience size expanded exponentially and management now looked upon television as a major source of revenue. Of all professional sports, football was the most adept in adapting to the new medium under the leadership of Commissioner Pete Rozelle. The so-called "Greatest Game Ever Played" proved to be the moment when television's vast economic potential was fully appreciated. The December 30, 1958, NFL championship game between the New York Giants and Baltimore Colts captivated an estimated 40 million viewers across the nation. As quarterback Johnny Unitas led the Colts to an exciting overtime victory, the long-struggling NFL came of age and stood on the cusp of an era that would be marked by spectacular expansion that has yet to run its course.[25]

Television's central role for the future of professional sports became evident in 1960 when the American Football League was launched based upon a business model that placed television revenues ahead of ticket sales. In 1964, the new league signed a stunning $42 million contract with NBC. The following year a Gallup Poll reported that football had replaced baseball, with it slow pace of play, as the nation's most popular spectator sport. Football made for compelling television viewing, combining athleticism and violence in a game based upon complex strategies. Advertisers willingly paid premium rates to become associated with the new national game. After the two leagues merged, the first Super Bowl championship game—ideally designed for television—was played at the end of the 1966 season, and within a few years it attracted the largest viewing audience of the year. For decades the NFL had played its games almost exclusively on Sunday afternoons, but in 1970 *Monday Night Football* became an instant sensation, setting viewing records. In 2015 it remained the longest continuous program on television.[26]

Propelled by television revenues that far outstripped ticket sales, the NFL launched an expansion program that resulted in its current size of 32 teams when the Houston Texans joined the league in 2002. The owners of the Texans had to fork over a $700 million admission fee simply to join the party. Seven years earlier, the Carolina Panthers and Jacksonville Jaguars were admitted after paying $140 million. Beginning in 2007, regular season games were scheduled in London, an indication that the league intended someday to expand across the Atlantic in search of new markets. In 1964 commissioner Pete Rozelle set the league on an upward trajectory when he shrewdly lured the three major networks into a highly publicized bidding war for television rights for the 1964–1965 seasons. The winning bid from CBS called for $14 million per year, a sharp increase over the $4 million for the previous year. As the years rolled by, the ever-increasing popularity of the NFL drove television revenues ever higher; in 2015, with three networks and two cable TV companies in the mix, revenues reached $6 billion. In 2014, the NFL had estimated revenues of $10 billion, and league officials predicted that by the year 2027 revenues would reach $25 billion.[27]

The other professional leagues expanded in a similar fashion. Between 1903 and 1953, Major League Baseball had remained static with 16 teams located in the same cities east of the Mississippi River and north of the Mason Dixon Line. It was inevitable that baseball would respond to the explosive population growth in the South and West. Thus in 1958, the Brooklyn Dodgers and New York Giants moved to Los Angeles and San Francisco in response to strong financial incentives offered by the two cities with prospects of lucrative television revenues. The offer by the city of San Francisco to construct a new ballpark for the Giants—the ill-fated windblown Candlestick Park—established a precedent that became the norm for financing stadiums: the taxpayer would bear the burden. Dodger Stadium, opened in 1961, would be one of the last ballparks paid for largely by its professional team occupant.[28]

Professional basketball made a modest appearance on the East Coast in the 1920s but interest remained minimal. It was not until 1949 that the National Basketball Association was cobbled together with 11 teams located in the upper Midwest and along the East Coast. The league gained momentum with increased television exposure that showcased two magnificent centers, Bill Russell of the Boston Celtics and Wilt Chamberlain of the Philadelphia Warriors. By 1990 the NBA had spread across the country by adding 21 new franchises, including four teams absorbed from the American Basketball Association when it dissolved in 1976 after nine years of precarious existence. Under Commissioner David Stern (who served between 1984 and 2014) the NBA enjoyed enormous growth and financial success. The NBA tended to feature a small number of superstars in its expansion, beginning with Magic Johnson and Larry Bird of the Los Angeles Lakers and Boston Celtics, soon followed by a host of others including Michael Jordan, Kobe Bryant, Shaquille O'Neal, and LeBron James.[29] The National Hockey League, which for nearly six decades had been content with just six teams, doubled in size in 1967 and continued to add franchises until it reached its present size of 30 teams, just 7 of which were Canadian. Few devoted fans bothered to question why a game played on ice would have appeal in such warm-climate cities as Tampa, Miami, Phoenix, and Los Angeles.

Skeptics publicly scoffed when a precariously financed 24-hour sports cable network was introduced in 1979, but it did not take long for the Entertainment and Sports Network (ESPN) to revolutionize the promotion and broadcast of sporting events. ESPN cleverly exploited the seemingly insatiable demand for live telecasts of sporting events. By the early 2000s, now owned by the Disney Corporation, ESPN produced nearly half of all its parent company's revenue as it dominated the American sports world. Its empire expanded to include seven cable television networks, a popular magazine, and sports restaurants, as well as a radio network. Within a few years, ESPN had effectively revolutionized sports television and flexed its muscle by dictating starting times of games so as to enhance its ratings. Its creative use of split-screens and ability to move from a lopsided game to a potential upset transformed the NCAA men's basketball tournament into the phenomenon of "March Madness." What had been a 16-team tournament grew into one with 68 entrants. Extensive coverage of college football by ESPN set off bidding wars with other networks that greatly increased the money that flowed into the NCAA and its "power conference" members, and all the while the network aggressively increased its coverage of the NFL, including taking over *Monday Night Football* from fellow Disney network ABC in 2005.[30]

Player salaries had remained depressed for all professional sports until the 1970s at which time a series of legal maneuvers masterminded by the head of the Major League Players

Association, Marvin Miller, led to the death of the reserve clause and the beginning of a new era of restricted free agency. Major league baseball salaries, which had averaged less than $20,000 per season in the mid-1960s, escalated to an average of $144,000 in 1980 and $891,000 in 1990. The NFL and NBA had no choice but to adopt their own versions of restricted free agency. The result was bidding wars for top players that tended to accelerate pay increases for all players, with much of the new money coming from ever-larger television contracts. In 2014 the average salary for a Major League Baseball player reached $3.3 million, but that paled in comparison the $5.5 million average salary paid by the NBA. Professional football trailed at an average of $2 million, although top quarterbacks commanded salaries above $20 million. At the extreme, in 2007 infielder Alex Rodriquez signed a 10-year contract with the New York Yankees for $275 million that stunned the sports world, but following the 2014 season the Miami Marlins of the National League, long recognized for an unwillingness to pay to keep top talent, reversed course and signed 25-year-old slugger Giancarlo Stanton to a 13-year $325 million contract. In sharp contrast, when superstar Mickey Mantle retired in 1969 on the eve of free agency, his highest salary was $100,000.

Television also contributed directly to the popularity and economic fortunes of so-called minor sports. During the 1970s and 1980s, women's and men's tennis elbowed their way on the front pages of sports pages because television highlighted the talents of such electrifying players as Arthur Ashe, Jimmy Connors, and John McEnroe. The long-running rivalry between Martina Navratilova and Chris Evert thrust women's tennis into the national spotlight, generating high viewer ratings. Golf benefitted from a similar rivalry during the 1960s between the aggressively charismatic Arnold Palmer and the cerebral craftsman Jack Nicklaus. In 1997, golf received a major boost when 21-year-old Tiger Woods astounded the sports world by winning the Masters by 12 strokes. When Woods was in contention in major tournaments, as he often was—he won his fourteenth major in 2008 in a dramatic playoff with Rocco Mediate—television ratings soared, and so did the prize money paid out by tournament sponsors.[31]

In this new era where commercialism reigned supreme, athletes were no longer evaluated simply by their performances. Charismatic star athletes like Tiger Woods, LeBron James, Derek Jeter, or Bret Favre greatly enhanced their annual salaries by endorsing a wide array of products. In 2013, James signed a $90 million contract to endorse a basketball shoe, but his endorsement income nonetheless paled in comparison to that of former NBA superstar Michael Jordan, whose spectacular NBA career (1983–1999) and magnetic personality enabled him to become fabulously wealthy by endorsing an eclectic collection of products, most notably an iconic sports shoe. Jordan's appeal extended to residents across the globe, prompting the historian Walter LeFeber to conclude that Jordan had become a living symbol of the transglobal nature of American capitalism, his personal wealth equal to that of some Third World countries.[32]

Major college football and men's basketball gladly joined in the bonanza and cut their own lucrative television deals. But, of course, under the guise that college athletes were "student-athletes," they did not pay their players other than waiver of tuition and fees. Instead, the millions that the NCAA and its individual members raked in fueled the rapid escalation of high paid coaches and administrators, which by 2014 saw nearly all major college head football coaches earning salaries ranging from $1 million to $7 million, with men's basketball coaches not far behind.

The reality was that with its football and men's basketball programs, American higher education now operated a multibillion-dollar athletic enterprise that rivaled the income levels of the biggest of professional leagues.[33]

Conclusion: Shadows on the Horizon

As professional sports moved into the second decade of the twenty-first century the future looked encouraging. With television revenues continuing to escalate and attendance stabilized, professional sports seemed impervious to a serious downturn. But that optimistic outlook overlooked the precipitous decline of two sports that had once enjoyed enormous popularity: horse racing and boxing. Horse racing began a steady decline in the 1950s when points spread wagering on football and basketball lured millions away from the track to a more attractive betting option. Boxing began losing its appeal in the late 1950s due to oversaturation of television coverage and disturbing revelations of the odious influence of organized crime, and growing awareness of retired fighters suffering from serious neurological impairment as a result of repeated blows to the head. Two deaths in the ring suffered by Benny Peret and Duk Koo Kim in 1962 and 1982 carried live on network television greatly damaged the image of the sport.

Increasingly boxing's appeal relied upon charismatic heavyweight champions and the melding of boxing with the culture of Las Vegas where the sport thrived with the explosive growth of the casino culture. Domination of the sport by promoter Don King, well known for his questionable ethics, raised damaging concerns about the ethics of the sport. A precipitous decline in popularity devastated the sport in the aftermath of the "Bite of the Century," when Mike Tyson chomped off a portion of Evander Holyfield's ear in a 1997 Las Vegas championship bout that generated millions of pay-for-view dollars. Coincidentally, the introduction and spectacular growth of mixed martial arts early in the twenty-first century siphoned off many fans, especially those under the age of 40, who apparently were interested in watching a more radical form of physical combat.[34]

By 2015, even the future of professional baseball and football had become somewhat cloudy. Baseball's slow and ponderous rate of play did not make for compelling television, especially compared to the much more frenetic action of basketball and football. Because baseball was not compatible with the points spread, it did not appeal to the large segment of sports fans that enjoy wagering on sports. Although baseball attendance remained high, disaffection of African Americans and younger fans was troubling to league officials. Critics warned of the long-term consequences of the reality that baseball increasingly appealed to those eligible for membership in the American Association of Retired Persons. Millions of Americans, born after 1975 and having played youth soccer rather than Pop Warner Football or Little League Baseball, also produced concern. The potential that professional soccer, already dominating the rest of the sporting world, would someday capture the loyalty of a large swath of a younger generation of American sports fans, now appeared possible.

Other issues also produced warning signs. After years of shameful denial and obfuscation, the NFL also had to confront the fact that many former players—estimated conservatively at 33 percent of its 34,000 retired players—suffered from some degree of chronic traumatic encephalopathy as a result of concussions and/or repeated blows to the head. Tragic suicides of several former players, most notably such stars as Mike Webster, Junior Seau, and Dave Duerson, sparked public awareness and the issue moved into federal court rooms.[35] Growing media reports of instances of professional athletes having engaged in illegal drug and steroid use, illegal possession and use of firearms, driving under the influence, sexual assault, and domestic violence, further tarnished the public image of professional sports. At what point such issues would lead to alienation of fans—with the potential of the loss of major corporate advertisers—remained an open, but very real question.[36]

Nonetheless, at the time of the writing of this chapter, the major established professional sports seemed capable of maintaining their popularity and financial well-being. As longtime professional football fan turned critic, Steve Almond, wrote in 2014: "Sports represent one of the few growth sectors for the corporate media. It's far more profitable to cover football as a glorious diversion than a sobering news story."[37] Perhaps, but an examination of the ebb and flow of the popularity of individual sports over the past 150 years suggests that far-reaching changes in professional sports nonetheless might loom just over the horizon.

Notes

1 Mike Ozanian, "The NFL's Most Valuable Teams," *Forbes*, August 8, 2014.

2 Mike Axisa, "Surprise! *Forbes* Ranks Yankees as Most Valuable MLB Franchise," *CBS Sports Web Site* (March 26, 2014); Ashlee Vance, "Steve Ballmer's New Life with the Clippers," *Bloomberg Businessweek*, October 16, 2014, 48–50.

3 Charles Alexander, *Our Game: An American Baseball History* (New York: Henry Holt, 1991), 26–129; Harold Seymour, *Baseball: The Early Years* (New York: Oxford, 1960), 307–324.

4 Connie Mack, *My 66 Years in the Big Leagues* (Philadelphia: Winston, 1950); William C. Kashatus, "Connie Mack," in *Scribner Encyclopedia of American Lives: Sports Figures, Vol. 2*, ed. Arnold Markoe (New York: Scribner, 2002), 89–91.

5 Warren Jay Goldstein, *Playing For Keeps: A History of Early Baseball* (Ithaca: Cornell University Press, 1989); Seymour, *The Early Years*, 35–72.

6 Seymour, *The Early Years*, 75–132.

7 Alexander, *Our Game*, 35–58; Seymour, *The Early Years*, 104–171.

8 Eugene Murdock, *Ban Johnson: Czar of Baseball* (Westport, CT: Greenwood, 1982); Seymour, *The Early Years*, 307–324; Harold Seymour, *Baseball: The Golden Age* (New York: Oxford, 1971), 3–37; Louis P. Masur, *Autumn Glory: Baseball's First World Series* (New York: Hill and Wang, 2003); Alexander, *Our Game*, 83.

9 Seymour, *The Golden Age*, 49–53; Alexander, *Our Game*, 108–155.

10 For an excellent overview of the history of boxing and its literature, see Randy Roberts and Andrew R.M. Smith, "'The Report of My Death Was an Exaggeration': The Many Sordid Lives of America's Bloodiest 'Pastime,'" *The International Journal of the History of Sport* Vol. 31: 1–2 (March 2014): 72–90; Jeffrey T. Sammons, *Beyond the Ring: The Role of Boxing in American Society* (Urbana: University of Illinois Press, 1990); Bert Sugar, *100 Years of Boxing* (New York: Routledge, 1982); Elliott Gorn, *The Manly Art: Bare-Knuckle Prize Fighting in America* (Ithaca: Cornell University Press, 1986); and Michael T. Isenberg, *John L. Sullivan and His America* (Urbana: University of Illinois Press, 1988).

11 Randy Roberts, *Papa Jack: Jack Johnson and the Era of White Hopes* (New York: Free Press, 1983); Charles Samuels, *The Magnificent Rube: The Life and Gaudy Times of Tex Rickard* (New York: McGraw Hill, 1957); Colleen Aycock and Mark Scott, *Tex Rickard: Boxing's Greatest Promoter* (Jefferson, NC: McFarland, 2012); and Richard O. Davies, *The Main Event: Boxing in Nevada from the Mining Camps to the Las Vegas Strip* (Reno and Las Vegas: University of Nevada Press, 2014).

12 Steven A. Riess, *The Sport of Kings and the Kings of Crime: Horse Racing, Politics, and Organized Crime in New York, 1865–1913* (Syracuse: Syracuse University Press, 2011); Steven A. Riess, "The Cyclical History of Horse Racing: The USA's Oldest and (Sometimes) Most Popular Sport," *The International Journal of the History of Sport* Vol. 31: 1–2 (March 2014): 29–54.

13 Robert Creamer, *Babe: The Legend Comes to Life* (New York: Simon and Schuster, 1974), and Marshall Smelser, *The Life that Ruth Built* (Lincoln: University of Nebraska Press, 1975).

14 Robert Peterson, *Only the Ball Was White: A History of Legendary Black Players and All-Black Professional Teams* (New York: Oxford University Press, 1992); Neil Lanctot, *Negro League Baseball: The Rise and Ruin of a Black Institution* (Philadelphia: University of Pennsylvania Press, 2004); Jules Tygiel, *Baseball's Great Experiment: Jackie Robinson and His Legacy* (New York: Oxford University Press, 1983).

15 Randy Roberts, *Jack Dempsey: The Manassa Mauler* (Baton Rouge: Louisiana State University Press, 1979), 267.
16 Roberts and Smith, "The Many Sordid Lives," 75–78.
17 Riess, "The Cyclical History of Horse Racing," 38–40.
18 Robert W. Peterson, *The Early Years of Pro Football* (New York: Oxford University Press, 1997); Jeff Davis, *Papa Bear: The Life and Legacy of George Halas* (New York: McGraw Hill, 2005).
19 John Sayle Watterson, *College Football: History, Spectacle, Controversy* (Baltimore: Johns Hopkins University Press, 2000), 143–218.
20 Randy Roberts, *Joe Louis: Hard Times Man* (New Haven: Yale University Press, 2010).
21 Charles Alexander, *Breaking the Slump: Baseball in the Depression Era* (New York: Columbia University Press, 2002).
22 Benjamin G. Rader, *In Its Own Image: How Television Has Transformed Sport* (New York: Free Press, 1984); Ronald A. Smith, *Play-by-Play: Radio, Television and Big-Time College Sports* (Baltimore: Johns Hopkins University Press, 2001).
23 Steve Almond, *Against Football: One Fan's Reluctant Manifesto* (Brooklyn: Melville House, 2014), 74–5.
24 Michael Oriard, *Brand NFL: Making & Selling America's Favorite Brand* (Chapel Hill: University of North Carolina, 2007); Andrew Zimbalist, *Baseball and Billions: A Probing Look Inside the Big Business of the National Pastime* (New York: Basic Books, 1992); 47–73.
25 Mark Bowden, *The Best Game Ever Played: Giants vs. Colts, 1958, and the Birth of the Modern NFL* (New York: Atlantic Monthly Press, 2008); Phil Patten, *Razzle-Dazzle: The Curious Marriage of Television and Professional Football* (Garden City: Dial Publishing, 1984); Benjamin Rader, *In Its Own Image: How Television Has Transformed Sport* (New York: Free Press, 1984).
26 Michael MacCambridge, *America's Game: The Epic Story of How Pro Football Captured a Nation* (New York: Random House, 2004), 153–291.
27 MacCambridge, *America's Game*, 103–107, 156–159, 171–174; Oriard, *Brand NFL*, 2–9, 250–257.
28 Neil Sullivan, *The Dodgers Move West* (New York: Oxford University Press, 1987); Zimbalist, *Baseball and Billions*, 123–146.
29 Terry Pluto, *Loose Balls: The Short, Wild Life of the American Basketball Association* (New York: Simon and Schuster, 1990); David Halberstam, *Playing for Keeps: Michael Jordan and the World He Made* (New York: Random House, 1999); Stephan Fox, *Big Leagues: Professional Baseball, Football, and Basketball in National Memory* (New York: William Morrow, 1994), 261–299, 426–436; Roland Lazenby, *Michael Jordan: The Life* (New York: Little, Brown, 2014).
30 Michael Freeman, *ESPN: The Uncensored History* (Dallas: Taylor Publishing, 2000).
31 Richard O. Davies, "Shootin' Irons: The Jack Nicklaus-Arnold Palmer Golf Rivalry," and "Friendly Foes: Chrissie and Martina," in *Rivals! The Ten Greatest American Sports Rivalries of the 20th Century* (Malden, MA: Wiley/Blackwell, 2011), 107–129, 181–204; David Owen, *The Chosen One: Tiger Woods and the Dilemma of Greatness* (New York: Simon and Schuster, 2001).
32 Walter LeFeber, *Michael Jordan and the New Global Capitalism* (New York: Norton, 2002).
33 Andrew Zimbalist, *Unpaid Professionals: Commercialism and Conflict in Big-Time College Sports* (Princeton: Princeton University Press, 1999).
34 Davies, *The Main Event*, 231–256.
35 Mark Fainaru-Wade and Steve Fainaru, *League of Denial: The NFL, Concussions, and the Battle for Truth* (New York: Crown Archetype, 2013).
36 Michael Oriard, *Brand NFL*, 105–109, 113–124, 192–196; Steve Almond, *Against Football: One Fan's Reluctant Manifesto* (Brooklyn: Melville House, 2014).
37 Almond, *Against Football*, 165–166.

23

SPORT IN AMERICAN FILM

Donald J. Mrozek

At the beginning of the age of motion pictures, some inventors such as Thomas Edison expected film to become a medium for preserving the greatest performances in elite culture—for example, scenes from the plays of Shakespeare performed by the greatest actors of the day. Few foresaw how "movies" would become an art form with their own special conventions and favored themes. Far from being elitist, film opened new opportunities for mass cultural expression keyed to popular taste. Thus films often give glimpses into the values and interests of people living when they were made. Many documentaries were produced, but narrative dramatic and comedic films predominated.

Encyclopedic websites help in exploring the thousands of films focused on sport. For example, Wikipedia includes entries featuring many hundreds of films focused on scores of sports.[1] The scope of sports included within the genre is vast, going beyond obvious ones such as American football, baseball, boxing, and basketball. Among other sports explored in movies are track and field athletics, auto racing, bobsledding, caving, figure skating, golf, gymnastics, rodeo, rowing, sailing, skateboarding, skiing, tennis, water polo, and wrestling.

The earliest films, dating to the 1890s, included "actualities"—generally, very brief captures of daily life such as military events and civic celebrations. The genre is usually dated to 1895 with the work of the Lumière brothers in France, but the Edison Company in the United States had been showing brief films by kinetoscope since 1893. Boat and yacht races were popular, and fight films were sufficiently numerous to be taken as a subgenre in their own right. Films such as Edison's *The Hornbacker-Murphy Fight* (1894) sometimes showed the actual events, but, for technical reasons, scenes were sometimes re-created in studios. Boxing "actualities" also had the special appeal of forbidden fruit because the sport was, at the time of the filming, illegal in most jurisdictions in the United States. By 1909, when American Biograph produced the first clearly identifiable documentary, the actuality was at an end. Many actualities remain available as contact prints, especially through the Paper Print Collection in the Library of Congress in Washington, DC.

By the 1910s, feature-length movies were common, aiming to give a sense of continuity that generally depended on narrative (or story line).[2] Sport was often treated with humor and irony in important early film treatments of the subject. At the start of *The Champion* (1915), for example, Charlie Chaplin's character is "meditating on the ingratitude of humanity" that has left him penniless.[3] Out of sheer desperation, he responds to a sign seeking "sparring partners who can take a punch." He shows surprising ability, trains for a championship bout, falls in love along the way, turns down a bribe to throw the fight, and ends up winning the title and the woman he loves. The last quarter of the film is the fight itself—likely a sign of continuing interest in an activity still widely forbidden in America. Strikingly, however, many early films about sport do not have "happy endings."

In *The Freshman* (1925), comic actor Harold Lloyd imagines himself accepted as an athlete when he is really "only the water boy."[4] He is even used to replace a damaged tackling dummy. Lucky accidents make him the key to victory in a crucial game. But in a sequel, *The Sin of Harold Diddlebock* (1947), the hero of the "big game" in the 1925 film has become a bored bookkeeper in a dead-end job. *College* (1927) is an especially good example of veiled melancholy.[5] Ronald, played by Buster Keaton, delivers his high school valedictory talk on "The Curse of Athletics." The young woman he loves insists that he must accept sport if she is to accept his attentions. The film records his complete failure in all sports except, largely by accident, as coxswain for a winning crew in a rowing event. Then, racing to save the young woman from another man, Ronald jumps, vaults, and otherwise succeeds in events at which he has failed miserably throughout most of the film. Seemingly, the demands of "real life" trump those of sport, and this impression is confirmed in an odd rush of scenes at the end of the film taking Ronald and his wife into old age and, literally, to their graves. In this earlier period, even comedy betrays underlying anxiety, questioning the value of pursuits presented to the young as if they were crucial.

In the 1930s, humor and harshness took turns. There was no completely light-hearted "age of innocence," followed by disillusionment decades later. Rather, complexity and internal contradiction were always present. The Marx Brothers played for humor, even to the point of slapstick, in *Horse Feathers* (1932) in which Groucho Marx plays Quincy Adams Wagstaff, president of Huxley College. The plot focuses on a coming showdown in football against arch-rival Darwin College. Some viewers might have had both Darwin and Huxley in active memory, thanks to the Scopes "Monkey Trial" of 1925. At the climax of the football game that dominates the late stages of the movie, Harpo Marx as Pinky drives the football into the end zone atop a horse-drawn garbage wagon, likely satirizing the epic film *Ben Hur* (1925). The film acknowledges the enormous popularity of football in particular and sport in general, while presenting the game subversively as a social double entendre. In *Maker of Men* (1931), directed by Edgar Sedgwick, Coach Dudley wants to save his job as a college football coach and must have a winning season, and he hopes to force his son to come to the rescue. Played by Jack Holt, Coach Dudley drives his players mercilessly, but they never complain because they accept it as one cost of being transformed into real he-men. Yet the "sensitive" son, Bob, hates athletics and shrinks from the game so deeply loved by his father. Seeing his own son as cowardly, the coach disowns his son, and the young man's sweetheart, Dorothy, does so as well. Driven by anger, Bob joins a competing college's team, and he proves himself by helping his own team defeat his father's. Fond words between father and son at the end of the movie do not conceal that a son's resentment and anger toward his father are shown as the price of victory. Are anger and revenge more powerful than love?

More light-hearted movies include *Pigskin Parade* (1936), implausibly featuring a husband and wife as de facto football co-coaches, who manage to get an exceptionally talented country boy to play for them as they seek entry into a bowl game. Hillbilly Amos, played by Stuart Irwin, wins the game by carrying the ball into the end zone, running barefoot. The film—a musical as well as a comedy—also features Judy Garland in her feature film debut. *The Big Game* (1936) deals with "under the table" money to players who come from modest backgrounds and with suspicion of games being thrown to get payoffs—a story curiously played for laughs. In *$1,000 a Touchdown* (1939), Joe E. Brown plays a man who inherits a college and proceeds to offer money to every football player who scores a touchdown.[6] Films such as these were generally produced and distributed by major firms such as RKO Radio Pictures, 20th Century Fox, Paramount, Warner Brothers, and Metro-Goldwyn-Mayer. The effectiveness of all such films as entertainment depended on widespread popular understanding of the sports featured in them and on some degree of possible empathy.

Challenging and more questioning films were also offered by these top companies in the industry. Among them were *College Coach* (1933), starring Pat O'Brien, which focused on academic favoritism and improper payments given to college athletes; *Over the Goal* (1937), in which a football star risks permanent injury to keep on playing for the team; *Navy Blue and Gold* (1937), starring James Stewart, in which a midshipman's chance to play in the Army-Navy game hinges on how rules violations and other problems are handled; and *Touchdown Army* (1938), in which Robert Cummings plays a cadet who must "shape up" to play in the annual meeting with Navy.

A similar mix of dramatic and comedic intent characterizes films of the 1920s and 1930s focused on other sports. Boxing movies with a serious turn include *The Champ* (1931), which won Wallace Beery an Oscar for portraying a "washed up alcoholic boxer" who tries to reestablish himself for the sake of his young and loving son; *Winner Take All* (1932), presenting James Cagney as a talented boxer recovering from too much alcohol and loose living, who seeks cosmetic surgery in trying to win the love of a fickle "society woman"; *Golden Boy* (1939), in which William Holden plays a talented violinist who risks sacrificing his hands to boxing; and *They Made Me a Criminal* (1939), with John Garfield as a boxer falsely accused of murder, who ends up running away and taking refuge where his training of young people may ruin his cover.[7] Among the comedies, *The Prizefighter and the Lady* (1933) stands out for casting champion heavyweight Max Baer opposite Myrna Loy. Supporting players included boxers Jack Dempsey and Primo Carnera, helping to turn "real life" into "reel life." Baer portrays a bouncer at a bar frequented by an alcohol-impaired former boxing manager, who sees potential in the boxer. Typical of many films of the time is a link with gangsters, as well as a focus on the problem of alcoholism, reflecting concerns of the day. A veteran of many films centered on sport, Harold Lloyd appears in *The Milky Way* (1936) as a milk delivery man who accidentally encounters the world middleweight champion in a bar brawl. The milkman ducks, the champ is knocked out by someone else's punch, but the milkman is promoted as a great boxing talent by a corrupt manager, who extends the fraud by fixing the milkman's fights. Whether serious in tone or comic, the films of the era put much emphasis on fraud and other problems widely ascribed to American society at large. *Kid Galahad* (1937), boasting an exceptional cast including Edward G. Robinson, Bette Davis, and Humphrey Bogart and directed by Michael Curtiz, shows yet another chance discovery of a previously unknown talent whose path to success is troubled by gangsters and other problems. In all, such films claim that personal achievement remains possible, yet the temptations to failure are many.

The use of sports figures as cast members and in other roles in films was an especially strong feature of sports movies in the early decades of the medium. For example, *Maker of Men* features several actors who later became stars in their own right, such as Ward Bond and John Wayne, who were hired for the film largely because of local notice they had won as football players.[8] Even the movie's director, Edward Sedgwick, had a fascinating career that says much about the growing place of sport in American culture. Before becoming a director, Sedgwick had been cast in films starting in 1915, often as a "zany baseball player," as one writer put it.

> Sedgwick's lifelong love of baseball came in handy as he helmed the ballpark sequences of Tom Mix's *Stepping Out* (1923), Buck Jones' *Hit and Run* (1924),

William Haines' *Slide, Kelly, Slide* (1927), Buster Keaton's *The Cameraman* (1928) and *Death on the Diamond* (1934).[9]

Even before film biographies of champions in sport became common, easily recognizable athletic stars proved immediately marketable as stars in film. Figure skating champion Sonja Henie bridged reality and fantasy in *One in a Million* (1936), which focused on the 1936 Winter Olympics.[10] But lighter fare such as *Thin Ice* (1937) and *The Ice Follies of 1939* (1939) gave her an extended life on screen. In 1943, in *Wintertime*, the displacements caused by World War II touched the plot, in which Henie's character must wed an American in order to stay in the United States and skate in New York. But even more enduring was the impact of the many athletes presented as the fictional heroic figure Tarzan.[11] Among the early Tarzans was James Pierce, who had been an all-American center for the Indiana University football team, later coached John Wayne at Glendale High School in California, and became the son-in-law of Edgar Rice Burroughs. Pierce starred in *Tarzan and the Golden Lion* (1927). Champion gymnast Frank Merrill (with 58 competitive titles to his credit) had been the body-double for Elmo Lincoln, the first to play Tarzan in the movies, and Merrill starred as Tarzan during the 1920s. In the 1930s, there were overlapping portrayals of Tarzan from Herman Brix, silver medalist in the Olympic shot put in 1928 and star of *The New Adventures of Tarzan* (1935). Brix had broken a shoulder while filming *Touchdown* (1931), and the producers hired Olympic swimming star Johnny Weissmuller to fill in, starting with *Tarzan the Ape Man* (1932).[12] His work in a dozen Tarzan movies helped to make the "swimmer's body" the default physical identity for Tarzan for more than just one generation. This was reinforced by Olympic swimmer Buster Crabbe's turn as Tarzan in *Tarzan the Fearless* (1933).[13] Also tapped to play Tarzan was the Olympic decathlon gold medalist from 1936, Glenn Morris, who appeared in *Tarzan's Revenge* (1938) for MGM.[14] After World War II, favorite body types would change, culminating in casting former professional football linebacker Mike Henry in the title role of *Tarzan and the Valley of Gold* (1966) and two other Tarzan movies. Decathlete Rafer Johnson costarred with Henry in *Tarzan and the Jungle Boy* (1968), also using sports accomplishments to validate "physical acting."[15] In time, crossing the line between the "real" world and the world on screen led to the emergence of Arnold Schwarzenegger in *Conan the Barbarian* (1982), which was actually his sixth credited role in film.[16]

Glenn Morris had first appeared in film when MGM produced a biographical short of him, prepared for theatrical release after the Berlin Olympics of 1936. Decades later, this scenario was repeated with Arnold Schwarzenegger and other bodybuilders being the focus of *Pumping Iron* (1977). This hinted at a hunger for full-length biographical treatments that pretended to present real lives while actually reshaping them for dramatic and societal purposes.

The enthusiasm for biographical treatment of sports figures was boldly shown in *Knute Rockne All-American* (1940), starring Pat O'Brien as the famous football coach of Notre Dame who died in an airplane crash in Kansas in 1931. The same sport yielded other focal figures, too, such as football star Tom Harmon in *Harmon of Michigan* (1941). The story of a boxer prematurely taken to the gates of heaven unfolds in *Here Comes Mr. Jordan* (1941), closely anticipating the angelic help to be given to a nonsportsman in *It's a Wonderful Life* (1946). Directed by Raoul Walsh and starring Errol Flynn as "Gentleman Jim" Corbett, *Gentleman Jim* (1942) also featured Ward Bond as John L. Sullivan, implying a theme of "progress" and generational change along with the thirst to see inside the lives of famous persons. Striking among wartime film biographies of sports figures was *The Pride of the*

Yankees (1942), starring Gary Cooper as Lou Gehrig and perhaps hinting in a time of world war that "good Germans" could be absorbed safely into American life. Moreover, the focus on biography suggested an essentially conservative understanding of how society operated—just as *How to Win Friends and Influence People* inferred that one's problems during the Great Depression ultimately came from one's own deficiencies and omissions.

Once established, the habit of focusing on a star athlete repeated itself. For example, football star Elroy Hirsch played himself in *Crazylegs* (1953). Boxer Coley Wallace played the title role in *The Joe Louis Story* (1953), and Bob Mathias, decathlon gold medalist at the 1952 Olympic Games, played himself in *The Bob Mathias Story* (1954). Paul Newman, near the start of his career in film, appeared as boxer Rocky Graziano in *Somebody Up There Likes Me* (1956). *The Stratton Story* (1949), with James Stewart and June Allyson, tells the story of Chicago White Sox pitcher Monty Stratton, who accidentally shoots himself in the right leg while on a hunting trip. Although the leg is amputated, he eventually fights back to play in the minor leagues—perhaps suggesting issues of adjustment for veterans of World War II.[17] Clearly, however, a blunt political statement animates *Strategic Air Command* (1955), directed by Anthony Mann. Again, Stewart and Allyson share the lead, Stewart portraying a Major League Baseball player whose career is twice interrupted by military service and who eventually decides that commanding a strategic bomber is as American as baseball and more important. Also important was the appearance of this expressive biographical form on television. A landmark event in this respect was the airing of *Brian's Song* (1971) with James Caan and Billy Dee Williams as Brian Piccolo and Gayle Sayers of the Chicago Bears.[18] *Brian's Song* mattered partly for its focus on interracial friendship, as well as the notion of sport could transcend the prejudices in the larger society, which was a striking theme after unrest and tension in the 1960s. The optimism of *Brian's Song* played counterpoint to *The Great White Hope* (1970), written by Howard Sackler and directed by Martin Ritt. Jack Jefferson, played by James Earl Jones, was clearly modeled on the experience of black boxing champion Jack Johnson from the early twentieth century.

Some works looked at more complex problems that matched the concerns of the day. Notable was *Fear Strikes Out* (1957), in which actor Anthony Perkins portrays baseball centerfielder Jimmy Piersall, tracing the compulsive pressures that led to his treatment for mental illness.[19] In one way, the film showed danger in the relentless pursuit of victory in sport. In another way, however, it bridged the distance between a professional athlete and "mere mortals," and, indeed, many Americans were now visiting psychologists, psychiatrists, and other mental health professionals. In 1956, the same subject had been dramatized for television with actor Tab Hunter as Piersall, again suggesting the deep interest in psychological motivation in sport. From time to time, movies featuring sport appeared that reflected new understandings, new challenges, and new issues. In *Fear Strikes Out*, for example, it was the individual and the family where remedy was needed. In *North Dallas Forty* (1979), however, the focus is on a system surrounding the sport of professional football that is itself the source of problems.[20] The fictional Dallas Bulls, modeled on the Dallas Cowboys, suffer from a measure of hypocrisy among some of the team's key personnel, including coaches and players. Use of drugs, sex, and alcohol by members of the team is deliberately overlooked by supposedly upright coaches and others, as long as the men play well while pretending to follow the team's rules about behavior off the field. The nonconformity of a player ultimately marks him for ruin, and he is forced into retirement despite his love for the game. The distinctive individual, however talented, is not saved by the system but rejected by it.

In the same decades, however, there was time for humor as well, as in the film version of the Broadway musical comedy *Damn Yankees* (1958). The premise is that avid Washington Senators baseball fan Joe Boyd says that he would sell his soul for his team to beat the New York Yankees. Like a twentieth-century answer to Faust, his opportunity soon comes. In fact, the middle-aged Boyd is transformed by a conman serving in the role of the devil into a young and amazingly talented player, who brings his team to the verge of a championship. Steps and missteps lead to a crisis—will Joe sacrifice his own real life with the woman he loves in order to have the pride of victory in a sport? The embrace of domestic life that brings the story to a climax is itself part of the cliché of the era.

The Bad News Bears (1976) is set in southern California with Walter Matthau as a former minor league baseball player Morris Buttermaker, an alcoholic who makes a living cleaning swimming pools. He is persuaded to become part of the solution to a legal case against Little League parents in the area who have been keeping the less talented children from playing. Buttermaker is given the least promising young players, but he looks elsewhere for a way to win. Child-actress Tatum O'Neal plays the daughter of Buttermaker's girlfriend, and the girl happens to be an amazingly talented pitcher.[21] The "Bears"—a team made up mostly of misfits plus a talented girl or two—prove to be better than almost anyone had expected, although it is also true to the spirit of the 1970s that the team does not win the championship. Also, the film took at least a few small steps in dealing with the increasingly important issue of gender in sport. The 1976 film inspired two sequels, a television series, and a remake in 2005.

In some ways, *The Bad News Bears* was playfully subversive in presenting females as figures of strength within American sport. But this was not an entirely new idea. Albeit with a measure of delicacy and grace, in *National Velvet* (1944), Elizabeth Taylor had portrayed a 12-year old girl in England who is a driving force behind preparing a horse for successful competition in steeplechase. Produced during World War II, the film links the English accents of actors such as Donald Crisp with the American tones of Taylor herself and of the highly popular Mickey Rooney, who plays an important supporting role.

Women athletes are also featured prominently in *Pat and Mike* (1952), directed by George Cukor and starring Katharine Hepburn and Spencer Tracy.[22] An able amateur athlete off the screen, Hepburn plays an exceptionally talented multisport athlete who breaks into professional ranks thanks to the efforts of her agent, played by Tracy.[23] Like many pre–World War II films, this one also enlisted real-life professional athletes such as Alice Marble, Gussie Moran, and Babe Didrikson Zaharias in small parts to establish an air of credibility. By the 1980s, it was possible to explore the realm of sexuality in unaccustomed ways, notably with Mariel Hemingway as an athlete seeking a place on the U.S. Olympic track and field squad in *Personal Best* (1982). The frustration of U.S. withdrawal from the 1980 Olympic Games for political reasons echoes the frustrations involved in the competing desires for same-sex and heterosexual relationships. Yet again, the fact of involvement (in this case, the involvement of women) was not new—but the manner in which it took place explored themes recently enlivened in the "real world," such as in the 1981 revelation of the same-sex identity of tennis champion Billie Jean King.

Arguably, *Rocky* (1976), directed by Sylvester Stallone, who also played the title role as a seemingly "washed up" boxer who ends up nearly a champion, enjoys special place for winning an Academy Award for best picture. Film critic Roger Ebert said that Stallone reminded him of "the young Marlon Brando," but some other critics were less flattering, seeing too much of the formulaic in the movie and too little of Brando in Stallone.[24] Some thought back to Terry Malloy, Marlon Brando's character in Eliza Kazan's *On the Waterfront*

(1954), who "could have been a contender" if he had not yielded to pressure to throw a fight. On the other end of the spectrum was evidence that winning did not guarantee a fulfilled and happy life. Sequels were commercially but, to some, not artistically successful—*Rocky IV* (1985) was once given the brief review "*Rocky IV*, audience nothing." To others, regardless of the dramatic development, movies such as those in the Rocky series focused much on tracking fighters' training, which was easier for viewers to emulate than was the attainment of a championship. In *Raging Bull* (1980), directed by Martin Scorsese, Robert de Niro played successful but sometimes obsessive and violent middleweight boxer Jake La Motta. De Niro won an Oscar as best actor for portrayal of La Motta as someone who was able to use his qualities—including those that were clearly destructive outside the boxing ring—to win championship status without ever having a conventionally satisfying personal life.[25] In *Prefontaine* (1997), Jared Leto explored the inner dynamic and social ties of Oregon runner Steve Prefontaine. By this time, running had already become a major phenomenon for a large segment of the U.S. population, and the film offered a kind of surrogate exploration of motivating oneself and of being "misunderstood."

Films focused on running took special notice with the release and widespread success of *Chariots of Fire* (1981), focused on the actual experiences of Scotsman Eric Liddell and Englishman Harold Abrahams in the 1924 Olympic Games.[26] The acclaim for the film, which won an Academy Award for best picture, was linked to the growing interest in running as a popular sport rather than as just a part of a fitness routine. This corresponded with the rise of running to high visibility, as well as broad participation, even in distances such as the marathon. Music at running events frequently included the theme music from *Chariots of Fire*.

The dynamic of *Chariots of Fire* was the contrast of two different motives for running as well as two different methods of preparing for it. One was systematic, scientific, and dedicated to the advancement of human achievement. The other was celebratory, focused yet peaceful, and aimed at realizing the glory of divine creation. Each approach ended with a gold medal. But the film *Running* (1979) with Kirk Douglas had already focused on achievement beyond winning medals—but not without some cost. The central character, Michael Andropolis, has focused on his sport—the marathon—to the point of losing his wife to divorce. It is debatable whether his daughters are more important to him than winning a spot on the U.S. Olympic team going to Montreal in 1976. He does eventually gain a spot on the team, but he suffers an injury during the race. Eventually, in great pain, he crosses the finish line. His ex-wife and his daughters greet him warmly. But the message is a curious reflection of the time and culture that produced it—obsessive pursuit of the medal was cause for divorce and even disdain, yet fighting through pain to finish an event regardless of "medal count" was taken as laudable.

Recognition was accorded to Native Americans as well, such as in *Running Brave* (1983) with actor Robby Benson as 1964 Olympic 10,000-meter gold medalist Billy Mills (Makata Taka Hela). His story took a conventional theme of seeking success and added to it the special leavening of renewed appreciation, at the time, for Native American accomplishments. Mills had left the reservation first to study (and run) at Haskell Institute (later Haskell Indian Nations University) in Lawrence Kansas, continued to run while in the U.S. Marines, and became the only man from the Western Hemisphere to win the Olympic 10,000-meter event.[27] A similar renewed interest was shown to African Americans, exemplified in *The Jesse Owens Story* (1985) with Dorian Harewood starring as the great track star of the 1936 Olympics in Berlin. It is not without relevance—suggestive of the way coverage in film reflects receptivity in the society at large—that Owens, himself a Republican throughout his adult life, had been embraced in film during the presidency of Ronald Reagan.

Seemingly single-handedly, Bruce Lee sparked interest in films focused on the martial arts. His hard work notwithstanding, Lee showed greater eloquence in "physical acting" than in dialogue. In *Game of Death* (1972), Lee took on the character Hakim, played by Kareem Abdul-Jabbar. *Enter the Dragon* (1973) further established Lee in memory, although this was the last film in his relatively short life.[28] In 1984, *The Karate Kid* stars Noriyuki "Pat" Morita as the older "master" who teaches the young Ralph Macchio lessons in life as well as in karate, helping the young man find strength and command of self while learning how to defend himself from others. In sequels in 1986 and 1989, the mainstreaming of Asian martial arts in America continued.

In some instances, whole careers were devoted to fictional films focused on martial arts. In 1986, Jean-Claude Van Damme appeared as a Russian fighter in *No Retreat, No Surrender*, taking on an American fighter supposedly trained by the ghost of Bruce Lee. More typical of films starring Van Damme and kickboxing champion Dennis Alexio is *Kickboxer* (1989), in which Van Damme plays Kurt Sloane, the brother of a martial arts champion whom he accompanies to a tournament in Thailand. His brother is beaten viciously and ends up paralyzed from the waist down. Then Kurt trains to take on the fighter who has deliberately brutalized his brother. The theme of innocence and honor triumphing over sinister misdeeds, even when trite in the execution, draws on a long-recognized tradition in "hero stories" in cultures across the world. It enjoyed new life in this period. Another example in martial arts was Chuck Norris, who took his skill in martial arts to film in *Way of the Dragon* (1972), *A Force of One* (1979), *The Octagon* (1980), and many others for more than two decades. Over time, the theme of the martial artist was combined with that of the Special Forces soldier, taking what had been exotic and making it almost a patriotic convention.[29]

Such films appeared regularly, continuing into the twenty-first century. In some instances, the storylines of the films focused on sport, but the appeal for much of the audience may have come more from the physical as opposed to strictly competitive appeal of the starring actors. In *Never Back Down* (2008), for example, actor Cam Gigandet starred as a ruthless and not entirely scrupulous fighter. He owed much of his real-life popularity to a regular role in the television program *The O.C.*, which risked making *Never Back Down* something of a "skin flick" for some part of the film audience. But Gigandet was a legitimate amateur athlete in his own right, holding a black belt in Krav Maga. By contrast, Channing Tatum was perhaps more widely known for a turn as a professional club dancer rather than as an athlete before starring in movies such as *Fighting* (2009). The impression was unfair, given his prior involvement in football, soccer, track, and baseball while in school as well as continuing practice in kung fu. In films such as these, the past experience in a sport helped to validate performance in roles as an active martial arts competitor.

Some movies from the 1970s pointed toward the return of sentiment, if not full-scale sentimentality. In *Bang the Drum Slowly* (1973), for example, talented pitcher Henry Wiggen of the New York Mammoths baseball team specially befriends catcher Bruce Pearson. Unknown to everyone on the team except Wiggen, Pearson has been diagnosed with Hodgkin's disease and does not have long to live. Wiggen has been holding out for a much more favorable contract but, in the end, surprises almost everyone by signing. It turns out that Wiggen has insisted that he and the far less talented (and mortally ill) Pearson come together or not at all. Even more, by happenstance, the team learns of Bruce's illness, and a positive shift in morale occurs, helping the team to win more games even as Bruce becomes too weak to play.

The team eventually wins the World Series, and, in the off-season afterward, Bruce dies. Is it possible that a friendly gesture has brought this highly prized reward?

Many films followed existing storylines, but some changed the plots outlined in their source materials. For example, love of a happy ending was evident in *The Natural* (1984), based on Bernard Malamud's first novel, which appeared in 1952. Robert Redford is cast as baseball player Roy Hobbs, who is wounded in an early incident that is left in a measure of mystery and, toward the end of the story, is induced to take a bribe to throw a game. Instead of following Malamud's line, in which Roy's final hit strikes Iris, the woman he loves, the ball strikes the overhead lights, winning the pennant. The final scene shows Roy playing ball with his young son. The tone of this distortion of Malamud's intent was in line with a campaign slogan in the Republican Presidential campaign of 1984 that "It's morning again in America."

Some films in which sport plays a crucial role actually devote only a small portion of their total time to presenting sport itself. For example, in *2001: A Space Odyssey* (1968), director Stanley Kubrick shows an astronaut jogging in the endless loop of a spacecraft that rotates as it presses toward Jupiter. It is exercise in isolation with little joy.[30] By contrast, in *One Flew Over the Cuckoo's Nest* (1975), patients in an asylum experience the spontaneous excitement and interest of basketball that they are encouraged by a fellow patient to play. In *The Deerhunter* (1978), a military veteran's true "coming home" from the American war in Vietnam is captured in his decision not to kill a deer that he has in his crosshairs. At almost the same time, *Apocalypse Now* (1979) showed a unit commander surfing with an enlisted man who had been a surfing champion in California before his induction into the military.[31] Is surfing in the midst of a war crazy, or is it the war itself that is crazy? In *A River Runs Through It* (1992), fishing in an environment of serene beauty serves as a kind of underlying truth, enduring in value regardless of what has happened in the often harsh dealings among men in society.

In the 1990s and in the first decades of the twenty-first century, many films that were focused on sport revived traditional emphases such as biography with touches of romance and reverie. Many showed a celebratory biographical style in use half a century earlier. Notable were *Ali* (2001) with Will Smith as Muhammad Ali and *Cinderella Man* (2005) with Russell Crowe, showing the comeback of fighter James J. Braddock. Notably, by the 1990s, Ali himself had been sufficiently "mainstreamed" to be given the honor of igniting the Olympic flame in Atlanta in 1996. At the edge of sentimentality, too, *We Are Marshall* (2006) with Matthew McConaughey explores the aftermath of the 1970 plane crash that caused the death of 37 members of the Marshall University football team along with five coaches, two athletic trainers, the athletic director, and 25 team boosters along with the five-member air crew. The message, in the end, was that football is too important to a social unit—in this case, the extended university community including alumni—for standing rules (such as the prohibition against having freshmen play on a varsity football team) to be left in force. On the other hand, the mere fact of fielding a team after such a disaster suggested the importance of the social and personal impact of a sport rather than just winning or losing. Another example of an established theme taking on a special guise in a new historical moment was Clint Eastwood's *Million Dollar Baby* (2004) with Eastwood starring as a boxing coach who reluctantly agrees to train a young woman, played by Hilary Swank.[32] The emergence of women in combative roles in American life offered new turns in dramatic lines favored in American film.

American sports films, then, evolved by continuing to touch on newer issues, yet doing so usually within largely accustomed frameworks. Sports films not only reflected elements of the society in which they were made but also entered into dialogue with it, playing a part in its evolution. Each new style or subgenre added to the options available to filmmakers, so that a century after the making of the first sports movies no one style predominated. Instead, sports films were as diverse as the sports culture itself and the opportunities it afforded its participants.

Notes

1 See "List of Sports Films" at Wikipedia.com. https://en.wikipedia.org/wiki/List_of_sports_films (accessed July 7, 2015).

2 See Scott Kirsner, *Inventing the Movies: Hollywood's Epic Battle Between Innovation and the Status Quo, From Thomas Edison to Steve Jobs* (Seattle, WA and Charleston, SC: CreateSpace Independent Publishing Platform, 2008); John Belton, *American Cinema/American Culture* 4th ed. (New York: McGraw-Hill, 2012); Philip C. DiMare, ed., *Movies in American History* (Santa Barbara CA: ABC-CLIO, 2011); Richard Maltby and Melvyn Stokes, eds., *American Movie Audiences: From the Turn of the Century to the Early Sound Era* (London: British Film Institute, 1999); and Steven J. Ross, *Movies and American Society* (Oxford, UK: Blackwell Publishing, 2002). Among the many fine explorations of American sport history are: Elliott J. Gorn and Warren Goldstein, *A Brief History of American Sport* 2nd ed. (Champaign, IL: University of Illinois Press, 2013); Gerald R. Gems, Linda J. Borish, and Gertrud Pfister, *Sports in American History: From Colonization to Globalization* (Champaign, IL: Human Kinetics, 2008); and Benjamin G. Rader and Pamela Grundy, *American Sports* 7th ed. (Boston MA: Pearson, 2014). Studies linking sport and film include: Ron Briley, Michael Schoenecke, and Deborah Carmichael, *All-Stars and Movie Stars: Sports in Film and History* (Lexington KY: University Press of Kentucky, 2008); Ray Didinger and Glen Macnow, *The Ultimate Book of Sports Movies: Featuring the 100 Greatest Sports Films of All Time* (Philadelphia PA: Running Press, 2009); Randy Williams, *Sports Cinema—100 Movies: The Best of Hollywood's Athletic Heroes, Losers, Myths, and Misfits* (Milwaukee WI: Limelight Editions, 2006); and Ronald Bergen, *Sports in the Movies* (Belleville, MI: Proteus, 1982).

3 See Kevin Brownlow, *Silent Traces: Discovering Early Hollywood Through the Films of Charlie Chaplin* (Solana Beach, CA: Santa Monica Press, 2006).

4 See John Bengtson, *Silent Visions: Discovering Early Hollywood and New York Through the Films of Harold Lloyd* (Solana Beach, CA: Santa Monica Press, 2011).

5 See John Bengtson, *Silent Echoes: Discovering Early Hollywood Through the Films of Buster Keaton* (Solana Beach, CA: Santa Monica Press, 1999). Also see Edward McPherson, *Buster Keaton: Tempest in a Flat Hat* (New York, NY: Newmarket Press, 2007).

6 See Wes D. Gehring, *Joe E. Brown: Film Comedian and Baseball Buffoon* (Jefferson, NC: McFarland, 2008).

7 John Garfield was interested in political matters, which eventually brought him into conflict with the House Un-American Activities Committee (HUAC). See Robert Noll, *He Ran All the Way: The Life of John Garfield* (Milwaukee, WI: Limelight Editions, 2003). Also see Larry Swindell, *Body and Soul: The Story of John Garfield* (New York: Morrow, 1975).

8 See, for example, Michael Munn, *John Wayne: The Man Behind the Myth* (New York: NAL, 2005) and Scott Eyman, *John Wayne: The Life and Legend* (New York: Simon and Schuster, 2015 [reprint]).

9 Celebrity and name recognition let some athletes go from sport to film regardless of aptitude as actors. See James E. Holbrook, *Athletes on the Stump and Stage* (Seattle, WA and Charleston, SC: CreateSpace Independent Publishing Platform, 2014).

10 An unflattering look at Sonja Henie may be found in Raymond Strait, *Queen of Ice, Queen of Shadows: The Unsuspected Life of Sonja Henie* (Lanham, MD: Scarborough, 1990).

11 See Gabe Essoe, *Tarzan of the Movies: A Pictorial History of More Than Fifty Years of Edgar Rice Burroughs' Legendary Hero* (New York: The Citadel Press [Kensington], 1968) and John F. Kasson, *Houdini, Tarzan, and the Perfect Man: The White Male Body and the Challenge of Modernity in America* (New York: Hill and Wang, 2002).

12 See David Fury, *Johnny Weissmuller: Twice the Hero* (Seattle, WA: Artist's Press through Amazon Digital Services, 2013) and Narda Onyx, *Water, World & Weissmuller: A Biography* (Los Angeles, CA: Vion, 1964).

13 See Jerry Vermilye, *Buster Crabbe: A Biofilmography* (Jefferson, NC: McFarland [reprint], 2014).

14 On athlete Glenn Morris, see Mike Chapman, *The Gold and the Glory* (Newton, IA: Culture House Books, 2003). Also see Leni Riefenstahl, *Riefenstahl Olympia* (Cologne, Germany: Taschen, 2002). Riefenstahl and Morris had an intimate relationship during the Berlin Olympics of 1936.

15 See Rafer Johnson, *Best That I Can Be* (Garden City, NY: Doubleday, 1998).

16 See Dave Saunders, *Arnold: Schwarzenegger and the Movies* (New York: I.B. Tauris, 2009).

17 Stewart and his films are explored in Michael Munn, *Jimmy Stewart: The Truth Behind the Legend* (New York: Skyhorse Publishing, 2013).

18 See the screenplay in William Blinn, *Brian's Song* rev. ed. (New York: Bantam, 1983).

19 See Jim Piersall with Al Hirshberg, *Fear Strikes Out* (Lincoln NE: Bison Books, 1999). The story was told in a television realization in 1956.

20 Peter Gent, *North Dallas Forty* (New York: Morrow, 1973).

21 See Tatum O'Neal, *A Paper Life* (New York: William Morrow, 2005).

22 The larger question is how much movies made sport seem "gendered"—and, specifically, mostly "masculine." By the end of the twentieth century, the accomplishments of women athletes made it hard to maintain this bias. The extent to which film may have reflected these biases is explored in Viridiana Lieberman, *Sports Heroines on Film: A Critical Study of Cinematic Women Athletes, Coaches and Owners* (Jefferson, NC: McFarland, 2014).

23 Concerning Tracy and Hepburn, see James Curtis, *Spencer Tracy: A Biography* (New York: Knopf, 2011) and Barbara Leaming, *Katharine Hepburn* (New York: Crown, 1995).

24 See Marsha Daly, *Sylvester Stallone* (New York: St. Martin's, 1986).

25 See Andy Dougan, *Untouchable: A Biography of Robert De Niro* (New York: Thunder's Mouth Press, 1997).

26 A study emphasizing Liddell's commitment to Christianity is David McCasland, *Eric Liddell: Pure Gold: A New Biography of the Olympic Champion Who Inspired Chariots of Fire* (Grand Rapids, MI: Discovery House, 2001).

27 Mills later explored the ways of linking tradition, character, and accomplishment in a co-authored novel. See Billy Mills, Nicholas Sparks, and Pat Mills, *Wokini* (Quincy, CA: Feather Publishing, 1990).

28 See Bruce Lee and John Little, *Bruce Lee: Artist of Life* (North Clarendon, VT: Tuttle Publishing, 2001).

29 See Chuck Norris with Ken Abraham, *Against All Odds: My Story* (Nashville, TN: B & H Books, 2008).

30 See Tatjana Ljujic, Peter Kramer, and Richard Daniels, eds., *Stanley Kubrick: New Perspectives* (New York: Black Dog Publishing, 2015).

31 See Peter Cowie, *The Apocalypse Now Book* (Boston: Da Capo Press, 2001).

32 See Michael Goldman, *Clint Eastwood: Master Filmmaker at Work* (New York: Harry N. Abrams, 2012).

24

HEGEMONY AND IDENTITY

The Evolution of American Women's Participation in Active Sport Tourism

Brenda P. Wiggins and Margaret J. Daniels

Introduction

Sport tourism integrates the separate but overlapping concepts of sport and tourism. As defined by sport tourism consultant Joy Standeven and professor Paul DeKnop, sport tourism includes "All forms of active and passive involvement in sporting activity, participated in casually or in an organized way for noncommercial or business/commercial reasons, that necessitate travel away from home and work locality."[1] Standeven and DeKnop further clarify that active sport tourists are a category of sport tourism where participants seek sport during travel as a primary goal or as an incidental part of the overall excursion, whereas, in comparison, passive sport tourists are observers who similarly may have the activity serve as a primary travel influence or secondary occurrence.[2] Although the origins of sport tourism have been traced to the first recorded ancient Olympic Games in 776 BCE, discussions today tend to delimit the conversation to coincide with the transportation innovations that resulted in mass tourism.[3] This boundary is reasonable when considering the history of sport tourism in America.

Both sport and tourism are economic development activities and, as such, sport tourism researchers tend to focus on financial indicators such as expenditures, growth potential, job creation, market share, and economic impact models.[4] Accordingly, when asked to write this chapter, our immediate thought was to provide an overview of business-centered forces. Upon further reflection, we came to understand that we were charged to consider the *history* of sport tourism, which inspired us to reflect on how individuals actively connect with the past in order to define the present.[5] We recognized that personal antecedents such as cultural influences, desires, motives, and constraints inform the nature and meaning of sport tourism experiences and therefore began to ponder how these variables may have shifted over time. Ultimately, this led to conversations about cultural hegemony and, specifically, how active sport tourism was and continues to be experienced differently by women and men.

Cultural hegemony is a contested term that broadly pertains to systems and institutions that strive to maintain social order through the establishment of consent formation via rules, policies, norms, values, and belief systems.[6] Hegemonic standards can be readily linked to institutions such as governments, schools, religious groups, the media, and families, where consistent messages are used that, if widely accepted as legitimate, create a worldview and public vocabulary that shape reality for the masses.[7] Those who comprise the political and social elite are the messengers, formulating viewpoints that enable them to maintain power while alternative opinions are marginalized or masked by the predominant voice.[8] When considering the history of women's access to sport tourism in America, evidence of hegemonic standards exists. These principles of order, power, and control maintain influence to differing degrees in many cultures today.

The central theme of this chapter is that the historical evolution of American women's participation in active sport tourism is embedded in cultural hegemony that over time has been challenged to increase access and disencumber identity formation. In this chapter, we will summarize hegemonic constraints placed on women that have influenced travel and sport participation, then merge the areas to demonstrate American women's early active sport tourism participation, allowing us to illustrate women's historic defiance of cultural norms while recognizing that a dominant ideology still exists.

Hegemonic Constraints to Travel

Constraints to travel are generally segmented into three hierarchical categories: intrapersonal, interpersonal, and structural, where intrapersonal constraints relate to an individuals' physical or psychological functioning, interpersonal constraints are based on social relationships and the dependency on others, and structural constraints pertain to operational factors such as access to transportation and finances.[9] For the purposes of this chapter, these barriers are considered in light of cultural hegemony and embedded within two travel access barriers that have particularly impacted women: freedom to travel and discretionary income.

Freedom to Travel

For travel to take place, the individual must be or feel permitted to do so. Prior to the 1820s, travel in Western countries was physically punishing and often dangerous. As a result, most travelers were young, male aristocrats who finished a "Grand Tour" for the purposes of education, curiosity, cultural enrichment, and career development.[10] Travel was also seen to be fraught with moral corruption, yet another reason to protect women from such excursions. "The young aristocrat went abroad also to grow up and to sow his wild oats. He could enjoy his rakish pleasures at a comfortable distance from home and reputation."[11] Beyond educational and cultural engagement, early travel was seen as a means to fulfill personal and social fantasies.[12] As explained by Lila Marz Harper, a professor of English, in her review of eighteenth-and nineteenth-century female science travel writers, ". . . to present oneself as essentially being alone invites questions about the traveler's morals."[13]

As accommodations, services, and transportation became formalized in the early 1820s and 1830s, mass travel evolved.[14] Transportation developments and enhancements during the industrial age, including travel by stagecoach, ship, and train, allowed tourism to become a commercial business and increased opportunities for individuals to travel purely for leisure and pleasure.[15] Luxury commercial sea tours to destinations across the globe became available by the late 1800s.[16] The emergence of the automobile and airplane, coupled with shorter workweeks, longer vacation times, increased income, and decreased family size, opened the door to mass tourism.[17] For Americans, ". . . until the end of the nineteenth century foreign travel (still mostly European travel) was the experience of the privileged few."[18] In North America, the automobile in particular "popularized travel, spreading the advantages of tourism from society's elite to the masses."[19]

Even under the guise of travel freedom, women remained constrained by their sex. Well into the nineteenth century, women who traveled abroad were seen as rebellious, conflicted, unacceptably extravagant, defiant spinsters who were doing the unthinkable, in particular if they traveled independently.[20] Solo travel, for instance, implied that a woman ". . . sought independence and solitude in a culture where such behavior was both highly suspect and difficult to obtain."[21] At the same time, honeymoon tourism became popularized and celebrated, thus offering an acceptable means of travel for women. Nonfiction writer Barbara Hodgson asserts that women were not always as helpless as they allowed themselves to be. In her analysis of female travel writers spanning the seventeenth to nineteenth centuries, Hodgson concedes that women were constrained by physical and emotional dependence on men and were constrained by family duties. She contends, however, that the sheer breadth of travel writing from that period suggests that travel-minded women simply waited until middle age and ". . . as soon as they could cut free, they did."[22] Eventually, capitalism trumped gender ideology as travel and transportation entrepreneurs increasingly targeted women: "The steam palace made it increasingly difficult to argue that the so called weaker sex belonged at home."[23]

Discretionary Income

A second precursor to travel is discretionary income. Assuming women had travel independence, they historically remained largely dependent on their male counterparts to provide the financial means to travel. Prior to the 1920s, women's workforce participation was minimal. Before marriage, women were almost universally fiscally reliant on their fathers; upon marrying, a woman's property was transferred to her husband, thus, making her financially dependent on her husband and solidifying his dominance.[24] The unmarried, unemployed adult woman found herself in a particularly unorthodox state that bestowed marginality, with the "ever-single" status making her appear to be "redundant" or "superfluous."[25]

Following the First Women's Rights Convention, held in Seneca Falls, New York, in 1848, much effort was given to squelching the possibility of women's rights, with the influential Reverend John Todd writing in 1867 that the "root of the great error of our day [to be] that woman is to be made independent and self-supporting."[26] Nineteenth-century American women were relegated to a different sphere, praised for piety and contributions to noneconomic functions while belying the business activities that were becoming and increasing the fabric of many women's daily lives.[27]

Longitudinal studies reflect changing lifecycle trends that have made female financial independence accessible. Sociologists Norella Putney and Vern Bengston studied and compared five generations of women, including 1920s women (born 1900–1915), Depression era women (born 1916–1930), silent generation women (born 1931–1945), baby boom women (born 1946–1964) and Gen X women (born 1965–1978).[28] Women's increased education level and participation in the workforce were clearly evidenced in this study. A more recently labeled generation, the echo boom women (born 1979–2002), is composed of children of baby boomers, also known as Generation Y and Millennials. Echo boomers are more highly educated than their predecessors, and their economic and residential independence has surpassed that of earlier generations.

The shifting landscape of women's educational attainment and career opportunities is perhaps best illustrated statistically. In the United States, the percentage of college-educated women in the workforce went from 11.2 percent in 1970 to 36.4 percent in 2010, whereas overall female labor force rates in the United States rose from 59.5 percent in 1980 to

70.2 percent in 2009.[29] Because American sport tourism includes both resident travel within the United States and international travel across the continent and abroad, it is important to note that these findings are not unique to the United States, with well-educated, career-oriented women entering the workforce in record numbers in countries such as Australia, Greece, Japan, the Netherlands, South Korea, and Switzerland.[30]

Hegemonic Constraints to Sport Participation

Two prominent hegemonic constraints that have applied to American women's sport participation over time include freedom to play and perceptions of femininity. Similar to travel barriers, these areas have concurrent intrapersonal, interpersonal and structural manifestations.

Freedom to Play

In the United States, the promotion of health and exercise for women gained momentum and formalization in the late nineteenth century, yet was strongly influenced by the cultural values of the time and did not routinely connect women and active sport.[31] Early physical education programs for women focused on improving hygiene, decreasing nervous tension, and medical supervision rather than training in rigorous exercise models.[32] Further, although hegemonic mandates for women's fitness focused on improving their procreative functioning and maintaining their vitality for raising children, the fashion options at their disposal did not allow for an optimal freedom of movement.[33] Women who did participate in sport did so as either a form of conspicuous consumption through involvement in upper-class social clubs allowing for activities such as fox hunting, golf, and tennis or, within the middle class, as a means of noncompetitive yet cost-effective social engagement such as bicycling and basketball.[34] Despite warnings of ". . . uterine displacement, spinal shock, pelvic damage, and hardened abdominal muscles," activities such as ". . . the bicycle merely whetted the appetite of many young women for more competitive activities."[35]

Opportunities grew for American women during the period loosely encompassing 1920 to 1940.[36] The women's model of sport and physical education at this time reflected ". . . democratic ideals for the new female athletic hero; that is, one who ought to be beautiful, strong and self-confident yet always fully cognizant of her delicate reproductive system."[37] Competition was still largely eschewed, although educational and professional institutions increasingly instituted women's teams in spite of legitimate concerns regarding exploitation and elitism.[38]

From 1940 to 1960, and particularly in the years following World War II, opportunities for American women to participate in sanctioned sport competitions grew as ". . . traditional philosophies concerning athletic competition were being swept aside."[39] Women were not only participants, but additionally were selected as coaches and officials.

The gradual build-up of American women's participation in sport accelerated during the "Female Athletic Revolution" that started in 1960 and culminated with the enactment of the United States' federal statute Title IX of the Education Amendments of 1972, widely considered to be ". . . the single most significant piece of legislation to affect the direction and philosophical tenets of women in sport."[40] As discussed in detail in Chapter 17, Title IX landmark cases opened the floodgates, resulting in an explosive increase in female participation in sport at all levels. A competitive orientation toward sport increased with participation.[41]

Perceptions of Femininity

"Decades of controversy over female competition, masculinization, and the sexual reputation of women athletes point to an enduring opposition between sport and womanhood."[42] Both subtle and overt analyses of what women play, how they play, and how they project their athletic selves point to hegemonic standards. The social construction of gender creates a collective understanding that grounds sport experiences and the description of athletes within the historic perception that "a female cannot be both an ideal woman and an ideal athlete because the characteristics that constitute a good athlete are inconsistent with the characteristics that constitute a good woman."[43] Psychologists Jennifer Knight and Traci Giuliano explain that "female athletes are required to overcompensate for their masculine behavior on the field by acting in traditionally feminine ways off the field," in part to assure people of their heterosexuality.[44]

In addition to concerns specific to sport impeding reproductive function, early American women athletes were hampered by criticisms that exercise resulted in broad shoulders and narrow hips, detracting from an ideal womanly form. Women were just as likely to actively denigrate female athletes as were men, signaling an "obsessive attention" to whether a female athlete displayed feminine characteristics on and off the field of play and causing female athletes to take on exaggerated feminine personas as a form of compensation or apologetics.[45]

Similar to encouraging participation, the enactment of Title IX signaled a change in perceptions of the female athlete. Female athletes are now status and sex symbols, and "girls and women see themselves being accepted as strong, effective, competitive, and skilled athletes."[46] Yet, research indicates that women continue to grapple with body image issues, with competing ideals of "thin and toned" and "fit and muscular."[47]

American Women's Active Sport Tourism Participation

Well before the conceptualization of leisure constraints as negotiable emerged; women were circumventing the sport tourism barriers linked to their sex.[48] Examples of active sport tourism follow to illustrate American women's historical defiance of hegemonic standards.[49] Using an informal chronological framework, we will focus on early female active sport tourism pioneers by showcasing their devotion to a variety of traditional and nontraditional sports, including climbing, angling, surfing, bicycling, polo, tennis, golf, trap shooting, barnstorming, open water swimming, table tennis, skiing, and more. Our goal here is not to offer a laundry list of legendary women and their personal sport accomplishments; instead, we highlight a breadth of sports and the participation profiles of women, many anonymous and some famous, some privileged and some not, whose passion for active sport and travel paved the way for American women sport tourists.

Appreciation for high-climbing skill competence has long been a pursuit for both sexes. Established in 1863, the Appalachian Mountain Club admitted both men and women on equal terms from its inception, quite opposite from their "man's club" English prototype.[50] The purpose of the Appalachian Mountain Club was then and continues to be scheduling tours for scientific study of the mountain's phenomenon while affiliating with individuals interested in preservation. By 1902 the club boasted 1,300 members. The Sierra Club, established in 1892 by John Muir, adopted the Appalachian Mountain Club's tenets, including membership by both sexes. Mazamas, a nonprofit Mountain Education Organization established in 1894 and based in Portland, Oregon, was formed on Mt. Hood, and members also chose to adopt the tenets established 30 years earlier.[51] America appeared ready to grant to "women more rights and privileges, recognizing their talents."[52] Women had begun to travel to participate in high-risk climbs alongside men.

During this same period angling became a popular sport for women. By becoming an angler, females were offered access to bodies of water, nature, and the social need of responsible conservation.[53] Angling was considered more respectable among middle- and upper-class fisherwomen who had earlier been constrained by cultural barriers.[54] Women were finally allowed to practice active sport tourism by traveling away from home, extending their independence, to pursue both an interest in and offer a public voice for conservation of natural resources.

Native Hawaiians for centuries embraced surfing as part of their culture and over time, tourists flocked to watch and attempt to learn the sport. "Surfing," noted roving freelance reporter Alexander Hume Ford in 1908, "has been one of the greatest assets toward bringing the confounded tourists to our over hospitable shores."[55] The evidence makes clear that not only were surfing chiefs, gods, and other men highlighted as surfers, but women also distinguished themselves on the Pacific Coast. According to historian Isaiah Walker, a local Hawaiian surfer, the society for generations talked of Hawaiian female surfers such as Kelea, Laieikawai, and Kailiokalauokekoa as empowered women in the waves who "inflicted mortal vengeance on male surfers who disrespected them in the surf."[56]

With the arrival of Captain James Cook, Europeans, and foreign missionaries in the late eighteenth century came criticism of the Hawaiian lifestyle. Surfing appeared barbaric to the missionaries who believed "wave riding" would only hinder the heathens' moral progress, especially since both women and men practiced the sport in little or no clothing.[57] Hawaiians began to adopt the Western cultural norms and a more modest behavior for women. Surfing became unacceptable because it was unladylike. Hawaiian women were faced with a moral predicament. They yearned to participate in an honored custom at the risk of being frowned upon by foreigners and natives alike. Whether women chose to surf or not, the historical vision of empowered female surfers was suppressed in order to assure tourists that Hawaii was a safe and respectable destination.[58] Instead of female surfers, for a time images on brochures and flyers portrayed hula girls in grass skirts. Surfing was viewed as a "men only" sport. But by the turn of the century, with tourists flocking to the islands, Hawaiian life that waned under missionary control experienced a resurgence of cultural pride, including surfing. Hawaiians formed a surf club, Hui Nalu, that included females like Mildred (Ladybird) Turner and Josephine (Jo) Pratt. Pratt was considered to be the most talented female surfer in Hawaii from 1909–1911.[59]

Another example of the expansion among active sport tourists in the United States was the bicycle craze. Not until the 1885 "ordinary" bicycle did women begin to ride.[60] This bike featured a large front wheel, smaller back wheel, and high seat evolved to a much easier mounting "safety" bicycle featuring two equal-size wheels and a drop frame to accommodate long full skirts.[61] Almost overnight accessible roads were important, attendance at racing events grew, and middle- and upper-class cyclists populated inns and hotels.[62] Importantly, the bicycle is considered the first active form of mass sport tourism for women, leading to personal freedom by offering them extended movement as well as geographic knowledge and the opportunity to engage in strenuous physical activity.[63]

In addition to providing women a degree of freedom and an activity that required a degree of physical exertion and geographical knowledge, the bicycle was partly responsible for dress reform. Mobility and function for active sport female tourists were limited until the bloomer garment came along. One of the first to support a new look for women was Amelia Bloomer, who at the time was not focused on cyclists, but a more comfortable way for women to dress. Bloomer wore a "Turkish-style trousers that gathered and frilled at the ankle with an elasticized cuff."[64] A year after Bloomer's death in 1895 women began sporting the bloomer fashion style, freeing the female cyclist.

Whereas middle-class women embraced the bicycle, many wealthy young women had the money to take their equestrian skills coast to coast by displaying cleverness and courage while playing polo.[65] Considered a dangerous sport, the constraints of riding with skirts and sidesaddles made it challenging, but what women seemingly had over men were their ability to ride lighter and the advantage of "better hands."[66] Traveling outside their home region, these active sport tourists would spend summers abroad playing teams from England and Ireland while becoming more knowledgeable about the sport, including how to ride cross-saddle. Women found excitement competing in polo, and one team in 1913 beat a men's team at Point Judith, Rhode Island, captained by Miss Emily Randolph.[67] Eleanora Sears, a national tennis and squash champion, was the first woman to play polo on a men's team and the first female multisport tourist of the twentieth century who also participated in golf, tennis, horseback riding, and long-distance walking.[68]

Active participation among women sport tourists continued to grow during World War I. President Woodrow Wilson emphasized that it was especially important to stay mentally and physically healthy while strained by war.[69] Women, whether ready or not, were tasked with taking over for men away at war; bringing job authority, challenging tasks, and long hours to their days. As a result, women were encouraged more than at any other time in America's history to become proactive through participation in sport. The Women's National Tennis Association in 1918 energized sport tourism by reestablishing a number of tournaments across the country.[70] By then, a quarter to half a million women played tennis, and prominent athletes rallied to help the war effort by setting up and competing in matches around the country.[71]

Margaret Abbott, winner of the Olympic golf championship in 1900 while on a sojourn to Paris, may be considered a sport tourist. Competition multiplied across America at the same time through golf tournaments benefiting relief organizations like the Red Cross. Women golfers in 1913, as an example, raised $60,000 from entrance fees toward a local Red Cross ambulance fund.[72] The acceptance of golf as an appropriate sport and its rise in participation among both men and women may have been due to media portrayals. The message depicted in a frame analysis of 250 articles from 35 magazines at the time included outcomes like game enhancement, physical and emotional benefits, and mythical nature of the game. According to researchers Robin Hardin and Carol Zuegner,

> a perfect incubator for golf and other sports that dominate popular culture today, the decade will always be the Golden Age to sports fans because the sports world produced perhaps the greatest collection of athletes of any decade before or since.[73]

The Golden Age introduced Annie Oakley, who was the ultimate active sport tourist. She traveled throughout the country and Europe delighting spectators with her sharpshooter skills and acting abilities.[74] During World War I, Oakley tried to organize a regiment of female sharpshooters. Her petition was ignored, so instead Oakley helped raise money for the Red Cross with exhibitions at Army camps.[75] Her dog, Dave, would tag along to sniff out money from the audiences and add to the fund. Until 1922, she taught shooting lessons and hosted exhibitions at the Carolina Inn while her husband Frank Butler managed the Pinehurst Gun Club.[76]

During this latter part of World War I and in the years to follow, the sport of trap shooting rose among American women. In 1917 less than 5 percent of the 600,000 trap shooters nationwide were women.[77] As the number of women trap shooters' grew at gun clubs like Butler's, so did the understanding that women possessed a number of skills perfect for the sport, including nerves of steel, an eye for the target, and confidence, all assets to successful participation. Women also joined men in hunting activities, including traveling to constructed remote areas that had been identified as hunters' paradises during this century.[78] One such destination was the Pacific Coast for organized rabbit hunts. From written accounts it appears that the female active sport tourists would take more chances while hunting than many men.[79] Their competencies included master at established hunts and efficiency as colony builders, an important aspect in sustaining the sport.

By the 1920s, women were mastering sports they had not been allowed to participate in 25 years earlier, such as barnstorming. Whether on the ground as baseball players or in the air on the wing of a plane, active sport tourists were traveling the country in the 1920s to the delight of sightseers. These traveling performances, usually from a farmer's field for a few days and then moving on to another field, were called a flying circus, and these daredevils included women.[80] Phoebe Fairgrave, owner of a Curtiss, JN-4 "Jenny," was both a pilot and acrobat, performing on the wing by dancing the Charleston and hanging by her teeth, and then falling toward the ground before opening her parachute. Along with her pilot, Vernon Omlie, who later became her husband, the couple performed for five years throughout Iowa, Illinois, and Minnesota.[81]

Bessie Coleman, later considered an early aviation hero, wanted to teach anyone how to fly as technology was improving, but especially African Americans like herself.[82] Once she had made enough money as a pilot and parachuter at air shows across the United States, Coleman's dream was to open a flight school. Training in France after no white pilot at home would agree to be her instructor, she received her pilot's license in 1921 and practiced her profession in Europe first.[83] In 1925 she appeared both in the air and on land at theaters in her home state of Texas.[84] Tragically, Coleman and her pilot William D. Wills died on April 30, 1926, preparing to perform for the Negro Welfare League of Jacksonville, Florida. Coleman, not wearing her seatbelt, was tossed from the plane when it took a dive at 1,000 feet and flipped over. Wills then died on impact seconds later.[85]

Active female sport tourist forerunners included long-distance open water swimmers. Upon completion of the fastest swim to date of any person in the English Channel, finishing in 14 hours and 30 minutes on August 6, 1927, Gertrude Ederle was asked at the water's edge for her passport.[86] Her dynamic freestyle and personally designed two-piece swimsuit, made to sustain the grueling 35-mile swim, did not deter officials from requiring the travel document that verifies identity and nationality. Ederle's swimming feat set off a craze, engaging other females.

Although not as daring as other ventures, women's participation in competitive table tennis brought international attention to Americans in a sport that was largely dominated by Europeans. Ruth Hughes Aarons was the first American to win the world singles table tennis championship in 1936.[87] A former tennis player who took up table tennis in a rainstorm that had cancelled her tennis match, Aarons perfected over time a shakedown grip that made her a defensive master of the game. She took sport tourism to a new level by performing a vaudeville routine centered on table tennis, both in the United States and England. Aarons had the consent of the United States Table Tennis Association (USATT) of which she was an active member. Aarons was paid for her performances, and the USATT honored her 30 years later, inducting her into the USATT Hall of Fame for contributions to and success in spreading the sport of table tennis.[88]

Also bringing an international audience to American women's active sport tourism was Gretchen Fraser, the first American skier to take gold in the slalom at St. Moritz, Switzerland, in the 1948 Winter Games.[89] Fitting the definition of a sport tourist, Gretchen was a native of Washington State and resident of Sun Valley, Idaho, then moved to Denver after marrying another skier, Don Fraser.[90] Fraser's intent in Colorado was to train for the 1940 Games, but due to World War II, the event never occurred. When her husband deployed, she moved back to Sun Valley where her venue had been repurposed for the Navy's wounded soldiers. When the war ended in 1945, training commenced for winter athletes but the women's team was expected to train on their own.[91] Although the men's team rotated their eight part-time coaches, all with different techniques, Fraser's team eventually hired at the eleventh-hour Swiss coach Walter Haensli. It paid off and she took home the first gold for an American man or women in the slalom at a Winter Olympics. Fraser's expertise in that technical event helped in winning a silver medal in the women's Alpine Women's Combined.[92]

Conclusion

Historians have long sought concrete ways to measure how individuals understand the past through their own lived experiences. Active sport tourism is a phenomenon in its own right with regard to how tourism and sport interrelate during different historical periods and in the development of diverse pursuits. The analysis of sport tourism participation by women provides a rich opportunity to analyze how women can ". . . take an active role in using and understanding the past—that they are not just passive consumers of histories constructed by others."[93]

Antecedents that are specific to cultural constraints, needs, and motives inform the nature and meaning of sport tourism experiences. In this research we analyzed precursors as associated with the meanings women derive from active sport tourism participation. Female athletes (participants), female officials and coaches (sporting infrastructure), and female spectators over time all benefitted from travel, as "Distance brings with it a sense of anonymity and fewer restrictions, and this is a lesson that women travelers eventually learn."[94] By separating themselves from their home environments, historically women were able to free themselves from cultural expectations and family obligations. They found a way to contribute and excel both extrinsically and intrinsically.

The history of American women pursuing sport tourism reflects that of women globally, many who are currently facing barriers that American women overcame a century ago. The women's team of the Afghan National Cycling Federation, for instance, must secure permission from male relatives to join the team, must wear full-length gear in even the hottest of weather conditions, and face "threats of violence in pursuit of their sport."[95] These women, "among the first generation of Afghan women to challenge deep-seated taboos," see themselves as pioneers, willing to face their fears, break cultural barriers, and risk their honor in order to race and compete in other countries.[96] Active sport tourism, then, remains a means of personal expression and political activism that can advance the cause of all women.

Notes

1 Joy Standeven and Paul DeKnop, *Sport Tourism* (Champaign, IL: Human Kinetics, 1999), 12.
2 Joy Standeven and Paul DeKnop, *Sport Tourism*, 12–13.
3 "Ancient Olympic Games." www.olympic.org/ancient-olympic-games (accessed November 5, 2014); Mike Weed and Chris Bull, *Sports Tourism* (Boston, MA: Elsevier, 2009), 27.
4 Douglas Michele Turco, Roger Riley, and Kamilla Swart, *Sport Tourism* (Indianapolis, IN: Cardinal Publishers Group, 2002), 53–72.
5 Roy Rosenzweig and David Thelan, *The Presence of the Past: Popular Uses of History in American Life* (New York: Columbia University Press, 1998), 3.
6 Celeste Michelle Condit, "Hegemony in a Mass-mediated Society: Concordance about Reproductive Technologies," *Critical Studies in Mass Communication* 11 (1994): 205–230.
7 Ibid.
8 Erika Engstrom and Beth Semic, "Portrayal of Religion in Reality TV Programming: Hegemony and the Contemporary American Wedding," *Journal of Media and Religion* 2 (2003): 145–163.
9 Duane W. Crawford, Edgar L. Jackson, and Geoffrey Godbey, "A Hierarchical Model of Leisure Constraints," *Leisure Sciences* 14 (1991): 309–320.
10 Shirley Foster, *Across New Worlds: Nineteenth-Century Women Travellers and Their Writings* (New York: Harvester Wheatsheaf, 1990), 33–34; John Towner, *An Historical Geography of Recreation and Tourism in the Western World 1540–1940* (Chichester, UK: John Wiley & Sons, 1996), Daniel J. Boorstin, *The Image: A Guide to Pseudo-Events in America* (New York: Macmillan, 1961), 81–83.
11 Boorstin, *The Image*, 81.
12 William W. Stowe, *Going Abroad: European Travel in Nineteenth-Century American Culture* (Princeton, NJ: Princeton University Press, 1994), 6.
13 Lila Marz Harper, *Solitary Travelers: Nineteenth-Century Women's Travel Narratives and the Scientific Vocation* (London: Associated University Presses, 2001), 17.
14 John Towner, "The Grand Tour: A Key Phase in the History of Tourism," *Annals of Tourism Research* 12 (1985): 297–333.
15 David Weaver and Laura Lawton, *Tourism Management* 2nd ed. (Milton, Australia: John Wiley & Sons, 2002), 62.
16 Chris Rojek, *Ways of Escape: Modern Transformations in Leisure and Travel* (Lanham: Rowman & Littlefield Publishers), 121.
17 Weaver and Lawton, *Tourism Management*, 62.
18 Boorstin, *The Image*, 83.
19 John A. Jakle, *The Tourist: Travel in Twentieth-Century North America* (Lincoln: University of Nebraska Press, 1985), xi.
20 Dea Birket, *Spinsters Abroad: Victorian Lady Explorers* (Gloucestershire: Sutton Publishing, 2004), 28; Foster, *Across New Worlds*, 6; Barbara Hodgson, *No Place for a Lady: Tales of Adventurous Women Travelers* (Berkeley: Ten Speed Press, 2002), 1–2; Mary Suzanne Schriber, *Telling Travels: Selected Writings by Nineteenth Century American Women Abroad* (DeKalb, IL: Northern Illinois University Press), xvi.
21 Harper, *Solitary Travelers*, 25.
22 Hodgson, *No Place for a Lady*, 2.
23 Schriber, *Telling Travels*, xv.
24 Thomas E. Will, "Weddings on Contested Grounds: Slave Marriage in the Antebellum South," *Historian* 62 (1999): 99–118.
25 Margaret H. McFadden, *Golden Cables of Sympathy: The Transatlantic Sources of Nineteenth-Century Feminism* (Lexington: The University Press of Kentucky, 1999), 151.
26 National Park Service, "Women's Rights." www.nps.gov/wori/index.htm (accessed December 28, 2014); In G.J. Barker-Benfield, *The Horrors of the Half-Known Life: Male Attitudes Toward Women and Sexuality in Nineteenth-Century America* (New York: Routledge, 2000), 190.
27 Lori D. Ginzberg, *Women and the Work of Benevolence: Morality, Politics, and Class in the Nineteenth-Century United States* (New Haven: Yale University Press, 1990), 53.
28 Norella M. Putney and Vern L. Bengtson, "Family Relations in Changing Times: A Longitudinal Study of Five Cohorts of Women," *International Journal of Sociology and Social Policy* 25 (2005): 92–119.

29 U.S. Bureau of Labor Statistics, "Educational Attainment of Women in the Labor Force, 1970–2010." www.bls.gov/opub/ted/2011/ted_20111229.htm (accessed February 11, 2015); US Census Bureau, International Statistics, "Female Labor Force Participation Rates by Country: 1980 to 2010." www.census.gov/compendia/statab/2012/tables/12s1368.pdf (accessed February 11, 2015).
30 Ibid.
31 Eileen Gree, Sandra Hebron, and Diana Woodward, *Women's Leisure, What Leisure?* (Houndsmills: Macmillan, 1990), 40–46.
32 Paul Atkinson, "The Feminist Physique: Physical Education and the Medicalization of Women's Education," in *From 'Fair Sex' to Feminism: Sport and the Socialization of Women in the Industrial and Post-Industrial Eras*, ed. J.A. Mangan and Roberta J. Park (Milton Park: Routledge, 1987), 38–57.
33 Jaime Schultz, *Qualifying Times: Points of Change in U.S. Women's Sport* (Urbana: University of Illinois Press, 2014), 15–17.
34 Mary A. Boutilier and Lucinda F. SanGiovanni, *The Sporting Woman* (Champaign, IL: Human Kinetics, 1983), 33–34.
35 Susan K. Cahn, *Coming on Strong: Gender and Sexuality in Twentieth-Century Women's Sport* (Cambridge, MA: Harvard University Press, 1994), 16.
36 Boutilier and SanGiovanni, *The Sporting Woman*, 33–34; Joan S. Hult, "The Story of Women's Athletics: Manipulating a Dream 1890–1985," in *Women and Sport: Interdisciplinary Perspectives*, ed. D. Margaret Costa and Sharon R. Guthrie (Champaign, IL: Human Kinetics, 1994), 88–91.
37 Hult, *The Story of Women's Athletics*, 89.
38 Nancy L. Struna, "'Good Wives' and 'Gardeners,' 'Spinners and Fearless Riders': Middle- and Upper-Rank Women in the Early American Sport Culture," in *From 'Fair Sex' to Feminism: Sport and the Socialization of Women in the Industrial and Post-Industrial Eras*, ed. J.A. Mangan and Roberta J. Park (Milton Park: Routledge, 1987), 237; Boutilier and SanGiovanni, *The Sporting Woman*, 33; Hult, *The Story of Women's Athletics*, 91–93.
39 Hult, *The Story of Women's Athletics*, 94.
40 Boutilier and SanGiovanni, *The Sporting Woman*, 33; Hult, *The Story of Women's Athletics*, 95. U.S. Department of Education, "Title IX and Sex Discrimination." www.2.ed.gov/offices/list/ocr/docs/tix_dis.html (accessed October 15, 2014); Diane Heckman, "Scoreboard: A Concise Chronological Twenty-Five Year History of Title IX Involving Interscholastic and Intercollegiate Athletics," *Seton Hall Journal of Sport Law* 7 (1997): 391–422.
41 Elaine M. Blinde, "Contrasting Orientation Toward Sport: Pre- and Post-Title IX Athletes," *Journal of Sport & Social Issues* 10 (1986): 6–14.
42 Cahn, *Coming on Strong*, 207.
43 Derek Hall, Margaret Byrne Swain and Vivian Kinnaird, "Tourism and Gender: An Evolving Agenda," *Tourism Recreation Research* 28 (2003): 7; Beth Ann Martin and James H. Martin, "Comparing Perceived Sex Role Orientations of the Ideal Male and Female Athlete to the Ideal Male and Female Person," *Journal of Sport Behavior* 18 (1995): 287.
44 Jennifer L. Knight and Traci A. Giuliano, "Blood, Sweat, and Jeers: The Impact of the Media's Heterosexist Portrayals on Perceptions of Male and Female Athletes," *Journal of Sport Behavior* 26 (2003): 273.
45 Patricia Vertinsky, "Body Shapes: The Role of the Medical Establishment in Informing Female Exercise and Physical Education in Nineteenth-Century North America," in *From 'Fair Sex' to Feminism: Sport and the Socialization of Women in the Industrial and Post-Industrial Eras*, ed. J.A. Mangan and Roberta J. Park (Milton Park: Routledge, 1987), 256–281.
46 Cahn, *Coming on Strong*, 207; Boutilier & SanGiovanni, *The Sporting Woman*, 109–110.
47 See, for example, Catherine Benton and Bryan T. Karazsia, "The Effect of Thin and Muscular Images on Women's Body Satisfaction," *Body Image* 13 (2015): 22–27; Ara Cho and Jang-Han Lee, "Body Dissatisfaction Levels and Gender Differences in Attentional Biases Toward Idealized Bodies, *Body Image* 10 (2013): 95–102; Tracy L. Tylka, "Evidence for the Body Appreciation Scale's Measurement Equivalence/Invariance between U.S. College Women and Men," *Body Image* 10 (2013): 415–418.
48 David Scott, "The Problematic Nature of Participation in Contract Bridge: A Qualitative Study of Group-related Constraints," *Leisure Studies* 13 (1991): 321–336. Mike Huggins, "Sport, Tourism and History: Current Historiography and Future Prospects," *Journal of Tourism History* 5 (2013): 108.

49 Mike Huggins, "Sport, Tourism and History: Current Historiography and Future Prospects," *Journal of Tourism History* 5 (2013): 108.

50 Charles Fay, "Mountain Climbing As An Organized Sport," *Outlook* 71 (June 7, 1902): 377–384; Thomas Girm-Hochberg, "Women Mountain Tourists," *The Chautauquan; A Weekly Newsmagazine* 25 (August 1897): 553–556.

51 "Mazamas, Who We Are." http://mazamas.org/about-us/ (accessed November 11, 2014); "Who We Are." www.sierraclub.org/about (accessed November 11, 2014); "About the AMC." www.outdoors.org/about/mission.cfm (accessed November 11, 2014).

52 Edgar Beall, "Fellowship Among Women," *The Phrenological Journal and Science of Health* 100 (September 1895): 138.

53 David McMurray, "The Charm of Being Loose and Free: Nineteenth-Century Fisherwomen in the North American Wilderness," *The International Journal of the History of Sport* 30 (May 2013): 826–852.

54 Ibid.

55 Scott Laderman, *Empire In Waves: A Political History of Surfing* (Berkeley and Los Angeles: University of California Press, 2014), 23.

56 "Isaiah Walker," *The Inertia.* www.theinertia.com/author/isaiah-walker/ (accessed July 13, 2015).

57 Scott Laderman, *Empire In Waves: A Political History of Surfing*, 11–12; Dinia Gilio-Whitaker, "Surfing as Sovereignty: How Native Hawaiians Resisted Colonialism," *Indian Country Today.* http://indiancountrytodaymedianetwork.com/2014/11/14/surfing-sovereignty-how-native-hawaiians-resisted-colonialism-157803 (accessed July 13, 2015).

58 Isaiah Walker, "Womentum, Rethinking the Women's Movement," *The Inertia.* www.theinertia.com/surf/women-movement-ancient-hawaiian-surf-lore/ (accessed July 13, 2015).

59 Louise Southerden, *Surf's Up: The Girl's Guide to Surfing* (New York: Ballantine Books, 2005), 13–14.

60 Richard Harmond, "Progress and Flight: An Interpretation of the American Cycle Craze of the 1890s," in *The American Sporting Experience: A Historical Anthology of Sport in America*, ed. S.A. Riess (Champaign: Human Kinetics, 1984), 191; Christina E. Dando, "Riding the Wheel: Selling American Women Mobility and Geographic Knowledge," ACME: An International E-Journal for Critical Geographies, 6 (2007): 184.

61 Christina E. Dando, "Riding the Wheel," 185.

62 Gary Allan Tobin, "The Bicycle Boom of the 1890's: The Development of Private Transportation and the Birth of the Modern Tourist," *The Journal of Popular Culture*, 8 (2004): 843.

63 Christina E. Dando, "Riding the Wheel," 175.

64 Paula Westin Thomas, "Rational Dress Reform Fashion History-Mrs. Bloomer," *Fashion-Era.* www.fashion-era.com/rational_dress (accessed July 30, 2015).

65 James Crowell, "Women in the Field of Sport," *The Spur* 17 (May 1, 1916): 17–19.

66 "Women Rival Men at Polo," *San Francisco Call* 112 (June 1912): 2.

67 Mrs. Thomas Hitchcock, "Women Riders Play Dashing Polo Against Men," *San Francisco Call* 113 (March 1913): 9; "Women Rival Men at Polo," *San Francisco Call* 112 (June 1912): 2.

68 Peggy Miller Franck, "The Mother of Title IX: Trailing Athlete Eleonora Sears," *The Daily Beast.* www.thedailybeast.com/articles/2012/06/22/the-mother-of-title-ix-trailblazing-athlete-eleonora-sears.html (accessed September 2, 2015).

69 James Crowell, "Women in Sport in Wartime," *The Spur* 21 (May 15, 1918): 24–25.

70 James Crowell, "How Women Have Carried On Sport," *The Spur* 23 (May 15, 1919): 32–33.

71 Ibid.

72 Ibid.

73 Robin Hardin, "Life, Liberty, and the Pursuit of Golf Balls: Magazine Promotion of Golf during the 1920s," *Journalism History* 29 (Summer 2003): 82–90.

74 Glenda Riley, *The Life and Legacy of Annie Oakley* (Norman and London: University of Oklahoma Press, 1994), 166–175.

75 Ibid., 187, 192–193; Shirl Kasper, *Annie Oakley* (Norman and London: University of Oklahoma Press, 1992), 212–215.

76 Glenda Riley, *The Life and Legacy of Annie Oakley*, 181–186; Shirl Kasper, *Annie Oakley*, 206–209.

77 Francis Scully, "Women in the Sport of Trapshooting," *The Spur* 19 (May 1, 1917): 23.

78 Karen Jones, "My Winchester Spoke to Her: Crafting the Northern Rockies as a Hunter's Paradise c. 1870–1910," *American Nineteenth Century History* 11 (2010): 183–203.
79 Francis Scully, "Women in the Sport of Trapshooting," 23.
80 Michael A. Salter, "Balloon Jumpers: An Early History of Parachuting," *South African Journal for Research in Sport, Physical Education & Recreation* 21 (1998–1999): 41.
81 George Wilson, "Phoebe and Vernon Omlie: From Barnstormers to Aviation Innovators," *Aviation History.* historynet.com (accessed November 1, 2014).
82 Kim Creasman, "Black Birds in the Sky: The Legacy of Bessie Coleman and Dr. Me Jemison," *The Journal of Negro History* (December, 1997): Vol. 82, pp. 158–159.
83 Amy Bix, "Bessie Coleman: Race and Gender Realities: Behind Aviation Dreams, *Digital Repository @ Iowa State University.* lib.dr.iastate.edu/history_pubs (accessed 2005).
84 Ibid.
85 Ibid.
86 Robert Bender, "Gertrude Ederle Sets Records with Fastest Swim of English Channel." *history.com* (accessed January 3, 2015).
87 Tim Boggan, "Ruth Hughs Aarons." www.usatt.net/organization/halloffame/aarons1.html (accessed February 13, 2015).
88 Ibid.
89 "Gretchen Fraser Goes Gold." www.legacy.com/news/legends-and-legacies/gretchen-fraser-goes-gold/112/ (accessed January 3, 2015).
90 Luanne Pfeifer, "The One and Only Gretchen," *Skiing Heritage* 6 (Fall 1994): 4–13.
91 Ibid.
92 Ibid.
93 Rosenzweig and Thelen, *The Presence of the Past*, 3.
94 Harper, *Solitary Travelers*, 18.
95 Peter Breslow, "Afghan Female Cyclists: Breaking Away and Breaking Taboos," *National Public Radio.* www.npr.org/blogs/parallels/2014/05/02/308353109/afghan-female-cyclists-breaking-away-and-breaking-taboos (accessed February 13, 2015).
96 Shannon Gaplin, "Essay: In Wake of Paris Attacks, Afghan Women Cyclists Offer Lesson in Courage—and Fear," *Adventure Journal.* www.adventure-journal.com/2015/02/essay-in-wake-of-paris-attacks-afghan-women-cyclists-offer-lesson-in-courage-and-fear/ (accessed February 13, 2015).

Part VI

MATERIAL CULTURE AND SPORT

25

PLAYGROUNDS, STADIUMS, AND COUNTRY CLUBS

Robert C. Trumpbour

Introduction

The origins of playgrounds, stadiums, and country clubs in America are rooted in models established in Europe, with the Industrial Revolution and Progressive Era as watershed moments in the respective evolution of each. The playground was heavily influenced by German culture, the stadium was rooted in construction practices that emanated from ancient Greece and Rome, and the country club borrowed heavily from British traditions. All three gained construction-related momentum in the United States as a result of the Industrial Revolution and expanded profoundly during the Progressive Era.

The initial concept for playground construction unfolded in 1812 as a result of Germany's Jahn Gymnastic Association. This well-known organization was the first formal school of play and part of a broader German commitment to structured physical education. The leaders of this organization and their supporters sought to counter the dangers presumed to be caused by urban living at a time when city populations were increasing rapidly.[1]

Predictably, the gymnasium and gymnastic-type equipment were integrated into the earliest aspects of playground design. However, over time, the equipment and materials introduced to such spaces became more varied. A turn-of-the-century playground, for example, might include gymnastic climbing equipment, ladders, sand boxes, shaded awnings, slides, swing sets, teeter boards, and perhaps tether poles. More sophisticated play areas might feature ball fields and courts, a merry-go-round, and shelter houses that contained restroom facilities and possibly storage areas for sports equipment.[2]

The Transition from Parkland to Playgrounds

Before the playground movement took full hold, urban leaders committed resources to the establishment of open parkland. The squalor of urban tenements and concerns about poor health and hygiene associated with cramped urban conditions prompted the use of public resources so that bucolic spaces could be provided for widespread and general advantage. The newspapers of the era argued that fresh air and open spaces would provide ongoing health benefits to urban residents, particularly benefiting working-class citizens who, unlike the wealthy, were unable to retreat to country and suburban enclaves.[3]

Fredrick Law Olmsted was a key leader in this movement. Beginning in 1858, he led the effort to design New York's Central Park in Manhattan, parkland that is still the most visited and utilized in America. Olmsted designed parkland in numerous other cities, including

Boston, Buffalo, Detroit, Louisville, Milwaukee, Montreal, and in the nation's capital. He further designed open spaces at various colleges and universities throughout the nation in a manner that similarly promoted open recreational spaces as a common element in campus design.

However, Olmsted was not committed to construction of playgrounds. He opposed creating spaces for competitive and strenuous activity and did not perceive installation of manufactured play equipment as part of what should be included in an urban parkland setting. Instead, Olmsted hoped to create a carefully structured natural environment that could serve as a civilizing influence and a beneficial retreat. The use of spaces for active sports and open play gradually evolved as urban residents ignored or otherwise flaunted Olmsted's initial plans that were predicated on the presumed benefits of passive recreation.[4]

In New York's Central Park, Olmsted aggressively pushed to retain a bucolic environment that was most desired by the elite, even engaging a police force disparagingly nicknamed "sparrow cops," to fend off play and undesirable activity. Olmsted wanted these enforcement officials to educate the public in his philosophy of park use. To ensure that the philosophy took hold, he was aggressive in officer training that would ensure vigorous enforcement. Olmsted created an elaborate set of guidelines that he labeled "Rules and Conditions for Service" and insisted that the officers employ the formality of military salutes while on duty.[5]

Such actions appear to have supported Olmsted's goals. In its early years, historians Roy Rosenzweig and Elizabeth Blackmar indicate that "wealthy New Yorkers defined the new public park as their own."[6] The six-day work schedule kept working-class families away from the park for all but Sunday; however, by the 1880s, these individuals "would begin to question the political and cultural boundaries" that had been established.[7] Such regulation had diverted numerous working-class families to the highly commercialized culture of places such as the nickelodeon or Coney Island in nearby Brooklyn. By the turn of the century, politicians began to relax various rules, with team sports commonplace by 1912 and, despite opposition from real estate and civic groups, permitted installation of Heckscher Playground in 1926. This construction introduced swings, jungle gyms, merry-go-rounds, and a wading pool to 4.5 acres of Central Park well after other cities had constructed park-based playgrounds.[8]

Chicago and Boston were pioneers in the early playground movement, with New York, San Francisco, and other major cities also playing a role. Edward B. DeGroot served as general director of field houses and playgrounds for Chicago's South Parks Commission, and he spoke widely as an advocate for the integration of play spaces in urban parks. In 1908, he advised the National Playground Congress that "not until we care for the relaxation of the nation can we boast of a permanent and virile civilization." He further cautioned that building urban playgrounds was not sufficient to achieve this goal, further advocating for "adequate maintenance and administration after the grounds are acquired."[9]

Public Support for Play Spaces

The playground movement gained considerable momentum as a result of Theodore Roosevelt's advocacy of a "strenuous life," and was further fortified by the writings of psychologist G. Stanley Hall. Hall advocated vigorous, masculine, and primal forms of play for childhood and adolescence as a way to counter fears that males were regressing and struggling to adapt as modern culture became more genteel and civilized.[10] Playgrounds served a secondary function of social control, providing public spaces in which supervision, instruction, and management of ethnic youth, whose demeanor was often perceived to be troublesome, could be inculcated with values that were deemed desirable by those in power.

Although playground construction was a decidedly local undertaking, the ideologies embraced during the Roosevelt administration were instrumental in fostering new construction and design. In 1900, before Roosevelt was president, only 11 of the nation's 100 most populous cities had playgrounds. By 1907 the number was 57, with the number of cities committing to playground construction rising to 77 by 1909.[11]

The public commitment to such construction was evident. At least 55 of these urban facilities were funded in some manner by municipal resources, with smaller cities committing to playground spaces with high levels of enthusiasm. Public referendums in cities such as Lynn, Massachusetts, for example, demonstrated the public's intense desire to provide such space. The town's 1908 vote tally of 11,122 to 1,083 to fund new playground construction demonstrated the public's desire to support such initiatives.[12]

The commitment to provide youth with play spaces maintained momentum in the decades that followed. In 1919, the Playground and Recreation Association of America reported that 423 American cities were maintaining nearly 4,000 playgrounds and recreation facilities, suggesting that World War I did not slow the momentum of recreational investment.[13]

Even with the severe challenges of the Great Depression, considerable resources were allocated to construction of playgrounds, sports fields, and other recreational spaces. Reflecting the sensibility of the era, in 1932 New York City Police Commissioner Edward Mulrooney confidently asserted, "[W]e know that where a boys club or playground flourishes, we have less delinquency."[14] Several Depression-era programs, most notably the Works Progress Administration, constructed recreational facilities, including playgrounds and ballparks for communities throughout the nation. By 1938, more than 1,200 cities were supervising operation of nearly 18,000 playgrounds and other recreational facilities.[15]

Although the momentum achieved in playground construction was laudable, some faulty design and maintenance practices undermined achieving playground safety. One playground designer, for example, lamented in 1917 that necessary maintenance was lacking because "the school trustees apparently finish the building and forget all about that playground." Worse, to avoid unwanted dust, the use of brick, concrete, sharp cinders, and asphalt surfacing were common design choices in the 1920s and 1930s in many playgrounds.[16]

The 1940s and 1950s marked a continuation of hard surface installations, with perhaps an increase in its overall usage. As an example, large cement sewer pipes were brought in and creatively shaped to look like rocket ships, turtles, and other objects. Concrete and asphalt was described by Joe Frost, a playground expert, as "the pride of maintenance personnel and administrators," yet its extensive use created a legacy that "we are still fighting . . . today."[17]

More modern playgrounds have transitioned to safer resilient surfaces, but limited resources and tight budgets have made playground-related expenditures an ongoing challenge. The postwar evolution of suburban communities has created numerous small playgrounds in a multitude of smaller communities. The flight of middle-class families from urban to suburban locales during the 1950s and 1960s, as well as the postwar baby boom, created a leisure economy that was less focused on the urban core. As a result, school locations, whether urban, suburban, or rural, became the site of much playground equipment.

The playground landscape has been complicated further by a wide range of market forces from the 1970s onward. Numerous factors have challenged the role of contemporary playgrounds in America. The increasing popularity of computer-based video games, particularly online variants that create virtual communities and web-based playgrounds is one complexity that has emerged, as is the rise of popular and brightly colored play spaces in unorthodox environments such as fast food restaurants, and the emergence of for-profit recreation and athletic facilities. All of these more recent developments create a complex political environment that muddies the waters for today's playground advocates.

School curriculum requirements predicated on raising standardized test scores further minimize in-school use of playground equipment, though a vibrant consumer marketplace has resulted in sales of playground-like equipment that is often installed in back yards of suburban and rural homes. Nevertheless, concerns about childhood obesity abound, with *Time* magazine, for example, suggesting in its June 23, 2008, issue that youth inactivity has emerged as a serious problem in America.

Stadium Construction in America

The stadium has followed a different trajectory than playgrounds, with little political desire to publicly fund such projects during the nineteenth century and the Progressive Era, but an intensely greater willingness more recently to do so. Early ballparks were austere structures that did not contain luxurious amenities. Some early ballparks were constructed by cheap hired labor and, on occasion, by players or team employees. The first ballpark to erect barriers and charge an admission fee was Brooklyn's Union Grounds, with entrepreneur William Cammeyer deciding in 1862 to convert a skating rink into a for-admission ballpark. After renovations in 1869, a press report suggested the venue could "prove to be very profitable" and might serve as "a credit to the section in which they are located."[18]

The popularity of eastern teams and the emergence of the 1869 Cincinnati Red Stockings, the first fully professional baseball team, resulted in larger crowds and the need for rudimentary ballpark construction elsewhere. Early ballparks were modest wooden structures that could be repaired, moved, or dismantled rather quickly. Teams tried to locate ballparks near transit hubs such as trolley lines, often favoring cheaper land outside of central city locations.[19]

Political leaders held great power over team owners, unlike today, with the ability to threaten the viability of a ballpark if not properly respected. In an extreme example, New York Giants team owner John B. Day was forced to move when an ill-advised political snubbing regarding game ticket distribution was followed by a punitive political measure to build a new road that would cut directly through his ballpark property.[20]

As time passed and team owners became increasingly entrenched in the urban economy, more sophisticated construction strategies were employed. The Polo Grounds in New York was among the most lavish and well known of the wooden structures, with on-site concessions provided by Harry M. Stevens, an Ohio native and hospitality industry pioneer. Eventually, concerns about fire safety, prompted by the popularity of tobacco products at ballparks, created a shift to more permanent brick and concrete construction.[21]

In 1902, Cincinnati's baseball team constructed a partially concrete facility that served as a harbinger of more lavish major league facilities to come. Nicknamed the "Palace of the Fans," the ballpark featured ornate Corinthian columns and a limited number of opera-style seating areas for select patrons. *The Cincinnati Enquirer*'s coverage on May 17, 1902, marked the first time a sizeable photograph, five columns in all, of a new ballpark's unveiling was featured on the front page of a major city newspaper.[22]

The next year, in 1903, Harvard University unveiled the first fully concrete and steel stadium. Reflecting the sensibilities of the time, the Harvard facility's construction was supervised by Ira Nelson Hollis, a Harvard professor, with faculty colleagues and select engineering students providing design expertise. Patterned after Greek athletic structures, the stadium was built with alumni support, most notably with donations from the class of 1879. A rail line was built to bring supplies to the construction site, and other efficient strategies were implemented as 200 hired laborers of Italian descent needed over 200,000 square feet of Portland cement to complete the project in a mere four and a half months.[23]

In time, other universities followed the model established by Harvard University, building massive concrete facilities for their respective institutions. As examples, the Yale Bowl was built in 1914 and Princeton's Palmer Stadium was unveiled in the same year. By the 1920s, state-supported institutions began to construct huge sports-related monuments, too, with the largest schools, including Ohio State, California, Illinois, and Michigan, erecting sports stadiums that remain to this day.[24]

Professional sports were also moving to upgrade their facilities. By 1909, Philadelphia and Pittsburgh's professional baseball teams moved into fully fireproof facilities. The Philadelphia Athletics christened Shibe Park, a brick and masonry facility, on April 12, 1909. The ballpark was assembled in a French Renaissance style that featured intricate masonry and brickwork as well as ornate archways.[25] The Pittsburgh Pirates opened an even more impressive venue, Forbes Field, on June 30, 1909. It was the first million-dollar facility and featured cutting-edge technology for that time. Though less ornate than Shibe Park, it featured an underground parking garage, pay telephones, and on-site laundry facilities.[26]

Fireproof facilities were built in other cities, with Boston's Fenway Park and Chicago's Wrigley Field as the last remaining ballparks in use from that era. Yankee Stadium, unveiled in 1923, marked the final move of a Major League Baseball team away from a wooden ballpark and into the modern era. Although not constructed for specific sports teams, the Rose Bowl, the Los Angeles Memorial Coliseum, and Chicago's Soldier Field were built in 1922, 1923, and 1924, respectively. They were and remain civic monuments intended to serve a multitude of purposes.

The Great Depression and World War II curtailed major stadium construction, particularly in professional sports, though some building did unfold. Cleveland erected a huge municipal stadium in 1931 with dreams of hosting the Olympic Games that never came to fruition. Red Sox Owner Tom Yawkey provided a major facelift to Fenway Park in 1934, but, in general, difficult economic times and resource limitations meant that team owners and universities were unable to undertake major sports-related projects. Yet anti-Depression government programs resulted in substantial ballpark construction on a lesser scale with the Works Progress Administration, an initiative of President Franklin Delano Roosevelt, responsible for construction of more than 2,500 smaller venues in communities throughout the nation.[27]

Ballpark construction did not rebound soon after World War II ended, but construction of Milwaukee County Stadium in 1953 ushered in a new era for ballpark planning and design. County Stadium was a departure from previous construction in several ways. First, it was positioned outside of the inner city's central core, with abundant parking near highway access, a clear concession to automotive culture and the postwar exodus to the suburbs. Second, and perhaps more significant, it was taxpayer funded, with a goal of attracting a major league team, philosophically changing the financing dynamic considerably. After its construction, the Boston Braves shifted operations to Milwaukee, and, as a result, increased their attendance by 750 percent.[28] Up to that point, major league teams typically funded their own ballpark construction, so the success of the Milwaukee project compelled other team owners to consider the allure of taxpayer-funded facilities.

As franchise relocations unfolded, stadium construction was a core component of team plans. Most notably, the Dodgers and Giants moved from the lucrative New York City market to profitable opportunities on the West Coast in 1958, with new ballpark construction woven into each of these teams' long-range plans. The construction of Dodger Stadium in Los Angeles and Candlestick Park in San Francisco was followed by further construction, including the erection of all-purpose ballparks in Washington, DC, and New York City in 1961 and 1964, respectively.

Cities that lacked major league teams planned new construction as a means of obtaining a coveted team, as major league presence was regarded as a cultural index of success and prosperity. New venues were constructed in Minnesota, Baltimore, and Houston, with the Houston project particularly revolutionary. Houston's Astrodome, unveiled in 1965, was a luxurious and massive indoor facility for baseball, football, and all-purpose entertainment. The Astrodome set the standard for stadium luxury for that decade. It contained luxurious skyboxes for private viewing, themed club-style restaurants, and cushioned theater-style seating.[29]

Additional all-purpose facilities, generally circular in shape to accommodate both football and baseball, were built in Atlanta, St. Louis, Cincinnati, Pittsburgh, Philadelphia, Oakland, San Diego, and elsewhere, though none featured all of the luxurious trappings of Houston's unique venue. The high cost of indoor construction made emulating Houston's indoor model prohibitive, but in 1975 New Orleans introduced the vast Superdome and other indoor stadia were unveiled in Pontiac, Michigan, as well as in Montreal, Seattle, Indianapolis, Minneapolis, and Toronto.

As these all-purpose venues aged, their novelty diminished, and team owners, in a push to maximize their revenues, lobbied to obtain taxpayer-funded sport-specific facilities that would not be shared with another sports team. Such a complex was constructed in Kansas City, with a football venue unveiled in 1972 and a nearby baseball park that was christened in 1973. However, the move to typically more economical multipurpose venues derailed this concept elsewhere until the 1990s.

During the 1990s, some NFL teams threatened to move without the assurance of a profitable stadium venue that would provide team owners skybox revenue and a greater share of parking and concession income. As examples, lucrative stadium deals prompted the Rams to move from Los Angeles to St. Louis in 1995 and the Cleveland Browns to move to Baltimore in 1996, to later be renamed the Ravens. Stadiums during this era were designed with an increasing focus on opulence, with club seating, skyboxes, and expansive retailing space prominent elements of the new design.

In baseball, the completion of Orioles Park at Camden Yards in 1992 prompted the construction of retro-style ballparks. These facilities were similarly designed with a premium on luxury and revenue-generating amenities, but were designed to reflect a nostalgic past. Use of brick, wrought iron, abandonment of artificial turf for natural grass, and early twentieth-century design features gave these ballparks an aura of a utopian past that helped boost attendance. Various retro parks were constructed in other cities throughout the United States. In addition, major renovations were provided to Fenway Park and Wrigley Field, old ballparks that reflect the nostalgic era that served as the inspiration for retro facilities.

As the twenty-first-century unfolded, posh stadiums for football and baseball were planned and constructed to replace older and less opulent venues. In several instances, over 1 billion dollars were allocated to such projects. The most expensive was MetLife Stadium, constructed in New Jersey for the New York Jets and Giants in 2010 at a cost of $1.6 billion.

Within close proximity, a new Yankee Stadium was unveiled a year earlier at a cost of $1.2 billion. Elsewhere, in 2009 the Dallas Cowboys moved into AT&T Stadium, a retractable-roof facility in Arlington, Texas, that cost $1.3 billion, and the San Francisco 49ers orchestrated the construction of Levi's Stadium in nearby Santa Clara. It opened in 2014, also at a cost of $1.3 billion. These stadiums included posh club facilities, luxurious skyboxes, upscale retailing spaces, massive digital scoreboards, and in-house wireless access.

To pay for such lavish and cutting-edge venues, fans were expected to pay higher ticket, parking, and concession prices. In addition, season ticket holders were asked to pay for personal seat licenses, a substantial one-time levy assessed by teams for the ability to purchase future season tickets. Taxpayer support was another dimension for facility financing, as was naming rights revenues, in-stadium advertising, and skybox rental fees.

The Country Club: Origins, Design, and Construction

Ballparks took approximately a century to evolve into luxurious venues that have become a playground for the wealthy, but country clubs began with a desire to achieve luxury as an overarching goal. Initially, private and exclusive social clubs were built in the urban environment, later moving to the suburbs and then classified as country clubs.

Such clubs were heavily influenced by British cultural mores, with a decided desire to emulate the wealthiest classes of that nation. In tracing the history of early inner-city clubs, private club historian Dianna Kendall asserted that

> U.S. elites built clubhouses in this country that looked (and many of which still look) very much like those in London, and by the same token they also adopted written (and unwritten) rules, policies, and procedures similar to those of British clubs.[30]

Yet simply having abundant wealth was not, in and of itself, an adequate marker for club membership. Historian James Mayo asserts that the membership's "roots lay in prominent colonial families that modeled themselves after the English gentry."[31] As such, maintaining prestige was a key aspect of membership, with clubs struggling to balance recruitment to raise funds necessary for operational needs and the limitation of membership to retain a sense of exclusivity.

According to Mayo, through location, function, and style, the London-based city clubs "reified their elite status" in a manner that was replicated in the United States. Boston's Temple Club, Pennsylvania's Philadelphia Club, and New York's Union Club were formed in the first half of the nineteenth century. Such clubs spawned imitation in other cities.[32] Although the city provided an origin for the exclusive club, unappealing inner-city conditions, including crime and squalor, prompted the affluent to move to nearby suburbs, giving rise to country clubs.

Before country clubs were created, spas, resorts, and sports clubs were established. Spas and resorts were enjoyed by the wealthy, but were commercial enterprises, and, as such, often lacked the exclusivity, permanence, and privacy that might be afforded within a more exclusive club setting.

Sports clubs emerged in the second half of the nineteenth century. One of the oldest, the Philadelphia Cricket Club, was formed in 1854, and its founding was a forerunner to the establishment of other cricket clubs around the nation. Clubs for other athletic endeavors, including cycling, tennis, squash, baseball, yachting, hunting, and equestrianism, were also established, some with an upper-class clientele, but others opened to less affluent enthusiasts. Ethnicity often drove the interests of these clubs, as was the case for several Boston-area clubs formed for hurling, a popular Irish sport. Class distinctions were a factor in club organization, formation, and structure, and, recognizing this, historian Stephen Hardy asserts that a "sorting function" was clear as membership rosters became more widely known.[33]

Most early sports clubs lacked permanent space and were forced instead to rent, if possible, or use public land as a meeting spot, as was the case with the Philadelphia Cricket Club. Without a central location, the organization held activities in various locales ranging from nearby Frankford to Camden, New Jersey, until 1883, when benefactor Henry H. Houston assisted the club in acquiring property in Philadelphia's Chestnut Hill neighborhood as a permanent base of operation.

Over time, land acquisition resulted in formation of what evolved into country clubs. Among the first was the Myopia Club, formed in 1879 from the combined membership of two Boston-based city clubs. Located eight miles north of Boston, the Myopia Club was a suburban retreat for the affluent that included a tennis court, baseball facilities, a billiards area, bedrooms, and a dining area, though its membership was particularly passionate about fox hunting and horse racing.[34]

Three years after the Myopia Club was established, several of its members decided to form a club that was named, appropriately, the Country Club. Located in Brookline, the Country Club is an institution that has been described as "the prototype of all later country clubs."[35] The Country Club's initial focus was the foxhunt and horse-related activities, though, like similar clubs of the time, other sports were featured, with golf and tennis eventually being introduced.

What made the Country Club, located just north of Boston, a model for others was its focus on exclusivity. The club was the brainchild of railroad magnate, merchant, and entrepreneur J. Murray Forbes. It was the domain of Boston's elite, with membership culled from a select group with prep school and Ivy League pedigrees. Of the 403 original members, 199 were Harvard graduates, with a majority also holding membership in Boston's exclusive Somerset or Union Clubs.[36]

These clubs created an opportunity for a city's wealthy to showcase their affluence, while demonstrating their patrician roots. Sociologist and economist Thorstein Veblen asserted in his analysis of wealth that "it is not sufficient to merely possess wealth or power. . . . [For esteem to be awarded,] the wealth or power must be put into evidence."[37] Although privacy was one element of the club environment, another dimension was to conspicuously showcase one's affluence among one's peers. As was the case with the urban city club, the clubhouse was generally a luxurious showplace and central focus of the private country club's social activities. Elaborate clubhouses with large meeting spaces, commercial-quality kitchen facilities, administrative offices, and comfortable locker rooms made the clubhouse an opulent and enjoyable retreat for club membership.

The introduction of golf as an integral part of a country club did not unfold until 1888 at St. Andrew's in Yonkers, a suburban community north of Manhattan, though records of golf in America can be found as early as 1786 in Charleston, South Carolina. Evidence also exists that golf was played before 1888 in West Virginia, Washington, Nebraska, Kansas, Minnesota, Vermont, and Pennsylvania. St. Andrew's, the oldest golf club in the United States, was formed when John Reid, a Scottish sportsman, turned a suburban New York cow pasture into a three-hole golf course. The emerging popularity of the game inspired purchase of new property elsewhere in Westchester County six years later.[38]

Boston's Country Club introduced golf in 1892, though golf's popularity took time to unfold. As was the case with many country clubs, infighting arose regarding use of valuable acreage for golf because such conversion tended to encroach on land used for the then-popular fox hunt. Over time, golf gained supremacy, in part because it was less resource intensive, as it did not require horse maintenance and the ongoing expense of stable operations.

The formation of the United States Golf Association in 1894 served as a catalyst to make golf a more popular sport and to formally sanction golf as a part of country club design. The organization's five charter members were St. Andrew's Golf Club, the Country Club, Shinnecock Hills Golf Club, the Newport Country Club, and the Chicago Golf Club. With the USGA in place, a governing body was established that allowed for codification of rules and expansion of the sport elsewhere.

As the country club evolved into a comfortable and elite suburban enclave, real estate development began to emerge as a factor. Pierre Lorillard IV was a pioneer in this regard with his development of Tuxedo Park, a development 40 miles north of New York City. Lorillard created a gated community that connected the country club to the bucolic town of which it was a part. In the late 1880s, Lorillard formed the Tuxedo Park Association, an autocratic governing entity that restricted entry and dictated what could and could not occur within the development's boundaries. Mayo describes the venture as one that "symbolized the transition from a summer resort to a permanent relationship between the club and home."[39]

As the Progressive Era unfolded, speculators and investors looked at strategies to lure wealthy investors, establishing country clubs as one way to do so, since the creation of such institutions could raise the value of their adjoining property. Edward H. Bouton's development of Roland Park in Baltimore, J.C. Nichols' creation of the County Club District in Kansas City, and William Hogg's investment in Country Club Estates in Houston were three examples, among many, where entrepreneurs utilized country clubs to attract an upscale clientele as a means of maximizing nearby property values.[40]

The exclusivity of country clubs brought with it discrimination against Jewish and African American citizens. Exclusion might be prompted by the bigotry of entrepreneurs, though some of it was inspired by concern that failure to discriminate might suppress profitability. To counter such discrimination, aspiring Jewish and African American investors created institutions that mirrored the opulence of other country clubs.

In response to anti-Semitism, affluent Jews planned, designed, and built numerous country clubs throughout the nation. By the 1920s New York had established 20 such clubs, leading the nation, with Illinois second with 7. Among the first to be built were the Century Club, created in 1898, and Inwood, unveiled in 1901, both in metropolitan New York.[41] In Illinois, the Lake Shore Country Club was established north of Chicago in 1908.[42] Although country club membership skewed heavily to a male clientele, several Jewish females distinguished themselves as championship-caliber athletes. Historian Linda Borish asserts that the Jewish country club provided such women and less skilled contemporaries "a setting to develop skills in golf, tennis, and swimming."[43]

In a similar reaction to discriminatory admission practices, African Americans established country clubs, too. For example, in 1921 a consortium of African Americans created the Shady Rest Golf and Country Club in Scotch Plains, New Jersey. The suburban New York enclave drew minority members from New Jersey, Brooklyn, and Manhattan. Its clubhouse later featured entertainment from such luminaries as Count Basie, Cab Calloway, Duke Ellington, and Ella Fitzgerald.[44]

Golf was considered a sport with European roots and heritage, but the surprising U.S. Open victory of Massachusetts native Francis Ouimet in 1913 at the Country Club gained widespread national attention and served to popularize the game in the United States. Then just 20 years old, Ouimet's surprising victory against a heavily favored British field sparked a public outpouring of excitement for golf in America. In reaction, more middle-class youth applied to serve as country club caddies and a greater overall investment in golf course design unfolded, including the creation of some public golf courses.[45]

By the 1920s, golf was a fixture of the American country club landscape, with other sports playing a secondary role. The postwar prosperity ushered in an era of opulent clubhouse construction and more systematic overall country club design as well. The establishment of Prohibition resulted in a tacit tolerance for alcohol on country club properties. Though formal bans may have been in place, private lockers and personal flasks ensured that wealthy patrons could imbibe as desired.

In addition, this era featured greater weaving of social and family events into the fabric of the country club. Despite the male dominance of country club governance, events such as debutante balls and holiday parties offered a veneer of inclusiveness. A recalibration of sports-related activities also unfolded. Golf was firmly entrenched, with many country clubs dropping such activities as billiards, croquet, and other throwbacks to the earliest era of country club development. Some clubs retained or added tennis, whereas others chose not to do so.[46]

Economic Challenges for the American Country Club

The Great Depression and World War II provided challenges for country club operations. The economic downturn challenged membership levels and revenue streams, forcing some country clubs to close, and others struggled to manage operations. Many country clubs cut staff and maintenance expenses, whereas some created different membership levels, including the offering of lifetime memberships and seasonal rates. Pools were used to bring in revenue and family-oriented social events were often increased, not for idealistic reasons, but as a way to generate restaurant income and other revenues. Outside groups were invited to book country club space as well.[47]

World War II provided its own set of challenges. With supply shortages, maintenance was often put on hold, and with a diminished labor pool, male staff was replaced in many instances by female workers. Little changed initially as the war ended, but as postwar prosperity encouraged more vibrant consumer spending, country clubs embarked upon new construction and worked to increase membership.

The civil rights movement spurred integration of major sports during the 1950s and 1960s, yet many country clubs retained all-white and male membership rosters even through the 1970s and 1980s. The prestigious Augusta National Golf Course, as an example, did not admit an African American to its club until 1990. Discrimination against women was yet another visible sign of some country clubs' insular governance, with Augusta finally admitting two female members in 2012.[48]

The country club remains a fixture in American culture, but new economic and cultural realities have provided this long-standing institution with a unique set of challenges. Dual-income families, economic uncertainties, and an on-demand digital culture are among the constraints that have drawn some individuals away from pursuit of country club membership. Reflecting these realities, the National Golf Foundation indicated that for eight straight years more golf courses have closed their doors than have been built. In 2013, for example, 160 courses were closed, whereas only 14 new ones were built.[49]

With many golf courses nestled in prime suburban locations, struggling country clubs may be regarded as attractive sites for developers to construct highly profitable residential or commercial ventures. In addition, more recently some environmental activists have been critical of golf course use of fertilizers and pesticides, asserting that such tactics reflect poor resource stewardship. Some struggling golf properties have been converted, in part, to parkland, though financial pressures have made commercial or residential development a much more common outcome.

Country clubs have tried to adjust to a variety of challenges by adapting to consumer desires. Some have retained their exclusivity and dues structure while attempting to focus more diligently on customer service. Others have installed digital game rooms, exercise areas, and numerous television monitors in locker rooms, social areas, and elsewhere, and many have offered high-speed wireless access for members' personal devices. Some have created tiered or seasonal membership categories, whereas others have opened their facilities to outside groups for special event-related rentals. As was the case during the Great Depression, strategies that are more inclusive and that might involve family members have also occurred. Similarly, recruitment drives have also been implemented that, unlike earlier eras, might specifically target women and minorities.[50]

Conclusion

Some individuals criticize the exclusive and rarified atmosphere that has been cultivated within the country club, but for others, it is the embodiment of a utopian dream that symbolizes upward mobility and success. Playgrounds, stadiums, and country clubs are unique American institutions that continue to evolve and adapt to the times. Despite the uncertainties and challenges that each of these areas now face, each is likely to remain an important part of the fabric of our culture for the foreseeable future.

Notes

1 Joe L. Frost and Susan C. Wortham, "The Evolution of American Playgrounds," *Young Children* 43, no. 5, (July 1988): 19.

2 Joe L. Frost, "History of Playground Safety in America," *Children's Environments Quarterly* 2, no. 4, (Winter 1985): 13.

3 Melvin Adelman, *A Sporting Time: New York City and the Rise of Modern Athletics, 1820–1870* (Urbana, IL: University of Illinois Press, 1990), 274.

4 Stephen Hardy, *How Boston Played: Sport, Recreation, and Community, 1865–1915* (Boston, MA: Northeastern University Press, 1982), 93.

5 Roy Rosenzweig and Elizabeth Blackmar, *The Park and Its People: A History of Central Park* (Ithaca, NY: Cornell University Press), 241–243.

6 Ibid., 212.

7 Ibid., 259.

8 Ibid., 393–395.

9 Everett Mero, ed., *American Playgrounds: Their Construction, Equipment, Maintenance, and Utility* (New York: Baker and Taylor, Co., 1909), 12–13.

10 Gail Bederman, *Manliness and Civilization: A Cultural History of Gender and Race in the United States, 1880–1917* (Chicago, IL: University of Chicago Press, 1995), 77–119.

11 Sarah Jo Peterson, "Voting for Play: The Democratic Potential of Progressive Era Playgrounds," *Journal of the Gilded Age and Progressive Era* 3, no. 2 (April 2004): 146.
12 Ibid., 145–146.
13 Roberta J. Park, "Setting the Scene—Bridging the Gap Between Knowledge and Practice: When Americans Really Built Programmes to Foster Healthy Lifestyles, 1918–1940," in *The Rise of Modern Stadiums in the United States: Cathedrals of Sport*, ed. Mark Dyreson and Robert Trumpbour (New York: Routledge, 2010), 12.
14 Ibid., 21.
15 Ibid., 22.
16 Frost, "History of Playground Safety in America," 14–16.
17 Ibid., 17.
18 Michael Benson, *Ballparks of North America: A Comprehensive Historical Reference to Baseball Grounds, Yards, and Stadiums* (Jefferson, NC: McFarland, 1989), 52–53.
19 Steven A. Riess, *Touching Base: Professional Baseball and American Culture in the Progressive Era* (Urbana, IL: University of Illinois Press, 1980), 12–51.
20 Benson, *Ballparks of North America*, 253–255.
21 Robert C. Trumpbour, *The New Cathedrals: Politics and Media in the History of Stadium Construction* (Syracuse, NY: University of Syracuse Press, 2007), 15–19.
22 John Erardi, "The Palace of the Fans," *Cincinnati Enquirer*, April 1, 1996, E13, E18–E20.
23 Craig Lambert, "First and 100: Harvard Stadium, With Its Storied Past Is Football's Edifice Rex," *Harvard Magazine*, September–October 2003, 42–53.
24 Trumpbour, *The New Cathedrals*, 15–17.
25 Rich Westcott, *Philadelphia's Old Ballparks* (Philadelphia, PA: Temple University Press, 1996), 99–111.
26 Robert Trumpbour, "Forbes Field and the Progressive Era," in *Forbes Field*, ed. David Cicotello and Angelo Louisa (Jefferson, NC: McFarland, 2007), 25–35.
27 Arthur MacMahon, John Millett, and Gladys Ogden, *The Administration of Federal Work Relief* (Chicago, IL: Public Administration Service, 1941).
28 Bob Buege, *The Milwaukee Braves: A Baseball Eulogy* (Milwaukee, WI: Douglas American Sports Publications, 1988), 14–16, 61.
29 Houston Sports Association, Inc., *Inside the Astrodome: Eighth Wonder of the World* (Houston, TX: Houston Sports Association, 1965), 8–94.
30 Dianna Kendall, *Members Only: Elite Clubs and the Process of Exclusion* (New York: Rowman & Littlefield, 2008), 20.
31 James M. Mayo, *The American Country Club: Its Origins and Development* (New Brunswick, NJ: Rutgers University Press, 1998), 12.
32 Ibid., 10–12.
33 Hardy, *How Boston Played*, 139.
34 Mayo, *The American Country Club*, 63.
35 Hardy, *How Boston Played*, 140.
36 Ibid., 140–141.
37 Thorstein Veblen, *Theory of the Leisure Class* (New York: New American Library, 1953 [1899]), 42.
38 Richard Moss, *Golf and the American Country Club* (Urbana, IL: University of Illinois Press, 2001), 22–24.
39 Mayo, *Golf and the American Country Club*, 118.
40 Ibid., 119–124.
41 Peter Levine, "'Our Crowd' At Play," in *Sports and the American Jew*, ed. Steven A. Riess (Syracuse, NY: Syracuse University Press, 1998), 160–183.
42 Mayo, *The American Country Club*, 131.
43 Linda J. Borish, "Jewish American Women, Jewish Organizations, and Sports, 1880–1940," in Riess, ed., *Sports and the American Jew*, 129.
44 Vicki Hyman, "Country Club Life: Shady Rest Was the First of Its Kind in the U.S., Offering African Americans Daytime Sports and Nighttime Socials," *Star-Ledger*, February 20, 2009, 37.
45 Moss, *Golf and the American Country Club*, 84–89.
46 Ibid., 152–157.

47 Ibid., 157–169.
48 Steve Hummer, "Payne's Master Stroke, Ushered in a New Era at Exclusive Club with Usual Diplomacy," *Atlanta Journal-Constitution*, August 26, 2012, C1.
49 Lindsey Rupp and Lauren Coleman-Lochner, "Golf Market Stuck in Bunker as Thousands Leave the Sport," *St. Louis Post-Dispatch*, May 24, 2014, A9.
50 Stephanie Akin, "Not Your Father's Country Club." *The Record*. December 6, 1912, S–1.

26

BUILDING AMERICAN MUSCLE

A Brief History of Barbells, Dumbbells, and Pulley Machines

Jan Todd and Jason Shurley

Introduction

In March 1861, Thomas Wentworth Higginson—minister, man of letters, and reformer—published a lengthy essay in the *Atlantic Monthly* titled, simply, "Gymnastics." The article toured readers through a New England gymnasium allowing them to observe a calisthenics class where no equipment was used; described the gymnastics area where ladders, rings, ropes, pommel horses, and parallel bars took pride of place; then led readers to the weight area with its "row of Indian clubs or scepters . . . giants of fifteen pounds to dwarfs of four," and then to the "masses of iron," or dumbbells, ranging from 4 to 100 pounds, placed in order of size on the floor.[1] The versatile dumbbell, wrote Higginson, was an ideal exercise implement. With just one 50-pound dumbbell—or a pair of 25—he explained, a man could exercise nearly every muscle in his body in just half an hour.[2] In fact, he enthused, the dumbbell is "a whole athletic apparatus packed up in the smallest space; it is gymnastic pemmican."[3]

Higginson was one of the mid-nineteenth century's most important proponents of the philosophy of Muscular Christianity, the ideology linking physical health, manliness, and spiritual well-being. As historians Clifford Putney and William J. Baker have documented, the rise of Muscular Christianity in the mid-nineteenth century led to the development and expansion of team sports, the invention of new forms of exercise, and the opening of a variety of public and commercial gymnasiums.[4] In these new gymnastic edifices many men, and some women, engaged in purposive exercise, training to enhance their physiques, improve their health, and build endurance and strength. Some did German-style gymnastics—climbing ropes and ladders, swinging on parallel bars, and using the pommel horse. Others followed the prescriptions of Boston's advocate of the "New Gymnastics," Dr. Diocletian Lewis, and met in virtually empty rooms for sessions of bean-bag throwing, marching, and group exercise employing wooden dumbbells, wands, and Indian clubs. Still others—including apparently Higginson—spent part of their time lifting heavy iron dumbbells, using large Indian clubs, and training on an array of primitive weight-lifting machines—machines inspired by the same drive toward industrialization and efficiency that built the cities of the nineteenth century.[5]

Although still somewhat rare at the time Higginson wrote "Gymnastics," progressive weight training would emerge by the end of the nineteenth century as the most popular form of gymnasium exercise for men. Boxing gymnasiums, dance studios, gyms in which one practiced German or Swedish gymnastics, gyms associated with schools and colleges, and, of course, a growing number of YMCA gymnasiums all existed by the turn of the twentieth century. However, for an adult male to say he was training, or practicing physical culture, meant a significant portion of his purposive exercise came from weight training. More than a century later that statement still holds true, only now women as well as men are equally familiar with the benefits of resistance exercise. In fact, according to the International Health, Racquet and Sportsclub Association, more than 63 million Americans trained in a gym or health club in 2014, and males and females are now equally represented as health club members.[6]

This chapter examines the American origins of several of the more popular forms of strength-building equipment: dumbbells, barbells, and pulley machines. The chapter does not pretend to be a comprehensive history of these pieces of equipment, but is, rather, an exploration of the early emergence of these training aids within an American context. Our focus, unfortunately, excludes other kinds of resistance-training equipment—Indian clubs, kettlebells, medicine balls, and handheld cable and spring expanders—that would rightfully be included if space permitted. Further, because historians Kimberly Beckwith and John Fair have written excellent histories related to the barbell in America, less space is devoted to the history of barbells here. Finally, for those interested in knowing more about rowers, health lift machines, movement cure apparatus, and other kinds of exercise machines, the works of Ellen Roney Hughes and Caroline de la Pena are highly recommended.[7]

Dumbbells

Higginson's familiarity and fondness for dumbbell training was not unusual in early America. In the late eighteenth century, Benjamin Franklin had also remarked on the efficiency of dumbbell training in a 1792 letter to his son. Franklin believed that exercise should be judged by the amount of warmth it produced in the body, and dumbbell training, he explained, was an excellent way to produce bodily warmth. "By the use of it, I have in forty swings, quickened my pulse from sixty to one hundred beats in a minute, counted by a second watch, and I suppose the warmth generally increases with quickness of pulse," he wrote.[8] As German-style gymnastics was introduced in New England in the 1820s and became a popular form of physical education, dumbbell training became increasingly familiar to Americans. Iron and wooden dumbbells were used in many antebellum exercise regimens, including those specifically designed for women.[9] Charles Beck even suggested in an 1828 book for Americans on German gymnastics that "these hand-held appliances are too well known to require a particular description."[10]

Higginson had not always been such an ardent fan of dumbbells. In 1858, in "Saints and Their Bodies," also published in the *Atlantic Monthly*, he wrote, "For the favorite in-door exercise of dumb-bells we have little to say; they are not an enlivening performance, nor do they task a variety of muscles."[11] Three years later, in his article "Gymnastics," Higginson told a different tale. "These playthings, he wrote, "suited to a variety of capacities, have experienced a revival of favor within a few years." The number of exercises one could do with a dumbbell, he explained, was now much larger, and "all exceedingly invigorating."[12] Higginson then discussed the lifting of Richard Montgomery (actually James L. Montgomery) of New York and suggested that Montgomery's putting overhead a 101-pound dumbbell inspired other men to also test their limits. The result, he explained, was that heavy dumbbell lifting had spread to other gymnasiums and "a good many persons in different parts of the country, now handle one hundred and twenty-five."[13] Boston's George Barker Windship held the greatest records in this lift. Windship, although a relatively small man, could put a 141-pound dumbbell overhead without bending his knees, wrote Higginson, but with a dip and a rapid jerk he could manage 180. The growing enthusiasm among gym members for setting dumbbell records and training with "very heavy ones," he further observed, "is so far as I can find, a peculiarly American hobby, though not originating with Dr. Windship."[14]

Higginson proved correct. Although historians have generally attributed the popularization of heavy lifting in the United States to Windship, he was clearly not the first American to pursue strength for its own sake.[15] That honor may more rightfully belong to the aforementioned James L. Montgomery, who, as a teenager became a habitué of Charles Ottignon's New York gymnasium. Montgomery was also an early member of the New York Knickerbockers baseball club.[16] New York was home to several gyms in the early part of the nineteenth century, and a surviving lithograph of Ottignon's gym from 1845 shows men fencing, sparring, doing one-legged squats, climbing ropes and ladders, and on the left, a single man training with a pair of "chest-weights" or wall pulleys. On the floor below him are several block weights, but there are no large dumbbells or barbells in evidence.[17]

When, where, and how heavy dumbbell users acquired and maximal lifting began to be pursued at Ottignon's gym is not known. However, in 1852, in a report of a gymnastics exhibition at the gym, Montgomery was listed as a prize winner in an event in which "great dumbbells were handled with perfect ease, while unpracticed men of twice their size could hardly lift these strong men's toys."[18]

Historians know relatively little about Montgomery's life before he began appearing in the newspapers in the 1850s. Through his lifting, however, he became a sport celebrity of sorts. The *New York Clipper* wrote in 1856 that Montgomery "may now be considered as one of the greatest gymnasts the world ever produced."[19] On May 10, 1856, a notice in the *New York Daily Tribune* proclaimed "James L. Montgomery has this day become a PARTNER in the GYMNASIUM and will give his personal attention to the business of the gymnasium." It is signed by C.E. Ottignon.[20] That same year, the *New York Clipper* heralded Montgomery as America's answer to Britain's famed club-swinging champion, Professor Harrison, whose bare, muscular torso had appeared in *New York Clipper* several months earlier. The *Clipper* wrote beneath their engraving of Montgomery lifting a dumbbell overhead that the image "represents a specimen of Young America . . . the strength displayed by him in his feats with his 101 lb. bell are truly astonishing, and should be witnessed by all fond of such exercises."[21] The *New York Daily Reformer* described Montgomery as a man of "prodigious power" and claimed he deserved credit for "introducing the fashion of using dumbbells" to America around 1856. Wrote the *Reformer* in 1865, "when he curled and put up the 100-pound bell, all New York wondered." The author then added, that although other men could now lift more overhead than Montgomery that no one—not even Windship—had been able to curl a 100-pound dumbbell so far, except him.[22]

By the early 1860s, the Eastern Seaboard was home to several gymnasiums where one could lift heavy dumbbells and unofficial records had begun to be kept.[23] One early advocate, William Wood, opened a commercial gym in New York City in 1835.[24] A native New Yorker, Wood began competing as an athlete at age 18, excelling in rowing, where he had a distinguished career as an athlete. After graduating from Yale, he opened a gym on Crosby Street in lower Manhattan that became a cultural nexus for boxers, pedestrians, businessmen, and those young, disaffected factory and office workers, who found in the gymnasium a band of big-armed brothers, a new vision for manhood, and a sense of physical empowerment.[25] When Wood died, his obituary in the *New York Times*, referred to him as the "Grandfather of

Athletics in the United States."[26] Weightlifting historian David Webster suggests that Wood's gym contained "many original pieces of equipment, including a unique rowing machine with a chest and shoulder exercising device." Webster also suggests that Wood was the first person to develop an "elastic exerciser" and the first inventor of spring cable expanders.[27]

Following in Wood's footsteps, historian Louis Moore suggests, were several African American "professors of pugilism," who also contributed to the evolution of physical culture and the commercial gymnasium scene in New England.[28] Aaron Molyneaux Hewlett, for example, opened a gymnasium in Worcester, Massachusetts, in 1855 that catered to white clients. Higginson also lived in Worcester at this time, which suggests, but does not prove, that Hewlett's gymnasium may be the one described in the *Atlantic Monthly*. Hewlett also served as the first gymnasium instructor at Harvard, joining the faculty in 1859.[29] Although few written records survive describing what kind of equipment existed in Hewlett's gymnasium, a photograph of him taken for the 1865 Harvard yearbook shows him surrounded with the tools of his trade: boxing gloves, a wooden wand, a medicine ball, heavy and light Indian clubs, and two iron dumbbells of significant size.[30]

Although not the first of these early strength seekers, Harvard-trained physician George Barker Windship was undoubtedly the most well known. Windship rose to national fame when he began demonstrating the benefits of heavy weight training in a series of lectures and public exhibitions in 1859. Newspapers widely reported these events across the United States; an account of an 1860 lecture in Philadelphia was even reprinted in the *Honolulu Polynesian*.[31]

Windship's personal quest for physical strength and greater muscularity began during his years as an undergraduate student at Harvard when he was embarrassed by his small size and general weakness. After German-style gymnastics failed to give him the physique and physical power he craved, Windship—one of the most inventive men in the history of the Iron Game—began experimenting with heavy weight-lifting movements, particularly those in which a large amount of weight moved just a short distance. He started by doing what we might now call a partial deadlift in which the weight was suspended below him, reaching 1,208 pounds by this method in 1860.[32] He then began experimenting with harness arrangements and built a special yoke to wear over his shoulders that eventually allowed him to lift more than 3,000 pounds according to contemporary reports.[33] Although he never weighed more than 155 pounds and so was an unprepossessing strongman, Windship's Boston Brahmin heritage, his visibly muscular body, and his ability to lift such enormous poundages—even though he did not move them very far—inspired dozens of other men to try heavy lifting in the years ahead. Windship's message that "Strength Is Health," and his avowal that the practice of "health lifting" was the fastest method to physical rejuvenation and lifelong health, proved to be a powerful motivation for men to start weight training.[34]

Following the Civil War, Windship opened a gym in Boston connected to his medical office where people practiced the health lift on machines he invented and trained with dumbbells and weighted pulley machines. By the early 1870s, other physical culture entrepreneurs were selling their own versions of health lift machines, and Windship's Boston rival, David P. Butler, had even begun franchising what he called "lifting cure" gyms branded with his name, machines, and methods.[35] The craze for health lifting became so large by the early 1870s that a stroll down Broadway Avenue in New York would take pedestrians past six different health lift studios. Boston, Brooklyn, Chicago, Cincinnati, and San Francisco all featured studios as well.[36]

As the practice of heavy lifting gained momentum at mid-century, the idea of adjustable dumbbells—rather than having to own a large number of dumbbells of different weights—prompted the application for America's first dumbbell patent. Daniel F. Savage's 1860 patent envisioned a "graduating dumbbell" made up of interlocking spheres and smaller internal pieces that allowed the dumbbell to retain the appearance of a solid weight.[37] In 1865, Windship, who may also have experimented with using lead shot to vary the weight of dumbbells, took out America's second dumbbell patent. Windship's patent was a major advance and used plates of different weights and size that allowed the dumbbell to vary from 8 to 101 pounds.[38] Although it is impossible to fully know what was happening in other parts of the world in this era, no evidence has been found that any Europeans were using disc plates before Windship.[39]

Barbells

Although both Savage and Windship stated that their patents would work with bars of any length—the barbell as we know it was not part of standard equipment in most nineteenth-century gyms. It is only in the 1890s, and no doubt inspired by the exhibitions of barbell-using professional strongmen like Eugen Sandow, that the now-ubiquitous barbell began to be more widely used by American weightmen.[40] Even then, according to Alan Calvert, America's first barbell manufacturer, fewer than 100 barbells a year were being sold in the United States and they were all custom made. Calvert was one of many Americans who became inspired to pursue physical culture after seeing Eugen Sandow perform during the 1890s. Once realizing the type of heavy equipment used by Sandow was not readily available for purchase, Calvert founded the Milo Barbell Company in 1902 and began manufacturing what he called a "bar-bell" consisting of cylindrically shaped canisters filled with lead shot. As Beckwith has demonstrated, he changed his design in 1908 to a globe-ended barbell that used both lead shot and plates to vary the weight.[41]

Barbells with exposed plates—like our modern barbells—did not become standard in the United States for several more decades. Although Samuel B. Stockberger of Canton, Ohio, was issued U.S. patent number 405,128 for what he called an "Exercising-Bar" that used plates, the bar in Stockton's device was wood, not metal, and so was not designed for heavy training.[42] True barbells were being used in Germany, however, and in 1901 Theodore Siebert began selling a plate-loading barbell. The next innovation came from Franz Veltum in 1905, who introduced a revolving sleeve that allowed the plates to rotate independently of the bar.[43] German manufacturer Kaspar Berg then improved Veltum's design in 1928, creating the first modern barbell with a seven-foot-long bar, a revolving sleeve, and plates of various heights and weights. The "Berg-Hantel" was used at the 1928 Olympic Games and regarded by those who used and saw it there as a great innovation.[44] Other companies copied it, including the York Barbell Company of the United States, whose "York Olympic Bar" then dominated the American market for barbells during most of the twentieth century.[45] No significant improvements have taken place in barbell design since this time.

Pulley Machines

Londoner James Chiosso reportedly began experimenting with weight-stack pulley machines in 1829. By 1855 he had designed what he called the Gymnastic Polymachinon, an eight-foot-tall, multistation machine housed within furniture cabinetry that he marketed for home and gym use.[46] Whether any Polymachinons—or just his book describing them—were actually sold in America is unknown. However, the basic mechanical concepts embodied by the machine—a stack of weights, a pin or other device to select only part of the stack at a time, and cables running over pulleys—reappeared in most other gyms in the nineteenth century. In fact, the Polymachinon seemingly is the forerunner of all the selectorized weight-pulley machines.[47] Windship was also an early user of pulley machines. Dudley Allen Sargent visited him in 1860s and saw the Roxbury Hercules train on several pulley machines he had invented. According to Sargent, Windship was "exceedingly strong" and did his pulley work with his back braced against the wall, seeing "how much he could pull this way, and that way."[48] David P. Butler, who also patented health lift machines, took out the first American patent for a pulley machine in 1865.[49]

Windship's visitor, Dudley Allen Sargent, born in 1849, would have the greatest impact on pulley machines in the nineteenth century. Sargent's introduction to physical training was Higginson's "Gymnastics" article in the *Atlantic Monthly*, which he cut out of the magazine and saved so he could follow its recommendations.[50] By the time Sargent reached young manhood, he was an excellent gymnast and for a brief time worked as a circus performer. Tiring of this peripatetic and aimless life, however, Sargent took a one-term job as the gymnasium director at Bowdoin College in 1869, where his continued employment was contingent upon the demonstration of physical improvement in his students.[51] Bowdoin had little in the way of gymnasium equipment when he arrived, and many of the students were not fit. Rather than use heavy dumbbells and gymnastics work as he had done, Sargent shaved down the school's Indian clubs and used window-sash weights, cotton rope, and wooden dowels to make light pulleys for his students; he later allowed the students to move on to heavier work on pulley machines he designed.[52] Sargent's approach succeeded. Bowdoin hired him full-time, and he started working on new ideas for machines.

In 1875, Sargent moved on to medical school at Yale and, shortly after graduating, migrated to New York where he opened a gym containing 30 pulley machines of his own invention.[53] In 1879 he met Harvard alumnus William Blaikie, who praised Sargent's machine-based fitness system in his influential book, *How to Get Strong and Stay So*, and helped Sargent become Director of Physical Culture at Harvard University.[54]

As Sargent rose to national prominence as a physical educator, interest in using pulley weights rose with him.[55] Harvard would not allow him to patent his inventions, so they were copied by many other companies.[56] Historian Ellen Roney Hughes has documented 24 different patents for pulley machines in the 1880s alone and concluded that the machines were the "most important exercise machines of the late nineteenth century."[57] Sargent-designed machines produced by the Narragansett Company, however, became the gold standard in outfitting university gymnasiums, largely because Sargent taught most of the prominent physical educators (men and women) who entered the field at the turn of the twentieth century.[58] Edward Hartwell of Johns Hopkins University, William Anderson at Yale, and R. Tait McKenzie of the University of Pennsylvania were all trained by Sargent, as was Luther Gulick, the preeminent physical educator at Springfield College, where the vast majority of YMCA directors were educated.[59]

In his 1923 text, *Exercise in Education and Medicine*, McKenzie praised Sargent's work on pulley weights, citing their effectiveness in providing exercise to those not strong enough for other gymnastic work and as a means for "all-around muscular development." According to McKenzie, pulleys, which could be set at floor, ceiling, or chest height and provided resistance from a variety of angles, enabled the isolation of specific muscle groups.[60] Weightlifting advocate and physical educator Father Bernard Lange of the University of Notre Dame noted the versatility of pulley weights. Wrote Lange, "[A]lmost every muscle of the body can be brought into play if one thoroughly masters all of the movements that can be executed with the aid of a chest-weight machine."[61] In his 1930 text *Physical Improvement*, Olympic weightlifting coach Mark Berry also discussed training with pulley weights. Although a barbell man, Berry nonetheless pointed out that a man could make do with the machines in a pinch and, as he correctly pointed out, they required "no degree of skill."[62]

Pulley machines fell into a brief decline during the Great Depression as America's physical culture community realigned itself. By the early 1930s, Sargent had been retired from Harvard for more than a decade, team sports and competitive games replaced gymnastics and physical training in most school physical education programs, and the loudest advocate for progressive weight training, Bob Hoffman, owner of the York Barbell Company, was just coming into his prime. Hoffman launched *Strength and Health* magazine in 1932, focusing it on training for competitive sport—especially Olympic weightlifting—and preferably on a York barbell. As the decade progressed, Sargent's ideal physique—the lightly muscled but balanced body—faded in the face of Hoffman's enthusiasm for serious strength and visible muscle.[63]

In the late 1930s, the Amateur Athletic Union (AAU), which sanctioned weight-lifting competitions and other sports, also began sanctioning physique contests. The first AAU Mr. America contest was held in 1939. As historian John Fair has documented, although the first AAU contests were open only to registered weightlifters, within a few years men began self-identifying as bodybuilders and physique-only contests were being sanctioned by both the AAU and the International Federation of Bodybuilders (IFBB).[64] Joe Peters, runner-up in the inaugural Mr. America contest, claimed that the event transformed the way barbell men thought about training by giving them a chance to focus specifically on physique development.[65] Physical culture magazines also began to be referred to as "muscle magazines" around this time, in part because their pages were increasingly filled with articles on muscle specialization aimed at producing big arms, broad shoulders, and washboard abs. Bodybuilders, like TV celebrity Jack LaLanne, soon realized in their quest for greater muscle that pulley weights with much heavier loads than Sargent ever imagined could stimulate specific muscles not reached by barbell training. LaLanne, who opened a gymnasium in Oakland, California, in 1936, is often credited as the inventor of the "lat" or upper back machine in which the cable ran over two overhead pulleys and then attached to a wide-handled bar. Peary Rader, publisher of *Iron Man* magazine, and a convert to heavy pulley work by 1946, wrote that pulley weights were "far superior" to barbells for developing some muscle groups.[66]

As bodybuilders used machines to hone their physiques, gyms also used the apparatus to appeal to a wider clientele. Noting that newcomers "tend to get bored" if only a few pieces of equipment are available, San Francisco gym owner Norman Fay added a variety of pulleys, incline and decline benches, a leg press, squat stand, and other equipment to his studio in the 1940s.[67] Fay went further, however, and provided chrome-plated equipment and even varnished all the visible wood.[68] Vic Tanny, often credited with the creation of the modern health club, copied Fay's use of chrome and elegant finishes as he established his chain of gyms in 1939.[69] Because Tanny's prime customers were women and businessmen, he relied heavily on various kinds of pulley machines to equip his gyms, placing them in rooms filled with brightly painted walls, carpeting, soft lighting, and background music. By the late 1950s, Tanny's gym chain stretched across the United States and consisted of more than 100,000 members.[70] Although he later went bankrupt, Tanny demonstrated that average Americans would frequent such sanitized, machine-centric facilities. His aesthetic vision would be copied by nearly all other successful gym chains in the latter half of the twentieth century.[71]

Muscle Beach alumnus Harold Zinkin is one inventor whose claim to originality cannot be disputed. Zinkin invented the multistation Universal Gym over several years in the late 1950s, building them one unit at a time until he began to mass produce the machines in 1963.[72] Like Chiosso's early Polymachinon, Universal machines included multiple stations allowing groups of exercisers to train simultaneously. Standard units came with a leg press, bench press, lat pull-down, a curling station, an overhead press station, and a chin-up bar. Although Universal machines appeared in YMCAs and dozens of commercial gyms in the 1960s, Zinkin's greatest impact was in helping high schools and universities feel comfortable with their sport teams practicing weight training.[73] Gene Mozee, his long-time friend, told the *Los Angeles Times*

> If a coach wants to move 30 athletes through training in a short period of time, he can do it on that machine . . . Harold did more for the acceptance of weight training by college athletes than anyone.[74]

Zinkin also recognized his impact on the world of sport. "If I'm proud of anything," he wrote in his memoir, "it's that machine and the fact that there probably isn't one professional athlete in the world who hasn't worked out on a Universal at least once."[75]

Whereas Zinkin's Universal machines consolidated many pulley movements into one large apparatus, Louisiana native Arthur Jones took a different approach for his line of Nautilus pulley-weight machines.[76] Jones noticed that when he trained on a standard pulley machine, it felt at some points in the range of motion as if he was pulling or pushing less weight than at other times. Jones believed that constant tension resulted in greater muscle gains, and so designed an asymmetrical pulley or cam that resembled the shape of a nautilus shell.[77] During the 1970s, Jones adopted Nautilus as his brand name and created a series of machines aimed at individually working the major muscles of the body.

Although Jones's first Nautilus creation consisted of a multistation machine designed to compete with Universal, the company did not begin taking off until 1970 when he sold his first "lat pullover machine" for $300.00. Jones soon followed it with a biceps/triceps machine, a leg and hip machine, an abdominal crunch machine, an overhead press machine, and others. Like Zinkin, it took Jones several years to get his new business into full production, but then, according to bodybuilder Bill Pearl, Nautilus sales skyrocketed; there was nothing else like it on the market.[78]

Nautilus succeeded for a number of reasons. For one thing, the machines looked and felt different than anything else ever marketed. They were large, heavily made, painted a metallic blue, and instead of cables, Jones used bicycle chains over the pulleys so that even the sound of training on Nautilus was different. Although the high prices Jones charged no doubt helped strengthen the public's belief that anything that expensive must be good, another major draw for the public was their time efficiency. Jones claimed that one needed only 30 minutes of training, as he recommended just one set per exercise. The notion that these futuristic machines would create dramatic physical changes in less than the time it took to watch a sitcom found a receptive audience. And, so, like David Butler's Health Lifting gyms of a century earlier, Jones began selling Nautilus Gym franchises. Because only Nautilus equipment was used in a Nautilus gym, the gyms were often located in strip malls and small storefronts. Inside these gyms, the blue machines were placed so individuals performed a prescribed circuit generally doing one set "to failure" at each station as Jones recommended. Combined with his enormous sales to pro and university athletic teams, the gyms helped Jones—who once ran a side-of-the-highway snake farm near Slidell, Louisiana, to make *Forbes* magazine's 1983 list of wealthiest Americans. After little more than a decade, he was reportedly worth $125 million.[79]

Although many decried Jones' "assembly line" approach to physical fitness, it is impossible to underestimate the impact of Nautilus machines on America.[80] As the *New York Times* put it in 2007, Nautilus machines "made weight lifting more attractive to a broader range of people and helped move the activity from the male-dominated domain of bodybuilders in dank YMCA basements, to today's well-lighted, fitness mega-complexes."[81]

Jones' idea of creating specialized weight-stack/pulley machines for different body parts would be copied by dozens of other American manufacturers in the latter decades of the twentieth century. The "rise of the machines" as the *New York Times* called the fitness evolution sparked by Nautilus, transformed the gymnasium experience of most Americans and made the 1980s and 1990s quest for fitness seem largely about engagement with resistance machines. However, as Arnold Schwarzenegger aged, leg warmers sagged, and bodybuilding became too freaky even for many of its fans, younger members of the fitness community began looking for new approaches and equipment.

Conclusion

The "new wave" in fitness is a return to older methods and equipment. Indian clubs, kettlebells, medicine balls, barbells, and dumbbells are, once again, found and used in many commercial gyms and by most athletic teams in the United States. This resurgence of interest in these early pieces of equipment is at the center of a new paradigm called functional training—an approach to fitness based on what the body can do rather than how it looks.

The most visible example of this new appreciation of functionality is the rise of the workout system known as CrossFit. Begun in 2001 by Greg Glassman, a former gymnast, CrossFit aims to create a level of physical competence not unlike that which Thomas Wentworth Higginson and George Barker Windship aspired to back in the 1860s.[82] CrossFit workouts consist of a wide variety of exercises performed for time. Typical exercises include variants on the Olympic lifts (the clean and jerk, and the snatch), powerlifts (squats and deadlifts), and body-weight movements like pushups, pull-ups, lunges, jumps, and burpees.[83] Implements incorporated into the workouts run the gamut from barbells, to dumbbells, to kettlebells, to tires, to monkey bars, to parallel bars, and to gymnastic rings. Like Arthur Jones' Nautilus circuit (or a Windship or Butler training session in the 1860s) one of the primary appeals of CrossFit is its relatively short but intense workout.[84]

CrossFit employs gymnastic and weight-lifting movements that have their roots in German gymnastic programs and some of the earliest contested barbell lifts. Functional programs seek to incorporate exercises that mimic activities of daily life, just as Dudley Allen Sargent did in the design of pulley machines that mimicked chopping, rowing, and sawing. Similarly, just as Sargent redesigned his pulleys to allow deconditioned individuals to train for strength, commercial gyms will always contain some machines as a point of entry for deconditioned or unskilled individuals.

Contemporary gyms are, therefore, a combination of modernity and nineteenth-century training methods. Although rows of treadmills and other cardiovascular equipment have video touchscreens that transport the user along mountain trails or plant them in the Tour de France route with pace riders, those runners and riders are sharing gym floor space with platforms holding Olympic barbells, kettlebells, Indian clubs, and medicine balls. If the IBIS World industry report is correct and the manufacture of exercise equipment exists in a phase of decline and "there will not be any new innovations," in the near future, it seems only reasonable to look toward the past for new inspiration. Perhaps Dr. Windship's Health Lift will be next to make a comeback.[85]

Notes

1 Thomas Wentworth Higginson, "Gymnastics," *Atlantic Monthly* 7 (March 1861): 289.

2 Ibid.

3 Ibid. Pemmican was concentrated food developed by Native Americans made of fat, dried meat, and berries.

4 Clifford Putney, *Muscular Christianity: Manhood and Sports in Protestant America, 1880–1920* (Cambridge, MA: Harvard University Press, 2001); William J. Baker, *Playing with God: Religion and Modern Sport* (Cambridge, MA: Harvard University Press, 2009); Linda J. Borish, "The Robust Woman and the Muscular Christian: Catharine Beecher, Thomas Higginson, and Their Vision of American Society, Health, and Physical Activities," *The International Journal of the History of Sport* 4 (September 1987): 139–154.

5 Higginson, "Gymnastics," 289–292; Jan Todd, *Physical Culture and the Body Beautiful: Purposive Exercise and the Lives of American Women, 1800–1870* (Macon: Mercer University Press, 2008); Peter Goheen, "Industrialization and the Growth of Cities in Nineteenth-Century America," *American Studies* 14, no. 1 (Spring 1973): 49–65.

6 "2015 Health Club Consumer Report." www.ihrsa.org/news/2015/9/28/ihrsa-releases-2015-health-club-consumer-report-the-story-be.html

7 Kimberly Beckwith, "Building Strength: Alan Calvert, The Milo Bar-Bell Company, and the Modernization of American Weight Training" (PhD. Diss., University of Texas at Austin, 2006); John D. Fair, *Muscletown USA: Bob Hoffman and the Manly Culture of York Barbell* (University Park, PA: Pennsylvania State University Press, 1999); Ellen Roney Hughes, "Machines for Better Bodies: A Cultural History of Exercise Machines in America, 1830–1950" (PhD. Diss., University of Maryland at College Park, 2001); and Carolyn Thomas de la Pena, *The Body Electric: How Strange Machines Built the Modern American* (New York: New York University Press, 2003). See also Jan Todd, "The Strength Builders: A History of Barbells, Dumbbells and Indian Clubs," *The International Journal of the History of Sport* 20, no. 1 (2003): 65–90; Shelly McKenzie, *Getting Physical: The Rise of Fitness Culture in America* (Lawrence, KS: University Press of Kansas, 2013).

8 Benjamin Franklin to his son, August 19, 1772, quoted in Albert Henry Smyth, ed., *The Writings of Benjamin Franklin, Vol. 5* (New York: 1905–07), 411–412.

9 Todd's *Physical Culture and the Body Beautiful* is a history of these early systems.

10 Charles Beck, *A Treatise on Gymnastics, Taken Chiefly from the German of F.L. Jahn*, (Northampton, MA: Simeon Butler, 1828), 123–124.

11 Thomas Wentworth Higginson, "Saints and Their Bodies," *Atlantic Monthly* 1 (March 1858): 84.

12 Higginson, "Gymnastics," 289.

13 Higginson is wrong about Montgomery's first name. See "Young America: Mr. Montgomery in His Exercises with the Dumb Bells," *New York Clipper*, 17 May 1856.

14 Higginson, "Gymnastics," 289. Windship's dumbbell lifts are described in "Physical Education," *Honolulu Polynesian*, July 14, 1860.

15 Jan Todd, "Strength Is Health": George Barker Windship and the First American Weight Training Boom," *Iron Game History: The Journal of Physical Culture* 3, no. 1 (September 1993): 3–14; Joan Paul, "The Health Reformers: George Barker Windship and Boston's Strength Seekers," *Journal of Sports History* 10 (Winter 1983): 41–57.

16 John Thorne, William J. Ryczek, and Peter Morris, "Lives of the Knickerbockers: Lesser Known Members of Baseball's Pioneer Club," *Base Ball: A Journal of the Early Game* 6, no. 2 (Fall 2012): 102–131.

17 "Charles F. Ottignon's Sparring Academy, 58 West 30th St, New York," *Circa 1845. Original at the City Museum of New York.* http://collections.mcny.org/Collection/Charles-F.-Ottignon's-Sparring-Academy,-58-West-30th-St,-New-York.-2F3XC5N5DC_B.html
18 "New York City: Gymnastics—The Advantages of Physical Training," *New York Times*, October 15, 1852. See also "New York City—Meeting of the Gymnasts," *New York Times*, April 15, 1853.
19 "Young America: Mr. Montgomery."
20 "Notice: Ottignon's Gymnasium," *New York Daily Tribune*, May 10, 1856.
21 "Young America: Mr. Montgomery."
22 "Miscellany: Strong Men," *New York Daily Reformer* (Waterton, NY), August 8, 1865, 1. Montgomery moved to Albany in either 1859 or 1860 where he worked as a postal clerk and managed the Albany gymnasium and he drifted away from public exhibitions. See *Albany Directory for The Year 1860.* www.mocavo.com/The-Albany-Directory-for-the-Year-1860-Containing-a-General-Directory-of-the-Citizens-a-Business-Directory-and-Other-Miscellaneous-Matter-Volume-1860/240635/186
23 See Ed James, *Practical Training for Running, Walking, Rowing, Wrestling, Boxing, Jumping and All Kinds of Athletic Feats* (New York: Ed James Publishing, 1877), 70; William Wood, *Manual of Physical Exercises, Comprising Gymnastics, Calisthenics, Rowing, Sailing, Skating, Swimming, Fencing, Sparring, Cricket, Base Ball. Together with Rules for Training and Sanitary Suggestions, Vols. 1 and 2* (New York: Harper & Brothers, 1867), 310.
24 "William Wood Dead: Had Trained Many Athletes," *New York Times*, September 22, 1900.
25 For a discussion of the bachelor subculture, see Elliott Gorn, *The Manly Art: Bareknuckle Prize Fighting in America* (Ithaca, NY: Cornell University Press, 1986), 141–142. See also "William Wood Dead." Wood's obituary states that his first gym was named Wood's and Attington's Gym. This is undoubtedly a misprint because no information on Attington has been found by the authors although there are numerous references to Ottignon. See "Bodily Exercise the Best Medicine: Ottignon and Montgomery's Gymnasium," *American Phrenological Journal* 25 (September 1857): 71; and H. Wilson (Compiler), *Trow's New York City Directory for the Year Ending May 1, 1859* (New York: John F. Trow's Publisher, 1859), 620.
26 "William Wood Dead."
27 Webster, *Iron Game*, 27–28.
28 Louis Moore, "Black Sparring Masters, Gymnasium Owners, and the White Body, 1825–1886," *Journal of African American History* 96, no. 4 (Fall 2011): 448–473.
29 Ibid., 466–469.
30 Photograph by George Kendall Warren in *Harvard Class of 1865 Photographic Year Book. Harvard College Photographs* (Cambridge, MA: Harvard University, 1865), 71.
31 "Physical Education," *Honolulu Polynesian.*
32 Webster, *Iron Game*, 27.
33 Ed James, *Practical Training for Running, Walking, Rowing*, etc. (New York: Ed James, 1877), 70; Jan Todd, "Strength Is Health: George Barker Windship and the First American Weight Training Boom," *Iron Game History* 3 (September 1993): 3–14.
34 Todd, "Strength Is Health," 8–9; George Barker Windship, "Autobiographical Sketches of a Strength-Seeker," *Atlantic Monthly* 9 (January 1862): 104.
35 Todd, *Physical Culture and the Body Beautiful*, 189–194.
36 Ibid., 195–198.
37 Patent #28505, Dumb-Bells, 29 May 1860, Daniel F. Savage, Boston, MA, United States Patent and Trademark Office (USPTO). www.uspto.gov/patft/index.html
38 Patent #46413, Improvement in Graduated Dumb-Bells, February 14, 1865, George B. Windship, Boston, MA. USPTO. www.uspto.gov/patft/index.html
39 "The Patent Graduating Dumb-Bell" [Advertising broadside] George Barker Windship Collection, Massachusetts Historical Society, Boston, MA; The first European plate-loaded equipment the authors have seen dates from 1889.
40 Todd, "Strength Builders," 83; Webster, *Iron Game*, 31. See also *Peck and Snyder Price List of Out & Indoor Sport and Pastimes* (New York: Peck and Snyder, 1886); *The 1902 Edition of the Sears and Roebuck Catalogue* reprint ed. (Avenal, NJ: Gramercy Press, 1993).
41 Beckwith, "Building Strength," 104–143.
42 Todd, "Strength Builders," 85.

43 Ibid.
44 Ibid.; Webster, *Iron Game*, 75.
45 Todd, "Strength Seekers," 85.
46 James Chiosso, *The Gymnastic Polymachinon* (New York: H. Balliere, 1855), 9.
47 David P. Butler recommended starting all workouts with pulley exercise. Todd, "Strength Is Health," 5.
48 Quoted in Todd, "Strength Is Health," 6.
49 Hughes, "Machines for Better Bodies," 249
50 L. Sargent, ed., *Dudley Allen Sargent: An Autobiography* (Philadelphia: Lea & Febiger, Philadelphia, 1927), 59.
51 Carolyn de la Pena, "Dudley Allen Sargent: Health Machines and the Energized Male Body," *Iron Game History: The Journal of Physical Culture* 8, no. 2 (October 2003): 4–6.
52 L. Sargent, ed., *Dudley Allen Sargent: An Autobiography*, 59, 93–95.
53 Ibid., 146.
54 Hughes, "Machines for Better Bodies," 257.
55 Sargent, *Dudley Allen Sargent*, 182.
56 de la Pena, "Dudley Allen Sargent," 8.
57 Hughes, "Machines for Better Bodies," 264, 267.
58 Sargent, Autobiography of *Dudley Allen Sargent*, 197, 199, 206.
59 de la Pena, "Dudley Allen Sargent," 14; Jack Berryman, *Out of Many, One: A History of the American College of Sports Medicine* (Champaign, IL: Human Kinetics, 1995), 4.
60 R. Tait McKenzie, *Exercise in Education and Medicine* (Philadelphia, PA: Saunders, 1923), 365.
61 B.H.B Lange, "How to Use a Gymnasium," *Strength*, February 1922, 27.
62 Mark H. Berry, *Physical Improvement Volume I: Exercises* (Philadelphia, PA: Milo Publishing, 1930).
63 Fair, *Muscletown USA*, 23–38. There was a sharp decline in patents according to Hughes, "Machines for Better Bodies," 288.
64 Ibid.
65 Fair, *Mr. America*, 73.
66 Peary Rader, "Get Those Pulley Weights Up," *Iron Man*, March 1946, 28–29.
67 Joseph Weider, "Fay's Fitness Studio of Health," *Your Physique*, January 1947, 10–11, 47. See also Peary Rader, "Editorial—Physical Culture as a Profession," *Iron Man*, July 1944, 3, 22–23.
68 Rader, "With Our P.C. Studios," 15.
69 Jonathan Black, *Making the American Body: The Remarkable Saga of the Men and Women Whose Feats, Feuds, and Passions Shaped Fitness History* (Lincoln, NE: University of Nebraska Press, 2013), 35–40; E.M. Orlick, "Vic Tanny, the Gym King of America," *Muscle Builder*, May 1958, 14–17, 32–35.
70 Orlick, "Vic Tanny," 34.
71 Thomas Buckley, "State Is Studying Vic Tanny Losses," *New York Times*, December 11, 1963, 1, 53; Roach, *Muscle, Smoke, and Mirrors*, 114; Black, *Making the American Body*, 35–40.
72 Mary Rourke, "Harold Zinkin, 82; Muscle Beach Pioneer Invented Weight Machine," *Los Angeles Times*, 24 September 2004.
73 "Universal Spartacus," *Scholastic Coach*, September 1974, 66.
74 Rourke, "Harold Zinkin, 82; Muscle Beach Pioneer."
75 Harold Zinkin, *Remembering Muscle Beach* (Los Angeles: Angel City Press, 1999), 20.
76 Arthur Jones, "The Total Omni-Directional Direct Exercise System: A Totally New Concept in Exercise and Equipment," *Iron Man*, September 1970, 30–32.
77 Arthur Jones, *Nautilus Training Principles: Bulletin No. 1* (Deland, FL: Arthur Jones Productions, 1970); Arthur Jones, *Nautilus Training Principles: Bulletin No. 2* (Deland, FL: Arthur Jones Productions, 1971).
78 Bill Pearl, "Arthur Jones: An Unconventional Character," *Iron Game History: The Journal of Physical Culture* 8, no. 4 (March 2005): 17–22.
79 "The Rise of the Machines," *New York Times*, September 2, 2007.
80 Howard Reich, "'Assembly Line' Physical Fitness Is a Draw at Area Nautilus Centers," *Chicago Tribune*, March 15, 1978, 5–3.

81 Benjamin Rader, "The Quest for Self-Sufficiency and the New Strenuosity: Reflections on the Strenuous Life of the 1970s and the 1980s," *Journal of Sport History* 18, no. 2, (Summer 1991): 255–266. See also "Rise of the Machines."

82 Stephanie Cooperman, "Getting Fit, Even If It Kills You," *New York Times*, December 22, 2005, G1; Cynthia Billhartz Gregorian, "Only the Fittest Survive," *St. Louis Post-Dispatch* (Missouri), September 10, 2007, H1.

83 Rebecca Dube, "No Puke, No Pain—No Gain," *The Globe and Mail (Toronto)*, January 11, 2008, L2.

84 Jill Barker, "CrossFit Is Fast and Furious," *The Gazette (Montreal)*, February 14, 2006, D4.

85 Black, *Making the American Body*, 154.

27

SPORT TRAINING, SPORT SCIENCE, AND TECHNOLOGY

Amanda N. Schweinbenz

Introduction

The motto for the modern Olympic Games is "Citius, Altius, Fortius; Faster, Higher, Stronger." The phrase conjures up images of an athlete sprinting down a track or a high jumper leaping through the air, or a weight lifter pressing a weighted barbell over their head. But behind these successes lay thousands of hours of training integrated with the most up-to-date technology and sport science. Athletes' bodies serve as objects to be scrutinized, tested, and evaluated. They are poked, prodded, measured, and tested constantly in order to optimize their training and ultimately their performance in order to win.

Because of the desire to win, athletic practices and training methods have dramatically changed since the inception of the modern Olympic Games in 1896. Athletes have become bigger, faster, and stronger as a result of intense training that has been specifically designed through sport science. It is no longer enough for an athlete to train a few times a week or even once per day. Rather, elite athletes will often train 30 hours per week, three to even four times per day. Training quality, intensity, and volume are strictly monitored by coaches and sport scientists to ensure that each athlete is meeting specified targets. Maguire has argued that sport scientists are "the technicians, and the athletes the cogs, in the machine" driven to win Olympic medals.[1] The athlete has become an efficient machine that has been medicalized and scientized, and laboratories around the world are in search of the "Holy Grail" that will produce optimal performance.[2] As Borish has explained, "sport in America expresses and constructs cultural meanings" and the athletic body serves as an important part.[3] We understand this meaning through material life—routines and processes that shape how Americans culturally construct their daily lives. Athletic excellence is an important part of American culture and as such, we must examine the material details affiliated.

Within minutes of waking in the morning, high-performance athletes immediately check their resting rate, check the app on their phone to see their previous night's sleep patterns, weight is checked, and in the morning sample urine is submitted to assess hydration levels. Throughout the day food is measured, weighted, and checked to see if it meets daily required caloric and nutrition requirements. A global positioning system (GPS) and heart rate monitor are worn, and blood is drawn to accurately account for the duration, intensity, and mileage of the day's training. Speed, strength, endurance, flexibility, and power are all routinely tested and measured against standards and norms specified for each sport. Nothing is left to chance, especially when you are in the hunt for athletic excellence. When did sport become so complicated? When did sport become so scientific?

This is not to say that sport science is new to the twenty-first century. Since the Ancient Games at Olympia, humans have tried to "strengthen their bodies through the intake of fortifying substances."[4] The use of oils, smelling salts, elixirs, etc., has been used to provide an athletic advantage over one's opponents. Although many might believe that the East Germans introduced ergogenic aids to sport, it was a common practice in Ancient Greece. Experts at Yale University experimented with various diets for its football players in the late nineteenth century;[5] hence, the training table was established. Amphetamine was first synthesized in 1887 by Lazăr Edeleanu, "simultaneously with the isolation of ephedrine."[6] Stimulants became commonly consumed in the last third of the nineteenth century, including strychnine, caffeine, alcohol, heroin, and even cocaine. Cyclists and endurance athletes believed that by ingesting these substances they could improve their performance. For example, at the 1904 Olympic Games in St. Louis, American athlete Thomas Hicks, the winner of the marathon, received injections of strychnine and drank brandy during his race to give him an advantage over his competitors.[7]

However, it was the politics of the Cold War that brought the importance of sport science into the forefront and forced the developed world to reconsider how to gain advantage in sport. Current training methods, physiological testing and measuring, coaching techniques, and sport technology, including doping methods, were revolutionized by the small former Eastern Bloc nations and now affect how high-performance and everyday people engage in sport and physical activity.

East German Sporting Machine

It was the potential to use international sporting achievement as a vehicle to communicate state ideology at home and on an international basis that took precedence in Eastern Bloc nations.[8] As Dennis observed, the successes in international competition and a high level of popular participation in sport were intended to demonstrate the superiority of the socialist system over capitalism.[9] Specifically, communist leaders regarded sport as a way to demonstrate the superiority of their ideology over leading capitalist nations, particularly the United States.[10] The regulation of sport received high priority in Eastern Bloc nations, and federal governments took it upon themselves to amply fund competitive sport during the Cold War. The German Democratic Republic (DDR, GDR in English) developed a centralized governmental bureaucracy that invested 2 billion American dollars a year into sport.[11] This was a staggering amount compared to its Western counterpart, the Federal Republic of Germany (FRD), a country that was four times the size of the GDR and spent a mere 70 million on sport each year.[12]

Sports doctors and sports scientists were central to the GDR's state-sanctioned sporting machine. Research was dedicated to developing advanced equipment and training and testing methods that would optimize each athlete's performance. Athletes within the system had their VO_{2max}, blood lactate thresholds, VO_2 kinetics, force production, strength endurance, flexibility, and anaerobic power and capacity, as well as body composition, all tested to ensure that the training plans prescribed were meeting the sport-specific requirements. During the 1960s through 1980s, access to these types of tests was a luxury for most Olympic hopefuls in North America, yet it was standard for all athletes in East Germany. The costs of these tests was often prohibitive for amateur athletes throughout most of the world, and only those who were deemed worthy of physiological testing (typically athletes who were on the verge of winning a gold medal) even had access to exercise physiologists and sport scientists.

Scientific testing on athletes was a major part of the state-run sports machine during the Cold War, but it was the initial talent identification process that laid the foundation for targeted athlete success. State sport representatives were assigned to visit schools and performed a series of anthropometric tests and measurements on young children. Sport historian Arndt Krüger has indicated that the scientific process of talent identification that was used in the GDR after 1968 was "the same anthropometric procedures developed by the [Nazi] racial scientists prior to 1945."[13] And it was the success of these early sport scientists that has motivated current talent identification programs across the world. The East German data have formed the basis for many of the current Western forms of athlete talent identification, testing the physiological characteristics of potential elite athletes.[14] The premise used by most countries worldwide is simple: "identify exceptionally gifted athletes at an early age so as to focus available resources on particularly promising individuals and to promote their development in a certain sport."[15] The top athletes in each sport have specific physiological characteristics. If these athletes follow a prescribed training and development regimen, they have the potential to become the best athletes in the world. For example, the ideal male rower is over six feet five inches tall, with a positive arm span (longer than their height), and has a strong cardiovascular capability and excellent strength. If a coach finds one of these athletes, this does not mean that he is guaranteed to win an Olympic gold medal, but it does mean that he has a physiological advantage over rowers who are only six feet tall.[16] Research has shown that current forms of talent identification are largely used by nations with relatively smaller populations, including Australia as they are attempting to access a small pool of gifted athletes. Whereas the United States has a large population and therefore national sport federations do not engage in the same forms of athlete identification.[17]

At a time when female athleticism was largely marginalized in the West, young girls and women were central to the development of the Eastern Bloc sporting machine, revolutionizing women's high-performance sport. Pfister has argued that "above all it was the top performances achieved by women, 'the diplomats in tracksuits,' that brought to the GDR the prestige of a world-class sports nation."[18] Female athletes made up a large proportion of communist teams compared to their Western counterparts. Riordan has noted:

> At the 1976 Olympics in Montreal, for example, Soviet sportswomen made up over a third (35%) of the Soviet team (overall women comprised 20.58% of all competitors) and contributed 36 of the 125 Soviet medals (almost 30%). The women of East Germany made up 40% of the GDR team and won more than half their team's gold and silver medals. By contrast, women comprised just over a quarter (26%) of the United States contingent, or 112 out of 425 competitors. British and West German women comprised slightly over a fifth (20.6% and 21% respectively) of their nation's teams; and French women less than a fifth (18.3%) of theirs.[19]

Eastern Bloc female athletes were expected to train like their male counterparts, a concept not prescribed or adhered to in the West. Eastern Bloc female bodies were in service of the nation; it was more important to lift weights than wear makeup. As such, the narrow Western definition of heterosexual femininity did not apply to these female athletes. This is not to suggest that their athletic experiences were unproblematic or that they were not objectified by the state. Rather, their bodies were used to reflect the strength and dominance of the state, and they promoted a different type of athletic womanhood. One East German sports official, Otto Schmidt, commented that "while other nations can produce men's teams as good as, if not better than ours, we beat them overall because they are not tapping the full potential of their women."[20]

These tactics revolutionized women's competitive international sport. Female athletes were now expected worldwide to be strong and athletic. Medical discourse historically argued that women are physiologically inferior to men and as such athletic performance should be restricted and monitored to prevent injury and disability.[21] Yet, Eastern Bloc nations provided very clear evidence that women proved in fact capable of enduring the requirements of high-performance training. If female athletes expressed a desire to win, female athletes were now required to adhere to training regimens that had previously been reserved for men. The myth of the fragile female body was certainly being debunked.

Doping

It was not only the state-of-the-art training regimens and testing measures that catapulted the East Germans to the top of the international sporting podium. As has been well documented, methodical doping measures fueled this emphasis on representing the nation. It is estimated that upwards of 10,000 East German athletes were given banned performance-enhancing substances to improve their athletic performances.[22] This state-sanctioned program, formally known as State Plan 14.25, revolutionized doping in sport.[23] For example, male hormones were injected into female athletes to increase their muscle power, thus improving performance. Chemists and sport scientists monitored urine samples to ensure that the drugs were "washed out" of the athletes' bodies before leaving for competition. The science was so advanced that chemists established masking agents prior to the implementation of any new performance-enhancing substance, a technique used even today.[24]

By the 1930s, amphetamines had replaced strychnine as a stimulant, but it was in 1935 when scientists were able to synthesize the hormone testosterone that sport performance enhancement changed.[25] Anabolic androgenic steroids, commonly referred to as "steroids," can be either naturally occurring, like testosterone, or synthetic, like danazol.[26] Anabolic steroids became an agent that supported the body's recovery after stress and exhaustion. It is not known when athletes first started using steroids to enhance their performance because testing did not become systematic for the International Association of Athletics (IAAF) until 1966 (although they had established antidoping regulations as early as 1928 but had no testing measures) and the Olympic Games in 1968. However, as early as 1954, former U.S. weightlifting coach Bob Hoffman reported that a Soviet colleague had informed him of the physiological benefits of athletes taking steroids. It has been argued that the athletes who benefit most from the use of steroids are those in power sports, primarily body builders and power lifters.[27]

In the two decades following World War II, synthetic analogs were designed to enhance the anabolic properties, and many U.S. patents were awarded to drug companies who established powerful synthetic testosterone used by elite athletes, including methandrostenolone to Ciba in 1959, oxymesterone to Farmitalia in 1960, and stanozolol to Sterling Drug in 1962.[28] Interestingly, although the drugs were clinically designed to promote protein anabolism without a strong androgenic effect, for example, reversing the catabolic state of severe burn patients or those with wasting diseases, their full potential was not realized and, as such, there remains a surplus of these steroids in the world.[29] The use of testosterone can provide a boost in performance if the right conditions are met, including proper diet and recovery; however, female athletes see a much greater benefit because they produce testosterone at a lower rate than men (0.1 to 0.4 mg per day vs. 3 to 7 mg per day).[30]

But it is not only steroids that are used to enhance performances. Chemists have broadened their scope and found alternative substances that can be used to target specific performance and training outcomes. For example, sprint athletes began using human growth hormone (hGH) to enhance their speed. hGH is a proteohormone that is secreted by the pituitary gland. When used by adults, hGH can help to decrease fat, increase power, and improve cardiovascular responses.[31]

For athletes in endurance sports, including cross-country skiing, cycling, distance running, biathlon, rowing, and triathlon, blood doping became a way to improve performance. Classical forms of blood doping included homologous or autologous blood transfusions. However, this became cumbersome, and sport scientists looked for more efficient ways to support endurance athletes' performances and thus erythropoietin (EPO) became the substance of choice.[32] Initial research on EPO dates back to the turn of the twentieth century, but in 1968 Goldwasser and Kung established a way to purify human EPO, and during the 1980s research at the Northwest Kidney Centers found a way to create a synthetic form of the natural human hormone.[33] EPO stimulates the growth of red blood cells and thus increases tissue oxygenation. With a half-life of six hours, EPO can clear the body within one to three days.[34] Although EPO was added to the banned substance list in 1990, there was no way to detect its use until 2000.

One of the issues related to doping is that testing lags behind the introduction of performance-enhancing substances. For many prohibited substances, there are masking agents. These drugs, including diuretics, epitestosterone, probenecid, and plasma expanders, are not considered performance-enhancing drugs. Their purpose, however, is to mask the administered doping agent. Athletes have gone to great lengths to prevent detection, including taking estrogen to "normalize" the increased levels of testosterone in the body, and those who want to prevent athletes from taking banned substances are constantly trying to find ways to detect those who intend to break the antidoping rules.

Arguably the most recognizable names related to doping in sport include Ben Johnson, Marion Jones, and Lance Armstrong. Johnson, the Canadian 100-meter sprinter who won gold at the 1988 Olympic Games in Seoul, South Korea, had his medal stripped after he tested positive for stanozolol.[35] The Canadian federal government established a commission to understand the prevalence of banned substance in sport, the Dubin Inquiry. Marion Jones was an incredible female athlete who won three golds and two bronze medals at the 2000 Olympic Games in Sydney, Australia. Jones was stripped of those medals and eventually went to prison, not for the use of performance-enhancing substances, but for lying to federal agents about her use of the illegal substances.[36] Jones was connected to the Bay Area Laboratory Co-operative (BALCO), when founder Victor Conte indicated that he had personally given the track star banned substances during the lead-up and throughout the 2000 Games.

Prior to 2012, Lance Armstrong was the American sports hero who beat cancer and won seven Tour de France titles between 1998 and 2005. Armstrong had long been accused of using banned substances, but he had always stated that he had never taken performance-enhancing substances. Yet, in 2013, after the United States Anti-Doping Agency (USADA) provided evidence that the cycling star had used banned substances throughout his cycling career, Armstrong admitted he had cheated. However, he argued that the culture of international cycling supported and reinforced the usage and that an athlete had to utilize performance-enhancing drugs to be competitive and ultimately win. It was argued by many that he was the ringleader of "the most sophisticated, professionalized and successful doping program that sport has ever seen."[37]

Sex Testing

An additional issue that arose out of the East German sporting machine was the concern over unfeminine-looking female athletes. East German and other Eastern Bloc female athletes dominated women's international sport throughout the 1970s and 1980s. Their strength and power were unmatched by their Western counterparts, which led to questions about the legitimacy of their femininity. Many observers were shocked by the physicality of the Eastern Bloc female competitors who appeared unconcerned with medical and aesthetic dogma that plagued Western women's sport participation throughout the Cold War period. Systematic sex testing of female athletes in international sport arose during the 1960s out of a contradiction: competitive sport for women had become more rigorous, which required female athletes to be stronger, faster, and increasingly more aggressive. Yet, at the same time these women were required to maintain their feminine appearance.[38] Those female athletes who excelled in sport were muscular and often times flat chested, and were targeted as sexually ambiguous.[39] Their bodies, although athletic and strong, did not conform to traditional heterosexist ideology. As such, competitors, sports officials, and the media questioned the eligibility of these apparently deviant athletes.

The Western print and television media feared that the superiority of female athletes from the Eastern Bloc ruined Western athletes' chances to win Olympic and world championship medals. They ridiculed the "strong Red ladies" and were instrumental in implying their deviance.[40] Western athletes were praised for their "good looks and charming ways," whereas competitors who opted to be "athletes first, girls second" were vilified for their "overdeveloped muscles and underdeveloped glands."[41] The media referred to Eastern Bloc female athletes as Amazons and frequently commented on their ambiguous sexual appearance. When successful Western female athletes, however, also possessed traditional masculine characteristics, Western journalists searched to find evidence of physical and/or social femininity as a means of justifying their "masculine physical ability."[42] The pervasive assumption that athletic excellence was incompatible with femininity was rampant. It was speculated that some Eastern Bloc female athletes were in fact men disguised as women. This form of questioning subliminally "symbolized the idea of male athletic superiority."[43]

This was not the first time that speculations over a female athlete's sex occurred at an international competition. At the 1932 Summer Olympic Games in Los Angeles, Polish sprinter Stanisława Walasiewicz, also known as Stella Walsh, won the women's 100-meter sprint and was poised to repeat her performance at the 1936 Games in Berlin, Germany. However, Helen Stephens of the United States bested Walsh in the final and captured Olympic gold in Berlin. Stephens' victory over Walsh proved a surprise to some, and her validity as a female competitor was questioned by the Polish track and field officials. As such, the American sprinter was forced to undergo sex testing to prove that she was in fact a woman. Ironically, after Walsh was murdered in 1980, her body was the subject of an autopsy and it was determined that she possessed both male and female genitalia, rendering her a "hermaphrodite," now known as intersex, which would have deemed her ineligible to compete as a woman in the Olympic Games.[44]

> The wide-spread concern that unfeminine female athletes dominated international sport prompted sport administrators to re-examine women's international sport competition. Lenskyj has stated: Clearly, sexual ambiguity, whether clinical or social, posed a threat to compulsory heterosexuality and male dominance.

> It is ironic, therefore, that subsequent developments in genetics and endocrinology reduced biological femininity to the single criterion of chromosomal count, while rendering the social and ethical questions increasingly complex.[45]

The intense rumors and rumblings about the "questionable" Eastern Bloc female athletes remained palpable, and those in decision-making positions in competitive international sport looked to the medical community to, as Ritchie argues, "delineate and contain female athletes' sex."[46] The legitimacy of the required medical certificates that had previously accompanied applications for competition were questioned when the visual appearance of some female athletes did not coincide with dominant hegemonic femininity.[47] In turn, medical research came to serve as the justification for this gendered social discourse, further reinforcing such notions as natural, biological "givens."

The emerging fields of genetics, endocrinology, physiology, and psychological sciences had experienced rapid change throughout the first half of the twentieth century, and many within these fields focused their research on explanations for sexual differences. In 1949, Western University researchers Murray L. Barr and Ewart G. Bertram published a paper that indicated that through the examination of cells of mature cats, they had identified sex chromatin—a substance made of DNA and protein—and concluded that this discovery now made it possible to determine the cellular sex of an adult individual.[48] In mammals, males are heterogametic (XY) and females are homogametic (XX). The heterochromatized X chromosome appears as darkly stained bodies attached to the nuclear membrane. These heterochromatin bodies, which later came to be known as Barr bodies, became easily detectable when in 1953 Keith Moore and Murray Barr devised what they determined to be a noninvasive method by which a chromosomal sex determination could be carried out from a skin biopsy in the human.[49] The oral mucosal smear test requires the scraping of the inside of an individual's cheek with a wooden spatula, and the obtained cells and saliva are spread on the surface of a clean dry slide.[50] A drop of stain is then placed on the center of the smear and the cell is visible under a microscope. It was argued that "[t]he chromosomal sex is perhaps closest to the 'true sex' of an individual."[51]

The IAAF and IOC were quick to reference this breakthrough research as a means of justification for the search of the "true" sex of competitors in women's events. However, the scientific community recognized that the Barr body test was problematic because of "errors of sex development" in some individuals.[52] Barr indicated in 1956 that "[c]ytological tests of sex have a useful role in indicating the presence of congenital error in sex development and in clarifying the nature of the abnormality."[53] Not surprisingly, those who have questionable or errors of sex development are pathologized and require diagnosis, treatment, and management, including individuals with gonadal dysgenesis, male pseudohermaphroditism, female pseudohermaphroditism, and true hermaphroditism. These people are found to be ill, wrong, out of order, and/or abnormal by the medical and scientific communities as they *suffer* from their sex afflictions rather than people who engage in a practice of self-determination and exercise autonomy.[54] Barr suggested that "[a] correct appraisal of the patient's status in early life, preferably within the first few months" and that surgical and hormonal treatment in infancy is desirable "before attitudes in the broad sexual sphere begin to develop" based on the external genitalia, which, he argued, "is the most important single guide to the more appropriate sex from the practical point of view."[55] What is interesting here is Barr's recognition of the cultural framing of sex and his steadfast commitment to assigning one's appropriate sex.

Despite Barr's early breakthroughs and development of buccal smear testing, international sport administrators did not immediately use this scientific evidence to form the basis for sex determination. Initially, the quest for sex determination in international sport focused on observable genitalia. Physicians identified "ladies" through a gynecological examine. Although scientific evidence showed that the presence of ambiguous external genitalia had the potential to lead to inaccurate sex determinations, this form of verification formed the basis for the first sex testing in competitive international sport. A panel of physicians required female athletes at the 1966 European track and field championships to undergo a complete gynecological examination. No thoughts occurred about the potential embarrassment that female competitors might experience or the ethical concern of systematically parading naked athletes before a panel of male "judges." Rather, male international sport officials justified their actions by arguing that they were protecting female athletes from those who would cheat and masquerade as women. Not until the 1968 Winter Games in Grenoble, France, was the buccal smear method of sex chromatin determination, or Barr body testing, introduced.

With the introduction of these tests, the female body served as an object for testing and measuring; a body with no rights. Between 1966 and 1999, all female athletes relinquished rights over their bodies when they signed the official waiver to compete at international competitions. In doing so, they agreed to subject themselves to doping control and gender verification. Failure to submit to testing resulted in an automatic positive result. Not surprisingly, the IOC publically claimed that female competitors willingly participated in the gender verification tests. "After having learned how simple the procedure is, the athletes submitted themselves to it with a smile."[56] The testing seemed so pleasant for the female competitors that the official report from the Albertville Games stated that the women enjoyed the atmosphere of the testing facilities and appreciated how the "centre was decorated."[57] The IOC consistently claimed that the tests did "not pose any major problem for the athletes" because of the medical commission's practices of confidentiality and respect for the "girls."[58] However, those who protested or questioned the validity of the process raised doubt about their own gendered identity. *True* women had no reason to question the tests and all *real* women submitted willingly. Once female athletes proved their chromosomal gender, the chair of the IOC Medical Commission gave them signed gender identity cards—this position has always been held by a white man.

By the 1990s, the medical community called not for the removal of gender verification testing, but rather a more accurate way to test one's sex. In 1991, the controversy regarding the barring of athletes from competition ultimately led to the IAAF removing mandatory and systematic sex testing in 1991. Finnish geneticist Albert De la Chapelle called for the IOC to remove all forms of sex testing or make significant revisions to its structure. The IOC's gender tests were implemented to detect and exclude male impostors or women who had conditions that caused masculine muscle development and therefore to confer a competitive advantage, and as such the sex chromatin test failed to serve the intended purpose. De la Chapelle argued that "women with certain congenital chromosome abnormalities and other abnormal conditions without increased muscle strength are found to have 'abnormal' sex chromatin" and the test failed to detect women with hormonal conditions that could give them a competitive advantage.[59] Clearly, the scientific community had begun to blur the definitions of gender and sex and use them interchangeably.

Indeed, the scientific community did not call for the removal of sex testing in the women's competitive international sport because it was humiliating, sexist, and degrading.

Rather, they called for better forms of testing that would be more accurate. It was even suggested that

> If the Medical Commission of the International Olympic Committee had wanted to please everyone, it is quite possible that several Olympic Games would have to be held to accommodate the different chromosomic groups. At such extremes, it would have been forgotten that the purpose of the Medical Commission of the International Olympic Committee is an investigation of femininity in order to establish equality among athletes in competition.[60]

For the IOC, "The issue of gender verification . . . [was] not at stake."[61] The IOC made the decision to continue sex testing, and vowed to improve "its reliability . . . Because this test is likely to deter anybody tempted to cheat . . . [and] is welcomed by athletes."[62] In 1999, the IOC formally removed sex testing for all female competitors from the Olympic Games. Now, however, female athletes must undergo sex testing if another competitor, coach, training, or official questions their validity.

The Modern Witch Hunt for Femininity

At the 2009 International Association of Athletics Federation (IAAF) Championships in Berlin, Germany, South African track sensation Caster Semenya eclipsed the field by winning the women's 800-meter race in a time of 1:55.45, more than two seconds faster than her competitors. Although her time was slower than the world record of 1:53.28, Semenya did post the fastest time of the year for this event. The 18-year-old crossed the line, caught her breath, flexed her biceps, and grabbed the South African flag to run her victory lap. When the television broadcast announcer claimed "we'll be hearing a lot more about her no doubt," he had no idea the media frenzy that was to erupt.[63]

Until the summer of 2009, no one had ever heard of this track star from Petrolia, South Africa. In June the 18-year-old won the African junior track and field championships, finishing in a time that was faster than any junior or senior runner that year. While her performance alone would have set off warning bells in Monaco, it was her physical appearance that alarmed international athletics officials. Semenya's ripped abs, muscular arms, narrow waist, deep voice, and chiseled jaw do not fit into heterosexist notions of appropriate femininity. Rather than have Semenya submit to doping control, IAAF officials requested that the South African athletics association begin the process of "gender verification." [64] IAAF spokesperson Nick Davies reassured the media that the international track and field federation was not suggesting that Semenya was a man masquerading as a woman, but that "she could suffer from a genetic disorder."[65]

Over the next 11 months, Semenya was subjected to numerous genetic and gynecological exams, all under the watchful eye of the international media. The public learned from the IAAF spokesperson that the testing that Semenya would undergo was extensive and would begin with a visual evaluation by a physician. In addition, "There is chromosome testing gyneacological investigation, all manner of things, organs, X-rays, scans . . . It's very, very comprehensive."[66] During the investigation, the IAAF banned Semenya from competition until she had been officially cleared to compete in women's events. No one could explain why the process took 11 months, but there was speculation that the IAAF was procrastinating and trying to avoid "dealing" with the case. It was even reported that Semenya had undergone medical treatment to "resolve her gender issue" and treat her "condition."[67]

> When the international track and field federation cleared the South African teen for competition, their press release read: The process initiated in 2009 in the case of Caster Semenya (RSA) has now been completed. The IAAF accepts the conclusion of a panel of medical experts that she can compete with immediate effect. Please note that the medical details of the case remain confidential and the IAAF will make no further comment on the matter.[68]

The assumption was made that because the sports federation refrained from commenting on the results of the tests that they respected the rights and privacy of the young track star. The sports federation provided no consideration, however, for the emotional and psychological trauma that Semenya had experienced during the 11-month ordeal; no apology from the media for terrorizing her, her friends, family, and colleagues in an attempt to garner the "truth"; nor was there recognition of the objectification she had endured. Her body had served as the object of scrutiny, testing, and evaluation because it did not conform to hegemonic feminine discourse. This young, athletic, strong female athlete performed fast, but too fast to be a woman.

Conclusion

Science and technology are intended to make aspects of our lives better. Within the world of sport, technology has created rubber balls and lighter poles and javelins, as well as faster and lighter hulls for boats and more buoyant suits for swimmers. We now have electronic timing, indoor artificial ice, domed stadiums, and instant replays. All of these technological inventions have helped to develop and enhance sport. Athletes can now throw farther, run faster, jump higher, swim faster, lift heavier weights, play a longer season, and achieve their optimal performance. However, with technological advances come consequences. Arguably, the age of a linear representation of performance improvement has come to an end and

> future limits to athletic performance will be determined less and less by innate physiology of the athlete, and more and more by scientific and technological advances and by the still evolving judgment on where to draw the line between what is 'natural' and what is artificially enhanced.[69]

Additionally, science is now being used to challenge ethical issues in sport, challenging what is natural and what is artificial. Sport scientists work endlessly to find ways to enhance an athlete's body within, and sometimes outside of, the rules and create advantages over competitors. In order to achieve athletic success at the international level, can an athlete ever rely on their own natural athletic abilities?

What is even more interesting is that this desire to optimize one's performance has extended beyond elite and professional athletes to less skilled everyday participants. Any individual can purchase a heart rate monitor, lactate testing strips, or GPS, and now cellular phones not only come with these capabilities but also apps to monitor and track daily performance and provide feedback. Is sport actually organic now? Are we all now striving for faster, higher, stronger?

Notes

1 Joseph Maguire, "Challenging the Sports—Industrial Complex: Human Sciences, Advocacy and Service," *European Physical Education Review* 10, no. 3 (2004): 300.
2 Ibid., 301–302.
3 Linda J. Borish, "Women at the Modern Olympic Games: An Interdisciplinary Look at American Culture," *Quest* 48, no. 1 (1996): 43.
4 Verner Møller, "Science and Technology," in *Routledge Companion to Sports History*, ed. S.W. Pope and John Nauright (London: Routledge, 2010), 188.
5 See Gerald R. Gems, *For Pride, Profit, and Patriarch: Football and the Incorporation of American Cultural Values* (New York: Scarecrow Press, 2000); Ronald A. Smith, *Sports & Freedom: The Rise of Big-time College Athletics* (New York: Oxford University Press, 1988).
6 Rudhard Klaus Müller, "History of Doping and Doping Control," in *Doping in Sport*, ed. D. Thieme and P. Hemmersbach (Heidelberg: Springer-Verlag, 2010), 5.
7 Terry Todd, "Anabolic Steroids: The Gremlins of Sport," *Journal of Sport History* 14, no. 1 (Spring 1987): 87–107.
8 Tara Magdalinski, "Sports History and East German National Identity," *Peace Review* 11, no. 4 (1999): 539–545.
9 M. Dennis, "Sport: GDR," in *Encyclopaedia of Contemporary German Culture*, ed. T. Dennis (London: Routledge, 1999), 576.
10 James Riordan, "The Rise, Fall and Rebirth of Sporting Women in Russia and the USSR," *Journal of Sport History* 18, no. 1 (Spring 1991): 194.
11 Allen Guttmann, *Sports: The First Five Millennia* (Massachusetts: University of Massachusetts Press, 2004), 303.
12 Ibid., 302.
13 Arnd Krüger, "Breeding, Rearing and Preparing the Aryan Body: Creating Superman the Nazi Way," in *Shaping the Superman: Fascist Body as Political Icon*, ed. J.A. Mangan (London: Frank Cass, 1999), 44.
14 See www.teamusa.org/US-Paralympics/Gateway-to-Gold
15 Arne Güllich Vaeyens, Chelsea R. Warr, and Renaat Philippaerts, "Talent Identification and Promotion Programmes of Olympic Athletes," *Journal of Sports Sciences* 27, no. 13 (November 2009): 1367.
16 See www.rowtopodium.ca/try-out.html
17 Vaeyens, Warr, and Philippaerts, "Talent Identification and Promotion Programmes of Olympic Athletes."
18 Gertrud Pfister, "Sport for Women," in *Sport and Physical Education in Germany*, ed. Roland Naul and Ken Hardman, International Society for Comparative Physical Education and Sport Series (London: Routledge, 2002), 172.
19 James Riordan, "The Rise, Fall and Rebirth of Sporting Women in Russia and the USSR," *Journal of Sport History* 18, no. 1 (Spring 1991): 194.
20 James Riordan and Hart Cantelon, "The Soviet Union and Eastern Europe," in *European Cultures in Sport: Examining the Nations and Regions*, ed. James Riordan and Arndt Kruger (London: Intellect Books, 2003), 95.
21 Patricia Vertinsky, *The Eternally Wounded Woman* (Chicago, IL: University of Illinois Press, 1994).
22 G. Spitzer, "Ranking Number 3 in the World: How the Addition to Doping Changed Sport in GDR (East Germany)," in *Doping and Doping Control in Europe*, ed. Giselher Spitzer (Oxford: Cardinal Publishers Group, 2007), 57–77.
23 Ibid.
24 Paul Dimeo and Thomas M. Hunt, "The Doping of Athletes in the Former East Germany: A Critical Assessment of Comparisons with Nazi Medical Experiments," *International Review for the Sociology of Sport* 47, no. 5 (2011): 581–593.
25 Yesalis and Bahrke, "History of Doping in Sport."
26 David A. Baron, David M. Martin, and Samir Abol Magd, "Doping in Sports and Its Spread to at-Risk Populations: An International Review," *World Psychiatry* 6 (2007): 118–123.
27 John A. Geddes, "Anabolic Steroids and the Athlete," *Canadian Family Physician* 37 (April 1991): 981; see Todd, "Anabolic Steroids: The Gremlins of Sport," 87–107.

28 David A. Cowan and Andrew T. Kicman, "Doping in Sport: Misuse, Analytical Tests, and Legal Aspects," *Clinical Chemistry* 43, no. 7 (1997): 1110.
29 Ibid.
30 Andrew T. Kicman, "Biochemical and Physiological Aspects of Endogenous Androgens," in *Doping in Sports*, ed. Detlef Thieme and Peter Hemmersbach (Heidelberg: Spinger, 2010), 25–64.
31 Martin Bidlingmaier and Christian J. Strasburger, "Growth Hormone," in *Doping in Sports*, eds. Detlef Thieme and Peter Hemmersbach (Heidelberg: Spinger, 2010), 187.
32 Christian Reichel and Günter Gmeiner, "Erythropoietin and Analogs," in *Doping in Sports*, ed. Detlef Thieme and Peter Hemmersbach (Heidelberg: Spinger, 2010), 252.
33 J.W. Eschback, J.C. Egrie, M.R. Downing, J.K. Browne, and J.W. Adamson, "Correction of the Anemia of End-Stage Renal Disease with Recombinant Human Erythropoietin. Results of a Combined Phase I and II Clinical Trial," *New England Journal of Medicine* 316, no. 2 (January 1987): 73–78.
34 Françoise Bressolle, Michel Audran, Raynald Gareau, Roy D. Baynes, Claudette Guidicelli, and Roberto Gomeni, "Population Pharmacodynamics for Monitoring Epoetin in Athletes," *Clinical Drug Investigation* 14, no. 3 (1997): 233–242.
35 John Hoberman, *Hybrid Athletes, Monstrous Addicts, and Cyborg Natures* (New York: The Free Press, 1992).
36 Daniel A. Nathan, "The Finish Line," *Journal of Sport History* 36, no. 1 (Spring 2009): 77–82.
37 "Lance Armstrong: USADA Report Labels Him 'A Serial Cheat'" *BBC News*, October 11, 2012. www.bbc.com/sport/cycling/19903716 (accessed July 25, 2015).
38 M. Ann Hall, *The Girl and the Game: A History of Women's Sport in Canada* (Peterborough, ON: Broadview Press, 2002).
39 Jennifer Hargreaves, *Sporting Females: Critical Issues in the History and Sociology of Women's Sports* (London: Routledge, 1994), 222.
40 Susan Cahn, *Coming on Strong: Gender and Sexuality in Twentieth-Century Women's Sport* (Cambridge, MA: Harvard University Press, 1994), 210.
41 Ibid., 207.
42 Ibid., 211.
43 Hargreaves, *Sporting Females*, 222.
44 Amanda N. Schweinbenz and Alexandria Cronk, "Femininity Control at the Olympic Games," *Thirdspace: A Journal of Feminist Theory & Culture* 9, no. 2 (2010). http://journals.sfu.ca/thirdspace/index.php/journal/article/viewArticle/schweinbenzcronk/329 (accessed July 30, 2015).
45 Helen Lenskyj, *Out of Bounds: Women, Sport and Sexuality* (Toronto, ON: Women's Press, 1986), 87.
46 Ian Ritchie, "Sex Tested, Gender Verified: Modern Sport and the Construction of Sexual Difference" (Doctoral Diss., Bowling Green State University, 1996), 159.
47 Arne Ljungqvist, Maria José Martinez-Patino, A. Marinex-Vidal, Luisa Zagalaz, Pino Diaz, and Covadonga Mateos, "The History and Current Policies on Gender Testing in Elite Athletes," *International Sports Medicine Journal* 7, no. 3 (2006): 277.
48 Murray L. Barr and Ewart G. Bertram, "A Morphological Distinction between Neurons of the Male and Female, and the Behaviour of the Nucleolar Satellite During Accelerated Nucleoprotein Synthesis," *Nature* 163 (1949): 676–677.
49 Walter Herrmann and Anna Marie Davis, "The Determination of Chromosomal Sex by Oral Smears," *Yale Journal of Biology and Medicine* 29, no. 1 (1956): 70.
50 Ann R. Sanderson and John S. Stewart, "Nuclear Sexing with Aceto-Orcein," *British Medical Journal* 2 (1961): 1065–1067.
51 Walter Herrmann and Anna Marie Davis, "The Determination of Chromosomal Sex by Oral Smears," *Yale Journal of Biology and Medicine* 29 (2000): 69.
52 Murray L. Barr, "The Sex Chromatin and Its Bearing on Errors of Sex Development," *The Canadian Medical Association Journal* 74 (1956): 419.
53 Ibid.
54 Judith Butler, *Undoing Gender* (New York: Routledge/Psychology Press, 2004), 76.
55 Barr, "The Sex Chromatin and Its Bearing on Errors of Sex Development," 419.
56 International Olympic Committee, *Newsletter No. 5* (Lausanne: International Olympic Committee, February 1968).

57 Albertville Olympic Committee, *Report on the XVI Olympic Winter Games in Albertville* (Lausanne: International Olympic Committee, 1992), 306.
58 Ibid.
59 Albert de la Chapelle, "The Use and Misuse of Sex Chromatin Screening for 'Gender Identification' of Female Athletes," *Journal of American Medical Association* 256, no. 14 (1986): 120.
60 Eduardo Hay, "Sex Determination in Putative Female Athletes," *Journal of American Medical Association* 221, no. 9 (1972): 998.
61 Bernard Dingeon, P. Hamon, M. Robert, P. Schamasch, and M. Pugeat, "Sex Testing at the Olympics," *Nature* 358, no. 447 (1992): 447.
62 Ibid.
63 See Jaime Schultz, "Caster Semenya and the 'Question of Too': Sex Testing in Elite Women's Sport and the Issue of Advantage," *Quest* 63 (2011): 228–243.
64 Alastair Jamieson "Caster Semenya Gender Row: What Is a Hermaphrodite?" *The Telegraph*, August 20, 2009) (accessed May 5, 2011).
65 Ibid.
66 Christopher Glarey "Gender Test after a Gold-Medal Finish," *New York Times*, August 19, 2009, www.nytimes.com/2009/08/20/sports/20runner.html (accessed August 25, 2015).
67 "Caster Semenya: Anatomy of Her Case," *The Telegraph*, July 6, 2010 (accessed May 5, 2011).
68 IAAF, "Caster Semenya May Compete." www.iaaf.org/aboutiaaf/news/newsid=57301.html (accessed May 5, 2011).
69 Giuseppe Lippi, Giuseppe Banfi, Emmanuel J. Favaloro, Joern Rittweger, and Nicola Maffulli, "Updates on Improvement of Human Athletic Performance: Focus on World Records in Athletics," *British Medical Bulletin* 87 (2008): 14.

Part VII

SOCIAL MOVEMENTS AND POLITICAL USES OF SPORT

28

"FASTER, HIGHER, STRONGER"—AND MORE PATRIOTIC

American Olympic Narratives

Mark Dyreson, Tom Rorke, and Adam Berg

Introduction: Presidential Election Cycles and Olympic Quadrennials

Every four years since 1796 the United States holds a presidential election. Every four years since 1896 the International Olympic Committee (IOC) stages an Olympic spectacle, or at least a summertime athletic extravaganza.[1] That U.S. election cycles and Olympic quadrennials fall in the same year is purely coincidental. That presidential contenders frequently invoke American Olympians to polish their populist bona fides, illustrate key aspects of their platforms, and bask in the reflected glow of golden triumphalism is no accident. The incorporation of narratives about American Olympians into presidential combat underscores the power of sport in U.S. political discourse.

Presidential hopefuls did not seize on the promises of Olympian political bounces for their campaigns instantaneously. In 1896 when American athletes voyaged to Athens for the inaugural modern Olympics, Democrat William Jennings Bryan and Republican William McKinley did not make a single mention of the Olympic dramas that unfolded in Greece. When Bryan invoked his "cross of gold" in the most famous oratorical episode of the campaign he was not referring to a Muscular Christian vision of American triumphs in track and field at Athens but to his opposition to the gold standard in the U.S. financial system. Four years later in 1900 during a lopsided rematch in which McKinley again bested Bryan by an even greater margin, neither candidate referenced the sterling performances of American athletes competing at the second Olympics in Paris. Four years later in 1904, however, President Theodore Roosevelt—who assumed the presidency after an assassin's bullet felled McKinley—cheered St. Louis' staging of the Olympics at the city's world's fair. Roosevelt was the first president to understand the value of the Olympics as a prime opportunity to wrap his candidacy in patriotic symbolism and cheer American exceptionalism. Roosevelt corresponded with IOC chieftain Baron Pierre de Coubertin, who encouraged the president to go to the Olympics during Roosevelt's quest to win election to a second term. In spite of Roosevelt's intense Olympic ardor, he did not bother to visit the 1904 Olympics, although he sent his daughter Alice to St. Louis for campaign photo opportunities.[2]

By the election of 1908, with Roosevelt in action as a powerbroker rather than a candidate, the Olympics had become an important electoral battleground. In the summer of that year as the presidential referendum between Roosevelt's hand-picked successor William Howard Taft and the perennial Democrat runner-up Bryan, President Roosevelt invoked American athletes as proof of American exceptionalism during an acrimonious series of rows with the British hosts at the London Olympics. On their return from England Roosevelt invited the American team to his Oyster Bay, New York, retreat and saluted them in the national press while touting his hand-picked successor "Solid Bill" Taft in the pages of the same sporting magazine that featured tales of American Olympic fortitude against dastardly British villains.[3] By the presidential election of 1912 all three of the leading candidates, Democrat Woodrow Wilson, Republican incumbent "Solid Bill" Taft, and the disgruntled Bull Moose insurgent Roosevelt, felt compelled to make the valedictory telegrams that they sent to the American team steaming home from the Stockholm Olympics available to the American press in order to publically highlight their commitment to the squad as an emblem of national pride and prowess.[4]

Since then presidential candidates of all parties, ideologies, and positions have made themselves cheerleaders for American teams. Like kissing babies and asking people for money, extolling American Olympians as avatars of national values has become a required component of presidential campaigning. The canniest American presidents have used the Olympics to burnish their patriotic credentials while steering clear of the fatal shores of Olympic controversy. Franklin Delano Roosevelt in 1936 kept key constituencies of his base—urban Catholics, mainline Protestant progressives, and Jewish advocacy groups—at bay while he danced around calls to boycott Berlin's "Nazi" Olympics as a protest against Adolf Hitler's anti-Semitic policies.[5] Ronald Reagan in 1984, the first sitting president to attend an Olympics in person, managed to link the Los Angeles celebration to his theme of American revival while scrupulously avoiding entanglements in his home state's battles over public funding for the event.[6] In contrast, in 1980 President Jimmy Carter issued a January ultimatum calling for a boycott of the Moscow Olympics if the Soviet Union did not withdraw from its incursion into Afghanistan. Carter's action squandered his efforts to capitalize on the red, white, and blue afterglow generated a month later by the "Miracle on Ice," the stunning upset by the U.S. hockey team over the Soviet's Red Army squad at the Lake Placid Winter Games. Unpopular with the public and even more detested by American athletes who vocally denounced the president's Olympic embargo, Carter's incursion into Olympic politics added to his political problems as he sought unsuccessfully to earn a second term in the 1980 race against the more Olympic-savvy Reagan.[7]

Presidential candidates, who by necessity must be shrewd interpreters of American popular culture in order to be competitive in the quest for the White House, quickly learned that the modern Olympics generated powerful narratives of American nationalism. Ronald Reagan mastered this traditional electoral genre. A few weeks after he presided over the 1984 games in his adopted hometown of Los Angeles, Reagan concluded his acceptance speech of the Republican nomination to run for a second term with a sequence of sound bites evoking U.S. Olympians as icons of American exceptionalism. Playing off a "melting pot" riff in which he observed that 140 nations had competed in the Olympics against a United States composed of "bloodlines of all those 140 countries and more," Reagan marveled that "only in the United States is there such a rich mixture of races, creeds, and nationalities, only in our melting pot." Seeking votes to hold his office, Reagan concluded his nomination speech by converting the Olympic torch into "Miss Liberty's torch" atop the great statue in New York City's harbor, "the lamp beside the golden door."[8]

Olympic Narratives and American National Identity

Even before Reagan and a host of presidential contenders before him dating back to Theodore Roosevelt discovered the power of the Olympics in evoking nationalist sentiment in their quests for their country's highest office, the American media had already discovered that potential. More than a century later the Olympics rank by many measures as the most common "shared experience" on earth. More people tune into the fortnight-long contests of winter and summer spectacles than watch any other event on global television.[9] Audiences estimated as large as 5 billion watched the 2008 Beijing and 2012 London games. Around the globe World Cup soccer telecasts rate as an equal contender to the Olympics for the "shared experience" title but in the United States where soccer has historically been viewed as a "foreign" endeavor, the Olympics clearly represent the global event that interests Americans far more than any other. Although another sporting contest, the annual Super Bowl of American football, ranks at the top of national televised "shared experiences" in the United States, in terms of American interaction with the world, nothing else comes close to the Olympics.[10]

Indeed, historically the Olympics have been the one major conduit through which the United States has interacted with the rest of the globe in an international sporting culture. Most American national pastimes, particularly the three that rank at as the most popular in the United States, are relatively parochial. The rest of the world rarely plays and only occasionally watches the American variant of the football codes. Baseball and basketball have over the course of the last century expanded their global reach, but the focus in the United States remains on American versions of these sports. For fans in the United States the annual "World Series" between U.S. professional teams remains far more significant than any world championships cobbled together by sporting federations. Both "March Madness," the intercollegiate basketball championship tournament, and the finals of the U.S.-based National Basketball Association attract the ardor of American audiences far beyond the myriad of global basketball competitions that have sprung up recently.[11]

The only place that the United States measures itself against foreign rivals in sporting venues that truly engage the American public's sustained attention is at the Olympics. Curiously, the troika of U.S. national pastimes, American football, baseball, and basketball, play relatively minor roles on Olympic programs. American football has never been more than an esoteric exhibition sport in a couple of Olympics that the United States has hosted: St. Louis in 1904 and Los Angeles in 1932. Baseball has a checkered Olympic history, appearing as an exhibition several times, finally gaining medal status at Seoul in 1992 and then suffering an ignominious removal from the program in the early twenty-first century.[12] The United States pushed basketball onto the Olympic program in 1936 and has won 14 gold medals since. The handful of games (five) that the United States has lost have been treated as national humiliations inflicted, especially in the 1972 gold medal final against the Soviets, by conniving foreign cheaters.[13]

Even though sports that many Americans consider "minor" pastimes such as track and field, swimming, and gymnastics have been the centerpieces of the modern Olympics, Americans have been drawn to Olympian spectacles far more than any other international events. The first two modern games, in Athens in 1896 and in Paris in 1900, drew national media coverage and elite participation.[14] The 1904 St. Louis spectacle, the first on American soil, vastly expanded the mass appeal of the Olympics among the U.S. public.[15] Thereafter, American audiences consumed Olympian festivals through newspaper and magazine accounts, over the radio waves, via newsreel compendiums, and, beginning with the 1960 Olympic Winter Games in Squaw Valley, California, on television. In 1964 the American Broadcasting Corporation (ABC), the struggling third-place contender among the "big three" U.S. networks, acquired the rights to the Olympics and made them a staple of their sports coverage as ABC catapulted by the 1970s to the top of the ratings heap. ABC lost their Olympic monopoly in 1988 when the National Broadcasting Corporation (NBC) won the bid for the Seoul summer games. Since then, NBC has dominated Olympic telecasting in the U.S. market while reaping huge ratings for the events.[16]

The roots of the popular media spectacles that Americans voraciously consume stretch back to the 1890s. From the beginning, the United States became enmeshed in the Olympics to a greater degree than practically any international movement of the modern era.[17] American teams have been at every Olympics, with the exception of the 1980 Moscow games that the United States boycotted. The United States holds a commanding lead in the overall medal count tabulating performances from Athens in 1896 to Sochi in 2014, with 2,680 gold, silver, and bronze medals, more than double that of the second-place nation, the Soviet Union (with 1,204), a seemingly secure lead given the now-extinct former Soviet state will presumably garner no more Olympic titles.[18] The United States has also staged more Olympic spectacles than any other nation, a total of eight (four summer and four winter episodes). The next closest rival in hosting is France, with five games (two summer and three winter versions).[19]

The Olympics and American Engagement with the World

Since 1896 the modern Olympic movement has provided one of the most important locations for the United States to engage the world. The Olympics create an international space where nations measure themselves against rivals, develop narratives that express their identities, and develop relationships with other nations. Built on the foundation of the older world's fair movement that blossomed in the middle of the nineteenth century, the Olympics make the nation the primary vehicle of identity. Just as in the world's fair movement, the nation stands at the core of the Olympic movement, and nationhood develops not in isolation but in sharp relief against other nations.[20] At the Olympics, the United States has articulated and argued about competing visions of their own national identity, designed and implemented programs for "Americanizing" the Olympic movement, and collaborated with and confronted other nations as well as the transnational agency that has long governed the movement—the International Olympic Committee (IOC).

The modern Olympic movement emerged at the end of the nineteenth century as schemes for a regular set of international sporting contests swirled through the global press. None of the many plans came to fruition until a French aristocrat, the Baron Pierre de Coubertin, managed to organize the modern Olympics. Inspired in part by the Greek Olympics of antiquity, Coubertin and his supporters constructed a thoroughly modern spectacle that embraced both internationalist and nationalistic dimensions. Like the world's fairs that both inspired Coubertin's plans and provided early meeting grounds for his organizing efforts, the Olympics sought to include participants from every corner of the globe—though the West thoroughly dominated the early events. Like the world's fairs, the Olympics made the nation the fundamental unit of organization, ensuring that the metrics of national prowess predominated. Nationalism suffused Coubertin's professions of internationalism in another way as well. Terrified like many of his caste and generation that France was bound for global insignificance, he sought to restore his nation's former grandeur. The Anglo-American sporting habits that had blossomed during the nineteenth century seemed to Coubertin the perfect antidote to French declension. He sought to inoculate his own nation against cultural torpor by seducing France into falling in love with the competitive sports that Great Britain and the United States adored.[21]

In spite of Coubertin's ardor for their traditions, the British initially ignored Coubertin's festivals, though imperial dominions such as Australia and Canada regularly sent teams.[22] In contrast the United States became a crucial founding member of the Olympic movement. An American academic who taught French history at Princeton University, William Milligan Sloane, served as an original delegate to the IOC that Coubertin organized in 1894. Sloane organized an American contingent headlined by Princeton athletes to compete in the inaugural 1896 Olympics in Athens. When Americans dominated track and field contests at the Olympics the U.S. media hailed their victories as symbolic of the youthful vitality, democratic institutions, and egalitarian character of the republic, thus inaugurating a tradition of defining Olympic success as an element in the folklore of American exceptionalism. Whether or not such interpretations conformed to actual social conditions, they provided a foundation for using the Olympics to tout American nationalism.[23] As James Connolly, the first U.S. Olympic champion who later became an international correspondent who covered the games, frequently proclaimed, Americans won Olympic victories not because they possessed superior athletes, but because they had built a superior society.[24]

Forging American Identities at the Olympics

Since 1896 the strains of American exceptionalism have dominated expressions of U.S. nationhood in Olympic arenas. Early chroniclers dubbed U.S. teams "America's athletic missionaries," emblems of the republic who personified national vitality.[25] American teams became avatars of social promise, comprised in popular depictions of every social class, ethnic group, and religious affiliation—and, beginning in 1920s when women gained official entry into Olympic sport, of female as well as male "athletic missionaries." The dominant version of these portraits depicted American teams as embodiments of a harmonious "melting pot" that mixed blacks and whites, immigrants and the native-born, and rich and poor, into a world-beating coalition. For more than a century American interpreters of the Olympics have insisted that triumphs in these contests signify not merely athletic superiority, but also the preeminence of American social constellations over the rest of the globe's social structures.[26]

When in the early decades of the twentieth century the European press condemned American teams as collections of "immigrant mercenaries," their American counterparts heralded the ethnic and racial diversity of U.S. teams as proof that the United States was an unbeatable "union of all races."[27] After World War I Americans celebrated the ethnic roots of Olympic stars such as the swimmers Gertrude Ederle (the daughter of German immigrants) and Johnny Weissmuller (the son of immigrants from the Austro-Hungarian Empire who was probably born in Romania though his nativity remains murky).[28] Revealing the remarkable durability of this theme, during the 2002 Salt Lake Winter Games those traditional "melting pot" canticles reappeared as African American, Asian American, and Hispanic American athletes earned medals for Team U.S.A. in sports previously considered the bastions of mainstream whites.[29] In 2008 at the Beijing Olympics the American media gushed when Sudanese immigrant and American distance runner Lopez Lomong earned the honor of carrying the "Stars and Stripes" in the opening parade of nations.[30]

The faith in American exceptionalism expressed in these melting pot narratives emerges in other Olympic tales as well. In Olympic forums the United States can magically transform itself from the wealthiest and most powerful nation on earth with vast resources that explain its long history of athletic success into underdogs who overcome nearly insurmountable odds to conquer bitter rivals. That script resides behind the 1980 manufacturing of the "Miracle on Ice" in which a supposedly ragtag collection of Americans defeated the mighty Soviet ice hockey machine on the way to winning an unexpected gold medal at the Lake Placid winter games. For more than three decades this Cold War "miracle" has generated an endless supply of "Star-Spangled" books, movies, and other popular culture artifacts that generate powerful visions of American nationhood.[31]

The avalanches of Olympic tales about American exceptionalism have ignited alternative narratives. Other nations point to American affluence as explanations for U.S. dominance rather than acceding to claims that the United States possesses a superior society. Nations as diverse as Jamaica and Norway have employed medal counts based on per-capita Olympic medal hauls or triumphs prorated by gross domestic product to construct different interpretations of national standing.[32] The Olympics also provide opportunities for a variety of communities within the United States to challenge claims about inclusion and equity. When during the early twentieth century Irish American athletes won a host of Olympic medals for the United States, Irish American commentators used their victories to challenge common stereotypes of Anglo-Saxon superiority.[33] At the 1936 Berlin Olympics in the face of tremendous racial hostility from Adolf Hitler and the Nazi regime, Jesse Owens won an unprecedented four gold medals in track and field. His fellow "black auxiliaries," as the German press labeled his African American teammates, added another four gold medals, three silver medals, and two bronze medals. Their performances unleashed a torrent of self-congratulatory devotionals that saw the medals as proof that black Americans could flourish in the United States. A determined cohort in both the black and white press dissented from incorporating Owens and his black teammates into the standard tapestries of racial exceptionalism. The dissenters pointed out that although Owens and the "black auxiliaries" had delivered a blow to Nazi racism in Berlin's Olympic Stadium, they were not in many places in the United States allowed to run, or jump, or go to school with, or eat in public, or engage in a host of other daily social activities with their fellow white citizens.[34]

Three decades later in 1968, two African American sprinters, Tommy Smith and John Carlos, dramatically repackaged this racial counternarrative to American exceptionalism when they donned black gloves and gave a "black power" salute on the medal podium after winning gold and bronze medals at the 1968 Mexico City Olympics. Their powerful dissent from the traditional American Olympic tributes represented the culmination of decades of challenges to racial barriers and sparked controversy not only in the United States but around the world. As members of the Olympic Project for Human Rights (OPHR) led by former athlete and racial justice advocate Harry Edwards, Smith and Carlos were engaged in a campaign to fight racism both in their own country and around the world. The OPHR condemned South African apartheid as well as American segregation. The silver medalist in the race who stood on the medal podium with Smith and Carlos, Australia's Peter Norman, joined in the protest by sporting an OPHR patch on his track suit, as well as publicly denouncing his homeland's "White Australia Policy."[35]

American nationalism and international conflicts overlapped not only in Mexico City but in other Olympic incidents. In the early twentieth century Irish American Olympians condemned the inclusion of their Irish kinsmen on Great Britain's Olympic squads rather than as a separate Irish team. American empathy for the plight of Ireland impelled an Irish American flag bearer, Ralph Rose, to refuse to dip the "Stars and Stripes" to an English monarch at the 1908 London Olympics.[36] Not only athletes but the U.S. government pressured the IOC to recognize American allies as Olympic "nations," including the U.S. protectorate the Philippines in the 1920s and 1930s. During the Cold War when questions of which of the "two" Germanys, "two" Koreas, and "two" Chinas the IOC should recognize precipitated international diplomatic crises, the United States consistently supported the inclusion of its protectorates, West Germany, South Korea, and the Republic of China (Taiwan) in the Olympic "family."[37]

Defining National Rivals at the Olympics

American Olympic narratives not only promoted the interests of allies and celebrated American exceptionalism, but confronted international rivals. In the early twentieth century Great Britain served as the American Olympic foil. Even the ardent Anglophile Theodore Roosevelt used his presidential "bully pulpit" to scold Britain for the poor sportsmanship that he thought it had displayed at the 1908 London games. When in the 1920s and 1930s the United States regularly surpassed Great Britain not only in Olympic medals, but also in many other measures of national prowess, new enemies appeared.[38] The American press routinely portrayed the Olympics during the 1930s as surrogate wars against the rising totalitarian powers, Italy, Japan, and Germany. When the totalitarian teams defeated their American rivals in Olympic arenas, the American media sometimes questioned the health of American culture but more frequently ascribed defeat to the nefarious strategies of their enemies. Japanese, German, and Italian Olympians became robotic warriors bent on winning at all costs, including cheating by ingesting performance-enhancing substances, presaging future criticisms of new American Olympic enemies that would appear after the defeat of the Axis in World War II.[39]

In the postwar world the United States played a central role incorporating the defeated Axis powers back into the community of "civilized" nations, even supporting hosting duties for Italy, Japan, and Germany (Rome in 1960, Tokyo in 1964, and Munich in 1972). In the Cold War that emerged at the end of World War II, a rival superpower emerged to challenge the United States in Olympic arenas. The Soviet Union and the United States engaged in four decades of Cold War Olympic clashes that began at Helsinki in the summer of 1952. The U.S.S.R. won the majority of these Olympian battles. Soviet teams reigned victorious in total medal counts and won the most gold medals at Melbourne in 1956, Rome in 1960, Munich in 1972, and Seoul in 1988. The United States triumphed in those two categories only at Helsinki in 1952 and Mexico City in 1968. The United States even finished third behind the U.S.S.R. and Soviet client-state East Germany in gold medals at Montreal in the American bicentennial year of 1976—though the United States did manage a second-place finish in the overall tabulation. In Tokyo in 1964 the United States won more gold medals, but the U.S.S.R. won the most total medals. In Cold War winter Olympics the Soviets claimed medal count victories in every game from their debut at Cortina D'Ampezzo in 1956 through the 1988 Calgary installment. The United States finished no higher than third and as low as ninth in Cold War–era winter medal counts.[40] In 1980 the United States boycotted the Moscow Olympics, and in 1984 the U.S.S.R. refused to compete in the Los Angeles Olympics, marking the apogee of hostile Olympic exchanges between the Cold War rivals.[41] In spite of the boycotts U.S.S.R. versus U.S. track meets in particular, as well as confrontations in other

Olympic sports such as gymnastics, wrestling, and swimming, remained Cold War staples through the 1980s.[42]

When the United States beat the Soviets in Olympic contests, Americans interpreted victory as a signal of social superiority. When the United States lost to the U.S.S.R.—more frequent occurrence—it raised fears of national decline. "Soft Americans," in the parlance of ardent cold warrior President John F. Kennedy, could not compete with their Soviet counterparts. The American media also raised the specter of Soviet-bloc Olympians as robotic automatons programmed to cheat whenever possible—resurrecting many of the old charges lobbed at Axis rivals. Routine claims that Olympians from the U.S.S.R., East Germany, and other client states won medals by creating state-sponsored doping programs that force-fed fistfuls of performance-enhancing drugs to their athletic minions added a new wrinkle to the charges. In fact, the ingestion of such substances represented a common feature of Olympic preparation by athletes from both the East and the West—with the United States and its allies generally at the cutting edge of the pharmaceutical arms race.[43]

The U.S.S.R. versus U.S. rivalry evaporated as the Soviet Empire dissolved during the late 1980s. New rivals emerged to confront the United States in world affairs and in Olympic venues. Beginning in the 1980s the People's Republic of China launched an ambitious athletic program to garner Olympic supremacy from the United States. At the 2008 Olympics, hosted by Beijing, China won the gold medal race, whereas the United States prevailed in the overall medal count. At the 2012 London Olympics the United States surged back into the lead in both categories. The Sino-American Olympic rivalry seems poised to continue for decades. A resurgent Russia, which hosted the 2014 Sochi Olympic Winter Games, portends a revival of an older rivalry.[44]

Conclusion: The Continuing Americanization and "Californization" of the Olympics

The United States has long sought not only to dominate Olympic medal counts, but also to control the machinery of Olympic production. Beginning in the early 1900s when the head of the American Olympic Committee James Sullivan and the head of the IOC Pierre de Coubertin engaged in more than a decade of struggle for control of the games to the current era where the U.S. Olympic Committee and the IOC quarrel over revenue sharing in the lucrative American market, the United States has sought to shape the Olympics as a vehicle for Americanization. American lobbyists sought to include their national pastimes on the Olympic program, unfruitfully in the case of American football and, ultimately, baseball, though a bit more successfully with basketball. Failing to put American national pastimes at the center of the program, entrepreneurs in the United States turned to other strategies. Beginning in the 1930s they cultivated swimming, a global pastime, as a sport with a distinctively American flair. Beginning in Los Angeles at the 1932 Olympics they advertised Olympic swimming through icons such as Johnny Weissmuller, branding the sport as the epitome of a sun-kissed, affluent, American way of life that would appeal to the globe's expanding consumer markets. Producers of American culture, from Hollywood filmmakers who made Weissmuller into a global cinema star as Tarzan, to fashion houses that made beach wear into a billion-dollar industry promoted swimming as a distinctively component of American lifestyles. This image of the American "good life" was primarily identified with California, the center of American beach culture and the capital of powerful American film industry.[45]

In the later decades of the twentieth century this trend toward Americanization of the Olympics through "Californization" dramatically increased. American interest groups successfully pitched California-incubated and California-styled "action sports" such as beach volleyball, triathlon, mountain and BMX cycling, snowboarding, and freestyle skiing to the IOC. The inclusion of these telegenic new sports not only produced an increased medal haul for the United States but created new markets in which U.S.-based corporations can sell products and promote California-inspired American lifestyles around the world.[46] In fact, this contemporary use of the Olympics to market American products and ways of life dates back to the origins of the modern Olympics when "America's athletic missionaries" won glory and A.G. Spalding and Brothers, an early manufacturer of sporting goods, outfitted the team and advertised its wares in Olympic stadiums.[47] A century later, Nike, Coca-Cola, and other companies have eclipsed Spalding and Brothers as the key Olympian advertisers for American lifestyles. The Olympics remain a beacon in American corporate and public imaginations as a crucial venue for crafting nationalistic narratives and for projecting American cultural power around the globe.

Notes

1 The quadrennial presidential elections have never been interrupted, but the Olympics have been cancelled during World Wars (in 1916, 1940, and 1944). Beginning in 1994 the IOC moved the Olympic Winter Games to a new calendrical cycle so that since that time a summer or winter Olympics takes place every two years.

2 John Watterson, *The Games Presidents Play: Sports and the Presidency* (Baltimore: The Johns Hopkins University Press, 2006); Mark Dyreson, *Making the American Team: Sport, Culture, and the Olympic Experience* (Urbana: University of Illinois Press, 1998); Mark Dyreson, *Crafting Patriotism for Global Domination: America at the Olympic Games* (London: Routledge, 2009).

3 Dyreson, *Making the American Team*. On "Solid Bill" Taft see Ralph D. Paine, "Taft at Yale," *Outing* 53 (November 1908): 135–150.

4 Dyreson, *Making the American Team*. For the telegram texts see James E. Sullivan, ed., *The Olympic Games: Stockholm 1912*, Spalding "Red Cover" Series of Athletic Handbooks No. 17R (New York: American Sports Publishing, 1912), 233–234.

5 Arnd Krüger and W.J. Murray, *The Nazi Olympics: Sport, Politics, and Appeasement in the 1930s* (Urbana: University of Illinois Press, 2003); Richard D. Mandell, *The Nazi Olympics* (New York: Macmillan, 1971); David Clay Large, *Nazi Games: The Olympics of 1936* (New York: W.W. Norton, 2007); George Eisen, "The Voices of Sanity: American Diplomatic Reports from the 1936 Berlin Olympiad," *Journal of Sport History* 11, no. 3 (Winter 1984): 56–78.

6 For historic overviews of the 1984 Los Angeles Olympics see the recent anthology by Matthew P. Llewellyn, John Gleaves, and Wayne Wilson, eds., *The 1984 Los Angeles Olympic Games: Assessing the 30-Year Legacy* (London: Routledge, 2015).

7 Nicolas Evan Sarantakes, *Dropping the Torch: Jimmy Carter, the Olympic Boycott, and the Cold War* (New York: Cambridge University Press, 2011).

8 "Transcript of Reagan's Speech Accepting GOP Nomination," *New York Times*, August 24, 1984. Mark Dyreson, "Return to the Melting Pot: An Old American Olympic Story," *Olympika: The International Journal of Olympic Studies* 12 (2003): 1–22.

9 Miquel de Moragas, Nancy K. Rivenburgh, and James F. Larson, eds., *Television in the Olympics, Vol. 13*, Acamedia Monographs (London: John Libbey, 1995), 207–218.

10 Andrew C. Billings, *Olympic Media: Inside the Biggest Show on Television* (London: Routledge, 2008); Peter Hopsicker and Mark Dyreson, "Super Bowl Sunday," in *The Historical Dictionary of American Holidays, Vol. I*, ed. Len Travers (Westport, CT: Greenwood Press, 2006), 30–55.

11 On the historic evolution of U.S. national pastimes see Mark Dyreson and Jaime Schultz, *American National Pastimes—A History* (London: Routledge, 2015).

12 Mark Dyreson, "Mapping an Empire of Baseball: American Visions of National Pastimes and Global Influence, 1919–1941," in *Baseball in America and America in Baseball*, ed. Donald Kyle and Robert R. Fairbanks (College Station: Texas A&M University Press, 2008), 143–188.

13 Carson Cunningham, *American Hoops: US Men's Olympic Basketball from Berlin to Beijing* (Lincoln: University of Nebraska Press, 2009).

14 Dyreson, *Making the American Team.*

15 Robert K. Barney, "Born from Dilemma: America Awakens to the Modern Olympic Games, 1901–1903," *The International Journal of Olympic Studies* 1 (1992): 92–135; Dyreson, *Making the American Team.*

16 Robert K. Barney, Stephen R. Wenn, and Scott G. Martyn, *Selling the Five Rings: The International Olympic Committee and the Rise of Olympic Commercialism* (Salt Lake City: University of Utah Press, 2002).

17 Dyreson, *Crafting Patriotism.*

18 "All-Time Olympic Games Medal Table." https://en.wikipedia.org/wiki/All-time_Olympic_Games_medal_table (accessed July 5, 2015).

19 Paris hosted the 1900 and 1924 summer games. Chamonix hosted the first winter games in 1924. Grenoble hosted in 1968 and Albertville in 1992. The United States had hosted winter games in Lake Placid in 1932 and 1980, Squaw Valley in 1960, and Salt Lake City in 1998. Summer U.S. hosts include St. Louis in 1904, Los Angeles in 1932 and 1984, and Atlanta in 1996.

20 The paradoxical conjunction of nationalism and internationalism dates to the origins of the Olympics and the ideology of its founder, the Baron Pierre de Coubertin. John J. MacAloon, *This Great Symbol: Pierre de Coubertin and the Origins of the Modern Olympics* (Chicago: University of Chicago Press, 1981); David Young, *The Modern Olympics: A Struggle for Revival* (Baltimore: The Johns Hopkins University Press, 1996); John A. Lucas, *The Modern Olympic Games* (New York: A.S. Barnes, 1980). For a fascinating comparative history of the Olympics to other contemporary transnational movements in the nineteenth century and early twentieth century, see John Hoberman, "Toward a Theory of Olympic Internationalism," *Journal of Sport History* 22, no. 1 (Spring 1995): 1–37. For a clear analysis of the links between the Olympics and the world's fair movement see Maurice Roche, *Mega-Events and Modernity: Olympics and Expos in the Growth of Global Culture* (London: Routledge, 2000). Solid chronicles of the national politics embedded in the Olympics include Allen Guttmann, *The Olympics: A History of the Modern Games* (Urbana: University of Illinois Press, 1992); Alfred Erich Senn, *Power, Politics, and the Olympic Games* (Champaign, IL: Human Kinetics, 1999), and Christopher R. Hill, *Olympic Politics* (Manchester: Manchester University, 1996). Two studies point to the power of Greek nationalism in the construction of the modern Olympics, Alexander Kitroeff, *Wrestling With the Ancients: Modern Greek Identity and the Olympics* (New York: Greekworks, 2004); and Konstantinos Georgiadis, *Olympic Revival: The Revival of the Olympic Games in Modern Times* (Athens: Ekdotike Athenon, 2003). For international perspectives see Boria Majumdar and Sandra S. Collins, eds., *Olympism: The Global Vision: From Nationalism to Internationalism* (London: Routledge, 2008); and J.A. Mangan and Mark Dyreson, eds., *Olympic Legacies: Intended and Unintended–Political, Cultural, Economic, Educational* (London: Routledge, 2010).

21 MacAloon, *This Great Symbol*; Young, *The Modern Olympics.*

22 Matthew P. Llewellyn, *Rule Britannia: Nationalism, Identity and the Modern Olympic Games* (London: Routledge 2012).

23 Richard D. Mandell, *The First Modern Olympics* (Berkeley: University of California Press, 1976); Dyreson, *Making the American Team.*

24 Connolly's serialized account of first modern Olympics in *Scribner's* magazine brilliantly displays these tropes. James B. Connolly, "An Olympic Victor," *Scribner's* 44 (July 1908): 18–31; James B. Connolly, "An Olympic Victor," *Scribner's*, August 1908, 204–217; and James B. Connolly, "An Olympic Victor," *Scribner's* 44 (September 1908): 357–370. For interpretations of Connolly's work see Dyreson, *Making the American Team.*

25 Edward Bayard Moss, "America's Athletic Missionaries," *Harper's Weekly* 56 (July 27, 1912): 8–9; Mark Dyreson, "'America's Athletic Missionaries': Political Performance, Olympic Spectacle and the Quest for an American National Culture, 1896–1912," *Olympika: The International Journal of Olympic Studies* 1 (1992): 70–91.

26 Dyreson, *Making the American Team*; Dyreson, *Crafting Patriotism*; Alan S. Katchen, *Abel Kiviat, National Champion: Twentieth-Century Track & Field and the Melting Pot* (Syracuse, NY: Syracuse University Press, 2009). On the inclusion of women on American teams see Mark Dyreson, "Icons of Liberty or Objects of Desire? American Women Olympians and the Politics of Consumption," *Journal of Contemporary History* 38, no. 3 (July 2003): 435–460; Linda J. Borish, " 'The Cradle of American Champions, Women Champions Swim Champions': Charlotte Epstein, Gender and Jewish Identity, and the Physical Emancipation of Women in Aquatic Sports," *The International Journal of the History of Sport* 21, no. 2 (February 2004): 197–235; Susan E. Cayleff, *Babe: The Life and Legend of Babe Didrikson Zaharias* (Urbana: University of Illinois Press, 1995).

27 The "union of all races" rhetoric appears first in "Race Questions at the Olympics," *The Independent* 73 (July 25, 1912): 214–215. See Mark Dyreson, "Melting Pot Victories: Racial Ideas and the Olympic Games in American Culture during the Progressive Era," *The International Journal of the History of Sport* 6, no. 1 (May 1989): 49–61.

28 Tim Dahlberg; Mary Ederle Ward; Brenda Greene, *America's Girl: The Incredible Story of How Swimmer Gertrude Ederle Changed the Nation* (New York: St. Martin's Press, 2009); Dyreson, *Crafting Patriotism*.

29 Mark Dyreson, "Return to the Melting Pot," 1–22.

30 Lopez Lomong, with Mark A. Tabb, *Running for My Life: One Lost Boy's Journey from the Killing Fields of Sudan to the Olympic Games* (Nashville, TN: Thomas Nelson, 2012).

31 Among the better artifacts that "Miracle" has produced are Wayne Coffey, *The Boys of Winter: The Untold Story of a Coach, a Dream, and the 1980 U.S. Olympic Hockey Team* (New York: Crown, 2005); and *Miracle*, Walt Disney Pictures, 2004. For an excellent analysis of the "Miracle on Ice" see Donald E. Abelson, "Politics on Ice: The United States, the Soviet Union, and a Hockey Game in Lake Placid," *Canadian Review of American Studies* 40, no. 1 (2010): 63–94.

32 Many nations have used the Olympics to project and refine national identity. Robert Edelman, *Serious Fun: A History of Spectator Sports in the USSR* (New York: Oxford University Press, 1993); Mike Dennis and Jonathan Grix, *Sport under Communism: Behind the East German "Miracle"* (New York: Palgrave Macmillan, 2012); Susan Brownell, *Beijing's Games: What the Olympics Mean to China* (Lanham, MD: Rowman & Littlefield, 2008); Guoqui Xu, *Olympic Dreams: China and Sports, 1895–2008* (Cambridge, Mass: Harvard University Press, 2008); John Hargreaves, *Freedom for Catalonia?: Catalan Nationalism, Spanish Identity, and the Barcelona Olympic Games* (Cambridge: Cambridge University Press, 2000); Arne Martin Klausen, *Olympic Games as Performance and Public Event: The Case of the XVII Winter Olympic Games in Norway* (New York: Berghahn Books, 1999); Barbara Keys, *Globalizing Sport: National Rivalry and International Community in the 1930s* (Cambridge, MA: Harvard University Press, 2006); Richard Mandell, *The Nazi Olympics* (New York: Macmillan, 1971); Victor D. Cha, *Beyond the Final Score: The Politics of Sport in Asia* (New York: Columbia University Press, 2009). Few nations, though, have used the Olympics for the projection of nationalism as consistently over time—at every Olympics contested since 1896—or as fervently as the USA with the possible exceptions of Greece and Australia. Kitroeff, *Wrestling with the Ancients*; Konstantinos Georgiadis, *Olympic Revival: The Revival of the Olympic Games in Modern Times* (Athens: Ekdotike Athenon, 2003); Daryl Adair and Wray Vamplew, *Sport in Australian History* (New York: Oxford University Press, 1997); Richard Cashman, *Sport in the National Imagination: Australian Sport in the Federation Decades* (Sydney: Walla Walla Press/Centre for Olympic Studies, the University of New South Wales, 2002).

33 Dyreson, *Making the American Team*; Dyreson, *Crafting Patriotism*.

34 William J. Baker, *Jesse Owens: An American Life* (New York: Free Press, 1986); David K. Wiggins, *Glory Bound: Black Athletes in a White America* (Syracuse, NY: Syracuse University Press, 2007); Mark Dyreson, "Jesse Owens: Leading Man in Modern American Tales of Racial Progress and Limits," in *Out of the Shadows: A Biographical History of the African American Athlete*, ed. David K. Wiggins (Fayetteville: University of Arkansas Press, 2006), 111–132.; John Gleaves and Mark Dyreson. "The 'Black Auxiliaries' in American Memories: Sport, Race, and Politics in the Construction of Modern Legacies," *The International Journal of the History of Sport*, 27, no. 16–18 (November/December 2010): 2893–2924.

35 Douglas Hartmann, *Race, Culture, and the Revolt of the Black Athlete: The 1968 Olympic Protests and their Aftermath* (Chicago: University of Chicago Press, 2003); Amy Bass, *Not the Triumph But*

the Struggle: The 1968 Olympics and the Making of the Black Athlete (Minneapolis: University of Minnesota Press, 2002); Kevin B. Witherspoon, *Before the Eyes of the World: Mexico and the 1968 Olympics* (DeKalb: Northern Illinois University Press, 2008).

36 On the history of flag-dipping see Mark Dyreson, "'This Flag Dips for No Earthly King': The Mysterious Origins of an American Myth." *The International Journal of the History of Sport* 25, no. 2 (February 2008): 142–162; and Mary Dyreson, "'To Dip or Not to Dip': The American Flag at the Olympic Games Since 1936," *The International Journal of the History of Sport* 25, no. 2 (February 2008): 163–184.

37 Senn, *Power, Politics, and the Olympics*.

38 Krüger and Murray, *The Nazi Olympics*; Sandra S. Collins, *The 1940 Tokyo Games—The Missing Olympics: Japan, the Asian Olympics and the Olympic Movement* (London: Routledge, 2007); Keys, *Globalizing Sport*.

39 Mark Dyreson and Thomas Rorke, "A Powerful False Positive: Nationalism, Science, and Public Opinion in the 'Oxygen Doping' Allegations against Japanese Swimmers at the 1932 Olympics," *The International Journal of the History of Sport* 31, no. 8 (May 2014): 854–870.

40 Guttmann, *The Olympics*; Senn, *Power, Politics, and the Olympic Games*; Hill, *Olympic Politics*; Cesar Torres and Mark Dyreson, 'The Cold War Games', in *Research in the Sociology of Sport: Olympic Journeys, Vol. III*, ed. Kevin Young and Kevin Wamsley (Amsterdam: Elsevier, 2005), 59–82.

41 Sarantakes, *Dropping the Torch*; Kenneth Reich, *Making It Happen: Peter Ueberroth and the 1984 Olympics* (Santa Barbara, CA: Capra, 1986); Peter Ueberroth, with Richard Levin and Amy Quinn, *Made in America: His Own Story* (New York: William Morrow, 1985).

42 Joseph M. Turrini, *The End of Amateurism in American Track and Field* (Urbana, IL: University of Illinois Press, 2010).

43 Thomas M. Hunt, *Drug Games: The International Olympic Committee and the Politics of Doping, 1960–2008* (Austin: University of Texas Press, 2011); Wayne Wilson and Ed Derse, eds., *Doping in Elite Sport: The Politics of Drugs in the Olympic Movement* (Champaign, IL: Human Kinetics, 2001); Steven Ungerleider, *Faust's Gold: Inside the East German Doping Machine* (New York: Thomas Dunne Books/St. Martin's Press, 2001).

44 Xu, *Olympic Dreams*; "Castles in the Sand: The Sochi Olympics," *The Economist*, July 13, 2013, 45–46; For an analysis of the West's intentions in the Olympic battles see Jules Boykoff, *Celebration Capitalism and the Olympic Games* (London: Routledge, 2014).

45 Mark Dyreson, "Johnny Weissmuller and the Old Global Capitalism: The Origins of the Federal Blueprint for Selling American Culture to the World," *The International Journal of the History of Sport* 25, no. 2 (February 2008): 268–283; Mark Dyreson, "Marketing Weissmuller to the World: Hollywood's Olympics and Federal Schemes for Americanization through Sport," *The International Journal of the History of Sport* 25, no. 2 (February 2008): 284–306; Mark Dyreson, "Crafting Patriotism–Meditations on 'Californication' and Other Trends," *The International Journal of the History of Sport* 25, no. 2 (February 2008): 307–311; Mark Dyreson, "Globalizing American Sporting Culture: The U.S. Government Plan to Conquer the World Sports Market in the 1930s," *Sportwissenschaft: The German Journal of Sport Science* 34, no. 2 (June 2004): 145–151.

46 Mark Dyreson, "The Republic of Consumption at the Olympic Games: Globalization, Americanization, and Californization," *Journal of Global History* 8, no. 2 (July 2013): 256–278.

47 Dyreson, *Making the American Team*.

29

AMERICAN MILITARY SPORT FROM COLONIAL TIMES TO THE TWENTY-FIRST CENTURY

Wanda Ellen Wakefield

The development of sports for American soldiers and sailors over the course of the past four centuries parallels the development of sports for the civilian population. Likewise, the growth of sports programs within the armed forces closely follows the general expansion and contraction of the numbers of men and women serving in the military at any particular time. For the bulk of the seventeenth and eighteenth centuries sports such as rounders and similar bat-and-ball games played by civilians and combatants alike were disorganized and spontaneous. Then during the nineteenth century the modernization of sport in the civilian world affected and was influenced by the experiences of the men who fought in the Civil War. By the end of the nineteenth century military commanders embraced the usefulness of sport as a mechanism to keep young soldiers busy with appropriate activities and as a way to ensure good unit order and discipline. The twentieth century witnessed the growth of military sports as the American armed forces organized to fight in the two World Wars. Soldiers were encouraged to demonstrate their physical prowess not only on the battlefield but also on the playing field. Even today, soldiers compete in sports offered at their forts and bases and against civilian athletes through the Army Master Athlete program.

Sport and the Colonial American Militias

The first English-speaking settlers in British North America brought with them many folk-ways and practices with which they had long been familiar. Englishmen celebrated their leisure time by engaging in casual sports testing each other's strength and coordination. They played various bat-and-ball games, bowled, and threw weights. Englishmen also believed that these casual sports were part of their preparation for military service. In fact, when King James I issued his famous proclamation ensuring the *Right to Sport*, he did so assuming that young men trained for sport would serve as good soldiers in His Majesty's Army. In the words of the king's Proclamation of 1618, if a ban occurred on Sabbath-day sport it would also bar "the common and meaner sort of people from using such exercises as may make their bodies more able for 'warre,'" creating an "inconvenience" should the King need them.[1] This connection between sport and war therefore was already apparent when the first settlers arrived in Jamestown in 1607.

For these adventurers, of course, the problem they faced was not what to do with their leisure time, but how to survive long enough to enjoy time off. The Jamestown settlement almost failed several times before the development of the trade in tobacco that led survivors in Virginia to neglect everything else in favor of growing the weed, which was much in demand in Europe because of its addictive qualities. While most of the Jamestown settlers, whatever their trade or social rank, pursued other activities, they always had to be available to fight the local Natives affiliated with the Powhatan Confederacy. Even with the need to maintain military fitness, most of the earliest settlers in Jamestown likely displayed extreme physical weakness, probably attributable to malaria, and experienced other sickness, likely due to drinking tainted water. Although we know that the men of Jamestown farmed and fought, little evidence exists that they played any sort of sport during the first few decades of settlement, especially sport intended to improve their soldiering.

When the Pilgrims arrived in New England to establish their Plymouth Colony in 1620 they faced similar challenges as they learned to live in what they viewed as a wilderness. They and the Puritan men and women who settled in the Massachusetts Bay Colony starting in 1630, struggled to maintain Sabbath holiness by banning leisure activities on Sundays, some of which might be characterized as sport.[2] Preachers and colonial governors commonly condemned play and playfulness that lacked any utilitarian value. However, they also knew that the people of Massachusetts Bay and Plymouth would have to defend themselves. Therefore, despite the general view that the Sabbath should be dedicated to worship and prayer, many communities began scheduling military drills on Sundays. The reliance on a well-trained militia rather than a standing army was a hold-over from England where men regularly trained with pikes, which were cheaper and easier to use than primitive muskets.[3] Military men then took advantage of the time after drill to play games and sports. Because the militia men conducted many of these casual activities outdoors, there remained the constant danger of property damage, such as was faced by communities during folk football games in the past. Within a few decades of settlement, therefore, colonial assemblies in New England began passing laws banning certain sports that political leaders believed led to mayhem and property damage.

During the eighteenth century little changed with regard to the types of leisure activities enjoyed by the colonists. Although a lively interest in spontaneous horse racing developed in Virginia, no connection between that activity and military preparedness ever appeared.[4] Elsewhere, militia training days continued providing young men with a chance to gather and test their athletic skills against one another. Most Americans remained committed to the idea that a standing army would inevitably lead to tyranny, and therefore rapid demobilization occurred after the Revolutionary War, the War of 1812, the Mexican War, and the various frontier struggles against the Natives. In other words, the development of military sports waited the development of large, professional armies—and the development of modernized sports with their own rules, administrative structures, and interested spectators.

Baseball and the Civil War

By the mid-1860s sports and athletics in both Great Britain and the United States underwent modernization. The Industrial Revolution brought changes in work life, communication, and technologies that allowed enthusiasts the time to experiment with older games and begin establishing formal rules for competitions. This was the case with football (soccer) as the Football Association was organized in London in 1861 and with baseball when the National League of Professional Baseball in was established in New York in 1876. The American Civil War also contributed to that modernization. For the first time in North America military leaders sent huge field armies into battle. For many of the men in arms on both sides of the conflict, hours of terror on the battlefield were counterbalanced by days and weeks of idleness as commanders planned the next campaigns. Although there was no formal institution in place to regulate idle time, soldiers apparently turned to playing baseball as well as boxing, wrestling, and other tests of their physical prowess.[5] Because no agreed-upon rules existed for the game of baseball, these men brought with them the "Boston" game, the "New York" game, and other iterations of the sport.[6] In order to ensure the best competition, the soldiers had to agree on some common features of baseball. Because of that George B. Kirsch argues in his seminal *Baseball in Blue and Grey: The National Pastime During the Civil War* that the war was critical to the development of the game.[7] He points to a growing understanding among commanders that by playing games together soldiers could improve their morale and, possibly, the unit cohesion necessary to battlefield success. Whether or not the Civil War made American baseball the *national* game, the game was clearly so important after the war that the Seventh Cavalry led by General George Armstrong Custer stopped to play a series of games on their way to the Little Big Horn using balls and bats purchased earlier by Captain Frederick Benteen's battalion.[8] This decision to play baseball on the way to war would eventually inform later commanders' belief that sport helped soldiers develop the good order and discipline necessary to military success.

America Acquires an Empire

By the 1890s sport went together with the development of the structures recognized elsewhere in American culture today. The British promotion of so-called "amateur" sport had been embraced by the Baron Pierre de Coubertin and the other white Victorian men who organized the first modern Olympics in 1896. De Coubertin believed that participation in sport would restore the masculinity of French soldiers after the disastrous loss of territory to the Germans following the Franco-Prussian War of 1870. To that end, invented sports such as the Modern Pentathlon emphasizing such military skills as shooting, fencing, running, and riding horses were added to the Olympic program. Indeed, the future American general George S. Patton competed in the Modern Pentathlon in the 1912 Games.

Alongside the development of sports adhering to the amateurism of the Olympic movement, soldiers in the United States and Great Britain familiar with the operation of sport introduced games and activities as they proceeded with their imperial projects in the Philippines and in the Caribbean after 1898, in the case of the Americans, and in Asia and Africa in the case of the British. For the Americans, various baseball games, boxing matches, and track meets staged in and around Manila were designed to keep the troops busy, but commanders also apparently hoped that athletic competition would demonstrate the superiority of the men sent to occupy the country.[9] For African American soldiers serving in the Philippines, the track meets presented an opportunity to compete on equal ground with soldiers of European descent. In fact, the great tennis champion Arthur Ashe suggested in his history of the black athlete that service sports were the sole occasion during the early years of the twentieth century for integrated competition.[10] As with the British and French in Africa, American troops also taught sports and games to the locals, whose successes against their occupiers seemed to disprove underlying Social Darwinist ideas about the superiority of white men in all facets of life.

Meanwhile supporters of a transformation in the U.S. Army from primarily a frontier constabulary to a modern fighting force turned to sports as a venue both to train civilians in the skills they would need should the country go to war and to identify those men who could potentially command troops in combat. The former football player and Army Chief of Staff, General Leonard Wood, was especially supportive of the notion that all American men, whether soldiers or not, should maintain a level of physical fitness that could be developed through sport.[11] Wood and others also believed that providing space for sports in young soldiers' lives represented, in the words of historian Steven W. Pope, "a moral commitment to the soldiers' welfare and [they] used sport initially to combat desertion, alcohol, and the lure of prostitution."[12]

When President Woodrow Wilson promised American mothers on the occasion of the American entry into World War I that their children would be returned to them morally pure, armed forces commanders took those words to heart. Working with the YMCA, the Knights of Columbus, the Jewish Welfare Board, and other social welfare agencies, the Army established an elaborate program of sports at the many training bases and camps that sprung up around the United States designed to keep the young soldiers of diverse backgrounds away from alcohol and prostitutes. For many men, this was their first acquaintance with modern coaching by men such as Yale's legendary football coach, Walter Camp, who introduced the "Daily Dozen" exercises for the military, and with new equipment. Pope argues that as a result after the war these men remained interested in sport as a result of their wartime experience.[13] Once the troops began arriving overseas they benefited from the chance to play in new baseball leagues in Paris and elsewhere in France. They were also introduced to boxing, a sport taught by professionals who analogized it to bayonet training. Again, boxing would become more significant and interesting to civilians after the war than it was before. Armed services teams drawn from the best athletes available were among the best in the country, as reflected in their play in the 1918 and 1919 Rose Bowls against other service teams. As these men played their games, the Army believed that they would tell a story about the quality of life in the United States and the significance of American sports such as baseball and bring European spectators to recognize the superior masculinity of the athletes themselves.[14] Military sports even became a part of the postwar settlement of new European boundaries. In 1919 the victors decided to celebrate the successful conclusion of the war with athletic competitions staged in Paris, called the "Inter-Allied Games." These games, open only to soldiers and sailors who had served with the Allies during the war, prohibited Germans from being invited. But representatives from new countries created at Versailles, such as Yugoslavia, were invited to play with the clear intention that any athletic success enjoyed by the Yugoslavs would translate into support for the new nation by its citizens.[15]

After the troops and their commanders returned to the United States, the Army invited Raymond Fosdick from the YMCA to the War College to discuss the successes and failures of the wartime sports program. Fosdick never wavered from his certainty that soldiers' athletics were good for morale, but he did argue in 1922 that in the future the military itself should handle sports and other social welfare activities. He pointed to the confusion that ensued when the YMCA; the Jewish Welfare Board, organized to assist Jewish soldiers; and the Knights of Columbus, seeking to assist Catholic soldiers, competed with one another to provide equipment and coaching.[16] Fosdick also told the assembled officers that the Army should concentrate in the future on sport programs for the masses of troops rather than for specialized athletes.[17] Brigadier General Edward L. King concurred and proposed that in the future all of the Army's sports activities should be handled internally to ensure the most efficient use of resources.[18] While the Army planned to develop sports programs should the need arise, the reality was that for most of the 1920s and 1930s the small size of the armed forces rendered concerns about soldier welfare irrelevant. Instead, most observers were only aware of service ball when West Point and Navy played their annual football game.[19] Active duty commanders meanwhile taught football as part of their Reserve Officers' Training Corps (ROTC) assignments or worked closely with young men assigned to Civilian Conservation Corps (CCC) camps to ensure their fitness.[20] Douglas MacArthur, as superintendent of West Point during the 1920s and as the leader of the American Olympic Committee, also encouraged the further development of sport for the troops.

World War II: Sport, Sport Everywhere

The transformation from a peacetime force to an army capable of taking on and defeating the Axis powers began in 1940 with the institution of a draft. As camps, forts, and bases throughout the United States expanded to accommodate the young men during their training, sports programs were established to entertain the draftees and promote unit cohesion. At least that was the theory. Although General King had called for maximum participation in sports and athletics before the war, that idea was eventually abandoned in favor of a process that culled the best athletes from companies to battalions and used them to represent the fort or base in competitions against excellent athletes from other locations. For commanders this seemed logical because at least a part of their annual fitness reports was dedicated to the quality of sport being played by their men.[21] Nevertheless, those athletic officers who attended the School for Special Services at Fort Meade, Maryland, learned from a recent technical manual how to create leagues and teams on bases that soldiers would want to join. Some officers therefore emphasized softball rather than baseball on the assumption that it was easier to play for less skilled athletes, whereas others embraced various versions of flag football to avoid the costs associated with tackle football.[22] In any event, the better athletes ended up being assigned to post and base teams that competed not only among themselves but against prominent college teams and professional clubs. One of the most famous of the service teams came from the Naval Air Station Camp Grant in Illinois, which played a schedule in 1942 that included the Universities of Wisconsin and Illinois as well as the Chicago Bears. Another powerful squad was the Ramblers from Randolph Field in Texas.[23] Because commanders wanted to win, they often fielded teams loaded with white and black athletes despite local rules requiring racial segregation. The decision to field integrated teams was praised by the *Baltimore Afro-American* reporting that it "took the Army to bring democracy to Virginia, where mixed competition is not sanctioned, except in rare instances, but the Camp Lee football knows no distinction."[24]

In addition to making sure there were sports opportunities at home, athletic officers met the challenge of providing athletics to soldiers overseas. One purpose was obviously to give young men just coming out of combat a chance to play, but another was to impress local men and women with the athletic achievements of those young men. To support that work, the government purchased an enormous quantity of balls (for football, baseball, and soccer), bats, boxing gloves, and table tennis sets during the war and shipped the equipment overseas along with weapons and other materiel.[25]

The United Service Organizations (USO) sent Broadway and Hollywood stars around the world to entertain the troops, but the Army had its own athletic entertainment as well. When the Army drafted heavyweight boxing champion, Joe Louis, commanders decided to use him not in combat, but as a roving ambassador meeting soldiers and putting on boxing exhibitions throughout Europe. The two famous bouts between Louis and the German champion

Max Schmeling were fresh in these men's minds as Louis had become a star not only in the black community, but in the white community as well when he defeated Schmeling at Yankee Stadium in 1938. As the war progressed athletic officers tried to make sporting events as similar as possible to what the men were used to back home. Because the soldiers were accustomed to listening to New Year's Day bowl games on the radio, athletic officers created a system of mock "bowl games" around the world. One of the most famous was the Arab Bowl played on January 1, 1944, at Oran in North Africa. The former professional baseball player, Master Sergeant Zeke Bonura, organized the game and arranged for prizes, but he also drew on the local community of Women's Army Corps (WACs) members to provide Bowl Queens and cheerleaders for the event. Other bowl games included the Lily Bowl, held in Bermuda; the Spaghetti Bowl, held in Florence; and the Mustard Bowl, staged in Dijon, France.[26] Making sure that soldiers overseas were connected with their relatives and other loved ones back home also included news and information about stateside baseball. The men enjoyed being able to "choose" a particular team to support and follow on the radio during the season. They also enjoyed receiving sport-themed gifts, as was the case with the VII Bomb Group in the China-Burma-India (CBI) theater who wore Boston Red Sox caps provided by the team during flights "over the hump" from India to China.[27] Finally, for many of the men in uniform, the connection between civilian and military life was reinforced by the conflation of the language of sport and war. The editors of the soldier newspaper, *Bom Bay*, for example, encouraged their readers to train for the fight with Hitler just as if they were training for an important baseball or football game.[28] And First Lieutenant William Scholl even ascribed his dogfight victory over a German pilot to the tactics he had learned while playing football at Cornell.[29] Although some soldiers doubted the value of sport, the majority seem to have accepted the idea that their sports experience helped them survive the war, whether they played baseball, football, or even table tennis.

Playing in Postwar Europe One More Time

As World War II came to an end, military planners realized that a large number of soldiers would need to remain in occupied Europe after hostilities ceased. They were needed to ensure the peace, provide for the survivors, and assist local authorities in rebuilding infrastructure destroyed by the war. In Austria, this meant that soldiers occupying the American zone around Salzburg fed local children at their mess halls, arranged for schools to reopen with a suitably vetted faculty, and helped in the reconstruction of various tourism facilities. The idea was that American troops and the Austrian people would be able to create an environment in which international tourism could resume, with the end result that Austria's economy would benefit by the acquisition of the hard currency that tourists could be expected to spend. Military commanders were determined to keep the occupying troops busy in a variety of ways. They encouraged young soldiers to attend classes offered by individual infantry divisions. They also encouraged young soldiers to sample the various recreational opportunities available in the Salzburg region and in the region of the Tyrol, occupied by French troops. They fished local lakes, hiked local trails, and skied local mountains. Apparently, commanders hoped that these young men and women might return to Austria after their military service ended to help build the Austrian economy with U.S. dollars.

Whereas Austria was treated as a victim of Nazi expansionism under an agreement made in Moscow in 1943, Germany was obviously not. The American troops who occupied Germany in the immediate aftermath of the war concerned themselves with de-Nazification and providing for the needs of displaced people. They also modeled and encouraged Germans to adopt the ways of democracy. Beyond that, as the Cold War emerged, military planners and civilians in Washington realized that thousands of American soldiers needed to remain in the Western part of Germany as a counterweight to the Soviet forces to the East. If these thousands of soldiers were to be stationed permanently on Germany soil, therefore, they would need to be entertained. And if they could establish good, friendly relationships with local Germans through sport, that would be even better. Although nobody in authority still believed that simply showing German youth how to play baseball would turn them into new people, as they had after World War I, everybody believed that the good behavior of American soldiers toward the German population would go far to ensure a lasting peace.

Within 10 years of the end of World War II, the situation in West Germany had stabilized. The growth and expansion of the West German economy meant that for the first time military officials allowed soldiers to bring their family members overseas without straining resources needed to improve the lives of the people facing the challenge of communism in East Germany. One of the major outfits assigned to the Federal Republic of Germany, the Eighth Infantry Division, moved into its headquarters at Bad Krueznach in 1957. Almost immediately the division's newsletter, the *Arrow*, began publishing articles about sporting opportunities on base and at various alpine resorts. In 1960, soldiers and their families discovered that if they traveled to Garmisch that January they could see, among other things, a night ski-jumping contest, the German speed skating championships, the European Figure Skating championships, and something called the "World Racing Sled Championships."[30] The soldiers could buy low-cost tickets for these many events courtesy of the Army and the local organizers.[31] Armed forces recreation continued to encourage soldiers to visit Garmisch and Berchtesgaden over the next several years, establishing a Skytop Sports Center in Berchtesgaden where soldiers could rent skis and sleds for a day playing on the snow.[32] American soldiers in Germany also had many chances to play among themselves and with local German athletes. As part of the German-American friendship events in 1960, teams from the Eighth Infantry Division faced German teams in both basketball and bowling. They also played a series of soccer matches against German teams.[33] To further cement friendly relationships between the Army and German civilians the Eighth Infantry Division ordered Sgt. Peter Ciminello to coach the Mannheim Knights, a local baseball team entered into a European tournament in Barcelona.[34]

Aside from competitions between German and American athletes, each autumn football players from the Eighth Infantry Division met teams from other American outfits in Europe to determine the European football champions. Unlike some of the mock football games played during World War II, in these games the athletes played in full gear, and such games became enormously popular among the men. Indeed, in December 1960 the *Arrow* was able to report the happy news that one of their own teams, the "Mainz Troopers," had captured the European Football Championship title, beating a team from SHAFE (Supreme Headquarters Allied Forces Europe).[35]

The year 1960 was also an Olympic year, and the men of the Eighth Infantry Division were encouraged to support the American teams headed for Rome in a variety of ways. Soldiers and their families were given a chance to buy tickets to the Rome Olympics through a special allotment extended to American forces in Europe.[36] Excellent athletes were also invited to participate in the Olympic trials in swimming, wrestling, and athletics, with the caveat that they must "be bona fide amateurs."[37] The Army's plan, created in January, was to establish an official "All-Army Training Camp" to select men to be entered into the Olympic trials back in the United States.[38] One of those men was weightlifter 1st Lt. Peter N. Talluio, who ended up not qualifying for the Olympics after finishing third in his weight class at the trials.[39] Four years later, another soldier stationed in Germany, the weightlifter James Millsap, would also try out for the Olympics scheduled to be held in Tokyo, Japan.[40] He was joined in this endeavor by the sprinter Willie Davenport who was rotated from Germany in May 1964 back to Fort Campbell in Kentucky to continue his pre-Olympic training.[41]

Finally, soldiers in Europe had yet another opportunity for competition in events organized by the International Military Sports Council (CISM). The CISM was an international governing body established to work alongside the Olympic movement, giving soldiers and sailors from military forces around the world a chance to play on a common field. In 1963, for example, fencers from the Eighth Infantry Division had the chance to compete at a CISM meet in Vienna, and Eighth Infantry Division wrestlers traveled to Egypt for another CISM event.[42] Nevertheless, the men of the Eighth Infantry Division could never forget that their sporting activities were simply a sideshow to the real dangers they were facing across the Fulda Gap. In that sense, just as had been the case since the end of the nineteenth century, soldiers' sports were not just about keeping the men fit and safely entertained, but also about maintaining their alertness and readiness for battle.

No "Spare Time" at All in Vietnam Really

Even as the situation in Germany stabilized, the situation in Vietnam became less stable. By 1965, hundreds of thousands of young American men began one-year rotations in and out of South Vietnam in an effort to stop the advance of communism in Southeast Asia. These one-year rotations meant that earlier military efforts to create strong unit cohesion through sport had to be abandoned. This seemed especially true as the fighting intensified throughout South Vietnam. And as the fighting consumed their days, soldiers found that they had little time to pursue leisure-time activities—assuming that they were able to find time for themselves at all. Therefore, most soldiers and Marines stationed in the country seem to have had to rely on themselves to organize pick-up basketball games and similar sports without the administrative structure for soldier sport that had developed during World War II and continued thereafter in Europe.

As an example, the *Arrow*, published by the Eighth Infantry Division in Europe during the late 1950s through the 1960s, regularly featured stories about division soldiers playing sports. On the other hand, the newsletter for the Air Cavalry Division published in Vietnam during 1968 and 1969 had very little reporting on in-country sports. Although one story discussed how Lt. Cameron Lee of the 41st Civil Affairs Co. (CA) "delighted children with his basketball antics," the story also made it clear that Lee's exhibition was not about competitive sport, but about efforts by Civil Affairs officers to win the hearts and minds of the Vietnamese.[43] Another article describes the typical night in Vietnam for soldiers at their base camps. While some troops were writing and reading cards and letters, others were "tossing basketballs through a hoop or pitching horseshoes or breaking into a sweat during a volleyball game."[44] Again, although the soldiers may have had the equipment and the short time to work on their "games," they were doing so without any formal leagues or rules.

Recently, the U.S. Army's Heritage and Education Center (USAHEC) has been releasing veteran surveys from the Vietnam conflict. Most survivors of that war who have responded to the USAHEC recall having little leisure time, even behind the wire. For example, E-4 Peter L. Cullen remarked that even at the base camps "they kept us busy," as did many of his colleagues.[45] With his limited spare time, LTC James R. Howard remembered drinking at the An Khe base, although that was not very often, and E-5 Lee T. McCann remembered reading and drinking "behind barbed wire."[46] Indeed, whereas few of the responding veterans remember playing sports, many recall spending their spare time drinking. Because the original justification for military sports as developed during World War I focused on keeping the men occupied and alcohol free, the fact that Vietnam veterans remember drinking or smoking "weed" rather than playing sports is remarkable.[47] Although SFCE 7 Robert D. Rizzard reported swimming and playing softball while in Vietnam, his account probably reflects his assignment to General Creighton Abrams' headquarters in Saigon rather than to a field outfit.[48] For most soldiers, the Army's assumption was that soldiers on the 365-day rotation would benefit more from time off spent in Australia or Thailand rather than playing organized sports inside Vietnam. This is reflected in articles published in the Air Cavalry Division newsletter encouraging men to take advantage of the surfing and waterskiing in Sydney and fishing, sailing, and swimming available in Bangkok.[49]

While American soldiers, sailors, and Marines were encouraged to spend their time off away from Vietnam, vacationing in Thailand, Australia, and other points of interest in the Far East, back home the complex system for military sports, which had existed two decades earlier, seems to have fallen by the wayside. At Fort Drum in the Adirondacks, leisure time activities for the soldiers stationed there in 1964 included movies, a disco, a pool tournament, and, of all things, croquet.[50] Eight years later, the sports program had been expanded to include a softball league with teams drawn from soldiers and airmen stationed at the base.[51] However, there seems to have been little to no effort by commanders to expand the scope and reach of Fort Drum athletics.

And Now We Are All Volunteers

The congressional decision to end the military draft and rely on an all-volunteer military force posed a particular challenge for the Army. Whereas Navy recruiters could extol the romance of the seas and Air Force recruiters could promise the romance of the air, Army recruiters had to find other ways to bring America's youth into the ranks. One way identified early on by recruiters was through sports. For example, in the early 1980s SPC Ed Budd, a black belt in tae kwon do, worked with five different karate clubs in the Concord, New Hampshire area, encouraging the young people he encountered to consider the Army as a career.[52] Similarly, the Army Reserves sponsored a nationwide scholar-athlete contest, both to publicize the exploits of young athletes and to create some good publicity for their organization.[53] The Army also sent serving athletes around the country to identify youths for further recruitment. Thus, SP5 Mike Shine, Olympic silver medalist in the 400-meter hurdles at Montreal in 1976, gave out awards at a Pittsburgh area track meet in 1980.[54] In fact, there were 17 soldiers on the American Olympic team at Montreal, a fact that Major Timothy Morgan always emphasized when talking to kids. As he put it, it was "amazing how interest in high school audiences rises when I casually mention that the Army trains Olympic athletes."[55] Recruiters also provided coaching to students interested in sports not offered at their high schools. For example, Massachusetts athletes interested in high school lacrosse benefited when two Army lieutenants were ordered to develop and coach teams in that state.

The Army Master Athlete Program

During the darkest days of the Cold War, American reporters often mocked the idea that Soviet and Soviet-bloc athletes were pursuing military careers. Certainly the suggestion that the tiny gymnast Olga Korbut somehow obtained the rank of sergeant in the Soviet Army before her sixteenth birthday raised eyebrows. As has already been demonstrated, the reality is that very often sport and military skills overlap. Learning how to shoot accurately, run efficiently, swim, and lift great weights has formed military training for centuries. Given that, in recent years the U.S. Army has encouraged world-class athletes to enlist and serve their country while competing. This World Class Athlete Program proved to be significant at the most recent Olympic Winter Games. At Sochi, Russia, in 2014 soldiers coached (SSgt. William Tavares and SFC Tuffield Latour), slid (Sgt. Nick Cunningham, Cpt. Christopher Fogt, Sgt. Preston Griffal, 1Lt Michael Kohn, Sgt. Matthew Mortensen, and Sergeant Justin Olsen), and guarded the goal in sledge hockey (SSgt. Jen Lee).[56] As Mortensen recently explained, as a member of the World Class Athlete Program he is expected to represent the United States in international luge competition. As an active-duty soldier he is also expected to keep up with his ongoing military training and be ready for call up when necessary. This program has allowed Mortensen to continue his competitive career while also preparing for his future outside of athletics.[57] Although the World Class Athlete Program is not intended to create a system of mass athletic participation, it is certainly intended to present the United States, its Army, and its athletes in the most favorable light.

Today the connection between sports and military skills seems well established. Although most civilians remain unaware of the time and effort dedicated by soldiers and sailors to athletic training and competition, commanders remain convinced that the best way to ensure good discipline and cohesion is to provide young men and women with the chance to become true team members.

Notes

1 "'The Kinges' Majesties Declaration Concerning Lawful Sports," in *The King's Book of Sports*, ed. L.A. Govett (London: Elliott Stock, 1890), in Steven A. Riess, ed., *Major Problems in American Sport History* 2nd ed. (Stamford, CT: Cengage Learning, 2015), 28.

2 "The Massachusetts Bay Colony," *Records of Massachusetts Bay* 3: 316–317, in the *Sabbath Recorder* 64, no. 12 (March 23, 1908), in ed. Riess, 29–30.

3 William T. Allison, Jeffrey Grey, and Janet G. Valentine, *American Military History: A Survey from Colonial Times to the Present* 2nd ed. (Boston: Pearson, 2013), 8.

4 Timothy Breen argues that the emergence of spontaneous horse races in Colonial Virginia was a reflection of the gentry's interest in gambling rather than an interest in the races themselves. See T.H. Breen, "Horses and Gentlemen: The Cultural Significance of Gambling Among the Gentry of Virginia," 34 *William and Mary Quarterly* (April 1977) 239–257.

5 Steven W. Pope, "An Army of Athletes: Playing Fields, Battlefields, and the American Military Sporting Experience, 1890–1920," *The Journal of Military History* 59 (July 1995): 436.

6 As an example of early rule making in baseball, see the New York Knickerbocker's Rules of Baseball from 1845 in ed. Riess, *Major Problems in American Sport History*, 93–94.

7 George B. Kirsch, *Baseball in Blue and Grey: The National Pastime During the Civil War* (Princeton: Princeton University Press, 2003).

8 Terry Bohn, "Nineteenth Century Base Ball in Bismarck, Dakota Territory," in *Baseball Research Journal* 43 no. 1, 2014, 48–53.

9 For more on the role of sport in advancing American imperialism see Gerald R. Gems, *The Athletic Crusade: Sports and American Cultural Imperialism* (Omaha: University of Nebraska Press, 2012). For how sport was used by other imperial powers to advance their interests see Heather L.

Dichter and Andrew L. Johns, *Diplomatic Games: Sport, Statecraft and International Relations Since 1945* (Lexington: University of Kentucky Press, 2014).

10 Arthur R. Ashe, Jr., *A Hard Road to Glory: A History of the African-American Athlete, 1619–1918, Vol. I* (New York: Warner Books, Inc., 1988), 14.

11 Wanda Ellen Wakefield, *Playing to Win: Sports and the American Military, 1898–1945* (Albany: SUNY Press, 1997), 6.

12 Steven W. Pope, "An Army of Athletes: Playing Fields, Battlefields, and the American Military Sporting Experience, 1890–1920," *The Journal of Military History* 59, no. 3 (July 1995): 436.

13 Ibid., 436.

14 See Wakefield, *Playing to Win*, Chapter 2.

15 Major George Whythe, Captain Joseph Mills Hanson, and Captain Carl V. Burger, eds., *The Inter-Allied Games, Paris 22nd June to 6th July, 1919* (Paris: The Games Committee, 1919) 17–20.

16 For more on the role of the Jewish Welfare Board's activities, see Linda J. Borish, "Athletic Activities of 'Various Kinds': Physical Health and Sport Programs for Jewish American Women," *Journal of Sport History* 26 (Summer 1999): 240–270. Borish is continuing her study of the Jewish Welfare Board as reflected in her recent presentation at the annual North American Society for Sport History Conference held in Miami in May 2015.

17 Raymond B. Fosdick, "Welfare Work," *War College Lecture*, March 3, 1922, delivered at Washington, DC.

18 Brigadier General Edward L. King, "The G-3 Division, War Department General Staff and its Present Outstanding Problems," *War College Lecture*, September 16, 1919, delivered at Washington, DC for G-3 Course #5.

19 For more see John Daye, *Encyclopedia of Armed Forces Football: The Complete History of the Glory Years*, (Haworth, NJ: St. Johann Press, 2014).

20 See the discussion in Wakefield, *Playing to Win*, 66–67.

21 Wakefield, *Playing to Win*, 82.

22 Ibid., 83.

23 For more on service football during the war, see Daye, *Encyclopedia of Armed Forces Football*.

24 *Baltimore Afro-American* quoted in Wakefield, *Playing to Win*, 128.

25 Wakefield, *Playing to Win*, 84.

26 Ibid., 88–89.

27 Ibid., 101.

28 Ibid.

29 Ibid., 103.

30 "Fun for Family at Garmisch," *Arrow*, January 8, 1960, 6. For more on the Allied interest in rebuilding the European economy through sport after World War II, see Wanda Ellen Wakefield, "Taking Back the Slopes," in Dichter and Johns, ed., *Diplomatic Games*.

31 "Garmisch Scene of European Figure Skating Championships," *Arrow*, January 30, 1960, 6.

32 "AFRC Offers Skiers Fun in Pleasant Surroundings," *Arrow*, February 23, 1963, 4.

33 "Snapshot Reflections of German-American Friendship Week," *Arrow*, May 14, 1960, 4–5, and May 21, 1960, 7.

34 "Sgt. to Coach German Team in World Series," *Arrow*, September 24, 1960, 3.

35 "The Mainz Troopers: 1960 European Football Champions," *Arrow*, December 10, 1960, 4–5.

36 "Olympic Ticket Requests Rise," *Arrow*, July 9, 1960, 8.

37 "Davis Aims for Discus Mark," *Arrow*, April 15, 1960, 3, and "DA Seeking Top Swimmers, Divers for Olympic Trials," *Arrow*, May 7, 1960, 6.

38 "USAREUR Matmen Sought by DA for Olympic Matmen," *Arrow*, January 23, 1960.

39 "20th Trains Weight Lifter—Heads for Trials," *Arrow*, June 4, 1960, 6 and "8th Division Lifter Grabs 3rd in Olympic Trials," *Arrow*, July 19, 1960.

40 W.W. Aucoin, "Weight Champ Tries for Japan's Games," *Arrow*, May 9, 1964, 6.

41 "Willie Davenport Off to Fort Campbell for 100 Meters," *Arrow*, May 16, 1964, 6.

42 "U.S. Fencers, Wrestlers Ready for May CISM Meet," *Arrow*, April 20, 1963, 4.

43 Photograph of Lt. Cameron Lee in *The Air Cavalry Division* Vol. 1 #1, April 1968, 24.

44 Tom Dotson, "Night in Vietnam: Air Cavalry Style," *The Air Cavalry Division*, Vol. 1 #4, January 1969.

45 E-4 Peter L. Cullen, Vietnam War, Veterans Survey Collection, Box 1, Folders 1–40, USAHEC, and E-5 James H. Minor, E-5 Michael McGregor.
46 LtC. James R. Howard and E-5 Lee T. McCann, Vietnam War, Veterans Survey Collection, Box 1, Folders 1–40, USAHEC.
47 For drinking, see E-5 Damon R. Kilmore and for smoking marijuana, see E-5 David Stark, Vietnam War, Veterans Survey Collection, Box 1, Folders 1–40, USAHEC.
48 SFCE 7 Robert D. Rizzard, Vietnam War, Veterans Survey Collection, Box 1, Folders 1–40, USAHEC.
49 Tom Dotson, "Holiday From a Warzone," *The Air Cavalry Division*, Vol. 1, #4, January, 1969 and James Dotson, "Holiday from a Warzone, Part Two," *The Air Cavalry Division*, Vol. 2, #1, Spring, 1969.
50 "Pine Plains Service Club," *Camp Drum Sentinel*, August 24, 1967, 8.
51 "TMP Nips Det 11, 8–7," *Fort Drum Sentinel*, July 30, 1975, 8.
52 "Karate Brings Results," *All Volunteer*, 33 #11, November, 1980, 14–15.
53 "Reserves Sponsor High School Awards for Nationwide Publicity," *All Volunteer* 35 #1, January, 1982, 26–27.
54 Russell Weiskircher, "Olympian Highlights High School Track Meet," *All Volunteer* 33, #9, September, 1980.
55 SPC Edward Cannato, "A Tale of Two Runners," *U.S. Army Recruiting and Reenlisting Journal*, 31 #6, June, 1978, 11.
56 For more see www.thearmywcap.com (accessed December 19, 2014).
57 Interview with Matthew Mortensen conducted by Wanda Ellen Wakefield, Lake Placid, New York, December 6, 2014.

30

A DIVIDED WORLD

The U.S., the U.S.S.R., and Sport during the Cold War

Chris Elzey

Introduction

In early December 1951, Richard B. Walsh, a U.S. State Department analyst, gave a talk at the national Amateur Athletic Union (AAU) convention in Florida. Earlier that spring, the Soviet Union had been admitted to the International Olympic Committee (IOC), paving the way for U.S.S.R. participation in the Games. Walsh was suspicious. "Reports from our embassies . . . afford positive proof that the Kremlin has mounted a gigantic cultural offensive," he told members. "It is designed to prove the Soviet line of supremacy in the arts as well as on the athletic field." Winning, it seemed, was all the U.S.S.R. cared about. A defiant Walsh remarked:

> We do not deny the prowess of the Soviet athlete. We are not boasting of American supremacy. . . . [B]ut we do not have to swallow the lie that the Soviet athlete is superior because he is a product of the Soviet regime.

Three weeks later, Walsh's talk was published in the *Department of State Bulletin.* In effect, America's top foreign policy agency had condoned his remarks.[1]

By late 1951, American officials were aware that the aim of Soviet sports had changed. In the years following World War II, the U.S.S.R. started competing widely in international events. Initially, the participation was more about assessing the caliber of Soviet athletes than it was about extolling the virtues of communism. But as U.S.S.R. victories piled up, the purpose of Soviet athletics shifted. Sport now had a political goal, as Walsh indicated in Florida.[2]

Until 1991, the two superpowers were locked in an athletic struggle of gargantuan proportions. Each measured success by defeating the other. The same remained true almost any time athletes from capitalist and communist nations met. Imbued with ideological significance, sport—particularly the Olympic Games and the dual track meets between the United States and the U.S.S.R.—symbolized the do-or-die competitiveness of the Cold War. Victory was the ultimate objective. Defeating one's ideological rival was often used as evidence to show that communism or capitalism was better. Fierce competition ensued. Sometimes relations were so strained that boycotts resulted. Politics defined how sport in the Cold War was played, organized, and viewed.

The Rivalry Starts

For almost 30 years after the founding of the Soviet Union in 1922, sporting relations between the United States and the U.S.S.R. were virtually nonexistent. In fact, the Soviets rarely competed against Western nations. The Kremlin believed that Western sport was immoral and nonutilitarian, a capitalist pursuit that undermined the goals of a socialist state. But in the aftermath of World War II, the U.S.S.R., realizing the propagandistic value of athletic victories, shed its isolationism and began competing against Western countries. The Soviets performed admirably and became America's chief athletic rival.[3]

The first major sporting event in which both countries participated was the 1952 Helsinki Olympics. Other communist nations had participated in the previous London Games with some success. But the Soviets sent only officials to London. The U.S.S.R. had not yet established a National Olympic Committee (NOC), a prerequisite for participation. "While the United States was running away with 1948 Olympic games, Russian observers spied diligently," *Newsweek* huffed in 1951. "They charted basketball plays. They took numerous pictures of track and field performers in action. They showed a distinct conversational interest in American weight lifters."[4]

By 1952, East-West relations were even icier. Mistrust was obvious. Helsinki planners had hoped that the torch relay could cross into the Soviet Union. The Kremlin, however, objected—which meant the relay had to be diverted farther north, into Sweden. Moreover, during the Games, competitors from communist countries were lodged in quarters near Helsinki, apart from other Olympians. For their part, American authorities tried unsuccessfully to have athletes who were opposed to communism and who had left the Soviet bloc participate in the Games as members of the newly established Union of Free Eastern European Sportsmen (UFEES). Assigned to the U.S. squad was an American official tasked with ensuring that U.S. Olympians were not put in politically comprising positions.[5]

During much of the Helsinki Games, U.S.S.R. newspapers published daily points tables showing the Soviet Union in the lead. But the United States would rally to draw even. (In a burst of overzealousness, *Pravda* prematurely reported that the U.S.S.R. had won.) In addition, the American method of scoring, which awarded three more points for first place, had the United States well ahead. The Soviets were not swayed. N.N. Romanov, who oversaw the U.S.S.R. Olympic effort in Helsinki, grumbled, "There is no doubt that given fair judging in all sports the athletes of the Soviet Union . . . would have been awarded considerably more prizes."[6]

Soviet success in the Games fanned U.S. animosity toward the communist nation's athletic system. "It should be clearly evident to those with eyes to see that the Communists . . . have their sinister eyes fixed upon the 1956 Olympic Games," Senator John Marshall Butler of Maryland said in 1955. "And their ulterior motive is to advance not the cause of fair play and sportsmanship, but international Communist domination." Butler continued: "[T]he Soviet athlete is not an amateur; he is a paid propaganda agent of the U.S.S.R. . . . one more slave in the hideous chain gang of brainwashed individuals slavishly advancing the Communist cause." Others agreed. In 1954, *U.S. News & World Report* observed, "In Russia, sports is a big, grim, production-line business, run from grade school to Olympic track by that supercoach (sic), the state."[7]

U.S.S.R. officials disputed the assertion. In a missive to IOC President Avery Brundage printed in the *Olympic Review* in 1960, Soviet NOC chair Konstantin Andrianov penned, in italics, "*There are simply no conditions for* [the] *existence of professionalism in Soviet sport.*" To Andrianov, communism was the wellspring of athletic success.

> Incessantly growing living standard[s] . . . *cutting down in working hours* . . . *increase of time for recreation* . . . excellent facilities for practising physical culture and sport . . . while working at industrial enterprises, collective farms and offices . . . [allow] Soviet people . . . enough time to make their health stronger and have all possibilities to reach the heights of sporting skill.

Andrianov added: "[athletes] are encouraged, *not with money* or . . . well paid (sic) jobs and luxurious flats"—all of which critics said Soviet athletes received—"but with . . . medals, diplomas, souvenirs and honorary titles."[8]

To many, the Soviet system was patently un-American. In a 1954 editorial titled "One Red Challenge We Should Not Meet," *Life* opined:

> It may sound like an advance alibi, but we say to hell with [competing all-out against the USSR]. . . . If sports are to be part of the cold war, they cease to be either hygiene or entertainment and become a form of mass biological experiment instead. . . . Sports to us are part of a way of life which holds that the human body is pretty well designed already, to be kept at its best by stress and strain, but not at the expense of mind and soul. If defending that idea means competing for second place, so be it.[9]

Aldo "Buff" Donelli, Columbia University football coach, concluded in *Amateur Athlete* in 1965 that American athletes

> have the incentive to become great and the opportunity to do so any way they wish. It is this incentive and this freedom of expression that gives them the one final burst of energy, the one extra second of determination that means victory. I think this is why it will be very difficult for the Soviets to catch [the US].[10]

But at the 1956 Melbourne Games, the U.S.S.R. outscored the United States, 622–497. Soviets rejoiced. *Sovetskii Sport* printed a chart whose title read: "Here it is, the table of success!" *Komsomolskaia Pravda* headlined on page one, "TRIUMPH FOR SOVIET SPORT." *Trud* published a cartoon of an athlete wearing a CCCP sweatshirt standing atop a medal dais; an American occupies second place, an Australian third.[11]

American commentators reconciled the defeat by reminding fans that many Soviet victories came in secondary sports. The American press also reported that several Hungarian athletes, whose homeland was occupied by Soviet troops after the Kremlin's crackdown on pro-democratic forces, had chosen to seek asylum in America. The implication was that the U.S.S.R. may have won the Olympics, but given a choice of which system to live under, communists preferred capitalism. For dispirited Americans, news of the defections was an Olympic salve.[12]

Controversy at the 1960 Rome Olympics

But if American pride took a hit in Melbourne, it was shattered four years later in Rome. At those Games, the U.S.S.R. scored its biggest victory to date, increasing its medal take from 98 in 1956 to 103 in 1960, and more than doubling its margin in total medals over the United States in the same two Olympics. Soviet papers had a heyday. "VICTORY!" a front-page headline in *Sovetskii Sport* shouted. *Pravda* ran the banner headline: "Glory to Soviet athletes—heroes of the XVII Olympiad." *Vecherniaia Moskva*, like many U.S.S.R. papers, reported the 683–463½ win. Soviet Premier Nikita Khrushchev boasted: "[T]he triumph of Soviet sportsmen means a victory for the man of the new socialist society, which has already given so much proof of its superiority in the field of science, technology, and culture." Three days after the Games, U.S.S.R. Olympians were honored before 100,000 people in Moscow's Lenin Stadium. *Izvestia* called the celebration "March of [the] victors."[13]

The defeat in Rome alarmed Americans. But unlike in 1952, they could not fall back on a more favorable method of scoring. The defeat—807½–664½, according to the U.S. method—was too great. Newspapers delivered the grim news. "Olympics End, U.S. 2nd-Best," the *Cleveland Plain Dealer* reported. Even the usually strong U.S. track squad had underperformed.[14]

Other situations in Rome revealed Cold War animosity. There was, for instance, the fractious relationship between nationalist China—in other words, the Republic of China (ROC)—and communist China, aka the People's Republic of China (PRC). The PRC had competed at the 1952 Helsinki Olympics, though only nominally (a swimmer was the lone entrant). But in 1958, the PRC, furious over the IOC's acceptance of nationalist China, pulled out of the Olympic movement. The PRC government considered itself to be the only lawful authority of the Chinese people, and it refused to let the IOC undermine that claim. So it quit. But in a surprise move in 1959, the IOC prohibited the ROC from calling itself "China" during the 1960 Games in Rome. Anticommunists in America and elsewhere were incensed.[15]

Political maneuvering began. According to writer David Maraniss, the American State Department, which backed the nationalists, not only tried to persuade the IOC to reverse its decision, it also attempted to convince ROC officials to withdraw their team. While U.S. authorities conducted sports diplomacy, the American press flayed IOC President Avery Brundage, labeling him an ally of communism. But the name calling and negotiations had no effect. Eager to have its star athlete—C.K. Yang—compete, the ROC agreed to the IOC's terms and sent a squad to Rome. The issue, though, was not over. When the ROC marched into the Stadio Olimpico during the opening ceremony, its delegation flashed a sign stating "Under Protest." Yang would be the sole ROC athlete to medal in Rome, finishing second to his friend and fellow UCLA Bruin, Rafer Johnson, the U.S. standard bearer in the Parade of Nations a few days earlier. Never before had an African American been selected for that privilege.[16]

A world-class athlete, Johnson knew what it was like to compete against the U.S.S.R. In an American-Soviet track meet in Moscow in 1958—the first time the two nations met in dual track competition—he won the decathlon and set a new world record. Even though Johnson had defeated Vasily Kuznetsov, a celebrated athlete in his own right, the Lenin Stadium crowd supported the American as if he were a member of the Soviet squad.[17]

The 1958 track meet was part of a bilateral pact between the United States and Soviet Union that instituted U.S.-U.S.S.R. exchanges in a wide range of activities, including sport. For years, American and Soviet sports officials had tried to organize athletic visits to one another's country, but Cold War politics always seemed to get in the way. For instance, in the 1950s both nations, fearing the exposure of sensitive geographical regions to spies, enacted regulations limiting the movement of the other's citizens. Such interdictions often thwarted sports visits.[18]

The bilateral agreement was culminated after the United States finally altered its policy of fingerprinting foreign visitors, as mandated by the Immigration and Nationality Act of 1952.

The Soviets, particularly Khrushchev, detested the law. But once it was repealed, serious parleying started. By January 1958, an agreement had been reached. But not much changed. Most U.S.-U.S.S.R. exchanges were still viewed through a Cold War prism.[19]

U.S.–U.S.S.R. Track and Field Competitions

The 1958 track meet between the two superpowers was so fraught with Cold War meaning that American and Soviet officials were unable to agree afterward on which nation had won. Like in Helsinki in 1952, scoring was the issue. Expressing sexist attitudes common in 1950s America, U.S. authorities refused to add the results of the men's events to those of the women's. The Soviets, however, with a much stronger women's team, tallied the scores together. In the meet, the U.S. men prevailed, 126–109, but the Soviet women outscored their American rivals, 63–44. Combined, the score stood 172–170—a victory for the U.S.S.R.[20]

To no one's astonishment, Soviets and Americans interpreted events differently. "Victory for Soviet track athletes," *Krasnaia Zvezda* proclaimed. Americans fired back. "U.S. and Russia agreed in advance on a scoring system to keep totals for men and women separate. U.S. men won," *U.S. News & World Report* declared, adding, "So Russia ignored the agreement, lumped all scores together and promptly announced a Soviet victory."[21]

The 1959 meet in Philadelphia was a replay of the Moscow competition: the American men achieved victory, but the Soviet women outdid their U.S. counterparts. Together, the scores gave the U.S.S.R. a 175–167 win. Which team won was, again, hotly debated. Radio Moscow called the meet "a great success for Soviet athletes and their trainers and our home sports as a whole." American officials had figured that the Soviets would view the outcome as they saw fit. Before the meet, an Associated Press (AP) story quoted Dan Ferris, longtime administrator of the AAU: "We're the host this year and we set the scoring rules. But they'll probably send it back to Russia the way they want."[22]

Why was it so difficult to decide the winner? One explanation is that the United States and the U.S.S.R. were directly pitted against one another. The head-to-head competition reflected Cold War hostility. Another reason was track and field itself. Admired on both sides of the Iron Curtain, track and field was something Americans and Soviets understood well and cared about. Politics, too, heightened the momentousness of the competitions. As East-West relations deteriorated during the early 1960s—caused in part by the construction of the Berlin Wall—the importance of the meets grew. The 1961 competition in Moscow drew 130,000 people—the most to attend the two-day affair at the time. The next year, the meet in Palo Alto, California, attracted even more. Friendliness between Soviet and American participants abounded, despite the animosities of the opposing governments.[23]

Before the 1961 meet, Soviet planners agreed that men's and women's results would be scored independently. U.S.S.R. officials even arranged to have gender-specific scoreboards placed inside Lenin Stadium. The cordiality soon disappeared. After the meet, the *San Francisco Chronicle* headlined, "U.S. Tracksters Top Russ, 124–111," forgetting that the United States had actually lost, 179–163, if women's results were included. By contrast, TASS, the main news organization in the U.S.S.R., said that the Soviets had won the combined meet.[24] Leonid Khomenov, head of U.S.S.R. track and field, stated:

> The United States is the only country where national championships are held separately for men and women. . . . [W]e made a concession to our American friends and this time kept a separate score for men's and women's teams. However, this is

> an exception and not the rule. . . . We believe that in this match, as was done in 1958 and 1959, an over-all score must be kept besides the separate scores.[25]

Harold O. Zimman, a U.S. Olympic official, wrote, "None but the most partisan Russian fans would consent to [combining scores], however."[26]

Khomenov's statement was precisely the kind American authorities feared the 1961 meet would spawn. A week before the Moscow competition, Senator Clair Engle of California warned:

> It seems to me that it is very bad business for our Government to help finance a trip to Moscow to compete with Russian athletes if we are not sending the strongest team we can put in the field. We may be supplying [the Soviets] with another opportunity of claiming superiority over the United States.

Weeks later, a State Department dispatch from Moscow confirmed Engle's fears. A writer for *Pravda*, the communiqué read, had "congratulate[d] the Soviet team on a 'new outstanding victory' in which the superiority of the Soviet side was even greater than in previous contests." An even bigger coup occurred in 1965 when the U.S.S.R. men downed the Americans in the meet in Kiev. The Soviet men had never won a dual meet against the United States.[27]

For Americans, the Kiev loss served as one more indication that the U.S.S.R. was a foe to be taken with deadly seriousness. Indeed, ever since the U.S.S.R. burst onto the athletic scene in the 1950s, U.S. authorities had issued ominous warnings about the prowess of Soviet teams and the propaganda that could be derived from it. Amid perceptions of American weakness resulting from Sputnik and other Cold War setbacks, the athletic progress made by the U.S.S.R. spurred Americans officials to reevaluate the U.S. sports system.[28]

During the 1960s, the National Collegiate Athletic Association (NCAA) and AAU came under fire for hampering America's international sports effort as each organization sought to prohibit its athletes from competing in events staged by the other. Many took exception to the noncooperation. When the American men lost in Kiev in 1965, U.S. officials pointed to the NCAA-AAU spat as the cause. The Amateur Sports Act of 1978, which consolidated power in the United States Olympic Committee (USOC) and sport-specific federations, finally settled the conflict. But it had taken a series of U.S.S.R. victories, most notably the Soviets' resounding win at the 1972 Munich Olympics, to help stir lawmakers to action.[29]

Another problem focused on the amount of government aid given to U.S. Olympians. Compared to the assistance lavished upon Soviet athletes, the support was meager. Lawmakers proposed changes. In 1964, after the United States finished a disappointing eighth at that year's Winter Games, Representative Frank Morse of Massachusetts submitted H.R. 10539, which "authorize[d] the appropriation of [public] funds to pay certain expenses of the U.S. Olympic team . . . in the 1964 [Summer] Olympic games." Morse said: "In my view the support of a group of outstanding amateur athletes carries with it no greater political overtones than any other program of cultural or educational exchange." Soon thereafter, a USOC plan to address recent Olympic defeats was made public. Overseen by Franklin L. Orth, erstwhile Assistant Secretary of War, the plan reflected American anxieties over Soviet power. Orth was quoted as "call[ing] the program 'our big test to determine whether democracy can compete with a regimented society as represented by the Soviet Union and its satellites.'"[30]

The USOC project garnered much support. Among the more enthusiastic backers was Minnesota Senator Hubert Humphrey. A year earlier, in 1963, *Parade* magazine had published an article by Humphrey entitled "Why we *must* win the Olympics." In the piece, he argued that Olympic success was a political necessity, in large part because it could be used to repudiate communist propaganda. Humphrey's recommendations included having better venues for "seemingly 'obscure' Olympic sports" and "find[ing] ways to raise the funds necessary to provide adequate training and facilities for our international competitors." Both Senator Abraham Ribicoff of Connecticut and AAU President Louis Fisher proposed holding "a national Olympics," a competition not unlike the Soviets' own sports festival, the *Spartakiad.* Many of the proposals were discussed at the inaugural National Conference on Olympic Development in Washington, DC, in May 1966.[31]

Ultimately, changes would be made. Meanwhile, the Soviets continued winning. At the 1960 Winter Olympics in Squaw Valley, they soundly defeated the United States. That summer, the Rome Games belonged to the communists too. Of the 11 countries to win at least three gold medals, five were from the Soviet bloc. Partly as a result, the then-national crisis in physical fitness among American youth acquired a distinct ideological hue. Charles "Bud" Wilkinson, the University of Oklahoma football coach who headed up the President's Council on Youth Fitness, wrote in the *Department of State News Letter* in 1962,

> Our opponents in the cold war welcome [reports of unsatisfactory youth health] and use them as propaganda to be spread in their attempt to convince citizens of other countries that we are not, as a nation, fit to meet our commitments abroad.

Athletic tours organized by the State Department were used to refute such claims. One American official noted in 1964, "Sport has become a vigorous force in international relations."[32]

Of course, that was one of the reasons why the American-Soviet track meets had been organized. Although goodwill prevailed at most, political disputes intervened. The 1966 meet in Los Angeles was planned for July 23 and 24. But 12 days before the competition, the U.S.S.R. announced that because of recent U.S. bombing attacks in North Vietnam, it would not be sending a team. According to TASS, Soviet athletes had "passed a protest resolution," which in part declared, "Our hatred for the American military which is perpetrating atrocities in Vietnam . . . does not permit us to take part in a match with sportsmen of a country from where this aggression comes." Two days after the Soviets' announcement, Polish authorities informed organizers of a U.S.-Poland meet in Berkeley, California, that Polish athletes, too, would not be participating.[33]

Americans decried the Soviets' decision. One columnist wrote, "It was pure, brazen, headline-grabbing propaganda."[34] Foy D. Kohler, American ambassador to the U.S.S.R., disputed the Soviet claim that athletes alone were responsible for the protest. In a July 11 cable to the State Department, Kohler wrote, tersely:

> MOSCOW TV TONIGHT CARRIED PROGRAM IN WHICH SOVIET TRACK TEAM ASKED TO EXPRESS VIEW RE PARTICIPATION IN LOS ANGELES TRACK MEET. ABOUT FOUR OF TEAM INDICATED CLEAR OPPOSITION . . . WHILE OTHERS FAILED TO QUESTION; WHEREUPON INTERLOCUTOR DECLARED TEAM UNANIMOUSLY OPPOSED TO PARTICIPATION. PATENT RIGGED NATURE OF DECISION APPARENT TO ANY VIEWER.[35]

American journalists were equally suspicious. The Kremlin attempted to deflect the skepticism. An AP story datelined July 14 reported,

> Gavriil Korobkov, head coach of the Soviet track and field, denied today that Russian athletes had obeyed instructions when they decided not to" participate in the meet. The story quoted part of a sentence Korobkov had penned in a Soviet daily. USSR sportsmen, the coach explained, "indeed had . . . 'instruction'—their conscience.[36]

The untimely withdrawal of the communist teams left planners of both meets scrambling. Fortunately, alternative competitions were organized. The one that replaced the American-Soviet meet fared particularly well. Renamed the LA Times International Games, it featured U.S., British, Norwegian, New Zealand, and Australian competitors. During the two-day event, which attracted almost 62,000 people, three world records were established. Two days after the meet, the Soviets and Poles held their own competition in the Byelorussian capital of Minsk. The U.S.S.R. won. The *New York Times*' Frank Litsky, measuring results in California against those in Minsk, found that the United States had outscored the U.S.S.R., 182½–149½.[37]

In the years before the 1966 meet, Americans, of course, had other reasons to cheer. After the United States smashed the U.S.S.R. in track at the 1964 Tokyo Olympics, Arthur Daley of the *New York Times* wrote:

> If [the Tokyo competition] was an eminently satisfactory meet for the Americans, it had to be close to disaster for the Red brothers. They have slipped back, and it has to be mortifying for them to realize that the American way is the better way. That's even harder to accept.

Greater US victories lay ahead.[38]

The 1968 Mexico City Games, for example, witnessed the United States' greatest Olympic victory yet over the Soviet Union. President Lyndon Johnson told U.S. Olympians: "Thanks to you, the world has witnessed once again the vitality, vigor and fair play which mark the American character." Demonstrating the close relationship between sport and politics, Americans commentators praised Czechoslovakian gymnast Vera Caslavska for her act of defiance during the medal ceremony in which she and a Soviet competitor were awarded first place. A proud Caslavska stood ramrod straight during the playing of the Czechoslovakian anthem. But for the Soviet hymn, she dipped her head and looked away, a mute yet determined stance against the U.S.S.R.'s suppression that August of the reform movement in Czechoslovakia known as the Prague Spring.[39]

Olympic Boycotts of 1980 and 1984

Geopolitical disputes would have more serious consequences. On Christmas Eve, 1979, the Kremlin dispatched thousands of troops to Afghanistan, a country whose pro-Soviet government had recently been taken over by forces less amenable to Moscow. In response, U.S. President Jimmy Carter proposed punitive measures, including a boycott of the 1980 Moscow Olympics. The Games had drawn attacks before. In 1977 and 1978, after reports of the maltreatment of dissidents and Jews in the U.S.S.R. surfaced, several American lawmakers demanded that the Games be relocated. The protests were largely ignored. Carter's, however, was not. For one thing, the country agreed with him. One poll showed that 75 percent of Americans backed a boycott. Congress had already voted for nonparticipation. On March 21, Carter declared that the United States would not be competing in Moscow. Three weeks later, the USOC cast its vote against participation.[40]

Meanwhile, the White House tried to persuade other nations not to participate. Some, like China, readily agreed. But the response was less than what Carter had hoped for. Several U.S. allies ended up competing, although a handful did stage some form of protest, such as not attending the opening ceremony. Among the countries that boycotted were Canada, Japan, Kenya, and, most significantly, West Germany, an Olympic force that had finished fourth at the 1976 Montreal Games. More than 60 countries opted not to participate.[41]

Anti-U.S.S.R. bias was prominent in several American accounts of the Games. Though some journalists praised the efforts of Moscow organizers, many discussed the heavy police presence in the Soviet capital; the poor quality of life for average Muscovites; and the decline in attendance, which, presumably, had been caused by the boycott. And, of course, there was the nonappearance of the U.S. squad. "An Olympics without the Americans," *Los Angeles Times* sportswriter Jim Murray quipped, "is like an Open without Nicklaus, a sail without a moonlight, a dinner without candlelight." Murray's colleague, Bill Shirley, began his piece summing up the Games: "It was a joyless Olympics. Color it gray."[42]

The Soviets, naturally, had other opinions. To them, the Games were a smash hit. Four days into the competitions, an AP story reprinted the views of the U.S.S.R. trade union publication *Trud*. "The Moscow Olympics have many exceptionally brilliant, unprecedented features," the organ gushed. "There are the remarkable palaces of sports . . . the unfeigned happiness of the city's eight million residents, and the expert organization of all events." (Perhaps conveying what it truly thought of the remarks, the AP story misidentified *Trud* as "the labor newspaper Turd.") After the Games, Soviet Olympic head Sergie Pavlov said, "There is every ground for believing that the Olympic Games in Moscow have won themselves a place in history for excellent organisation, their packed calendar of events and the absorbing contests that were witnessed in all sports."[43]

As could be anticipated, the boycott was assailed in the U.S.S.R. A writer for *Pravda* believed:

> The real reason behind the . . . boycott ploy . . . was an attempt by US ruling circles and other imperialistic forces to prevent the . . . Games from being held in the first socialist country, so that the truth about our country, which is persistently hushed-up by bourgeois propaganda, would not become known to the international community.[44]

A substitute competition in the United States for boycotting countries was also denounced. A journalist for TASS termed the patriotic-sounding Liberty Bell Track and Field Classic, which was held before more than 20,000 fans at Franklin Field in Philadelphia, a "gross anti-Olympic farce" and "disgraceful failure."[45]

Four years later, the Soviets boycotted the Games in LA. Only one Warsaw Pact nation—Romania—defied the boycott. Most Westerners figured that the communist withdrawal was retribution for the 1980 boycott. Peter Ueberroth, chair of the Los Angeles Olympic Organizing Committee (LAOOC), stated as much. Similarly, a Harris poll revealed that 69 percent of respondents believed that "a major reason" why the U.S.S.R. had pulled out was to get even with the United States, whereas only 14 percent attributed the boycott to Soviet anxieties over "the safety of [U.S.S.R.] athletes at the Games." Earlier, U.S.S.R. officials had voiced concerns about "the flagrant anti-Soviet campaign" in Los Angeles. *Literaturnaia Gazeta* grimly predicted that "[athletes would] be seized and whisked away to clandestine hide-outs. And there all conceivable methods will be used to extort from them betrayal of their motherland." Americans brushed aside the claims as Soviet propaganda.[46]

In reality, the Kremlin had serious qualms about the wellbeing of U.S.S.R. Olympians. As historian Robert Edelman has shown, such fears proved to be more than just hype. Specifically, U.S.S.R. officials were concerned about an ad-hoc group known as the Ban the Soviets Coalition (BSC). In September 1983, after the U.S.S.R. attacked a Korean Airlines jet in mid-flight, which resulted in 269 deaths, several LA residents organized the BSC, whose purpose was to prevent the U.S.S.R. from competing at the Los Angeles Olympics. Among Americans, the BSC seemed to find a sympathetic ear. Not long after the destruction of the Korean airliner, a Soviet basketball squad's tour of the United States was shelved, as was a trip by a U.S.S.R. hockey team.[47]

Malice toward the Soviet Union lingered. But Ueberroth was adamant: the U.S.S.R. would be invited. According to the Olympic Charter, all nations in good standing with the IOC—and the Soviet Union was—were to be admitted. Nevertheless, three months before the Games, an organization with ties to the BSC announced that it would help Soviet Olympians defect. U.S.S.R. authorities accused the U.S. government of aiding the group, adding, "Open threats of physical victimization and provocative actions [have been] made to sportsmen and officials of the U.S.S.R. and other Socialist countries." On May 8—VE Day—the U.S.S.R. declared that it would be skipping the Olympics. Fourteen other nations, the vast majority of which were communist, did the same. Once again, sport had fallen prey to Cold War politics.[48]

Whether the LA Olympics were considered a success depended upon one's ideological perspective. In general, Americans touted the smooth operation of what they believed were well-hosted Games. The opening ceremony, with its showbiz theatrics and rousing musical accompaniment, was especially admired. Much, too, was made of the 140 countries that took part—an Olympic record, despite the Soviet boycott. Commentators also noted that the record number of tickets (5.5 million) bought in Los Angeles was 200,000 more than the number purchased in Moscow.[49]

In contrast, U.S.S.R. journalists informed readers back home that Los Angeles was lawless and dangerous, that LAOOC planners were "putting crude pressure on foreign judges" to ensure American wins, that Ueberroth and his staff had cheapened the Games by running them like a corporation, and that Olympic venues were too spread out. What Americans praised, Soviets derided. "The opening ceremonies were an overtly political performance whose organizers strenuously propagandized for the notorious 'American way of life,'" TASS stated. The overall quality of athletic performances was also impugned. One Soviet magazine called the LA Games "THE OLYMPICS THAT WERE LACKING."[50]

But the greatest attack was leveled at the displays of American patriotism. With the United States winning 83 gold medals, the most ever won by a single nation, there were plenty of opportunities to fly the American flag. (After the Americans famously upset the Soviets in hockey at the 1980 Winter Olympics, Pete Axthelm of *Newsweek* wrote, "I loved the comment of a fan who said she hadn't seen so many flags since the 1960s. When we were burning them.") Critics in the West carped that ABC-TV, which carried the Games, focused too much on U.S. victories. To sportswriter Frank Deford, ABC meant "Always Be Cheerleaders."[51]

The Soviets seized upon the self-aggrandizement. "The Los Angeles Olympic Games," *Pravda* reported, "were held to the roar of such a jingoistic cannonade that one could think that those were not international competitions but a protracted celebration of Independence Day by America." U.S.S.R. commentators also suggested that the Games had been infused with patriotism to aid President Ronald Reagan in his reelection bid that November. Two days after the Games, American Olympians were celebrated on Capitol Hill. Earlier, onlookers chanting "USA, USA" had thronged Pennsylvania Avenue as team members paraded by. During the Hill ceremony, U.S. Olympians were given S.J. Resolution 338, which, in part, recognized "[American] athletes . . . [for] achiev[ing] great success personally and for the Nation."[52]

Conclusion

The collapse of the Soviet Union in 1991 sounded the death knell for the Cold War in sports. But the demise was not sudden. The athletic rivalry between the superpowers had been losing energy ever since the Kremlin instituted the reformist policies of *perestroika* and *glasnost* in the mid-1980s. Not long after, the ill will generated by the two Olympic boycotts gave way to cautious understanding.[53]

Emerging from this newfound collegiality was a return to large-scale contests in which both nations competed. Picking up where the Friendship Games—a series of athletic events held in communist countries as an alternative to the 1984 Los Angeles Olympics—left off, the Goodwill Games in Moscow in 1986 were, in the words of the *New York Times*, "the first multisport competition between the United States and the Soviet Union since the 1976 Montreal Olympics." A collaborative venture between American television tycoon Ted Turner and U.S.S.R. media agencies, the Goodwill Games proved to be a financial failure. The 1986 Games finished $26 million in debt. The next Games, in 1990 in Seattle, were even more of a flop. All of which suggests that by the late 1980s, the Cold War held less sway over fans.[54]

Still, some longed for the days when sport was construed as a proxy battle of the Cold War. As the *Wall Street Journal* asked on the eve of the 1992 Winter Olympics in Albertville, France, "Who'll We Root Against Now?" More often than not, however, political realities trumped wistful remembrances. After the former Soviet Union competed for the first time as the Commonwealth of Independent States (CIS) at the 1992 Albertville Games, a journalist for *Izvestia* observed: "Before, the Soviet team used to provoke admiration, but at the same time it seemed to be a mighty and soulless machine, whose screws were called on to submissively serve the glory of the Land of the Soviets." It is difficult to imagine those words being uttered during the Cold War. Times had indeed changed. And so, too, had sport.[55]

Notes

1 *Department of State Bulletin*, December 24, 1951, 1007, 1010. For USSR and Olympics, see Allen Guttmann, *The Olympics: A History of the Modern Games* (Urbana, IL: University of Illinois Press, 1992), 86–90.

2 Robert Edelman, *Serious Fun: A History of Spectator Sports in the USSR* (New York: Oxford University Press, 1993), 121–122, and Henry W. Morton, *Soviet Sport: Mirror of Soviet Society* (New York: Collier Books, 1963), 17–18.

3 James Riordan, *Sport in Soviet Society: Development of Sport and Physical Education in Russia and the USSR* (Cambridge, UK: Cambridge University Press, 1977), 161–182, 363–367.

4 *Newsweek*, May 7, 1951, 80.

5 Alfred E. Senn, *Power, Politics, and the Olympic Games: A History of the Power Brokers, Events, and Controversies That Shaped the Games* (Champaign, IL: Human Kinetics, 1999), 100–102. Nonaffiliated athletes in Toby C. Rider, "Political Warfare in Helsinki: American Covert Strategy and the Union of Free Eastern European Sportsmen," *The International Journal of the History of Sport* 30, no. 13 (2013): 1493–1507. Official in Barbara Keys, "The Early Cold War Olympics, 1952–1960: Political, Economic and Human Rights Dimensions," in *The Palgrave Handbook of Olympic Studies*, ed. Helen Jefferson Lenskyj and Stephen Wagg (New York: Palgrave Macmillan, 2012), 78.

6 *Pravda*, August 4, 1952, 4. Romanov in *Soviet News*, August 14, 1952, 4.

7 Butler in *Congressional Record*, June 14, 1955, 8209. *US News & World Report*, August 20, 1954, 35.

8 Andrianov letter in *Olympic Review*, November 1960, 71–72.

9 *Life*, August 2, 1954, 24.

10 *Amateur Athlete*, July 1965, 7.

11 *Sovetskii Sport*, December 11, 1956, 6. *Komsomolskaia Pravda*, December 9, 1956, 1. *Trud*, December 9, 1956, 4.

12 *Sports Illustrated*, December 17, 1956, 14–18.

13 *Sovetskii Sport*, September 13, 1960, 1. *Pravda*, September 13, 1960, 4. *Vecherniaia Moskva*, September 12, 1960, 4. Khrushchev in *Daily Report, Foreign Radio Broadcasts*, September 13, 1960, BB10. *Izvestia*, September 16, 1960, 6.

14 *Cleveland Plain Dealer*, September 12, 1960, 31.

15 Christopher R. Hill, *Olympic Politics* 2nd ed. (Manchester, UK: Manchester University Press, 1996, 1992), 44–46.

16 David Maraniss, *Rome 1960: The Olympics That Changed the World* (New York: Simon & Schuster, 2008), 56–60. A good source on the Chinese dispute is Richard Espy, *The Politics of the Olympic Games* (Berkeley, CA: University of California Press, 1979), 36–38, 62–66.

17 *Sports Illustrated*, August 11, 1958, 10–11, and *Chicago Defender* (daily edition), July 30, 1958, 24. For more on the meets, see Joseph M. Turrini, "'It Was Communism Versus the Free World': The USA-USSR Dual Track Meet Series and the Development of Track and Field in the United States, 1958–1985," *Journal of Sport History* 28 (Fall 2001): 427–471.

18 For agreement, see Yale Richmond, *Cultural Exchange and the Cold War: Raising the Iron Curtain* (University Park, PA: Pennsylvania State University Press, 2003), 14–20, 68, 123–127, 133–135. *New York Times*, January 4, 1955, 1, 10.

19 Full agreement in *Department of State Bulletin*, February 17, 1958, 243–247.

20 Victor Peppard and James Riordan, *Playing Politics: Soviet Sport Diplomacy to 1992* (Greenwich, CT: JAI Press, 1993), 76–80.

21 *Krasnaia Zvezda*, July 29, 1958, 4. *U.S. News & World Report*, August 8, 1958, 37.

22 Radio Moscow in *Washington Evening Star*, July 21, 1959, D1. Ferris in *Chicago Sunday Tribune*, July 12, 1959, sec. 2, 5.

23 Edelman, *Serious Fun*, 75–76, 119–120. For coverage of meets, see *Track & Field News*, August 1961, 1, 3–4, and *Pravda*, July 23, 1962, 4.

24 *San Francisco Chronicle*, July 17, 1961, 13. TASS in *New York Times*, July 17, 1961, 15.

25 Khomenov in *New York Times*, July 17, 1961, 15.

26 Zimman in *Amateur Athlete*, August 1961, 6.

27 Engle in *Washington Post*, July 8, 1961, A11. Dispatch in RG 59, CDF, 1960–63, Box 2642, Document: 861.453/7–2161, National Archives II (hereafter NARA), College Park, MD.

28 *Congressional Record*, August 9, 1954, 13762–13763; May 9, 1955, 5907–5908; and June 4, 1956, A4393–A4394.

29 Thomas M. Hunt, "Countering the Soviet Threat in the Olympics Medals Race: The Amateur Sports Act of 1978 and American Athletics Policy Reform," *The International Journal of the History of Sport* 24, no. 6 (2007): 796–818.

30 Resolution in *Congressional Record*, March 23, 1964, 5921. Morse in Ibid., 5904. *New York Times*, May 5, 1964, 58.

31 *Parade*, 11–12, in *Boston Sunday Globe*, January 6, 1963. Ribicoff in *Congressional Record*, July 10, 1963, 12395–12397. Quote from Ibid., 12396. Fisher in *Amateur Athlete*, October 1963, 11, 37. *Proceedings of National Conference on Olympic Development*, May 18–26, 1966.

32 Wilkinson in *Department of State News Letter*, June 1962, 10. Official in *Amateur Athlete*, August 1964, 18.
33 TASS in Foreign Broadcast Information Service (hereafter FBIS), *Daily Report, USSR and Eastern Europe*, July 11, 1966, bb22.
34 *Oakland Tribune*, July 12, 1966, 39.
35 RG 59, Central Foreign Policy Files, 1964–66, Box 350, Cul 16 USSR, NARA.
36 AP story in *Washington Post*, July 15, 1966, D1.
37 *New York Times*, July 27, 1966, 31.
38 Ibid., October 23, 1964, 47.
39 Johnson in *Boston Globe*, October 31, 1968, 31.
40 *ABC News-Harris Survey*, February 14, 1980, vol. II, no. 20, 2. For more on the boycott, see Nicolas Evan Sarantakes, *Dropping the Torch: Jimmy Carter, the Olympic Boycott, and the Cold War* (Cambridge, UK: Cambridge University Press, 2011); Derick L. Hulme, *The Political Olympics: Moscow, Afghanistan, and the 1980 U.S. Boycott* (New York: Praeger, 1990); and Allen Guttmann, "The Cold War and the Olympics," *International Journal* 43 (Autumn 1988): 554–568.
41 Sarantakes, *Dropping the Torch*, 196–213.
42 *Los Angeles Times*, July 18, 1980, sec. 3, 14, and August 3, sec. 3, 1.
43 *Trud* in *Hartford Courant*, July 23, 1980, 48. See also *Boston Globe*, July 23, 1980, 63. Pavlov in *Sport in the USSR*, November 1980, 3.
44 *Pravda* in *Current Digest of the Soviet Press*, September 24, 1980, 15.
45 TASS in FBIS, *Daily Report, USSR International Affairs*, July 21, 1980, A6. Liberty Bell Classic in *Philadelphia Inquirer*, July 18, 1980, C1, C6.
46 *Harris Survey*, May 21, 1984, 2. *Current Digest of the Soviet Press*, May 2, 1984, 10. *Literaturnaia Gazeta* in *Los Angeles Times*, April 20, 1984, sec. 2, 1.
47 Robert Simon Edelman, "The Russians Are *Not* Coming! The Soviet Withdrawal from the Games of the XXIII Olympiad," *The International Journal of the History of Sport* 32, no. 1 (2015): 9–36.
48 *New York Times*, April 10, 1984, B15.
49 *Wall Street Journal*, August 14, 1984, 44.
50 FBIS, *Daily Report, Soviet Union, USSR International Affairs*, August 7, 1984, CC1. TASS in *Current Digest of the Soviet Press*, August 29, 1984, 6. *Sport in the USSR*, September 1984, 10.
51 *Newsweek*, March 10, 1980, 69. *Sports Illustrated*, August 13, 1984, 38.
52 *Pravda* in *Los Angeles Times*, August 14, 1984, sec. 8, 34. Chant in *Los Angeles Times*, August 15, 1984, sec. 3, 4. Resolution in *Congressional Record*, August 3, 1984, 22349.
53 Peppard and Riordan, *Playing Politics*, 115–130.
54 *New York Times*, June 29, 1986, sec. 5, 3. Goodwill Games debt in *Business Week*, July 23, 1998, 73.
55 *Wall Street Journal*, February 7, 1992, A11. *Izvestia* in *New York Times*, February 25, 1992, B12.

Part VIII

FACETS OF SPORT IN RECENT AMERICAN CULTURE

31

ACTIVE RADICALS

The Political Athlete in the Contemporary Moment

Amy Bass

Introduction

In 1999, Brandi Chastain ripped her shirt off to celebrate her successful shoot-out penalty kick, which secured the World Cup championship for her team, brought 90,000 fans in California's Rose Bowl (and the 40 million watching at home) to their feet, and sent home a powerful Chinese squad. Chastain's form of celebration is common on the pitch, so the response came as a surprise. She made the covers of *Sports Illustrated* ("YES!") and *Newsweek* ("Girls Rule!") and, more recently, of Jane Gottesman's book *Game Face: What Does a Female Athlete Look Like?* and Jaime Schultz's *Qualifying Times.*[1] "It was a crowning moment for women everywhere, a moment of freedom, of liberation," observed Marlene Bjornsrud, then general manager of Chastain's professional team, the San Jose CyberRays. "It was casting off the burden of everything that kept us down and said, 'You can't do that because you are a woman.' It was a moment that screamed, 'Yes, I can.'"[2]

Not everyone saw the empowerment in Chastain's action. Some saw inappropriate titillation, whereas others conspired it was a marketing ploy by the bra's manufacturer, Nike. Sportswriter Jere Longman described it as "a sort of Rorschach test," and scholar Mary Jo Kane rued how "it immediately got turned into 'Brandi Chastain took her shirt off,' rather than 'what fabulous athletes these women are!'" Sales of sports bras skyrocketed and, according to one fashion analyst, the trend began of women wearing underwear as outerwear.[3]

As Chastain's image fluctuated between feminist emblem and corporate sell-out, one thing was certain: the action of an elite athlete simultaneously sparked thoughtful conversation and heated controversy. Intentionally provocative or not, Chastain's merriment got marked as a radical turning point in women's sports, a sealing of the deal that Title IX began almost 30 years earlier, and further evidence of the already well-documented political potential of athletes, whether in terms of performance, dedicated action, or both. As has been clear time and again, from the line drives of Jackie Robinson to the black-gloved fists at the Mexico City Olympics, from the forehand of Billie Jean King to the court battles of Curt Flood, from the Brazilian protests against the 2014 World Cup budget to the citizens of Oslo demanding its 2022 Olympic host bid be withdrawn, politics do not cease to exist when players step onto the field, the track, the court, or the pitch. Indeed, it is quite often the sports spotlight that pushes a political platform to the next level.

The End of the Crewcut

Sport provides a critical window into the politics of the world we live in, with athletes becoming political actors for a variety of reasons. For some, their mere presence, their performance, is reason enough to hold political value. Jesse Owens' four gold medals at the Berlin Olympics in 1936 demonstrated athletic perfection as well as a symbolic defeat of white supremacy, and Jackie Robinson's breakthrough at bat in 1947 marked the start of a career that was as full of, in the words of historian Rob Ruck, "uncanny baseball intelligence and unrivaled intensity" as historic worth to the fight for integration of U.S. society.[4]

Others have committed to bringing direct political action into their games, mining the politics of the social movements in the postwar period to create change within the sports world. At the height of his career, and well within the context of U.S. labor movements, Curt Flood went to the Supreme Court to fight baseball's reserve clause in the hopes that he could make the game fairer for future players, despite the toll he knew it would take on his own livelihood.[5] In a similar vein, Billie Jean King led the "Original Nine"—players who pushed for the creation of a women's tour in tennis with the launch of the Houston Virginia Slims tournament, paving the way for economic equality between men and women on the tennis court—and sits well within second-wave feminism in the early 1970s, although without the same consequences on her overall career; as a woman, she did not have as much to lose as Flood.[6]

Perhaps no one was as central to the politicization of the athlete as boxer Muhammad Ali. Ali's engaging charisma, athletic prowess, and biting political wit cannot be undervalued in the political coming of age of athletes in the post–World War II period. Compared to competitors such as Floyd Patterson, a devout Christian and card-carrying NAACP member who Ali once described as "the Technicolor white hope," Ali's Black Muslim identity ostracized and alienated some fans while at the same time lending power to civil and human rights activists throughout the world. "I'm no longer a Cassius Clay, a Negro from Kentucky," Ali told sportswriter Robert Lipsyte. "I belong to the world, the black world."[7]

Ali lost his title not at the hands of another boxer, of course, but when he refused to fight in Vietnam, a moment that exemplifies how an athlete can politically use his or her celebrity. "I have searched my conscience," Ali stated, "and I find I cannot be true to my belief in my religion by accepting such a call."[8] The consequences for Ali came fast and furious: he lost his title immediately and was mired in legal proceedings for three years before returning to the ring. Ali knew his title was at stake when he made his decision and chided the boxing powers for their action: "I have the world heavyweight title not because it was 'given' to me, not because of my race or religion, but because I won it in the ring through my own boxing ability," he wrote in his prepared statement.

> Those who want to "take" it and hold a series of auction-type bouts not only do me a disservice but actually disgrace themselves. I am certain that the sports fans and fair-minded people throughout America would never accept such a "title-holder."[9]

Ali personified a turning point in the radical potential of the athlete. While Owens made his mark with his unprecedented athletic performance, and Robinson broke the color line through a well-orchestrated at bat, Ali's overtly political stance inspired others to follow. As civil rights movements in the United States evolved from the increasingly mainstream tactics of the Southern Christian Leadership Conference to the more militant Black Power stances of the Student Non-violent Coordinating Committee and objections to the U.S. involvement in Vietnam gained momentum in the wake of the Tet Offensive's horrors, radical politics became increasingly visible in the late 1960s. Because of its central role in popular culture, one that had grown more dominant in the postwar period with television, sport was an arena ripe for political questions to be asked of it, through it, and within it, particularly those that connected to the various machinations of identity that became hammered out in the various social movements of the day.

The rise of what *Newsweek* magazine called "the angry black athlete" in 1968, then, fit well within the context of civil rights movements transitioning from models of nonviolence into more combative forms.[10] While one sportswriter christened the 1960s a "slum of a decade,"[11] for many, including athletes, it offered a seemingly unprecedented moment to effect change. Ali's decision in 1967 to refuse the draft had not only secured his own legacy; he demonstrated how an athlete could popularize political issues and exert modes of political resistance, critiquing not just sport, but country—and beyond.

If Ali personified the political stance an individual athlete could take, the Olympic Project for Human Rights (OPHR), largely inspired by Ali, represented how collective action by athletes could take place. Created to boycott the Mexico City Olympic Games if its list of civil and human rights demands were not met, including the reinstatement of Ali's title, the OPHR had precursors that predated the rebel boxer. At the same time that A. Philip Randolph and Bayard Rustin predated King's March on Washington by a few decades with their intent to protest segregation in wartime manufacturing plants in October 1940, students at New York University (NYU) launched a series of protests against racial discrimination in college sports. The fight began when the NYU administration told Leonard Bates, a black football player, that he could not travel with the team to face the University of Missouri because of segregation laws. As detailed by historian Donald Spivey, some 2,000 NYU students marched in support of the "Bates Must Play" campaign, bringing the so-called Gentlemen's Agreement, in which Northern schools did not bring black players to the segregated South, in sports into question. The administration suspended seven members of the newly formed Council for Student Equality for passing around a petition in support of Bates, which only brought more attention to the matter. A number of prominent organizations and figures, from the NAACP to Paul Robeson, came out in support of the students, who had brought to the forefront the idea that perhaps nowhere did segregation conflict more directly with democratic principles than in sport, an allegedly level playing field.[12] In 2001, the university finally admitted that suspending the "Bates Seven" had been wrong and honored the students at a dinner, although it never issued an apology because, according to NYU spokesman John Beckman, "we can't put ourselves in [that administration's] shoes, and we can't turn back the hands of time."[13]

Although the NYU protest brought about no institutional change, it firmly established a means for collective civil rights action to take place within the world of sports, something that would prove critical to the creation of the OPHR in 1967. As early as 1960, comedian Dick Gregory—a former track star at Southern Illinois University—advocated boycotts by black athletes, a call taken up later by triple Olympic medalist Mal Whitfield, who urged "every Negro athlete eligible to participate in the Olympic Games in Japan . . . boycott . . . if Negro Americans by that time have not been guaranteed full and equal rights as first-class citizens."[14] After having been suspended from San Jose City College for trying to draw attention to the predicament of black student basketball players who had been denied some of the perks of their recruiting packages, Ken Noel, a nationally ranked runner, landed in graduate school at San Jose State University, where he joined forces with sociologist Harry Edwards to create the OPHR.[15]

Although the Olympic boycott never came to fruition, over the course of just a few months the organization created a critical national gaze on the ability of athletes to create effective political statements, culminating in the Black Power action taken by sprinters Tommie Smith and John Carlos during the medal ceremony for the men's 200-meter event in Mexico City. Within a matter of days, as the now-iconic photograph of the two Americans with black gloved fists raised high over their bowed heads circulated around the globe, a heated discussion took place regarding whether or not the duo had abused their privileged space as athletes. Forced out of the Olympic Village by the U.S. and International Olympic Committees, the duo returned home, disinherited by the Silent Majority that would soon elect Richard Nixon, but embraced by members of the counterculture who continued to burn draft cards in the streets.

Sports reflected this political tension, appearing to work within more traditional American values but increasingly finding that its athletes were not always on board. "When the country changed, the athlete didn't stay crew cut," remembers hockey star Derek Sanderson, known as much for his flamboyant style off the ice as his killing penalties on it. "The athlete didn't stay where sports told him to stay."[16]

For NFL linebacker Dave Meggyesy, that meant critiquing the sport he played. His controversial memoir, *Out of Their League*, first published in 1970, focused on what he called the dehumanizing impact of the sport on its players, detailing the drugs, racism, and violence that led him to quit at the height of his career. In a similar vein, baseball's Jim Bouton published *Ball Four* the same year, provocatively exposing the reality of life as a player, and—like Meggyesy—bringing the wrath of the sports industry down on his head.

Other athletes used marquee events to attempt change, exemplified by Kathrine Switzer's battle to open distance running to women. On April 19, 1967, Switzer became the first woman to officially run the Boston Marathon, creating a tense situation when race official Jock Semple attempted to physically remove her from the course, screaming "Get the hell out of my race and give me those numbers!"[17] Although women had run Boston before, she was the first to wear a number and therefore record a finish. Her action led to her immediate dismissal from the Amateur Athletic Union for running a distance farther than one and a half miles, "the longest distance allowable for women"; fraudulently entering a race by signing in only with her initials; running a marathon with men; and running a marathon unchaperoned.[18] Switzer, however, continued running, winning the New York marathon in 1974, and working to get the women's marathon into the Olympics, the first of which occurred in Los Angeles in 1984, won by American Joan Benoit.

In the 1960s and 1970s, examples such as the OPHR, Bouton, Meggyesy, Ali, Flood, and Switzer represent only a few of those who created critiques of and rebellions within sport. From Bill Russell to Jim Brown, Billie Jean King to Kareem Abdul Jabbar, athletes from all walks of life found themselves challenging not just the rules and prescriptions of sport, but, more broadly, societal and political norms, hoping to change the playing field for future athletes, as well as society writ large.

The Republic of Nike

Yet as sweeping social movements faded in the last decades of the twentieth century and the counterculture took a backseat to the "Greed Is Good" mantra of the Reagan Era, a political identity became too risky for many athletes, with extraordinary celebrity and riches available to a lucky few in the increasingly dominant culture industry of sports. Basketball star Michael Jordan, dubbed "the Greatest Endorser of the Twentieth Century" by Walter LeFeber, personified this transformation, in which bringing politics onto the court threatened the opulent livelihood that sports had the potential to provide.[19]

Jordan wielded much power throughout his career. His time on the so-called Dream Team at the Barcelona Olympics epitomizes how past political stances wilted as the commercial stock of sport grew, with an athlete's profit potential recognized by sneaker manufacturers and fast food chains. A select few became richer than any of their predecessors could have imagined, but with wealth came complications. In Barcelona, Jordan's commercial obligations directly conflicted with his role on the U.S. delegation when he balked at wearing the official Team USA warm-ups, issued by Reebok, because of his contract with Nike. "When you hire 12 Clint Eastwoods to come in here and do a job," he said, "don't ask them what bullets they're putting in the gun."[20]

Although the team played its games wearing uniforms made by Champion, never considered a direct a competitor to Nike, the problem came to a head at the medal ceremony. The solution for Jordan (and Charles Barkley and Magic Johnson) was far easier to come by than what Smith and Carlos had to do just a few decades before: they left their jackets unzipped, obscuring the Reebok logo, and threw an American flag over their right shoulders. "Everyone agreed we would not deface the Reebok logo on the award uniform," said Jordan. "The American flag cannot deface anything. That's what we stand for. The American dream is standing up for what you believe in. . . . If I offended anyone, that's too bad."[21] Draped in patriotism, the flag-wearing athletes claimed freedom of expression to stand in allegiance with a corporate sponsor, demonstrating how a logo had replaced the black-gloved politics of the past.[22]

Conversely, just a few years after the Dream Team's "protest," the NBA suspended Denver's Mahmoud Abdul-Rauf for refusing to stand during the national anthem. Abdul-Rauf claimed the anthem conflicted with his Muslim beliefs, but the NBA contractually requires players to stand "in a dignified posture . . . during the playing of the national anthem." As the debate raged on talk radio and sports pages, it was clear few supported the player's stance. A notable exception, columnist Harvey Araton, called the NBA out for its hypocrisy, observing that the league did nothing when "Jordan, Charles Barkley and other Republic of Nike pitchmen shamelessly used the flag to cover competing corporate logos on the Olympic medal stand in Barcelona, Spain, four years ago."[23]

The economic viability of the famous black athlete, something that simply did not exist in the era of the OPHR, lent an increasingly hostile tone to any athlete, such as Abdul-Rauf, who dared to take a political stance, portraying him as ungrateful for the opportunities sports created and creating a false assumption that in a country where someone like Jordan existed, the missions of civil rights movements were complete. Such assumptions created political complacency, at best, and a dangerous ignorance, at worst, begging the question: If a large part of twentieth-century American sport had such a rich history of protest and critique, could the same be said of what came next?

Sport in the Age of Obama

The social movements of the earliest decades of the twenty-first century evolved far differently from those of the 1960s. The Occupy Wall Street movement issued a powerful call from Zuccotti Park for the end of social and economic inequality, but its visibility was short term. On the opposite end of the political spectrum, the so-called Tea Party movement attempted to shift the conversation further to the right, racially codifying its constant attack on the presidency of Barack Obama.[24]

Sports both reflected and shaped this ambiguous political context. Whereas many athletes continued to reach for the prizes that Jordan had laid the foundation for, others, such as basketball star Steve Nash, used their spotlight in much the same way as those in the 1960s and 1970s. Nash's refusal to set aside his political perspectives, including his belief in socialism and a well-publicized bedside reading list that includes *The Communist Manifesto* and Che Guevara's autobiography, led *Esquire* magazine to dub him the "Karl Marx of the Hardwood."[25] In 2003, Nash wore a tee-shirt throughout All-Star weekend that read "No War. Shoot for Peace," causing a terrific amount of backlash that deemed the Canadian unpatriotic.[26] Flash-forward a few years, and he was one of the most ardent supporters of his team, the Phoenix Suns, wearing "Los Suns" jerseys during the Western Conference semifinals to protest Arizona's restrictive immigration laws. The idea for the shirts came from team owner Robert Sarver, who left it up to the players as to whether they wanted to wear them. "I think it's fantastic," Nash said at the time.

> "I think the law is very misguided. . . . I think it's very important for us to stand up for things we believe in. As a team and as an organization, we have a lot of love and support for all our fans. The league is very multicultural. . . . our Latino community here is very strong and important to us."

The NBA agreed, releasing a statement that expressed support for the symbolic move against "the misguided efforts of Arizona lawmakers."[27]

Based on past precedent, the league's support for the players came as something of a surprise. The NBA had grown increasingly conservative regarding the racial and ethnic identities of its players under the powerful hand of Commissioner David Stern, who saved the league from disarray when he took the post in 1984. After the infamous "Malice at the Palace" incident in 2004, a bench-clearing brawl between the Pacers and the Pistons during which Ron Artest entered the stands to square off against fans, Stern indicated a need to counter the sport's declining popularity in the United States with a change in the culture of the sport, which, according to David Leonard, meant "deracializing the league."[28] One such measure was the implementation of a mandatory dress code, which required players to wear business attire and barred medallions, chains, and do-rags. Many players vocally objected: "They're targeting my generation—the hip-hop generation," said Allen Iverson. "You can put a murderer in a suit and he's still a murderer."[29]

But these kinds of style politics could also be put to symbolic—and political—use. In the wake of the shooting death of Trayvon Martin in 2012 by George Zimmerman, some players used their celebrity to shed light on what happened to the unarmed black teenager. Miami Heat star Dwyane Wade took to social media, posting photographs wearing a hooded sweatshirt, which was what Martin was wearing the night of his death. Soon after Wade's posts, LeBron James posted a photograph of the entire team wearing "hoodies," heads bowed, hands in pockets, accompanied by the hashtag "WeWantJustice."

In a similar vein, days after the grand jury failed to indict police officer Darren Wilson for the shooting death of unarmed teenager Michael Brown in 2014, members of the St. Louis Rams took to the field in the "hands up, don't shoot" pose, symbolizing the position many eyewitnesses claim Brown took when Wilson pulled his gun. "There has to be a change," said tight end Jared Cook, "that starts with the people who are most influential around the world." Teammate Kenny Britt agreed: "I don't want people in the community to feel like we turned a blind eye to it."[30]

Outside the stadium, protesters chanted "No Justice, No Football!" while an increased police presence watched.[31] In response to the players' action, the St. Louis Police Officers Association, historically the city's "white" police fraternal organization, demanded that the players be disciplined and both the team and NFL apologize.[32] The group condemned the team, "who chose to ignore the mountains of evidence . . . and engage in a display that police officers around the nation found tasteless, offensive, and inflammatory." The SLPOA's Jeff Roorda went so far as to threaten the sport itself. "I'd remind the NFL and their players that it is not the violent thugs burning down buildings that buy their advertiser's products," he said. "It's cops and the good people of St. Louis and other NFL towns that do."[33]

That both team and league management expressed support for the athletes' actions is significant. In the case of the Heat, coach Erik Spoelstra not only knew about the team photo, he deemed it "a powerful move" to commemorate "a tragic story," and the front office expressed sympathy for the Martin family and support for the players, "hoping that their images and our logo can be part of the national dialogue and can help in our nation's healing."[34] In terms of the Rams' action on behalf of Brown, the NFL's vice president of communications, Brian McCarthy, said simply "We respect and understand the concerns of all individuals who have expressed views on this tragic situation"; Rams chief operating officer Kevin Demoff said, "We do believe it is possible to both support our players' First Amendment rights and support the efforts of local law enforcement as our community begins the process of healing"; and Rams coach Jeff Fisher reinforced that the players would not be disciplined in any way.[35]

Of course, not everyone proved as understanding. In Galesburg, Illinois, Knox College suspended junior Ariyana Smith for one game after she made a "hands up, don't shoot" gesture before a game against Fontbonne University, located in Clayton, Missouri, where the grand jury announced its decision on Wilson. Smith fell to the ground and lay on the court for almost five minutes before being forced off by her coach. A day later, under national scrutiny, the college reversed its decision, allowing Smith to "resume all basketball activities" and thanking "the many viewpoints expressed by the women's basketball team and their thoughtful dialogue."[36]

Days later, after a grand jury in New York failed to indict a police officer in the chokehold death of Eric Garner, protests increased throughout the United States, including at sporting venues. Outside a basketball game at the University of Maryland, protesters held a "die-in" and Terrapin football player Deon Long held a sign that asked "Are We Still 'THUGS' When You Pay to Watch Us Play Sports?"[37] A few days later, Chicago Bulls star Derrick Rose warmed up before a game against Oakland wearing a t-shirt that read "I CAN'T BREATHE," the last words Garner allegedly said before his death. Rose's handmade shirt appeared to be the tipping point. Soon after, LeBron James, now with the Cleveland Cavaliers, donned a slick version of the shirt alongside teammate Kyrie Irving before a game against the Brooklyn Nets. Building on the position he had taken on behalf of Trayvon Martin, speculation swirled about what seemed like an increasingly political persona. "If it feels important to me, then I respond," James said. "If it doesn't, I don't. There's a lot of issues I haven't talked about. For me it's about knowledge, it's about the gut feeling."[38]

Although James had little to lose by donning the shirt, the behind-the-scenes story demonstrates some of the logistical complications of getting an athlete of his caliber to take a political stance. Encouraged by James' statement that Rose's shirt was "spectacular," Justice League NYC, which had been staging protests for Garner throughout New York City, leapt into action, reaching out to Nets owner Jay-Z, who planned to be at the game with his wife, Beyoncé (as well as the Duke and Duchess of Cambridge). Jay-Z asked James if he would wear the shirt, while organizers found a security guard who was willing to sneak the shirts into the Barclays Center without anyone from the NBA noticing. As the players began to warm up wearing the shirts, protesters wearing the shirts outside the arena began to cheer.[39] "Obviously we're not on the front line of this movement," said Kevin Garnett. "But I think it's important to give to these communities and support these communities."[40]

Although the league affirmed it would take no action against the players for the shirts, Commissioner Adam Silver indicated he wished they would reconsider: "I respect Derrick Rose and all of our players for voicing their personal views on important issues but my preference would be for players to abide by our on-court attire rules."[41] Silver, according to William Rhoden, was "trying to walk a thin line between protecting the business interests of the league and its sponsors and not appearing to mute the voices of its athletes." Nets guard Jarrett Jack, who wore a shirt, understood Silver's position. "Obviously, these are business hours, so I get the angle that he is coming from," Jack said. "But this is something that was very, very important to us. . . . almost like a civic duty. We want people to know that we are not oblivious to what is going on around us."[42]

In contrast to the discomfort apparent within the front office, Nets coach Lionel Hollins expressed unwavering support for his players. "They should be political," he said.

> They should be about social awareness. Basketball is just a small part of life. If they don't think there is justice, or they feel like there is something they should protest, then they should. That is their right as citizens of America, and I have no problem with that at all."[43]

Michele A. Roberts, executive director of the National Basketball Players Association (NBPA), also expressed support:

> Our players are members of the community. They see, hear and are affected by events—just like the rest of us. That some have chosen to give voice to recent unfortunate events and communicate their support to the Garner family is yet another reason why I and my colleagues on staff at the N.B.P.A. are proud to serve them.[44]

College athletes took a cue from their professional counterparts as the "black lives matter" campaigns turned into a widespread protest movement. At the University of Oregon, basketball players Dwayne Benjamin and Jordan Bell made the "hands up, don't shoot" gesture during the national anthem to the dismay of Coach Dana Altman: "I think every player has a right to express their opinion, however, I didn't think this was the time or place for it."[45] Georgetown's men's basketball team put on the shirts before a game against Kansas, and Notre Dame became the first women's squad to wear them, with Coach Muffet McGraw and the university administration in support.[46] "I was really proud of our team," said McGraw. "The accountability doesn't end when they leave the locker room . . . I want them to be strong, confident women, who are not afraid to use their voice and take a stand."[47] At the University of California, the women's squad donned handmade "BlackLivesMatter" shirts and made the "hands up, don't shoot" gesture during the national anthem. Coach Lindsay Gottlieb understood the players' desire to make a statement, particularly after a black man hanged in effigy at the campus entrance gates. "The entire team came to me," Gottlieb said. "They were compelled to act . . . As a group, they decided to wear shirts that brought attention to lives lost—recently and throughout history—and to stand and say that black lives matter; all lives matter."[48]

On the football field, Reggie Bush and Johnson Bademosi also wore shirts with the phrase, and the Rams' Davin Joseph wrote it on his cleats, and Andrew Hawkins of the Cleveland Browns wore a shirt asking for justice for Tamir Rice and John Crawford, both of whom had been killed by Cleveland police in separate incidents.[49] Bush, arguably the highest profile of the group and the son of a deputy sheriff, said he had no regrets. "I just felt like I do have a voice," he said. "It's OK for me to say how I feel. . . . I feel like we can all be role models and lead by example." Detroit Lions coach Jim Caldwell expressed support. "I grew up in the '60s where everybody was socially conscious," he said.

> I believe in it. I'd be a hypocrite if I stood up here and told you differently 'cause more than likely, some of those protests that Dr. King and some of the others that took part in non-violent protest is the reason why I'm standing here in front of you today.[50]

Sports, it seems, were echoing yet again the political tenor of the times, with athletes recognizing that they could use their privileged and rare public spotlight to get involved in thornier political issues instead of their usual charity circuits. Basketball great Magic Johnson supported the radical turn, telling sports stars to get more "involved socially" and to use their celebrity in more overtly political ways.

> They have to because it affects them, too. . . . They grew up in these situations; they must not forget that. They [were] once poor, they went to inner-city schools . . . A lot of their cousins are still going through that, so they must not forget that. I hope that they would do more.[51]

Johnson was not alone. Kareem Abdul-Jabbar, who had been one of the few athletes in 1968 to shun the Olympics, took up the cause of college athletes in the wake of controversies regarding the NCAA. In an article for radical *Jacobin* magazine, Abdul-Jabbar writes that he stayed home from Mexico City in order to earn enough money to get through his senior year and play basketball. "I was walking out on the court a hero, but into my bedroom a pauper," remembers Abdul-Jabbar. "Naturally, I felt exploited and dissatisfied . . . The worst part is that nothing much has changed since my experience as a college athlete almost forty years ago." One difference? The NCAA's enormous profit margin—almost $1 billion from its March Madness network contract alone. The solution, Abdul-Jabbar posits, is for college athletes to unionize, rather than continue in "indentured servitude," language reminiscent of when Curt Flood dubbed baseball a form of slavery.[52]

Abdul-Jabbar also publically supported athletes wearing "I Can't Breathe" shirts. His stance was particularly significant because he made it after the shooting deaths of New York City police officers Rafael Ramos and Weinjian Liu, which stopped the "BlackLivesMatter" movement in its tracks and created an enormous amount of backlash and, incredibly, blame. Abdul-Jabbar argued that the movement was not an antipolice crusade and that Attorney General Eric Holder, President Barack Obama, and New York City mayor Bill de Blasio were not responsible because of their support of the protests, regardless of what some, including former New York governor George Pataki, might claim. Abdul-Jabbar wrote:

> This phony and logically baffling indignation is similar to that expressed by the St. Louis County Police Association when it demanded an apology from the NFL when several Rams players entered the field with their hands held high in the iconic Michael Brown gesture of surrender . . . Or when LeBron James and W.R. Allen wore his "I Can't Breathe" shirts echoing Eric Garner's final plea before dying.[53]

It is critical to understand that Abdul-Jabbar's historic sports career provided him with a safe space to take part in the conversation. This was not true for all athletes, especially those who go beyond wearing a political shirt. Chris Kluwe, for example, former punter for the Minnesota Vikings, asserts that management cut him after his very vocal stances on marriage equality. Kluwe became involved with Minnesotans for Marriage Equality to defeat a bill designed to define marriage as a commitment between a man and a woman. Kluwe says he got approval from the team as long as it remained clear that he was acting on his own and not as a team representative. That support soon diminished.[54]

For Kluwe and others—including Jason Collins, the first "out" player in the NBA, and Michael Sam, the first "out" player to be drafted into the NFL—movements for gay rights and marriage equality seemed to recapture some of the political ethos of the 1960s. And although Collins and Sam became the most high-profile athletes to publically confront sexuality (indeed, Collins found himself on the cover of *Sports Illustrated*), according to Outsports, some 109 athletes, coaches, and sports administrators came out in 2014 alone, meaning that sports had overtaken Hollywood in numbers alone.[55]

Conclusion: Commercial and Political Consequences

Much like the impact civil rights movements had on athletes in the 1960s, issues such as marriage equality and movements like "Black Lives Matters" demonstrated that there were still viable political platforms in sports. Athletes recognized ways in which they could use their spotlight to, minimally, support others or, more importantly, create modes of empowerment to exact changes both within sports and within broader society. Yet many questions remain. Can an athlete be radical and make productive political contributions in the post-Jordan era? Has the commercial viability of the athlete—especially, perhaps, the black athlete—weakened the political stakes of sport not only because it makes political action riskier, according to Chris Kluwe, but also because it has commercialized and, thus, tamed, the image of the athlete writ large? Has sport hit a level of commercial viability that weeds out the bold political athlete before he or she gets to the show? To answer such questions, they must be put to society more broadly. The imperatives of social movements in the decades that followed World War II have not been replicated in this century, or even in the waning decades of the last. With sports so deeply embedded in American culture, can we expect more of athletes than we do from anyone else?

Notes

1 Jane Gottesman, *Game Face: What Does a Female Athlete Look Like?* (New York: Random House, 2003); Jaime Schultz, *Qualifying Times: Points of Change in U.S. Women's Sport* (Urbana: University of Illinois Press, 2014).

2 Quoted in Jere Longman, "The Sports Bra Seen Round the World," *The New York Times*, July 5, 2003. www.nytimes.com/2003/07/05/sports/soccer-thesports-bra-seen-round-the-world.html (accessed October 7, 2014).

3 Mary Jo Kane, "Playing Unfair: The Media Image of the Female Athlete," Media Education Foundation, 2002; transcript accessed at www.mediaed.org/assets/products/208/transcript_208.pdf; Longman, "The Sports Bra Seen Round the World."

4 Rob Ruck, *Raceball: How the Major Leagues Colonized the Black and Latin Game* (Boston: Beacon Press, 2012), 99.

5 Allen Barra, "How Curt Flood Changed Baseball and Ruined His Career in the Process," *The Atlantic*, July 12, 2011; Brad Snyder, *A Well-Paid Slave: Curt Flood's Fight for Free Agency in Professional Sports* (New York: Plume, 2007).

6 *Billie Jean King: Portrait of a Pioneer*, HBO Documentary Film (2006); Tony Collins, *Sport in a Capitalist Society* (New York: Routledge, 2013), 112; Susan Ware, *Game, Set, Match: Billie Jean King and the Revolution in Women's Sports* (Chapel Hill: University of North Carolina Press, 2011).

7 Mike Marqusee, *Redemption Song: Muhammad Ali and the Spirit of the Sixties* (London: Verso, 1999), 70–93; 175.

8 Robert Lipsyte, "Clay Refuses Army Oath; Stripped of Boxing Crown," *New York Times*, April 29, 1967. www.nytimes.com/books/98/10/25/specials/ali-army.html

9 Ibid.

10 Pete Axthelm, "The Angry Black Athlete," *Newsweek*, July 15, 1968.

11 Amy Bass, *Not the Triumph but the Struggle: The 1968 Olympic Games and the Making of the Black Athlete* (Minneapolis: University of Minnesota Press, 2002), 32.

12 Donald Spivey, "'End Jim Crow in Sports': The Protest at New York University, 1940–1941," *Journal of Sport History* 15 (Winter 1988): 283–285, 300–301.

13 Edward Wong, "NYU Honors Protesters It Punished in '41'," *New York Times*, May 4, 2001. www.nytimes.com/2001/05/04/sports/college-football-nyu-honors-protesters-it-punished-in-41.html (accessed July 13, 2015).

14 Spivey, "Black Consciousness and Olympic Protest Movement: 1964–1980," in *Sport in America: New Historical Perspectives*, ed. Donald Spivey (Westport, CT: Greenwood Press, 1985), 240.

15 Bass, *Not the Triumph but the Struggle*, 85.

16 Quoted in Ibid., 32.

17 Kathrine Switzer, *Marathon Woman: Running the Race to Revolutionize Women's Sports* (Cambridge: De Capo Press, 2007), 91.

18 Ibid., 117.

19 Walter LeFeber, *Michael Jordan and the New Global Capitalism* (New York: Norton, 2002), 27.

20 Mike Littwin, "Jordan Hid Allegiance under Flag," *The Baltimore Sun*, August 9, 1992.

21 Ibid.

22 Ibid., 347.

23 Bass, *Not the Triumph but the Struggle*, 310–313.

24 Jill Lepore, *The Whites of Their Eyes: The Tea Party's Revolution and the Battle Over American History* (Princeton: Princeton University Press, 2010).

25 Chuck Klosterman, "The Karl Marx of the Hardwood," *Esquire*, October 31, 2005.

26 Marc Stein, "Nash Not Backpedaling from Anti-War Stance," *ESPN*, April 3, 2003. http://sports.espn.go.com/nba/columns/story?id=1527038 (accessed July 13, 2015).

27 "'Los Suns' Jerseys Set for Cinco de Mayo," *ESPN*, May 4, 2010. http://sports.espn.go.com/nba/playoffs/2010/news/story?id=5162380 (accessed July 13, 2015).

28 See David Leonard, *After Artest: The NBA and the Assault on Blackness* (Albany: SUNY Press, 2012), 10.

29 Mike Wise, "Opinions on the NBA's Dress Code are Far from Uniform," *Washington Post*, October 23, 2005. www.washingtonpost.com/wp-dyn/content/article/2005/10/22/AR2005102201386.html (accessed July 13, 2015).

30 R.B. Fallstrom, "Rams Raise Arms in Show of Solidarity," *Associated Press*, November 30, 2014. http://bigstory.ap.org/article/932105fca3b342c69b115ef9da77402f/rams-raise-arms-show-solidarity (accessed July 13, 2015).
31 Timothy Burke, "Rams Players Enter Field With 'Hands Up, Don't Shoot,'" *Deadspin*, November 30, 2014. http://deadspin.com/rams-players-enter-field-with-hands-up-dont-shoot-1664860731 (accessed July 13, 2015).
32 Shaun King, "Police Organizations in St. Louis Have Separate Predominantly White and Black Organizations," *The Daily Kos*, December 1, 2014. www.dailykos.com/story/2014/12/01/1348628/-St-Louis-has-two-police-associations-one-for-white-officers-and-one-for-black-officers (accessed July 13, 2015).
33 Tom Boggioni, "St. Louis Police Officers' Group Demands Players Be Disciplined," *RawStory*, November 30, 2014. www.rawstory.com/rs/2014/11/st-louis-police-officers-group-demands-rams-players-be-disciplined-for-hands-up-dont-shoot/ (accessed July 13, 2015).
34 "Heat Dons Hoodies After Teen's Death."
35 Sally Jenkins, "St. Louis Rams' 'Don't Shoot' Gesture Was Free Speech, and the Police Should Know It," *Washington Post*, December 1, 2014; Cindy Boren, "Rams, St. Louis County Police at Odds Over Whether Team Apologized for Ferguson Protest," *Washington Post*, December 1, 2014; Oren Yaniv, "St. Louis Rams Deny 'apology' to Local Law Enforcement," *Daily News*, December 2, 2014.
36 Jackson White, "Knox College Women's Basketball Player Delays with Protest," *Galesburg Register-Mail*, December 2, 2014. www.galesburg.com/article/20141202/NEWS/141209945/?Start=1 (accessed July 13, 2015).
37 Kevin Draper, "UVA-Maryland Basketball Game Site Of Protest," *Deadspin*, December 4, 2014. http://deadspin.com/uva-maryland-basketball-game-site-of-protest-and-no-me-1666572025 (accessed July 13, 2015).
38 Zach Schonbrun, "For LeBron James and Other Stars, the Political Is Personal," *The New York Times*, December 8, 2014.
39 Scott Cacciola, "At Nets' Game, a Plan for a Simple Statement Is Carried Out to a T," *New York Times*, December 9, 2014.
40 Schonbrun, "For LeBron James and Other Stars, the Political Is Personal."
41 Nia-Malika Henderson, "LeBron James Wore an "I Can't Breathe" Warmup Shirt Tonight. That's a Very Big Deal," *The Washington Post*, December 8, 2014; Julie Miller, "Jay Z Outfits LeBron James and Brooklyn Nets in T-Shirts Supporting Eric Garner's Family," *Vanity Fair*, December 8, 2014; Chris Strauss and Nate Scott, "LeBron James, Kyrie Irving and Nets Players Wear 'I can't breathe' shirts before Cavs game," *USA Today*, December 8, 2014.
42 William Rhoden, "Social Convictions Don't Tuck Neatly into NBA's Interests," *New York Times*, December 9, 2014.
43 Rhoden, "Social Convictions Don't Tuck Neatly Into NBA's Interests."
44 Cacciola, "At Nets' Game, a Plan for a Simple Statement Is Carried Out to a T."
45 Rob Dauster, "Dana Altman Says Oregon's Hands Up Don't Shoot Protest Not 'Appropriate Time,'" NBC Sports Talk, December 11, 2014. http://collegebasketballtalk.nbcsports.com/2014/12/11/dana-altman-says-oregons-hands-up-dont-shoot-protest-not-appropriate-time/ (accessed July 13, 2015).
46 Jasmine Watkins, "Notre Dame Becomes First Women's Team to Wear 'I Can't Breathe' Shirts," *The Sporting News*, December 13, 2014. www.sportingnews.com/ncaa-basketball/story/2014–12–13/notre-dame-womens-basketball-i-cant-breathe-shirts-eric-garner (accessed July 13, 2015).
47 Rodger Sherman, "Notre Dame Women's Hoops Wears 'I Can't Breathe' Shirts," *SB Nation*, December 13, 2014. www.sbnation.com/lookit/2014/12/13/7388169/notre-dame-womens-hoops-wears-i-cant-breathe-shirts (accessed July 13, 2015).
48 Raphielle Johnson, "California Women's Basketball Team Wore Handmade #BlackLivesMatter T-Shirts Saturday," *NBC Sports*, December 14, 2014. http://collegebasketballtalk.nbcsports.com/2014/12/14/california-womens-basketball-team-wore-handmade-black-lives-matter-t-shirts-saturday/ (accessed July 13, 2015).
49 Martin Pengelly, "Reggie Bush and Other NFL Players Wear Eric Garner Protesters' 'I Can't Breathe' Slogan on Clothing," *The Guardian*, December 7, 2014. www.theguardian.com/us-news/2014/dec/07/reggie-bush-and-other-nfl-players-wear-i-cant-breathe-slogan-on-clothing

(accessed July 13, 2015); Adam Ferrise, "Cleveland Police Union President: Browns' Receive Andrew Hawkins Justice for Tamir Rice Shirt 'Disprespectful', *The Cleveland Plain Dealer*, December 14, 2014. www.cleveland.com/metro/index.ssf/2014/12/cleveland_police_union_preside_1.html (accessed July 13, 2015).

50 Jeff Seidel, "Reggie Bush Says a Lot with 'I Can't Breathe,'" *Detroit Free Press*, December 8, 2014. www.freep.com/story/sports/columnists/jeff-seidel/2014/12/08/seidel-reggie-bush-makes-statement-breath-shirt/20078225/

51 Nick Friedell, "Derrick Rose Wears Protest Shirt," *ESPN.com*, December 6, 2014. http://espn.go.com/chicago/nba/story/_/id/11990119/derrick-rose-chicago-bulls-wears-breathe-shirt-reference-eric-garner (accessed July 13, 2015).

52 Kareem Abdul-Jabbar, "College Athletes of the World, United," *Jacobin*, November 12, 2014. www.jacobinmag.com/2014/11/college-athletes-of-the-world-unite/ (accessed July 13, 2015).

53 Kareem Abdul-Jabbar, "The Police Aren't Under Attack. Institutionalized Racism Is," *Time*, December 21, 2014.

54 Chris Kluwe, "I Was an NFL Player Until I Was Fired by Two Cowards and a Bigot," *Deadspin*, January 2, 2014. http://deadspin.com/i-was-an-nfl-player-until-i-was-fired-by-two-cowards-an-1493208214 (accessed July 13, 2015).

55 Outsports, December 18, 2014. www.outsports.com/2014/12/18/7341179/gay-lgbt-athletes-coaches-2014 (accessed July 13, 2015).

32

ALTERNATIVE, EXTREME (AND *AVANT-GARDE*) SPORT

Robert E. Rinehart

Introduction—Proem: Coming to Terms

Alternative. The word conjures up all manner of related images: "oppositional" to Raymond Williams; "deviant" for Howard Becker.[1] Or perhaps "alternative" posits new possibilities, novel approaches, and solutions and combinations: thus, it re-forms anew, as a creative impulse that imagines heretofore unremembered formations. The meanings, delineations, and characteristics of these activities, for a chapter on these kinds of so-called "extreme pursuits,"[2] make quite a difference: they have been variously named *lifestyle*, *alternative*, *extreme, action*, *adventure*, and even *outdoor challenge* "sports" by several different scholars[3] (or, in the case of "extreme" and "X," largely by multinational corporations) over the past 20 years.

Generally, "alternative" means to be oppositional to something, to push against some sort of border. In terms of alternative sport, "alternative" can be characterized in terms of lifestyle, argot, value structures—something not "normative," and yet not necessarily as "deviant" the way Becker and Hughes and Coakley may see it.[4] The motivation of those who practice such "extreme pursuits" really does matter—in naming them, but also in characterizing where and how they fit within contemporary American, and, increasingly, global sport relative to patterns of docility and resistance, individuality and the collective, and multinational and grassroots activity.

In terms of some of these pursuits—that is, nonmainstream, nondominant sports—"alternative" may not work. As well, "extreme," in the sense of physical action pursuits, first made salient to masses of consumers by ESPN, lacks.[5] "Extreme" has stuck as a label, despite its obvious inaccuracies: "extreme" implies risk and overconformity to danger, yet "participants define their own level of risk, and an activity that one individual defines as risk free, another may consider high risk."[6] The naming of such limitations, however, helps to contextualize what it is being discussed by sport historians regarding alternative and extreme sport.

Having depicted how problematic the terminology is for these activities, I next briefly sketch an argument I made nearly 20 years ago. My contention then, and even more now, is that sports scholars need to explore the salience of an avant-garde element within contemporary sport.[7] After briefly discussing the avant-garde element in sport studies within the first section of this chapter, I refer back to the concept of the "alternative" as a form of the avant-garde.[8] I discuss the trajectories of avant-garde sport forms new, unseen, and perhaps unimagined. I classify sporting pursuits in rough categories initially named by Booth and Thorpe: air sports, climbing sports, combative sports, ice and snow sports, terrestrial pursuits, water sports, and wheeled sports.[9] Finally, I conclude by speculating about contemporary and historical issues of avant-garde sport forms.

The Avant-Garde as "New" Sport

The "alternative" is a cultural and sportified formation that always evolves and is concerned with and politically confrontational to established forms of mainstreamed, dominant sport: the "alternative" is, however, *not* a monolithic structure. Thus, I characterize forms of alternative sport as moving targets, antisnapshot historiographical entities whose major abstractions remain interesting, vibrant, and alive, rather than as concrete exemplars. Many of the concrete exemplars of contemporary extreme sport will likely become mainstreamed and dominant forms, themselves opposed in the future by new oppositional formations. The contemporary avant-garde operates this way: it eschews classification, fixing, and, in the case of avant-garde sport, commodification. In this sense, then, these constantly evolving, constantly involuted "becomings," in the view of Deleuze and Guattari, are "rhizomatic" in that they re-form and re-formulate, creatively, as amalgams of themselves and as formulations of the known and the as-yet-known.[10] They are like locally formed archipelagos, rising out of the cultural bedrock when the conditions are right.

Deleuze and Guattari's "becoming" works alongside the performative sporting avant-garde—creatively—to reconstitute new formations from old and unthought-of formulations. As they write,

> . . . there is a self-movement of expressive qualities.
>
> . . . In effect, *expressive qualities or matters of expression enter shifting relations with one another that 'express' the relation of the territory they draw to the interior milieu of impulses and exterior milieu of circumstances.*[11]

In the case of a sporting avant-garde, some of the "points in the territory that place the circumstances of the external milieu in counterpoint"[12] include the very physical constituents of earth. The so-called "invention" of new sport forms aligns nicely with the physical bounds of gravities, frictions, surfaces, and fluids.

The avant-garde within contemporary sport works as an ideal, as a virtual becoming in itself. Dominant, mainstream, and traditional sports tend to be conservative propositions, comforting and safe within their own logics. Nostalgia, patriotism, nationalism, capitalism, and other "past-looking" tropes both reinforce and entrench sport formations into solidified, naturalized, seamless entities that protect and reinstitute their status quo positioning. However, nothing remains static in lived life.

In the 1990s, I discussed the avant-garde in terms of a postmodern moment relative to contemporary sport forms.[13] By classifying dominant sport as the only type of sport forms worthwhile of notice, sport scholars (and publics) denied fresh, new, spatially and temporally different alternative and/or extreme sports. I see the terms "alternative" and "avant-garde" interchangeably, demonstrating what is actually happening in lived experiences of sports people who are pushing limits, inventing new forms, and challenging reified assumptions.

In localized units,[14] by recovering "involutions" such as self-control of activities, inventions of new pursuits, and demand for novelty, players are moving forward in new, unimaginable ways to truly continue to create "alternative"/ "avant-garde" sport formations. This means that at the local level, groups of individuals may create their own variations, their own argot, style, and values.

Thus, we can glean some tenets from the modernist avant-garde movement to better understand some of the trajectories of new sport forms today and in the future. In insisting on change, on audience involvement in the whole of the performance itself,[15] on the pastiche (both in art and in sport), on a variety of values redefining "sport," the postmodern/poststructuralist avant-garde sport formation exemplifies the rhizomatic "becoming" that Deleuze and Guattari suggest.

I draw on the work of Booth and Thorpe's *Berkshire Encyclopedia of Extreme Sports* to delineate historical categories: air sports, climbing sports, combative sports, ice and snow sports, terrestrial pursuits, water sports, and wheeled sports. However, no single list can encompass the ever-expanding and growing types of contemporary so-called "risk" sport formations pursued.

This discussion, with the caveat that these activities fall under the larger rubric of avant-garde, is not meant as a synchronic snapshot of what these pursuits will "mean" contemporaneously and in the future. Rather, these descriptions—and accompanying issues—outline the rough historical edges of the growing forms (thus rapidly mainstreamed, according to the logics of the avant-garde) of so-called "extreme," "action," "lifestyle," or "alternative" sport forms.

Air Sports and Technology

Air sports are those that primarily rely upon "air" as a fluid "surface" for participants to mark themselves against, with, and among. Human fascination and creativity with air as a milieu in which to operate has probably increased since the beginning of "manned [sic] flight," but certainly indications of such interest goes back as far as the "flight ship" drawings of Leonardo Da Vinci to the "sci-fi" dreamings of writers regarding such devices as a jetpack.[16] Some air sports that currently exist: paragliding, parasailing, gliding, hang gliding, parachuting, sky surfing, wingsuit flying, kite surfing, speed flying, ultralight, ultralight trike, and vertical wind tunnelling.

The World Air Sports Federation (FAI) governs most of these activities. (FAI stands for "Fédération Aéronautique Internationale," based in Lausanne, Switzerland, and founded in 1905). The genesis of the organization began accordingly:

> On 10 June 1905, Count Henri de la Vaulx, Vice President of the Aero Club of France, Major Moedebeck of the German Airship League and Fernand Jacobs, President of the Aero Club of Belgium, gave a presentation to the Olympic Congress of Brussels on their proposal for a "Fédération Aéronautique Internationale.[17]

Though there was no official incorporation of the proposal, within six months, the Olympic Congress urged countries throughout the world to form national associations, which would then feed into the "Universal Aeronautical Federation," as the Olympic Congress termed it.[18]

As with many of these 100-plus-year-old organizations, keeping up with technological growth of the activities means that the federations, associations, or organizations must remain relatively flexible. But there are contemporary, avant-garde movements afoot as well: the "Space Games," founded in 1997 by Olav Zipser and lasting until 2006, had many events meant to "interrogate" human free flight in a competitive setting.[19] Zipser, too, has been working on a project—the FreeFly Astronaut Project—which tests the limits of human adaptation to space.[20] Also, nonhuman forms of "virtual" air sports include rocket racing (and its league), controllable slope soaring, and, of course, drone flying.[21]

The Rocket Racing League, abetted by new technology, a public thirst for spectacle, and extremely wealthy entrepreneurs, is currently forming to take advantage of the successes of auto racing and air shows. The Red Bull Air Race World Championships is another facet of an avant-garde, invented sport form whose synergistic reach reflects both a commercialized and an entrepreneurial aspect to new sport forms.

Rocket Racing League (RRL)

Currently being formed by CEO and President Ramy Weitz, the RRL, according to its online advertising, is meant to include five teams flying "rocket powered racing plane[s]" in contests ranging from drag racing to a "4-lap, multiple elimination heat on a 5-mile Formula One-style Raceway-In-The-Sky™." The vehicles currently used are "a Velocity airframe and a single-thrust liquid oxygen (LOX) and ethanol rocket."[22]

An interesting adjunct to this marketable marketing ploy includes the incorporation of the gamelike, sportlike aspects of rocket racing with iPhone and iPad technology. RRL applications will exist for these devices. Clearly, this is intended as a new-age spectator sport and virtual participation sport.

Red Bull Air Race World Championships

The Red Bull Air Race, although an actual event as well, capitalizes on its synergy with the iTunes- and Android-promoted Red Bull Air Race Game.[23] The actual championship event, promoted as a seven-race series at "courses" across the globe, promises (for the Texas Speedway event) pilots "navigating 82 feet high pylons at speeds of up to 230 mph."[24] These amalgams of auto racing (and its knowledge and fan base), air flight of some sort, and twenty-first-century technology provide examples of entrepreneurs utilizing their imaginations for creative presentations of new sport.

Technological advancements characterize contemporary air sports. Use of rocket fuel and boosters, new-age social media platforms, virtual gaming, and so forth have advanced many of the air sports classifications beyond what their inventors first envisioned.

Climbing Sports and the Concept of Risk

Climbing sports include caving and offshoots like underwater caving and bouldering; more frequently these sports consist of mountaineering and various forms of rock climbing. Buildering, another derivative of these pursuits, draws upon bouldering for its ethos and style: it is "climbing human-made structures designed for purposes other than climbing."[25] The Union Internationale de Spéléologie (UIS) is considered the international organization for caving and speleology; the International Climbing and Mountaineering Federation (UIAA) was founded in 1932.[26] The International Federation of Sport Climbing (IFSC) was founded in 2007 and oversees lead climbing, speed climbing, and bouldering.

These organizations, supported by national member institutions, seek to provide stability; consistency; and standardization of rules, record keeping, and other bureaucratic issues within the climbing pursuits. Important issues within climbing sports seem to be twofold: their emphases on ecological and environmental impacts, and the "selling" of safety/risk.

Caving

Caving, also known as spelunking, has been characterized as an "extreme" sport, largely due to the countercultural values orientation of its practitioners. Pólus-Thiry and Rédei examined three groups of extreme participants, and found that their "perception of [a] risk level . . . is related to special situations provoked by action sports."[27] Thus, perceptions of risk for cavers seem to be based upon situational variations.

Bouldering

Bouldering is a form of climbing "in which the athlete performs short, powerful, gymnastic-type movements on rocks or cliff bands 7–8 meters high."[28] Bouldering is considered a relatively safe sport. Appleby claims that the decade of the 1970s, when John Gill and others "devised a simple rating system that determined the difficulty" of various boulder "problems,"[29] was the formal start of the sport. Bouldering's claim to "extreme" is due to the "fringe" (e.g., alternative) aspects of its subculture: its emphasis on hedonism, youth, and historical connection to nature. Bouldering competitions in the United States are conducted under the auspices of USA Climbing, with the American Bouldering Series (ABS) conducted annually.[30]

Mountaineering/Rock Climbing

Mountaineering has a long history—and, in terms of "risk," the challenges and honor of first achieving a summit made it one of the original "extreme" sports. With the late twentieth-century environmental movement, climbing sports aficionados also recognized their place in the degradation of the very environment they cherished, and new forms of climbing began to pop up.

Originally founded in 1932 in Chamonix, France, the Union Internationale des Associations d'Alpinisme (UIAA) serves as the liaison to the International Olympic Committee, and also is seen as the arbiter of international safety and cultural meaning-making regarding ethical and sustainable mountaineering practice.[31] As new forms of climbing grew in critical mass and popular appeal, the UIAA created "the ICC—International Council for Competition Climbing . . . to guarantee sufficient autonomy to [sport climbing] and to provide it with the tools required for growth and development."[32] In 2006, the UIAA relinquished its governance of competitive (indoor) climbing to the International Federation of Sport Climbing (IFSC)—who has advocated for the inclusion of sport climbing in the World Games, the Olympics, and recognition by the Association Générale des Fédérations Internationales de Sports (General Association of International Sports Federations, or AGFIS)[33]—and the International World Games Association.[34]

Climbers may have been one of the first groups to see the impact they had on the environment. Partially as a result, climbing "styles" became broken into these types: sport climbing, in which the climber establishes *permanent* anchors in rock; traditional climbing, in which climbers utilize safety gear *during* the climb; "free solo climbing," in which the climber eschews *any* devices, ropes, or gear to assist in the climb; and speed climbing (and indoor speed climbing), in which the major goal is to climb as quickly as possible. These generally cover most climbing situations, although variations occur. The ethics of climbing without damaging the rock face or climbing surface have taken on more importance in the last 20 to

30 years, largely due to a recognition by many climbers and environmentalists that mountains are not invulnerable.[35]

As the emphasis on "leave no trace" principles grows, so, too, has the increased stress on safety (less "risk") and the mass mountaineering participation for novices (aka "tourism mountaineering"). Indoor sport climbing—and speed climbing in particular—epitomize the emphasis on safety as the skills of climbing, techniques of belaying and providing safety backups, and use of current technology reduce the statistical risk for these types of climbers.

Concomitant with the increased safety for those with means (e.g., Western mountaineers who have Sherpas carry oxygen bottles):

> . . . many Western climbers now prophylactically dose themselves with dexamethasone, a powerful steroid, when they ascend above twenty-two thousand feet, which has proven to be an effective strategy for minimizing the risk of contracting high-altitude cerebral edema (HACE) and high-altitude pulmonary edema (HAPE), potentially fatal ailments that are common on Everest.[36]

Safety for these mountaineering Western tourists has improved in large part due to technology. But it has not for the Sherpas.

Although there exists, generally, an ecological waste from sport tourism, mountain adventure tourism has flourished. Catherine Palmer (2002) details the emerging advent of a class of "executive adventurers":

> Despite the relatively high levels of skill, athleticism, and technical nous that are needed to master these 'frontier challenge activities', such pastimes are nonetheless constructed in very particular ways, so as to attract an amateur, tourist-based clientele, with little or no experience in the activity they are undertaking.[37]

Such amateurs not only undercut the capital of practiced and skilled mountaineers, they also put fellow mountaineers at risk. On April 18, 2014, 16 Sherpas were killed while "laboring slowly through the Khumbu Icefall" beneath Mt. Everest. This tragedy highlights the increasing risks to non-Westerners (e.g., locals like the Sherpa, Gurung, Tamang, and Hindu Chhetri caste), in part due to more tourist pressure on the mountain,[38] and demonstrates a market-based decision-making process towards mountain "adventure tourism."

Combative Sports and "Extreme" Violence

I do not include such agon-intensive activities as jousting, ultimate fighting, and professional wrestling. They are only extreme in their potentiality for death, and their ethos are most decidedly anti-alternative: as blood sports, they are heightened, dominant sport forms that simply reproduce dominant ideologies of authoritarian, ego- and product-oriented, instrumental, capitalist, and outcome-based sports models. These sport forms do not contain any of the salient elements of most so-called extreme or alternative sports. They lack anti-authoritarian ethos; task and process-orientations; and socialist, hedonistic, and reflexive philosophies.

"Extreme" as a term for these pursuits really has no value. Combative sports seem to be extreme only in the sense that they reproduce transnational and multinational corporate marketing campaign rhetorics.

Ice and Snow Sports and Corporatization

Gliding across the surface of ice and snow has been a goal for humankind for eons. Humans have devised many creative ways to negotiate ice and snow, some of which are cumbersome and require great stamina and some of which are quicker, with shorter bursts of energy. The former might include snowshoeing and Nordic, or cross-country, skiing (though, in keeping with the thesis of avant-garde sporting types, these "slower" activities have been amalgamated with tenets of the faster events to produce new formations like ski skating). Alpine skiing, snowboarding, ice yachting, telemark skiing, extreme helicopter skiing ("heli-skiing"), and many of the more recent Winter X Games' (ESPN) types of events comprise some of the faster-paced events.

The X Games' sports have included snowboarding (slopestyle, superpipe, X, big air); skiing (big air, slopestyle, superpipe); snowmobile (speed and style, long jump, hill cross); adaptive events (mono skier X); and a non-ice-related activity, an eSport electronic gaming Invitational: Counter Strike: Global Offensive.[39] A key issue for ice and snow sports is the synergy between the activities and corporate and globalized sponsors.

Other corporate-aligned events included the World Snowboard Tour (with 14 sites in 2012–2013, including resorts in Europe, North America, China, and Scandinavia,[40] and up to 24 sites for the 2014–2015 season[41]), the Winter Gravity Games 2005,[42] and the Winter Dew Tour, sponsored by Mountain Dew.

NBC Sports Group (aligned with Alli Sports since 2008) recently announced it was changing its format to three yearly events: a "Beach" event, a "City" event, and the "Mountain" event, which consolidates the winter sports sponsored by Mountain Dew and Alli into a one-event winter tour.[43] The Dew Tour event will include "snowboard (superpipe and slopestyle) and freeskiing (superpipe and slopestyle)," in addition to a "Nike snowboarding streetstyle" contest.[44] All these events are promoted by private industry/multinational corporations, rather than, for example, government-funded educational systems.

Although dominant forms of ice skating, snowboarding, skiing, and "adaptive" ice and snow events have become legitimized through inclusion in the Winter Olympics and the Paralympics, snowmobiling and many nontraditional offshoot versions of the previous pursuits have not. Red Bull has established a massified, amalgamated ice skating event, called Crashed Ice:

> Call it a combination of ice-skating, downhill skiing, moguls, and throw in a dash of hockey for good measure. Crashed Ice is definitely an extreme sport. Competitors usually have a hockey background, and they race four at a time down a mountain through a city on an icy track.[45]

Some of the more interesting sport forms of traversing oneself on ice or snow end up being highly influenced by an agon component.[46] In the case of Crashed Ice, the change from one skier/snowboarder racing against the clock to four competitors in a massed pack vying for position, hurtling down a steep incline, reinforces the importance of competition to competitors and audience.

By modifying the formats of these activities, promoters and "inventors" of new sports are acceding to the dominant cultural values that will gain them the most audience. These activities may be "extreme," as Red Bull insists, but they are certainly neither alternative nor avant-garde. In the case of these examples, corporatization has trumped individualism.

Terrestrial Pursuits and Creative Play

Bound to the earth, and yet dependent upon the physical concepts of friction, gravity, transfer of energy, spatial orientation, place and landscape ensembles,[47] kinesthetic awareness, magnetism, solar energy, flow and transport, force, and grace and balance, those who engage in terrestrial pursuits both play with these concepts and test their limits. Such activities as parkour, triathlon, ultra (marathon, pedestrianism), bungee jumping (considered both air and terrestrial sport), ecochallenge/adventure racing, orienteering, "outdoor" games and sports, and other modifications of typical activities comprise terrestrial pursuits. Modifications might include distance, intensity, rest, or time constraints (the DIRT principle), with the prefix "ultra" added to signify extraordinary excesses. Parkour enthusiasts have played with both gravity and force, balance and spatial awareness, power and transfer of energy. Such creative play with physical laws appears to be one of the defining aspects of terrestrial pursuits.

Parkour

The World Freerunning Parkour Federation (WFPF) was envisioned in 2007 by a group of individuals who had been involved in the Red Bull Art of Motion Tournament. In 2009, MTV gave WFPF an hour time slot to present parkour to a television audience: "Would MTV get it? . . . Would the message of Parkour have a chance in the middle of all the hype?"[48]

Freerunners practice parkour; they are also known as traceurs.[49] In fact, according to Ameel and Tani, the term "freerunning" stems from Sébastien Foucan's intent to "emphasise the aesthetic values in the movements and connect . . . them to Asian philosophies and the martial arts."[50]

Coined after the 2001 film *Yamakasi: Les Samouraïs des Temps Modernes*, "Traceur means 'bullet' and was chosen because of the emphasis [David] Belle and his contemporaries put on achieving direct, efficient and fast movement over any terrain."[51] The initial "players" of parkour were David Belle and Yann Hnautra, but, with others, "They began to develop and refine a fundamental set of movements: vaults, jumps, climbs, rolls. They taught themselves to be athletes, moving through their environment in a way never before seen in an urban setting."[52] "Parkour" was started in the 1980s, and with the encouragement of David's father Raymond, termed "l'Art du Deplacement."

Whichever of the historical mythos regarding parkour's inception one wishes to believe, clearly this sport pursuit has stemmed from a ludic spirit articulated by cityscapes, natural and constructed elements, and physical laws. As Paula Geyh points out, in parkour "the urban space is re-embodied—its rigid strata effectively 'liquified.'"[53] Further, parkour creates a playful city, inspiring its participants.

Water Sports and Competitiveness

What constitutes a sport in the extreme/alternative or sporting avant-garde sense? Allen Guttmann recharacterized Max Weber's seven aspects of historical epochs for sport.[54] However, one of the most obvious, naturalized features of contemporary sport—including these types of extreme pursuits—has become the overarching ethos of competition. Some of the newer—perhaps avant-garde—formations for these "extreme pursuits" deliberately have opposed overt competition. How we determine what constitutes "sport" determines our orientation to these avant-garde pursuits.

Many of the water sports/pursuits, like most of the other types of activities, have, in varying degrees, dominant values of capitalism, individuality, self-aggrandizement, and/or competitiveness. Some activities might include so-called "barrel jumping" (dropping down natural waterfalls in a barrel),[55] surfing, cave diving, free diving, jet skiing, open water swimming, outrigger/waka boat or canoe racing, paragliding, endurance yacht racing, kiteboarding (freestyle, freeride, downwinders, speed, course racing, wakestyle, jumping, kite surfing), wakeboarding, wakeskating, waterskiing, windsurfing, SCUBA diving, and whitewater negotiation in various crafts. The criteria for competitions appear quite wide ranging. However, as many of these pursuits become commoditized, their regional differences, like language dialects, tend to flatten out into a global lexicon. One interesting case representing water sports is kiteboarding.

Kiteboarding

Kiteboarding consists of a boarder atop a kiteboard (like a wakeboard), attached or unattached, and gripping onto a harnessed kite to propel them up and across the water's surface. According to the International Sailing Federation (ISAF), kiteboarding interest has grown relatively quickly: "App. 60000 [sic] persons start kiteboarding every year. App. 180000 kites and 75000 [sic] hulls are sold every year with a yearly growth of 10%."[56] The ISAF, formed in Paris in 1907, and the International Kiteboarding Association teamed together to campaign for inclusion of kiteboarding in the 2016 Rio de Janeiro Olympics, but wakeboarding retained the slot.[57]

The range of beginner to professional kiteboarder exemplifies much of the competitive ranges of avant-garde pursuits. Marc Jacobs, whose personal website—embedded with SwitchKites, Mystic waterwear, Ronix wakeboards and boots, Skull Candy headphones, and Balance (Ultimate Body Performance) protein supplement brandings—claims that he has won "2 New Zealand Junior National titles, 2 New Zealand Open Men's titles," is a professional kiteboarder/kitesurfer.[58] Mark Symonds interviewed 50-year-old Glenn Bright, who switched to kiteboarding from windsurfing. Although his children are winning championships, Bright sees kiteboarding as more of a lifestyle activity: "It's not scary to kite anymore. . . . Now the kites have got so much control and wind range, teaching has become fun."[59]

Wheeled Sports and Gendered Branding

Wheeled pursuits include skateboarding, BMX (bicycle motocross), inline skating (Rollerblade), motocross, street luge, mountain bike racing, motor sports, even "land sailing" (aka, sand yachting, land yachting): in other words, any kind of activity in which human beings traverse across a surface on a wheel or wheels. There are a number of ways these activities can be characterized.

The surface varies within wheeled activities (such as in land yachting, where contestants race across packed sand). Mud, dirt, macadam, asphalt, concrete, bricks, or mixed surfaces also are typical. The attachments that join humans to the actual device vary in wheeled sports. For example, motor sports generally mean that the driver is sitting in some sort of seat within or on a frame; skateboarding usually requires good footwear, as the skater is not attached by bindings to the board; inline skating, by definition, means that the skater is bound to the skate itself. Locomotion determines some of the facets of these wheeled sports. In land yachting, the wind provides propulsion: this is an example of the use of natural energy (solar-powered wheeled sports may be one of the next things!). Skating types of wheeled pursuits may rely primarily on human-propelled locomotion: skateboards, inline skates, unicycles, bicycles, tricycles, quad-cycles, and OrbitWheels pursuits depend upon human effort for propulsion.

Other pursuits depend upon motors. These, like motorcycles, automobiles, motobikes, tricycles, motorized scooters, go-karts, and quads, gain their propulsive force from human-designed motors that often rely upon an outside element for movement (e.g., steam, electricity, petrol, jet fuel). The quality, size, and number of wheels also discriminate many of these wheeled pursuits, even within categories. Finally, the number of humans operating and engaging in these activities may vary from one to many comprising a "team."

Team building leads to the concept of sponsorship, gaining support for one's efforts. Thus, within many of these wheeled sports, seeking branding contracts, sponsorship, and support systems at an early age seems to have become a naturalized part of the lifespan of sports. Examples of two stars follow.

The Path to "Success": Two Motocross "Stars"

Motocross has been a sport for many years, but its spectatorial interest has blossomed. The first cited off-road event was in 1924: ". . . the Scrambles was held at Camberley in Surrey [UK]."[60] As the growth of motorized wheeled sports has grown, so, too, has the sponsorship interest in them.

Vicki Golden: Monster Energy Supercross

In 2015 Vicki Golden, aged 22, challenged the hegemony of males in the 250 (cc) Supercross.[61] She has "earned" the chance for "Supercross" based upon her previous record:

> Golden, with three X Games gold medals in Women's Moto X Racing and a bronze in Moto X Best Whip, will ride for the Mississippi-based Hanson Racing Team (HRT) aboard a Suzuki.[62]

She rides a Suzuki because Suzuki is one of her major sponsors. The Hanson Racing Team (HRT)—her team—has *allowed* her to compete on her Suzuki motorbikes, despite the fact that HRT is sponsored by KTM Sportmotorcycle AG (from Austria). Other Golden sponsors include One Industries, "The Talking Frog, Metal Mulisha (clothing), Mandingo Pickles, and Mind-FX Energy."[63]

Though she has been riding motorbikes since age seven, her sponsorship is tenuous. She is in a privileged position, yet she constantly has to struggle for sponsors. She has moved from team to team in order to remain viable.

Unlike Travis Pastrana—discussed next—Golden struggles a bit for sponsorship—and sometimes is criticized for gaining it—in part because of her being photogenic and a gender "trailblazer"). Such backlash is not atypical to mainstream sports, but in so-called "extreme" sports, where rejecting mainstream society is often celebrated, this gendered discourse is ironically conformist.

Travis Pastrana: Nitro Circus

Travis Pastrana, whose estimated net worth varies from $15 to 30 (US) million, was sponsored "by Suzuki at eight years old."[64] According to his website, he is largely sponsored now by Roush Racing, Red Bull, KMC wheels, Suzuki, DC shoes, Samsung, Boost Mobile, Smith Optics, Nixon watches, Kicker Car audio, Ethika, Alpinstars, AC, AGV, and Action Shot cams.[65] In an interview, Pastrana claimed

> . . . When you're good enough in your sport, you have the option to choose your sponsors. Sometimes you pass up a lot of money to support the people you like and the products you want to use but in the end it's worth it! I've been fortunate [in] that when I was at the top of my game I was really loyal to the brands and sponsors that I liked. In turn, most of them have stuck with me through the many injuries and down the years I've had in my career.[66]

In this story, Pastrana fails to note his gendered privilege. Sponsor perceptions of ability, how an athlete resonates with an existing public/consumer appetite, covert forms of sexism, and conformity to dominant views of celebrity may be reasons that the status quo positions remain fixed within a so-called patriarchy.[67]

Branding and mediatization aspects are writ large in wheeled sports—from logos on uniforms, to affiliations of sponsored athletes, to the actual naming of events. In fact, in a recent piece on Formula One drivers, Sturm writes, ". . . transnational corporations purchase a degree of influence through sponsorship [of this]. . . corporate spectacle."[68]

Conclusion

In this chapter, I suggest the use of the term "avant-garde" sports to describe many of these newly hatched forms. Here, I revisit two main points: 1) the presence and rough identification of life cycles within these new sport forms and 2) a reinforcing of the types of issues that many of these sport forms may exhibit. The sense of "becoming" within these avant-garde sports insists on their constant change and movement toward incorporation into the mainstream.

Many of these avant-garde forms often follow distinctively predictable life cycles. Some of them—like snowboarding, in the Winter Olympics—are late avant-garde sports. That is to say, they may start out as "grassroots"-type activities; move to more critical mass pursuits; achieve heightened critical mass; reach a tipping point; and eventually become mainstreamed, normalized, and sometimes dominant activities or sports.

The grassroots level may mean that a few inventive individuals (scattered around the world spurred by technological advances) begin "playing" with new invented forms of amalgamated pursuits. Achieving critical mass means, in one sense, that endemic products supporting these sports' future mass appeal begin to crop up. People talk about the activities, and a few will sample them. Heightened critical mass is demonstrated when finite resources are fought over—as in ocean waves. The tipping point of these once-avant-garde sports means mass acceptance, more instances of a normalized acceptance than overt resistance. 1998 snowboarder Ross Rebagliati, who won, lost, and re-won a gold medal,[69] represented the last vestiges of snowboarding's claim to be an avant-garde sport. His rebellious attitude, personified by his use of marijuana, became emblematic of a pre-mass-appeal snowboarding ethos.

Becoming mainstreamed, these sports take on many of the aspects of modernist sports that Guttmann proposed many years ago.[70] When these sports eventually reach a global audience, gain thousands of practitioners, support world championships, and foster "celebrities," by definition, they are no longer alternative, extreme, or avant-garde. Soon, ironically, new forms will replace them. The only term that currently works for these oppositional sport forms is "avant-garde."

In closing, I have demonstrated that several themes exist within these stages of avant-garde sport formations. These themes are air sports, with its technological advancements; climbing sports, both in terms of ecological impact and safety/risk factors; combative sports, with a push toward extreme/X/spectatorial aspects;[71] ice and snow sport, with its corporatization and globalization; terrestrial pursuits, with its creative play with physical laws; water sports, with its competitiveness and professionalization; and wheeled sports, in terms of branding and mediatization. The examples I have provided have been specific, but my caution to readers is that these examples may be applied across the various groups—that it is the stages of formation, from so-called grassroots to highly commercialized, that determine what issues and concerns any particular sport form may exhibit.

Notes

1 Raymond Williams, *Marxism and Literature* (Oxford: Oxford University Press, 1977); Howard Becker, *Outsiders: Studies in the Sociology of Deviance* (New York: Free Press, 1963).

2 Douglas Booth and Holly Thorpe. "The Meaning of Extreme," in *Berkshire Encyclopedia of Extreme Sports*, ed. Douglas Booth and Holly Thorpe (Great Barrington, MA: Berkshire Publishing Group LLC., 2007), 181.

3 For "lifestyle," see, e.g., Belinda Wheaton, ed., *Understanding Lifestyle Sport: Consumption, Identity and Difference* (London: Routledge, 2004); Wheaton, "Introducing the Consumption and Representation of Lifestyle Sports," *Sport in Society: Cultures, Commerce, Media, Politics* 13, no. 7–8: 2010, 1057–1081. For "alternative," see, e.g., Robert E. Rinehart and Synthia Sydnor, "Proem," in *To the Extreme: Alternative Sports, Inside and Out*, ed. Robert E. Rinehart and Synthia Sydnor (Albany: State University of New York Press, 2003), 1–17. For "adventure" see, e.g., Joan Ormrod, 2009. "On the Edge: Leisure, Consumption and the Representation of Adventure Sports—Introduction," in *On the Edge: Leisure, Consumption and the Representation of Adventure Sports*, ed. Joan Ormrod and Belinda Wheaton (University of Brighton: Leisure Studies Association, 2009), v-xix. For outdoor challenge sport and similar terms, see, e.g., Barbara Humberstone and Ina Stan, "Nature and Well-Being in Outdoor Learning: Authenticity or Per-Formativity," *Journal of Adventure Education & Outdoor Learning* 12, no. 3 (2012): 183–197; Brian Wattchow and Mike Brown, *A Pedagogy of Place: Outdoor Education for a Changing World* (Victoria, Australia: Monash University Publishing, 2011); Luděk Šebek, Developing the Ability of Adventure (Unpublished manuscript, nd.). For an overview of these name challenges, see, e.g., Robert E. Rinehart, "Anhedonia and Alternative Sports," *Revue STAPS* 104, no. 2 (2014): 9–21.

4 Cf., Becker, *Outsiders*. See also Robert Hughes and Jay Coakley, "Positive Deviance Among Athletes: The Implications of Overconformity to the Sport Ethic," *Sociology of Sport Journal* 8, no. 4 (1991): 307–325.

5 See Rinehart, "Inside of the Outside: Pecking Orders Within Alternative Sport at ESPN's 1995 *The eXtreme Games*," *Journal of Sport & Social Issues* 22, no. 4 (1998): 398–415.

6 Booth and Thorpe, "The Meaning of Extreme," 181.

7 The major problem, of course, with *avant-garde* as a modifier for these sports or pursuits is that it has very little cultural capital within sport studies and beyond.

8 Rinehart, *Players All: Performances in Contemporary Sport* (Bloomington, IN: Indiana University Press, 1998).

9 Booth and Thorpe, eds., *Berkshire Encyclopedia of Extreme Sports* (Great Barrington, MA: Berkshire Publishing Group LLC., 2007).

10 Gilles Deleuze and Félix Guattari, *A Thousand Plateaus: Capitalism and Schizophrenia*, trans., Brian Massumi (Minneapolis: University of Minnesota Press, 1987), 240.

11 Deleuze and Guattari, *A Thousand Plateaus*, 317, emphasis in original.

12 Ibid., 317.

13 Rinehart, "Dropping Hierarchies: Toward the Study of a Contemporary Sporting Avant-Garde," *Sociology of Sport Journal* 13, no. 2 (1996): 159–175; Rinehart, *Players All*.

14 The "sporting avant-garde" works best at the local level, where grassroots participants create sports that challenge the status quo of larger organizational structures.

15 Cf., Henry M. Sayre, *The Object of Performance: The American Avant-Garde Since 1970* (Chicago: University of Chicago Press, 1989).

16 In 1981, New Zealander Glenn Martin began research for a personal jetpack. The twelfth incarnation of this jetpack received "authorisation from New Zealand Civil Aviation Authority for manned test flights," with a projected availability to the public of 2017. "Company." www.martinjetpack.com/company (accessed December 27, 2014).

17 "History, FAI." www.fai.org/about-fai/history (accessed January 26, 2015), 3.

18 "About FAI." www.google.co.nz/url?sa=t&rct=j&q=&esrc=s&source=web&cd=5&ved=0CDQQFjAE&url=http%3A%2F%2Fwww.fai.org%2Fdownloads%2Ffai%2Fabout_fai&ei=N_3FVPCzEsbt8gWLzIHACw&usg=AFQjCNFcU8zW68WWaCnuArdoDx4yYlrdog&bvm=bv.84349003,d.dGc (accessed January 26, 2015).

19 "Space Games." http://en.wikipedia.org/wiki/Space_Games#History (accessed February 1, 2015).

20 Matteo Emanuelli, "Interview with Olav Zipser—Freefly Astronaut Project," January 10, 2014. www.spacesafetymagazine.com/aerospace-engineering/red-bull-stratos/interview-olav-zipser-freefly-astronaut-project/ (accessed February 1, 2015).

21 "World Air Games." http://en.m/wikipediaorg/wiki/World_Air_Games (accessed December 23, 2014).

22 "Rocket Racing," Rocket Racing League. www.rocketracingleague.com (accessed December 23, 2014).

23 "Red Bull Air Race Game." www.redbullairrace.com/en_INT/article/red-bull-air-race-game-voted-one-best (accessed December 12, 2014).

24 "Red Bull Air Race," "Red Bull Air Race," Red Bull Air Race Championship: Texas Motor Speedway. www.texasmotorspeedway.com/upcoming-events/special-events/red-bull-air-race-world-championship (accessed December 23, 2014).

25 Ivo van Hilvoorde, "Buildering," in *Berkshire Encyclopedia of Extreme Sports*, ed. Douglas Booth and Holly Thorpe (Great Barrington, MA: Berkshire Publishing Group LLC, 2007), 50–54.

26 "UIAA," International Climbing and Mountaineering Federation. www.theuiaa.org (accessed January 1, 2015).

27 Éva Pólus-Thiry and Csaba Rédei, "Value Orientation of People Involved in Action or Extreme Sports in Hungary," *European Journal for Sport and Society* 9, no. 1+2 (2012): 115.

28 Karen M. Appleby, "Bouldering: North America," in *Berkshire Encyclopedia of Extreme Sports*, ed. Douglas Booth and Holly Thorpe (Great Barrington, MA: Berkshire Publishing Group LLC, 2007), 47.

29 Ibid., 48.

30 "USA Climbing." http://usaclimbing.net/about (accessed January 2, 2015).

31 "UIAA."

32 "Climbing Competitions History." www.ifsc-climbing.org/index.php/about-ifsc/what-is-the-ifsc/history (accessed November 27, 2014).

33 "Climbing Competitions History."

34 "IWGA," International World Games Association. www.theworldgames.org/the-iwga/association (accessed October 27, 2014).

35 Yvon Chouinard, *Let My People Go Surfing: The Education of a Reluctant Businessman* (New York: Penguin, 2006).

36 Jon Krakauer, "Death and Anger on Everest," *The New Yorker*, April 21, 2014. www.newyorker.com/news/news-desk/death-and-anger-on-everest (accessed December 12, 2014); Mark Jenkins, "Historic Tragedy on Everest, with 13 Sherpas Dead in Avalanche," *National Geographic*, April 19, 2014. http://news.nationalgeographic.com/news/2014/04/140418-everest-avalanche-sherpa-killed-mountain/ (accessed June 12, 2015).

37 Catherine Palmer, "'Shit Happens': The Selling of Risk in Extreme Sport," *The Australian Journal of Anthropology* 13, no. 3 (2002): 324.

38 Krakauer, "Death and Anger on Everest."

39 "Counter Strike," Counter-Strike: Global Offensive. www.majorleaguegaming.com/competitions/83 (accessed January 5, 2015).
40 "World Snowboard Tour (2012–13)." www.redbull.com/nz/en/snow/events/1331578845675/spring-battle (accessed January 7, 2015).
41 "World Snowboard Tour (2014–15)." www.worldsnowboardtour.com (accessed January 7, 2015).
42 "Winter Gravity Games," March 3, 2005. www.ecolips.com/news-and-events/winter-gravity-games (accessed January 7, 2015).
43 "Changing Dew Tour." http://xgames.espn.go.com/article/7823954/dew-tour-scale-three-yearly-events (accessed January 7, 2015).
44 "Dew Tour." www.gobreck.com/events/dew-tour (accessed January 7, 2015).
45 Miranda Lightstone, "Extreme Sport Red Bull Crashed Ice: Downhill Skating." www.watchmojo.com/video/id/9543/ (accessed December 23, 2014).
46 Cf., Roger Caillois, *Man, Play and Games* (New York, Free Press, 1958).
47 Cf., Karl B. Raitz, "Perception of Sports Landscapes and Gratification in the Sport Experience, *Sport Place* 1, no. 1 (1987): 4–19.
48 "The WFPF Idea," The WFPF idea—October 2007. www.wfpf.com/history-wfpf/ (accessed February 1, 2015), 4.
49 Cf., Michael Atkinson, "Parkour, Anarcho-Envionmentalism, and Poiesis," *Journal of Sport and Social Issues* 33, no. 2 (2009): 169–194; Michael Atkinson, 2013. Heidegger, Parkour, "Post-Sport, and the Essence of Being," in *A Companion to Sport*, ed. David L. Andrews and Ben Carrington (London: Blackwell Publishing Ltd., 2013), 359–374.
50 Lieven Ameel and Sirpa Tami, "Everyday Aesthetics in Action: Parkour Eyes and the Beauty of Concrete Walls," *Emotion, Space and Society* 5, no. 3 (2012): 164.
51 "Parkour History," "Parkour History—Parkour Generations," August 22, 2014. http://parkourgenerations.com/parkour-history/ (accessed February 1, 2015), 13.
52 Ibid., 11.
53 Paula Geyh, "Urban Free Flow: A Poetics of Parkour," *M/C Journal* 9, no. 3 (2006). http://journal.media-culture.org.au/0607/06-geyh.php (accessed February 1, 2015), 10.
54 Allen Guttmann, *From Ritual to Record: The Nature of Modern Sports* (New York: Columbia University Press, 1978).
55 Cf., Ellen Staurowsky, "Barrel Jumping," in *Berkshire Encyclopedia of Extreme Sports*, ed. Douglas Booth and Holly Thorpe (Great Barrington, MA: Berkshire Publishing Group LLC, 2007), 15–20.
56 "ISAF Kiteboarding," "ISAF kiteboarding format trials (PDF, 2012)." www.sailing.org/tools/documents/EC8bKiteboardingTechnicalReport-%5B12451%5D.pdf (accessed January 28, 2015).
57 Duncan Mackay, "Windsurfing to Stay in Rio 2016 Olympics After Kiteboarding Decision Overturned," *Inside the Games*, November 11, 2012. www.insidethegames.biz/sports/summer/sailing/1011620-windsurfing-to-stay-in-rio-2016-olympics-after-kiteboarding-decision-overturned (accessed January 28, 2015).
58 "Marc Jacobs." www.marcjacobswake.com/index.html (accessed January 28, 2015).
59 Quoted in Mark Symonds, "The sky's the limit," *Uno 12* (Bay of Plenty, NZ) (2008): 21.
60 "History of Motocross," "Freestyle motocross: History of motocross." www.freestyle-motocross.net/info/guide/fmx/history (accessed January 30, 2015), 1.
61 In fact, Golden ". . . isn't the first female to compete in supercross [sic]. That honor goes to Dorene Payne who attempted to qualify for the 1983 San Diego Supercross at Jack Murphy Stadium. In 2000, Italian Stefy Bau attempted four events in what was then called the 125 class (now 250SX)" ("Vicki Golden," 2015, 10).
62 "Vicki Golden," "Vicki Golden to race 250 Supercross." http://xgames.espn.go.com/rally-moto-x/article/12161214/vicki-golden-race-men-250-monster-energy-supercross (accessed January 30, 2015), 2.
63 Michael Antonovich, "She races: Vicki Golden," *TransWorld Motocross*, August 8, 2013. http://motocross.transworld.net/1000151296/features/she-races-vicki-golden/ (accessed January 30, 2015).
64 Quoted in Damien Ashenhurst, "Travis Pastrana interview—The return of Nitro in 2015" (2014). http://dirtaction.com.au/travis-pastrana-interview-the-return-of-nitro-in-2015/ (accessed January 30, 2015), 2.

65 "Travis Pastrana Sponsors." www.travispastrana.com/m/sponsors.php (accessed January 30, 2015).
66 Quoted in Ashenhurst, "Travis Pastrana interview," 3.
67 Cf., Rebecca Finkel, "Broadcasting from a Neutral Corner? An Analysis of the Mainstream Media's Representation of Women's Boxing at the London 2012 Olympic Games," in *Sports Events, Society and Culture*, ed. Katherine Dashper, Thomas Fletcher, and Nicola McCullough (Oxon: Routledge, 2015), 89–90.
68 Damion Sturm, "A Glamorous and High-Tech Global Spectacle of Speed: Formula One Motor Racing as Mediated, Global and Corporate Spectacle," in Dashper, Fletcher, and McCullough, eds., *Sports Events, Society and Culture*, 80.
69 Ross Rebagliati, *Off the Chain: An Insider's History of Snowboarding* (Vancouver: Greystone Books, Ltd., 2009).
70 Guttmann, *From Ritual to Record.*
71 Cf., Guy Debord, *The Society of the Spectacle*, trans., Donald Nicholson-Smith (New York: Zone Books, 1994[1967]).

33

NOT QUITE A SLAM DUNK

Globalization and American Team Sports

John Nauright

Introduction

For many decades the United States has been actively involved in international sports with many early influences coming from the British Isles, particularly England. English settlers and their American offspring established horse racing, boxing, pedestrianism, and cricket as major pastimes in the period before the American Civil War (1861–1865). After the war, other sporting influences emerged, including the arrival of football, in the forms of soccer and rugby, which were codified in England in 1863 and 1871, respectively. During the 1870s and 1880s baseball began to replace cricket as the leading summer bat-and-ball sport, though pockets of cricket popularity remained, and English and Australian cricket teams continued to tour the United States until the 1920s.[1] Baseball became so popular that Albert Goodwill Spalding, former player and sporting goods pioneer, financed a world baseball tour in 1888.[2] Though the world did not take to baseball as easily as Spalding had hoped, neither did Cuba take up cricket as Winston Churchill famously predicted.[3]

Though Spalding's tour did not lead to baseball storming the world, it and other endeavors did begin to put an American stamp on the global sports marketplace, particularly in areas where American imperialist interests were strong, such as Cuba, Dominican Republic, Mexico, and the Philippines, or where American missionaries promoted the spread of sport in addition to emerging trading interests in Japan, Taiwan, and Central America as Gerald Gems outlines in his work.[4] American missionaries were partly responsible as well for the spread of soccer in sub-Saharan Africa as they believed it to be a good sport for urbanizing Africans to play.[5] Despite this initial flurry and spread of sporting interests, most particularly baseball, the role of American sports globally has been far less dominant compared to other areas of American mass culture such as movies, television, popular music, or fast food restaurants. The late British-based American commentator Mark Marqusee pointed out in 2000 the relative weakness of American global sporting dominance. Compared to popular music, cinema, and television, he asserted American sports were much weaker in global influence.[6] Despite Marqusee's assertion there is no doubt that American sports such as basketball and volleyball have spread across the globe, becoming the second and third most widely played team sports, respectively, and the NFL is watched in over 100 countries around the world.

The global popularity of Michael Jordan (developed in partnership with the Nike shoe and sports apparel company)[7] in the 1990s launched a new era of American sporting engagement globally as U.S. sports expanded business interests around the world and U.S. investors began to take an interest in international sports team ownership.[8] Top American soccer players began to appear regularly for leading European clubs,[9] hundreds of former college basketball players earned a living playing basketball professionally around the world, and countless athletes from around the world were recruited for the U.S. intercollegiate sports system. Although the case of Michael Jordan in the 1990s has been well documented, perhaps equally important for U.S. sport in the global marketplace was the bringing of Chinese star Yao Ming to the NBA as American sports began to tap the largest potential sports marketplace in the world.

The Last Frontier: Yao Ming and Selling U.S. Sport to China[10]

On October 30, 2002, Yao Ming made his debut in the NBA for the Houston Rockets. Yao Ming was not the first Chinese player to don an NBA uniform, but he was by far the most significant in terms of both pure basketball skill and commercial potential. This historic contest against the Indiana Pacers not only marked his first NBA game, but it was the culmination of a long-planned relationship between the NBA and China. Yao made a difference on the court for his team, but his impact has been far grander and wider reaching in terms of international marketing and business. Sponsors viewed Yao as the gateway to the Asian market; as such he became the NBA symbol for globalization there. An estimated 500 million Chinese tuned into Yao's NBA debut on television.[11] In October 2004 Yao was ranked nineteenth in the *Sports Business Journal*'s listing of the 20 most influential people in professional basketball. Yao was one of only two then active players on the list, along with mega-superstar Shaquille O'Neal.[12] Both China and the United States shared the same capitalist dream for Yao. The Yao situation was compared by a Chinese diplomat as similar to that of the United States–China "Ping-Pong" diplomacy of the 1970s, when the two countries started to build relations through sport; they would build business interests through sport in the 2000s.[13]

The case of Yao Ming details the relationship that the NBA worked so hard to cultivate with the Chinese in anticipation of becoming a major player in the region. It is now exemplified by Major League Baseball in several countries in Latin America and the Caribbean and in Asia, as well as the National Hockey League (NHL) in Eastern and Northern Europe. Since 2008, Major League Soccer (MLS) has followed suit bringing in English stars David Beckham and Steven Gerrard and French icon Thierry Henry, among others, to attract wider interest to its competition. Yao Ming represents how globalization has been a two-way street in the expansion of North American sports leagues internationally and serves as a useful case study to understand how globalization and U.S. professional sports business interests have worked in tandem. The NBA, in its pursuit of Yao Ming, was at the forefront of a newly aggressive U.S. professional sport engagement with global markets.

In October 2002, the NBA opened a regional office in Beijing, China, to grand fanfare.[14] This occurred right before Yao took the court for the Houston Rockets for the first time. However, as far back as 1979, the NBA had its eye on the Asian market and the huge opportunities for development and marketing that were virtually untapped by any American sport save pockets of baseball interest in Japan, Taiwan, and South Korea. That summer, the league's Washington Bullets (now the Wizards) visited China and competed in two exhibition games against the Chinese National team and the Bayi Rockets, a team in the Chinese Basketball Association (CBA).[15] This was the first key event in the relationship between the NBA and China. This event set in place a chain of other events that led to what would have been unthinkable at the time—Chinese players in the NBA. Six years later, the NBA-China

Friendship Tour was formed. The Chinese National team came to New York to participate in training and practice against NBA teams and receive instruction from such legendary NBA figures as Red Auerbach and Pete Newell.[16] There were then no significant developments with the Chinese until 1994 when events and contacts between the two parties started occurring on a regular basis; however, in the interim the NBA opened its first Asian office in Hong Kong in 1992.[17] That same year, developments with the Chinese community in the United States began. In November 1994 a radio station in Los Angeles broadcast the game between the Los Angeles Lakers and Los Angeles Clippers in Mandarin Chinese, marking the first broadcast in Chinese of an NBA game within the United States.

In June 1994, CCTV, the state-run television network in China, broadcasted the entire NBA Finals series between the Rockets and New York Knicks live. This marked the first time that the Chinese people had the opportunity to witness all of the games without delay.[18] Today, NBA games can now be seen in over 400 million homes in China, and more Chinese are now acquiring televisions for the first time.[19] China quickly became the league's largest television base outside of the United States and recently surpassed the United States in total numbers of viewers.[20] In 1997, prominent NBA players David Robinson and Joe Smith held multiple basketball clinics for thousands of children in Beijing. In early 1999, *NBA Shi Kong*, the Chinese version of *Hoop* magazine, debuted in China. *Hoop* is the official NBA magazine and it is sold as a program at game venues.[21] In August 2000 an NBA Legends Tour traveled to China to play exhibitions against the Chinese national team. By the time Yao was drafted by the Houston Rockets in June 2002, the NBA had launched a Mandarin-language website in preparation for his arrival.[22]

The China/NBA relationship came full circle in October 2004, as Yao and the Rockets played in two exhibition games in Shanghai and Beijing dubbed the "China Games" against their Western Conference foes the Sacramento Kings. This marked the first time NBA teams competed in China. Not surprisingly, both games featuring Yao were sold out, and NBA Commissioner David Stern said, "[I]t is like the Beatles on tour."[23] Appearances by Yao were not disclosed publicly before they occurred so crowds of Chinese supporters and well-wishers would not mob him. Fans waited over 40 hours to see their hometown hero, and courtside seats inside went for more than $2,500, which was more than the annual income of the average Chinese citizen at the time.[24] The Kings roster also featured roster hopeful Liu Wei, who played in China for the Shanghai Sharks, Yao's former team. The NBA brought along former league stars as well as WNBA players for this tour across China to help with promotion.[25] Of course, the tour was marketed by the league as a homecoming for Yao, but the NBA really looked at it as an opportunity to promote itself, its products, and their sponsors in China. It was more of an investment in the future by the NBA and the six high-level American multinational corporate sponsors (McDonald's, Anheuser-Busch, Reebok, Eastman Kodak, Disney, and Coca-Cola), who jumped at the chance to pick up the bill for the trip across the globe.[26]

China has a history of emphasizing sport as a way to boost national morale. This started in 1949 when the communist People's Republic of China was founded and continues through today.[27] The backbone of the sporting system in China is their "sports schools." Yao is a product of these programs, as he was selected at a young age to be a basketball player because of his height and genes (his parents were both basketball players). Thus, because the Chinese players are trained by the government, they have been viewed by the regime as property of the state.[28] These thoughts were evident when you look at how they handled the Yao Ming situation and the case of Wang Zhizhi, another Chinese basketball star.

In 1999, the Dallas Mavericks drafted Wang Zhizhi. Wang was the second Chinese player drafted by the NBA, and he became the first Chinese player with a legitimate chance to play in the NBA. (In 1987 the Atlanta Hawks drafted Sung Tao in the seventh round, but he never even traveled to the United States.) At the time he was drafted, Wang's official position in China was not as a member of the national basketball team, but it was as a "regimental commander" for the P.L.A., the Chinese army.[29] It took over two years for Mavericks management to convince Wang's bosses at Bayi to allow him to play in the United States. After his second NBA season in which he averaged around five points a game, Wang requested permission from the Chinese to stay in the United States so he could compete in the NBA's summer league in 2002. Wang had previously agreed to travel home every summer to fulfill commitments for the national team. The Chinese government denied his request, but Wang would not return to China to compete for the national team. Showing how delicate their relationship with China was, the Mavericks refused to offer Wang a new contract; they did not want to tarnish the bond they, and by extension the NBA, had formed with the Chinese. That fall, the Los Angeles Clippers signed Wang to a new contract, and they were promptly banned from appearing on Chinese television. Wang's military passport expired, and he did not return to China after the summer of 2001, in between his first and second professional seasons.[30]

Before this incident the Chinese embraced Wang. Just a few months after his Mavericks debut, he participated in a coaching clinic that took place throughout China and was treated like a hero by the Chinese government upon his return.[31] Then in April 2002, the first NBA Asian media tour was arranged. The tour focused on Wang and the second NBA player from China, Mengke Bateer (a good player, but nowhere near the skill level of Yao or Wang), but the NBA was still intently focused behind the scenes on bringing Yao to the United States.[32] He was still the number-one prize in China.

On June 26, 2002, the Rockets selected Yao Ming as the first player chosen overall in the NBA draft. The Wang Zhizhi situation directly influenced Yao. After Wang did not return, Chinese officials became even more protective of their coveted star center. "Yao Ming is China's (Michael) Jordan. We don't want to lose him," said Li Yaomin, the vice general manager of the Sharks.[33] These officials wanted to be sure that Yao would not repeat the actions of Wang, and the negotiation process was a very difficult one. Yao was considered by just about every basketball scout to be a top prospect ready for the NBA by 2001, but his Chinese Basketball Association team, the Shanghai Sharks, wanted to win a title first and they would not permit Yao to leave (the team did win the championship that next season). These same officials also were wary of relinquishing any control they had over Yao; they had said he would be able to be drafted by the NBA in 2001, but then changed their stance. Scouts from virtually every NBA team visited Shanghai in 2002 to observe Yao in person when they finally felt the Chinese would let him go. When the Houston Rockets stumbled upon the NBA's first pick through the draft lottery they decided to negotiate with the Chinese separately from the NBA, whose efforts had not been going well.[34] They knew exactly who they were going to draft, and they wanted to make sure Yao was going to become a Rocket. The Sharks were willing to let Yao go, but they wanted more than a small piece of the pie in exchange.

Almost immediately after his team had won the first pick in the draft, Rockets general counsel Michael Goldberg traveled to Shanghai. When he got there, he met with Mr. Li in order to establish a relationship right away. The Sharks immediately started listing off their demands, none of which could be granted under NBA collective bargaining rules.[35] After hard negotiations, a deal was reached the morning of the 2002 NBA draft, with the Chinese receiving assurances that Yao would be able to (and would) compete for China in the Olympics. When Yao was finally drafted, he put on the hat of his new team, which is an American draft day tradition. However, in a symbol of just how peculiar the entire situation was, the newest member of the NBA did it from a television studio in Beijing, not from the Madison Square Garden stage with his fellow draftees.

Indeed, China could have refused to release Yao to the United States. There is a lot of speculation as to why China allowed their prized sports star to leave the country. The most probable explanation is the fact that Beijing was to host the 2008 Summer Olympics. China viewed their Olympics as a major chance to continue building relations with the United States and the rest of the world both diplomatically and commercially. The country recently had been admitted to the World Trade Organization and their gross domestic product (GDP) grew at a rate of nearly 10 percent annually in the first decade of the 2000s.[36] China also had long had an unfavorable human rights reputation. Secrecy also is synonymous with the country, as much of the world is dominated by more open societies. Permitting Yao to pursue a career elsewhere was perceived as a sign the Chinese were willing to open up and be trusted by the United States and the world as a whole. China was eager to be seen as an open nation, but at the same time it still seemed unwilling to give up too much control over its prized athletes.[37] In this way, Yao was a political symbol. During a visit to Houston in September 2002, the Chinese ambassador to the United States mentioned Yao's situation as an example of "constructive engagement" between the United States and China.[38] However, the mixed signals they sent regarding their "ownership" of Yao raised questions about how much the Chinese wanted to open up before the 2008 Games.[39]

Before he was allowed to travel to Houston, Yao had to promise to fulfill his commitments to the national team during the NBA off-season, and in 2004 he represented China at the Summer Olympics in Greece. He had to agree to pay the CBA between 5 and 8 percent of his annual salary from the Rockets for the duration of his career. That was not all, as Yao also had to pay the Sharks a buyout that ranged from 8 to 15 million dollars (the final price was to be set by the length of his career and endorsements).[40] NBA rules did not allow for any of Yao's contract money to go directly back to China, but players' union official Billy Hunter said that "after he has received his money, that's on him," implying that Yao could send the money back if that is part of his separate deal with the Chinese government.[41] If Yao did not abide by the rules of this contract, extreme penalties from the Chinese regime were possible. It promised to impose drastic measures, such as huge fines, expulsion from the national team, and would invalidate all of Yao's overseas contracts.[42] It never became public exactly how much of Yao's earnings had to be sent home, but sources close to his old team, the Shanghai Sharks, put the number at around one third.[43] No matter how much money Yao had to send back to China, he was still far better off than the average Chinese basketball player, who made the equivalent of $12,500 yearly in 2002.[44]

The Marketing Machine Takes Over

Once Yao was in the league, the NBA put their Asian marketing efforts into full throttle. Yao is exactly the star the NBA desperately wanted to assist with overseas branding. The NBA was well aware of the grand potential for sponsorship and new television viewers that came with the arrival of Yao. In addition to the Beijing office and the Chinese NBA website where Yao is prominent, the 2003 NBA All-Star ballots were developed in Chinese for the first time. Voters were also allowed to vote online—resulting in a huge surge of Yao votes from his home country and all of Asia. By allowing the fans to vote online, the NBA funneled millions of Chinese to their website. This allowed the NBA put a premium on corporate logos placed on their Internet home. The second Asian media tour, which featured exclusive interviews with Yao for the Chinese media, was launched in March 2003. The tour followed Yao around for a span of eight games during his rookie season.[45]

There is virtually no way the China games would have occurred without Yao.[46] The China games exposed the NBA product to many more Chinese, but that was not all gained by the league's trip overseas. In the early 2000s, the NBA generated less than 10 percent of its revenue internationally, something it desperately wanted to change. Global business was still in its infancy in China when Yao Ming was drafted, and the NBA knew a good opportunity when it saw one. The NBA, along with many other sport organizations, now views the international market as the place to expand their product most effectively and profitably. The common outlook among professional sports leagues in North America by 2000 was the market in the United States was close to its saturation point. "We are a mature business in the U.S. and the growth is outside the U.S.," said Heidi Ueberroth, executive vice-president of global media properties for the NBA.[47] Many NBA and Yao Ming sponsors, such as Reebok, traveled to China in order to leverage their investment in the league and the player.

Yao took in over $10 million in revenues from endorsements per year by 2003, which put him on the same level as Kobe Bryant, Shaquille O'Neal, Jeff Gordon, and Venus Williams.[48] Even though Yao did not see all of the money he "earned" from endorsements because he had to send a percentage back to China, his take for a still relatively unproven center was staggering. As the entire situation surrounding Yao is out of the ordinary, it should come as no surprise that the way endorsements are determined regarding the 7'5" center was also unconventional. From the very beginning, "Team Yao" carefully planned out an endorsement plan based on a study by students at the University of Chicago. Team Yao was made up of sports agent Bill Duffy, Bill Sanders (marketing director for BDA Sports Management), distant Yao cousin and University of Chicago graduate student Erik Zhang, and University of Chicago business school deputy dean John Huizinga.[49] Duffy had been wooing Yao since 1998 when he played on a San Diego summer league team during his first trip to the United States.[50]

Yao became so popular by 2005 that Team Yao feared he would be overexposed. They were determined to not let that occur, no matter how much of an icon he became. Team Yao stuck to their secretive, five-year marketing plan. According to *Business Week*, a former student at the University of Chicago business school, Aaron Abraham, said, "We were interested in protecting him as a brand." Abraham would not provide more details, as he had to sign a confidentiality agreement when he left the school. Reebok CEO Paul Fireman chimed in, saying that so far "Yao's handlers have done a good job of not rushing him out to every company, not prostituting him."[51] Yao would not be seen pitching goods for a regional company or small-town businesses to earn a few quick dollars.

Yao signed a major deal with PepsiCo in February 2003 that was worth seven figures. This deal primarily had Yao working with the makers of the sport drink Gatorade, a subsidiary of PepsiCo. The deal paid dividends very early for PepsiCo; sales were up 30 percent in China the following year.[52] Sales is really the only way to gauge the value of a sponsorship deal in China right now, as media market research was only just beginning at the time Yao Ming's career began.[53] PepsiCo (17 percent current market share) has always trailed chief rival Coca-Cola (33 percent current market share) in the Chinese market and was looking to Yao to help them gain ground.[54]

Yao did have an endorsement with Nike, which predated his arrival with the Rockets (he saw no money from this deal; only the team benefited financially). The company signed Yao to a five-year deal in 1998 after watching him play on their own sponsored summer league team in San Diego. The deal provided Yao with the large shoes he needed at the time; he wears a size 18.[55] Nike CEO Phil Knight had had his eye on the Asian market for a long time before Yao came along, but he was seen as the perfect fit for Nike (basketball is the main money maker for the company).

Nike's long-range plans were evident from as far back as the 1970s when Knight incorporated a Nike subsidiary started in Taiwan under a different name. This both calculating and forward-looking move was made because China considers Taiwan a breakaway province, and Nike did not want to alienate the Chinese in any way. During the 1990s and early 2000s basketball's popularity skyrocketed in China (as well as all of Asia). The actions taken by Nike and Knight were a major factor, if not the biggest, in this equation. The company had been building basketball courts in both China and Taiwan, while at the same time launching leagues to play on them.[56] During summer months (the NBA off-season), Nike brought NBA superstars Kobe Bryant (2001) and Vince Carter (2002) to China to visit large cities and to donate basketball equipment.[57] One of the biggest obstacles facing the Chinese desire to become the world's dominant sports power has been their lack of quality facilities.[58] Nike's actions were an effort to help China upgrade their basketball facilities while gaining advantage in the market, as well as with Yao and his handlers specifically.

In what must have been an extremely dismal development to Nike officials, Yao signed a deal with Reebok in late 2003 when his five-year contract with Nike ended. Reebok planned to use Yao for the same reason as other firms. The NBA marketing gurus jumped on the bandwagon of the Rockets' center: to tap into the huge marketing possibilities in China and all of Asia.[59] Immediately after signing Yao, Reebok quickly launched their NBA Enigma shoe endorsed by the Rockets' center. The company also hired famous basketball scout Sonny Vaccaro to develop a plan to win over Chinese consumers.[60] Reebok CEO Paul Fireman said he could envision his company earning 25 percent of the estimated $1 billion sporting shoe business in China by the time the Beijing Olympics came around. Reebok at the time only did $30 million a year in sales in China.[61]

Another global power able to bring Yao on board was McDonald's. McDonald's is the world's most popular and recognizable fast food chain and was the "Official Restaurant of the 2004 Olympic Games." Yao became the first "global ambassador" of McDonald's when he signed his deal with the company in early 2004. Yao's initial McDonald's television spot is part of the company's "Big Mac Rolling Energy" campaign, which features athletes from various sports explaining that McDonald's will be feeding Olympians like Yao.[62] The ads were shot in both Houston and Shanghai and started airing in China in September 2004. Yao's image also began to appear inside of McDonald's restaurants both in China and the United States.[63] Like most multinational corporations, McDonald's also had its eye on the expanding Chinese market. It is likely not a coincidence that McDonald's announced in Beijing it had extended its Olympic partnership through the 2012 Games. McDonald's described the Chinese market as "one of our priority growth markets in the world."[64] Clearly Yao was the man McDonald's wanted to represent them in China; he is a powerful draw that has a very high profile and is admired by sports fans all over the nation, as shown by the countrywide reaction during the China Games.

Some entities are legally using Yao's image without paying him endorsement money to move their product. One example of this can be seen by looking at the recent move of *ESPN*

The Magazine. *ESPN The Magazine* sees China as a prime location to sell their publication. Beginning in December 2004, the magazine published biweekly in Chinese in both China and Hong Kong, with an initial print run of 60,000. The cover choice for the preview edition was not a difficult one for the *ESPN* editors: Yao Ming. This preview edition was timed to coincide with the Rockets' exhibition games in Beijing and Shanghai. The general manager of the magazine proclaimed this move would "reflect well on the brand."[65] Companies such as Coca-Cola, Anheuser-Busch, Adidas, and Kodak have also been running NBA-themed promotions in China without using Yao's image—only that of the league.[66] Kodak sales in China jumped 30 percent in digital-printing volume once their China Games promotion began in September 2004.[67]

By drafting Yao, the Rockets transformed from a forgotten NBA franchise to a prominent one. The asking price for their arena, which opened in 2003, was boosted.[68] Sponsorship revenue increased by over 300 percent since the team drafted Yao. The number of corporations partnering with the team also doubled. The Rockets sold a record number of season tickets for the 2004–2005 season.[69] The Rockets also boosted Asian American attendance not only for home games, but also when they visit other cities.[70] Yanjing, a Chinese beer company, signed a $1 million a year deal with the team upon the drafting of Yao.[71] Yao frequently played in the NBA All-Star Game, making eight appearances.

Not everything worked out quite so smoothly once Yao arrived in the United States. Shaquille O'Neal, then of the Los Angeles Lakers, said in an interview, "Tell Yao Ming 'Ching chong yang wah ah so'." This incident sparked a media firestorm, and O'Neal was later forced to apologize after he was seen as being insensitive to Asians—not how the NBA wanted him or the league to be perceived. After the two first met on the court O'Neal said, "Yao Ming is my brother. The Asian people are my brothers." Later that season, Yao caused quite a stir when he arrived for his first All-Star Game press conference wearing an old Chinese national team sweatshirt. Yao simply said it was comfortable, but the Chinese media hounded him for the other possible reasons he was wearing it.[72]

Future Outlook

Long-range plans included bringing more NBA games to China, including possibly regular season contests.[73] This seems almost assured based on the early returns the NBA, league sponsors, and companies promoted by Yao have seen. More corporations soon wanted to be involved with the NBA in order to tap into the Chinese and Asian markets. Over 50 million Chinese watched the 2002 NBA Finals on television, even though Yao and the Rockets did not even qualify for the playoffs that season.[74] In just the first two years after Yao arrived in Houston:

- The NBA brought the NBA Jam Session to Shanghai in September 2003 and 2004.
- Two more Asian media tours were launched.
- Thirteen provincial networks reaching 314 million households in China picked up NBA programming in 2003–2004, showing 170 games, 30 of which involved the Rockets.
- American coach Del Harris coached the Chinese national team at the 2004 Athens Olympics.
- A new NBA office in Shanghai opened.
- Michael Jordan toured China for Nike.

- The NBA championship trophy toured Chinese cities.
- McDonald's sponsored a joint American-Chinese coaching camp in Beijing.[75]

There is no question that sponsors of the NBA and Yao capitalized on the 2008 Beijing Olympics and tied the Rockets center to the event. Beijing 2008 was especially attractive for a company like Reebok even though it was not a global TOP Olympic sponsor. With Reebok featuring Yao in ads in China leading up to the Beijing Olympics, basketball and associated products increased in popularity. "Kids are going to want to be like Yao now," said NBA Commissioner David Stern.[76] As Yao himself said, "The sponsors are helping me and I am helping them. It is mutually beneficial."[77]

The Yao Ming case is emblematic of post-2000 American sport expansion into new global markets. It has not been all smooth sailing for American sporting enterprises, however. The NFL's attempt to set up a permanent league in Europe under different names, most recently NFL Europe, ultimately failed. The league began in 1991 as the World League of American Football, lasting two seasons with some European teams. The league relaunched in Europe only in 1995 and lasted until 2007 but was mostly sustained in cities near U.S. military bases in Germany. When the league folded in 2007 the only non-Germany-based team was Amsterdam. The NFL rebooted its global strategy, focusing, like the more successful NBA, on support of locally controlled leagues and promotion of NFL games globally. Additionally, the NFL began to play regular season games in London at Wembley Stadium, with the Jacksonville Jaguars becoming a regular participant and by 2015 making London a second home city by playing multiple games a year there. The NHL began playing exhibition preseason games in Europe in the 1990s, but with the beginning of a heavily financed Russian-led European League, the Kontinental Hockey League (KHL) in 2008, the NHL responded by playing regular season games in Europe as well, with four teams opening their 2008–2009 seasons in Europe (New York Rangers, Ottawa Senators, Pittsburgh Penguins, and Tampa Bay Lightning). The NHL suspended regular season games in Europe in 2012, however.

With expanded pay television and online platforms for viewing, playing large numbers of games overseas diminished in significance for the NHL particularly as it faced several internal challenges. Most European hockey arenas are far smaller than NHL ones, whereas the NFL can generate massive media hype in one country and fill stadiums of 80,000 plus in places like London or Barcelona.

The NCAA got in on the global market as well, beginning in 1988 with the Emerald Isle Classic in Dublin between Boston College and Army. The 1996 game between Notre Dame and Army significantly was the first non–Gaelic Athletic Association sporting event ever held at its iconic Croke Park stadium. Subsequent games returned to Ireland in 2012 with Notre Dame and Boston College, the two Catholic universities with the most Irish links, visiting in rotation biennially. Irish airline company Aer Lingus, which flies several routes to the United States, took naming sponsorship of the games from 2016.[78]

MLS teams regularly play touring European teams, which frequently tour to the United States during the summer off-season in Europe. The European teams see the American marketplace as one of their most lucrative, and MLS benefits from demonstrating it can play with the best in the world. The best-attended soccer match in the United States, however, was held at the University of Michigan stadium on August 4, 2014, between Real Madrid and Manchester United, attracting over 109,000 spectators and selling out the stadium.[79] MLS is attracting increasing global interest, as the Seattle Sounders have had several of their home games (especially against arch-rivals the Portland Timbers) rank in the top five of weekly attendance globally. With a surge in support surrounding the U.S. men's team in the 2014 FIFA World Cup in Brazil and the United States winning the Women's World Cup title for the third time in Canada in 2015, the United States' position in soccer accelerated at break-neck speed. Perhaps the most audacious move by the United States into the political economy of global sport began in May 2015, however.

When Two Worlds Collide: The United States vs. FIFA

The revelations by the Federal Bureau of Investigation (FBI) and the U.S. Justice Department in May 2015 involving the arrest and indictment of Fédération Internationale de Football Association (FIFA) officials left many nonsoccer media experts stunned. Those who have worked in and researched soccer for many years, however, wondered why it took so long for someone to topple FIFA's house of cards. Academics from the University of Brighton, John Sugden and Alan Tomlinson, exposed corrupt practices within FIFA going back to the 1990s in a groundbreaking 1998 book. Investigative journalist Andrew Jennings, who originally exposed corruption in Olympic bidding in *Lords of the Rings*, similarly exposed this culture within FIFA. We all knew, yet the world allowed the charade to continue.[80]

Although most assessment has concentrated on a culture of corruption, which has developed inside the corridors of footballing power, what this particular situation demonstrates is the growing significance of soccer in the United States and the increasing influence of American geopolitical interests in the global game. Aston Villa, Liverpool, Manchester United, and Arsenal, among others, have American owners and investors.[81] Major American transnational corporations such as Nike, Visa, and Coca-Cola are major sponsors of FIFA and other football organizations. However, there are many more companies and interests who want to profit from the international football marketplace. Declan Hill, Canadian investigative journalist and Oxford PhD, now also working with the University of Brighton, has published two books exposing the level of corruption in international soccer, including World Cup matches, linked to match fixing, a global practice just beginning to infiltrate U.S. professional sport.[82] Trinidad and Tobago official Jack Warner, when president of Confederation of North, Central American and Caribbean Association Football (CONCACAF) and a vice-president of FIFA, allegedly sold votes to potential hosts of World Cups.[83] Many others, both inside and outside of FIFA, have been attempting to profit, often by what the American legal system views as illegitimate means.

As the largest single sports marketplace and largest market within CONCACAF, the United States is positioned to play a significant role in global football in the twenty-first century. Although many laws in the United States protect corporate interests, these laws also have strong provisions against openly corrupt business practices. Leverage and influence are one thing; overt bribery and money laundering are something quite different according to U.S. business practice.

Sports have been recognized for quite some time in the United States as "more than a game." Major League Baseball (MLB) had for over a century exemption from provisions of American antitrust law. This has been challenged in recent years. Congress intervened in the illegal drug use in baseball when it felt the sport was not fully addressing the issue. Although MLB is a private organization, the companies and doctors supplying performance-enhancing substances fell under medical and health care acts, and individual players were called to testify. It was U.S. efforts that forced the International Olympic Committee to address corrupt practices, at least in part, in the scandals surrounding the 2002 Salt Lake City Winter Olympics whose organizational committee was headed by Mitt Romney. At the same time, Utah congressmen planted plenty of "pork-barrel" funding by attaching infrastructural monies to other bills, which would assist Utah in holding the Games. American congressional legislators also challenged the right of National Football League (NFL) teams to relocate to other cities as they sought better stadia and deals from host cities and states. (Under the guise of protecting taxpayers, the league was forced to take action allowing Cleveland, Ohio, to keep the Browns name and history and to put a new franchise there after the former team relocated to Baltimore, whose original team fled to Indianapolis in 1984.) When a lockout of referees by the NFL was thought to have led to a blown call changing the result of a game, politicians, including President Obama, spoke out and pushed the NFL to resolve the dispute.[84] President Obama and others realize the increasingly global links of U.S. sport, actively supporting U.S. World Cup soccer teams and continuing to back State Department sports diplomacy programs.

The challenge for global sports organizations, businesses, and other interests is to understand the climate in which they operate, but first and foremost to operate in a transparent manner. In this, they have to exceed standards applied in normal global business practices because regulation is even weaker in sport. In a revealing article about the power of the World Anti-Doping Agency (WADA), Verner Moeller asked "who is watching the watchers?"; in other words, who is able to hold FIFA or the International Olympic Committee or WADA accountable for its actions?[85] FIFA has declared itself custodian of the "people's game," "the beautiful game," a sport popular among all ages around the world; as such it (as well as FIFA officials) must be held accountable for the management of the sport or be replaced by other group(s) who will practice ethical standards of good stewardship. The FBI and U.S. Justice Department may not be everyone's choice for holding FIFA accountable, but through American action supported by Swiss investigations, we may learn how pervasive and widespread is the culture of corruption haunting the world's favorite sport.

Conclusion

Although American sport history is often written without much reference to the rest of the world, it is clear that modern sports in the United States, although unique in many respects, cannot be viewed with an isolated lens any longer. For at least 150 years, American sporting stars have tested themselves against international competition; migrants have integrated themselves into the American melting pot through sports participation; and sporting entrepreneurs have sought to profit from the sports marketplace, both domestically and internationally. For 50 years or more, a migrant labor system has become increasingly important within NCAA competitions, and international players have become stars in baseball and basketball in particular. Many international golf and tennis players base themselves in the United States. The United States exports sporting talent all over the world, and American sporting business interests play significant roles in the global sports business marketplace. The Boston Red Sox have invested in the Japanese professional baseball league, and its parent company also controls Liverpool Football Club (soccer) in England. The New York Yankees sponsor the Chinese Baseball League. The NFL plays regular season games in London, England. Major League Baseball does so in Asia, and the NHL does the same in Europe. MLS teams compete in the CONCACAF Gold Cup tournament, which is a regional version of the Champions League in Europe.

With American political and economic interests spanning the globe, there is no doubt sport will continue to play an important role. The U.S. Department of State has long recognized this, running sporting ambassador programs since the 1960s. Government-sponsored sports ambassador and development programs fly in the face of the reluctance of the U.S. government to become directly involved in American sports programs. The United States remains the only advanced capitalist society without a ministry responsible for domestic sport. Despite partial American "exceptionalism" in sport, there is no doubt American sport is enmeshed in the global sports system and is likely to be more and more engaged globally throughout the twenty-first century and beyond, particularly as U.S. leagues play regular season games overseas and European elite soccer teams tour the United States regularly in their off-seasons. American-based companies are key sponsors of sport globally, but the United States faces challenges internationally, as there is a seductiveness of American culture and sports, while many have serious concerns about the Janus-faced approach of American "interests" throughout the world.

Notes

1 I outline the history of British sports in the United States from 1865 to 1930 in a forthcoming work, *Sport and the Making of the British World.* An initial version of this work was presented at the Lives and Deaths of American Sporting Pastimes at Pennsylvania State University in 2012 entitled "The Comparative Failures of Cricket, Soccer and Rugby to become National Pastimes in the USA."

2 Mark Lamster, *Spalding's World Tour: The Epic Adventure That Took Baseball Around the Globe—And Made It America's Game* (New York: Public Affairs Books, 2006); Gerald R. Gems *The Athletic Crusade: Sport and American Cultural Imperialism* (Lincoln: University of Nebraska Press, 2012).

3 For the best discussion of globalization and baseball, see Alan Klein, *The Globalization of Major League Baseball* (New Haven: Yale University Press, 2006).

4 Gems, *The Athletic Crusade.*

5 See John Nauright, *Long Run to Freedom: Sport, Cultures and Identities in South Africa* (Morgantown, WV: Fitness Information Technology, 2010); Alan Gregor Cobley, *Rules of the Game: Struggles in Black Recreation and Social Welfare Policy in South Africa* (Westview, CT.: Greenwood Press, 1997); Ray Phillips, *The Bantu Are Coming* (London: Student Christian Movement Press, 1930).

6 Mike Marquese, "Global Sport, American Sport" *Colourlines* (2000). www.mikemarqusee.com/?p=58 (accessed July 7, 2015).

7 The role of Nike in the global marketplace is outlined by George Sage, *Globalizing Sport: How Organizations, Corporations and Media are Changing Sport* (New York: Paradigm Press, 2010). Nike, founded in Oregon by Phil Knight, was a pioneer in off-shore production of sporting footwear, building its early reputation through controversial sports stars such as John McEnroe and Andre Agassi in tennis and Charles Barkley in basketball. With Jordan, Nike began to mainstream its marketing image more fully and did much to create him as the first real U.S. global mega-star athlete. Also see, Walter LaFeber, *Michael Jordan and the New Global Capitalism* (New York: W.W. Norton, 2002).

8 John Nauright and John Ramfjord, "Who Owns England's Game? American Professional Sporting Influences and Foreign Ownership in the Premier League," *Soccer and Society* 11, no. 4 (2010): 428–441.

9 For example, the two leading goalkeepers for the United States in World Cup 2014 were Tim Howard, who played for Everton, and Brad Guzan, who played for Aston Villa, both in the Premier League in England.

10 This section is developed from an earlier paper; see Ben Keeler and John Nauright, "Team Yao: Yao Ming, the NBA and Selling Sport to China," *American Journal of Chinese Studies* 12, no. 2 (2005): 203–218.

11 Stefan Fastis, Peter Wonnacott, and Maureen Tkacik, "Chinese Basketball Star Is Big Business for NBA: NBA and Nike Are Banking Yao Ming Will Open a Huge Chinese Market," *The Wall Street Journal*, October 22, 2002.
12 John Lombardo, "The Twenty Most Influential People: Professional Basketball," *Sports Business Journal* 7, no. 25 (2004): 19.
13 Peter Hessler, "Home and Away: Yao Ming's Journey from China to the NBA," *The New Yorker*, December 1, 2003, 65–81.
14 "Grooming the Game: NBA's Relationship with China, *National Basketball Association*. www.nba.com/china2004/timeline.html (accessed October 17, 2004).
15 Ibid.
16 Hessler, "Home and Away."
17 "Grooming the Game."
18 Ibid.
19 "The Yao Crowd," *The Economist*, August 9, 2003, 55.
20 Frederik Balfour, "Game Plan B: Sponsors Find Sports Marketing in China Is No Slam Dunk," *Business Week*, September 15, 2003, 56.
21 "Grooming the Game."
22 Balfour, "Game Plan B."
23 Peter Wonacott, "Yao-mania: Hoop Star's China Visit Evokes Beatles, 1964," *The Wall Street Journal*, October 15, 2004, B1.
24 Ibid.
25 Stephanie Hoo, "NBA Brings Its Game to Beijing," *Associated Press Online*. www.theapn.com/newap/D85O6R2O1.html (accessed October 17, 2004).
26 John Lombardo, "Global Trade," *Sports Business Journal* 7, no. 25 (2004): 21–25.
27 Robert H. Van Horn, Jr., "Sports Development and Training in China," *Mankind Quarterly* 29, no. 1/2 (1988): 143–162; John Nauright, "China and Global Soccer," *World Football Forum*, Moscow, May 2015; "Awakening the Sleeping Giant: China and Global Football," *FC Business Magazine*, August 2015.
28 Craig S. Smith and Mike Wise, "Eying NBA: China Will Make Athletes Pay," *The New York Times*, April 25, 2002, A1.
29 Hessler, "Home and Away."
30 Ibid.
31 Ibid.
32 "Grooming the Game."
33 Fastis et al., "A Global Journal Report."
34 Ibid.
35 Ibid.
36 Tom Lowry and Dexter Roberts, "Wow! Yao!," *Business Week*, October 25, 2004, 86.
37 Smith and Wise, "Eying NBA."
38 Fastis et al., "A Global Journal Report."
39 George Vecsey, "Chinese Still Stuck in the Past," *The New York Times*, May 1, 2002, D1.
40 Hessler, "Home and Away."
41 Smith and Wise, "Eying NBA."
42 Ibid.
43 Lowry and Roberts, "Wow! Yao!"
44 Alkman Granitsas and Ben Dolven, "Show Me the Money", *Far Eastern Economic Review* 165, no. 14 (2002): 38–41.
45 "Grooming the Game."
46 Lombardo, "Global Trade."
47 Lombardo, "The Twenty Most Influential People."
48 Rick Fisher, "Selling Yao: Corporate America Is Impressed with the 7-Foot 5-Inch NBA Star's Marketability," *The Washington Times*, February 7, 2003, C1.
49 Tom Fowler, "Yao's Ad Potential Bears Fruit with Apple TV Spot," *The Houston Chronicle*, January 8, 2003, B1, B5.
50 Fastis et al., "A Global Journal Report."
51 Lowry and Roberts, "Wow! Yao!"

52 Ibid.
53 Balfour, "Game Plan B."
54 Peter Wonacott and Betsy McKay, "Yao Is a Pitchman Torn Between Two Colas," *The Wall Street Journal*, May 16, 2003, B1.
55 Smith and Wise, "Eying NBA."
56 Fastis et al., "A Global Journal Report."
57 "Grooming the Game."
58 Van Horn, "Sports Development and Training in China."
59 Fastis et al., "A Global Journal Report."
60 S. Holmes and F. Arner, "A New Game Afoot for Adidas and Reebok," *Business Week Online*, December 5, 2003.
61 Lowry and Roberts, "Wow! Yao!"
62 Liz Clarke, "McDonald's Goes for Gold with Olympic Sponsorships," *The Washington Post*, August 30, 2004, E1.
63 Arun Sudhaman, "Yao Ming Stars in First McDonald's ad Spots," *Media*, June 4, 2004, 13.
64 Clarke, "McDonald's Goes for Gold."
65 Robert Adams, "ESPN Magazine Sets Its Sights on China," *Sports Business Journal* 7, no. 24 (2004): 7.
66 Fastis et al., "A Global Journal Report."
67 Wonacott, "Yao-mania."
68 Fastis et al., "A Global Journal Report."
69 Lowry and Roberts, "Wow! Yao!"
70 Chih-Ming Wang, "Capitalizing on the Big Man: Yao Ming, Asian America, and the China Global," *Inter-Asia Cultural Studies* 5, no. 2 (2004): 263–278.
71 Fastis et al., "A Global Journal Report."
72 Hessler, "Home and Away."
73 Lombardo, "Global Trade."
74 Balfour, "Game Plan B."
75 Fowler, "Yao's Ad;" "Grooming the Game;" Wonacott, "Yao-mania."
76 Fastis et al., "A Global Journal Report."
77 Wonacott, "Yao-mania."
78 For more on Irish NCAA games, see http://collegefootballireland.com
79 www.telegraph.co.uk/sport/football/teams/manchester-united/11005513/Manchester-United-v-Real-Madrid-109000-sell-out-highlights-extent-of-footballs-breakthrough-into-the-USA.html
80 John Sugden and Alan Tomlinson, *FIFA and the Contest for World Football* (London: Polity Press, 1998); Andrew Jennings, *Foul!: The Secret World of FIFA: Bribes, Vote Rigging and Ticket Scandals* (London: HarperSport, 2008).
81 Nauright and Ramfjord, "Who Owns England's Game."
82 Declan Hill, *The Fix: Soccer and Organized Crime* (Toronto: McClelland & Stewart, 2010), reprint edition; *The Insider's Guide to Match-Fixing in Football* (Toronto: Anne McDermid & Associates, 2013).
83 See John Nauright and Anand Rampersad, "Reform or revolution: The future of sport governance, organisation and business in Caribbean after the fall of Jack Warner." Paper presented at the Play the Game Conference, Aarhus, Denmark, October 2015. www.playthegame.org
84 www.washingtontimes.com/news/2012/sep/25/politicians-grab-political-football-run-with-it/
85 Verner Moeller, "One Step Too Far—About WADA's Whereabouts Rule," *International Journal of Sport Policy and Politics* 3, no. 1 (2011): 177–190.

SUGGESTED FURTHER READINGS

I. Introduction to American Sport History: Perspectives and Prospects

Adelman, Melvin L., "Academicians and American Athletics: A Decade of Progress." *Journal of Sport History*, 10 (Spring 1983): 80–106.

Baker, William J., *Sports in the Western World*. Urbana, IL: University of Illinois Press, 1988.

Booth, Douglas, *The Field: Truth and Fiction in Sport History*. London: Routledge, 2005.

Borish, Linda J., "Transformations in Recent American Sport History." *Journal of Sport History*, 36 (Fall 2009): 401–410.

Borish, Linda J. and Murray Phillips, "Sport History as Modes of Expression: Material Culture and Cultural Spaces in Sport and History." *Rethinking History: The Journal of Theory and Practice*, 16 (October 2012): 465–477.

Cox, William R. and Michael A. Salter, "The IT Revolution and the Practice of Sport History: An Overview and Reflection on Internet Research and Teaching Resources." *Journal of Sport History*, 25 (Summer 1998): 283–302.

Davies, Richard O., *Sports in American Life*. Malden, MA: Blackwell Publishing, 2007.

Dyreson, Mark and Jaime Schultz, eds., *American National Pastimes—A History*. London: Routledge, 2014.

Gems, Gerald R., Linda J. Borish, and Gertrud Pfister, *Sports in American History: From Colonization to Globalization*. Champaign, IL: Human Kinetics, 2008.

Gorn, Elliott J. and Warren Goldstein, *A Brief History of American Sports*. Urbana, IL: University of Illinois Press, 2013.

Grundy, Pamela and Benjamin Rader, *American Sports: From the Age of Folk Games to the Age of Television Sports*. New York: Pearson, 2014.

Hardy, Stephen, "The City and the Rise of American Sport, 1820–1920," *Exercise and Sports Sciences Review*, 9 (January 1981): 183–219.

Noverr, Douglas and Lawrence E. Ziewacz, eds., *Sport History: Selected Reading Lists and Course Outlines from American Colleges and Universities*. New York: Markus Wiener Publishing, Inc., 1987.

Osmond, Gary and Murray Phillips, eds., *Sport History in the Digital Era*. Urbana, IL: University of Illinois Press, 2015.

Phillips, Murray, ed., *Deconstructing Sport History: A Postmodern Analysis*. Albany, NY: State University of New York Press, 2006.

Pope, S.W., "Sport History: Into the 21st Century." *Journal of Sport History*, 25 (Summer 1998): i–x.

Pope, S.W., ed., *The New American Sport History: Recent Approaches and Perspectives*. Urbana, IL: University of Illinois Press, 1997.

Pringle, Richard and Murray Phillips, eds., *Examining Sport Histories: Power, Paradigms, and Reflexivity*. Morgantown, WV: Fitness Information Technology, 2013.

Rielly, Edward J., ed., *Baseball in the Classroom: Essays on Teaching the National Pastime*. Jefferson, NC: McFarland, 2006.

Riess, Steven A., ed., *A Companion to American Sport History*. New York: Wiley-Blackwell, 2014.

Riess, Steven A., ed., *Major Problems in American Sport History: Documents and Essays*. Boston, MA: Houghton Mifflin, 1997.

Riess, Steven A., "Sport and the American Dream: A Review Essay." *Journal of Social History* 14 (December 1980): 295–301.

Rosenzweig, Roy, "Sport History on the Web: Towards a Critical Assessment." *Journal of Sport History*, 31 (Fall 2004): 371–376.

Schultz, Jaime, "Sense and Sensibility: Pragmatic Postmodernism for Sport History" in Pringle, Richard and Murray Phillips, eds., *Critical Sport Histories: Paradigms, Power and the Postmodern Turn.* Morgantown, WV: Fitness Information Technology, 2013, pp. 59–76.

Struna, Nancy L., "Reframing the Direction of Changes in the History of Sport." *The International Journal of the History of Sport*, 18 (2001): 1–15.

Vanderwerken, David J., ed., *Sport in the Classroom: Teaching Sport-Related Courses in the Humanities*. Cranberry, NJ: Associated University Presses, 1990.

Wiggins, David K., *Sport in America: From Colonial Leisure to Celebrity Figures and Globalization.* Volume II, Champaign, IL: Human Kinetics, 2010.

II. Sport and Education

Anderson, Ryan K., *Frank Merriwell and the Fiction of All-American Boyhood.* Fayetteville, AR: The University of Arkansas Press, 2015.

Austin, Brad, *Democratic Sports: Men's and Women's College Athletics During the Great Depression.* Fayetteville, AR: The University of Arkansas Press, 2015.

Barnett, Robert, *Hillside Fields: A History of Sports in West Virginia.* Morgantown, WV: West Virginia University Press, 2013.

Berryman, Jack W., "From the Cradle to the Playing Field: America's Emphasis on Highly Competitive Sports for Pre-Adolescent Boys." *Journal of Sport History*, 2 (Fall 1975): 112–131.

Bundgaard, Axel, *Muscle and Manliness: The Rise of Sport in American Boarding Schools*. Syracuse, NY: Syracuse University Press, 2005.

Carriere, Michael H., "A Diamond Is a Boy's Best Friend: The Rise of Little League Baseball, 1939–1964." *Journal of Sport History*, 32 (Fall 2005): 351–378.

Clotfelter, Charles T., *Big-Time Sports in American Universities*. New York: Cambridge University Press, 2011.

Gildea, Dennis, *Hoop Crazy: The Lives of Clair Bee and Chip Hilton*, Fayetteville, AR: The University of Arkansas Press, 2013.

Grundy, Pamela, *Learning to Win: Sports, Education, and Social Change in Twentieth-Century North Carolina.* Chapel Hill, NC: University of North Carolina Press, 2001.

Ingrassia, Brian M., *The Rise of Gridiron University: Higher Education's Uneasy Alliance with Big-Time Football.* Lawrence, KS: University Press of Kansas, 2012.

Kaliss, Gregory J., *Men's College Athletics and the Politics of Racial Equality: Five Pioneer Stories of Black Manliness, White Citizenship, and American Democracy.* Philadelphia, PA: Temple University Press, 2012.

Kemper, Kurt Edward, *College Football and American Culture in the Cold War Era.* Urbana IL: University of Illinois, 2009.

Lester, Robin, *Stagg's University: The Rise, Decline, and Fall of Big-Time Football at Chicago.* Urbana, IL: University of Illinois, 1995.

Oriard, Michael, *Bowled Over: Big-Time College Football From the Sixties to the BCS Era.* Chapel Hill, NC: University of North Carolina Press, 2009.

Oriard, Michael, *Reading Football: How the Popular Press Created an American Spectacle*. Chapel Hill, NC: University of North Carolina Press, 1993.

Pruter, Robert, *The Rise of American High School Sports and the Search for Control, 1880–1930*. Syracuse, NY: Syracuse University Press, 2013.

Schmidt, Raymond, *Shaping College Football: The Transformation of an American Sport*. Syracuse, NY: Syracuse University Press, 2007.

Smith, John Matthew, *The Sons of Westwood: John Wooden, UCLA, and the Dynasty that Changed College Basketball*. Urbana, IL: University of Illinois Press, 2013.

Smith Ronald A., *Pay for Play: A History of Big-Time College Athletic Reform*. Urbana, IL: University of Illinois Press, 2010.

Smith, Ronald A. *Sports and Freedom: The Rise of Big-Time College Athletics*. New York: Oxford University Press, 1988.

Smith, Ronald A., *Wounded Lions: Joe Paterno, Jerry Sandusky, and the Crisis in Penn State Athletics*. Urbana, IL: University of Illinois Press, 2016.

Sperber, Murray, *Shake Down the Thunder: The Creation of Notre Dame Football*. New York: Henry Holt, 1993.

Watterson, John Sayle, *College Football: History, Spectacle, Controversy*. Baltimore, MD: The Johns Hopkins University Press, 2000.

Zimbalist, Andrew, *Unpaid Professionals: Commercialism and Conflict in Big-Time College Sports*. Princeton, NJ: Princeton University Press, 1999.

III. Race, Ethnicity, American Sport, and Identity

Baker, William J., *Jesse Owens: An American Life*. New York: The Free Press, 1986.

Bloom, John, *To Show What an Indian Can Do: Sports at Native American Boarding Schools*. Minneapolis, MN: University of Minnesota Press, 2000.

Borish, Linda J., "'An Interest in Physical Well-Being Among the Feminine Membership': Sporting Activities for Women at Young Men's and Young Women's Hebrew Associations," *American Jewish History*, 87 (March 1999): 61–93.

Borish, Linda J., "Jewish Women in the American Gym: Basketball, Ethnicity and Gender in the Early Twentieth Century" in Greenspoon, Leonard, ed., *Jews in the Gym: Judaism, Sports, and Athletics*, Vol. 23, Studies in Jewish Civilization. West Lafayette, IN: Purdue University Press 2012, pp. 213–237.

Burgos, Jr., Adrian, *Playing America's Game: Baseball, Latinos, and the Color Line*. Berkeley: University of California Press, 2007.

Early, Gerald, *A Level Playing Field: African American Athletes and the Republic of Sports*. Cambridge, MA: Harvard University Press, 2011.

Eisen, George and David K. Wiggins, eds., *Ethnicity and Sport in North American History and Culture*. Westport, CT: Greenwood Press, 1994.

Fisher, Donald M., *Lacrosse: A History of the Game*. Baltimore, MD: The Johns Hopkins University Press, 2002.

Gems, Gerald R., *Sport and the Shaping of Italian-American Identity*. Syracuse, NY: Syracuse University Press, 2013.

Gould, Todd, *For Gold & Glory: Charlie Wiggins and the African-American Racing Car Circuit*. Bloomington, IN: Indiana University Press, 2002.

Hartmann, Douglas, *Race, Culture, and the Revolt of the Black Athlete: The 1968 Olympic Protests and Their Aftermath*. Chicago, IL: University of Chicago Press, 2003.

Hofmann, Annette, *The American Turner Movement: A History From Its Beginning to 2000*. Indianapolis, IN: Max Kade, 2010.

Iber, Jorge and Samual O. Regalado, eds., *Mexican Americans and Sports: A Reader on Athletics and Barrio Life*. College Station, TX: Texas A&M University Press, 2007.

Isenberg, Michael T., *John L. Sullivan and His America*. Urbana, IL: University of Illinois Press, 1988.

Jenkins, Sally, *The Real All Americans: The Team That Changed the Game, a People, a Nation*. New York: Doubleday, 2007.

Kaye, Andrew, *The Pussycat of Prizefighting: Tiger Flowers and the Politics of Black Celebrity*. Athens, GA: The University of Georgia Press, 2004.

King, Richard and Charles Fruehling Springwood, *Beyond the Cheers: Race as Spectacle in College Sport*. Albany, NY: State University of New York Press, 2001.

Lanctot, Neil, *Negro League Baseball: The Rise and Ruin of a Black Institution*. Philadelphia, PA: University of Pennsylvania Press, 2008.

Lansbury, Jennifer H., *A Spectacular Leap: Women Athletes in Twentieth-Century America*. Fayetteville, AR: The University of Arkansas Press, 2014.

Levine, Peter, *Ellis Island to Ebbets Field: Sport and the American Jewish Experience*. New York: Oxford University Press, 1992.

Lomax, Michael E., *Black Baseball Entrepreneurs, 1902–1931: The Negro National and Eastern Colored Leagues*. Syracuse, NY: Syracuse University Press, 2014.

Lomax, Michael E., ed., *Sports and the Racial Divide: African American and Latino Experience in an Era of Change*. Jackson, MS: University Press of Mississippi, 2008.

Martin, Charles H., *Benching Jim Crow: The Rise and Fall of the Color Line in Southern College Sports, 1890–1980*. Urbana, IL: University of Illinois Press, 2010.

Miller, Patrick B. and David K. Wiggins, eds., *Sport and the Color Line: Black Athletes and Race Relations in Twentieth-Century America*. New York: Routledge, 2004.

Mooney, Katherine C., *Race Horse Men: How Slavery and Freedom Were Made at the Race Track*. Cambridge, MA: Harvard University Press, 2014.

Oxendine, Joseph B., *American Indian Sports Heritage*. Lincoln, NE: University of Nebraska Press, 1995.

Power-Beck, Jeffrey, *The American Indian Integration of Baseball*. Lincoln, NE: University of Nebraska Press, 2004.

Redmond, Gerald, *The Caledonian Games in Nineteenth-Century America*. Cranbury, NJ: Associated University Presses, 1971.

Regalado, Samuel O., *Nikkei Baseball: Japanese American Players From Immigration and Internment to the Major Leagues*. Urbana, IL: University of Illinois Press, 2013.

Regalado, Samuel O., *Viva Baseball! Latin Major Leaguers and Their Special Hunger*, 3rd ed. Urbana, IL: University of Illinois Press, 2008.

Riess, Steven A., ed., *Sports and the American Jew.* Syracuse, NY: Syracuse University Press, 1998.

Roberts, Randy, *Joe Louis: Hard Times Man*. New Haven, CT: Yale University Press, 2010.

Roberts, Randy, *Papa Jack: Jack Johnson and the Era of White Hopes*. New York: The Free Press, 1983.

Ross, Charles K., ed., *Race and Sport: The Struggle for Equality on and off the Field*. Jackson, MS: University Press of Mississippi, 2004.

Ruck, Rob, *Sandlot Seasons: Sport in Black Pittsburgh*. Urbana, IL: University of Illinois Press, 1987.

Runstedtler, Theresa, *Jack Johnson, Rebel Sojourner: Boxing in the Shadow of the Global Color Line*. Berkeley, CA: University of California Press, 2012.

Schultz, Jaime, *Moments of Impact: Injury, Racialized Memory, and Reconciliation in College Football*. Lincoln, NE: University of Nebraska Press, 2016.

Swanson, Ryan A., *When Baseball Went White: Reconstruction, Reconciliation, & Dreams of a National Pastime*. Lincoln, NE: University of Nebraska Press, 2014.

Thomas, Damion L., *Globetrotting: African American Athletes and Cold War Politics*. Urbana, IL: University of Illinois Press, 2012.

Tygiel, Jules, *Baseball's Great Experiment: Jackie Robinson and His Legacy*. New York: Oxford University Press, 1983.

Wiggins, David K., "'Black Athletes in White Men's Games': Race, Sport, and American National Pastimes." *The International Journal of the History of Sport*, 31 (January 2014): 181–202.

Wiggins, David K., *Glory Bound: Black Athletes in a White America*. Syracuse, NY: Syracuse University Press, 1997.

Wiggins, David K., ed., *Out of the Shadows: A Biographical History of Black Athletes*. Fayetteville, AR: The University of Arkansas Press, 2006.

Wiggins, David K., "Symbols of Possibility: Arthur Ashe, Black Athletes, and the Writing of a Hard Road to Glory." *The Journal of African American History*, 99 (Fall 2014): 379–402.

Wiggins, David K. and Patrick B. Miller, *The Unlevel Playing Field: A Documentary History of the African American Experience in Sport*. Urbana, IL: University of Illinois Press, 2003.

Yep, Kathleen S., *Outside the Paint: When Basketball Ruled at the Chinese Playground*. Philadelphia, PA: Temple University Press, 2009.

Zang, David W., *Fleet Walker's Divided Heart: The Life of Baseball's First Black Major Leaguer*. Lincoln, NE: University of Nebraska Press, 1995.

IV. Gender and American Sport

Adams, Mary Louis, *Artistic Impressions: Figure Skating, Masculinity, and the Limits of Sport*. Toronto: University of Toronto Press, 2011.

Bederman, Gail, *Manliness and Civilization: A Cultural History of Gender and Race in the United States, 1880–1917*. Chicago, IL: University of Chicago Press, 1995.

Borish, Linda J., "Benevolent America: Rural Women, Physical Recreation, Sport, and Health Reform in Ante-Bellum New England," *The International Journal of the History of Sport*, 22, 6 (November 2005): 946–973.

Borish, Linda J., "'The Cradle of American Champions, Women Champions Swim Champions': Charlotte Epstein, Gender and Jewish Identity, and the Physical Emancipation of Women in Aquatic Sports." *The International Journal of the History of Sport*, 21 (March 2004): 197–235.

Borish, Linda J., "Jewish Women, Sports, and Chicago History," in Gorn, Elliott J., ed., *Sports in Chicago*. Urbana, IL: University of Illinois Press, 2008, pp. 62–77.

Borish, Linda J., "The Robust Woman and the Muscular Christian: Catharine Beecher, Thomas Higginson, and their Vision of American Society, Health, and Physical Activities." *The International Journal of the History of Sport*, 4 (September 1987): 139–154.

Borish, Linda J., "Settlement Houses to Olympic Stadiums: Jewish American Women, Sports and Social Change, 1880's–1930's." *International Sports Studies*, 21 (2001): 5–24.

Cahn, Susan K., *Coming on Strong: Gender and Sexuality in Women's Sport*, 2nd ed. Urbana, IL: University of Illinois Press, 2015.

Cayleff, Susan E., *Babe: The Life and Legend of Babe Didrikson Zaharias*. Urbana, IL: University of Illinois Press, 1995.

Davies, Richard O. *The Main Event: Boxing in Nevada from the Mining Camps to the Las Vegas Strip*. Reno, NV: University of Nevada Press, 2014.

Englemann, Larry, *The Goddess and the American Girl: The Story of Suzanne Lenglen and Helen Wills*. New York: Oxford University Press, 1988.

Festle, Mary Jo, *Playing Nice: Politics and Apologies in Women's Sports*. New York: Columbia University Press, 1996.

Fields, Sarah K., *Female Gladiators: Gender, Law, and Contact Sport in America*. Urbana, IL: University of Illinois Press, 2005.

Gems, Gerald R., *Boxing: A Concise History of the Sweet Science*. Lanham, MD: Rowman & Littlefield, 2014.

Gorn, Elliott J., "Gouge and Bite, Pull Hair and Scratch: The Social Significance of Fighting in the Southern Backcountry." *American Historical Review*, 90 (February 1985): 18–43.

Gorn, Elliott J., *The Manly Art: Bare-Knuckle Prize Fighting in America*. Ithaca, NY: Cornell University Press, 1986.

Grundy, Pamela, "From Amazons to Glamazons: The Rise and Fall of North Carolina Women's Basketball, 1920–1960." *Journal of American History*, 87 (June 2000): 112–146.

Grundy, Pamela and Susan Shackelford, *Shattering the Glass: The Remarkable History of Women's Basketball*. Chapel Hill, NC: University of North Carolina Press, 2007.

Guttmann, Allen, *Women's Sports: A History*. New York: Columbia University Press, 1991.

Liberti, Rita, "'We Were Ladies, We Just Played Like Boys': African-American Womanhood and Competitive Basketball at Bennett College, 1928–1942." *Journal of Sport History*, 26 (Fall 1999): 567–584.

Liberti, Rita and Maureen M. Smith, *(Re)Presenting Wilma Rudolph*. Syracuse, NY: Syracuse University Press, 2015.

O'Reilly, Jean and Susan K. Cahn, eds., *Women and Sports in the United States: A Documentary Reader*. Boston, MA: Northeastern University Press, 2007.

Park, Roberta J., "Contesting the Norm: Women and Professional Sports in Late Nineteenth-Century America." *The International Journal of the History of Sport*, 29 (2012): 730–749.

Peiss, Kathy. *Cheap Amusements: Working Women and Leisure in Turn-of-the-Century New York*. Philadelphia, PA: Temple University Press, 1986.

Putney, Clifford, *Muscular Christianity: Manhood and Sports in Protestant America, 1880–1920*. Cambridge, MA: Harvard University Press, 2000.

Schultz, Jaime, *Qualifying Times: Points of Change in U.S. Women's Sports*. Urbana, IL: University of Illinois Press, 2014.

Suggs, Welch, *A Place on the Team: The Triumph and Tragedy of Title IX*. Princeton, NJ: Princeton University Press, 2005.

Titman, Nathan, "Taking Punishment Gladly: Bill Tilden's Performances of the Unruly Male Body." *Journal of Sport History*, 41 (Fall 2014): 447–466.

Tucker, Ross and Malcolm Collins, "The Science of Sex Verification and Athletic Performance." *International Journal of Sports Physiology and Performance*, 5 (June 2010): 127–139.

Verbrugge, Martha H. *Able-Bodied Womanhood: Personal Health and Social Change in Nineteenth-Century Boston*. New York: Oxford University Press, 1988.

Verbrugge, Martha H., *Active Bodies: A History of Women's Physical Education in Twentieth-Century America*. New York: Oxford University Press, 2012.

Ware, Susan, *Game, Set, Match: Billie Jean King and the Revolution in Women's Sports*. Chapel Hill, NC: University of North Carolina Press, 2011.

Ware, Susan, *Title IX: A Brief History with Documents*. Long Grove, IL: Waveland Press, Inc., 2014.

V. The Business of Sport

Alexander, Charles, *Our Game: An American Baseball History*. New York: Henry Holt, 1991.

Banner, Stuart, *The Baseball Trust: A History of Baseball's Antitrust Exemption*. New York: Oxford University Press, 2013.

Briley, Ron, Michael Schoenecke, and Deborah Carmichael, *All-Stars and Movie Stars: Sports in Film and History*. Lexington, KY: University Press of Kentucky, 2008.

Burk, Robert, *Much More Than a Game: Players, Owners, and American Baseball Since 1921*. Chapel Hill, NC: University of North Carolina Press, 2001.

Chandler, Joan, *Television and National Sport*. Urbana, IL: University of Illinois Press, 1998.

Coenen, Craig, *From Sandlots to the Super Bowl: The National Football League, 1920–1967*. Knoxville, TN: University of Tennessee Press, 2005.

Crepeau, Richard, *NFL Football: The Rise of America's New National Pastime*. Urbana, IL: University of Illinois Press, 2014.

Elzey, Chris and David K. Wiggins, eds., *DC Sports: The Nation's Capital at Play*. Fayetteville, AR: The University of Arkansas Press, 2015.

Fainaru-Wade, Mark and Steve Fainaru, *League of Denial: The NFL, Concussions, and the Battle for Truth*. New York : Crown Archetype, 2013.

Fox, Stephen, *Big Leagues: Professional Baseball, Football, and Basketball in National Memory*. New York: William Morrow, 1994.

Gems, Gerald R., *For Pride, Profit, and Patriarchy: Football and the Incorporation of American Cultural Values*. Lanham, MD: Scarecrow Press, 2000.

Goldstein, Warren. *Playing for Keeps: A History of Early Baseball*. Ithaca, NY: Cornell University Press, 1989.

Gorn, Elliott J., ed., *Sports in Chicago*. Urbana and Chicago, IL: University of Illinois Press, 2008.

Grow, Nathaniel, *Baseball on Trial: The Origin of Baseball's Antitrust Exemption*. Urbana, IL: University of Illinois Press, 2014.

Halberstam, David, *Playing for Keeps: Michael Jordan and the World He Made*. New York: Random House, 1999.

Korr, Charles, *The End of Baseball as We Know It: The Players Union, 1960–1981*. Urbana, IL: University of Illinois Press, 2002.

LeFeber, Walter, *Michael Jordan and the New Global Capitalism*. New York : Norton, 2002.

Levine, Peter, *A.G. Spalding and the Rise of Baseball: The Promise of American Sport*. New York: Oxford University Press, 1985.

Lieberman, Viridiana, *Sports Heroines on Film: A Critical Study of Cinematic Women Athletes, Coaches, and Owners*. Jefferson, NC: McFarland, 2014.

Lunsford-Neal, Jeff, "Sport in the Land of Television: The Use of Sport in Network Prime-Time Schedules, 1946–50." *Journal of Sport History*, 19 (Spring 1992): 56–76.

Moore, Kenny, *Bowerman and the Men of Oregon: The Story of Oregon's Legendary Track Coach and Nike's Co-Founder*. New York: Rodale, 2006.

Nathan, Daniel A., ed., *Rooting for the Home Team: Sport, Community, and Identity*. Urbana, IL: University of Illinois Press, 2013.

Nathan, Daniel A., *Saying It's So: A Cultural History of the Black Sox Scandal*. Urbana, IL: University of Illinois Press, 2003.

Oriard, Michael, *Brand NFL: Making & Selling America's Favorite Sport*. Chapel Hill, NC: University of North Carolina Press, 2007.

Oriard, Michael, *King Football: Sport & Spectacle in the Golden Age of Radio & Newsreels, Movies & Magazines, The Weekly & The Daily Press*. Chapel Hill, NC: University of North Carolina Press, 2001.

Powers, Ron, *Supertube: The Rise of Television Sports*. New York: Coward-McCann, Inc., 1984.

Rader, Benjamin G., *In Its Own Image: How Television Transformed Sports*. New York: The Free Press, 1984.

Riess, Steven A., *The Sport of Kings and the Kings of Crime: Horse Racing, Politics, and Organized Crime in New York, 1865–1913*. Syracuse, NY: Syracuse University Press, 2011.

Riess, Steven A. and Gerald R. Gems, eds., *The Chicago Sports Reader: 100 Years of Sports in the Windy City.* Urbana, IL: University of Illinois Press, 2009.

Rondinone, Troy, *Friday Night Fighter: Gasper "Indigo Ortega" and the Golden Age of Television Boxing.* Urbana, IL: University of Illinois Press, 2013.

Smith, Ronald A., *Play-By-Play: Radio, Television, and Big-Time College Sport*. Baltimore, MD: The Johns Hopkins University Press, 2001.

Snyder, Brad, *A Well Paid Slave: Curt Flood's Fight for Free Agency in Professional Sports*. New York: Viking, 2006.

Standeven, Joy and Paul DeKnop, *Sport Tourism.* Champaign, IL: Human Kinetics, 1999.

Staudohar, Paul, and James Mangan, eds., *The Business of Professional Sports.* Urbana, IL: University of Illinois Press, 1991.

Swanson, Ryan A. and David K. Wiggins, eds., *Philly Sports: Games, Athletes, and Teams from Rocky's Town.* Fayetteville, AR: The University of Arkansas Press, 2016.

Thayer, Gwyneth Anne, *Going to the Dogs: Greyhound Racing, Animal Activism, and American Popular Culture*. Lawrence, KS: University Press of Kansas, 2013.

Vogan, Travis, *ESPN: The Making of a Sports Media Empire*. Urbana, IL: University of Illinois Press, 2015.

Vogan, Travis, *Keepers of the Flame: NFL Films and the Rise of Sports Media*. Urbana, IL: University of Illinois Press, 2014.

Zimbalist, Andrew, *In the Best Interests of Baseball? Governing the National Pastime*. Lincoln, NE: University of Nebraska Press, 2013.

VI. Material Culture and Sport

Baker, William J., *Playing with God: Religion and Modern Sport*. Cambridge, MA: Harvard University Press, 2009.

Berryman, Jack, W. and Roberta J. Park, eds. *Sport and Exercise Science Essays in the History of Sports Medicine*. Urbana, IL: University of Illinois Press, 1992.

Black, Jonathan, *Making the American Body: The Remarkable Saga of the Men and Women Whose Feats, Feuds, and Passions Shaped Fitness History*. Lincoln, NE: University of Nebraska Press, 2013.

Borish, Linda J. "American Jewish Women on the Court: Seeking an Identity in Tennis in the Early Decades of the Twentieth Century" in Zuckerman, Bruce, ed., Sclar, Ari F., Guest ed., and Lisa Ansell, *Beyond Stereotypes: American Jews and Sports*, the University of Southern California Casden Institute for the Study of the Jewish Role in America Life, Annual Review, Volume 12. West Lafayette, IN: Purdue University Press, 2014, pp. 43–72.

Borish, Linda J. "Women at the Modern Olympic Games: An Interdisciplinary Look at American Culture," *Quest*, 48, 1 (February 1996): 43–56.

Cavallo, Dominick, *Muscles and Morals: Organized Playgrounds and Urban Reform, 1880–1920*. Philadelphia, PA: University of Pennsylvania Press, 1981.

Chapman, David L., *Sandow the Magnificent: Eugen Sandow and the Beginnings of Bodybuilding*. Urbana, IL: University of Illinois Press, 1994.

Corzine, Nathan Michael. *Team Chemistry: The History of Drugs and Alcohol in Major League Baseball*. Urbana, IL: University of Illinois Press, 2016.

Dyreson, Mark and Robert Trumpbour, eds., *The Rise of Modern Stadiums in the United States: Cathedrals of Sport*. New York: Routledge, 2010.

Ernst, Robert, *Weakness Is a Crime: The Life of Bernarr Macfadden*, Syracuse, NY: Syracuse University Press, 1991.

Fair, John D., *Mr. America: The Tragic History of a Bodybuilding Icon*. Austin, TX: University of Texas Press, 2015.

Fair, John D., *Muscletown USA: Bob Hoffman and the Manly Culture of York Barbell*. University Park, PA: Pennsylvania State University Press, 1999.

Green, Harvey, *Fit for America: Health, Fitness, Sport and American Society*. Baltimore, MD: The Johns Hopkins University Press, 1988.

Grover, Kathryn, ed., *Fitness in American Culture: Images of Health, Sport, and the Body, 1830–1940*. Rochester, NY: The Margaret Woodbury Strong Museum, 1989.

Hoberman, John, *Hybrid Athletes, Monstrous Addicts, and Cyborg Natures*. New York: The Free Press, 1992.

Hoberman, John, *Mortal Engines: The Science of Performance and the Dehumanization of Sport*. New York: The Free Press, 1992.

Kuklick, Bruce, *To Everything a Season: Shibe Park and Urban Philadelphia*. Princeton, NJ: Princeton University Press, 1991.

Mayo, James M., *The American Country Club: Its Origins and Development*. Philadelphia, PA: Temple University Press, 1998.

McKenzie, Shelly, *Getting Physical: The Rise of Fitness Culture in America.* Lawrence, KS: University Press of Kansas, 2013.

Moore, Louis, "Black Sparring Masters, Gymnasium Owners, and the White Body, 1825–1886." *Journal of African American History*, 96 (Fall 2011): 448–473.

Moss, Richard, *Golf and the American Country Club.* Urbana, IL: University of Illinois Press, 2001.

Mrozek, Donald J., *Sport and American Mentality, 1880–1920.* Knoxville, TN: The University of Tennessee Press, 1983.

Osmond, Gary, "Photographs, Materiality and Sport History: Peter Norman and the 1968 Mexico City Black Power Salute," *Journal of Sport History*, 37 (Spring 2010): 119–137.

Plymire, Darcy, "Positive Addiction: Running and Human Potential in the 1970s," *Journal of Sport History*, 31 (Fall 2004): 297–315.

Rader, Benjamin G. "The Quest for Self-Sufficiency and the New Strenuosity: Reflections on the Strenuous Life of the 1970s and the 1980s." *Journal of Sport History*, 18 (Summer 1991): 255–266.

Raitz, Karl B., *The Theater of Sport.* Baltimore, MD: The Johns Hopkins University Press, 1995.

Rosenzweig, Roy and Elizabeth Blackmar, *The Park and Its People: A History of Central Park.* Ithaca, NY: Cornell University Press, 1992.

Todd, Jan, *Physical Culture and the Body Beautiful: Purposive Exercise in the Lives of American Women, 1800–1875.* Mercer, GA: Mercer University Press, 1998.

Todd, Jan, "Strength Is Health: George Barker Windship and the First American Weight Training Boom." *Iron Game History: The Journal of Physical Culture*, 3 (September 1993): 3–14.

Todd, Jan, "The Strength Builders: A History of Barbells, Dumbbells, and Indian Clubs." *The International Journal of the History of Sport*, 20 (2003): 65–90.

Trumpbour, Robert, C., *The New Cathedrals: Politics and Media in the History of Stadium Construction.* Syracuse, NY: Syracuse University Press, 2007.

Westcott, Rich, *Philadelphia's Old Ballparks.* Philadelphia, PA: Temple University Press, 2007.

Whorton, James, C., *Crusaders for Fitness*. Princeton, NJ: Princeton University Press, 1982.

Wiltse, Jeff, *Contested Waters: A Social History of Swimming Pools in America.* Chapel Hill, NC: University of North Carolina Press, 2007.

Zinkin, Harold, *Remembering Muscle Beach.* Los Angeles: Angel City Press, 1999.

VII. Social Movements and Political Uses of Sport

Abelson, Donald E., "Politics on Ice: The United States, the Soviet Union, and a Hockey Game in Lake Placid." *Canadian Review of American Studies*, 40 (2010): 63–94.

Anderson, Sheldon, *The Politics and Culture of Modern Sports*. New York: Lexington Books, 2015.

Barney, Robert K., Stephen R. Wenn, and Scott G. Martyn, *Selling the Five Rings: The International Olympic Committee and the Rise of Olympic Commercialism.* Salt Lake City, UT: University of Utah Press, 2002.

Bass, Amy, *Not the Triumph But the Struggle: The 1968 Olympics and the Making of the Black Athlete.* Minneapolis, MN: University of Minnesota Press, 2002.

Dahlberg, Tim, Mary Ederle Ward, and Brenda Greene, *America's Girl: The Incredible Story of How Swimmer Gertrude Ederle Changed the Nation.* New York: St. Martin's Press, 2009.

Dichter, Heather and Andrew J. Johns, eds., *Diplomatic Games: Sport, Statecraft, and International Relations Since 1945.* Lexington, KY: University of Kentucky Press, 2014.

Dyreson, Mark, *Crafting Patriotism for Global Domination: America at the Olympic Games.* London: Routledge, 2009.

Dyreson, Mark, *Making the American Team: Sport, Culture, and the Olympic Experience*. Urbana, IL: University of Illinois Press, 1998.

Dyreson, Mark, "Mapping an Empire of Baseball: American Visions of National Pastimes and Global Influence, 1919–1941" in Kyle, Donald and Fairbanks, Robert R. eds., *Baseball in America and America in Baseball.* College Station, TX: Texas A&M Press, 2008, pp. 143–188.

Guttmann, Allen, *The Olympics: A History of the Modern Games*, Urbana, IL: University of Illinois Press, 1992.

Hoberman, John, "Toward a Theory of Olympic Internationalism," *Journal of Sport History*, 22 (Spring 1995): 1–37.

Hulme, Derick L., *The Political Olympics: Moscow, Afghanistan, and the 1980 U.S. Boycott*. New York: Praeger, 1990.

Hunt, Thomas M, "Countering the Soviet Threat in the Olympics Medals Race: The Amateur Sports Act of 1978 and American Athletes Policy Reform," *The International Journal of the History of Sport*, 24 (2007): 796–818.

Llewellyn, Matthew P., John Gleaves, and Wayne Wilson, eds., *The 1984 Los Angeles Olympic Games: Assessing the 30 Year Legacy*. London: Routledge, 2015.

Morris, Andrew D., *Colonial Project, National Game: A History of Baseball in Taiwan*. Berkeley, CA: University of California Press, 2011.

Pope, S.W., *Patriotic Games: Sporting Traditions in the American Imagination, 1876–1926*. New York: Oxford University Press, 1997.

Reich, Kenneth, *Making it Happen: Peter Ueberroth and the 1984 Olympics*. Santa Barbara, CA: Capra, 1986.

Roche, Maurice, *Mega-Events and Modernity: Olympics and Expos in the Growth of Global Culture*. London: Routledge, 2000.

Sarantakes, Evan Nicolas, *Dropping the Torch: Jimmy Carter, the Olympic Boycott, and the Cold War*. New York: Cambridge University Press, 2011.

Shimizu-Guthrie, Sayuri, *Transpacific Field of Dreams: How Baseball Linked the United States and Japan in Peace and War*. Chapel Hill, NC: University of North Carolina Press, 2012.

Soares, John, "Cold War, Hot Ice: International Ice Hockey." *Journal of Sport History*, 34 (Summer 2007): 207–230.

Turrini, Joseph M., "It Was Communism versus the Free World: The USA-USSR Dual Track Meet Series and the Development of Track and Field in the United States, 1958–1985," *Journal of Sport History*, 28 (Fall 2001): 427–471.

Wagg, Stephen and David L. Andrews, *East Plays West: Sport and the Cold War*. London: Routledge, 2007.

Wakefield, Ellen Wanda, *Playing to Win: Sports and the American Military, 1898–1945*. Albany, NY: State University of New York Press, 1997.

Watterson, John, *The Games President's Play: Sports and the Presidency*. Baltimore, MD: The Johns Hopkins University Press, 2006.

Witherspoon, Kevin B., *Before the Eyes of the World: Mexico and the 1968 Olympics*. DeKalb, IL: Northern Illinois University Press, 2008.

Zeiler, Thomas W., *Ambassadors in Pinstripes: The Spalding World Baseball Tour and the Birth of the American Empire*. Lanham, MD: Rowman & Littlefield, 2006.

Zimbalist, Andrew, *Circus Maximus: The Economic Gamble Behind Hosting the Olympics and the World Cup*. Washington, DC: Brookings Institute Press, 2015.

VIII. Facets of Sport in Recent American Culture

Andrews, David L. and Ben Carrington, eds., *A Companion to Sport*. London: Blackwell Publishing, 2013.

Booth, Douglas and Holly Thorpe, eds., *Berkshire Encyclopedia of Extreme Sports*. Great Barrington, MA: Berkshire Publishing Group, LLC, 2007.

Dyreson, Mark, "Marketing Weismuller to the World: Hollywood's Olympics and Federal Schemes for Americanization Through Sport." *The International Journal of the History of Sport*, 25 (2008): 284–306.

Gems, Gerald R., *The Athletic Crusade: Sport and American Cultural Imperialism*. Lincoln, NE: University of Nebraska Press, 2006.

Keeler, Ben and John Nauright, "Team Yao: Yao Ming, the NBA and Selling Sport to China." *American Journal of Chinese Studies*, 12 (2005): 203–218.

Keys, Barbara, "Spreading Peace, Democracy, and Coca-Cola: Sport and American Cultural Expansion in the 1930s." *Diplomatic History*, 28 (April 2004): 165–196.

Klein, Alan, *Sugarball: The American Game, the Dominican Dream*. New Haven, CT: Yale University Press, 1991.

Laderman, Scott, *Empire in Waves: A Political History of Surfing*. Berkeley, CA: University of California Press, 2014.

Markovits, Andrei and Lars Rensmann, *Gaming the World: How Sports are Reshaping Global Politics and Culture*. Princeton, NJ: Princeton University Press, 2010.

Miller, Toby, Geoffrey Lawrence, Jim McKay, and David Rowe, *Globalization and Sport: Playing the World*. London: Sage, 2001.

Nathan, Daniel A., "Review Essay: Traveling: Notes on Basketball and Globalization; or Why the San Antonio Spurs are the Future." *The International Journal of the History of Sport*, 25 (2008): 737–750.

Nauright, John and John Ramfjord, "Who Owns England's Game? American Professional Sporting Influences and Foreign Ownership in the Premier League." *Soccer and Society* 11 (2010): 428–441.

Ormond, Joan and Belinda Wheaton, eds., *On the Edge: Leisure, Consumption, and Representation of Leisure Sports*. University of Brighton: Leisure Studies Association, 2009.

Rinehart, Robert E., "Dropping Hierarchies: Toward the Study of a Contemporary Sporting Avant-Garde." *Sociology of Sport Journal*, 13 (1996): 159–175.

Rinehart, Robert E. "Inside of the Outside: Pecking Orders Within Alternative Sport at ESPNs 1995 the Extreme Games." *Journal of Sport and Social Issues*, 22 (1998): 398–415.

Rinehart, Robert E., *Players All: Performances in Contemporary Sport*. Bloomington, IN: Indiana University Press, 1998.

Rinehart, Robert E. and Synthia Sydnor, eds., *To the Extreme: Alternative Sports, Inside and Out*. Albany, NY: State University of New York Press, 2003.

Ruck, Rob, *Raceball: How the Major Leagues Colonized the Black and Latin Game*. Boston, MA: Beacon Press, 2012.

Sage, George, *Globalizing Sport: How Organizations, Corporations and Media Are Changing Sport*. New York: Paradigm Press, 2010.

Switzer, Katherine, *Marathon Woman: Running the Race to Revolutionize Women's Sports*. Cambridge, MA: DeCapo Press, 2007.

Wheaton, Belinda, ed., *Understanding Lifestyle Sport: Consumption, Identity and Difference*. London: Routledge, 2004.

INDEX

CPSIA information can be obtained
at www.ICGtesting.com
Printed in the USA
JSHW041736090622
26866JS00001B/2